# THE NIV APPLICATION COMMENTARY

## EZRA, NEHEMIAH

# THE NIV APPLICATION COMMENTARY SERIES

# THE NIV APPLICATION COMMENTARY

## EZRA, NEHEMIAH

BRINGING THE ANCIENT MESSAGE OF THE BIBLE INTO YOUR WORLD

DONNA PETTER AND THOMAS PETTER

ZONDERVAN ACADEMIC

*Ezra-Nehemiah*


Published in Grand Rapids, Michigan, by Zondervan. Zondervan is a registered trademark of The Zondervan Corporation, L.L.C., a wholly owned subsidiary of HarperCollins Christian Publishing, Inc.

Requests for information should be addressed to customercare@harpercollins.com.

Zondervan titles may be purchased in bulk for educational, business, fundraising, or sales promotional use. For information, please email SpecialMarkets@Zondervan.com.

ISBN 978-0-310-22543-0 (hardcover)
ISBN 978-0-310-49288-7 (ebook)



*Printed in the United States of America*

25 26 27 28 29 30 31 32 33 24 35 /TRM/ 16 15 14 13 12 11 10 9 8 7 6 5

Donna dedicates the book of Ezra to Ron and Judy Smith, founders and directors of the School of Biblical Studies in Youth With A Mission. Thank you for teaching me the Scriptures. Because of your example, I am continuing in what I have learned and have become convinced of (the power and relevance of the sixty-six books of the Bible), because I know from whom I've learned it (2 Tim 3:14)!

Tom dedicates the book of Nehemiah to the members and attendants of Trinitarian Congregational Church in Wayland, Massachusetts, who model attentiveness to the Scripture coupled with a deep love for the Lord. Thank you for giving me this incredible privilege to feast on the Word, week after week!

# Contents


*Series Introduction* . . . . . 9
*General Editor's Preface* . . . . . 13
*Authors' Preface and Acknowledgments* . . . . . 17
*Abbreviations* . . . . . 19

Introduction . . . . . 21
Maps and Timeline . . . . . 34
Outline . . . . . 39
Select Bibliography . . . . . 43
Text and Commentary . . . . . 49

*Scripture Index* . . . . . 483
*Subject Index* . . . . . 501
*Author Index* . . . . . 511

THE NIV APPLICATION COMMENTARY SERIES

**Old Testament Volumes**

*Genesis,* John H. Walton

*Exodus,* Peter Enns

*Leviticus, Numbers,* Roy Gane

*Deuteronomy,* Daniel I. Block

*Joshua,* Robert L. Hubbard Jr.

*Judges, Ruth,* K. Lawson Younger Jr.

*1 and 2 Samuel,* Bill T. Arnold

*1 and 2 Kings,* August H. Konkel

*1 and 2 Chronicles,* Andrew E. Hill

*Ezra-Nehemiah,* Donna Petter and Thomas Petter

*Esther,* Karen H. Jobes

*Job,* John H. Walton

*Psalms Volume 1,* Gerald H. Wilson

*Psalms Volume 2,* W. Dennis Tucker Jr. and Jamie A. Grant

*Proverbs,* Paul E. Koptak

*Ecclesiastes, Song of Songs,* Iain Provan

*Isaiah,* John N. Oswalt

*Jeremiah, Lamentations,* J. Andrew Dearman

*Ezekiel,* Iain M. Duguid

*Daniel,* Tremper Longman III

*Hosea, Amos, Micah,* Gary V. Smith

*Jonah, Nahum, Habakkuk, Zephaniah,* James Bruckner

*Joel, Obadiah, Malachi,* David W. Baker

*Haggai, Zechariah,* Mark J. Boda

**New Testament Volumes**

*Matthew,* Michael J. Wilkins

*Mark,* David E. Garland

*Luke,* Darrell L. Bock

*John,* Gary M. Burge

*Acts,* Ajith Fernando

*Romans,* Douglas J. Moo

*1 Corinthians,* Craig L. Blomberg

*2 Corinthians,* Scott J. Hafemann

*Galatians,* Scot McKnight

*Ephesians,* Klyne Snodgrass

*Philippians,* Frank Thielman

*Colossians, Philemon,* David E. Garland

*1 and 2 Thessalonians,* Michael W. Holmes

*1 and 2 Timothy, Titus,* Walter L. Liefeld

*Hebrews,* George H. Guthrie

*James,* David P. Nystrom

*1 Peter,* Scot McKnight

*2 Peter, Jude,* Douglas J. Moo

*Letters of John,* Gary M. Burge

*Revelation,* Craig S. Keener

## NIV APPLICATION COMMENTARY

# Series Introduction

THE NIV APPLICATION COMMENTARY SERIES IS UNIQUE. Most commentaries help us make the journey from our world back to the world of the Bible. They enable us to cross the barriers of time, culture, language, and geography that separate us from the biblical world. Yet they only offer a one-way ticket to the past and assume that we can somehow make the return journey on our own. Once they have explained the *original meaning* of a book or passage, these commentaries give us little or no help in exploring its *contemporary significance*. The information they offer is valuable, but the job is only half done.

Recently, a few commentaries have included some contemporary application as *one* of their goals. Yet that application is often sketchy or moralistic, and some volumes sound more like printed sermons than commentaries.

The primary goal of the NIV Application Commentary Series is to help you with the difficult but vital task of bringing an ancient message into a modern context. The series not only focuses on application as a finished product but also helps you think through the *process* of moving from the original meaning of a passage to its contemporary significance. These are commentaries, not popular expositions. They are works of reference, not devotional literature.

The format of the series is designed to achieve the goals of the series. Each passage is treated in three sections: *Original Meaning*, *Bridging Contexts*, and *Contemporary Significance*.

THIS SECTION HELPS YOU UNDERSTAND THE meaning of the biblical text in its original context. All of the elements of traditional exegesis—in concise form—are discussed here. These include the historical, literary, and cultural context of the passage. The authors discuss matters related to grammar and syntax and the meaning of biblical words.[1] They also seek to explore the main ideas of the passage and how the biblical author develops those ideas.

After reading this section, you will understand the problems, questions, and concerns of the *original audience* and how the biblical author addressed those issues. This understanding is foundational to any legitimate application of the text today.

THIS SECTION BUILDS A BRIDGE BETWEEN THE world of the Bible and the world of today, between the original context and the contemporary context, by focusing on both the timely and timeless aspects of the text.

God's Word is *timely*. The authors of Scripture spoke to specific situations, problems, and questions. The author of Joshua encouraged the faith of his original readers by narrating the destruction of Jericho, a seemingly impregnable city, at the hands of an angry warrior God (Josh 6). Paul warned the Galatians about the consequences of circumcision and the dangers of trying to be justified by law (Gal 5:2–5). The author of Hebrews tried to convince his readers that Christ is superior to Moses, the Aaronic priests, and the Old Testament sacrifices. John urged his readers to "test the spirits" of those who taught a form of incipient Gnosticism (1 John 4:1–6). In each of these cases, the timely nature of Scripture enables us to hear God's Word in situations that were *concrete* rather than abstract.

Yet, the timely nature of Scripture also creates problems. Our situations, difficulties, and questions are not always directly related to those faced by the people in the Bible. Therefore, God's word to them does not always seem relevant to us. For example, when was the last time someone urged you to be circumcised, claiming that it was a necessary part of justification? How many people today care whether Christ is superior to the Aaronic priests? And how can a "test" designed to expose incipient Gnosticism be of any value in a modern culture?

Fortunately, Scripture is not only timely but *timeless*. Just as God spoke to the original audience, so he still speaks to us through the pages of

---

1. Please note that in general, when the authors discuss words in the original biblical languages, the series uses a general rather than a scholarly method of transliteration.

Scripture. Because we share a common humanity with the people of the Bible, we discover a *universal dimension* in the problems they faced and the solutions God gave them. The timeless nature of Scripture enables it to speak with power in every time and in every culture.

Those who fail to recognize that Scripture is both timely and timeless run into a host of problems. For example, those who are intimidated by timely books such as Hebrews, Galatians, or Deuteronomy might avoid reading them because they seem meaningless today. At the other extreme, those who are convinced of the timeless nature of Scripture but who fail to discern its timely element may "wax eloquent" about the Melchizedekian priesthood to a sleeping congregation or worse still try to apply the holy wars of the Old Testament in a physical way to God's enemies today.

The purpose of this section, therefore, is to help you discern what is timeless in the timely pages of the Bible—and what is not. For example, how do the holy wars of the Old Testament relate to the spiritual warfare of the New? If Paul's primary concern is not circumcision (as he tells us in Gal 5:6), what *is* he concerned about? If discussions about the Aaronic priesthood or Melchizedek seem irrelevant today, what is of abiding value in these passages? If people try to "test the spirits" today with a test designed for a specific first-century heresy, what other biblical test might be more appropriate?

Yet, this section does not merely uncover that which is timeless in a passage but also helps you to see *how* it is uncovered. The authors of the commentaries seek to take what is implicit in the text and make it explicit, to take a process that normally is intuitive and explain it in a logical, orderly fashion. How do we know that circumcision is not Paul's primary concern? What clues in the text or its context help us realize that Paul's real concern is at a deeper level?

Of course, those passages in which the historical distance between us and the original readers is greatest require a longer treatment. Conversely, those passages in which the historical distance is smaller or seemingly nonexistent require less attention.

One final clarification. Because this section prepares the way for discussing the contemporary significance of the passage, there is not always a sharp distinction or a clear break between this section and the one that follows. Yet, when both sections are read together, you should have a strong sense of moving from the world of the Bible to the world of today.

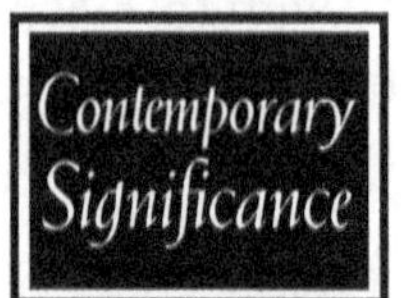


THIS SECTION ALLOWS THE BIBLICAL MESSAGE TO speak with as much power today as it did when it was first written. How can you apply what you learned about Jerusalem, Ephesus, or Corinth to our present-day needs in Chicago, Los Angeles, or London? How can you take a message originally spoken in Greek, Hebrew, and Aramaic and communicate it clearly in our own language? How can you take the eternal truths originally spoken in a different time and culture and apply them to the similar-yet-different needs of our culture?

In order to achieve these goals, this section gives you help in several key areas.

(1) It helps you identify contemporary situations, problems, or questions that are truly comparable to those faced by the original audience. Because contemporary situations are seldom identical to those faced by the original audience, you must seek situations that are analogous if your applications are to be relevant.

(2) This section explores a variety of contexts in which the passage might be applied today. You will look at personal applications, but you will also be encouraged to think beyond private concerns to the society and culture at large.

(3) This section will alert you to any problems or difficulties you might encounter in seeking to apply the passage. And if there are several legitimate ways to apply a passage (areas in which Christians disagree), the author will bring these to your attention and help you think through the issues involved.

In seeking to achieve these goals, the contributors to this series attempt to avoid two extremes. They avoid making such specific applications that the commentary might quickly become dated. They also avoid discussing the significance of the passage in such a general way that it fails to engage contemporary life and culture.

Above all, contributors to this series have made a diligent effort not to sound moralistic or preachy. The NIV Application Commentary Series does not seek to provide ready-made sermon materials but rather tools, ideas, and insights that will help you communicate God's Word with power. If we help you to achieve that goal, then we have fulfilled the purpose for this series.

—The Editors

# General Editor's Preface

THE BOOKS OF EZRA AND NEHEMIAH tell the story of Israel's return to Zion during a hundred-year period from 539 BC to 433 BC. The return was led first by a scribe and priest, Ezra, who brought a group of Babylonian exiles back to Jerusalem, and later by a governor appointed by the Persian ruler Artaxerxes, an Israelite politician named Nehemiah. In keeping with their complementary roles as religious and political leaders, Ezra emphasized the need to reestablish the law of Moses while Nehemiah advocated and oversaw the rebuilding of the gates and walls of the city.

Both Ezra and Nehemiah were responding to a 559 BC proclamation by Cyrus the Great, King of Persia. Cyrus, whose heart was moved by the Lord (Ezra 1:1), announced that the God of heaven had appointed him to build a temple in Jerusalem—not only build it but raise the funds to pay for it. Ezra and Nehemiah ended up being Cyrus's proxies in fulfilling this divine command.

Yet, there was an even bigger motivation at work here. In the commentary that follows, Donna Petter and Thomas Petter emphasize that for both Ezra and Nehemiah, law keeping and wall building were manifestations of a larger purpose, a purpose larger even than Cyrus's proclamation. Both Ezra and Nehemiah believed that a successful return from Babylon to Jerusalem was predicated on a theological task: the renewal of the worship of Yahweh.

Does this sound at all familiar? God's people forced into exile, opposition to true belief at every turn, quixotic political rulers mouthing orthodoxy while practicing hedonistic excess? More than you might think, I say—but before jumping to any conclusions about how this story might have meaning for those of us who live in the twenty-first-century West, we should note some pretty dramatic cultural differences between our day and the Middle East in the sixth century BC.

For starters, we are not physically exiled, looking for a way to get back to our promised land. God's people had been militarily conquered and physically removed from their land and lived in exile in Babylon. Our predicament today as religious people is that we are being culturally exiled even as we continue to live on the same streets that once showcased our churches and provided places for our food banks, clothes pantries, and shelters in stormy times.

And we are not looking for a return to a religiously-homogeneous culture (if we ever had one). We are not looking for endorsement of our particular religious views. To paraphrase Ruth Bader Ginsburg who quoted women suffragette Sarah Grimké in an argument before the Supreme Court, "We ask no favor for our particular religion—all we ask of our law-makers is that they take their feet off our spiritual necks."

To be sure, some resonances can be discerned in each of the tasks taken on by the triumvirate of returners—Cyrus's reconstruction of the temple, Ezra's reestablishment of the law, Nehemiah's rebuilding of the walls. That is, we can easily identify a current need for church revitalization that can learn from Cyrus's burden. We need a strong church and, according to a recent Pew survey, Americans are turning away from the Christian church in record numbers.[1] In fact, the most energetic Western "institutions" seem to be Facebook, Google, and Twitter.

And although our Western cultures are far from being lawless, they certainly are lawlite. The laws having to do with religion today are not the carefully thought out restrictions by all sectors of society that allow us to live together in peace and harmony, but laws that follow political and cultural fashion. Given our almost 50/50 division between "red" and "blue," we have laws favorable to half our neighbors and anathema to the other half. The kind of cooperation and compromise that enable true civic harmony has all but disappeared from our law-making process.

And where, we might ask, can one find a safe context in which to practice her or his religion? Certainly not in our public schools, where even a hint of Christian prayer or practice is considered a threat to civic society. And it is difficult to decide which is worse—the old status quo where politicians running for office felt obligated to trot out a pean to God and church no matter how insincere, or the more current obligation to take some kind of pot-shot at religion no matter how crude.

Yet, behind each of these resonances lies a deeper vacuum, a loss of a sense of Homo sapiens as worshiping beings. What is missing from public discourse and private convictions alike is a constant awareness

---

1. "In U.S., Decline of Christianity Continues at Rapid Pace: An Update on America's Changing Religious Landscape." https://www.pewforum.org/2019/10/17/in-u-s-decline-of-christianity-continues-at-rapid-pace/.

that we are created beings, creatures of a creator beyond time and space, all powerful and totally good. This awareness of God can only be nurtured by congregations in worshiping churches, by law-making that looks far beyond immediate political advantage to laws that encourage what Emile Durkheim called events of "collective effervescence," and by the contextual safety of a country that sees its citizens' devotion to transcendence as a strength rather than a weakness. Ezra and Nehemiah demanded that this be the foundation of the recivilization of the promised land; we need to learn the lesson again.

—Terry C. Muck

# Authors' Preface and Acknowledgments

WE BOTH WISH TO THANK THE TRUSTEES of Gordon-Conwell Theological Seminary for the sabbaticals given to the writing of this commentary. Tom wishes to thank Trinitarian Congregational Church in Wayland, MA, for the yearly study leaves, which have allowed the completion of the work. A heartfelt thank you also goes to the editors of the series, especially Terry Muck and Nancy Erickson for their patience in overseeing the completion of this project. We are also thankful for the ministry of the late Verlyn Verbrugge at Zondervan who put us on the right track early on to "keep it simple."

In this regard, the scope of this commentary is intentionally limited with respect to its interaction with secondary literature. Likewise, we address matters pertaining to Hebrew (and Aramaic) only when deemed absolutely relevant to the interpretation of the received text or where the NIV translation fails to convey the precise sense of the original text. Consequently, footnotes are kept at a minimum, which will inevitably frustrate students of the text who expect more in-depth dialogue with voices in past and present scholarship. We especially are sympathetic to those who come to the text with training in the higher-critical arts. Our constant appeal to the text in its final form will leave out many scholarly discussions regarding current and past theories on the possible formation and editorial processes. Instead, our approach reflects a long-standing tradition in commentary writing that seeks to elucidate the text as it was received rather than focus on the pre-history of the text. Many will recognize the influence of several influential academic streams in our work, including literary (structural) and syntactical analysis of the Hebrew and Aramaic text, ancient Near Eastern history and archaeology, Old Testament, New Testament, and biblical theologies. Our lives as missionaries, as professors of Old Testament in a seminary, and (for one of us) as a full-time pastor, have deeply shaped us. Several illustrations in the contemporary significance section will be drawn directly from these experiences.

In every part, and as much as possible, we strive for succinctness, clarity, and plain meaning of the text. One deliberate strategy from the outset included the creation of obvious links between the three main parts of each section that are a hallmark of the NIVAC series: original meaning, bridging contexts, and contemporary significance. We hope we have achieved a measure of success in this challenging task. It is fair to say that it is a lot easier for biblical scholars to be content to interact with the ancient context and to simply "outsource" the application of the text to others. The strength of the NIVAC series is that the writer is compelled to think for herself and himself as to what this text actually means and its value from an eternal perspective. One needs to be a firm believer in the sufficiency and relevance of Scripture to engage in such practice. Again, we will leave it to the reader to decide whether we have achieved this or not.

A note about authorship and the editorial process of the commentary writing itself seems in order. Donna Petter is the author of the book of Ezra's commentary and Tom Petter is the author of Nehemiah's commentary. We have deliberately tried not to interfere with each other's "voice" while at the same time took time to edit the complete work together so that inconsistencies would be removed.

In conclusion, the explanation of the book of the law in the assembly in Nehemiah 8 serves as a vivid witness to the importance not only of hearing the Word but of understanding and applying it. Thus, the task is upon the modern "Ezras" among us not only to know the Scripture but also to explain it so that people who hear it can also understand it. Our prayer is that this commentary will serve in the propagation of the gospel throughout the world. May his word be fruitful and multiply until the knowledge of the glory of the Lord covers the earth as the waters cover the sea.

—Donna and Tom Petter

# Abbreviations

| | |
|---|---|
| ASOR | American Schools of Oriental Research |
| *ABD* | *Anchor Bible Dictionary*. Edited by David Noel Freedman. 6 vols. New York: Doubleday, 1992 |
| *ANET* | *Ancient Near Eastern Texts Relating to the Old Testament.* Edited by James B. Pritchard. 3rd ed. Princeton: Princeton University Press, 1969 |
| *AP* | Cowley, A. E. *Aramaic Papyri of the Fifth Century B.C.* Ancient Texts and Translations. Eugene, OR: Wipf & Stock, 2005 |
| *BAR* | *Biblical Archaeology Review* |
| HAT | Handbuch zum Alten Testament |
| *JETS* | *Journal of the Evangelical Theological Society* |
| *JBL* | *Journal of Biblical Literature* |
| *LW* | *Luther's Works* |
| LXX | Septuagint |
| MT | Masoretic Text |
| NAC | New American Commentary Series |
| NICOT | New International Commentary on the Old Testament |
| NIVAC | New International Version Application Commentary |
| OTL | Old Testament Library |
| PNTC | Pillar New Testament Commentary |
| THOTC | Two Horizons Old Testament Commentary |
| TOTC | Tyndale Old Testament Commentaries |
| *VT* | *Vetus Testamentum* |
| VTSup | Supplements to Vetus Testamentun |
| WBC | Word Biblical Commentary |

# Introduction

## Literary and Historical Setting

Ezra-Nehemiah (traditionally considered originally one book)[1] should be viewed in four distinct parts,[2] spanning a period of about one hundred years (539 BC–433 BC) during the period in Judah (Aramaic *Yehud*), the Persian province "beyond the river" (Euphrates).[3] In light of this long span of history, it is no surprise that modern scholars have debated the context(s) of the composition and redaction(s) of the volume. Recent approaches built upon the classical German school[4] now include sophisticated models involving a complex process of composition and redaction.[5] Other critical scholars find contentment in approaches that, while allowing for some measure of diversity in the redactional process, also embrace an overall unity and the notion that Ezra the scribe and Nehemiah the governor had a hand in the process, as well.[6]

Our focus in this commentary is on the ancient text in its syntactical, semantic, and historical context, rather than an attempt to provide another model to elucidate the compositional process of Ezra-Nehemiah. By anchoring the text in its syntactical and literary context; this, in turn, provides the signposts for application of the text in the contemporary context. As such, this commentary belongs to the long-standing school of interpretation that upholds the view that the ancient text of the Bible deserves a fair hearing just like any other ancient or modern text in terms of the intent of the received text. Matters pertaining to the formation/

---

1. For a recent summary of the debates on the question, see Nissim Amzallag, "The Authorship of Ezra and Nehemiah in Light of Differences in Their Ideological Background," *JBL* 2 (2018): 271–97.

2. For further treatment on the unity of Ezra-Nehemiah see H. G. M. Williamson, *Ezra, Nehemiah*, WBC 16 (Waco, TX: Word, 1985), xxi–xxiii.

3. See chart, "Return of the Exiles 539 BC–444 BC."

4. Wilhelm Rudolph, *Ezra and Nehemia*, HAT 20 (Tübingen: Mohr, 1949).

5. See Jacob L. Wright, *Rebuilding Identity: The Nehemiah-Memoir and its Earliest Readers* (Berlin: de Gruyter, 2005).

6. See Mark J. Boda and Paul L. Redditt, eds., *Unity and Disunity in Ezra-Nehemiah: Redaction, Rhetoric, and Reader* (Sheffield: Sheffield Phoenix, 2008).

pre-history of the text are addressed only if these significantly affect the interpretation of the text and its impact upon the contemporary milieu (a hallmark of the NIV Application Commentary Series). However, lest a false dichotomy between historical and literary pursuits is created, we recognize the complexities attached to the historical process of composition and redaction (which in this case spans over one hundred years!); nevertheless, from a syntactical-structural standpoint, we find some of the critical arguments to dislodge the text from its intended literary-historical moorings unconvincing.

The ancient writers' intent was not to mislead the reader. What they said and how they said it presents itself in a developed literary-theological framework. The traditional critical triggers to recover multiple redactional hands are well known: discrepancies, contradictions, stylistic variations, repetitions, and inconsistencies (whether literary or historical). In the specific case of Ezra-Nehemiah, there exists a certain linguistic and topical integrity to the text in its final form that perhaps should be taken at face value. We find that the evidence collected to support a multi-layered editorial process can be explained with reasons other than the presence of an editor(s) who intentionally smoothed the seams between the different texts brought together to make Ezra-Nehemiah as we have it today.

Another assumption that is affirmed in our approach is that a deeply confessional and theistic reading of the text reflects the intent of the writers. Consequently, a theistic reception of the text was equally expected by the writers.[7] These writings were considered sacred and therefore

---

7. Some confessional scholars who embrace the idea of multi-authored and long-term editorial activities (the assumption of critical scholars) make the case that it does not negate divine superintendence of the received text (e.g., John Goldingay is probably the main proponent. *Theological Diversity and the Authority of the Old Testament* [Grand Rapids: Eerdmans, 1987]). While this idea a priori seems to have merit since it would retain the notion that the final text is a reliable carrier of theological truths through the ages (the essential idea of a Sacred text), we are still left wondering precisely why would the authors/editors engage in such complex undertaking of reworking the original sources? Why does the *Sitz Im Leben* of the formation of the text need to be far apart from the events it describes? The originators of the text, the prophetic guild (to which we must include the main protagonists in Ezra-Nehemiah), did not share this approach. In their mind, they were carriers of the Word of God through their writing, not the initiators of an evolving document containing literary and historical errors left for others at a time quite separate from the setting of the text to fix as best they could in an open-ended sort of way (until the said errors are

reliable in the eyes of the ancient.[8] This is true of the writers/editors of Ezra-Nehemiah as well. They do not hide their intent to implicate the "God of heaven" as the main actor of this narrative. His motives are pure and good, not suspicious, unfair, or reprehensible. For Nehemiah, it is an account of events as they occurred in real time and space.[9] Some may or may not appreciate or embrace this God-centered narrative strategy, but in fairness to the text and in order to be true to the exegetical process, the meaning of the text as we have it is our first priority in this commentary. Some segments of Ezra-Nehemiah also function as an official record in the Persian court, since it emanates from officials of the Persian administrative apparatus (Nehemiah) or persons directly delegated by the Persian Empire (Ezra). It is therefore highly unlikely Persian authorities would have appreciated fabrications and historical inaccuracies.

Consequently, it is our conviction that the final edition of Ezra-Nehemiah reflects a higher degree of compositional and editorial clarity than is sometimes discussed (speculated?) by some scholars.

---

uncovered some two millenia later by modern scholars). From a historical standpoint, factoring errors in the narrative is on an exponential trajectory as more and more time elapses between the eyewitnesses and the first written transcription (historical oral memory notwithstanding, see Andrew Shryock's work in the tribes of Jordan [*Nationalism and the Genealogical Imagination* (Berkeley: University of California, 1997)]). From the perspective of the proclamation and the applicability of the text in the modern setting in both the minority and majority world of Christianity, such processes cast serious doubt whether we are really dealing with God's Word given in a particular time and space directly connected to the events describes (e.g., the prayers of Ezra 9 and Neh 9) or not. After all, the God of the Hebrews as understood by its New Testament interpreters is a God who, unlike the perennially deceitful Cretans, "does not lie" (Titus 1:2, 12). Scripture is forever "God-breathed" (2 Tim 3:16) and a reliable guide to the one who is himself the way, the truth and the life. In Ezra-Nehemiah, we find remarkable candor on the part of the writers to state clearly when events do not follow the assumed chronological trajectory (Ezra 4, see commentary). When two events could be misconstrued to be one and the same, the text interjects enough clues for the reader to understand there were not one but two reforms regarding foreign wives (see commentary on Neh 8–9).

8. The precise opposite is true in mainstream critical scholarship: the theological underpinnings of the narrative of the Bible is what render the received text highly suspicious. In *On the Reliability of the Old Testament* (Grand Rapids: Eerdmans, 2006) Kitchen argues, successfully in our opinion, that attempts to dichotomize ancient and modern historiographies with the implication that modern "truth" standards are somehow more sophisticated than what ancients viewed as truthful remain unconvincing in light of the corroborating ancient Near Eastern data.

9. See Luther's Bible, *Geschichte*, on Neh 1:1.

We find no compelling reason not to uphold the earliest available Second Temple and Christian traditions that attributed the origins of the account principally to Ezra whenever he is involved and Nehemiah when he is involved, or both. In turn, they relied on the sources provided by Zerubbabel and others in the first return, along with attachments from official Persian records (some of them preserved in Aramaic in the Hebrew text of Ezra-Nehemiah).[10]

## A Tale of Three Kings

EZRA-NEHEMIAH SPANS THE EARLY PART of the Achaemenid/Persian period (early sixth century BC) through the mid-fourth century (433 BC), when a young Macedonian general, Alexander the Great, would stun the world and topple the mighty Persian Empire. The Persian culture was known for its horses. They were expert breeders and supplied the constant equestrian needs of the Assyrian and Babylonian armies in the Mesopotamian lowlands. The Persians were also known for their massive ceremonial cities and columned halls. Spectacular archaeological remains are attested at Anshan (Tall-i Malyan), Pasargadae, Persepolis (including a one-hundred-column hall), and Susa.[11]

Ezra-Nehemiah interacts with three kings and emphasizes their direct intervention in providing the opportunity for the Jews to return to Zion: Cyrus II (also known as Cyrus the Great), Darius the Great, and

---

10. Ezra 4–6 is written in Aramaic in the Hebrew text of Ezra. For a thorough discussion of the Hebrew text and other major textual witnesses (Greek and Aramaic) of Ezra-Nehemiah, see Williamson (*Ezra, Nehemiah*, xxiv–xxxiii). By way of summary, the Hebrew and Aramaic texts emanating from the Ben Asher Tiberian tradition (the "Leningrad Codex") reflect a stable tradition. Therefore, text-critical questions are not addressed unless a significant issue with the MT is encountered, which is not the case in Ezra-Nehemiah. The LXX (the Greek translation of the Old Testament) contains a formal equivalent translation of Ezra-Nehemiah designated 2 Esdras. The well-known matter of significant discrepancies between the account in MT and 2 Esdras does not affect the interpretation of the received text, since these two should be treated as separate traditions.

11. Iran was first excavated by the French in the late 1800s, until other expeditions joined them (the university of Chicago at Persepolis, among others). For a good summary of the history of ancient Iran, See T. Cuyler Young Jr., "The Iranian Migration into the Zargos," *Iran* 5 (1967): 11–34, for an essay on the origins of the Iron Age culture in Iran and the emergence of the Iranian/Median tribes in the Highlands of the Zagros and the lowlands of the Khuzistan plain starting in the mid-second millennium BC.

Artaxerxes.[12] Cyrus the Great (559–530 BC)—the unifier of the Mede and Persian tribes and the conqueror of Babylon (539 BC)—provides the initial impetus with his famous decree (Ezra 1:1–4) that allowed indigenous peoples freedom of religion (within limits) throughout the provinces of the empire. Populations were allowed to worship their gods and rebuild their temples. In his own words: "I returned them unharmed to their cells, in their sanctuary to make them happy." Of course, there were strings attached to this arrangement: "May all the gods whom I settled in their sacred centers ask daily of Bêl and Nâbu that my days be long and may they intercede for my welfare. May they say to Marduk, my lord: 'As for Cyrus, the king who reveres you, and Cambyses, his son, . . .'"[13]

The second Persian king whose involvement had direct impact on the community is Darius the Great (522–486 BC), the great builder of Persepolis and Susa and whose decree (Ezra 6:6–12) jumpstarted and funded the completion of the temple in Jerusalem. The third Persian king of note is Artaxerxes (465–425 BC). He singlehandedly stopped the work of the rebuilding of Zion and singlehandedly decreed its resumption and completion via his trusted servant Nehemiah.[14] King Xerxes (or Ahasuerus; 486–465 BC), the main Persian king in the book of Esther who decrees the annihilation of the Jews, only gets a nod in Ezra-Nehemiah (see 4:6). The mention of the three primary kings and their decrees magnifies the fact that God is truly the King of kings, since these Persian rulers end up doing precisely the bidding of Yahweh to restore worship in Zion.

## Authorship and Date

THE QUESTION OF AUTHORSHIP SEEMS STRAIGHTFORWARD, at least initially. From a literary perspective, since the Hebrew Bible (Masoretic Text)[15] shows Ezra-Nehemiah as one book, it is best that authorship issues treat both books as one. From a chronological perspective the story unfolds

---

12. See chart, "Return of the Exiles."

13. See "Cyrus Cylinder Translation," Livius, https://www.livius.org/sources/content/cyrus-cylinder/cyrus-cylinder-translation/.

14. See commentary on Neh chapter 2. Cf. Amélie Kuhrt, *The Ancient Near East, C. 3000–330 BC*, vol. 2 (New York: Routledge, 1995), 648.

15. Along with the Talmud (b. B. Bat. 15a), and many medieval commentators. N. Amzallag, "Authorship of Ezra and Nehemiah," 271.

naturally with Ezra arriving in Jerusalem first (457 BC) followed by Nehemiah (444 BC) roughly thirteen to fourteen years later. Accordingly, tradition assigns Ezra the authorship of Ezra-Nehemiah, which includes a section commonly designated as the memoirs of Ezra. This includes about two chapters written in the first-person perspective (7:28–9:15) along with the third person (7:1–26; 10). These memoirs of Ezra, as they are commonly designated, therefore, provide some guidance. These facts alone, however, are not enough to assign authorship to Ezra.

As a scribe (7:6) Ezra's profession caused him to deal with documents. Indeed, the book includes various sorts of legal paperwork/archival materials that a scribe/priest such as Ezra could have been supplied by temple or government personnel. Three official pieces of Aramaic correspondence are woven into the narrative with, what appears to be, the intentionality of a careful scribe (4:8–24; 5:1–6:18; 7:12–26). The incorporation of numerous lists with information important to the storyline indicates accessibility of a priest and scribe to such materials. In addition, the first three verses of Ezra are linked with the last two verses in 2 Chronicles.[16] This, likewise, conveys deliberate scribal activity. At the very least, and without compelling evidence to the contrary, applying authorship to Ezra on the internal evidence outlined above certainly seems reasonable.

Likewise, in the book of Nehemiah, the first-person accounts (his memoir) also provide a reasonable clue that these texts came from the hand of Nehemiah (via a secretary). Other texts that do not mention his name could easily belong to him as well but only as official court records, since Nehemiah ultimately answered to the king of Persia for his mission in Yehud (the list in Neh chapter 3 for example). The situation becomes more complex after the memoirs end in Nehemiah 6. Chapter 7 essentially is a recap taken from archives dating back to the time of Zerubabbel. Chapters 8–11 belong to the restoration of worship in Zion, and here the hand of Nehemiah is clearly felt at critical moments (e.g, Neh 8:9; 10:1[10:2]; 12:31). The resumption of the memoir in Nehemiah 13 provides a suitable bookend to the eponymous record: "remember me for *good*," which was

16. Note that the ending of 2 Chr 36:22–23 is repeated word for word in Ezra 1:1–3. There seems to be intentionality in such a repetition linking the story line by a careful writer. For an excellent summary of the relationship between the account in Chronicles and Ezra-Nehemiah, see J. Blenkinopp, *Ezra-Nehemiah*, OTL (Philadelphia: Westminster, 1988), 37–54.

the impetus of chapter 1, where the *good* hand of the Lord was upon him. It seems reasonable to assign a place of preeminence for both Ezra and Nehemiah in the compositional and editorial process that resulted in the final form of the books (around 430 BC) not long after the events.[17]

## Audience: Purpose in Writing

THE TARGET AUDIENCE OF EZRA-NEHEMIAH and the purpose in writing depend on knowing when the book was written. Since we can only surmise when it was written, we must rely on internal evidence as a guide relative to the audience. In general terms, after the return Ezra anticipated that generations of Israelites would benefit from hearing his theological perspective on the historical events that unfolded during this hundred-year period. More specifically, one gets a strong sense that perhaps the renewed worship of the postexilic Jewish community faced challenges as to their way of worship (see Themes below). To that end, the book seems to present not just a record of the events for posterity, but it also seems to offer a defense of sorts. For those in the audience potentially viewing things with a critical eye, Ezra clearly demonstrates to such an audience that the community had the "right" and "authority" to do what they were doing (e.g., Ezra 3:2–4, 7; 4:1–5). The author wants his audience to know that, years of exile notwithstanding, the markers of identity of God's people—possessing the promised land, temple, and torah—were still valid for them.

## Structure and Outline

EZRA 1–6 NARRATES THE FIRST RETURN under Zerubbabel and Joshua (539 BC) through the events leading to the completion of the temple in 515 BC.[18] The first generation, with fits and starts and under the

---

17. For alternate views, we recommend David Noel Freedman, ed., *The Anchor Bible Dictionary*, "The Books of Ezra-Nehemiah" and "Esdras," vol 2 (New York: Doubleday, 1992). We also suggest the exegetical and theological commentary by Mervin Breneman on *Ezra, Nehemiah, Esther* in the New American Commentary series (Nashville: Broadman & Holman, 1993) for a clear presentation of the material. Lastly, H. G. M. Williamson's *Ezra, Nehemiah* (WBC; Nashville: Nelson, 1985), remains a classic to this day in terms of discussion of the critical issues.

18. See chart, "Return of the Exiles 539 BC–444 BC."

prophetic impetus of Haggai and Zechariah, lay the initial foundation of the temple (Ezra 3) culminating in the rebuilt temple (Ezra 6). Renewed worship could not get underway without a rebuilt temple.

The next part of the story takes place some half-century later with the second return under Ezra, the priest and scribe (Ezra 7–10), in 458 BC. His return entailed a reinstatement of the law of God. The temple had been completed, but the people seemed to stagnate without any real sense of purpose. As a student of the law, Ezra frames the return as a new conquest for the reestablishment of worship in Zion. The connection to conquest narratives and the theme of Canaanization at the time of the judges come to a head when Ezra (Ezra 9–10 and Nehemiah) has to deal with marriages with foreign wives (Judg 2–3).[19] Unless the people live in holiness in obedience to God's law, the danger of a new exile and expulsion from Zion is real. Renewed worship cannot be reestablished without a rebuilt temple *and* reestablishment of God's law.

The third part of the Ezra-Nehemiah story focuses on the coming of Nehemiah, the governor emerging on the scene in 444 BC about a decade after Ezra's return to rebuild the city's wall and the sanctity of the city. The setback described in Ezra 4 should be seen as a prime reason for Nehemiah to seek a commission from the king of Persia (the very same king who ordered the work to be stopped in chapter 4!) to rebuild the walls and gates and provide a boost to a demoralized community. To focus solely on the wall rebuilding would be to miss the bigger picture of what Nehemiah, together now with Ezra, is doing in the book: by restoring the sanctity of the acropolis in Jerusalem, Nehemiah is further paving the way for the restoration of worship, the primary theme of Nehemiah 8–12. He builds on the accomplishments described earlier with Zerubbabel and Ezra. The story takes on a decidedly official tone with long lists of carefully vetted Levites, priests, and temple attendants so that the worship of Yahweh can be restored as "prescribed by David the man of God" (Neh 12:24, 36). This tripartite structure of the story shows a panoramic view of renewed worship.

The final part of Ezra-Nehemiah (Neh 13), an epilogue of sorts, is a sad note of failure on the part of Nehemiah (Ezra has by now disappeared from the narrative): the organizational efficiency, unity, and the people's

---

19. Daniel I. Block, *Judges, Ruth*, NAC 6 (Nashville: Broadman & Holman, 1990), 9–14.

commitment not to "neglect the house of our God" (Neh 10:39)—all that good will has now vanished. Nehemiah returns to the province in 432 BC (after his twelve-year term as governor had ended) only to find the people in blatant violation of Sabbath laws, in direct compromise with non-Yahwists (even among the family of the high priest), and engaged in illicit marriages with non-Yahwists (Neh 13). Yet this epologue ends on a note of hope as Nehemiah appeals to Yahweh for "good" (*tobah*, best translated "favor" in this context). Nehemiah's faith-filled hope is that Yahweh will not forget the "good" that he bestowed on Nehemiah, Ezra, and all of what the returnees experienced in rebuilding Zion.

## Themes

### Renewed Worship

EZRA-NEHEMIAH RECORDS ANOTHER RESCUE MISSION not unlike that of the Exodus. Yahweh "saves" Israel from the Persians and brings her back to himself (Ezra 9:9; Ezek 34:12, 22; 36:24–29). Through the assistance of a benevolent foreign king and the surrounding neighbors, this rescue mission unfolds (Ezra 1:6; Exod 12:38). What constitutes the purpose of yet another rescue mission? In a word, worship. As with the first rescue mission in Exodus (e.g., Exod 3:12, 18; 4:23; 5:3; 15:1–21), so here in Ezra, worship of Yahweh remains the goal (e.g., Ezra 1:3; 3:4; 3:10–13). As long as Israel remained in Babylon under Persian rule her service was to a master other than Yahweh (Ezra 9:9; Neh 9:36). Servitude to another master was not an option. In this act of restoration, God is rescuing them for reestablishing relationship. The latter culminates in renewed worship, something powerfully visualized throughout Ezra-Nehemiah, commencing with the rebuilt altar (Ezra 3) and culminating with the rebuilt wall (Neh 12).

At the outset in Ezra, a hunger in their hearts for worship manifests itself with the zeal to give offerings to the Lord even though the temple foundation was not finished. Evidently, this longing for Zion was never fulfilled in exile (Ps 137). Even with the mere completion of the temple foundation, we get a glimpse of what the first worship service was like after exile. Yahweh receives the praise due Yahweh's name, and the witness of their worship was heard from afar (Ezra 3:11,14). Likewise, at the dedication of the completed temple they worshiped by celebrating Passover (6:19–22). The mention of their joyous Passover celebration at this juncture provides further insight relative to the ultimate outcome of the rescue mission: Yahweh at long last receives credit and the honor due Yahweh's name for making it all possible.

Renewed worship, however, requires more than a temple; it demands the law. When Ezra returns, not unlike Moses the first lawgiver, he reinforces *torah* in Jerusalem, and the picture of restoration continues to unfold. On a few occasions the awareness of the law and its standards led the community to a confession of sin. As evidenced by Ezra's and Nehemiah's own actions, true worship incorporates confession (Ezra 9:5–15; 10:1–2; Neh 9:2–37). On another occasion, the awareness of the law gained through Ezra's recitation of it to the community produced worship as well as the celebration of the Feast of Tabernacles (Neh 8:1–8, 18). The reestablishment of the law of God regulates people in their worship.

Finally, the picture of renewed worship would not be complete without securing the sanctity of Zion. The holiness of God is a prevailing theme in Ezra-Nehemiah and will govern the actions of both Ezra and Nehemiah at every turn. To be sure, Nehemiah's efforts with rebuilding the wall provide some measure of protection and safety from physical threats, but one quickly gets the sense that the protection of the sanctity of the precinct supersedes other interests. Accordingly, a substantial role is attributed to the Levitical priesthood (and other "guardians of holiness") at key junctures of the restoration. The fitting climactic end to the project is a priestly led procession (in effect, a large praise and worship service) at the dedication of the wall (Neh 12:27–46). The witness, through worship, reverberated beyond Jerusalem (Neh 12:43). Thus, rebuilding the temple, reinstating the law, repairing the wall, and rebuilding the gates all serve to renew the authentic and pristine worship of Yahweh once again (the ultimate purpose of God's rescue mission in Exodus and now here).

The concern for renewed worship has several sub-themes. The eagerness of "all the people" (see Neh 8:1) to do things by the book surfaces (i.e., "in accordance with the Law of Moses," and "as prescribed by David king of Israel"; see Ezra 3:2, 4, 10; Neh 12:36; 45–46). The sacred tradition legitimizes the present worship. Seldom in Israelite history do we have recorded moments when the Israelites are trying to do things "by the book," let alone weeping when hearing words from the *torah* (Ezra 10:1; Neh 8). Thus, if anyone would challenge the form of worship adopted by the returnees, they are grounded in the traditions of the past. When authority issues do appear in the narrative (mostly by the enemies of Zion), we are repeatedly reminded that actions taken (both physical and spiritual) were in fact backed by both the highest temporal and spiritual authorities in the land (the king of Persia and the "King of kings," Yahweh).

The sub-theme of exclusion versus inclusion likewise fits within the larger context of the restoration of sacred worship in accordance with the equally sacred written traditions. Some of the drastic measures taken to restore the sanctity of Zion are congruent with the need for purity and holiness in worship. In fact, the way Ezra and Nehemiah allow for the handling of the unfaithfulness in Ezra 10 and the harsh "separation" of the women and children parallels the warning connected with failure to remove the land of its uncleanness (Deuteronomy 7:1–11). While the context is evidently quite different, some of the actions taken can be framed as a reenactment of possessing the land according to the trajectory of Deuteronomy 30. Only now, the project is limited to the restoration of the cult in Zion, rather than a full program of territorial conquest, as was the case in the original mandate.

## Renewed Worship and the Promise of Zion

THE THEOLOGICAL IMPETUS FOR RENEWED WORSHIP in Ezra-Nehemiah falls in line with the initial intervention of Yahweh in causing Cyrus to issue his decree in 539 BC. This follows the divine plan for the reestablishment of Zion as forecasted by the prophets, among whom the prophecies of Isaiah find preeminence with all things pertaining to the restoration of Zion (see Isa 1–2).[20] Isaiah places a strong emphasis on the sovereignty of Yahweh over kings, both during the Neo-Assyrian period of domination in the eighth century (the beginning of the emergence of Babylon with Merodach-Baladan; see Isa 39), and in the distant future (the advent of *koresh* [Heb.]/Cyrus, who is presented as the temporal liberator of Zion; see Isa 44:28; 45:1).

The prophetic vehicle kept the hope of renewed worship alive and closed the gap between their difficult circumstances and the realities tied to their theological history. Israelite history portrayed in Ezra-Nehemiah represents fulfilled prophecy (Ezra 1:1) because of the sovereignty of God (i.e., 1:1, 5; 5:5, 6:14; 7:27; Neh 2:8; 20, 4:15, 20; 6:16).

---

20. For a helpful introduction to the Zion tradition, see Jon D. Levenson, *Sinai & Zion: An Entry Into The Jewish Bible* (San Francisco: HarperCollins, 1985).

Ezra-Nehemiah grounds that hope in the reestablishment of worship in Zion by restoring the sanctity of the site that has been defiled by a broken-down temple, enclosure, and the reproach of the people (Isa 58:12). This advances God's promises. The actions of Zerubbabel, Joshua, Ezra, and Nehemiah in the ensuing events betray a profound awareness of Zion's place in redemptive history. By restoring pure worship now, the leaders in Judah are by implication preparing for the future of Zion, when the Davidic King will return to Zion (Jer 33).

### Renewed Worship and Opposition

ALTHOUGH RENEWED WORSHIP BECOMES A REALITY and fulfills prophetic expectations for Zion, it entails serious opposition from the enemies of God's people. Ezra-Nehemiah reveals a series of starts and fits giving way to a dominant theme of opposition. Although the temple was rebuilt (Ezra 6:14–15), a conclusion to the events of chapters 1–6, it entailed great opposition and took a long time. While acceleration relative to God's promises has taken place, overcoming external obstacles remained a reality; so the plot thickens and includes stories showing serious setbacks. In this regard the external opposition emphasized in several chapters (4–6) plays a key role in the story line. The outcome of the return and rebuilt temple (renewed worship) must be understood against the backdrop of opposition. Indeed, triumphing through opposition only served to magnify the sovereignty of God and underline the victory. There was triumph and advancement but through opposition.

Although the law was restored in Jerusalem under Ezra's leadership as both priest and scribe it, likewise, involved opposition. The shock, however, concerns the internal nature of the opposition and another conflict in the plot. The returnees, by their marriage alliances with foreigners, directly opposed the law of God and Ezra's efforts to end that. The outcome of the law being restored in Jerusalem must be understood against the background of opposition. While the law was going forth from Jerusalem once again, another critical marker of identity, some of God's people opposed it by their actions. The irony is that despite the physical restoration graciously afforded them, theologically and spiritually speaking God's people were still in exile. Indeed, a renewed threat about the promises of God looms large in the book's closing scene. Some of the leadership were involved in an unexcusable faithlessness to God's law (Ezra 9:1–2; 9:13–15; 10:14). The future of God's people hangs in the balance yet the unresolved threat paves the way for more of redemptive history to unfold.

Although the city wall was completed, the work done with the help of God under Nehemiah's leadership (Neh 6:15–16), it too entailed fierce external opposition from the outset (Neh 2:19). The goal, as with the temple, was to stop the work on the wall through intimidation, fear, and threats of violence (Neh 4:1–3, 7–8, 11). The climate of opposition continues in earnest during Nehemiah's leadership. The opposition by neighboring governors and officials underscores how isolated and precarious the situation of the community of God's people was during the Persian period: they are literally surrounded and opposed on all sides. Any attitude or action that represents a threat to their neighbors is sure to elicit a prompt and sometimes forceful response (Ezra 4). Like Ezra, Nehemiah faced internal opposition with the slide again toward disobedience to God's law (Neh 13:23, 29). Nehemiah's official role as the new governor completes what Ezra, the priest and scribe, started. Thus the book highlights both internal and external opposition to restoration of the temple, law, and walls in Jerusalem. Progression and regression, advancement and obstacles provide an interpretive framework for the reader.

Although advancement of God's promises is achieved, resistance in the restoration process was likewise a reality and to be expected. In the context of articulating blessings to Abraham, God also warned of outward opposition toward those goals, that there would be those who curse his people (Gen 12:1–3). With the warning, though, came God's assurance that he would personally deal with all opposition. Thus, the theological history of Israel's restoration described in Ezra-Nehemiah does not downplay resistance but shows that God met human resistance with divine resistance and assistance enabling God's people to prosper and God's promises to advance.[21] Yet as good as these advancements were, more was needed. God's people still have sin and guilt issues even though serious "house cleanings" took place. The exile really did not fix much. The heart remains a problem, and there exists no king. Ezra-Nehemiah prepares the way for the return to Zion of the King who alone establishes an eternal, pure, and holy worship of the living God (Revelation 21–22).

21. This represents fulfilled prophecy (Ezra 1:1).

# Persian Empire

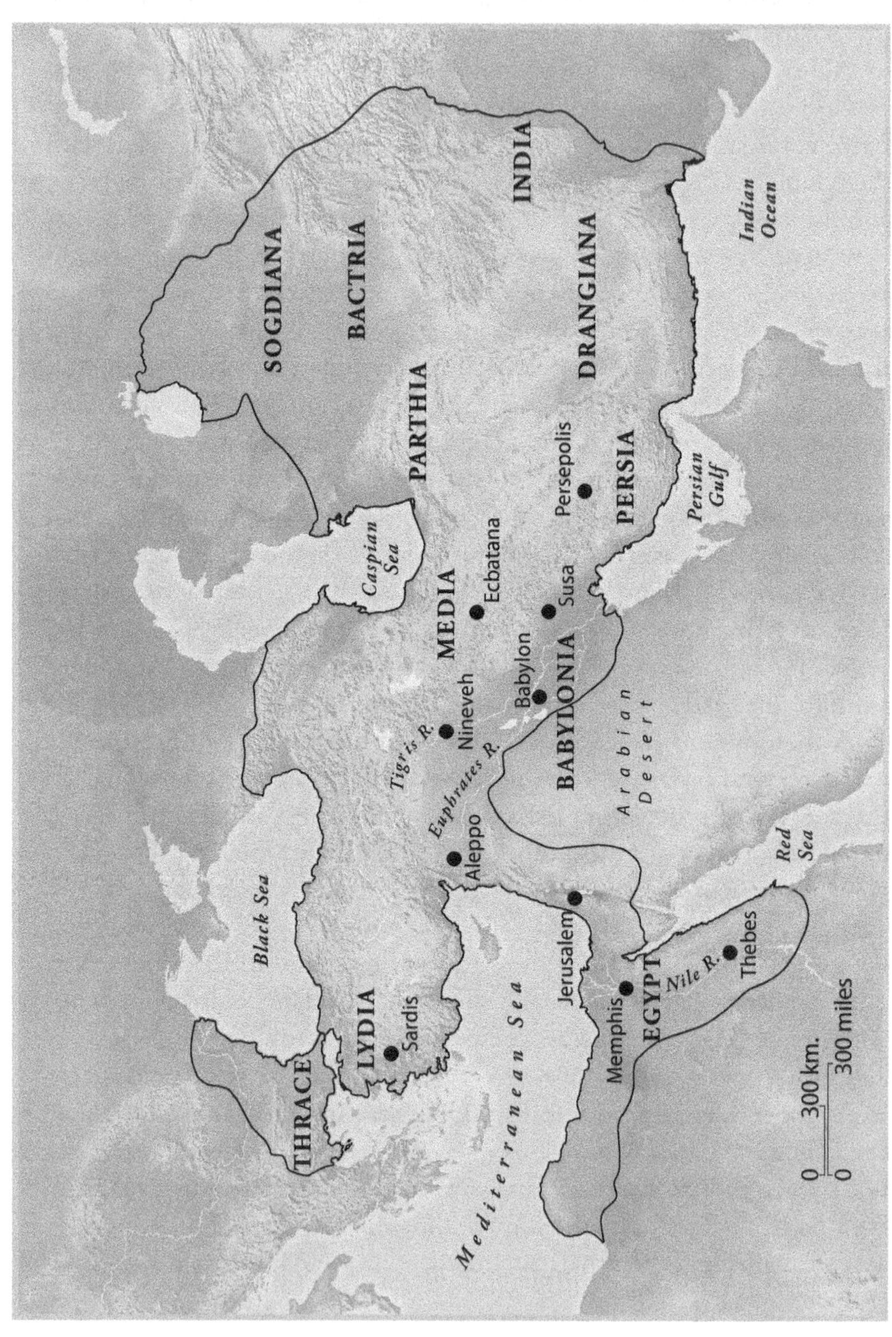

# Province of Yehud

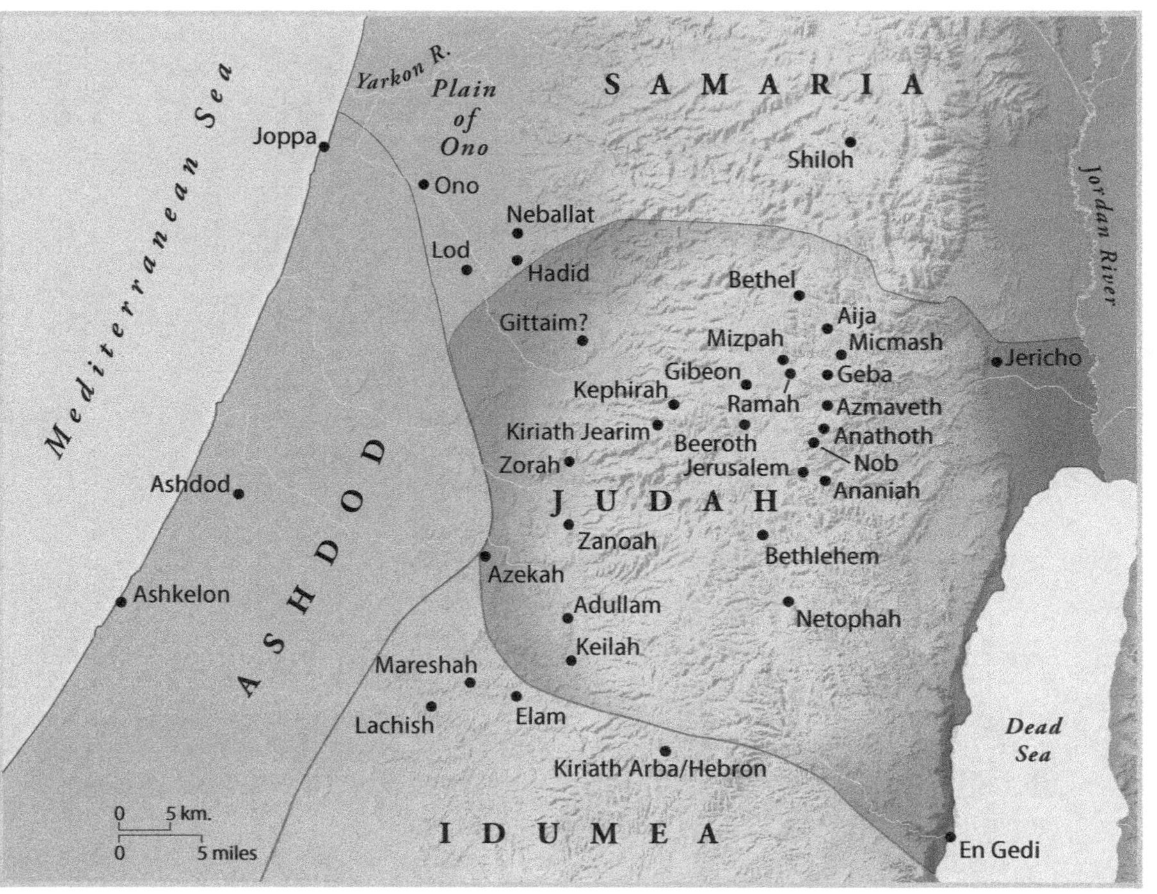

# Nehemiah's Walls

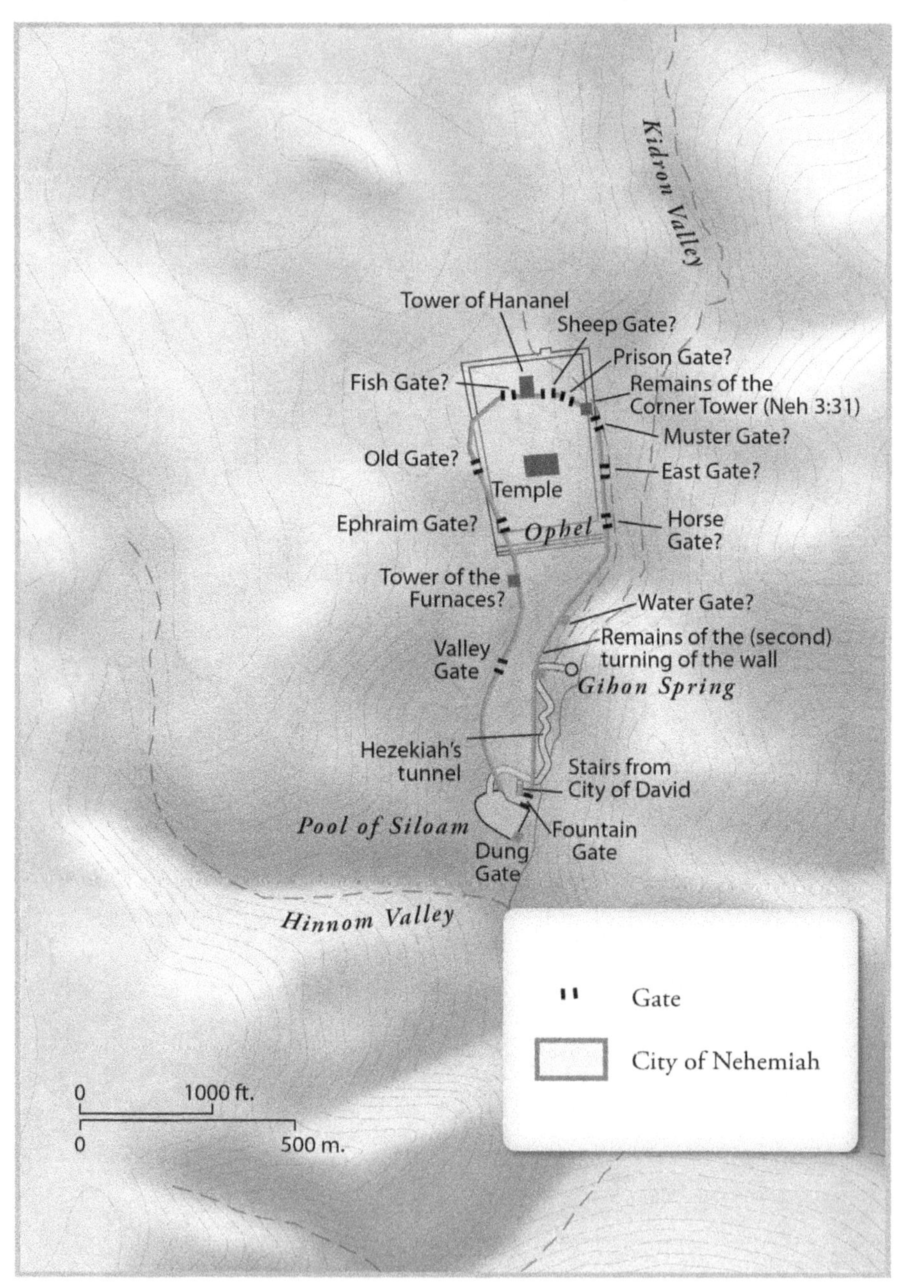

# Jerusalem at the time of Nehemiah

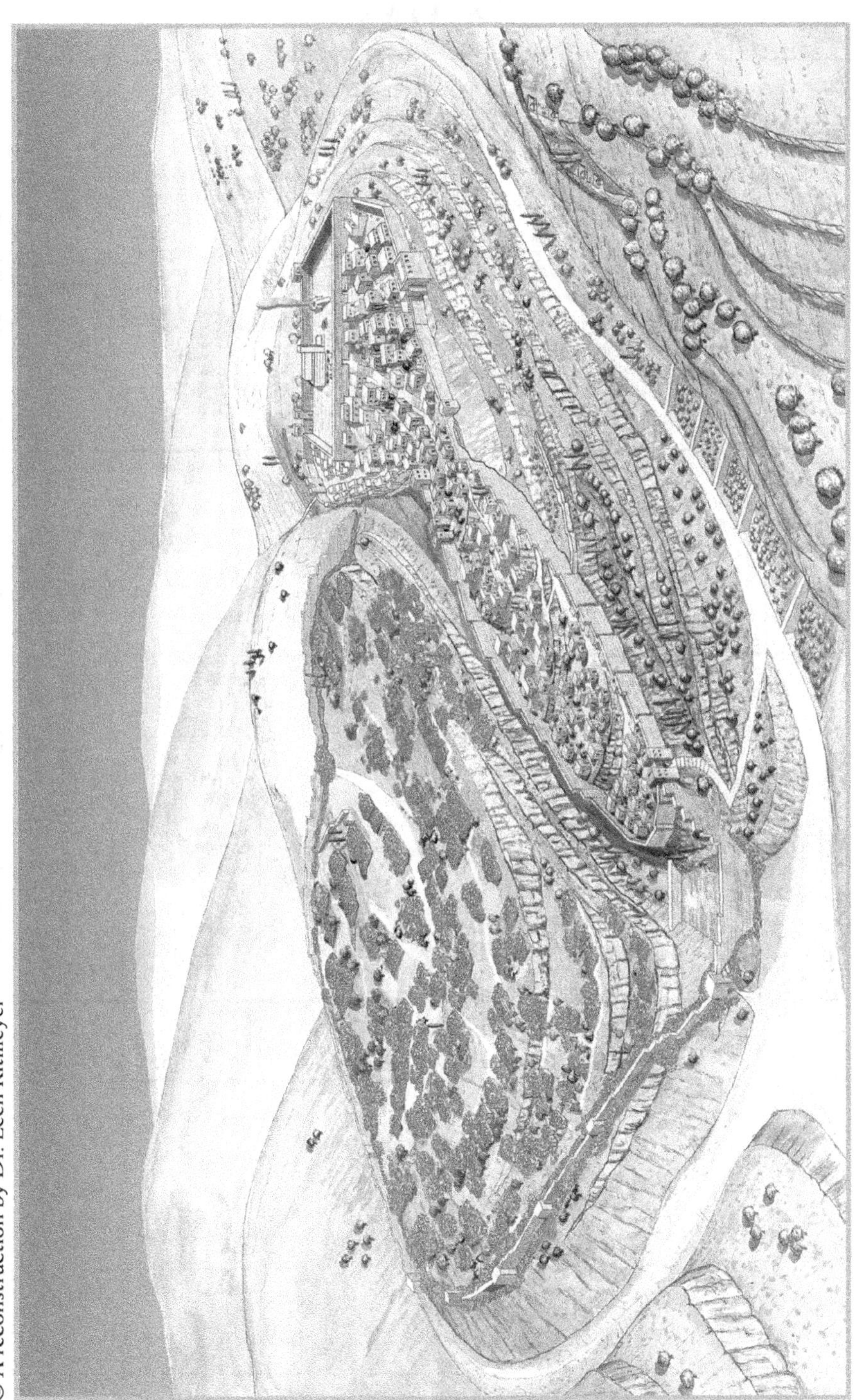

# Timeline: The Return of the Exiles
# 539–444 BC

| 560–530 | | 530–520 | 520–490 | 480–470 | 460–450 | 450–440 | 430 |
|---|---|---|---|---|---|---|---|
| FIRST RETURN<br>Exiled living in Persia<br>Cyrus Issues Decree 539 BC<br>For exiled to return to Jerusalem and rebuild the temple (the Cyrus Cylinder)<br>**Sheshbazzar**<br>Governor of Judah Ezra 5:14<br>Brought up People Ezra 1:11<br>42,360 exiles plus 7,337 servants<br>Laid temple foundation 537 BC<br>Ezra 5:16<br>**Zerubbabel**<br>-Also came on first return<br>-Rebuilt altar Ezra 3:2<br>-Feast of Tabernacles<br>-Laid temple foundation 537 BC<br>Ezra 3:8<br>Opposition 536 BC<br>People of land frustrate their purpose until reign of Darius<br>Ezra 4:4–5 | | OPPOSITION<br>Temple restoration ceases for 16 years (536–520 BC)<br>People of the land discourage Jews from building Ezra 4:4<br>Jews become preoccupied with building own houses and commerce Hag 1:4 | BUILDING RESUMES<br>**Haggai and Zechariah**<br>Prophets urge Yehud to complete the task<br>During this time the people are more concerned with building their own homes and pursuing their commercial endeavors than with building and finishing God's house<br>In 510 BC they prophesy: Finish the temple Ezra 5:1<br>Building begins 520 B.C. Ezra 5:2<br>Tatteni sends letter of opposition to Darius Ezra 5:3<br>Search for original documents<br>Cyrus edict found Ezra 6:1–5<br>Darius issues decree for Yehud to complete the rebuilding Ezra 6:6–12<br>Temple completed 516 BC Ezra 6:14<br>Temple dedicated Ezra 6:16–17<br>Passover<br>Unleavened bread Ezra 6:19–22 | ESTHER<br>The story of Esther and King Ahasuerus/Xerxes 483–471 BC<br>Ahasuerus divorces Vashti<br>King marries Esther<br>Haman, ancestral enemy, promoted by Xerxes<br>Decree to annihilate Jews<br>Esther- counter decree<br>Mordecai promoted<br>In the beginning of Ahaseurus's reign, the people of the land wrote an accusation against Judah and Jerusalem<br>Ezra 4:6 | 2[ND] RETURN 458 BC<br>**Ezra** Returns with:<br>-1500<br>-38 Levites<br>-220 helpers<br>-Journey 8½ months<br>Ezra's Mission:<br>-Make inquiries of Judah<br>-Deliver gold and silver<br>-Avert wrath of God from king and sons<br>Ezra 7:14<br>-Judge and appoint judges<br>Ezra 7:25<br>-Bring Law and teach people<br>Ezra 7:10, 25<br>-Dissolve mixed marriages<br>Ezra 10 | OPPOSITION<br>Opposition to building wall<br>-Sometime between Ezra and Nehemiah 458–444 BC (closer to 444 BC)<br>Ezra 4:7-23<br>Letter sent to king<br>Walls being rebuilt<br>Jerusalem a rebellious city, Artaxerxes orders building of walls to stop<br>Hanani and men of Judah tell Nehemiah of the condition of the walls<br>Neh 1:1–3 | 3[RD] RETURN<br>445 BC<br>**Nehemiah** prays and fasts for God's favor in regard to Jerusalem<br>Nehemiah gets permission to return to Jerusalem<br>444 BC<br>Nehemiah returns to rebuild walls of Jerusalem<br>444 BC<br>Walls are completed in 52 days<br>Post 432 BC<br>Final Reforms |
| **Cyrus** 559–530 BC | | **Cambyses** 530–522 BC | **Darius** 522–486 BC | **Xerxes** 486–465 BC | **Artaxerxes I Longimanus** 465–425 BC | | |
| 559 BC King of Anshan<br>550 BC Controls Median territories<br>547 BC Conquers Lydia<br>539 BC Controls Babylon<br>-Restored gods to their temples and exiles back to their homelands<br>-Dominated Mesopotamia<br>-Died in battle in northern frontier<br>-Isaiah prophesied his reign 200 years prior (Isa 44:45) | | Inherited throne from Cyrus<br>Conquered Egypt<br>Committed suicide on return to Babylon | Served in army under Cyrus and Cambyses<br>Suppressed rebellion within Persian empire<br>Great law giver of the Persians<br>Reorganized empire<br>Susa and Persepolis building projects<br>Granted permission to resume building temple in Jerusalem<br>Persia's most capable leader | Son of Darius<br>Also called Ahasuerus<br>Defeated by Greece<br>Inferior military leader<br>City builder<br>Assassinated by Artabanus<br>Husband of Esther | Seized father's throne through assassination disposed of other aspirants to the throne<br>Suppressed rebellion in Egypt and Syria<br>Negotiated treaty with Athens<br>Released Ezra and Nehemiah to Journey back to Jerusalem during his reign | | |

Adapted from and used by permission of the School of Biblical Studies, University of the Nations.

# OUTLINE

- **I. The First Return: Zerubbabel/Sheshbazzar Restore the Temple (1:1–6:22)**
  - A. Fulfillment of Prophecy (1:1–11)
    1. Cyrus's Proclamation: The Hope and Help (1:1–4)
    2. The Response to Cyrus's Proclamation (1:5–11)
  - B. The People Returning to Jerusalem (2:1–70)
    1. Those with Documentary Proof of Descending from Israel (2:1–58)
    2. Those without Documentary Proof of Descending from Israel (2:59–70)
  - C. The Rebuilding Begins (3:1–13)
    1. The Altar Rebuilt (3:1–6)
    2. The Temple Foundation Rebuilt (3:7–13)
  - D. Opposition to the Rebuilding (4:1–24)
    1. Opposition under Cyrus's Reign (4:1–5, 24)
    2. Later Opposition under Xerxes and Artaxerxes: Work Ceases (4:6–24)
  - E. Rebuilding Resumes and Temple Completed (5:1–6:22)
    1. Haggai and Zechariah Motivate People: Work Resumes but Is Challenged (5:1–5)
    2. Investigation Pursued (5:6–17)
    3. Evidence Found and Response to Investigation by Darius (6:1–12)
    4. The Temple Rebuilt and Celebration (6:13–22)
- **II. The Second Return: Ezra Restores the Law (7:1–10:44)**
  - A. Ezra Comes to Jerusalem (7:1–28)
    1. Ezra's Background and Commission (7:1–10)
    2. A Letter Legitimizing Ezra's Return (7:11–28)
  - B. The People Returning with Ezra and the Journey (8:1–36)
    1. List of Returning Families (8:1–14)
    2. The Journey: Problems and Preparations (8:15–20)
    3. The Solution about Safety and Finances and their Safe Arrival (8:21–36)

C. Marriage Problems and Ezra's Response (9:1–15)
    1. Ezra Mourns and Confesses Corporate Sin (9:1–15)
D. The People's Response to Ezra's Prayer of Confession (10:1–44)
    1. Confessions of Unfaithfulness in Community and Action Taken (10:1–17)
    2. The Guilty Parties (10:18–44)

**III. The Third Return: Nehemiah Restores the Walls and Sanctity of Zion (Neh 1:1–13:31)**

A. Nehemiah's Prayer (1:1–11)
    1. The Setting (1:1–4)
    2. The Prayer (1:5–11)
B. Nehemiah's Commission (2:1–8)
C. Initial Impressions in Jerusalem (2:9–20)
D. The Rebuilding of the Gates and Repairing the Walls (3:1–32)
    1. Sheep Gate (3:1–2)
    2. Fish Gate (3:3–5)
    3. Jeshanah Gate (3:6–12)
    4. Valley, Dung, and Fountain Gates (3:13–15)
    5. Wall Repairs (3:16–32)
E. Physical Threat (4:1–23)
    1. Sanballat's Brinksmanship (4:1–3)
    2. Nehemiah's Corporate Prayer (4:4–6)
    3. Escalation of the Crisis (4:7–9)
    4. Nehemiah's Address to the Community: Remember and Fight! (4:10–15)
    5. Total Commitment (4:16–23)
F. Internal Threat (5:1–19)
    1. Three Famine-Related Problems (5:1–5)
    2. Nehemiah Resolves the Dispute with the Tribal Leadership (5:6–13)
    3. Two Examples of Nehemiah's Integrity as Governor (5:14–19)
G. Personal Threat (6:1–19)
    1. Intimidation and Distraction Tactics from Sanballat and Geshem (6:1–4)
    2. Accusation of Sedition (6:5–9)
    3. Tobiah the Godfather (6:10–15)

4. Victory (6:16)
5. Post-Scriptum: Letters of Intimidation by the Nobles of Judah (6:17–19)

H. Genealogical Record (7:1–73a)
1. Completing the Task of Securing Zion (7:1–3)
2. Divine Initiative to Register People (7:4–5)
3. List of Returnees (7:6–73a)

I. Covenant Renewal (7:73b–8:18)
1. Reading of the Law (7:73b–8:8)
2. Holy Day of Celebration (8:9–12)
3. The Feast of Booths is Observed (8:13–18)

J. Historical Retrospective (9:1–37)
1. Call to Worship (9:1–6)
2. The Covenant with Abraham (9:7–8)
3. Exodus (9:9–11)
4. Sinai (9:12–15)
5. The People's Arrogance and Yahweh's *Hesed* (9:16–18)
6. Wilderness (9:19–21)
7. Conquest and Settlement (9:22–25)
8. The Time of the Judges as Paradigm of Israelite History (9:26–31)
9. Confession: We Have Acted Unfaithfully While You Have Been Righteous (9:32–35)
10. Petition: We Are Slaves! (9:36–37)

K. Covenant Ratification (9:38–10:39)
1. The Binding Agreement (9:38)
2. The List of Signatories (10:1–27)
3. The Rest of the People Join in (10:28–29)
4. Promise to Maintain their Own Sanctity (10:30–31)
5. Promise to Maintain the Sanctity of Zion (10:32–39)

L. Resettling the Land (11:1–36)
1. Summary of the Resettlement of the Holy City and the Land (11:1–3)
2. Judah and Benjamin (11:4–9)
3. The Priests (11:10–14)
4. The Levites and the Gatekeepers (11:15–19)
5. Other Temple Attendants (11:20–24)
6. Allotments in the Province (11:25–36)

M. Lineage of Priests and Levites (12:1–26)
N. Dedication of the Wall and Restoration of Worship (12:27–13:3)
   1. Celebration and Dedication of the Walls (12:27–43)
   2. Securing the Ongoing Support for the House of the Lord (12:44–47)
   3. One Final Warning about Their Hostile Neighbors (13:1–3)
O. Nehemiah's Final Attempts at Reform (13:4–31)
   1. Dealing with Eliashib (13:4–9)
   2. Restoring the Support of the House (13:10–14)
   3. Restoring the Sanctity of Zion and of the Sabbath (13:15–22)
   4. Restoring the Sanctity of Marriage (13:23–27)
   5. Restoring the Sanctity of the Priesthood (13:28–31)

# Select Bibliography


### Commentaries

Allen, Leslie C. and Timothy S. Laniak. *Ezra, Nehemiah, Esther.* UBCS. Grand Rapids: Baker Books, 2003.

Beale, G. K. *Revelation: A Shorter Commentary.* Grand Rapids: Eerdmans, 2015.

Blenkinsopp, Joseph. *Ezra-Nehemiah.* OTL. Philadelphia: Westminster, 1988.

Block, Daniel I. *Judges, Ruth.* NAC 6. Nashville: Broadman & Holman, 1990.

Boda, Mark J. *Haggai, Zechariah.* NIVAC 9. Grand Rapids: Zondervan, 2004.

Breneman, Mervin. *Ezra, Nehemiah, Esther.* NAC 10. Nashville: Broadman & Holman, 1993.

Carson, D.A. *The Gospel According to John.* PNTC. Leicester: Apollos, 1991.

Hill, Andrew. *1 & 2 Chronicles.* NIVAC. Grand Rapids: Zondervan, 2003.

Keil, Karl F, and Sophia Taylor. *The Books of Ezra, Nehemiah, and Esther.* Sydney, Australia: Wentworth Press, 2016.

Kidner, Derek. *Ezra and Nehemiah.* TOTC 12. Downers Grove, IL: InterVarsity Press, 1979.

Kline, Meredith G. *Genesis: A New Commentary.* Peabody: Hendricksen, 2016.

Rudolph, Wilhelm. *Esra and Nehemia.* HAT 20. Tübingen: Mohr, 1949.

Selman, Martin J. *1& 2 Chronicles.* TOTC. Downers Grove, IL: InterVarsity Press, 1994.

Shepherd, David J. and Christopher J. H. Wright. *Ezra and Nehemiah.* THOTC. Grand Rapids: Eerdmans, 2018.

Smith, Gary V. *Ezra, Nehemiah, Esther.* CBC. Carol Stream, IL: Tyndale House, 2010.

Steinmann, Andrew E. *Ezra and Nehemiah.* Concordia Commentary. St. Louis, MO: Concordia, 2010.

Wenham, Gordon J. *Genesis 1–15.* WBC 1. Waco, TX: Word, 1987.

Williamson, H. G. M. *Ezra, Nehemiah.* WBC 16. Waco, TX: Word, 1985.

### Other Studies

Albertz, Rainer. *Israel in Exile: The History and Literature of the Sixth Century B.C.E.* Atlanta: Society of Biblical Literature, 2004.

Alexander, T. Desmond. *From Paradise to the Promised Land: An Introduction to the Pentateuch.* Grand Rapids: Baker Academic, 2012.

Baltzer, Klaus. "Moses Servant of God and the Servants: Text and Tradition in the Prayer of Nehemiah (Neh 1:5–11)." Pages 125–29 in *The Future of Early Christianity.* Edited by Birger A. Pearson. Philadelphia: Fortress, 1991.

Beaulieu, Paul-Alain. "Yahwistic Names in Light of Late Babylonian Onomastics." Page 247 in *Judah and the Judeans in the Achaemenid Period: Negotiating Identity in an International Context.* Edited by Oded Lipschits, Gary N. Knoppers, and Manfred Oeming. Winona Lake, IN: Eisenbrauns, 2011.

Boda, Mark J., and Paul L. Redditt, eds. *Unity and Disunity in Ezra-Nehemiah: Redaction, Rhetoric, and Reader.* Sheffield: Sheffield Phoenix, 2008.

Brecht, Martin. *Martin Luther: A Bibliography.* 3 volumes. Philadelphia: Fortress, 1993–1999.

Briant, Pierre. *From Cyrus to Alexander: A History of the Persian Empire.* Winona Lake, IN: Eisenbrauns, 2002.

Bunyan, John. *The Pilgrim's Progress.* New York: Penguin, 2008.

Burge, Gary M., and Andrew E. Hill, eds. *The Baker Illustrated Bible Commentary.* Grand Rapids: Baker Books, 2012.

Carter, Charles E. *The Emergence of Yehud in the Persian Period: A Social and Demographic Study.* JSOT 294. Sheffield: Sheffield Academic, 1999.

Casting Crowns. *Lifesong.* Beach Street/Reunion, 2005, CD.

Corey, Barry H. "Anchored in the Word." *Biola* (Winter 2018): 6.

______. "Conviction, Courage and Civility: Three Virtues for a Virtriolic Age." *Biola* (Summer 2016): 6.

Cowles, C. S, Eugene H. Merrill, Daniel L. Gard, and Tremper Longman. *Show Them No Mercy: 4 Views on God and Canaanite Genocide.* Edited by Stanley N. Gundry. Grand Rapids: Zondervan, 2003.

Cunningham, Loren, with Janice Rogers. *Is That Really You, God? Hearing the Voice of God.* Grand Rapids: Chosen Books, 1984.

______. *The Book that Transforms Nations: The Power of the Bible to Change Any Country.* Seattle, WA: YWAM Publishing, 2007.

Currid, John D. and David P. Barrett. *Crossway ESV Bible Atlas.* Wheaton: Crossway, 2010.

De Wette, Wilhelm Martin Leberecht. *Beitrage zur Einleitung in das Alte Testament*. 2 vols. Halle: Schimmelpfennig, 1806, 1807.

Dearman, John Andrew. *Studies in the Mesha Inscription and Moab*. Atlanta: Scholars Press, 1989.

Dobbs-Allsopp, F. W. *Weep O Daughter of Zion: A Study of the City-Lament Genre in the Hebrew Bible*. Rome: Biblical Institute Press, 1993.

Fee, Gordon D. and Douglas Stuart. *How to Read the Bible for All Its Worth*. 3rd ed. Grand Rapids: Zondervan, 2003.

Fensham, Charles. *The Books of Ezra and Nehemiah*. NICNT. Grand Rapids: Eerdmans, 1982.

Fried, L. S. "Something There is That Doesn't Love a Wall: The Crisis Created by the Wall Around Jerusalem." *Transeuphratène* 39 (2010): 83–84.

Grabbe, Lester L. *A History of the Jews and Judaism in the Second Temple Period Volume I*. New York: T&T Clark, 2004.

Green, J. "Did God Dwell in the Second Temple? Clarifying the Relationship Between Theophany and Temple Dwelling." *JETS* 61.4 (2018): 767–84.

Greer, Jonathan S., John W. Hilber, and John H. Walton, eds. *Behind the Scenes of the Old Testament: Cultural, Social, and Historical Contexts*. Grand Rapids: Baker Academic, 2018.

Jenson, Philip P. *Graded Holiness: A Key to the Priestly Conception of the World*. JSOT 106. Sheffield: JSOT Press, 1992.

Johnson, M. D. *The Purpose of the Biblical Genealogies*. Cambridge: Cambridge University Press, 1969.

Jones, S. *The Archaeology of Ethnicity*. London: Routledge, 1997.

Kaiser, Walter C. and Paul D. Wegner. *A History of Israel. From the Bronze Age through the Jewish Wars*. Revised Edition. Nashville: Broadman and Holman, 2016.

Kitchen, K. A. *On the Reliability of the Old Testament*. Grand Rapids: Eerdmans, 2003.

Klein, Ralph W. "Ezra-Nehemiah, Book of." *ABD* 2. New York: Doubleday, 1992.

Kline, Meredith G. *By Oath Consigned: A Reinterpretation of the Covenant Signs of Circumcision and Baptism*. Grand Rapids: Eerdmans, 1968.

Knoppers, Gary N. "Intermarriage, Social Complexity, and Ethnic Diversity in the Genealogy of Judah." *JBL* 120.1 (2001): 15–20.

________. *Jews and Samaritans: The Origins and History of Their Early Relations*. Oxford: Oxford University Press, 2013.

Kooiman, W. J. *Luther and the Bible*. Translated by John Schmidt. Philadelphia: Muhlenberg, 1961.

Kuhrt, Amélie. *The Ancient Near East, C. 3000–330 BC*. Vol. 2. New York: Routledge, 1995.

Levenson, Jon D. *Sinai and Zion: An Entry into the Jewish Bible*. San Francisco: HarperCollins, 1985.

Lints, Richard. *Identity and Idolatry: The Image of God and Its Inversion*. Downers Grove, IL: IVP Academic, 2015.

Livius, "Tacitus on the Christians," *Livius*, http://www.livius.org/sources/content/tacitus/tacitus-on-the-christians/.

MacDonald, Burton. *East of the Jordan: Territories and Sites of the Hebrew Scriptures*. Alexandria, VA: American Schools of Oriental Research, 2001.

Marshall, Paul, Lela Gilbert, and Nina Shea. *Persecuted: The Global Assault on Christians*. Nashville: Nelson, 2013.

McConville, J. G. "Ezra-Nehemiah and the Fulfillment of Prophecy." *VT* 36 (1986): 205–24.

McRaven, William H. *Spec Ops Case Studies in Special Operations Warfare: Theory and Practice*. New York: Random House, 1995.

Metaxas, Eric. *Martin Luther: The Man who Rediscovered God and Changed the World*. New York: Viking, 2017.

Motyer, J. Alec. *The Revelation of the Divine Name*. London: Tyndale Press, 1959.

Na'aman, Nadav. "Text and Archaeology in a Period of Great Decline: The Contribution of the Amarna Letters to the Debate on the Historicity of Nehemiah's Wall." Pages 20–30 in *The Historian and the Bible: Essays in Honour of Lester L. Grabbe*. Edited by Philip R. Davies and Diana V. Edelman. LHBOTS 530. New York: Bloomsbury, 2010.

Petter, Thomas. *The Land Between Two Rivers: Early Israelite Identities in Central Transjordan*. Winona Lake, IN: Eisenbrauns, 2014.

________. "Tribes and Nomads in the Iron Age Levant" in *Behind the Scenes of the Old Testament*. Edited by Jonathan S. Greer, John W. Hilber, and John H. Walton. Grand Rapids: Baker, 2018.

Pittman, Holly. "Susa." Pages 106–10 in *The Oxford Encyclopedia of Archeology in the Near East*. Edited by Eric M. Meyers. New York: Oxford University Press, 1997.

Pratico, Gary D., and Miles V. Van Pelt. *Basics of Biblical Hebrew*. Grand Rapids: Zondervan, 2001.

Pritchard, James B., ed. *The Ancient Near East: An Anthology of Texts and Pictures*. Princeton: Princeton University Press, 2011.

Revell, E. J. *The Designation of the Individual: Expressive Usage in Biblical Narrative*. Kampen: Kok Pharos, 1997.

Sakenfeld, Katharine D. *The Meaning of Hesed in the Bible: A New Inquiry*. Eugene, OR: Wipf & Stock, 2002.

Shryock, Andrew. *Nationalism and the Genealogical Imagination: Oral History and Textual Authority in Tribal Jordan*. Berkeley: University of California Press, 1997.

Smith, Ron. *Hooked on the Word: Changing Your Life through Bible Meditation*. Lakeside, MT: West Shore Books, 1994.

Sparks, Kenton. *Ethnicity and Identity in Ancient Israel*: Prolegomena to the Study of Ethnic Sentiments and Their Expression in the Hebrew Bible. Winona Lake, IN: Eisenbrauns, 1998.

Vincent, L.-H. "L'étendue de Jerusalem." Page 121 in *La Palestine A L'Epoque Perse*. Edited by E.-M. Laperrousaz and A. Lemaire. Paris: Editions du Cerf, 1994.

Warfield, Benjamin B. "Our Seminary Curriculum." *The Presbyterian* (September 15, 1909): 7–8. Repr., Page 369 of Vol. 1 in *Benjamin B. Warfield: Selected Shorter Writings*. Edited by John E. Meeter. 2 Vols. Phillipsburg, NJ: Presbyterian & Reformed, 2001.

Wright, Jacob L. *Rebuilding Identity: The Nehemiah-Memoir and its Earliest Readers*. BZAW 348. Berlin: de Gruyter, 2005.

Young, T. Cuyler "The Iranian Migration into the Zagros." *Iran* 5 (1967): 11–34.

# Ezra 1:1–11

1 In the first year of Cyrus king of Persia, in order to fulfill
the word of the LORD spoken by Jeremiah, the LORD moved
the heart of Cyrus king of Persia to make a proclamation
throughout his realm and also to put it in writing:

> 2 "This is what Cyrus king of Persia says:
> "'The LORD, the God of heaven, has given me all
> the kingdoms of the earth and he has appointed me to
> build a temple for him at Jerusalem in Judah. 3 Any of
> his people among you may go up to Jerusalem in Judah
> and build the temple of the LORD, the God of Israel, the
> God who is in Jerusalem, and may their God be with
> them. 4 And in any locality where survivors may now
> be living, the people are to provide them with silver
> and gold, with goods and livestock, and with freewill
> offerings for the temple of God in Jerusalem.'"

5 Then the family heads of Judah and Benjamin, and
the priests and Levites—everyone whose heart God had
moved—prepared to go up and build the house of the LORD
in Jerusalem. 6 All their neighbors assisted them with articles
of silver and gold, with goods and livestock, and with valuable
gifts, in addition to all the freewill offerings.

7 Moreover, King Cyrus brought out the articles belonging
to the temple of the LORD, which Nebuchadnezzar had carried
away from Jerusalem and had placed in the temple of his god.
8 Cyrus king of Persia had them brought by Mithredath the
treasurer, who counted them out to Sheshbazzar the prince
of Judah.

9 This was the inventory:

| | |
|---|---|
| gold dishes | 30 |
| silver dishes | 1,000 |
| silver pans | 29 |

| | |
|---|---|
| 10 **gold bowls** | **30** |
| **matching silver bowls** | **410** |
| **other articles** | **1,000** |

11 **In all, there were 5,400 articles of gold and of silver.**
**Sheshbazzar brought all these along with the exiles when they**
**came up from Babylon to Jerusalem.**

THE BOOK OF EZRA-NEHEMIAH OPENS WITH A profound hope for the displaced people of God. After experiencing the wrath of God through roughly seventy years of exile, after seeing the rise and fall of the Babylonians, and after the loss of their national identity as the people of God (temple and land defiled) the author makes it clear that advancement with respect to God's covenantal promises is imminent.

What we are about to see is that Yahweh initiates the restoration and rebuilding phase of Israelite history by giving the exiles tangible hope (fulfilled prophecy) and tangible help (the kings of Persia). The entire phase covers approximately one-hundred years and involves three distinct movements.[1] Ezra chapters 1–6 record the first return of the exiles under the leadership of a man named Zerubbabel. It mainly involves a physical rebuilding process with a focus on the temple (539–458 BC). Ezra 7–10 charts the second return of the exiles under the leadership of a priest named Ezra. In this movement the reader is first introduced to Ezra, where the focus is a spiritual rebuilding process (457 BC). Finally, a third return takes place with Nehemiah leading the way to rebuild the walls (Neh 1–14), achieving both a physical and spiritual renewal (444 BC).[2] The sum of all of this represents a return to the pure worship of Yahweh. To the first movement involving chapters 1–6 we turn our attention.

Chapter 1, especially verses 1–3, provides a literary hinge with the closing verses of Chronicles (2 Chr 36:22–23). The mention of Cyrus's

---

1. For a discussion on the history of this period see Introduction.

2. See Timeline: The Return of the Exiles for a chronological overview of this period.

proclamation allowing the Jews to return to Jerusalem to rebuild the temple points backward from a literary perspective. The author of Chronicles ended his recollection of Judah's history on a positive note by speaking of Cyrus's proclamation. The author of Ezra opens his history of the nation's restoration and directly connects it to Cyrus; thus, Cyrus's decree provides a literary link that points the reader forward and fleshes out the positive storyline. Although chapter 1 is technically a unit, it does divide logically. Ezra 1:1–4 introduces Cyrus's Proclamation, while Ezra 1:5–11 highlights the responses to Cyrus's proclamation. In the chapter we learn that God keeps his word to restore his people and simultaneously judges his enemy. Fulfilled prophecy sets the stage and both the decree by Cyrus and the responses to it provide evidence. In fact, God sovereignly intervenes in time and space to keep his word to restore. In so doing, the human and divine work in tandem.

## The First Return: Zerubbabel/Sheshbazzar Restore the Temple (1:1–6:22)

### Cyrus's Proclamation: The Hope and Help (1:1–4)[3]

**FULFILLED PROPHECY (1:1).** The first year of Cyrus, king of Persia, was eventful for international politics. In 539 BC the Persians together with the Medes diverted the waters of the Euphrates and marched into well-fortified Babylon[4] on a night King Belshazzar and all the city were making merry (Dan 5).[5] With a bloodless transition the Babylonian Empire fell to the Persians.[6]

Shortly after this takeover, a verbal proclamation was made by the new king of Persia and put into writing, as noted in 1:1; the contents of the writing are partially preserved both in Hebrew (Ezra 1:2–4; 2 Chr 36:22–23) and in Aramaic (Ezra 6:3–5).

---

3. See also J. G. McConville, "Ezra-Nehemiah and the Fulfillment of Prophecy," *VT* 36 (1986): 205–24; and Breneman, *Ezra, Nehemiah, Esther*, 56–58.

4. Babylon was considered impregnable due to its system of double defenses. It had an inner wall of twenty-one feet thick reinforced with towers and an outer wall eleven feet wide. See Herodotus, *The Histories*, book 3.

5. The date here refers to Cyrus's control over Babylon and Judah and not his rule that commenced in 550 BC when he took over the Median Empire. See Introduction and Timeline.

6. See Introduction.

The archaeological record offers evidence of Cyrus's capture of Babylon and his subsequent edict. A clay barrel, designated the Cyrus Cylinder, is a cuneiform text that was found in the vicinity of Marduk's temple in Babylon.[7] The textual information on the cylinder corroborates both the biblical record and ancient historians' record about Cyrus. Indeed, one named Cyrus did conquer Babylon, . . . "without any battle, he (Marduk) made him (Cyrus) enter his (Marduk's) town Babylon, sparing Babylon any calamity."[8] In addition to this bloodless takeover, the text indicates that Cyrus returned the gods held captive in Babylon by previous conquerors to their sacred cities. This was accomplished by allowing for the rebuilding of the earthly sanctuaries of the deities.[9] Cyrus hoped to gain spiritual blessings (peace and long life) as a result: "May all the gods whom I have resettled in their sacred cities ask daily Bel and Nebo for long life for me."[10]

The author, however, wants the reader to see that Cyrus's first year and the corresponding edict was not business as usual. It was not to be interpreted merely from the vantage of international politics, eventful as Cyrus's rise to power was for the latter. Instead, it was much more. The notification of Cyrus's first year and the mention of his edict in verse 1 envelops the real rationale for the unfolding events. With the sole purpose of keeping his word through Jeremiah, God takes action and intervenes. The grammatical construction "in order to" indicates purpose and is fronted in Hebrew for emphasis. God's purposes and intentions are clear, and there can be no misunderstanding: the time has come to make good on his word. It is this intent, therefore, that sets the story line of restoration into motion in Ezra. It is for this purpose the LORD takes deliberate action; God "moved the heart of Cyrus" in a very specific direction—one that would advance covenantal promises for the people of God, as evidenced in the edict that follows (1:2–4).

The divine purpose gains further traction through divine intervention. While the NIV reads "the LORD moved the heart of Cyrus" (1:1a), another way to reflect the language is by rendering it as "the LORD *caused*

---

7. See Introduction.

8. James B. Pritchard, ed., *The Ancient Near East: An Anthology of Texts and Pictures* (Princeton: Princeton University Press, 2011), 283.

9. Ibid., 284.

10. Ibid.

the heart of Cyrus to be stirred." The use of this causative verbal action communicates unequivocally that God caused Cyrus's benevolent plan. It infers that not even Cyrus the Great[11] had a say in the matter.[12]

In fact, Jeremiah used this language with the same verb and object in 51:11, "The LORD has stirred up the kings of the Medes, because his purpose is to destroy Babylon. The LORD will take vengeance, vengeance for his temple."[13] This text indicates that the LORD caused Cyrus's rise to power, which resulted in the defeat of the Babylonian Empire. From the divine perspective this defeat satisfied God's anger for the desecration of the temple, a punishment from God on Babylon (Jer 25:12). The stirring directly and positively benefited the LORD. The same stirring directly and positively affected God's people, as seen by Ezra 1:1 and what follows. Therefore, without this divine stirring Babylon would not have been defeated, Cyrus would not have risen to power, and his edict would not have been written. God's word to Jeremiah would remain incomplete relative to Babylon. The stirring was one way that God kept God's word spoken by Jeremiah, particularly the word pertaining to Babylon.[14]

There is more involved, however, with God keeping his word to Jeremiah and the divine stirring. While the author undoubtedly had the prophecies about Babylon's judgment in view due to the "stirring" language in both Ezra 1:1 and Jeremiah, there are two other prophecies from Jeremiah likely at the forefront of the author's mind. The prophet also announced that Israel's servitude to the king of Babylon would be a duration of seventy years[15] (Jer 25:11), a prophecy that the exiled Jews would have embraced now that Jeremiah was proven to be a true prophet, given the reality of Jerusalem's fall. The prophet promises a positive visitation from God for God's people when seventy years are

---

11. See Introduction concerning this title.

12. This perspective also surfaces on the Cyrus Cylinder. Marduk *declared* Cyrus as ruler of the entire world; Marduk *ordered* Cyrus to march against Babylon and *made* Cyrus enter Babylon without a battle.

13. See also Jer 51:1, 50:9 and also Isa 13; 17; 41:12, 25 without the use of *nephesh*.

14. One cannot forget that the prophet Daniel was in Babylon at this critical time (Dan 1:21; 6:28; 10:1). Daniel 9:1–19 reflects his prayers and pleas to restore and build Jerusalem, as well as Gabriel's assurance that Daniel's prayers were heard.

15. A seventy-year time span typically refers to a period of judgment (2 Chr 36:21; Isa 23:15,17; Dan 9:2, 9:24; Zech 7:5), but it can also refer to a period of mourning (Gen 50:3).

completed for Babylon: "I will come to you and fulfill my good promise to bring you back to this place" (Jer 29:10). This defined period of time indicates that an end of servitude for sin would be a reality for God's people (so, too, Isa 40:1–2). It meant that God's anger against Israel had chronological limits. It indicated that movement forward relative to God's good promises would be a reality. An exiled Israelite would have clung to such hopes; indeed, the community was anxiously waiting for their fulfillment (Ps 42–43, 74, 137).

The duration of time indicated in Jeremiah's prophecies, then, represents another aspect of God keeping his word—a word that is linked to the outcome relative to Babylon and depends on the stirring of God.[16] In context, then, God keeping his word is very specific. Primarily, God is keeping his word relative to the time of Israel's restoration. Secondarily, he is also keeping his word relative to the time of Babylon's destruction, Israel's enemy.[17] Therefore, the two promises are intricately related.

What is stunning here is how the author does not want the reader to miss the theological interpretation of Cyrus's first year as king of Persia. He puts the spotlight on the real issue, one that would have had deep significance to the exilic community. The fact that the underpinnings of the stirring and its purpose are tied to God's concern for fulfilling his word comes out strongly in the passage. Keeping his word to Jeremiah has implications for God, God's people, and God's enemy (Babylon). Thus, in the opening verse, the first year of Cyrus represents a providential event and a tangible hope for God's people. It is a joyful announcement

---

16. The calculation for seventy years of exile derives from the first captivity of Judah by Babylon c. 606/5 BC, where Daniel is taken away (2 Kgs 24:1–7; Dan 1:1–3). It ends with Cyrus's decree issued in 539 BC. The second captivity of Judah by Babylon takes place in 597 BC where the prophet Ezekiel is taken away (2 Kgs 24:8–17; Ezek 1:1–2). The fall of Jerusalem occurs in 586 BC (2 Kgs 24:25:1–21). Still others consider the fall of Jerusalem in 586 BC to the temple's completion in 516 BC as another way to figure the seventy years.

17. Although Jeremiah's prophecies are the focal point for the author (probably due to mention of the seventy-year duration and its correspondence with Cyrus'srise to power) the prophet Isaiah should also be noted. Exceptional for the range of this prophecy, Isaiah speaks of the Persian liberator by name and says that Cyrus will fulfill the LORD's purposes as God's shepherd and anointed one (Isa 44:24–28; 45:1–6). He speaks this word about 150 years before it comes to pass. This view assumes the unity of Isaiah with a single author whose predictions were generated in the eighth/seventh centuries.

of fulfilled prophecy! Prophecy fulfilled sets the stage for the entire narrative of Ezra-Nehemiah.

The results, then, of the LORD stirring Cyrus's heart translate into a verbal and written proclamation that went out to his kingdom. This is the practical side of fulfilled prophecy (1:1).

After making it clear from verse 1 that Yahweh sovereignly ordained this hopeful moment in Israel's history, the reader is given a portion of Cyrus's decree, perhaps as documentary evidence of fulfilled prophecy. The proclamation reveals important details about Cyrus's perception as the new king over Babylon and his own interpretation of the unfolding events of his first year.

**The acquisition (1:2a).** First, Cyrus acknowledges that his successful military acquisition of "all the kingdoms of the earth" derives from "The LORD, the God of heaven (1:2a)." This precise designation appears only one other time in Ezra-Nehemiah and it comes from the praying lips of Nehemiah as he cries out for mercy to his God (Neh 1:5).[18] A modified or more generic version of "the God of heaven" without Yahweh's covenantal name surfaces several times in both the Hebrew and Aramaic sections of the book.[19] In these texts both Persian kings Darius and Artaxerxes, as well as the elders of the Jews addressing a Persian king, appeal to the deity with this designation.[20] One wonders, then, why Cyrus does not use the more generic designation when acknowledging divine military help. This question can be more fully answered after considering the latter part of verse 2 where the author continues to provide the reader with more of Cyrus's perspective of the events.

**The appointment (1:2b–3).** Second, Cyrus acknowledges that this military achievement directly corresponds to an unavoidable religious appointment, namely, the task of [re]building Yahweh's earthly dwelling in Jerusalem (1:2b). This would include financial backing and any other resources to make it happen.

---

18. Elsewhere the designation is used in the oath that Abraham prompts his servant to take (Gen 24:3,7) and by Jonah when identifying himself to the mariners in the midst of the mighty tempest (Jonah 1:9).

19. Ezra 5:11, 12; 6:9, 10; 7:12, 21, 23 and Neh 1:4, 5; 2:4, 20.

20. Such is true of Daniel at King Nebuchadnezzar's court (Dan 2:18, 37, 44). It is possible, therefore, that the term "god of heaven" was widely used and acceptable in the Persian religious context. See Bezalel Porten, *Elephantine Papyri in English: Studies in Near Eastern Archaeology*, rev. ed. (Atlanta: SBL Press, 2011).

Yahweh is addressed in the designation (1:2a) because the temple is for the god associated specifically with territory in Jerusalem. Building Yahweh's temple in Jerusalem will bring about religious restoration and reestablish his cult there. It will require full cooperation and participation, financially and otherwise, given the appointment. This is not insignificant, since Yahweh's people currently dwell on foreign soil. Therefore, the gracious invitation for "his people" to go up and build "the temple of the LORD, the God of Israel, the God who is in Jerusalem" (1:3) recognizes this deity's territory. In so doing Cyrus hopes for favor among his subjects and placation of the gods of his subject peoples. To his newly-conquered peoples, notably the Israelites, he proclaims himself as Yahweh's choice for the task:[21] "the LORD, the God of heaven, . . . has appointed me to build a temple for him." Thus Cyrus's use of the designation "Yahweh" has to be understood together with the building of the temple and the ethos attached to it. Hence, he attributes his military victory to Yahweh, the God of heaven.

Cyrus's surprising use of the covenantal name Yahweh is not an acknowledgement that Cyrus knew and had experienced Yahweh in the same way as an Israelite. Rather it is an acknowledgement that Yahweh is Israel's God who resides in Jerusalem. Such acknowledgement is altogether appropriate given the possibility that Cyrus could have understood the various deities in different regions as manifestations of one supreme god.[22] It thus explains why Cyrus esteems Yahweh the way he does in the edict.[23]

In Ezra 1:3, Cyrus solicits Judean support. He commissions the Jews for a special building project, "Any of his people among you may go up to Jerusalem and build the temple[24] of the LORD." Although Cyrus puts out a kingdom-wide proclamation (1:2), he specifically addresses the Jews,

---

21. Lester L. Grabbe, *A History of the Jews and Judaism in the Second Temple Period, Volume I* (New York: T&T Clark, 2004), 272.

22. Ibid.

23. As God of heaven (1:2); his temple is in Jerusalem (1:2, 3[2x]); the God of Israel (1:3); the God in Jerusalem (1:3–4).

24. Literally the word is "house" (*bayit*) in all its occurrences here—not "temple" (*hekal*). Because a temple was understood as the earthly dwelling place of a deity, the biblical writers also used the word for house when speaking of the deity's dwelling as in "house of God" or "house of the LORD." In the passage the NIV is not consistent in translating (*bayit*) as "temple" and switches to "house of the LORD" in 1:5 for unclear reasons.

the people who belong to Yahweh ("his people"), he names their deity, and he acknowledges Yahweh's earthly habitation as a political preface to the expression of the king's will in the edict.

Embedded in the edict are two important factors for the successful execution of the project. On the one hand it depends upon the willingness of some people to leave Babylon. That is, Cyrus is not forcing his will on the Jews to return to their homeland but allowing them the opportunity to do so if they wish. On the other hand, it depends entirely on divine presence/favor, as Cyrus states, "May their God [the LORD] be with them" (1:3). Cyrus acknowledges and wishes, as is appropriate for one in the milieu of the ancient Near East, that the divine presence alone would grant such victory. Although this was a common theological construct in the ancient Near East, the notion of the divine presence was particularly a hallmark of Israelite religion (i.e., Gen 26:3; 31:3; Exod 3:12; Josh 1:5).

Moreover, given the fact that the temple is mentioned five times in seven verses, rebuilding this architectural structure seems to be a key point of the narrative from a thematic point of view and not merely a reflection of Cyrus's desire to win political and religious favor.[25] The repetition reveals the significance of the temple for the process of restoration. To the mind of an exiled Israelite, restoration and temple rebuilding would be synonymous. It would indicate a return to all of what was lost through exile. Those of the exilic community returning to the land would be reconnecting with their past; therefore, they would have hope for a brighter future grounded in the promises of their God.

**Cyrus solicits community-wide support (1:4a).** The king further enables those who wish to go up by rallying support, first from those Jews who wish to stay but also from the non-Judean community. The Hebrew of verse 4 is not straightforward and needs clarification on a few issues that most English translations inadequately address. The NIV rendering of verse four suggests that those Jews living in Babylon who survived Jerusalem's destruction and want to return are to receive

25. Three times "temple" is used in two verses. The temple is for the LORD, the God of heaven (1:2), the LORD, the God of Israel, the God who is in Jerusalem (1:3), and the God (*'elohim*) in Jerusalem (1:4). In addition to these three citations the text also speaks of the temple in 1:5,7 in reference to articles belonging to temple of the LORD and a final time in 1:7; however, the latter refers to Marduk's temple.

support: "the people of any place where survivors may now be living are to provide." With this translation the NIV takes the Hebrew "survivors" as referring to survivors of Jerusalem's destruction. Another reading of the Hebrew, however, is to understand "survivors" as those who remained in Persia, those who did not want to return should offer assistance.

The question posed by the different readings of "survivors" concerns who is giving or receiving assistance. Is it those who survived destruction/exile and want to return that should be given assistance? Or is it those who remain, who do not want to return, that should offer assistance? The latter rendering seems more likely since remaining or staying provides a logical contrast to the going up mentioned in 1:3. Thus the Jew, or in Hebrew, "the one who remained," also designated later in verse 4 in the original as the "resident foreigner," is to support the Jew who decides to go. This is not unlike what took place when God's people left Egypt (Exod 12:35) and seems to best account for the syntax of 1:3–4.

And yet the Hebrew phraseology here suggests that the nature of the support is broader than just the Jewish community. Verse 6 clearly states that "all their neighbors assisted them with articles of silver and gold, with goods and livestock, and with valuable gifts." Moreover, Cyrus himself contributed (1:8–9; see also 6:2–4), and his edict is addressed to people "throughout his realm" (1:1). Hence, Cyrus seems to be soliciting community-wide support for the building project. The appeal for such support, coming from a non-Yahwistic leader, regardless of his own motivations, enhances what is already an amazing extension of kindness toward God's people. It is the author's implicit way of showing that the LORD is with his people.

**Cyrus solicits needed resources (1:4b).** The building project required not only willing souls but also money and materials. It included practical items, such as silver, gold, and goods. The kind of support spoken of here is similar to that generated by Hiram, king of Tyre, who offered material goods and money to Solomon for building the temple in Jerusalem (1 Kgs 9:11). The list also includes animals. The latter would provide sustenance as well as suitable sacrifices once worship was reinstated in Jerusalem. The giving was also to be spontaneous. The term used here refers to a voluntary offering, such as the money that helped support the construction of the tabernacle (Exod 35:29; 36:3) and the offering of the prince mentioned in the new spiritual center

Ezekiel envisions (Ezek 46:12). Just as going up to Jerusalem should be spontaneous, so the giving should be also.

Thus the part of the edict preserved here in Ezra 1:2–4 gives the human perspective on the events of Cyrus's rise to power, whereas Ezra 1:1 gives the divine perspective. In this way the spiritual and practical align. Cyrus's edict represents the needed help, the practical side of fulfilled prophecy. God's people can return to the promised land, rebuild the temple of Yahweh, and hope afresh in the promises of their God. Likewise, God's people who stay back can participate by giving rather than going. Stated another way, the edict meant the tangible removal of major obstacles (Babylon/foreign captors) relative to God's promises.

## The Response to Cyrus's Proclamation (1:5–11)

THE SECOND PART OF THE CHAPTER OUTLINES the various responses to the king's edict. The proclamation received a positive response. The author notes several categories of people who decided to take on the challenge outlined in the edict, along with a summation of the total provisions given.

**Leaders respond (1:5).** The first responders (those rising to action) were leaders (NIV "family heads") from the tribes of Judah and Benjamin. Before the exile of 586 BC these two tribes constituted the Southern Kingdom, what remained of Israel after the downfall of the Northern Kingdom in 722 BC. After Jerusalem's demise, the sociopolitical leaders of these tribes (extended family units) are quick to identify with their important past. To these belonged the promises of God. Yet, as the numbers in chapter 2 make clear, not many chose to return. In fact, it seems likely that more stayed back. Regardless, an effort was made by these key people to rally together for such a purpose.

The author deliberately mentions that priests and Levites were among a second group who also responded. These are highlighted because they are the needed cultic personnel for restoring and revitalizing Israelite worship at the rebuilt temple. Put another way, without these spiritual leaders in particular, the renewal process would not have been possible.

These responders, however, are not limited to sociopolitical and spiritual leaders from the Judean community. The text in 1:5 summarizes all responders, a broad group consisting of "everyone whose heart God had moved." The term "everyone" expresses totality. It includes those already mentioned in 1:5a, but also those who will be mentioned, "all their neighbors" and even Cyrus (1:6–7). In this summary statement the author explicitly tells the reader that those responding were doing so because of divine activity. The same causative verb used above in 1:1a that brought about Cyrus's decree is used here with respect to people's responsiveness. God "stirred" the hearts of certain people, obviously not all, which resulted in positive first steps for the stated project. Clearly, the author wishes to foreground the theological reasons for the positive response.

**Neighbors respond (1:6).** Another group of responders were "[a] ll their neighbors." In Hebrew the subject "all their neighbors" is placed at the beginning of the clause. Rather than commence the clause with the typical word order of verb, subject, object ("they assisted them, all their neighbors"), the subject is put before the verb to call attention to this particular group; thus, "All their neighbors assisted them." As noted above, this reference need not exclude non-Judean members of the community. Indeed, it would be unrealistic to imagine that the exiled Jews were able to live apart from the established peoples of the lands when they were deported.

What exactly did these neighbors do? The Hebrew literally says "they strengthened their hands." Since hands are often used figuratively in the Bible for symbols of power and strength, this related idiom suggests the ability to enable someone in need (Isa 35:3; Jer 23:14). The way the neighbors enabled those going to Jerusalem was through giving. The neighbors "assisted" and encouraged those going up to Jerusalem with a tangible expression of support. They helped fund God's renewal and restoration mission in Jerusalem with money and materials. In so doing the neighbors were following Cyrus's edict as outlined in 1:4.

The show of support to go and to give (1:5–6) is both expected and unexpected. On one hand, one would expect subjects of Cyrus's kingdom to respond to his edict. On the other, one does not expect that non-Yahwistic followers would actually help fund the project! Under the umbrella of religious tolerance and the hope of divine favor, the assistance and support become understandable.

**Cyrus responds (1:7–8).** Finally, another responder, perhaps unexpected as well, was King Cyrus himself. Beyond the response from the surrounding Judean and Babylonian community (1:6), God also moved the Persian king further to action. As with "all their neighbors" in verse 6, "King Cyrus" as subject of the clause is placed before the verb, giving added attention to Cyrus.

Cyrus possessed a stash of beautiful "articles" from Solomon's temple that the Babylonian king, Nebuchadnezzar, plundered and placed in Marduk's temple, "the temple of his god."[26] This was because, in typical ancient Near Eastern fashion,[27] Nebuchadnezzar attributed his victory over Jerusalem to divine favor from his god, Marduk. Marduk defeated Yahweh and was more powerful, as the Babylonians understood it, when Yahweh's temple was razed in 586 BC. In declaration of Marduk's sovereignty, Nebuchadnezzar, therefore, placed these costly items in the earthly home of his god.

Several decades after these events, and in declaration of Yahweh's sovereignty over Jerusalem, Cyrus, by contrast, wanted to return these cultic objects to their rightful place—to Yahweh's rebuilt house in Jerusalem. Driven by pleasing his subjects and a tolerance for their religious beliefs, Cyrus also responds to his own edict (v. 7 by returning the temple vessels), albeit for self-serving purposes. The other side to the story, however, concerns a previous prophecy of Isaiah. Roughly two hundred years earlier, Isaiah prophesied that God's people would return to Jerusalem and that "the articles of the Lord's house" would be involved (Isa 52:11–12).

Cyrus gives the items to Mithredath, the Persian treasurer, who stewards the items by counting them to Sheshbazzar, Judah's leader (NIV "prince"), who had the responsibility for the return of both the temple vessels (1:8, 11) and the exiles to Jerusalem (1:11). We learn only a bit about Sheshbazzar from Ezra 1. He bore a title that came with a huge leadership responsibility. Slightly more information, however, can be gleaned about him from Ezra 5:14–16, the Aramaic correspondence confirming that the Jews had the right to rebuild the temple, when questioned by their opponents. That letter states that Cyrus made Sheshbazzar "governor," the Aramaic equivalent for "leader" or "prince" in Hebrew. Accordingly, Sheshbazzar was not a self-appointed leader. Cyrus placed Sheshbazzar in the role in the Persian satrap of Judah, territory beyond the Euphrates, as the king's representative (see comments below on Ezra 5:14). In this capacity he oversaw the return

---

26. These articles are further identified in the inventory noted in 1:9–11 and will be discussed below.

27. Jeffrey J. Niehaus, *God at Sinai: Covenant and Theophany in the Bible and Ancient Near East* (Grand Rapids: Zondervan, 1995).

of the temple vessels (5:15). In addition, he was involved with laying the temple's foundation (5:16). Beyond these responsibilities, the author does not further discuss Sheshbazzar's involvement.[28]

Thus, even Cyrus was a responder to his own decree. All these responses in 1:5–8 resulted in the appointment of necessary leadership to care for the collection of cultic items gathered.

**Cultic provisions (1:9–11).** The chapter closes with a tally based on the numbering in verse 11[29] of the items collected, but these are not just any items. The Hebrew shows four categories of items that Cyrus brought out:

1. 1,030 gold and silver "dishes" or possibly "containers full of gold and silver"
2. 29 "silver pans," perhaps "knives" or "offering basins"
3. 440 gold and silver bowls
4. 1,000 miscellaneous items or "other articles"

A precise translation and corresponding identification of the items in numbers 1 and 2 is not possible given the ambiguities of the vocabulary used. Also, because of the generic nature of those items in number 4, we are hard pressed to offer a tight description of the provisions. Based on 1:7 it seems reasonable that the list encompasses items specifically used in the temple service. Further evidence derives from the reports

---

28. Some suggest that Shesbazzar appears in 1 Chr 3:18 in a variant form Shenazzar. According to the record in 1 Chr. 3:18, Shenazzar was the son of Jehoiachin, king of Judah (598–97) who was taken into captivity by Nebuchadnezzar. If Shenazzar is a variant of Sheshbazzar, this would tie him to royal ancestry, a key member in the Davidic line. Such a tie would legitimize his leadership role with the exiles and the temple-building project. There is no proof, however, that Shenazzar is a variant of Sheshbazzar. As a Persian representative in Judah, regardless of his possible ties to royal ancestry, he was a key person because of carrying out the word of the Lord. For a cogent discussion see Derek Kidner, *Ezra and Nehemiah*, TOTC 12 (Downers Grove, IL: InterVarsity Press, 1979), 153.

29. The itemized list totals 2,499 objects. However, the total number of articles computes to 5,400 in verse 11. The discrepancy can easily be accounted for. This list, as is so common with biblical lists in general, is not meant to be exhaustive. The author's calculation of 5,400 articles obviously includes objects not enumerated in that list. Given the fact that verse 11 is a summary statement concerning all collected "articles of gold and silver," the larger number seems to include non-cultic "articles of gold and silver" contributed by generous neighbors as indicated in (1:6).

in 2 Kings (25:13–14) and Jeremiah (52:17–18) of Jerusalem's fall. In both of these accounts, the objects Nebuchadnezzar whisked away from Solomon's temple are designated as temple-service items. In fact, Belshazzar's feast as recorded in Daniel mentions that party participants were actually drinking wine from vessels belonging to Solomon's temple (perhaps the small bowls used for drink offerings, Dan 5:1–5, 23). Given the holy use of these items in Yahweh's temple, Belshazzar's unholy use was an insult. The items are not insignificant and represent a tangible hope of restoring worship. The summary statement in verse 11 captures it best by referring to all the items generically as "articles of gold and of silver," precious items symbolizing holiness.

Regardless of the stated ambiguities relative to the specific identification of the objects and their exact numbers, it seems that the author does not want the reader to miss the point. The hand of God orchestrated both the decree (1:1–4) and certain responses to it, especially the mobilization of the people to go up to Jerusalem and to give (1:5–11). Responses derive from inside as well as outside the covenantal community. The success of the project appears inevitable now that all obstacles are removed and things are in place practically. Indeed, proper provisions (cultic and non-cultic) have been secured, people are willing to return, and the necessary leadership emerged to oversee the process. Chapter 1 concludes by indicating that the journey from "Babylon to Jerusalem" could officially begin (1:11). All of this empirical evidence, even before the building project gets underway, affirms Cyrus's best wishes, ". . . may [their] God be with [them]" (1:3). It is the author's implicit way of showing that the LORD is with his people, thus practically fulfilling his word spoken by Jeremiah.

THE MAIN POINT OF THE PERICOPE, THAT GOD keeps his word (fulfilled prophecy) to restore his people and simultaneously judge his enemy and that he sovereignly intervenes in time and space to do so, becomes evident given the emphases noted above. The action the LORD takes here in Ezra 1:1 by stirring up Cyrus is nothing less than divine intervention. Unwittingly, a non-Yahwistic leader like Cyrus acts in accordance with what God has willed to take place. God controls all history according to his plan, but it would have been understood as more than prophecy fulfilled from the exilic and postexilic community. In keeping this specific word to Jeremiah, it harkens back to God keeping his word to Moses (Lev 26:41–45; Deut 30:1–5), which also harkens back to the inviolable promises and oath God made to Abraham (Gen 12, 15). Ultimately, keeping his word to Jeremiah means God is remembering his covenant with Abraham, Isaac, and Jacob.

The Mosaic law promised that, upon seeing humbled hearts, God would remember his covenant with Jacob, Isaac, and Abraham (Lev 26:42, 45) and remember the land (26:42). The law also acknowledges that God would neither spurn nor abhor them, and that he would not destroy them by breaking covenant with them (Lev 26:43–44). This remembering of both their ancestors and the land translates into action—God would allow for a repossession of the promised land (Deut 30:1–5).

God is remembering Abraham by acting favorably to restore a people to their place, part of the promises outlined in Genesis 12:1–3. In Genesis, God promised the patriarchal father a nation of people and a land as their inheritance. Implicit in these blessings was also the promise of the divine presence.[30] The restoration of God's presence, however, is not addressed until later in the book (Ezra 6:19–22). The edict clearly allowed for restoration of the people to their place.

The significance of Jeremiah's word being fulfilled is that it corresponds to previous promises and ones with greater longevity than Jeremiah's prophecy. The exiles would have understood the broader implications of God keeping his word to Jeremiah. The option for a physical return to the land via Cyrus's decree demonstrates divine action and favor on their behalf. Given the background of God's previous covenantal loyalties, this moment would have been understood as having profound spiritual implications.

What was clearly a timely word for the exiles might seem to have little abiding value at first glance. After all, it was a word fulfilled for them. Our situation does not remotely compare with that of the exiles in Babylon. How are we to understand this? Perhaps it is a promise that God will stir the leadership of your township to commission you to build a church in the area to bring about spiritual restoration? Or that

---

30. See also T. Desmond Alexander, *From Paradise to the Promised Land: An Introduction to the Pentateuch* (Grand Rapids: Baker Academic, 2012).

God will finance your church building project through your unbelieving friends and neighbors? However tempting these approaches might be, the exegesis done previously does not allow for such specifics. It does, however, allow us to connect with our ancient audience on a broader, timeless concept.

God has, indeed, kept his word to restore his people and simultaneously judge his enemy. When the Word became flesh and blood, God was keeping his word, not just to one but to all the prophets of old to restore humanity unto himself. In the incarnation, God came to us in the person of Christ. God came at his own initiative and at the perfect time (Gal. 1:4; 4:4). Just as the exiles were waiting for God to come to them and fulfill his good promises to return them to the land (Jer 29), humankind was waiting for God to come to fulfill his good promises relative to our complete spiritual restoration (Isa 59:21; Rom 8:23). The fact that the Word became flesh and blood and that God made his abode with humankind demonstrated his desire to relate to people (John 1:14). Through Jesus, a temple not built with human hands, God created sacred space (John 2:21). In him one could achieve and aspire to proper worship and devotion to God. The incarnation was a tangible expression of the LORD's long-term loyalty to bringing restoration to his relationship with humankind.

But the incarnation, which led to the cross, expressed his loyalties even more vividly. Through his death on the cross and the shedding of his blood, he became sin so we could know righteousness. As a result, we have received spiritual restoration, an end of servitude to sin became a reality for God's people (Isa 40; John 1; Col. 2:14–15). Accordingly, we have been transferred from the kingdom of darkness to the kingdom of light and have been given an inheritance (1 Pet 1:11). The cross was both a visual aid of God keeping his word to restore humanity unto himself and a judgment on his enemy (e.g., Gen 3:15, fulfilled prophecy). At the cross, Colossians reminds us that Christ triumphed over the devil and made a public spectacle of him (2:15). Thus, the ultimate act of God keeping his word to bring restoration to his people and judge the enemy is found in the incarnation and at the cross. The incarnation and the cross, therefore, were both profound actions/expressions of God's long-term loyalty, revealing that God is remembering his word to Abraham to give him a people with an inheritance.

This overarching exile-restoration model represented in Ezra thus repeats itself in the course of redemptive history. Like the exiles of Cyrus's day and the Christians of the first century, Peter and other New Testament authors remind us that we, too, are exiles and aliens on this earth because we are away from our true homeland, a displaced people. In our earthly exile (1 Pet 1:1; 2:11; Heb 11:13) we have to contend with "Babylon," the world empire opposed to God and his people (Rev 17–19).

But God will keep his word and come again at his own initiative and timing! Titus reminds us that we are waiting for "the blessed hope," the second appearing of our great God and Savior Jesus Christ and the fulfillment of redemptive history (Titus 2:13). In New Testament parlance this refers to the coming Day of the Lord, the second coming (e.g., 2 Pet 3:12–13; 1 Thess 5:2; 2 Thess 2:2). It will be God's final and tangible expression, not only to us but also to the world, concerning the longevity of God's loyalty to restore people to himself. Christ's return will represent the consummation of the covenantal relationship, where all the promises to Abraham will find their amen! As exiles and aliens on this earth, we long for that day of complete spiritual restoration. We are waiting for the fulfillment of God's word, which promises that our servitude to the god[s] of this world will have a definitive end. Likewise, we are awaiting the fulfillment of God's word that promises judgment will come to the enemies of God and God's people (this world system called Babylon/the great harlot who stands in opposition to God) discussed in the book of Revelation.

But what do we do while we wait? What do we do in this interim period between the first act of restoration and the second/final act of restoration yet to come? Are we to hold our breath, groping for daily or ongoing restoration in our lives and world? No, we are to be hopeful and anticipate divine intervention in the waiting room of life. God has also kept his word to restore and empower his people, particularly after Christ's resurrection, with the Holy Spirit, a tangible expression of his continued loyalties to look after us. Once again, God sovereignly intervenes in time and space to restore his people and simultaneously judge the enemy by the coming of the Holy Spirit. Because of the ongoing, daily work of the Holy Spirit in our lives and world, restoration remains possible for believers while we await our ultimate restoration.

Although our situation does not mirror that of the author and his audience, and though their problems clearly are not ours, we can identify with the exiles of Ezra's day because of the exile-restoration motif that encompasses us this side of the cross.

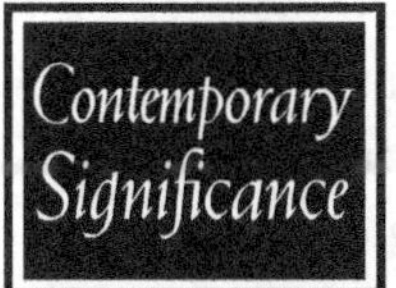


GOD IS GOING TO KEEP HIS WORD NO MATTER what obstacles are stacked against him! This means God acts not only at the level of international politics but also at the personal level to restore all things unto himself and his kingdom's purposes. It means God sovereignly intervenes (in tangible ways) in time and space to do so. It also means the tangible removal of all obstacles to achieving those purposes. The significance of knowing that God keeps his word to restore all things unto himself, especially in times of separation from him due to sin's consequences or on account of living in this world, is critical. Without such a worldview, we lose our view and perspective on life.

The author of Ezra draws us behind the curtain, gives us a backstage pass, and makes us privy to the workings of the divine drama that give perspective and interpretation to the international politics of the day. Cyrus's "word" proclaimed in his edict aligns itself with the fulfillment of Yahweh's word. Rather than the two realms colliding with each other, the two worlds actually correspond to fulfill God's purposes. Behind the scene of international politics is a sovereign God using the nations *and* individuals for the fulfillment of his purposes. The sovereign God is remembering his promises and covenant to Abraham.

The biblical writer, therefore, intentionally connected the two worlds. The writers of Holy Scripture—particularly the author of Ezra-Nehemiah[31]—had a theological lens that guided the interpretation of certain events in world politics as related to the people of God. The ability to connect the two worlds, however, is directly related to the writer's deep awareness of the ancient word itself.

This is a wake-up call for us to be likeminded and to do no less than the biblical writers while situated in our earthly exile. Rather than intentionally disconnect the two worlds and see them in opposition to each other, we are encouraged to connect the two by bringing them into a theological focus.

It is also an invitation for us to ask ourselves: what interpretive lens do we wear as we attempt to grapple with life and the events unfolding in our world? There are many lenses from which one may choose to view life. If, however, the lens is something other than the abiding word of

31. See Introduction.

God, this is an invitation to discard that lens. As God's people we should understand that the present events we read about in the newspapers involving the nations of the world, as well as future events, are determined not by powerful leaders and their strategies, either for ill or good.

Instead, the living God, who is carefully planning and guiding humankind's destiny in accordance with his kingdom purposes, *is* determining world events. He guides not just his people, but also those outside the covenantal community, to bring things in alignment with his plans. Such a theological lens not only anchors the church and gives us confidence, but it should also drive us to our knees in petition for all who are in high positions, that we may lead a peaceful and quiet life, godly and dignified in every way (1 Tim. 2:1–2): "thy kingdom come, thy will be done on earth as it is in heaven" (Matt 6:10).

Accordingly, the living God who is carefully planning and guiding humankind's destiny relative to world events does the same with personal events. We should apprehend the hope involved in this reality: that God will again keep his word in order to restore us to himself today. But this is also difficult to hold on to in times of isolation due to sin's consequences. One might ponder why God would initiate restoration?

The good news is this: While living in sin's consequences, God will make something happen to give hope to our hopeless hearts. Perhaps a phone call from a friend, a note in the mail, a billboard driving down the road, something on the radio or television. God will stir the circumstances. He is the trigger in our story line of restoration! He will bring relief at a time of his designation. When this happens, we need to know and remember it is *the living God* who is approaching us, who is coming to us through those circumstances. He is relentlessly pursuing us for relationship. God's long-term loyalty is *the only* explanation and rationale for his ongoing acts of restoration in our lives!

Many years ago, I was alone having breakfast at a local restaurant. Across the room was an old friend of mine that I previously worked with. She did not notice me. But as soon as I saw her, I felt prompted and compelled to do something I have never done since! The whisper in my ear was, "Write her a note with Hebrews 3:15 on it." This verse reads, "Today, if you hear his voice, do not harden your hearts as you did in the rebellion." My first reaction was "Oh, no, there must be some mistake, God?" My heart was beating so fast and so hard that I thought my chest was going to explode. Knowing the inevitable lay ahead, I took my napkin, the only piece of paper available, and called over my waitress to do the deed for me. Once the waitress took the note, I wanted to dart out of the restaurant in hopes I would not be seen; sadly, I had not yet paid for my breakfast! Once the delivery was made, I saw my friend read the napkin note and then immediately she looked up just in time for our eyes to meet. She approached my table and we exchanged greetings. I admitted that my note was truly a strange way to say, "Hi," but that I was compelled to do so. To my great surprise the woman sat down in my booth and began to tell me about her personal struggle with sin; she was doing something she knew was wrong. As she read my note, she felt God was tugging at her heart to make a lifestyle change! She thanked me profusely for reaching out in this way and we parted ways. I sat in stunned silence, overcome by the situation.

Because of the Holy Spirit we have been promised ongoing, daily restoration. God stirred my heart to write this note; it was the trigger in my friend's story line of restoration. The note was a tangible expression of God coming to her via the Holy Spirit; he intervened in time and space, and one of his daughters was restored. We would do well to maintain an unshakable and immovable awareness that a chronological limitation does exist for such things to come to pass, and, at a time period of his choosing, God will act. Indeed, we can trust that God will intervene and act again to move redemptive history to its completion, thereby fulfilling the prophetic word. The longevity of his loyalties to the sons and daughters of Abraham should encourage us and humble us at the same time. Truly the steadfast love of the LORD is never ceasing.

# Ezra 2:1–70

1 Now these are the people of the province who came up
from the captivity of the exiles, whom Nebuchadnezzar
king of Babylon had taken captive to Babylon (they
returned to Jerusalem and Judah, each to their own town,
2 in company with Zerubbabel, Joshua, Nehemiah, Seraiah,
Reelaiah, Mordecai, Bilshan, Mispar, Bigvai, Rehum
and Baanah):

The list of the men of the people of Israel:

| | |
|---|---|
| 3 the descendants of Parosh | 2,172 |
| 4 of Shephatiah | 372 |
| 5 of Arah | 775 |
| 6 of Pahath-Moab (through the line of Jeshua and Joab) | 2,812 |
| 7 of Elam | 1,254 |
| 8 of Zattu | 945 |
| 9 of Zakkai | 760 |
| 10 of Bani | 642 |
| 11 of Bebai | 623 |
| 12 of Azgad | 1,222 |
| 13 of Adonikam | 666 |
| 14 of Bigvai | 2,056 |
| 15 of Adin | 454 |
| 16 of Ater (through Hezekiah) | 98 |
| 17 of Bezai | 323 |
| 18 of Jorah | 112 |
| 19 of Hashum | 223 |
| 20 of Gibbar | 95 |
| 21 the men of Bethlehem | 123 |
| 22 of Netophah | 56 |
| 23 of Anathoth | 128 |
| 24 of Azmaveth | 42 |
| 25 of Kiriath Jearim, Kephirah and Beeroth | 743 |
| 26 of Ramah and Geba | 621 |

| | |
|---|---|
| 27 of Mikmash | 122 |
| 28 of Bethel and Ai | 223 |
| 29 of Nebo | 52 |
| 30 of Magbish | 156 |
| 31 of the other Elam | 1,254 |
| 32 of Harim | 320 |
| 33 of Lod, Hadid and Ono | 725 |
| 34 of Jericho | 345 |
| 35 of Senaah | 3,630 |

36 The priests:

| | |
|---|---|
| the descendants of Jedaiah (through the family of Jeshua) | 973 |
| 37 of Immer | 1,052 |
| 38 of Pashhur | 1,247 |
| 39 of Harim | 1,017 |

40 The Levites:

| | |
|---|---|
| the descendants of Jeshua and Kadmiel (of the line of Hodaviah) | 74 |

41 The musicians:

| | |
|---|---|
| the descendants of Asaph | 128 |

42 The gatekeepers of the temple:
the descendants of
Shallum, Ater, Talmon,
Akkub, Hatita and Shobai 139

43 The temple servants:
the descendants of
Ziha, Hasupha, Tabbaoth,
44 Keros, Siaha, Padon,
45 Lebanah, Hagabah, Akkub,
46 Hagab, Shalmai, Hanan,
47 Giddel, Gahar, Reaiah,
48 Rezin, Nekoda, Gazzam,
49 Uzza, Paseah, Besai,

[50] Asnah, Meunim, Nephusim,
[51] Bakbuk, Hakupha, Harhur,
[52] Bazluth, Mehida, Harsha,
[53] Barkos, Sisera, Temah,
[54] Neziah and Hatipha

[55] The descendants of the servants of Solomon:
the descendants of
Sotai, Hassophereth, Peruda,
[56] Jaala, Darkon, Giddel,
[57] Shephatiah, Hattil,
Pokereth-Hazzebaim and Ami
[58] The temple servants and the descendants of
the servants of Solomon 392

[59] The following came up from the towns of Tel Melah,
Tel Harsha, Kerub, Addon and Immer, but they could
not show that their families were descended from Israel:
[60] The descendants of
Delaiah, Tobiah and Nekoda 652

[61] And from among the priests:
The descendants of
Hobaiah, Hakkoz and Barzillai (a man who
had married a daughter of Barzillai the
Gileadite and was called by that name).

[62] These searched for their family records, but
they could not find them and so were excluded from
the priesthood as unclean. [63] The governor ordered
them not to eat any of the most sacred food until
there was a priest ministering with the Urim and
Thummim.

[64] The whole company numbered 42,360,
[65] besides their 7,337 male and female slaves; and
they also had 200 male and female singers. [66] They
had 736 horses, 245 mules, [67] 435 camels and 6,720
donkeys.

**[68] When they arrived at the house of the LORD in Jerusalem, some of the heads of the families gave freewill offerings toward the rebuilding of the house of God on its site. [69] According to their ability they gave to the treasury for this work 61,000 darics of gold, 5,000 minas of silver and 100 priestly garments.**

**[70] The priests, the Levites, the musicians, the gatekeepers and the temple servants settled in their own towns, along with some of the other people, and the rest of the Israelites settled in their towns.**

IN THIS CHAPTER THE AUTHOR INCLUDES A LIST of roughly 50,000 people (2:64–66) who were stirred by the Lord to return to Jerusalem (1:5). This list, one among several in the book,[1] serves a distinct purpose when observing its literary structure, theological content, and placement in the book. Chapter 1 focused on fulfilled prophecy, specifically through Cyrus's decree. Part of that fulfilled prophecy involved restoration of Abraham's seed (a people) and their repossession of the land (a place) after the exile, according to the promises of God. The genealogy of chapter 2 puts a zoom lens on the people side of those promises. The main point of the pericope, therefore, becomes evident: genealogy defines the true people of God, whose identity and inheritance are rooted in a relationship; that relationship entails the promises of God.

As mentioned above, the chapter's structure is important. Although not divided evenly with respect to literary space, it divides topically into two lists or groups of people returning to Jerusalem. The first group consists of those "who came up" (v. 1) who could prove their descent was from Israel. Ezra 2:2b–58 concerns a list of lay people and ministers who have legal connections with the past; that is, they have documentary proof that their families descended from Israel.[2]

The second group consists of "the ones who came up" (v. 1) who could not prove their descent was from Israel (vv. 59–63). The contrasting

1. Ezra 1:9–10; 10:18–44; Neh 7:5–73; 10:1–27; 11:1–36; 12:1–26.

2. The keeping and compilation of family records or registers is assumed on the basis of Neh 7:5ff and 1 Chr 1:1–9:44.

language used in Ezra 2:59–63 leads to a natural division of the material. Ezra 2:59–63 concerns a list of lay people and ministers who have questionable connections with the past. These folks could not show documentary proof that their families descended from the true seed of Israel (v. 59). The chapter then concludes with a summary about the arrival of these groups and subsequent settlement into their towns (vv. 64–70).

## The People Returning to Jerusalem (2:1–70)

### Those with Documentary Proof of Descending from Israel (2:1–58)

**The people and the leadership (2:1–2).** In 2:1 the people are designated first as "the people of the province"[3] and as those "who came up from the captivity of the exiles." The former identifies the people with Persia and the latter identifies the people with Babylon.[4] Both designations reveal the painful reality of the past seventy years for God's people. Instead of belonging to and being members of national Israel, Judah was enveloped as part of Persia with no authority of her own. Rather than enjoy the privileges associated with their homeland, they were identified as captives. Indeed, the designation "the people of the province who came up from the captivity of the exiles" makes clear that they were cut off from the promises of God and alienated from the commonwealth of Israel, like strangers relative to the covenant of promise, without hope and God's presence.

These captive people, however, are returning to their homeland of Jerusalem and Judah. In this regard another exodus is taking place, one promised by the prophet Isaiah: "Leave Babylon, flee from the Babylonians! . . . The Lord has redeemed his servant Jacob" (Isa 48:20–22). Those "who came up from captivity" are journeying from Babylon to Jerusalem (Ezra 1:11) as decreed by God. Moreover, the author says they are returning "each to their own town" (2:1). This geographical specificity is the first of several reminders in the chapter that, although captives

---

3. Under Persian hegemony this refers to the returned people lived in Yehud, a new Persian administrative territory or province.

4. In this one verse alone the author repeats words that connect the people to their previous hardships: the mention of King Nebuchadnezzar (1x), Babylon (2x), *golah* or "exile" (2x in Hebrew but translated the second time in the NIV as "captive"); and the word for captive or captivity, *shabah* (1x in Hebrew).

and cut off for these many years, they still have an inheritance in the land; therefore, a covenantal connection with the preexilic community is maintained.

The opening verse (2:1) forms an inclusio with the closing verse of the chapter (2:70). In 2:1 the people are designated as captives, but in 2:70 they are designated as "Israelites." In 2:1 they are returning, but in 2:70 they are residing. Once they take up residence and repossess the promised land, the "captive" designation is no longer used to describe the people. In both texts the author highlights their geographical ties to the land, another side to the promises of Abraham.

In Ezra 2:2 the people returning came with a "leadership team" or "company" of eleven according to the list of names in 2:2, and together with Sheshbazzar, already named in 1:8 and 11, these "twelve," a possible allusion to the twelve tribes, constitute the new leadership of the renewed community of Israel.[5]

As the ensuing narrative in Ezra-Nehemiah makes clear, both Zerubbabel and Joshua, the first two names on the list, emerge as key players in the restoration and rebuilding process. In six instances they are mentioned together (3:2, 8; 4:3; 5:2; Neh 7:7; 12:1).[6] Of these six instances, on only one occasion is Joshua's name given first (3:2). The fact that Zerubbabel's name appears first in five of six instances is not surprising given

---

5. A parallel list of returnees is also found in Neh 7 with a leadership team of twelve, but the list does not mention Sheshbazzar as part of the first return. This has led some to assume and infer the following: (1) the two names refer to the same person; (2) Ezra speaks of a leadership team led by Sheshbazzar under Cyrus (Ezra 1:1–4; 5:13–16) and a second team led later by Zerubbabel under Darius (2:1–70). These assumptions call into question Ezra's own record of a return under Sheshbazzar. As a priest and scribe, and as one who utilizes primary source documents throughout the work to tell the story, scribal inaccuracy on his part seems highly unlikely. If one takes the text at face value, the easiest way to understand this is that Ezra shows the two as contemporaries and both as leaders, but that Zerubbabel took on a different and more prominent role over time. For similar conclusions and a full discussion see Andrew Steinmann, *Ezra and Nehemiah: A Theological Exposition of Sacred Scripture*, Concordia Commentary (St. Louis: Concordia Publishing, 2010), 29–39. The Nehemiah list will be discussed in the commentary below, especially with respect to its placement and function within the context of the restoration of the walls and the renewal of the covenant (Neh 8–10).

6. The same is true of these individuals when addressed by the prophets Haggai and Zechariah (Hag 1:1, 12–13; 2:2, 4; Zech 6:9–15). Both prophets intersect with the narrative of rebuilding the temple and are key to the success of the project (see Ezra 5:1–2; 6:14). On one occasion, however, Haggai speaks only to Zerubbabel (2:21). In Zechariah, the word of the Lord is reserved for Zerubbabel alone in chapter 4.

his responsibility. As Judah's later governor,[7] he apparently succeeded Sheshbazzar's initial leadership role as "prince of Judah" and "governor" (1:8; 5:14) for reasons not stated. In this way Zerubbabel gives solid administrative leadership to the project. In addition, as the grandson of King Jehoiachin (Ezra 3:2; Matt 1:11–12; Luke 3:27), Zerubbabel has a position in the Davidic line, a hope of reestablishing kingship, which is why both Matthew and Luke list him in the ancestry of Jesus.[8] However, due to the curse on Jehoiachin, which prohibited anyone from his line to sit on David's throne (Jer 22:28–30), Zerubbabel would not serve as Israel's king. Thus, as a governor with past ties to royalty, Zerubbabel is prominent in the narrative.

Joshua, as Judah's high priest,[9] gives solid spiritual leadership and is noted first when rebuilding the altar is in view (3:2). As high priest, he was uniquely qualified to give oversight in this area and thus is named first in that context. In addition, he is the great-great-grandson of Hilkiah (1 Chr 6:13). Hilkiah was the high priest who found the book of the law in the temple and aided King Josiah with religious reforms (2 Kgs 22:4–14; 23:4; 2 Chr 34:9–22). Like Hilkiah his great-great-grandfather, Joshua brings religious reform to the postexilic community and helps revive worship of Yahweh at a critical juncture in the nation's history. Together with Zerubbabel, these two men exercise leadership for the community.

The remaining names on the list, including Nehemiah and Mordecai, are people not as prominent but whose names match other biblical characters. Nehemiah cannot be, due to obvious reasons of chronology, the famous cupbearer who built the walls and was Judah's governor at a later time (Neh 1:11; 5:14). Such is also true of Mordecai, who is known for his involvement with the story in Esther, which dates much later.

On the one hand, in 2:1–2a the author tells us about the people and the leadership going up in very general terms. On the other, they are designated "the men of the people of Israel" (2:2b). This is the first of three occurrences of the designation "Israel" in chapter 2.[10] Moreover, in

---

7. We know from the prophet Haggai (1:1; 2:2, 21) that Zerubbabel was Judah's governor at the time of Darius, the Persian ruler following Cyrus.

8. 1 Chronicles 3:19 lists Zerubbabel as the son of Pedaiah, the brother of Shealtiel.

9. We know from the prophet Haggai (1:1, 12; 2:2, 4) that Joshua was Judah's high priest. The prophet Zechariah singles out the high priest Joshua and gives him the word of the Lord in Zech 3;1, 6, 8; 6:11.

10. See also 2:59, 70.

the list that follows in 2:2b–70 he will elaborate, offering important and deliberate content about the identity of these "people of Israel."

**Lay People: Connections with the past by family of origin (2:2b–20).** The list commences with a broad umbrella category of lay people designated as "the men of the people of Israel" (vv. 2b–35). From a practical point of view, the designation distinguishes these from the ministers noted in 2:36–58. From a theological point of view, the fact that the returning remnant from exile is called "the people of Israel" has significance. Although the designation "Israel" on its own can indicate one of several collective entities in the Bible,[11] its use with "people" may help narrow the options. It probably refers to God's chosen people, the ethno-religious community that the LORD established when he rescued his people for relationship with him through the exodus and covenant at Sinai (Exodus 6:7–9; 12–24). The imagery attached to this would be of vital importance to people detached from such realities. The use of "the people of Israel" is a second reminder of the ties and connections these people have to a past that defined them.

In Ezra 2:3–20, eighteen family names emerge on the list. The expectation, based on a typical genealogy (see 1 Chr 1–9), is to have the present heads of the families mentioned (see 1:5 or 7:1–6; 8:1–14). Instead, the family name of an important ancestor in preexilic Israel is cited. Using the ancestral name rather than the current family head is the author's implicit way of stating that these people have a legal connection to the land. It is the third reminder that the people stirred by God to go up to Jerusalem have special covenantal connections to the land based on their ancestors or family of origin.

Within this list the author highlights two families in particular who have a connection with notable people of the past. The family of Pahath-Moab is noted because their ancestry intersects with that of Jeshua and Joab (v. 6). Likewise, the family of Ater is noted because their ancestry intersects with Hezekiah (v. 16).

The attention drawn to Jeshua and Joab in 2:6 and Hezekiah in 2:16 may not be an intentional case of name-dropping, especially since clear identification of these individuals is not possible. The latter is particularly true with respect to the quite common name Jeshua, a shorter version of

11. See commentary below on Ezra 2:70.

Joshua used mainly, although not exclusively, before the exile.[12] However, at the very least, a common thread with these three names has to do with associations to the tribe of Judah. Furthermore, both Joab[13] (if referring to David's sister's son and captain of his host) and Hezekiah[14] (if referring to Judah's great reformer king) could potentially boast of royal descent. Through this emphasis the author might be suggesting that not only do these two families going up to Jerusalem have ancestral ties to the land, but these ties may be royal.

**Lay People: Connections with the past by city of origin (2:21–35).** In Ezra 2:21–35, twenty-one geographical names emerge on the list. The list associates the people who are going up to Jerusalem and Judah with towns in the region, not an ancestor. Starting with "the men of Bethlehem," the folk listed are connected to the past by their city of origin or birthplace. Some of these place names are well known, but others are not. Regardless, people have land allocations based on specific towns and cities connected to their past. Again, this official covenantal connection is the fourth reminder that this group of returnees unequivocally has a stake in the land.

**Ministers: Connections with previous personnel (2:36–58).** After enumerating lay people (vv. 3–35), the author lists five distinct categories of ministers who return (priests, Levites, musicians, gatekeepers, and temple servants). Four families of priests are noted first (vv. 36–39). Of these priestly families, special attention is given by way of another parenthetical statement[15] to those descending from "Jedaiah (through the family of Jeshua)" (v. 36). The special mention again of one named Jeshua in the register of priests proves the common nature of the name as stated above. However, as a name associated with the head of one of the classes of priests, Jedaiah may have been prominent.

In the ministerial hierarchy, the high priest, priests, and Levites form a tripartite division, with the high priest at the highest level and the Levites at the lowest. Knowledge of these ministries derives mainly from the Pentateuch in reference to the building of the tabernacle. When the more

12. Per the NIV note Joshua is a variant of Jeshua. We see the transliteration of the name in English as Jeshua in 1 Chr 24:11; 2 Chr 31:13.

13. For Joab see 2 Sam 8:16; 20:23; 1 Chr 11:6.

14. For Hezekiah see 2 Kgs 18–20.

15. This was already seen in the Hebrew and English concerning Jeshua, Joab, and Hezekiah in Ezra 2:36; 6, 16.

permanent structure of the temple replaces the tabernacle, David develops these positions in accordance with the new worship situation in Jerusalem.

The priests, hailing from the tribe of Levi (Gen 49:5; 29:34), were responsible for services pertaining to God's house (1 Chr 23:32 cf. Num 8:11, 15). Likewise, they were to "do the work at the tent of meeting on behalf of the Israelites" (Num 8:19). God, however, first established the appointed duties of the priests through Aaron (Exod 28:1). The priesthood was reserved for the descendants of Aaron, and only they could minister at the sacrifices of the altar (Num 16:40). All priests, therefore, were Levites and descendants of Aaron by divine design (Exod 24–40). The list of priests does not mention anyone explicitly as descending from Aaron, however. According to David, who administratively and financially facilitated the building of the temple before his death, the priests (those in the middle of the tripartite structure noted above) were sacred officers of God (1 Chr 24:5).

Along with the priests, two families of Levites are named (2:40). Again, special parenthetical attention is given to those descending from "Jeshua and Kadmiel (of the line of Hodaviah)." These two families of Levites are associated with one named Hodaviah. Not much is known of him except that he might have been a chief Levite (1 Chr 5:24).

The Levites who occupied the lowest level in the ministerial hierarchy minded the service of the sanctuary as assistants to Aaron (Num 3:5–6). Their appointed duties were also established at God's command (Num 3–4). Because of their positive response to the golden calf incident, the Levites ordained themselves for the LORD'S service (Exod 32:29). David organized the Levites before his death and recommissioned them "in the service of the temple of the LORD," in place of carrying the tabernacle (1 Chr 23:24–32). They were also responsible for offering praises to God with instruments crafted by David for worship (1 Chr 23:5). As the numbers reveal, though, not many Levites were among the returnees.[16]

The list also includes musicians associated with the "descendants of Asaph" (v. 41). Asaph was a Levite appointed as chief worship leader/musician by David (1 Chr 6:39). Besides sounding the cymbals before

---

16. In fact, later when Ezra journeys toward Jerusalem with the second wave of exiles, he notices that none of the sons of Levi are in the group. As a result, he asks capable leaders to go and try to gather people from the tribe of Levi so that their mission might be successful upon arrival in Jerusalem (Ezra 8:15–20).

placing the ark in its resting spot (1 Chr 16:5–6; 2 Chr 5:12), his charge was the service of song; to play loudly on musical instruments and raise sounds of joy (1 Chr 15:16–17). The "sons of Asaph" did the same (1 Chr 6:39). Under the influence of God's Spirit and through ecstatic song and music, they were to offer thanksgiving and praise to God with lyres, harps, and cymbals at the time of Solomon (1 Chr 25:1–8; 2 Chr 20:14). Their duties were both small and great (1 Chr 25:8). As will be discussed below, "the sons of Asaph" were key for Israel's renewed worship experience when the temple foundation was laid (see commentary on Ezra 3:10).

There is mention also of six families of gatekeepers (2:42). As with the musicians, David organized the gatekeepers. He considered them as ministers in the house of the LORD, with tasks small and great alike (1 Chr 26:12–13). The gatekeepers were positioned as guards, east, west, north, and south on the four sides of the house of the LORD (1 Chr 9:23–25) so that nothing unclean would enter (2 Chr 23:19). The gatekeepers gave oversight to the treasures of the house of God (1 Chr 9:26–27; 12:25).

The list concludes with thirty-five families of temple servants and an additional ten families associated with the servants of Solomon (2:43–58). The former group, "temple servants" (NIV), reads literally in Hebrew as "the giving ones" or "the devoted /dedicated ones."[17] They are mentioned a total of fourteen times in Ezra-Nehemiah and once in Chronicles (1 Chr 9:2). The only concrete information about their identity comes from a statement made later in Ezra: they were people that David set apart specifically to attend the Levites (8:20). They devoted themselves daily to temple-related tasks, tasks that can only be assumed since no further information is given.

The mention twice of the descendants of the servants of Solomon should not go without notice (2:55, 58). Attaching people to this king's reign, along with the entire list of temple personnel and the isolation of their respective duties, serves to legitimize the task at hand, even if no descendant of Solomon would ever reign in Judah as king during the restoration period (539 BC–AD 70; Jer 22:28–30). Since Ezra 2:58 tallies the two groups together, the assumption is that they functioned together. Thus, this first division of the chapter ends with the list of Solomon's servants.

The list of lay people in 2:3–34 has significance. Those mentioned have the legal right to go up to Jerusalem and to renew their association

---

17. The typical Hebrew word for "servants" is *'avadim* not *nethinim*.

with promises and privileges of the past, either through family ties or place of origin. Likewise, the priests, Levites, musicians, gatekeepers, and temple servants have significance as well. They are legitimate personnel because David reestablished their positions relative to temple worship.[18] Isolating these ministerial categories and temple personnel reconnects postexilic Israel to preexilic Israel. Although few, these ministers bear a heavy weight of responsibility. They will reestablish and legitimize worship of the LORD in Jerusalem once the temple is built. All of these, both lay people and ministers, have proven through various means that they were of the true seed of Israel.

### Those Without Documentary Proof of Descending from Israel (2:59–70)

THE LIST NOW TURNS TO THOSE LAY PEOPLE and ministers "who came up" (2:1) but could not prove their descent was from Israel because of lost paperwork (2:59, 62). This is the second of three occurrences of the term "Israel" in chapter 2.[19] There exists a stark contrast with the previous material, providing a natural thematic division to the chapter. Unlike the list above that evidenced unequivocally that the people were from Israel, this short list acknowledges that no such documentary evidence existed to determine if they were truly part of the people of God.

Although relatively few were unable to show their Israelite descent by comparison with the previous group, three lay families are named first (v. 60). Next, three priestly families are mentioned (v. 61). In this group, Barzillai is parenthetically highlighted as Jeshua, Joab, Hezekiah, and Hodaviah were previously (vv. 6, 16, 36). The author deems further identification is necessary for Barzillai. Barzillai, the father of this family with questionable priestly descent, apparently married and took his name from his wife's family. Although separated by centuries, his wife's father was related to Barzillai the Gileadite. When King David was fleeing from Absalom, this wealthy man brought supplies to David and his men and provided an escort service for David after he defeated Absalom

---

18. That is, prior to the building of the temple, the tabernacle was Israel's means to commune with God. The requirements for worship and the necessary priestly personnel were already established by God's command outlined in Mosaic legislation. Thus, with the new and permanent structure of the temple, David is merely reestablishing that worship, but he also develops aspects of it as well.

19. See also Ezra 2:2b, 70.

(2 Sam 17:27–29; 19:31–39). In gratitude, David offered him a home in the palace and charged Solomon to show kindness to this man's sons (1 Kings 2:7). The point of the parenthetical information seems apparent: although this family will not get any special treatment, as indicated below, their remote connection to the court of David raises an eyebrow.

In Ezra 2:62–63 the outcome for the priests without records is given. Regardless of the search for their family records, no evidence surfaced to clarify the matter as it pertained to the priests. Ezra 2:62 states that "[t]hese searched for their family records, but they could not find them and so were excluded from the priesthood as unclean." Although family records were apparently lost for both lay people and priests (vv. 59, 62), the wording of the latter verse draws attention to the specific search pertaining to the priests since "exclusion" from the priesthood is mentioned as a result of the unsuccessful search.[20]

At the command of the governor of Judah, either Sheshbazzar or Zerubbabel, the priests had orders not to partake of the priestly meal. In Hebrew, Ezra 2:62 reads, "[t]hey were desecrated from the priesthood" or were deposed. The NIV does not fully capture the nuance of the term with the translation "excluded." An immediate, even abrupt response is in view with the use of this verb in Hebrew.[21] Accordingly, the desecration meant they were immediately unable to eat from the priestly food. The use of the verb, together with the entire incident, shows both the urgency and necessity of purity in the priesthood.

However, this "exclusion" is part of a larger process. Although God's will for these people could not be determined decisively by the legal paperwork, the Urim and Thummim would ultimately determine God's intentions for them once a priest was again officiating with these sacred instruments. According to pentateuchal references, the high priest's breastplate contained a pocket where these small objects were placed. Their purpose was to ascertain God's will in some situations, the

20. The lay people without records mentioned in 2:59–60 do not seem to be in view.

21. "Excluded. . . . as unclean" is one verb (*ga'al*) in the original, which can also be translated as "polluted" (see also Mal. 1:7 [2x], 12). In the passive form (*niphal* conjugation), the translation typically becomes "stained" or "defiled" (cf. Isa 59:3; Lam. 4:14; Zeph 3:1; see also Dan 1:8 for the reflexive, "defile oneself"). The underlying theme of sanctity/holiness in Ezra-Nehemiah warrants such a strong stance against that which is not viewed as holy and therefore unworthy to participate in the restoration of the worship of Yahweh. See discussion below on chapters 9–10 and Neh 13.

equivalent of providing a yes or no answer (Exod 28:30; Lev 8:8; Num 27:21; Deut 33:8; 1 Sam 23:9–12).

During the monarchy, it seems the Urim and Thummin fell into disuse (along with many other neglected sacred duties).[22] Ezra 2:63 suggests that after the exile these objects were available again, but due to lack of appropriate personnel, were not accessible for determining God's will. The larger point of the account here is that, in spite of the re-instatement of the Urim and Thummin ritual (see 1 Sam 30:7–8 for a "real-time" application of the ritual), it remains unclear whether the priests under scrutiny could be consecrated for the LORD's work. The author is also silent concerning the lay people and the outcome there.

Thus, this division in Ezra 2:59–63 ends on a dissatisfying note relative to the decisive standing and status of these individuals. Regardless, the author has made a clear point. This small group of people was not deemed Israelite enough. Reestablishing true worship in Israel cannot effectively be done if lay people and ministers of the LORD have questionable identity as the people of God.[23]

**Summary and conclusion (2:64–70).** Verse 64 functions as a numerical summary. The chapter concludes with what appears to be a total head count of people and their possessions, including servants and animals, that set out and eventually settled in Jerusalem. However, the total of the "whole company" listed in 2:64 does not mathematically equate when adding the numbers together, but that is not surprising as often lists are incomplete without intending to be exhaustive. Moreover, it is impossible to determine if the non-Israelite lay people and ministers noted in 2:59–63 were factored in the final head count. Overall, the numbers returning are not high when compared to the numbers of people exiled. This reveals that not everybody in exile wanted to return to his or her homeland of Jerusalem. Regardless, God stirred the few that went and they, no doubt, set out in faith, hoping in the promises of God.

The first thing that happened upon their arrival was the receiving of additional funds for the project. The leadership that welcomed the returnees also contributed financially. Their generosity supplemented

---

22. Besides 1 Sam 14:41, where the Urim and Thummin were used to establish guilt, the biblical record does not mention use after this time.

23. On the importance of genealogies, see M. D. Johnson, *The Purpose of the Biblical Genealogies* (Cambridge: Cambridge University Press, 1969), 43–44.

the donations already given, by those who stayed in Babylon (1:4–6) and Cyrus's gift (6:4). They gave, not under compulsion but as they were able. The whole scene is reminiscent of both David and the "leaders of families" who willingly gave for the work on the first house of the LORD (1 Chr 29:1–9), and the giving done by the people of Israel when the tabernacle was constructed (Exod 25:2–9; 35:21–29). They give willingly and according to their abilities. The financial abilities of the people are mixed, as noted in Ezra 2:65–66. Some are poor or of smaller means. This is seen by the fact they possess donkeys. Others are wealthy and of greater means as they possess slaves and horses. After the pain of sin's consequences suffered by the exile, giving to re-enable Israelite worship was no small victory. Regardless, this joyous occasion of giving marks the first act of worship the community takes toward reaching the goal of erecting God's house and prepares us for chapter 3.[24]

Verse 70 functions as a personnel summary of those who settled in their towns. Instead of starting with the lay people, the list starts by summarizing ministry personnel first, the reverse order of Ezra 2:2. As mentioned above, 2:70 forms an *inclusio* with the material in 2:1. The narrative has progressed so that those who "returned . . . each to their own town" (v. 1) have now "settled in their towns" (2x in v. 70). They re-inherited the promised land.

The author discards the negative labels used earlier to describe the people, because their fortune had changed (v. 1). This is the third and final time the Israelite designation appears in chapter 2. The fact that "the rest of the Israelites" dwelt in their towns shouts a return to national identity. Using the Israelite designation immediately calls to mind the descendants of Jacob as a group: those who were legal heirs to the promises, including a land to possess and a special relationship with the LORD. Moreover, the term unifies the exilic community with the preexilic community, particularly to the unified community established in the reigns of David and Solomon. It must be kept in mind that even before the exile the nation was divided as a result of Jeroboam's influence. The Northern Kingdom was designated as Israel and the Southern Kingdom was designated as Judah (1 Kgs 12). Previously the kingdom had unity

24. This recalls the first act of worship that entailed giving for building the tabernacle prior in Exodus (Exod 25:1–7) as well as the act of worship that entailed giving for the building of the temple (1 Chr 29:1–9).

under David's and Solomon's rules. The use of the Israelite designation, therefore, speaks of a unified ("reunified") people of God who dwell in their land and yet are to be distinguished from the people of the land. Although from the Persian political point of view they are "the people of the province" (v. 1), they are, from a theological point of view, God's people, and their return to the promised land constitutes proof. The chapter ends on a high note of hope.

Thus the author carefully and deliberately communicates to the reader through this thematically structured genealogy. Through the structure, the author tells us who is a part of Israel and who is not. Important theological content or reminders emerge that legitimize the connection these people have to their rich past. Their legitimate connection, therefore, authorizes them for the task assigned by Cyrus. In this way, the literary placement of the genealogy, at the beginning of the narrative, makes sense. The task could not be accomplished without the proper people and temple personnel returning. The zoom lens that has been placed on the people via the genealogy is the author's way of showing the restoration of Abraham's seed. Thus, combined with Cyrus's edict in chapter 1, the genealogy provides further evidence of fulfilled prophecy.

The main point of the pericope, therefore, stands out. The genealogy defines the true people of God whose identity and inheritance are rooted in a relationship; that relationship entails the promises of God. The picture is a remnant returning, receiving, and residing in the land. This identity and inheritance are not subject to change even after years of ruin and devastation.

## Identity and Inheritance: Who Is in and Who Is Out and Why

THIS GENEALOGICAL ACCOUNT OF INCLUSION and exclusion represents the first "shot across the bow" in Ezra-Nehemiah regarding what constitutes a true member of the community in Yehud. The standards of ethnic identity during the postexilic period follow the expected patterns of primordial (bloodlines) ethnic identity established during the patriarchal/ancestral period and through the time of the emergence of Israel in Canaan and the monarchy. Established primordial identities through the tracing of bloodlines is foundational in forging Israelite identity throughout its history.[25] Nevertheless, and following anthropological, ethno-historical, and ethnographic research, ethnic markers do shift depending on the variables of the socio-historical setting in view (what anthropologists call the instrumental/circumstantial dimensions of ethnic identities[26]). Thus, identities will emphasize either instrumental or primordial traits in different ways depending on the context. This sense of shifting dynamics is especially true in tribal settings.[27] For instance, the period of the emergence of Israel in Canaan (Late Bronze/Iron Age I period, 1400–1200 BC) represents a time that reflects variability and includes certain instrumental/circumstantial traits (i.e., shifting tribal loyalties toward Yahwism as in the case of Rahab [Josh 2, 6], Ruth, and Jael [Judg 5]) in addition to the expected primordial markers of identity, such as genealogies/bloodlines, language, territory and other "fixed" categories.

However, the return to the land under Persian occupation—now as a clear ethnic minority—draws the focus back to primarily ancestral (primordial) traits of what constitutes an "Israelite." Gone are the days of being able to claim the land as their own (see Ezra 9 and Neh 9, e.g., "we are slaves to this day"). Gone are the days when they can claim the majority status among the people of the land (even if they could never truly take control of the "promised" land; see Judg 1 for a well-known catalogue of the failure of the conquest as envisioned in Josh 1). Instead, the returnees are weak, under threat from their hostile immediate neighbors to the north, east, and south (a point made particularly poignant during the tenure of Nehemiah; see Neh 4:1–14). To keep the identity "pure" (through genealogical proof) is paramount and key to their survival. The point is all the more obvious to the postexilic community in light of the devastating effect of the exile. As the story unfolds in Ezra-Nehemiah, we are confronted with the sense of tremendous fear and

---

25. There is an abundance of literature on ethnic identity in the past. A strong theoretical framework to understand the dynamics of identities is offered by S. Jones (*The Archaeology of Ethnicity.* London: Routledge, 1997). Discussions usually summarize and adapt the same ideas to their particular foci, e.g., K. Sparks on ethnic identity in ancient Israel (*Ethnic Identity in Ancient Israel* [Winona Lake, IN: Eisenbrauns, 1996]). K. Southwood (*Ethnicity and the Mixed Marriage Crisis in Ezra 9–10* [Oxford: Oxford University, 2012]) focuses on the question of marriage in Ezra (see discussion below).

26. Cf. Jones, *Archaeology of Ethnicity.*

27. T. Petter, "Tribes and Nomad in the Iron Age Levant" in *Behind the Scenes of the Old Testament.* J. Greer, J. Hilber, J. Walton, ed. (Grand Rapids: Baker [2018]), 391–95.

pressure on the part of the principals not to fall back on the sin-patterns of the past (especially intermarriage with foreigners, i.e., non-Yahwists in the context of Ezra-Nehemiah).

Thus, during the postexilic period one's identity and inheritance are critical and directly related to a relationship that entails receiving the promises of God as enshrined in the identity of the family. The "given" (primordial) trait of historical identity predominates. The appeal to the authority of the ancestors, especially Moses, becomes particularly significant (see discussion below in Ezra 3 and Neh 8). Thus, only if they can truly demonstrate their identity can they be the true people of God. Only the true people of God can inherit the promises of God. Only the true people of God can fulfill his purposes and carry out his work in the land, namely, the restoration of the worship and sanctity of Zion.

Who the true people of God are during the postexilic period must be answered unequivocally and categorically. They must be tied to ancestral history, and the genealogies must provide incontrovertible evidence of inclusion (and exclusion). The success of the mission is at stake. Anyone who is found to be defiled will compromise the restoration of the worship (and create a new pathway to exile). The presence of unqualified temple personnel will also seriously compromise the mandate by the Persian authorities to both Ezra and Nehemiah to restore the correct worship of Yahweh (see Ezra 7 and Neh 1–2). In this socio-historical setting, bloodlines speak loud and clear and forge firm relational ties to "Israel," one of the chief patriarchal fathers (Jacob). This means inheritance rights are restricted to those who are Israelites. As the remnant returns under the edict of Cyrus, only those who can demonstrate legitimate relational ties to ancestral Israel are allowed to, as it were, "repossess the land" (the theme of "conquest" will be picked up in Ezra 9–10).

According to this model of ethnic identity during the postexilic period, the concept of an elect group of people inheriting and possessing a land strikes at the very heart of the promises to Abram (Gen 12:1–3, 7). Inheriting the land, however, was tied to a relationship with God: "The whole land of Canaan . . . I will give as an everlasting possession to you and your descendants after you; and I will be their God" (Gen 17:8). The people of Yehud are reappropriating for themselves the narrative of their ancestors in terms of promise-fulfillment. In the book of Exodus God conducts a rescue mission: "I will take you as my own people, and I will be your God" (Exod 6:7). God rescued Israel from Pharaoh and

Egypt and arranged Israel's itinerary to be with him. As a result of that rescue mission, God gives them inheritance rights: "And I will bring you to the land I swore with uplifted hand to give to Abraham, to Isaac and to Jacob" (Exod 6:8). God then tells Moses that with his help, Moses will take them out of Egypt and into Canaan, the promised land. They will reside in this land, which is God's, with the status of foreigners and strangers (Lev 25:23). In the book of Joshua, the story moves forward to that end (of inheritance) in a profound way. God charges Joshua to go into the land because God is about to give it to his people (Josh 1:2–6). This required faith in the promises of God. Indeed, Joshua and Israel acquire the land through no merit of their own (13:1–19:51), and the entire narrative is summed up in Joshua 21:43: "So the LORD gave Israel all the land he had sworn to give their ancestors, and they took possession of it and settled there." Thus here, along with geneaology, the all-important primordial category of "land" is upheld as well (though now limited largely to Zion itself, as the narrative will reveal).

In this recollection of their past, the community of Yehud takes the threat of idolatry extremely seriously, since the idolatry of their fathers compromised their identity to the core and ended up canceling their inheritance rights altogether. Because of idolatry they were unidentifiable as God's people—"you are not my people, and I am not your God" (Hos 1:9). The covenantal curse of Deuteronomy 28:63 became a reality. If not careful to obey the words of the law, God promised they would be "uprooted from the land" which they were entering to take possession. Ironically, Israel polluted the land in like manner of the Canaanites who previously possessed it (e.g., Judg 2:11–13). Israel's destiny was precisely like the Canaanites' (hence the term "canaanization" applied to Israel's waywardness). Just as the Canaanites were forcefully removed, the Israelites experienced the same fate: "So Israel was exiled from their own land to Assyria until this day" (2 Kgs 17:23 ESV). "For because of the anger of the LORD it came to the point in Jerusalem and Judah that he cast them out of his presence" (2 Kgs 24:20 ESV). Both their identity and inheritance were lost. One gets the sense that this sad narrative is a constant focus of Ezra-Nehemiah. Events will show that both men are not about to allow this history of idolatry to repeat itself, along with the certain outcome of exile.

Now through Cyrus's decree, the charge is to go back to the land and rebuild (Ezra 1:1–4). This required renewed faith in the promises of

God as in the times of Joshua. This faith dimension, as the people of Yahweh, crucially connects their identity to that of their forefathers. Prior to the significance of bloodline and land, there was the all-important circumstantial/instrumental dimension of faith (Gen 15:6). The faith of the postexilic community as a circumstantial marker is also reflected in Ezra-Nehemiah. God is graciously giving them back the land and, indeed, the Israelites repossess it in Ezra 2 through no merit of their own. Thus, their "kingdom" markers of identity are being restored and strongly connect to the key traits of Israelite identity markers of the past. Their core kingdom markers of identity (election and response of faith) stand the test of time because not only did God initially arrange Israel's itinerary to be with him (Exodus), but he renews their itinerary (a *new* exodus, just as Isaiah foretold, cf. Isa 40) by bringing them back to the land, so he can continue in relationship with them and cause them to (begin to) receive their inheritance: "I will surely gather them from all the lands where I banish them in my furious anger and great wrath; I will bring them back to this place and let them live in safety. They will be my people, and I will be their God" (Jer 32:37–38).

The conception of their identity, in preexilic times and now at the time of Ezra-Nehemiah, comes together: it was all about relationship then, and it is all about relationship now. The Lord says, "I will say to those called 'Not my people,' 'You are my people'; and they will say, 'You are my God'" (Hos 2:23). The restoration that takes place in Ezra-Nehemiah reestablishes their identity and inheritance rights as the people of God. Even though they appear to have ceased to exist as God's people, he never stopped being their God, and the return to the land of their inheritance is further evidence of this reality.[28] Thus, in Ezra 2:70, where both lay and priestly/levitical Israelites "settled" in their towns, one finds a striking similarity in wording to Joshua, where "the Lord gave Israel all the land he had sworn to give their ancestors, and they

---

28. In this regard, the magisterial and dynamic *longue durée* shifting patterns in ethnic conceptions in Israel follow documented patterns in other tribal settings. Tribal identities appear and then disappear from the pages of history, only to reemerge later on. The history of the postexilic period as anchored in Ezra-Nehemiah provides yet another example of this phenomemon, now superintended by divine providence since God was not about to abandon his "holy race" (*zer'a haqodesh* Ezra 9:2, see discussion there; a phrase itself taken from Isa 6:13 "holy seed" [*zer'a qodesh*]), from whom the Savior of the world would come (Rom 1:3; 9:5).

took possession of it and settled there" (Josh 21:43). The settlement in their towns reflects tangible proof of God's faithfulness to his people.

This postexilic conception of identity, then, is consistent with the preexilic markers of loyalty to Yahwism and descent, with the accompanying privileges that are also material—namely, the restoration of worship in Zion in the province of Yehud. Nevertheless, the option for inclusion of other nations is no longer described as it was during the formative years of Israelite identity (e.g., "many other people went up with them" in the exodus, Exod 12:38 ). It must be noted at the outset of our discussion on the question of exclusion and inclusion (see Ezra 9–10 and Neh 13 in particular) that, a priori, the option to join the community of faith for non-Israelite descent entities remains open since it is enshrined in the law of Moses (e.g., all the laws regulating the outsiders within Israel) and actualized in preexilic history. However, and this is perhaps the most important contextually driven shift in conceptions of identity during the postexilic period, the postexilic community has precious little margin for error as they seek to rebuild Zion and its worship. This sense of urgency is reflected at critical junctures in the rest of the corpus of Ezra-Nehemiah. Clearly the inclusion of the outsider, while most probably readily known by Ezra and Nehemiah, who are both keen readers and interpreters of the law of Moses (see Ezra 7, 9, Nehemiah 1, 13), cannot be factored into the restoration of worship by the priestly and Levitical class. In this regard the standards are equally strict in preexilic settings. It is one thing to recognize the legitimacy of Rahab's presence among Israel "to this day" (Josh 6:24); it is quite another to have compromised Levites and priests involved in the cult of Yahweh (see Ezra 9:1 and commentary below).

### Returning to the Core: NT Conceptions of Identity and Inheritance

PAUL TAKES THIS DISCUSSION OF IDENTITY head on in the book of Romans, especially chapters 4 and 9–11. The apostle reminds his Jewish and Gentile audience that identity in its origin was not primordial but circumstantial/instrumental. The "instrument" was Abram's faith, and the primordial origin of Abraham came second (who is "ungodly," Rom 4:5; cf. Josh 24:2). Spiritual descent is what matters rather than primordial descent. Even when Paul's argument weighs heavily toward the primordial benefits of ancestry (e.g., "the adoption to sonship; theirs the divine glory, the covenants, the receiving of the law, the temple worship and the promises," Rom 9:4–5), he also reminds his audience that not even this legitimate genealogical and historical connection (Abraham's descendants) provided guaranteed access to the promises associated with Abraham: "For not all who are descended from Israel are Israel" (Rom 9:6). His point, "it is not the children by physical descent who are God's children, but it is the children of the promise who are regarded as Abraham's offspring" (Rom 9:8), affirms that the circumstantial dimension of identity prevails in the end.

In Galatians, he argues that in Christ Jesus we are all children of God through faith (Gal 3:26) and that those who have faith are the true genealogical children of Abraham (Gal 3:7). If one belongs to Christ, then we are Abraham's seed, and heirs according the promise (Gal 3:29). God's children are made his heirs (Gal 4:7; Rom 8:17). Thus because of Jesus "the Gentiles are heirs together with Israel, members together of one body, and sharers together in the promise in Christ Jesus" (Eph 3:6). It is all about relationship. In this way, the New Testament returns to the core marker of Old Testament identity as the "people of the LORD" (*'am Yahweh*, e.g., Judg 5:13): faith. This is the definition of identity embedded in the very life of Abraham, Moses, Ruth (the Moabitess-turned-Israelite who becomes David's ancestor), Uriah the Hittite (2 Sam 11:6, 11), and so on. As Paul returns to this definition, he of course follows in the footsteps of his Lord, who schooled his own at Capernaum (see Luke 4:16–30) that faith, not ancestry, determines who is "in" and who is "out" (the people's reaction—"furious," v. 28—makes it quite clear whether they themselves are in or out).

Accordingly, the New Testament authors, then, also redefine the nature of what is inherited. Far greater than a piece of real estate on the Eastern Mediterranean coastline, God has blessed us with every spiritual blessing in the heavenly places because of our position "in Christ" (Eph 1:3). In God's great mercy we have been given an imperishable inheritance kept in heaven (1 Pet 1:4). The proof? God sent his son that we might receive adoption to sonship: "Because you are his sons, God sent the Spirit of his Son into our hears, the Spirit who calls out, '*Abba*, Father'" (Gal 4:6). As God's children, therefore, God has made us heirs (Gal. 4:7). The adoption paperwork is official! Thus Paul gives new meaning typologically to this concept of identity and inheritance, the consummation of which takes place at the end of the age.

The precursors to restoration that we see in the return to the land, the rebuilt temple, and the incarnation find ultimate fulfillment in Revelation. This book provides *the* evidence that God restores and resurrects our identity and inheritance! The heavenly anthem that resounds in the book testifies to the accomplishment of God's goal. Here is the picture: besides the four living creatures, the twenty-four elders, and myriads upon myriads of angels (Rev. 7:11), John sees a crowd of people, a concert of sorts peopled by a multitude, where participants surround the throne of God, his seat of sovereignty over the universe (Rev. 7:9).

More specifically, Revelation shows that the results of God's rescue missions were successful! People from every nation—all tribes and peoples and languages—were there, standing before the throne. Their "concert" attire? They are adorned in white robes with palm branches in their hands, symbolism of purity. The "concert" music? John mentions that they are all making a very loud declaration! Their praise is exclusive; it recognizes that God alone possesses salvation, and that salvation could come by no other means *except* by God: "Salvation belongs to our God, who sits on the throne, and to the Lamb" (7:10). These are those God took for himself as a people, and they recognize him as their God! They recognize God as *savior* at this world-wide worship service! Hence, their unending song serves God by giving him the glory and honor he deserves. God never stops being our God, and we never stop being his people!

Finally, John sees a new heaven and earth. He sees the new Jerusalem, coming down out of heaven from God, prepared as a bride adorned for her husband (Rev 21:2). It is a permanent place of inheritance where the relationship will continue and never suffer loss. John hears "a loud voice from the throne saying, 'Look, God's dwelling place is now among the people . . . They will be his people, and God himself will be with them and be their God!'" (Rev. 21:3). The voice affirms the permanent nature of the situation. God has indeed arranged and rearranged our itinerary and brought us to himself. Our identity and inheritance remain secure. The faith dimension of identity prevails in the end, a faith populated by people of various ancestry and language (i.e., primordial markers). This is the endgame, the 30,000 ft view. But now, back with feet on the ground in the the fifth century BC, the pressure to rebuild Zion from the ground up and restore worship of Yahweh is tremendous. The imposition of hostile neighbors and the community's own complacencies (see Hag 1) all weigh heavily on the minds of the architects of the restoration (first Zerubbabel and Joshua, then Ezra and Nehemiah). The need is for a clean break from the past and a fresh start with a new identity. Only then can the wheels of redemptive history turn again toward this awesome fulfillment envisioned by John, himself in exile, on the Isle of Patmos.

As we journey in becoming the people of God, we need to be reassured that when we lose our spiritual markers of identity because of our own wrongdoing or life's circumstances, we are *still* God's! The fact of the matter is this: we make our own markers of identity as a result of trying to figure out who we are. Some of us make our markers of identity by preserving and emphasizing the physical. Others of us identify our identity by education, achievements, professions, titles, by being a wife, husband, mother, or father. Still some of us make our markers of identity by the wrong things we have done (abortion, sex offender, etc.), or with adverse health issues and disorders (I am a cancer patient, I have ADD, I am a single mom, widower, etc.).

The problem with the markers of identity that we establish is that they do not stand the test of time, because they are of human origin. Another problem with the markers of identity that we create is this: If who we are is what we have, and what we have is taken away, then who are we? If who we are is our profession, education, health, family, beauty, reputation, country, and if those things are taken away, then who are we? We feel empty and like nobodies as a result. We need, therefore, to have a purpose that is not grounded in ourselves. Essentially, it might be summed up this way: we don't know who we are until we know *whose* we are! Therefore, as those who have been taken directly into the loving and safe arms of God, we are not just any people, but we are people of the living God! We have an identity based on this common experience. We belong, are legitimate, have been cared for, and are included. The cross tells us that a relationship with God is what defines us. God has told us who we are. We are his. This is the most secure marker of identity we can have. The cross also tells us he is our God. Since no other has done what Christ has done, he is our God, the master and maker of our identity and destiny. Our relationship with Christ ensures our provision, protection, and guidance.

As our God, he gives us incredible privileges and rank. We have inheritance rights. God grants us privileges that outrank our human existence. We are the people of God, and with this comes great perks. We are all blue bloods because of his shed blood. Everything is not lost; we are still somebody even when what we have is taken away from us. We still have everything, because he never stops being our God. The challenge is to exchange our markers of identity for his, especially the negative markers. Likewise, we need to put into better perspective our markers of identity, vis-á-vis the kingdom marker of identity.

Although a true heir, I did not inherit a penny when my father passed away. To be sure, the inheritance would have been minimal given the blue-collar background of his employment. Regardless, the issue that pained me was not the money that might have been involved; it was my legal right to inherit based on being his daughter. The issue was one of identity.

Ten years after my mother died of cancer, my father remarried, happily, a woman with three older children. Although he promised to put a will together before they wed, it never happened. The state law where he resided, however, guaranteed that in the event of death without a will, inheritance rights belong to the blood children, regardless of remarriage or the relationship of the children to the new spouse. This law consoled me, because internally I was fighting a deep loss of identity, through the death of my mother many years previous and my dad's remarriage. Without a will, the state would affirm my identity, something I was desperately seeking to achieve. I had nothing to worry about, or so I thought. In the intervening years, not long before my dad died, I was informed that a living trust was set up that, for some reason, excluded me and my sister. I was devastated. The paperwork confirmed my worst fears—the complete loss of my identity. My identity seemed stolen, and I felt I was a victim of identity theft. How and why all this transpired remained a mystery, as I was very close to my dad.

I was faced with deeper, soul-searching questions, questions that I thought were already answered as a result of walking with God for many years. Where does my true identity come from? What is my true inheritance? Perhaps I did not quite yet know who I was in God? No doubt, these facts about my faith were put to the test. My true identity and true inheritance in Christ became the anchor for my soul in the pain of such a loss. I told myself over and over again that God was my inheritance. My self-talk was reliant on the cross. This saying is so true, that we do not know who we are until we know whose we are. Even though I had the legal right to inherit, it was taken away from me—and there was nothing I could do about it. I realized the only rights I had were granted to me through God's grace. As John says, "to those who believed in his name, he gave the right to become children of God" (John 1:12). I am a daughter of the living God. I legally belong to him and bear his name. My identity is secure. God is my inheritance along with the riches of heaven. Neither my identity nor inheritance is subject to change. My heart was at peace.

A few months after my dad's death, a curious letter came in the mail from the U.S. government. Apparently, my dad took out a life insurance policy when he worked for the VA Hospital. It was in the amount of $10,000. There were two lines that read:

| | | | |
|---|---|---|---|
| **Beneficiary #1** | **My sister's name** | **Relationship: Daughter** | **Amount $5,000** |
| **Beneficiary #2** | **My name** | **Relationship: Daughter** | **Amount $5,000** |

This was documentary proof that I was my father's daughter and that he was looking out for me! It was my father's desire to be sure his daughters were looked after. Even though my true identity and inheritance were strangely denied to me through the circumstances of his remarriage, I felt vindicated, elated, and affirmed at the same time. Although in many ways I was a victim of identity theft, the truth about who I was (this side of heaven) could not be denied. I actually had the legal right to receive what was due me. The U.S. Government validated it, too! In fact, I made a file with a copy of the document declaring the truth about my identity as a stone of remembrance. While my identity was secure knowing I belonged to God's family, it was nice to be reminded that at one time I belonged to a loving earthly family of four, graciously given to me by God. As a result of this correspondence, together with the work of God, the deep loss of identity I experienced through my mother's death and my dad's subsequent remarriage became a gain. Indeed, it was God's sweet way of acknowledging an end of the pain of the past. The issue is identity. We do not know who we are until we know whose we are!

# Ezra 3:1–13

1 When the seventh month came and the Israelites had
settled in their towns, the people assembled together as one
in Jerusalem. 2 Then Joshua son of Jozadak and his fellow
priests and Zerubbabel son of Shealtiel and his associates
began to build the altar of the God of Israel to sacrifice burnt
offerings on it, in accordance with what is written in the
Law of Moses, the man of God. 3 Despite their fear of the
peoples around them, they built the altar on its foundation
and sacrificed burnt offerings on it to the LORD, both the
morning and evening sacrifices. 4 Then in accordance with
what is written, they celebrated the Festival of Tabernacles
with the required number of burnt offerings prescribed
for each day. 5 After that, they presented the regular burnt
offerings, the New Moon sacrifices and the sacrifices for all
the appointed sacred festivals of the LORD, as well as those
brought as freewill offerings to the LORD. 6 On the first day
of the seventh month they began to offer burnt offerings to
the LORD, though the foundation of the LORD's temple had
not yet been laid.

7 Then they gave money to the masons and carpenters, and
gave food and drink and olive oil to the people of Sidon and
Tyre, so that they would bring cedar logs by sea from Lebanon
to Joppa, as authorized by Cyrus king of Persia.

8 In the second month of the second year after their
arrival at the house of God in Jerusalem, Zerubbabel son of
Shealtiel, Joshua son of Jozadak and the rest of the people
(the priests and the Levites and all who had returned from
the captivity to Jerusalem) began the work. They appointed
Levites twenty years old and older to supervise the building
of the house of the LORD. 9 Joshua and his sons and brothers
and Kadmiel and his sons (descendants of Hodaviah) and the
sons of Henadad and their sons and brothers—all Levites—
joined together in supervising those working on the house
of God.

[10] When the builders laid the foundation of the temple of
the LORD, the priests in their vestments and with trumpets, and
the Levites (the sons of Asaph) with cymbals, took their places
to praise the LORD, as prescribed by David king of Israel.
[11] With praise and thanksgiving they sang to the LORD:

"He is good;
his love toward Israel endures forever."

And all the people gave a great shout of praise to the
LORD, because the foundation of the house of the LORD was
laid. [12] But many of the older priests and Levites and family
heads, who had seen the former temple, wept aloud when
they saw the foundation of this temple being laid, while many
others shouted for joy. [13] No one could distinguish the sound
of the shouts of joy from the sound of weeping, because
the people made so much noise. And the sound was heard
far away.

CHAPTER 1 ANNOUNCED THE PLAN TO REBUILD the Jerusalem temple through Cyrus's edict. Chapter 2 focused on the people returning to the land who would realize the plan. Now in chapter 3 the actual building project commences. It contains a literary symmetry, whereby the chapter naturally divides into two sections relative to what is built. The first section commences with building the altar of burnt offering (3:1–2) followed by responses at its completion (3:3–6). The second section discusses the rebuilding of the temple foundations (3:7–9) followed by responses at their completion (3:10–13). The entire chapter, however, is part of the larger literary unit encompassing Ezra 3:1–6:22 that envisions the completion of the temple. Far from merely describing the building project, the chapter reveals that true worship of Yahweh is underway for God's people once again. The main point reflects that the returned people of God, even after years of exile, can worship again because of God's goodness to them. Their markers of identity as the people of God (discussed in ch. 2) have been resurrected.

## The Altar Rebuilt (3:1–6)

**Rebuilding the altar (3:1–2).** The rebuilding of "the altar of the God of Israel" commences with the arrival of the seventh month, or early fall (September/October). The seventh month is significant for several reasons.

First, the author reports by way of introduction (v. 1) and conclusion (v. 6) that the activities surrounding the rebuilding of the altar take place in the seventh month, providing a literary framework for this section (3:1–6). The seventh month seems to suggest the passing of a period of time (2:70). The returned Israelites have been back in the land now for several months. They are, perhaps, more "settled" in their towns. Accordingly, it was a time to commence with what they were commissioned by Cyrus to do: build and care for the things of God.

Second, for a Jewish person the seventh month (Tishri or September/October) marks three mandatory celebrations in their calendar year.[1] The first day of the seventh month is the New Year and Festival of Trumpets (Lev 23:23–25; Num 29:1). It kicks off and inaugurates the important events of the seventh month whereby the ninth, tenth, and fifteenth days all required something special of the people. On the ninth day they were to keep their Sabbath (Lev 23:32). The tenth day was the Day of Atonement (Lev 23:26–32); and the fifteenth day was the Festival of Tabernacles (Lev 23:33–43). The latter extended for seven days longer and concluded roughly on the twenty-second/third day of the month. In all of these celebrations, sacrifices were needed and offered. The seventh month was a time of enthusiasm and deep reflection.

Without a rebuilt altar, the approaching seventh month and the associated events related to their rich religious past would not be possible, much like their experience in exile. The emphasis is not merely on rebuilding the altar, but on the altar's purpose. The altar is vital and tied to reestablishing their relationship to the Lord via the sacrificial system.

Third, given the religious weight of this calendar month, one understands the rally to Jerusalem that takes place in 3:1b. The seventh month rallies people in a unified way to Jerusalem. This unity is evidenced by the fact that literally "the people were gathered as one man to Jerusalem" (author's translation). The idiomatic language is reminiscent of the

---

1. The religious activity and fervor of the seventh month would correspond to the religious activity and fervor of the month of December in the mind of a Christian.

people of God who gathered previously with a unified voice for various occasions (Judg 20:1, 8, 11; see also Neh 8:1).

Unity of purpose, however, is further evidenced in that the gathered people are designated in the original as "the sons of Israel" (*beney yisra'el*) or "Israelites" (NIV). The use of this designation continues to confirm the point made previously (see commentary on 2:70); namely, that postexilic Israel is connected and unified to preexilic Israel. Perhaps more significant, the designation confirms that their identity as the people of God is restored.

The rally to Jerusalem in the seventh month was for the unified purpose of reestablishing worship to the LORD, something years of exile had suspended. In this way the seventh month represents so much more than a chronological peg. From a literary perspective, it structures the unit of thought in Ezra 3:1–6. It also signals movement forward from both a practical point of view (to rebuild the temple) and a theological perspective (to rebuild worship).

**Joshua and Zerubbabel (3:2).** From the midst of this unified group, two main leaders from the larger list of leaders previously noted (2:2) emerge to oversee the entire project, Joshua and Zerubbabel (3:2). Zerubbabel's name typically appears first when the two are mentioned together (i.e., Ezra 3:8; Hag 1:1, 12, 14). However, Joshua's name precedes here because the focal point of Ezra 3:1–6 pertains to rebuilding "the altar of the God of Israel" (v. 2), the piece of furniture central for the work of a priest such as Joshua. It is understandable that the high priest of the new community, together with his fellow Levites, is given prominence.

As high priest, Joshua was the nation's spiritual leader, providing access to God. His spiritual leadership would, perhaps, be best exemplified once the annual observance of the Day of Atonement was reinstated, after the temple's completion. On this solemn day, Joshua alone would have had access to the holy of holies. Upon entering he would sprinkle the blood of the sin offering over the mercy seat in order to cover the sins of the nation (Lev 16:1–34). Until this day, ceremonial purity was demanded of him as Israel's new spiritual leader, since he represented the people before God (Exod 28:29).

The role of high priest, the most prominent position in the priesthood before the exile, not only bears the same weight of responsibility but the role also reaches new heights after the exile given the absence of a reigning king.[2] Since no king would sit on the throne again in Jerusalem as in preexilic times, the influence of the high priest was even greater. Joshua's leadership goes uncontested and is affirmed by the prophets Haggai and Zechariah respectively (Hag 1:1–2:9; Zech 3:1–10).[3]

As Joshua and Zerubbabel provide spiritual and administrative leadership, verse 2 orients the reader to the specific goals of this covenantal community. Ezra 3:2 announces the stated project, "to build the altar of the God of Israel," but the verse also reflects the stated purpose for building the altar, "to sacrifice burnt offerings on it." Furthermore, Joshua and company have the stated authority backing their efforts, "in accordance with what is written in the Law of Moses, the man of God." This threefold statement merits further analysis.

First, the stated project: "to build the altar of the God of Israel." The "altar" spoken of here is "the altar of burnt offering" first discussed in Exodus and found in the courtyard of the tabernacle (Exod 27:1–8; 38:1–7) and noted also by the Chronicler (1 Chr 6:49; 16:40; 21:29). Solomon's "altar of bronze," a much larger rendition found in the courtyard of the temple, was the equivalent of this altar (2 Chr 1:5–6; 4:1). The name of the altar suggests its primary purpose, a point discussed below. The altar of burnt offering is distinct from the smaller altar of incense (Exod 30:1–10), which was placed before the veil that screened the holy of holies and functioned differently.

Moreover, the author notes the altar about to be rebuilt belongs to "the God of Israel." While the phrase "the God of Israel" is used panbiblically, Ezra 3:2 has the only occurrence of the specific designation "the altar of the God of Israel." The designation makes a purposeful and needed distinction.[4]

This altar should not be confused with altars presently in the land from the neighboring peoples and their respective gods. Given Israel's

---

2. The prophets Haggai and Zechariah show this reality.

3. More will be said concerning the prophets Haggai and Zechariah since they surface as dominant voices relative to the temple's completion (see commentary on Ezra 5:1; 6:14).

4. This mention of the altar in Ezra 3:2 is similar to the designation, "the glory of the God of Israel" used in Ezekiel's vision of abandonment (Ezek 8:4; 9:3; 10:19; 11:22) and the distinction made between the "image of jealousy" and God's glory at the temple's entrance. True ownership is emphasized in Ezekiel, as in Ezra with the altar.

past record[5] and affinities for religious pluralism and syncretism, the designation makes this distinction and is necessary upon returning to the land. The designation reinforces that centrality of worship belongs to Israel's God alone (Deut 12:4–7). It fits squarely within the purpose of Ezra-Nehemiah to restore the sanctity of Zion with the theme of holiness and separation. Sacrifices are to be holy unto the LORD, and they are to be separate from the people of the land. In fact, Joshua and Zerubbabel are obligated to reinforce this distinction by refusing help from the people of the land. Only people who could prove both Israelite ancestry and willingness to worship Israel's God were, in their minds, qualified to build alongside the returned exiles (Ezra 4:1–3).

Next, the stated purpose: "to sacrifice burnt offerings on it." As noted above, it is the altar's purpose, not its construction, that the author emphasizes. This emphasis is seen by the repetition of the terms "to sacrifice" "sacrifices" and "burnt offerings," found nine times in Ezra 3:1–6.[6] In addition, when the same altars were previously built at the time of Moses and Solomon, the biblical writer customarily[7] gave the size of the object for practical purposes, but also to highlight the grandeur of the building project. The latter is especially true of Solomon's temple. There is, however, no mention of the size of the new altar in Ezra 3:1–6, a point that seems to suggest that the author wants to underscore its important purpose.[8]

As the name suggests, the use of the altar was for offering up various sacrifices to the LORD. Israel's daily, weekly, monthly, and annual festivals all required sacrifices, but the rhythm of such practices was temporarily interrupted in exile. The burnt offering in particular was vital, since it was the most frequently offered sacrifice in the community.

Burnt offerings (Lev 1:3–17; 6:8–13[6:1–6]) come under the category of consecratory offerings along with cereal and drink offerings (Lev 2; 6:14–23[6:7–11]); Num 15:1–10). In very general terms, the sacrifice

---

5. Ezekiel 20:1–44 provides a stunning historical recollection of the nation's idolatrous behavior that commenced in Egypt and continued even into the exile.

6. Ezra 3:2 (2x); 3:3 (3x); 3:4 (1x); 3:5 (2x); 3:6 (1x). In Ezra 3:5 the NIV adds the term sacrifice (2x) for the sake of clarity, something not found in the Hebrew.

7. See Exod 27:1–8; 2 for the tabernacle altar and 2 Chron 4:1 for the temple altar.

8. Note, however, that in Ezra 6:3–4, when the rebuilding of the temple is under scrutiny at the time of Darius's reign, measurements are noted in the communication from Cyrus's decree.

made with this type of offering represented an act of full surrender and commitment to God. Furthermore, the burnt offering played a primary role in the festivals of the sacred calendar and was associated also with atonement. When a person offered a sheep, goat, or bird, the entire offering was consumed by the fire and deemed a pleasing odor to the LORD.

Thus, by building and sacrificing on the burnt altar, Israel is given the opportunity once again to access the divine presence and experience atonement for sins. The nation and individuals can devote themselves entirely to the LORD. These sacrifices officially reinstate their relationship to their God, the God of Israel, the one to whom the altar belongs, and the one to whom all worship rightfully belongs. God's people are free to offer to him their worship in an unhindered way.

Lastly, the stated authority: "in accordance with what is written in the Law of Moses, the man of God." The final clause of Ezra 3:2 mentions the weighty authority that backed the stated project and its purpose, the third element related to the goals of the community. This phrase appears only here in Ezra-Nehemiah. That authority, however, is not only the law of Moses, but that which is written in the law of Moses. The biblical writer is stressing the fixed, unchangeable, and even inerrant nature of the law of Moses by mentioning the written component, since through writing aspects of reality are communicated (so, too, the scroll in Ezek 2:10; Jer 36:1–22). The theme will continue in earnest elsewhere in Ezra-Nehemiah, especially during the covenant renewal ceremony in Nehemiah 8.

The phrase, "in accordance with what is written" is used numerous times in the historical books and functions as a justification for certain actions taken by the covenantal community. For example, they built an unhewn stone altar ("according to what is written"; Josh 8:31); the Passover had not been celebrated in large numbers, "according to what was written" (2 Chr 30:5; 2). Moreover, some "ate the Passover, contrary to what was written" (2 Chr 30:18).[9] Of note is the fact that the postexilic

9. Other actions include walking in God's ways (1 Kgs 2:3); not putting to death the children of a murderer (2 Kgs 14:6; 2 Chr. 25:4); sacrificing firstborns (Neh 10:34); celebrating Feast of Booths (Neh 8:15). Although the phrase "in accordance with what is written" is standard in the historical books, the prepositional phrase that typically follows it various significantly. Sometimes the reference is to that which is written in the "Law of Moses" (1 Kgs 2:3; 2 Chr. 23:18; 25:4 "the Law, the Book of Moses"). At other times

historical books (Ezra-Nehemiah; Chronicles) utilize the phrase the most. Since returning to proper worship practices after exile is in view throughout Ezra-Nehemiah, the community can only achieve this by making every effort to rely on God's fixed and unchangeable word, to do that which is "in accordance with what is written." The use of this phrase is, therefore, comprehendible and provides proper justification for their actions.

Although initially it was that which was written by decree of Cyrus that sanctioned the building project, it is only that which is written in the Law of Moses that can sanction their worship. This written authority is far more relevant to the covenantal community than the decree of Cyrus, king of Persia. Their mandate and emphasis as it pertains to rebuilding is to do it all "in accordance with what is written in the Law of Moses" (3:2; 7:6).

The mention of the "Law" with Moses' name attached to it is key. It is an appeal to Mosaic authority. As the figurehead and founder of the nation, it not only signifies the supreme authority by which they are reestablishing worship, but it reunites and connects them to their ancestral/primordial past, particularly Sinai and the supreme event of God giving the law to Moses. Their worship to the LORD is rooted and grounded in the word of God. This initial appeal on doing things according to the Law of Moses, however, prepares the reader for the roles of both Ezra and Nehemiah, but especially the former.

Later in the book when the reader is introduced to Ezra, he is described as a ready scribe in the law of Moses (7:6), the second instance of this authority. His mandate and emphasis as a scribe pertain to rebuilding the community's conduct according to Ezra's supreme example and authority, the law of Moses, to regulate the community's values and actions through it (7:25–26). The mention of the law with Moses's name here validates and authorizes Ezra's entire mission in a way no Persian king's laws could do. The law of Moses identifies and unifies them as a people, makes them separate, and distinguishes them afresh. Thus, as both these examples reveal, not only their worship but also their whole way of life

---

it is the "Book of the Law of Moses" (Josh 8:31; 2 Kgs 14:6); just "the book of Moses" (2 Chr. 35:12); or "the Book of the Covenant" (2 Kgs 23:2). One also finds reference to "the Law of the LORD" (2 Chr. 30:18; 31:3; 35:26). Finally, a few verses merely say, "as it is written" (Ezra 3:4; Neh 8:14–15).

will once again be centered on the law of Moses, an authoritative voice of the past that has relevance for the present.

Beyond these two instances (Ezra 3:2; 7:6), Nehemiah's reforms, mandated as they were by the Persian king, also have as their authority from either the "Law" (Neh 8:14; 10:34, 36) or the "Law of God" (*torat ha'elohim*, Neh 8:8; 10:29).[10] In sum, the law with or without Moses's name appears a total of seven times in Ezra-Nehemiah. The purpose seems evident. Only the law of Moses can recalibrate and anchor the community's actions on the heels of exile. As the ensuing story unfolds, it also anchors the people, in the face of their own fears and of fierce opposition from the local residents, for a time (3:3; 4:4–5). Thus, the Law (i.e., the Pentateuch) takes on a central authoritative role at the beginning of the rebuilding phase, even before the time of Ezra but in anticipation of the reforms he will bring.

The author appeals to Mosaic authority, however, not just by speaking of Moses's close association with the law. He also appeals to Mosaic authority in 3:2 by referring to him as "the man of God." Elsewhere Moses is also designated as a "man of God" by the narrator of Deuteronomy (33:1), the Chronicler (1 Chr 23:14; 2 Chr 30:16), the superscription to Psalm 90, and by Caleb (Josh 14:6).[11]

The designation "man of God," rather than a reflection of character, is a title that indicates another role Moses had in the preexilic covenantal community, a role similar to that of three non-writing prophets.

The designation "man of God" (*'ish ha'elohim*, not "prophet," *nabi'*) is used of the prophets Samuel, Elijah, and Elisha (1 Sam 9:9; 1 Kgs 17:18; 2 Kgs 4:7). Since Moses considered himself a prophet (*nabi'* is used in Deut 18:15, not "man of God"), perhaps the author is also appealing to Moses's prophetic voice of authority. The lawgiver is also a prophet. The mention of Moses as the man of God obligates them further to follow

10. Similarly, the postexilic book of Chronicles refers to this authoritative document as either the law (2 Chr 25:4), the law of Moses (2 Chr 23:18), the law of the LORD (1 Chr 16:40; 2 Chr 31:3, 4;35:26), or his law referring to Elohim (2 Chr 31:21). See Andrew Hill, *1 & 2 Chronicles*, NIVAC (Grand Rapids: Zondervan, 2003).

11. The texts in Chronicles (especially 2 Chr. 30:16), due to similar context and usage of the designation in Ezra 3:2, may betray Ezra's authorship of both documents as is customarily assumed. Authorship issues, therefore, might partially explain the repeated use of the term in those related books. For further consideration, see Martin J. Selman, *1& 2 Chronicles*, TOTC (Downers Grove, IL: IVP Academic, 1994).

the written word. Both Moses's written and prophetic voices of authority seem to be in view in the latter part of verse two. The final clause of the verse, therefore, appeals to Mosaic authority and is meant to mobilize, legitimize, and energize Joshua's and Zerubbabel's project.

In sum, verse two highlights the stated project and its purpose. Moreover, Joshua the high priest, his Levitical associates, and Zerubbabel were not acting on their own accord when they commenced the building. Indeed, they have the stated authority undergirding their rebuilding project. The remaining verses of this section (3:3–6) transition to internal responses surrounding the altar's completion.

**Context of rebuilding: Fear and outcome (3:3).** The outcome of being rightly motivated (via the law of Moses) is noted immediately in verse 3. The outcome of rebuilding pertains immediately to daily worship.

With the altar rebuilt according to Mosaic specifications, the people were ready to reengage worship of Yahweh on a daily basis. Regardless of their ongoing fears, they commenced with sacrificing to the LORD burnt offerings on the rebuilt altar for both the morning and evening sacrifices (Exod 29:38–42; Num 28:1–8). This daily routine, probably coupled with morning, noon, and evening prayers (Ps 55:17), was a symbolic act of dedicating the day fully to the LORD and consecrating it unto him; an act of worship that the exile had prohibited. The first aspect of the building project was completed. Although they built the altar motivated and energized by the Mosaic authority and resumed daily sacrifices, the context remains one of fear.

For reasons not specified, the locals or "peoples around them" caused terror among the returned exiles. Who were these people? The author identifies them later as adversaries using tribal eponymous terminology: "enemies of Judah and Benjamin" (4:1). More specifically, these were linked to historical enemies of preexilic and exilic Israel: Ammonites, Moabites, Edomites, and Samaritans, people living in Judah as foreigners (4:2; cf. 2 Kgs 17:33). Thus, these foreigners (non-Yahwists) are identified as the people of the land who initially made them afraid to build the altar (3:3; 4:4). Furthermore, the same opponents also intermarried with some members of the ancestral (primordial in anthropological terms) Israelite community (Ezra 9:1; 12; 10:2, 11; Neh 10:30; 13:23–27; see discussion in Ezra 2 and commentary below). Thus the designation either in the singular or plural, "peoples around them" or "neighboring peoples," carries nothing positive. It spells opposition, trouble, ritual defilement, and compromised worship. These illegitimate "peoples" represents a direct threat to the strategic mission in Yehud to restore the legitimate worship of Yahweh. A compromised form of Israelite worship would also violate Persian law as reflected in Cyrus's edict.

How this group of hostile people brought fear among the exiles at the time of rebuilding the altar is unstated here. However, Ezra 4:4 gives some indication, since fear was a tactic used by this same group when Zerubbabel and Joshua refused their offer to help build the temple. Through bribery they hired people to intimidate God's people (4:5) as the result of Zerubbael's blatant refusal to allow their assistance in the rebuilding project (4:2–3). In fact, this overall strategy of intimidation on the part of the enemies of Zion takes on a paradigmatic function in the rebuilding process and will continue in earnest during the period of the rebuilding of the wall at the time of Nehemiah.

In the context of chapter 3, one thing is clear, however. Although the returnees labored under adverse conditions, they were not paralyzed so as to stop the work altogether on the altar. Perhaps for this reason no further information is given in 3:3 on how or why the peoples around them brought fear. In fact, the scenario here greatly contrasts a later situation, when they labored in the context of fear, trouble, and discouragement, which led to a sixteen-year delay of the project's completion (4:4–5.) The Hebrew idiom "weakening the hands" (*merappim yedey*) reflects the problem that led to paralysis (4:4–5).

Despite genuine fear, a discernible authority/action pattern emerges in 3:2–4 that typifies events in the book of Ezra. Cyrus's decree is issued, and the ensuing action is that the Jews returned to Jerusalem. Authority is granted via the law of Moses, and the ensuing action is that the altar is rebuilt and sacrifices offered. Then the author introduces the peoples of the lands. They represent a competing authority in that they instill fear in the Jews; regardless, the ensuing action of the Jews is to finish the altar.

In contrast, in Ezra 4:4–23 the "people of the land" become the authority, and the ensuing action of the Jews is to stop working on the temple. Then, after a sixteen-year hiatus, a new authority emerges: the prophets Haggai and Zechariah, bearing Mosaic authority. They prophesied to the Jews in Judah and Jerusalem (5:1) and freshly motivated the Jews to take action and commence rebuilding. Finally, authority is granted by decree of Darius, and the ensuing action is that the Jews complete the temple! In this way Ezra 3:2–4 introduces an important cycle that dominates the book. Although fear was their context, the effect was inconsequential. Fear and working in the face of fear is the context in which the altar is rebuilt.

**Outcome of rebuilding: Yearly and monthly worship (3:4–5).** In verse 4, the author quickly moves from the daily sacrifices offered (3:3) in the seventh month to the sacrifices offered on the fifteenth day of the seventh month (Num 29:12–38), those associated with the start of the Feast of Tabernacles. By advancing to the fifteenth day, he bypasses the requirements for the first, ninth, and tenth days of the same month also outlined in the law (Num 29:1–11). This de-emphasis seems deliberate. In an effort to emphasize that God's people have reestablished a worship routine and rhythm, he gives pride of place to one of the three great annual Jewish festivals.

He announces that the community of Yehud offered appropriate sacrifices in order to celebrate the Festival of Tabernacles.[12] He prefaces his statement about this celebration with the familiar phrase "in accordance with what is written" (v. 4), an abbreviated version of 3:2 that does not mention the law or Moses. Regardless, pentateuchal authority is reasserted, justifying the celebration and what appears to be a strict attempt to do what is required.

The Feast of Tabernacles was a festival characterized by joy and great celebration deriving from the fact that God graciously protected and provided for their ancestors when they lived in tents during their forty-year desert discipline. As a way to commemorate this, following in the footsteps of their forefathers, the postexilic community was required to live in tents and to offer up numerous burnt offerings for a set period of seven days (Num 29:12–38). The celebration was to begin on the fifteenth day of the seventh month. The seventh month will also serve as a chronological anchor for the restoration of the sanctity of Zion in Nehemiah 8–9.[13]

By giving emphasis to this feast, the tone of their worship is set.

12. This is also known as the Festival/Feast of Booths/Shelters or Ingathering (Exod 23:14–17; Lev 23:33–43; Deut 16:13–16). It was one of the three main religious celebrations, along with Passover and Feast of Weeks or Pentecost (Exod 34:22–23; Deut 16:16; cf. Acts 2:1).

13. See commentary on Neh 7:73b; 8:2, 14–18. Second Chr 5:3; 7:8–10 also emphasize the seventh month.

Moreover, celebrating this communal festival first, after years of exile, would have been particularly meaningful. It is hard to imagine that the returned community would not have likened their own exilic and postexilic situations to that of their forebears as they commemorated the feast. In fact, likening the present to the past and the strong sentiment attached as a result is something acknowledged later in the chapter (3:12–13). Therefore, although the author draws no intentional parallels (brought out of Egypt//brought out of exile), their parallel experience would have allowed them to contextualize the feast and give it fresh meaning.

After distinguishing the seventh month and the Feast of Tabernacles, the author now discusses the remaining sacrifices that were offered following the list of festivals prescribed in the law (cf. Lev 23:1–32; Num 28:1–29:11). The sacrifices for the new moon celebration were to be performed monthly; therefore, the seventh month naturally included this festival (Num 10:10; 28:11–15). The sacrifices for all the "appointed sacred festivals of the LORD" (v. 5) were not confined necessarily to the seventh month. Likewise, sacrifices for freewill offerings could be brought to the LORD any time. In this way (apart from the new moon festival), verse 5 functions as a summation of the beginning of sacrificial activity to show that regular, ongoing worship of the LORD is not only reestablished and possible, but also demanded by the law. Thus, the law would once again regulate their relationship to the LORD and serve as another marker of continuity with the past. The people are reconnecting with their ancestral identity.

With the altar rebuilt, the people were ready to engage the LORD with all the required sacrifices built into their calendar year. Once the priest or high priest stood at the newly built altar, it would have been a great visual aid and opportunity to forget their oppression under the foreign yoke of Persia. It would also rekindle their hopes in the LORD; he had not forgotten them and was extending to them his *hesed*/steadfast love (Ezra 9:9).

**Summary of activities in the seventh month (3:6).** Ezra 3:6 provides a conclusion to the entire section. In the seventh month the altar was rebuilt; most of their sacrificial system was in place; both fear and celebration characterized the emotional landscape of the people; and all this happened not long after their return to Jerusalem (3:1) but prior to the building of the temple ("though the foundation of the LORD's temple had not yet been laid").

This parenthetical information is not insignificant and informs the reader of several things. It explains that true worship is possible even without the temple. The former idolatry associated with the LORD's temple, described vividly before Jerusalem's fall by Jeremiah (ch. 7) and Ezekiel (ch. 8), seems to be in check after years of exile. The fact that most aspects of the sacrificial system were reinstated, even without the temple, shows a new awareness about the availability of God's presence. Clearly, the exiles embraced these truths from the painful experience of exile. Although commissioned by Cyrus to rebuild the temple, they commence with the altar, the smaller of the two tasks but the one that provided the quickest route to reestablishing the religious norms of the community. The significance they placed on their cult is evidenced in this first task.

The phrase also reveals that true worship is their priority. Mosaic legislation demanded strict adherence to the sacrificial system as a way to approach God. Rather than wait for the temple to be rebuilt, their eagerness to approach him is demonstrated by targeting the seventh month to start the process. Clearly, the exiles' readiness and desire to approach God after years of exile is evident.

Thus, verse 6 functions as a literary hinge. On the one hand it sums up the main event associated with the seventh month, sacrificing on the rebuilt altar. But on the other, it serves as an introduction to Ezra 3:7–13, the main event associated with the second month of the second year after their arrival: rebuilding the temple foundation.

## The Temple Foundation Rebuilt (3:7–13)

### *Supplies and Personnel (3:7)*

After completing the altar, they immediately turn their attention to preparations for rebuilding the temple, starting with the foundation. The preparation includes securing building supplies as authorized by Cyrus. Here, too, the authority/action pattern seems obvious.

Their actions to hire workers and to import cedar logs from the Mediterranean coast has the authority of Cyrus, king of Persia, in addition to his original edict (1:2–4). The author wishes to assure the reader that the actions of the people are legitimate and in keeping with Persian law. Moreover, their actions to hire personnel and to import cedar logs from Sidon and Tyre are reminiscent of actions taken by Solomon to start building his temple (a common practice by ancient Near Eastern potentates as well[14]). Per Solomon's request, the king of Tyre authorized his servants to cut and transport cedar and cypress timber for the building. After the logs from the Lebanon were cut, they were made into rafts, floated along the Mediterranean coast, dismantled once they reached Solomon's desired destination, and used for construction (1 Kgs 5:7–10; 1 Chr 22:4; 2 Chr 2:3–8).

This is the first of what appears to be deliberate attempts by the author to draw comparisons in this chapter between the two building projects. Although the returned exiles were doing what was natural, relying on the experts for their supplies and personnel needs, more is going on. There seems to be an attempt by the author to show continuity with the past and to normalize the exiles' situation. The author has already noted that continuity with the past is key, but this statement, as well as other obvious ones below (3:8–10), reflects persistence in wanting to front this idea, the purpose of which will be explored in the ensuing discussion.

### *Attaining Supervision and Workers (3:8–9)*

With ample supplies and contracted workers from abroad in place, they prepare further by establishing local supervision for the project, allowing the designated workmen to get underway.

**Work begins (3:8).** The start of the work takes place in the second month of the second year after their arrival, approximately mid-spring, 537 BC. A chronological indicator heads off this section (3:8–13), as was done in 3:1–6. The year is included here, unlike Ezra 3:1. This raises the question, why did the work begin in the second month and not any other month of the second year? Rather than randomly select the second month, there seems to be intentionality. The second month, the month of Ziv (April/May), was the month Solomon began work on the house of the Lord (1 Kgs 6:1). Although the selection could be coincidental, it seems unlikely given the continuous efforts of the author to bridge the gap caused by the exile. This is the second comparison/parallel with the circumstances of the first edifice.

In addition, verse 8 makes it clear that all hands were on deck to work (a recurring theme in the larger program of restoration of the worship in Zion (see also Neh 3:1–32). The administrative and spiritual leaders

---

14. Phoenician King Hiram of Tyre sent wood from Lebanon to build David's palace in Jerusalem (2 Sam 5:11). He did the same for Solomon (1 Kgs 5:20; 2 Chr 2:3, 7).

(Zerubbabel and Joshua, respectively), as well as the priests, Levites, and "all who had returned from the captivity" (v. 8), worked. The parentheses noted in the NIV is an attempt to unpack the more literal rendering of the Hebrew, "the rest of their brothers" (*sh'ar ahehem*). As such, this statement, along with that in Ezra 3:1, is yet another declaration expressing a unified purpose.

This unified group was carefully organized. The Levites who were age twenty and older were appointed to supervise all the work. This appointment parallels that of King David to some degree (1 Chr 23:4–32). David updated the service of the Levites, given the new worship conditions (a permanent temple in Jerusalem rather than a portable tent shrine used in the wilderness). Those Levites whom he appointed to service and care for the new temple had to be twenty years and older. Here in Ezra 3:8, a similar situation prevails. The leadership updated the service of the Levites, given the new worship conditions after the exile. But rather than select people twenty-five or thirty years of age and older as mandated by Mosaic law (Num 4:3, 8:24), the returned exiles reinforced the age requirement established by David (see also commentary on Neh 12 below). The lowering of the age would ensure there were enough Levites to get the job done. The intentionality here of the author to make connections with the past seems evident. Thus, the age requirement is the third comparison/parallel made with Solomon's temple.

**Levitical families (3:9).** Verse 9 continues the discussion and gives the specific names of Levitical families leading the way to organize the unified group of workers. What is especially striking is the language of verse 9. Literally, the Hebrew reads that these families are "as one" (*ke'ehad*), or joined together to supervise the work, just as the Israelites "gathered as one man (*ke'ish ehad*) in Jerusalem" for building the altar in Ezra 3:1. The language expresses unity of purpose once again.

Thus, with the proper supplies, personnel, and supervision, this unified group is moving toward the goals for which they were commissioned. That the rebuilt structure is important to rebuilding their identity is seen by the fact that three times in two verses one finds "house of the LORD" or "house of God" (3:8–9).

### *Temple Foundation Completed: Responses (3:10–13)*

In the final section of this chapter, one does not read about the completion of the temple, as might have been hoped for, but the completion of its foundation, along with various responses to it. It is likely that the old foundation was exposed from the ground beneath and repaired after destruction and years of decay. In this regard, "the builders laid the foundation of the temple of the LORD" (3:10).

In between verses 9 and 10 an undesignated amount of time passed, and the author informs us that the foundation was laid on the temple (*hekal*) of Yahweh. This building report, quick as it was, functioned as a primer for the real announcement that immediately follows: Israel celebrates her first worship service after exile. The author vividly describes this scene in the closing verses of chapter 3. In terms of literary space, he gives more attention to rebuilding worship than to rebuilding the temple foundation. It is the worship that serves as the focal point.

**The scene: First worship service after exile (3:10–11).** The personnel took their places with the sole purpose of offering up praises to the Lord. The worship personnel included the priests, who were adorned with garments and trumpets. It also included the Levites, adorned with their cymbals. This arrangement, however, was not random. It was "prescribed by David, king of Israel" (v. 10). Here again the authority/action pattern appears. Their act of worship, particularly the dress and arrangement of the priests and Levites, is an action sanctioned by another reputable authority:[15] David, king of Israel (1 Chr 23–25; see Neh 12:36, 45–46).

Notice, however, how the author refers to David. This prescription for worship did not derive from "King David" but "David king of Israel." The former designation highlights the person as king, but the latter highlights the person as king of a nation. The titular title "king of Israel" shouts of unity. Although the circumstances are very different, postexilic Israel is unified as in former days and is experiencing a measure of unity that she once fully enjoyed under David's leadership. The author attempts to view this worship service like old times. In addition, the mention of David in connection with the temple and music speaks of a joyous worship celebration. Indeed, David was known as the sweet psalmist of Israel (2 Sam 23:1). Thus, dropping David's name, along with his specific designation as king of Israel, is important and gives special meaning to the worship service. It represents the fourth attempt to draw lines of correspondence with the former edifice.

---

15. Before it was Cyrus in 3:7 and Moses in 3:1–6.

The scene here is vivid and is easy to imagine which, due to the descriptive language, seems to be part of the author's objective. This continues in verse 11. First, they sang with praises and thanksgiving. The word translated "sang" (v. 11) is literally (*'nah*) "answered," in reference to responsive singing or antiphonal choral singing. In other words, they are giving an answer or response to the completion of the temple foundation. Praise and thanksgiving form the content of their response. They direct their response toward the LORD. The NIV translates Yahweh, the name of Israel's deity and one that resonates with covenant, as LORD. This name is used approximately fifty-one times in Ezra-Nehemiah, more than the generic *'elohim*, which is found thirty-five times in the book.

Due to the exodus event, the name Yahweh resonates with covenant.[16] The revelation of God in the book of Exodus revealed an aspect of his character that was previously unknown, that he was/is a god who rescued people for relationship. Yahweh acted, and continues to act, on behalf of his people. Therefore, directing their praise to Yahweh is specific and altogether appropriate, given that Yahweh is continuing his relational obligations by rescuing them from exile in order to renew a relationship with them.

Second, their praises and thanksgiving contained a specific declaration lauding the twofold nature of the LORD's character: The Hebrew literally reads, "*For* He is good *for* forever is his covenantal loyalty (*ki tob ki le'olam hasdo*) in verse 11. The NIV does not reflect the two causal clauses each commencing with "for" in Hebrew. That is, the cause for their praise is due to the fact that God is inherently good! And because God is good, he manifests covenantal loyalty or relational loyalty (NIV "love") without end! God's goodness and "love" are evident because the foundation of the temple was laid. They laud God for his exclusive character. Indeed, Israel knew him and experienced him to be a God "abounding in covenantal" or (*rab hesed*, Exod 34:6–7); an experience that commenced on the heels of the golden calf incident (Exod 34:1–7) and right up to this moment when the foundation was laid.[17]

Third, their song of praise identifies the recipient of his goodness. The text clearly indicates this, "for forever is his covenantal loyalty *toward Israel*" (author's translation)—the only occurrence where the object

16. See Exod 3:13–15; 6:2–8; 20:1–2; 34:6–7.

17. See Ezra 9 for further discussion about God's character.

"Israel" is stated. Typically, when this refrain "for forever is his covenantal loyalty" appears elsewhere in the biblical text, often the object of his covenantal loyalty is not stated (for example, 1 Chr 16:34; Pss 106:1; 107:1; 118:1; 136:1–26). The added object here says something about their present self-awareness, to be sure. The returned exiles consider themselves the new Israel. They have a renewed sense of belonging once again to the LORD. They are aware that they are his people (Israel) and he is their god (Yahweh). The assembled community is, therefore, unified in their declaration of praise, which is an affirmation of the LORD's ongoing providence. Perhaps most important is how the song provides a corporate affirmation of God's enduring character. His goodness and loyalty in the relationship pave the way for the restoration underway.

Thus, their answer to such a display of God's goodness and love was not just a shout of praise but "a great shout of praise" (v. 11)! Their praise was rooted in a keen awareness of Yahweh's strong and unshakable character, without which the return from exile and the completion of the temple foundation would not have been possible. Although the historical circumstances are drastically different—there is no ark and the second temple is not yet built—their outburst of praise at this moment represents the fifth connection with first edifice (2 Chr 5:2–14; 7:3).

**Contrasting Experience (3:12).** The scene in Jerusalem seems almost electrifying. In the closing two verses, the author continues the description of the worship celebration. The focal point concerns all the sounds associated with the celebration. Together with the "great shout of praise" (v. 11), others "wept aloud" and still others "shouted for joy" (v. 12). These sounds were indistinguishable because the people "made so much noise" (v. 13). Moreover, the sound traveled ("the sound was heard far away"; v. 13). Numerous times in these few verses, the author references the sound at the construction site. As a result, the reader gets pulled into the emotion of it.

Although the environment is joyful and great strides have been made toward reestablishing Israelite worship, those who recalled the glorious realities of the past experienced contrasting emotions (v. 12). There were those in the crowd who had seen the "the former temple" (v. 12). Why Solomon's temple is designated generically as "the former temple" is not entirely clear. It might have to do with the fact that "this temple" (v. 12) being built by the exiles is not associated with any Israelite superstar, simply because there was none. Regardless, the eyewitnesses of Solomon's temple (aging senior citizens) were underwhelmed at what they saw and wept loudly.[18] The mention of these people who saw the first edifice is yet another connection to the past that the author establishes.

Thus emotions were high (whether loud laments or shouts of joy). Rather than mute the deep sadness of some present, the author captures the dual sentiment of the crowd, almost as if an eyewitness himself. In fact, depending on one's position in this crowd, only an eyewitness of this worship celebration would be able to distinguish between the two sounds.[19]

**Praise to the LORD (3:13).** For those in the immediate larger group and those in earshot of the event, parsing the sound of the rallied crowd would not be possible. Regardless, the point of such descriptive language is that the author wants the reader to know that not only was the sound of Israel's praises to the LORD loud (indicative of a renewed heart), but also the sound reverberated outside the community (indicative of a renewed and unified witness; Ps 126). In fact, their renewed witness in the land sets the stage for the trouble described in the chapter that follows (Ezra 4:1–24).

In this chapter, the ancestral identity of the people of God has been resurrected. Out of loss comes life. The united worship service makes this evident. In essence, the kingdom markers of identity associated with the promises of God are mostly in place, a process that started in chapters 1 and 2. A united people of God reemerge, and the Israelites have Yahweh at the center of their lives once again. The historic and distinct conception of their identity as the *'am Yahweh* ("people of Yahweh") is reestablished, defined in contrast to other identities. In the context of Yehud, a strong "consciousness of differences"[20] is developed: the newly re-consituted *'am Yahweh* cannot collaborate in any way with "the peoples around them" (3:3), that is, "the enemies of Judah and Benjamin" (4:1). These foes function as a sort of resurrected Canaanites in the land. They represent a constant and direct existential threat to the restoration of the proper worship of Yahweh according to the ancestral/primordial[21] givens of identity: bloodlines (Judah, Benjamin, and Levi), land (Zion), and ancestral authority (the law, redemptive history itself [new exodus; new

---

18. See Hag 2:3. Zechariah 4:10 seems to suggest that some dismissed the moment as merely one small step toward a new beginning.

19. David J. Shepherd and Christopher J. H. Wright, *Ezra and Nehemiah*, THOTC (Grand Rapids: Eerdmans, 2018), 20, also suggest this.

20. Jones, *Archaeology of Ethnicity*, 97.

21. See Ezra 2.

conquest; new temple], Moses, David, and other key figures in Israelite lore). Within these ethnic traits, the emphasis on *ritual purity* should be added to the list. Without holiness and purity in worship (including establishing the altar in postexilic Zion), the identity of the people will be diluted, just as it had been in the past[22] (per Levitical regulations).

THE MAIN EXEGETICAL POINT, ON THE BASIS OF the textual analysis above, seems to be that the returned people of God, even after years of exile, can worship their God once again because of his goodness to them. After years of separation, they can draw near to God through proper sacrifices and corporate worship. Through reinstating sacrifices, their relationship to God becomes a reality and their access to God has opened up once again. Through reinstating worship, their devotion to the one true God likewise becomes a reality. The significance of this reinstated worship in Israelite history, even without the temple's full reconstruction in place (6:14ff), should not be overlooked.

As with Ezra 1:1–6 the author's theological lens continues to surface. Just as the word of the LORD through Jeremiah was fulfilled via Cyrus's decree and the return of the exiles in Ezra 1:1, so, too, Jeremiah's word relative to restored worship finds fulfillment here in chapter 3. Jeremiah foretold that God would "bring Judah and Israel back from captivity and rebuild them as they were before" (Jer 33:7). At such a time, the LORD says, the city will bring him "renown, joy, praise and honor" (33:9). For in the streets will be heard "the voices of those who bring thank offerings to the house of the LORD saying, 'Give thanks to the LORD Almighty, for the LORD is good, for his steadfast love endures forever'" 33:11). In other words, Jerusalem's fortunes would be restored, and the visible manifestation of that would be the shift from silence to celebration, from

22. Perhaps one of the most vivid and sad expressions of a diluted identity comes from the prophet Hosea. Hosea's marriage to Gomer produced three children, two whose names reveal much. "Lo-Ruhamah (which means 'not loved'), and Lo-Ammi (which means 'not my people'), for you are not my people, I am not your God" (Hos 1:6, 8). These names show how idolatry made God's people unidentifiable. "The holy nation" (Exod 19:6) was far from holy; and the exclusive covenantal relationship, "I will take you as my own people, and I will be your God" (Exod 6:7) was far from exclusive.

mourning to dancing, from weeping to worship in the cities of Judah and Jerusalem (33:10–11).

That day has indeed come, for now Jerusalem's desolate streets are again full of joyful, thankful, and worshipful inhabitants because of the rebuilt altar and temple foundation in Jerusalem.

The significance of this moment of worship should not be overlooked given the backdrop and mournful tone of the exile. On the basis of Psalm 137, we know of the painful reality of no worship in Babylon: "There on the poplars we hung our harps, for there our captors asked us for songs, our tormentors demanded songs of joy; they said, 'Sing us one of the songs of Zion!'" (vv. 2–3). In response to the taunt of their enemies was a self-imposed silence: "How can we sing the songs of the LORD while in a foreign land?" (v. 4). But now, in glaring contrast and with the same emotional intensity as that of Psalm 137, the author captures the worshipful tone after the exile. The strong sentiment of the people manifested itself in an extremely loud and unified worship service heard from a distance. The exiles understood and were proclaiming God's character as result of his favorable actions.

The significance of the moment is further felt by the fact that the Israelite community last assembled to sing this song when the ark of the covenant was brought into the holy of holies upon completion of Solomon's temple (2 Chr 5:2–14; 7:3). Prior to that, David, Israel's sweet psalmist, instructed thanksgiving to be conducted after the ark was brought to Jerusalem; indeed, David was no stranger to vibrant worship (2 Sam 6:3–16; 1 Chr 16:1–7; see Neh 12:45–46). The basis of David' s exhortation to give thanks at that moment derived from this profound theological truth: "For he is good, for his steadfast love endures forever!" David understood God's character.

The impetus for the rich theological claims about God's goodness, highlighted in the anthem sounded first by David, preexilic Israel, and now by the returned exiles here in Ezra 3:11, goes all the way back to Moses in the book of Exodus. In response to Moses's request to see God's glory (Exod 33:18), the LORD declares that he will show Moses his total goodness (33:19). This goodness refers to God's character, his essence (33:19; 34:5–7), a description of who God is. One experiences it through covenantal relationship with Yahweh (34:5–7). One knows it by the LORD'S direct and ongoing involvement in the lives of his people as he manifests his nature for their benefit. God's goodness was immediately manifested in that he forgave Israel after the golden calf incident. Moses and Israel understood God's character.

This was not a limited manifestation. Ongoing manifestations of his goodness were revealed all throughout their early history. The Psalter provides evidence. In numerous preexilic psalms, the cause for the command to praise/give thanks to the LORD was rooted in an understanding of the LORD's character of goodness and unwavering loyalty (Pss 100:5; 106; 107; 136.). For this reason, the Psalmist, in reference to corporate Israel or an individual worshiper, often says, "Give thanks to the LORD, for he is good, for his steadfast love (*ḥesed*) endures forever" (118; 136). In fact, Psalm 136 uses the phrase as a liturgical refrain (26x) alongside recitations of Israel's early history and the Lord's ongoing providence. This song was on the tongue of the nation and people who individually experienced God's deliverance from a personal crisis. Only one who truly believes can say this. Thus, the rationale, and the call to praise and to give thanks, derives from the theological reality that God in his very essence is good—that his goodness knows no limits. The people of God understood God's character.

From the perspective of the biblical writer in Ezra-Nehemiah, the manifestation of his goodness is apparent with the temple foundation laid. Although the historical circumstances are different (no ark, and the second temple is not yet rebuilt), their outburst of praise at this moment represents hearts of worship, hearts that recognize the very essence of God's being as good. The former exiles knew their sordid history, but they also knew the God of their history. The former exiles understood God's character (2 Chr 5:13; 7:3, 6).

Accordingly, in various psalms after the exile, this song of praise became a standard expression of praise in the community of believers based on the return from exile. Psalm 126 states that, indeed "[t]hose who sow with tears will reap with songs of joy. Those who go out weeping, carrying seed to sow, will return with songs of joy, carrying sheaves with them" (vv. 5–6). The psalmist recognizes that bringing back the captives is God's work of restoration and, for this reason, laughter and songs of joy are on their tongues (126:2). Indeed, this was a work not only significant for Israel, but one that captured the attention of those looking on: "Then it was said among the nations, 'The LORD has done great things for them'" (126:2). God demonstrated his power to bring his people back from exile and, as a result, his people extol his character of goodness and the nations recognize the LORD.

Ezra 3 paints a picture of unified corporate worship after tangible evidence of God's goodness to them. The only appropriate response to being on the receiving end of God's undeserved goodness is worship. In other words, to attribute this favorable outcome in their lives (after a time of hardship brought on by their own wrongdoing) to a natural set of circumstances is to deny God the praise he deserves. Restoration is supernatural, and all depends on God's unshakeable and unchangeable character.

Isaiah's prophecies also spoke about this moment in Israelite history, when the temple foundation would be laid, with incredible precision. Approximately 150 years before the events that unfold in Ezra 1–3, Isaiah announced, in his polemic against the trustworthiness of idols, that the LORD could be trusted because of his abilities to know the future: who says of Cyrus, "He is my shepherd and will accomplish all that I please; he will say of Jerusalem, 'Let it be rebuilt,' and of the temple, 'Let its foundation be laid'" (Isa 44:28). As a demonstration of God's power over idols, God tells Isaiah that Jerusalem will be inhabited, rebuilt, and restored (Isa 44:26). God even offers the specific name of the human instrument who will accomplish this. God raised up Cyrus to "rebuild my city and set my exiles free" (45:13).

With the temple foundation laid and the accompanying worship service that immediately followed, both the aforementioned prophecies of Isaiah and Jeremiah have come to pass. These prophecies would have been known to the exiles. Attributing the events of the day to a mere set of natural circumstances (Cyrus's decree) was not on their radar. They knew and acknowledged through their declaration of praise that the events that transpired were because of God's character. Thus, the content of their praises was nothing less than Israel's spiritual anthem, an anthem that rang throughout Israelite history, but one that also anticipates a future worship service.

"GOD IS GOOD, ALL THE TIME; ALL THE TIME, God is good!" The pastor or worship leader exclaims, "God is good," and the congregation responds, "all the time!" The pastor/or worship leader proclaims, "all the time," and the congregation responds, "God is good!" You may have heard this declared or even declared it yourself at one time. In the movie *God's Not Dead*, two pastors, one from America and the other from Nigeria, greet each other using this line throughout the movie. This greeting or call to worship derives from Nigeria but was introduced in America through a prison ministry in the 1980s. The inmates taught this praise response to the visiting Methodist minister, and he in turn introduced it to the United Methodist Church.[23] The phrase was and is typically used during and after times of turmoil and distress.

This is especially true of the Liberian church,[24] whose people have for years experienced the horrors of civil war. Instead of shaking their fists at God and pointing the finger at him for all the bad things they experienced, they were constant. Rather than say, "If you are good, God, then how can you let such bad things happen?" they rejected doubt. They endured hardships by living in the blessed assurance that God is good all the time. By clinging to this reality, one understands the thriving and exuberant nature the Liberian church boasts today. If believers do not toe the line on this belief, the world has nowhere to turn in times of devastation. The church must take the lead here; doubting the very character and essence of God is not an option.

The "God is good" statement derives from an awareness of God's very nature. Moses asked to see more of God and his glory (Exod 33:13, 18), and he got a revelation of God's goodness (Exod 33:19). His glory is his goodness, which equates to a revelation of his character (Exod 34: 6–7), a God gracious, merciful, slow to anger, abounding in steadfast love, forgiving iniquity, transgression, and sin. We, too, can see more of God and his glory, we also get a revelation of God's goodness expressed in the person of Jesus. God's character is manifested, experienced, and seen in Jesus. In Jesus, we experience and see a manifestation of God's glory (John 1:14).

Therefore, knowing Jesus and experiencing his involvement in our lives is the only way one can say with conviction that God is good all the time. Knowing Jesus means knowing the Good Shepherd, the one who guides, provides, protects, and lays down his life for his sheep (John 10:1ff). Knowing the divine Shepherd means we "lack nothing," and it means his goodness and love pursues us *all*, not just some, of the days of

---

23. See sermoncentral.com. A message by R. David Reynolds, September 6, 2005.
24. Ibid.

our lives (Psalm 23). Thus, like David in the twenty-third psalm, we can laud God's good character in spite of our circumstances. Indeed, as Jesus himself says, "No one is good—except God alone" (Luke 18:19; Mark 10:18). If this is so, we ought not expect to find goodness elsewhere.

But we cannot attribute goodness and subsequent praise to somebody we do not know. We cannot state somebody is good if we have not experienced that goodness in relationship. Believers are quick to affirm that God is good when things are good. But we need to affirm with equal passion that God is *still* good even when things are not good. If the latter is not the case, then God's goodness is conditional; in fact, it is not "all the time." In other words, either God is good all the time or he is not. He does not change when our circumstances change. His goodness becomes the constant in our lives. We need something constant with life's ups and downs. We find that in the character of God. Ultimately, we find our constant in knowing Jesus.

This fact about God's character enables us to look at life's difficulties (self-imposed or otherwise) and see God presently is good. But it also enables us to look forward with great assurance when we face life's difficulties (self-imposed or otherwise) and see that God will still be good. Rather than a trite platitude, the praise explodes from our hearts to our lips because of a staunch and unwavering assurance of knowing God's nature.

The ability to praise and worship God after a demonstration of power/undeserved grace in our lives derives from the belief that God is good all the time, and all the time God is good. In other words, to attribute favorable outcomes in our lives, after a time of hardship brought on by our own wrongdoing, to merely a natural set of circumstances is to deny God the praise he deserves. Restoration is supernatural, and all depends on God's unchangeable character.

# Ezra 4:1–5

[1] When the enemies of Judah and Benjamin heard that the
exiles were building a temple for the LORD, the God of Israel,
[2] they came to Zerubbabel and to the heads of the families
and said, "Let us help you build because, like you, we seek
your God and have been sacrificing to him since the time of
Esarhaddon king of Assyria, who brought us here."
[3] But Zerubbabel, Joshua and the rest of the heads of the
families of Israel answered, "You have no part with us in building
a temple to our God. We alone will build it for the LORD, the
God of Israel, as King Cyrus, the king of Persia, commanded us."
[4] Then the peoples around them set out to discourage
the people of Judah and make them afraid to go on building.
[5] They bribed officials to work against them and frustrate their
plans during the entire reign of Cyrus king of Persia and down
to the reign of Darius king of Persia.

IN ORDER TO UNDERSTAND THIS CHAPTER, SEVERAL introductory comments are in order. First, the chapter consists of both Hebrew and Aramaic. For the latter, it commences in Ezra 4:8 and concludes in Ezra 6:18, and also involves Ezra 7:12–26. Aramaic was used for the diplomatic correspondence of the day. Second, the chapter is topical, not chronological. It discusses the topic of opposition that the Jews faced in rebuilding, not just the temple but also the walls of the city at a later period. The opposition discussed in chapter 4, therefore, spans the reign of not one, but several Persian rulers (Cyrus, Darius, and Artaxerxes). Accordingly, it is helpful to read Ezra 4:1–5 and then skip down to verse 24 as a conclusion to section one.

## Opposition to the Rebuilding (4:1–24)

### Opposition under Cyrus's Reign (4:1–5, 24)

THIS FIRST UNIT (4:1–5, 24; SIX VERSES ONLY) talks about opposition from Cyrus's reign through Darius's reign, which resulted in a standstill of the work on the temple. The second unit is 4:6–23, which is best read as a parenthetical statement about other waves of opposition involving different Persian kings (4:6; 4:7; 4:8–23). Apparently, while recounting the story of current temple building opposition (4:1–5),[1] the narrator interrupted himself to recall other periods of opposition that the Jews faced before finishing his thoughts about the temple. The storyline of opposition to building the temple then continues in Ezra 5:1–6:12, with further events that unfold in Darius's reign.[2]

Thus, the bigger picture of opposition to God's goal for the community unfolds in the following manner and is tied contextually to the theme of restoration, found in the broader section of Ezra 1–6.

- God raised up Cyrus (1:1). Cyrus's favor and decree allowed for the people to return to Jerusalem and for the *work to start* (1:1–3:13).
- In chapter 4, severe opposition leading to complacency caused the *work to stop* (4:24).
- God raised up the prophets Haggai and Zechariah and, through the prophetic word, the *work begins again* (5:1–2). Their work on the temple is subsequently *challenged and evidence demanded for the work*, but the work was not stopped (5:3–5).
- God raised up Darius. Darius's favor and decree allowed for *zero interference with the work* (6:7).
- All these cumulative efforts combined resulted in the *finished work* (6:14–15).
- The *work was celebrated and dedicated* (6:16), and there was acknowledgment that God assisted them in this work (6:22). Clearly the repeated term "work" indicates the focal point of the narrative.

The biblical writer intentionally gives a lot of literary space (roughly three consecutive chapters, 4:1–6:12) to this topic of opposition and only ten verses to narrate the completion and celebration of the rebuilt

---

1. Other scolars recognize Ezra 4:6–23 as a parenthetical point emphasizing later persecutions. See D. Kidner, *Ezra and Nehemiah*, 56–59; F. Charles Fensham, *The Books of Ezra and Nehemiah*, NICNT (Grand Rapids: Eerdmans, 1982), 70.

2. For a different view of the chronology, see Williamson, *Ezra, Nehemiah*, 43–60.

temple (6:13–22). The point is that one must understand the completed task in light of its opposition. As one sees the longevity and severity of the opposition, it makes the completion of the project even sweeter (Ezra 6:13–22).

As the story line of restoration progresses in the narrative, chapter 4 is pivotal, especially 4:1–5, 24. Not long after the unhindered building of the altar and dedication of the new temple foundation, still early in Cyrus's reign, the Jews had to run interference in their building project. For the first time, the Jews faced serious, external opposition from the locals or "peoples around them" (4:4) in regard to rebuilding. Although we are told that the Jews feared "the peoples around them" as they built the altar (3:3), chapter 4 unpacks the rationale for such fear as it reveals more about these people.

The narrator further identifies these locals as "the enemies of Judah and Benjamin" (4:1). But in the recorded speech, they self-identify as exiles, people also carried away from Assyria to Samaria by King Esarhaddon (4:2). Although Assyrian kings were known for repopulating a conquered land with those from other conquered nations (2 Kgs 17:24), the mention of an exile by Esarhaddon (681–669 BC) is not observed in the Bible. These people likely descended from those brought to Samaria previously by the Assyrians (4:10; Neh 4:2). In addition, these exiled locals claim to seek and worship the same God (4:2). Accordingly, the boast "like you, we seek your God" becomes their rationale for offering assistance. Perhaps a sense of entitlement based on the long residence in the land prompted the offer of help.

Regardless, Israel's leaders respond with a united voice demonstrating discernment and uncompromising theological conviction. Although these neighbors may consider themselves exiles, Cyrus's decree was not issued to them (4:3, cf. 1:2). And while they may be seeking and worshiping Yahweh, their system likely involved other religious practices in addition to the worship of Yahweh (2 Kgs 17:24ff).[3] As such, they were

---

3. Based on the story that unfolds in 2 Kgs 17:24–41, these were folks not exclusively devoted to Yahweh. They were people from foreign territories who were forced to repopulate the land when the king of Assyria deported the Israelites in 722 BC. They did not know the nature of Yahweh worhip and had to be taught by an Israelite priest (vv. 27–28). In spite of these efforts, "To this day they persist in their former practices. They neither worship the LORD nor adhere to the decrees and regulations, the laws and commands that the LORD gave . . ." (v. 34).

not wholly and exclusively devoted to the LORD (Exod 15:1–21). The conclusion was simple. They had neither legal nor religious grounds to participate and were, therefore, excluded. The identity of the renewed community was fragile. Serious measures had already been taken to ensure this (cf. chapters 2 and 3). Purity, for the sake of preserving the identity of the people of God, was the premise of rebuilding the new community. It was not a time to be "neighborly" and to hope that these neighbors could be won over to the worship of Yahweh alone. A lack of purity could not be tolerated given their sordid past, but especially in light of this second chance. The leadership demonstrated courage, conviction, and sober-mindedness about the offer of help. They discerned the threat to this premise, and, as a result, flat out rejected additional help in the rebuilding project. For these reasons, religious intolerance needed to be upheld. It was a time to draw a line in the sand and say no.

The wise decision to exclude these folks because of legal and theological convictions was not without a cost for the reestablished community. Those excluded most likely felt angry and rejected, which led to retaliation. Since the neighbors could not help, they hindered the process with unidentified tactics that were ongoing, troublesome, and may have included bribes to pay for interference (4:4–5). They took targeted measures to harm the community, ones that did not entail violence but nonetheless amounted to persecution. The goal of their tactic was to "set out to discourage" or, more literally, "weakening the hands (*merappim yedey*) of the people of Judah" (v. 4). When this phrase appears elsewhere in the Bible, it describes a crippling effect caused by deep despair and dismay (see 2 Sam 4:1; Isa 13:7; Jer 38:4). Indeed, the enemies' tactic, whatever it was, produced fruit. Eventually the Jews, worn out by the opposition, voluntarily stopped their work on the house of God for sixteen years (536–520 BC; 4:24; cf. Hag 1:4).

THE PEOPLE OF GOD HAVE ALWAYS HAD ENEMIES and external opposition attempting to thwart the advancement of God's purposes (e.g., Pharaoh, the Canaanites). The timing of the opposition in Ezra, however, is delicate. The community is barely on its feet, and their identity as the renewed people of God remained fragile. The offer of help at such a time might have been appealing, a chance to get done faster and more efficiently. In addition, the offer of help under the guise of being likeminded spiritually could have been a temptation to which the leadership succumbed. But here in Ezra, in a joint council session, Zerubbabel and the other leaders surprise the reader as they respond with discernment and a firm theological conviction for the sake of purity.

This narrative is without parallel in the entire Old Testament! With few exceptions in the annals of Kings and Chronicles,[4] Israel's leaders are not lauded for their discernment or an uncompromising stance against syncretism or idolatry. Their tendency was to be tolerant and inclusive rather than intolerant and exclusive. This lack of passion for purity defiled the people of God and eventually led them into exile. The leaders in Ezra 4:3 may be trying to avoid the mistakes of the past by taking a hard line with those proposing help as they rebuild the covenantal community. Regardless of the unfavorable, costly results of retaliation that crippled the project for years, their courage and conviction took precedent.

This is not unlike what the leaders of the early church felt and faced as they worked to build and rebuild their covenantal community in the New Testament. The identity of the early church was at stake in much the same way. They wanted to get it right and had a united voice about working or partnering with false brethren. No one led with more uncompromising theological conviction in this area than Paul the apostle. When his enemies appeared to have had the same message as he did and claimed to be like him theologically, he was not fooled nor swayed (e.g., Gal 2:1–21). As a leader, Paul knew the nature of his opponents (2 Cor. 11:26). He knew their tactics. Indeed, their tactics were subtle and deceptive for the disciples in young churches (Acts 20:30). He warns of such opponents and guards against falling prey to them (1 Tim 4:1–5; 2 Tim 4:14–15). His response was always exclusivity, which produced, at times, even stronger opposition and delays in moving forward with building the kingdom of God. His exclusivity, however, was an attempt to preserve the purity of God's people to whom he was called. Aware that a theological purity would naturally lead to purity in one's ethic, most of his writings show the connection between pure doctrine and

4. Eight Judean kings—Asa, Jehoshaphat, Joash, Amaziah, Azariah, Jotham, Hezekiah, and Josiah—have positive records (see 2 Chr 14–32).

behavior.[5] For this reason, Paul did not tolerate religious syncretism. Neither a blend of Judaism, Gnosticism, or mystery religions with Christianity was to be tolerated.[6]

The same posture was also taken by other writers such as John, Jude, and Peter. First John 2:19 warns that those who were once brothers are now deceivers. "They went out from us, but they did not really belong to us" (see also 1 John 4:1–6). Those appearing as legitimate brethren ended up becoming false teachers and enemies of the gospel, as their actions and teachings make clear. Second John describes a shut-door policy as it relates to offering hospitality to those who appear to uphold the gospel message but are really deceivers (7, 9). The conviction that the leaders demonstrate in Ezra also compares to Jude's exhortation to "contend for the faith" (Jude 3). Thus, the New Testament writers took a separatist stance because the stakes were too high to embark in the wrong kind of partnerships when building a covenantal community.

THE PEOPLE OF GOD TODAY FACE SERIOUS EXTERNAL opposition as we seek to build/rebuild the church and advance God's kingdom on earth. Our identity and purity as a people of God is being challenged more than ever. Radical shifts in culture (whether militant secularism or persecutions in cultures hostile to the Christian faith) have paved the way for confusion at times about what it means to be Christian and who Jesus is. These may come from appealing offers of partnership from a variety of sources under the guise of sharing the same kind of faith. Other appealing offers of help may come also at times of need and vulnerability. We need to know who our "enemies" are. We need to know who we are. Church leaders need to have crisp discernment about the nature of such help and must have a united voice with offers that come from a theologically compromising place. This short narrative invites the reader, but especially a leader, to lead with

---

5. For example, this is true of the Pastoral Epistles (1 and 2 Timothy and Titus). With regard to Titus, Paul teaches that sound doctrine and behavior go hand in hand (Titus 2:11–14). Likewise, Romans highights the need to understand the doctrine of sin and justification so that they would live free of racial biases and in harmony one another (Rom 15:5–6).

6. This refers to the books of Galatians, Colossians, and Ephesians, respectively.

conviction and to count the cost of conviction. It shows that such a thing exists as a theology of saying no! There is a time for religious intolerance, but what does this look like for us?

The decision to reject needed help in favor of keeping separate for theological reasons demonstrates an important leadership precedent that remains timeless, especially in times of rebuilding a covenant community. Exercising true leadership in such a context includes decisions that are, for the sake of the gospel, exclusive. Exercising true leadership includes leading out of deep theological convictions, not cultural consensus or accommodation. This kind of leadership, focused on a passion for purity and identity, is particularly pertinent when reestablishing a community of believers after a time of great upheaval.

Leading with conviction in such circumstances means making enemies, not friends. If you have the "disease to please" and are in such a leadership role, you will feel the challenge. Making enemies invites retaliation, trouble, suffering, and persecution. It could even entail a halt in moving forward with the things of God. Moreover, this passage shows that such hindrances may not be short-lived, but can potentially drag on for years (4:24). So, expect delays, opposition, and a crippling effect on your kingdom work—the direct fruit of having the courage to have convictions.

In a short note titled Conviction, Courage and Civility: Three Virtues for a Vitriolic Age,[7] Biola University President Barry H. Corey gives his perspective on how to handle disagreements as Christ followers in today's polemical culture. Although Corey's note does not reference our text specifically, it clearly exemplifies how the principles of this text in Ezra might be applied today. It emphasizes how we need "a soul of conviction, a voice of courage"[8] in the face of opposition.

The university often hosts symposiums designed to tackle topics that engender conversation with Christian speakers of different backgrounds. Two events in particular, one entitled, "Love No Matter What: Politics, Sex, Race and the Way of the Cross," and the other symposium designated "Disagree" Conference reflect the university's efforts. The following excerpts from Corey illustrate well.

---

7. Barry H. Corey, "Conviction, Courage and Civility: Three Virtues for a Virtriolic Age," *Biola* (Summer 2016): 6.

8. Ibid.

How do we winsomely engage with those who may not share our faith in conversations on worldviews, social issues, politics, race, economics, war, immigration, gun control and even the existence of God? We need modelers who show how we can flourish in the context of disagreement. . . . This takes Christians who embody the virtues of courage, conviction and civility. Conviction is the virtue that binds us to our most cherished and least changing beliefs. It grounds us in biblical truth and forms our core. Courage is the virtue that calls us to bold action, reaching beyond the horizons of possibility. As Christians, we are called to be a present witness within our culture. We do this by melding conviction with courage, guided by civility that bears witness to the gospel. Only with all three do I believe we'll make progress on the seemingly intractable challenges of our day.

In my nine years as president of Biola University I have become convinced that we need a generation of Christians with deep convictions regarding what is true, grounded in the word of God. We need a generation of Christians courageous in their faith, empowered by the Spirit of God. And we need a generation of Christians whose demeanor is civil, kind and compassionate, modeled by the Son of God. Even within the church, the days of going it alone or fostering a spirit of competition need to give way to fresh partnerships and collaborations that stretch beyond our theological and denominational differences.[9]

---

9. Ibid.

# Ezra 4:6–24

6 At the beginning of the reign of Xerxes, they lodged an
accusation against the people of Judah and Jerusalem.

7 And in the days of Artaxerxes king of Persia, Bishlam,
Mithredath, Tabeel and the rest of his associates wrote a letter
to Artaxerxes. The letter was written in Aramaic script and in
the Aramaic language.

8 Rehum the commanding officer and Shimshai the secretary
wrote a letter against Jerusalem to Artaxerxes the king as follows:

> 9 Rehum the commanding officer and Shimshai the
> secretary, together with the rest of their associates—
> the judges, officials and administrators over the people
> from Persia, Uruk and Babylon, the Elamites of Susa,
> 10 and the other people whom the great and honorable
> Ashurbanipal deported and settled in the city of Samaria
> and elsewhere in Trans-Euphrates.
>
> 11 (This is a copy of the letter they sent him.)
>
> To King Artaxerxes,
>
> From your servants in Trans-Euphrates:
>
> 12 The king should know that the people who came
> up to us from you have gone to Jerusalem and are
> rebuilding that rebellious and wicked city. They are
> restoring the walls and repairing the foundations.
>
> 13 Furthermore, the king should know that if this city
> is built and its walls are restored, no more taxes, tribute or
> duty will be paid, and eventually the royal revenues will
> suffer. 14 Now since we are under obligation to the palace
> and it is not proper for us to see the king dishonored, we
> are sending this message to inform the king, 15 so that a
> search may be made in the archives of your predecessors.

In these records you will find that this city is a rebellious city, troublesome to kings and provinces, a place with a long history of sedition. That is why this city was destroyed. [16] We inform the king that if this city is built and its walls are restored, you will be left with nothing in Trans-Euphrates.

[17] The king sent this reply:

To Rehum the commanding officer, Shimshai the secretary and the rest of their associates living in Samaria and elsewhere in Trans-Euphrates:

Greetings.

[18] The letter you sent us has been read and translated
in my presence. [19] I issued an order and a search was
made, and it was found that this city has a long history of
revolt against kings and has been a place of rebellion and
sedition. [20] Jerusalem has had powerful kings ruling over
the whole of Trans-Euphrates, and taxes, tribute and duty
were paid to them. [21] Now issue an order to these men
to stop work, so that this city will not be rebuilt until I
so order. [22] Be careful not to neglect this matter. Why let
this threat grow, to the detriment of the royal interests?

[23] As soon as the copy of the letter of King Artaxerxes was read to Rehum and Shimshai the secretary and their associates, they went immediately to the Jews in Jerusalem and compelled them by force to stop.

[24] Thus the work on the house of God in Jerusalem came to a standstill until the second year of the reign of Darius king of Persia.

THE STORY OF OPPOSITION THAT COMMENCED IN 4:1–5 continues in Ezra 4:6–23. We are introduced to two other instances of opposition that the Jews faced in their rebuilding efforts. The author steps aside from telling the story of the temple (4:1–5, 24) and informs the reader of further complaints leveled against God's people in Jerusalem as they attempted to rebuild, with particular attention to the city walls (4:12–23).

## Later Opposition under Xerxes and Artaxerxes: Work Ceases (4:6–24)

**Ezra 4:6.** The first of the two instances concern an accusation leveled at the people early in the reign of Xerxes, another name for Ahasuerus (486–465 BC), the king with whom Esther's story unfolds. The author offers no information about the nature of this complaint but merely lists it first.

**Ezra 4:7.** The second instance concerns a piece of correspondence. The author mentions several things about this letter by way of introductory matters (4:7–10) and then quotes the actual letter in 4:11–22. In the introduction the reader learns about both the recipient and the writers of the letter. The recipient is King Artaxerxes of Persia.[1] Here the author does not date the opposition to a specific year in Artaxerxes's reign but is more general, "in the days of Artaxerxes" (4:7).

The actual scribe of the letter is Shimshai (v. 8), who was authorized by Rehum, the commanding officer (vv. 8 and 9), to file the legal complaint contained in the letter. The complaint derives from trustworthy sources: the testimonies of the king's top provincial associates/advisors, Bishlam, Mithredth, and Tabeel. Moreover, the complaint has the backing of other people of rank, the rest of their associates including judges and officials (4:9), and it is geographically widespread (Tripolis, Persia, Erech, Babylon, and Susa (4:9–10). Finally, the complaint derives from others who have been in the land, with legal ties to it, since the time the Assyrian king Ashurbanipal (669–633 BC) deported them.[2] Although no record exists for either of these deportations, Assyrian kings were well known for such conduct. [3] Name-dropping two Assyrian kings, however, smacks of political appeal. The appeal to Artaxerxes

---

1. Artaxerxes ruled 465–424 BC (see Introduction). During Artaxerxes's seventh year, Ezra (whom we have not yet met in the story but will in 7:1) was sent to Jerusalem (7:6–7). During Artaxerxes's twentieth year Nehemiah was sent to Jerusalem (Neh 2:1).

2. Ashurbanipal (literally "Osnappar," an Aramaic variant) succeeded Esarhaddon (681–669 BC), who is mentioned in verse 2.

3. Joseph Blenkinsopp, *Ezra-Nehemiah*, OTL (Philadelphia: Westminster, 1988), 112–13.

concerning ties to Ashurbanipal found in the letter reveals the tug of war about who has ultimate authority. Put another way, the complaint verbalized in the letter carries some weight, is legitimate, and is not merely a provincial squabble confined to a small group of disgruntled people. The other introductory matter (v. 7) states that the letter is written in Aramaic and translated (following the NIV note here, cf. 4:18) into the Persian language for the king.

After the salutation (v. 11), the formal complaint begins. The Jews are engaged in rebuilding the city's walls and foundations. The point, however, is that unlike Cyrus's decree that allowed for the temple's reconstruction, no Persian king sanctioned this specific project (4:21). To be sure, they do not yet have legal grounds to rebuild the walls.[4]

Moreover, the heart of the complaint pertains to loyalty (4:14–16). Those crafting the letter prop themselves up and appear to have a staunch loyalty (probably overstated) expressed by the idiomatic expression, "Now since we are under obligation to the palace" (or my translation, "now since we have eaten/salted the salt of the palace," v. 14). Salt could be used to ratify the relational obligations between two parties (Lev 2:13; Num 18:19; 2 Chr 13:5).[5] Put another way, since they are in the service of/receiving a salary from the palace, they are honoring the king by being his loyal informants (vv. 14, 16). Their pledge of allegiance with respect to the revenue of the palace, the king's reputation, and his power abroad, however, seems overstated. Regardless, since rebuilding a city wall is akin to gaining strength and independence, it was viewed as a compromise of loyalties, posing a serious threat to the empire. Searching the archives of previous political administrations (the Assyrians and Babylonians) concerning the past conduct and reputation of the Jews would provide further evidence demanding a verdict from the king.

Even before the king issues a formal search and the evidence is properly assessed (vv. 19–22), the informants describe Jerusalem's interactions with past political administrations as rebellious, wicked, and a place of sedition (vv. 12, 15 [2x]). Rebellion here means a political revolt against international powers whereby the vassal breaks allegiance with the suzerain.[6] And indeed, such rebellion happened with Hezekiah

---

4. Nehemiah will provide the impetus for this later, however, cf. Neh 1.
5. Blenkinsopp, *Ezra-Nehemiah*, 114.
6. See 2 Kings 17:1–4; 24:1.

against Assyria (Isa 36–39) and with Jehoiakim and Zedekiah against Babylon (2 Kgs 24–26). Thus, according to the king's informants, the city was destroyed on account of such rebellion (Ezra 4:15), and they are justified in their complaint. Their human perspective, however, contrasts with the divine perspective about the city's fall (2 Chr 36:15–19).

The section closes with a record of the king's response and action to the supposed threat (Ezra 4:17–23). It speaks of three orders: one to look into the matter, another to stop the work, and a hypothetical order that might grant rebuilding at a future time. The king's findings corroborated the informants' concerns. Indeed, the reputation of the Jews and their past conduct was deemed a genuine concern and threat for the present administration. The result of the political inquiry process, "they went immediately to the Jews in Jerusalem and compelled them by force to stop" (v. 23). The force used to stop them is not stated, but little is left to the reader's imagination: Someone forcefully intervened. Indeed, the opposition was such that it would be sixteen years before the people of God would finish rebuilding the temple (Ezra 4:24; 6:13–15). This literary interlude (4:6–23) fills out the bigger picture of opposition that the Jews faced. The author then returns to the subject at hand, the temple building project, and will complete his thoughts on that topic in what follows (5:1–6:22).

EZRA 4 CONTAINS DESCRIPTIONS OF TWO INSTANCES of opposition against the Jews. In 4:1–5, we see personal oppostition raised against those who are rebuilding the temple. Here in 4:6–23, we see political opposition against those rebuilding the walls. Yet, both types of opposition, personal (4:1–5) and political (4:6–23), produced similar results: a halt in the work of the kingdom, not to mention psychological ramifications. With rebuilding the temple, the Jews were not legally bound to stop their work. They stopped as a result of fears caused by their neighbors (4:4–5, 24). However, due to the supposed political threat and the king's official order, the Jews were legally bound to stop working on the walls until further notice (see discussion in Neh 1).

Scripture tells us that governments and political entities have always been threatened (whether real or imagined) by the power and numbers of God's people. In fact, God warned and promised as early as Abram that "whoever curses you I will curse" (Gen 12:3). *In other words, expect opposition, but God will eventually deal with that opposition, too.* Threatened by political concerns that the Hebrews might bring (Exod 1:10), the king of Egypt issued an order to have male Hebrew babies thrown into the Nile (Exod 1:15–16, 22). The king of Moab, Balak, was threatened by the military power of Israel over the Amorites, so he hired Balaam to curse God's people (Num 22:1–6). Threatened by the lack of loyalty displayed to him by Mordecai, Haman, "the enemy of the Jews" (Esth 3:10), seeks to destroy all the Jews in Susa (Esth 3:6). He frames his complaint to King Ahasuerus (483–471 BC) as a lack of loyalty by all Jews to the laws of the land—indeed a political threat to the king. With such royal interests at stake, the king issues a decree to annihilate all Jews living in his provinces (Esth 3:12–15).

As redemptive history moves forward, we see similar events in the opening pages of the New Testament. Herod the Great was threatened by the birth and worship of "the king of the Jews" (Matt 2:2–3). He ordered all male children up to two years of age to be slain in order to end the threat (Matt 2:16). In Acts, Paul met Aquila and Priscilla at Corinth because "Claudius (Roman emperor from AD 41–54) had commanded all Jews to leave Rome" (Acts 18:2). This edict was made because he was threatened by the loyalty that Jewish converts had to Christ in Rome and was a huge setback for Christianity there.

A couple of universal principles emerge here. First, the nature of the complaint about God's people cuts across time and space. The complaint entailed a perceived lack of loyalty to the laws of the land. God's people are portrayed as unsubmissive rebels posing a serious threat to governments. The main criticism from the enemy concerned the question of loyalty to governments and the fear of what could happen if such loyalties were compromised. As noted by Marshall, Gilbert, and Shea, "Christians while usually loyal citizens, have repeatedly said with Peter that they must obey God rather than man, and are obliged to serve 'another King' (Acts 17:7). This denies that the state is all encompassing or the ultimate arbiter of human life. The claim that *Caesar is not God* challenges every authoritarian regime, ancient Romans and modern totalitarians alike, and draws their angry and bloody response."[7] The goal, therefore, was to

---

7. Marshall, Paul, Lela Gilbert and Nina Shea, *Persecuted: The Global Assault on Christians* (Nashville: Thomas Nelson, 2013), 17.

eliminate the threat, then and now. In this regard, serious accusations of apostasy and/or blasphemy sometimes go together in parts of the Muslim world that target Christ followers especially.[8] For example, "In Pakistan, Christians and Ahmadis are disproportionately charged—typically with no evidence to support but the accusation itself—with defacing or burning the Qur'an or insulting the Muslim prophet."[9] This leads to another universal principle.

The second universal principle is that in the canon of Scripture evil kings have routinely issued formal decrees against God's people. Through their political prowess, they attempt to stop God's work. Whether they are aware of it or not, they are attempting to stop the history of redemption from moving forward. The power of these political entities provides huge setbacks, the work of God gets hampered, God's people are treated unfairly, and the opposition seems endless. God's people face persecution.

In sum, God's people threaten political entities in a land. Such a threat leads to unfair criticisms. The unfair criticism in turn leads to unjust treatment. The unfortunate fruit of these realities produces frustrating complications and hurdles. Ezra helps give us a sobering perspective about such opposition.

INDEED, THE NATIONS OF THE WORLD TODAY have it out for God's people. The application, therefore, of these principles just discussed is readily seen in the contemporary context. The reputation of Christians and their past conduct has been deemed a genuine concern and threat for contemporary political administrations in the twentieth and twenty-first centuries, and in the pages of church history. In the book *Persecuted: The Global Assault on Christians*, the authors have as their goal to focus on "an underreported fact: Christians are the single most widely persecuted religious group in the world today."[10] This includes Catholics, Protestants, Orthodox, liturgical, evangelical,

8. Ibid., 287.
9. Ibid.
10. Ibid., 4.

charismatic, and hundreds of no-name sects related to those who embrace the belief that Jesus Christ is their Lord and Savior.[11]

For a variety of reasons, but especially the desire for total political or religious dominance, governments and political entities in nations such as China, India, North Korea, Vietnam, Iran, and elsewhere have interfered and opposed the advancement of God's work.[12] In this regard, Christian suffering entails real oppression (not mere discrimination or slight offenses) from serious violations of religious freedom which include torture, rape, imprisonment, death, and church buildings attacked or destroyed.[13] The goal has been and will continue to be to stop and thwart, and to curse, the work of God by the enemies of God's people. But what really lies behind these powerful human agencies' attempts to stop the work of God?

The staunch opposition and nasty accusations faced by the Jews in their effort to rebuild reflect what we know, this side of the cross, to be spiritual warfare. What looks like a fight against flesh and blood really *is* a fight against the principalities and powers in the heavenly places (Eph. 6:10–12). We often forget, and perhaps even deny, that theologically speaking we are in a time of war, *not* peace. War was declared on God's people described in Revelation 12 as a fight between the dragon and woman (12:17).[14] The dragon gave the "beast out of the sea" his power

11. Ibid., 4–5.

12. Ibid., 9.

13. Ibid.

14. In actual fact, the opposition goes as far back as Genesis 3:15. On account of the events in the garden, God promises the serpent that enmity will exist "between your offspring and hers" (Gen 3:15). Revelation reminds "that ancient serpent called the devil, or Satan, who leads the whole world astray" is ultimately behind the opposition. We are alerted to a clash of kingdoms from the very beginning between the seed of the woman (or Jesus) and the serpent, the devil (Gen 3:15). The whole OT shows the conflict and opposition, previous warfare against Christ before his appearance.

The conflict comes to a head with the birth and life of Jesus and is described in Rev 12 and summarized here. Satan tries to kill the seed of the woman; he looks successful with Jesus's death on the cross, but up from the grave he rose again! This humiliating victory angered the devil, so he turns his fury to the church and individual believers. He tries to hurt the witness of the church, water down its testimony of Jesus through persecutions, accusations, and much more. He attempts to deceive the world and win people to his side. He tries to usurp God's sovereignty and God's exclusive claim to the throne. He raises havoc throughout the world in various ways, as in the past and is presently doing so.

The outcome of this cosmic battle for the church and individual believers is positive, yet we are in the crossfire of the conflict. We experience pain and suffering while we

and authority (13:1–2), and the beast was given power to wage war against God's holy people and to conquer them (13:6–7). The threat is verbalized in the rhetorical question, "Who can wage war against it?" (13:4). For this reason, John gives the needed wartime exhortation, "This calls for patient endurance and faithfulness on the part of God's people" (13:10).

The nature of opposition is such that it is no respecter of persons or time. It is often both overt and subtle, individual and corporate, varied and yet painfully real. We need to understand opposition from a theological perspective to properly face it. Again, it is not a time of peace, but of war. From Genesis to Revelation, but especially in the New Testament, we learn there is a clash of ages. With Jesus's resurrection, the age to come has broken into this present age. We have a taste of it (Acts 2:17–21). But the present age is not benign. It is the present *evil* age (Eph. 6:12). This is why some receive salvation and others do not. This is why we see some healings, but not all the time. This is why we ultimately experience opposition, individually and corporately as the church. This is the reason why the nations are not yet reached for the Gospel. This is why some nations remain closed to Christianity. This is why evil prevails. This is why the church looks defeated, thwarted, and even stopped! We are living in the age of tension.

We should expect delays, opposition, and all the forces of the evil one to stop us from advancing anything pertaining to the kingdom of God. When evil prevails, our mindset must align itself with the realities of the spiritual world, realities we do not see with the natural eye. In this regard, the Lord's Prayer helps, because it acknowledges evil and our need to be delivered from it, "deliver us from evil/the Evil One" (Matt 6:13).

Jesus faced intense opposition to the kingdom work assigned him by the Father. In fact, the escalated opposition was directly related to his personhood, his identity. The operative questions in the Gospels concern Jesus's identity. "Who are you?" Jesus is asked (John 8:25). "By what authority do you do these things?" or "Who gave you this authority?" asked the religious leaders (Mark 11:28; Luke 20:2; Matt 21:23). Jesus himself asked his disciples, "Who do people say I am?"

---

are in this world but are protected. The devil declared war at the cross, but the cross declares the victory! We need to be reminded of this back story to opposition.

(Matt 16:13–16; Mark 8:27–29; Luke 9:18–20). How did Jesus handle opposition? He knew he was God's servant (Matt 12:15–21). He had a strong self-identity and authority that were not his own. He did not quit but kept on demonstrating the kingdom through his actions (healing, casting out demons, etc.).[15] The greatest opposition Jesus faced was death. But death could not hold him nor oppose him! He triumphed through opposition due to the power of God (Phil. 2:9)! He allowed God to handle his opposition and make the final move. Jesus encountered, handled, and moved on from opposition and triumphed through God's power. Because of his ascension to heaven and the descent of the Holy Spirit, the age to come was ushered into this present evil age. And so, the context then and now is the age of tension for doing kingdom work. We need to have this as our framework in life and for ministry. A colleague of mine rightly said, "Often as Christians we sometimes want to get to the light at the end of the tunnel but not notice that it is because of the experience of the tunnel that we are able to see the light!"[16] Through Jesus's death and resurrection, God fulfills part of his promise to Abraham: "I will curse those who curse you" (Gen 12:1–3).

---

15. See Matt 9:35 as a summary statement of Jesus's kingdom work as it pertains to healings. Matthew 8:28–34 and Mark 5:1–17 illustrate his ministry with the demonic.

16. Thanks to my colleague at Gordon-Conwell Theological Seminary, Dr. Jacquelyn Dyer.

# Ezra 5:1–17

1 Now Haggai the prophet and Zechariah the prophet, a
descendant of Iddo, prophesied to the Jews in Judah and
Jerusalem in the name of the God of Israel, who was over
them. 2 Then Zerubbabel son of Shealtiel and Joshua son of
Jozadak set to work to rebuild the house of God in Jerusalem.
And the prophets of God were with them, supporting them.

3 At that time Tattenai, governor of Trans-Euphrates,
and Shethar-Bozenai and their associates went to them and
asked, "Who authorized you to rebuild this temple and to
finish it?" 4 They also asked, "What are the names of those
who are constructing this building?" 5 But the eye of their God
was watching over the elders of the Jews, and they were not
stopped until a report could go to Darius and his written reply
be received.

6 This is a copy of the letter that Tattenai, governor of
Trans-Euphrates, and Shethar-Bozenai and their associates, the
officials of Trans-Euphrates, sent to King Darius. 7 The report
they sent him read as follows:

To King Darius:

Cordial greetings.

8 The king should know that we went to the district of
Judah, to the temple of the great God. The people are
building it with large stones and placing the timbers in
the walls. The work is being carried on with diligence
and is making rapid progress under their direction.

9 We questioned the elders and asked them,
"Who authorized you to rebuild this temple and to
finish it?" 10 We also asked them their names, so that we
could write down the names of their leaders for your
information.

11 This is the answer they gave us:

"We are the servants of the God of heaven and
earth, and we are rebuilding the temple that was built
many years ago, one that a great king of Israel built and
finished. 12 But because our ancestors angered the God of
heaven, he gave them into the hands of Nebuchadnezzar
the Chaldean, king of Babylon, who destroyed this
temple and deported the people to Babylon.
13 "However, in the first year of Cyrus king of
Babylon, King Cyrus issued a decree to rebuild this
house of God. 14 He even removed from the temple
of Babylon the gold and silver articles of the house
of God, which Nebuchadnezzar had taken from the
temple in Jerusalem and brought to the temple in
Babylon. Then King Cyrus gave them to a man named
Sheshbazzar, whom he had appointed governor, 15 and
he told him, 'Take these articles and go and deposit
them in the temple in Jerusalem. And rebuild the house
of God on its site.'
16 "So this Sheshbazzar came and laid the
foundations of the house of God in Jerusalem. From
that day to the present it has been under construction
but is not yet finished."
17 Now if it pleases the king, let a search be made
in the royal archives of Babylon to see if King Cyrus
did in fact issue a decree to rebuild this house of God
in Jerusalem. Then let the king send us his decision in
this matter.

THE NARRATOR NOW RETURNS TO THE TOPIC AT hand: the work on rebuilding the house of God, the subject of Ezra 4:24, after an aside about opposition. In what follows, chapter 5 is thematically connected to chapter 4 but also to the broader section that includes chapter 6 (5:1–6:22) relative to the building report and the work on the house of God. Under the prophets Haggai and Zechariah (520 BC), after a hiatus of sixteen years of not working on the temple (4:4, 24; 536 BC), the people find motivation and the work on the temple resumes (5:1–5). Their work is further challenged, and an investigation is encouraged and conducted per a letter to King Darius (5:6–17). The outcome of this investigation with Darius's response immediately follows in Erzra 6:1–12.[1]

## Rebuilding Resumes and Temple Completed (5:1–6:22)

### Haggai and Zechariah Motivate People: Work Resumes but Is Challenged (5:1–5)

PROPHETIC PLAYERS (5:1) Chapter 5 can be divided into two sections. The first is 5:1–5, which serves as an introduction to the piece of correspondence contained in the second section, 5:6–17. Ezra 5:1–2 reintroduces the prophetic word as a critical dynamic in this period of restoration. The author's purposes are clear. He wants to communicate that God intervened after the long, sixteen-year hiatus to fulfill the intended goal of rebuilding the temple (Ezra 1:1–11). Through the prophetic word, the Jews were given divine reauthorization resulting in a recommissioning of their work. The fact that two individuals prophesied "in the name of the God of Israel, who was over them" (5:1) forcefully suggests a needed stamp of authority, given the circumstances.

**Prophetic response (5:2).** Ezra 5:2 provides the outcome of the prophetic messages given by Haggai and Zechariah. The outcome stuns the reader. Simply put, prophets prophesy and the leaders listen! The leaders listen to the prophets, and together the prophets and leaders lead the way for the entire community to finish the work on the temple (see also Hag 1:12–15). These verses in Ezra demonstrate how true prophecy was meant to motivate, bring change, and work in the lives of God's covenantal people.

**Persian officials (5:3–5).** Once again Persian officials challenge the Jews about the rebuilding process but with an entirely different spirit. Several factors make it clear their challenge is not necessarily to deter,

1. Darius conducts the investigation, which concludes decisively in favor of allowing the Jews to continue the work, evidenced in the second of two letters in this section (6:1–12). Darius's formal decree re-enables the process that Cyrus's decree enabled initially, a major win for the people of God. Finally, work on the temple is completed and a great celebration takes place, concluding this section of the book (6:13–22).

but to do things according to government regulations. First, the tone of Tattenai's letter to Darius (5:6–10) is not harsh, in contrast to the letter sent to Artaxerxes (4:12–16). Second, the phrase "and their associates, the officials" can also be read "and his companions, the inspectors" (5:6). One understands that building inspectors inspect; thus, the neutral nature of the inquiry seems justified. Regardless of the benign nature of the question, it still represented a competing, secular authority for the Jews, and it could have derailed them. The fact that it did not reflects how deeply the prophetic word took root in their hearts.

In addition, the fact that they were not stopped for a second time pertains to God's sovereignty. Ezra 5:5 reveals the heart of the matter: "But the eye of their God was watching over the elders of the Jews and they were not stopped." The "eye" and "hand" of God feature prominently in the book. God's seeing eye leads to protection from harm.[2] That God is portrayed anthropomorphically (as a human with body parts) creates a sense about the reality of his presence. He is present, not absent. He is near, not far. In the book, the narrator's interests clearly lie with the divine protection, provision, and providence about the rebuilding process. Regardless of human interference or political policies (no lack here), God superintends the situation. Ezra 5:5 provides another indicator.

## Investigation Pursued (5:6–17)

**SPECULATIONS (5:6–10).** The second section of chapter 5 (5:6–17) concerns the first of two pieces of royal correspondence in Ezra 5:1–6:12, Tattenai's letter of inquiry to Darius. Although a challenge was posed once again to the Jews in their rebuilding process (5:3), the tone of the letter investigating the situation confirms the benign nature of the challenge (5:8–10). The main question looming in the minds of the officials was whether the Jews ever received official permission to rebuild the temple prior to Darius's rise to the throne under Cyrus, and if they were building with government stipulations (5:3, 9). These officials, too, are loyal informants of the king but of a different stripe from those mentioned in 4:12–16. They simply wish to obtain government clearance

2. A significant theme in Nehemiah (e.g., 1:6; cf. 2 Chr 6:20; Pss 33:18; 34:15). But God can refuse to see, with the notion that help will not be available (Isa 1:15–16). For other examples of the eye(s) of God, consider Prov 15:3; Ps 32:8; 2 Chr 16:9. For other examples of the hand of God, see Pss 63:8; 89:13; Isa 48:13.

on the building project, labeled here "the temple of the great God" (NIV) or "the great house of God" (v. 8).[3] Given the context the former is preferred.

With this designation the Persians are not acknowledging Israel's God as *the* God, but as one among many (see Ezra 1:1–3). He was, however, chief God for the Israelites.The mention of the greatness, though, has to do with the knowledge of the international prestige Israel achieved in the past due to historical interactions with nations in the ancient world. Likewise, it was customary for the Persians to use the religious labels of those they conquered, out of respect and in hope of divine favors.[4] No malice seems intended in the investigation. In fact, the Persian officials affirmed both the workers and the work (5:8). In addition, these officials also wanted to know names of those from the Jewish community who initially gave leadership to the successful project that was carrying on "under their direction" (v. 8). Possessing the names of their leaders would only help the investigation; the more information, the better in bringing the matter to a conclusion.

**Jews' response (5:11–17).** Ezra 5:11–17 gives the confident response by the Jews to the inquiry of the Persian officials. The letter not only summarizes the events that unfold in Ezra 1–4, but it also provides historical background to the situation not mentioned in Ezra. The letter defines who they are, "we are the servants of the God of heaven and earth" (v. 11). The fuller designation "God of heaven and earth" emphasizes the stature of the God they humbly work for (see Ezra 1:2), the divine authority ultimately commissioning their work. The letter gives indirect information about the original builder of the temple and its completion, "a great king of Israel" (v. 11). This "great king" did the biddings of the great and lofty God (5:11). The letter also shows why the building was destroyed—"our ancestors angered the God of heaven, he handed them over to Nebuchadnezzar." (v. 12). The statement reveals a correct perspective on the temple's destruction and the exile by the Babylonians. Although they do not disclose the behavior leading to the deity's anger, it resulted in divine abandonment (v. 12).

---

3. The syntax of the Aramaic allows for the adjective (*raba'*) to modify either God or house.

4. M. Dunand, "Byblos, Sidon, Jerusalem. Monuments apparentes des temps achemenides," VTSup 17 (1969): 64–70.

The letter seeks primarily to show that their present work has historical precedent. It stretches back some 440 years but also includes more recent official authorization under Cyrus (vv. 13–16), here designated "king of Babylon" and not "king of Persia" (1:1), to show the progression of the events mentioned in verse 12. King Cyrus's decree authorized the work (Ezra 1:2–4; 6:3–5) and enabled the Jews to return, rebuild, refinance, and replenish the temple with previously confiscated vessels (Ezra 1:7–11). By this authorization, Cyrus did what was typical in the ancient Near East. It was customary for kings, having won a great victory or after acquiring new territory, to refurbish or rebuild broken-down temples and restore their divine images to the rebuilt shrine. In the mind of a person in the ancient Near East, the latter was understood as returning the divine presence to his/her earthly home. In so doing the king was acknowledging the deity who gave them victory. Cyrus was seeking to return the divine presence to Jerusalem and, because no image existed for Yahweh, he returns temple vessels. Cyrus's rise to power and his decree functioned this way (see 1:1).

In sum, the Jews confidently provide Darius with a historical sketch about the temple. Although not mentioned by name, the builder, designated "a great king of Israel" (v. 12), refers to the accomplishment of Solomon (1 Kgs 5–8; ca. 960 BC). The sketch also mentions its destruction (586 BC), its reauthorization to be rebuilt under Cyrus (539 BC), and the completion of the second temple's foundation under Sheshbazzar (536 BC). Ezra 5:16 mentions that Sheshbazzar laid the temple foundations, not Zerubbabel (3:8–10; Zech 4:8–10) as other texts inform, and Zerubbabel's name is a curious omission here. By comparison, Solomon's name was also omitted above in reference to the first temple (Ezra 5:12). Perhaps this reveals a deliberate strategy of the Jews for Darius's investigation? The Jews may have put forward only the names of those who could be traced in the official documents. Clearly, Solomon's name (tenth century BC) would not be found in Persian documents of the sixth century, and thus it would be moot to mention his name. Zerubbabel's name, too, would not likely appear in the Persian records since Cyrus himself appointed Sheshbazzar "governor of Judah" (5:14). For this reason, perhaps, it would seem logical to give priority to Sheshbazzar. It assumes, and does not contradict, that both worked on the temple foundations together and that, indeed, as other texts indicate, Zerubbabel had a key role. The focus on chapter 3 pertains to the building, but here in chapter 5 the focus is on the evidence allowing them to build.

Finally, the sketch concludes with the present state of the project: "not yet finished," according to the report of Darius's officials (v. 16; 520 BC). They also provide Darius with a reason to follow the policies of his predecessor and allow the work to continue to its completion. With this set of concrete facts now articulated by the Jews and inserted in the letter, the Persian officials invited a formal governmental investigation "in the royal archives of Babylon" for corroboration of these facts during Cyrus's reign (v. 17).

IN ORDER TO UNDERSTAND THE FULL FORCE OF this pericope, a brief note on how prophecy functioned in the Old Testament is helpful, as well as usual outcomes of the prophetic word in the nation's past. In general, prophecy entailed both foretelling and forthtelling.[5] Ezra 5:1–2 is an example of foretelling. In this situation, the prophet interpreted the present circumstances of the people to motivate them toward right action rather than predict something about their future as a nation (forthtelling). One must read the separate books of Haggai and Zechariah to get a fuller picture of those circumstances. In brief, one can observe some of the emotional, economic, and spiritual demeanors of Zerubbabel, Joshua, and the entire community from the respective messages of the prophets (Hag 1:6, 9–11; 2:20–23; Zech 3–4). After intense opposition that brought the work to a standstill, it seems complacency set in. The people of the province of Judah/Yehud put their priorities elsewhere; namely, with building their own homes and pursuing commercial endeavors rather than building God's house (Hag 1:4). The leadership, too, lost all motivation and may have even doubted that God still wanted them to rebuild the temple (Hag 1:13; 2:20–23; Zech 3–4). *With this mindset, the Jews now posed an internal threat to their own rebuilding process.*

Haggai and Zechariah speak directly into these specific circumstances by telling complacent folks to get busy with God's project (Hag

5. For further reading on prophetic genre, see Gordon Fee and Douglas Stuart, *How to Read the Bible for All its Worth*, 3rd ed. (Grand Rapids: Zondervan, 2003).

1:1–11) and by assuring them of God's presence (Hag 1:13; 2:5; Zech 4:10) with the hope they would move toward the intended goal of temple completion. This is how the prophets interpreted the present circumstances of the people in order to motivate them toward right action.

But this is not a new thing. Prior to the exile, God persistently raised up prophets to steer Israel in the right direction relative to his holy standards as outlined in the covenant (2 Chr 36:15–16; see also 2 Kgs 17:13–14). These texts in Kings and Chronicles underscore God's character in raising up prophets. His deep compassion for his people drove him to do so. The fact that the prophets appeared on the scene (sixteen with books attached to their names; numerous others mentioned in the narrative without a book) was a visual aid of God's grace and mercy to his people, undeserved extensions of grace. He was relentless in pursuing them, and the prophets demonstrate that. The typical response, however, to the prophetic word was met with relentless resistance leading to the exile of both kingdoms (2 Chr 36:16; see also 2 Kgs 17:13–14; Neh 9:30; Zech 1:1–6; 7:11–14). Moreover, the nation's leaders were scrutinized and held accountable for the demise of the nation (Ezek 13 and the whitewashing prophets).

In vivid contrast to previous responses and outcomes of the prophetic word in Israelite history, Ezra 5:1–2 demonstrates a different outcome. Mobilization of the entire community takes place because the leaders listened to God's word through the prophets. Both clergy and laity united to accomplish previously established God-given goals (Ezra 1:1–6). One could account for this surprising and out of character responsiveness with speculations of various sorts, not the least of which is that a long period of discouragement softened them. Ultimately, Haggai says it was God's Spirit that stirred the people to action (Hag 1:14). This is not unlike Paul's proclamation of the prophetic word about Jesus and the ensuing response in Thessalonica. The gospel came to them with words "but also with power, with the Holy Spirit and deep conviction" (1 Thess 1:5). Their lives were transformed by the word and they "became imitators of us and of the Lord . . . in the midst of severe suffering" (1:6). Even in the face of strong opposition, "with the help of our God we dared to tell you his gospel" (2:2). The Thessalonians understood that the word they received from Paul was not a human word, but the word of God (2:13). The word "worked" in their lives and they were transformed, becoming imitators of God (2:14).

Thus, from this section of the book, the author wants his audience to see that a sovereign God resolves even potential interference (Ezra 5:5) in the restoration process. From beginning to end, divine intervention through the prophetic word (5:1–2), the prevention of God's watching eye (5:5), and the intentional stirring of people to action by God himself brought the desired results (Hag 1:14). He raised up those from among the covenantal community who listened to God and thereby intervenes to achieve his purposes.

Tattenai's letter to Darius reveals that the work of God's people is under constant scrutiny, and potential interference always looms large. It represents a benign challenge, but a challenge no doubt. Noteworthy is how the people respond to this challenge and the legal investigation that ensued. They are not threatened but produce the necessary evidence for the officials. They give an account for their actions. Their response here drastically contrasts the earlier time when the enemies of Judah discouraged them and hired counselors to frustrate their plans (4:4). After being "rebooted" by the prophetic word (5:1–2), they face the challenge with confidence. Not only did the prophetic word motivate them to start building again, but also it enabled them by renewing their confidence. Their renewed confidence displays itself beautifully in the letter and has timeless nuggets imbedded in it.

The first nugget concerns a deep awareness of their true identity as "servants of the God of heaven and earth" (v. 11). Their service to God corresponds to working for God by building the temple. The term "servant," although seeming counterintuitive, can imply leadership,[6] not just one serving under the authority of another. In fact, some of Israel's brass (Abraham, Isaac, Jacob, Moses, Joshua) have such a title,[7] as does Isaiah's messianic servant who is tasked with restoration and salvation (Isa 42:1–6; 42:1; 49:5–7; 52:13–53:11). The main factor in carrying out God's work is having one's identity firmly established in God. Their identifying statement comes first in the letter, and not without reason. They realize they are doing God's bidding, first and foremost. Their leadership in this regard connects to God's leadership; they lead under

6. For a helpful discussion on the topic of leadership in the Bible, see Benjamin Forrest and Chet Roden, eds., *Biblical Leadership: Theology for the Everyday Leader* (Grand Rapids: Kregel, 2017).

7. Deuteronomy 9:27; Judg 2:8.

God's leadership, a higher power and authority. When God's people are under scrutiny, reaffirming this will continue to anchor the work. Whether such a claim has an appeal to those investigating is not as important as it is to those being investigated. It serves as a reminder of where one's true loyalties must lie.

The people also advocate for themselves on a legal and historical basis, not just a spiritual one. The second nugget is that when under scrutiny, God's people need not be afraid to stand up for themselves. They knew the facts, that they legally had the right to do what they were doing. Although they did not possess the documents, the assumption is that the government would, so they appeal to that documentation. The legal documents provide yet another level of confidence as God's people withstand investigation. But this remains secondary to the confidence produced from the awareness of one's identity as God's servant, when working in/for his kingdom.

Thus, scrutiny and potential interference is to be expected, especially when doing kingdom work. The way to withstand the pressure of being scrutinized is with an acute awareness of the spiritual (God has called us to this) as well as the legal (we have tangible evidence) component to the work. Even with such confidence in place, favorable results are not guaranteed. The results of the investigation must be left in the hands of a sovereign God. Ezra makes this extremely clear as he brings the story of the temple to a conclusion in the following section.

WHILE IT IS TRUE THAT POTENTIAL GOVERNMENT interference looms, legal restrictions are increasing, and battles for religious freedom are now being waged here in courts and legislatures as well as in the public square, the church in the USA enjoys a blessed freedom of religion. We can advocate for ourselves on the basis of our First Amendment rights. Not unlike the Israelites under Persian rule, US residents have legal recourse to protect their First Amendment rights (freedom of speech). Free debate is encouraged, and there is an ability to seek help and reform through democratic means. Historically and legally, freedom of speech allows one to defend the Christian worldview. On this basis, it would appear a Christian in the USA (and other parts of the Western world) may be able to stand somewhat secure in her or his rights and freedom to worship (unlike the suffering and persecuted underground church elsewhere in the world). Nevertheless, this sense of security is false in many aspects, since our confidence and freedom must stem from something surer than political constitutional rights.

Indeed, Peter reminds us that we have the prophetic word made surer in the person of Jesus (2 Pet 1:12–19). In a manner like Old Testament prophets, the book of Hebrews teaches us that "[i]n the past God spoke to our ancestors through the prophets at many times and in various ways, but in these last days he has spoken to us by his Son, whom he appointed heir of all things" (Heb 1:1). His message to us spoken through the Son, the incarnate word, remains critical. Jesus, the last prophet of the old covenant, and the first of the new covenant, gives us the ultimate interpretive lens for life and how to navigate opposition. He also provides us with a model for motivation to do kingdom work. How one understands the prophetic role and its intended outcome today is critical for needed security in our lives.

First, the regular proclamation and exposition of the word of God via pastors and teachers fulfills a foretelling role not unlike the prophets of old. Pastors and teachers interpret God's covenantal instructions found in the Bible for present day circumstances by exhorting and motivating their audiences to live by those instructions. The pulpit provides the platform.

Second, among other things, pastors and teachers are visual aids that show God is relentlessly pursuing people for kingdom purposes and work. The key role of pastors and teachers as interpreters of God's word is apparent, especially when opposition faces individual covenantal communities. When this happens, it is hard to hang on to God's goals. Complacency, lack of motivation, loss of focus, and discouragement become issues beside the initial obstacle that triggered the problem in the first place. Accordingly, the church looks to its leaders with expectation, and rightly so. The church needs more of the word, not less, in such conditions. Perhaps, for a pastor/teacher in a similar context to that of Ezra's audience, it might be helpful to think of oneself as a Haggai or Zechariah, a motivational speaker raised up for the mission of God. In other words, we should understand that the pastorate and the prophetic (as in both forthtelling and foretelling, i.e., the second coming and the impending judgment of this present evil age) merge. Often the real issue is not what one sees on the surface. Complacency, lack of motivation, and even fear of opposition, for example, are symptoms of something else; in the case of Ezra, it goes back to disobeying God's initial word. The pastor's task, therefore, is to provide a spiritual reboot to get to the real issue. Is the congregation receiving the word from the pastor/teacher as a human word or as the word of God? If the former, movement forward cannot happen. But if they understand that through the preaching, they are receiving the word of God working in their lives, then kingdom work will get on track again.

Church leaders, regardless of one's church governance, should lead by heeding the word of God themselves. As they lead by heeding, they pave the way for the entire community so that together they unite for kingdom purposes. In other words, they might consider rolling up their sleeves and getting to work themselves. One should not only give the word but also follow through with it. That said, it must be remembered that the mobilization of leaders and lay people to respond depends on God. We have the ability for mobility toward kingdom concerns (whatever it might be) because of God's indwelling Spirit. Through the work of the Holy Spirit, the word gets rooted in our lives, and we are stirred to action. Ezra reminds the reader that, in such circumstances, God remains sovereign. God intervenes to encourage the flock in the right direction again through pastors and teachers. God delights in intervention, which ultimately reflects his gracious character. God intervenes, and because of his watchful eye (his presence), prohibits further opposition. Because God's intention is having his will done on earth, God enables the audience by the Spirit for the work.

# Ezra 6:1–12

1 King Darius then issued an order, and they searched in the
archives stored in the treasury at Babylon. 2 A scroll was found
in the citadel of Ecbatana in the province of Media, and this
was written on it:

Memorandum:

3 In the first year of King Cyrus, the king issued a
decree concerning the temple of God in Jerusalem:

Let the temple be rebuilt as a place to present
sacrifices, and let its foundations be laid. It is to be sixty
cubits high and sixty cubits wide, 4 with three courses of
large stones and one of timbers. The costs are to be paid
by the royal treasury. 5 Also, the gold and silver articles
of the house of God, which Nebuchadnezzar took from
the temple in Jerusalem and brought to Babylon, are to
be returned to their places in the temple in Jerusalem;
they are to be deposited in the house of God.

6 Now then, Tattenai, governor of Trans-Euphrates,
and Shethar-Bozenai and you other officials of that
province, stay away from there. 7 Do not interfere with
the work on this temple of God. Let the governor of the
Jews and the Jewish elders rebuild this house of God on
its site.

8 Moreover, I hereby decree what you are to do for
these elders of the Jews in the construction of this house
of God:

Their expenses are to be fully paid out of the royal
treasury, from the revenues of Trans-Euphrates, so
that the work will not stop. 9 Whatever is needed—
young bulls, rams, male lambs for burnt offerings to
the God of heaven, and wheat, salt, wine and olive
oil, as requested by the priests in Jerusalem—must be
given them daily without fail, 10 so that they may offer

sacrifices pleasing to the God of heaven and pray for
the well-being of the king and his sons.
[11] Furthermore, I decree that if anyone defies this
edict, a beam is to be pulled from their house and they
are to be impaled on it. And for this crime their house
is to be made a pile of rubble. [12] May God, who has
caused his Name to dwell there, overthrow any king
or people who lifts a hand to change this decree or to
destroy this temple in Jerusalem.

I Darius have decreed it. Let it be carried out with diligence.

## Evidence Found and Response to Investigation by Darius (6:1–12)

THE TENSION ABOUT THE INVESTIGATION'S OUTCOME (Ezra 5:17) is immediately relieved in Ezra 6:1–12, especially the opening verses (6:1–2). Evidence is found (6:1–5), and Darius's response to the investigation is recorded (6:6–12). Darius's favorable edict enabled the completion of the work (6:8–12), just as Cyrus's favorable edict enabled the start of the work several years prior (Ezra 1:1–5). For these reasons, the narrator highlights the legal nature of the investigation in 6:1–12 by attaching two pieces of official correspondence (6:3–5; 6–12) and through the repetition of a key term, *sim*, which the NIV does not always translate it as "decree." It is "order," "decree," and "edict," not always following the one distinction in the Hebrew. Through this, the narrator continues to build the case for the legitimate nature of what the Jews were doing, his goal from the beginning (cf. Ezra 2–3), but now under different circumstances.

Earlier, their return, rebuilding, and offering of sacrifices were sanctioned by Cyrus (1:1–11) and done "in accordance with what is written in the law of Moses" (Ezra 3:2; 4). Both externally and internally, the Jews played by the rules (the law of Moses and the laws of the land). The Jews continue to rebuild and presently have the internal spiritual backing from God via the prophets (5:1–2), but they also have the external backing of the government (6:6–12). The laws of the land authorized and reauthorized the work. The law of Moses and God through the words of the prophets, respectively, authorized and reauthorized the Jews spiritually. The spiritual aligns with the natural set of circumstances. Both tracks intersect, underscoring the legitimate nature of the project from its inception and for its continuation and completion.

Ezra 6:1–12 also concludes the storyline of temple building opposition that the narrator commenced in Ezra 4:1, a rather long literary slice covering waves of opposition (see commentary on 4:1–5), but one that ends with an ironic twist.[1] King Darius promises severe opposition to any who interfere and oppose the work of God's people, presently and in the future!

**Scroll of Ecbatana (6:1–5).** In Ezra 6:1–5, the needed documentary evidence, "a scroll," was found in Ecbatana, neither in the "royal archives" nor in the "treasury" at Babylon (5:17; 6:1), as was expected. Ecbatana was the summer residence of Persian kings. The part of the scroll quoted here gives different information from that found in 1:2–4 but is not contradictory. The narrator quotes only what is necessary information from the edict to continue the present storyline. The officials investigating had two main objectives: who authorized the project and the building methods employed (5:8–10). Accordingly, the injunction in the scroll—not only to build but also how to build (6:3b–4a), provisions for building (v. 4b), and the return of articles to the house of God (v. 5)—functions as the needed building permit authorized originally by Cyrus.

Both the measurements, "sixty cubits high and sixty cubits wide" (v. 3), and the materials, "three courses of large stones and one of timbers" (v. 4), give governmental specs. In this way, the Jews were in the clear. They are following governmental guidelines, plus the testimony of the elders about the articles of silver and gold (5:14–15) finds confirmation in the edict.

**Darius's response (6:6–10).** Ezra 6:6–10 contains Darius's letter of response to Tattenai. Three statements in 6:6–7 reflect the king's definitive word; two are stated in the negative, "stay away from there" and "do not interfere with the work" (6:6b, 7a), and one in the positive, "Let [them] rebuild this house" (6:7b). The repetition reinforces the king's decision and underscores the serious tone. He prohibits interference physically (6:6b). In addition, Ezra 6:8 suggests that the king prohibited any financial interference. Lack of finances could potentially interfere

---

1. To be sure, the author does mention more opposition in Ezra 7–10, but in those chapters the opposition comes largely from within the ranks of the exiles and their unfaithful conduct, with one exception (8:22).

and stop the work, but, more importantly, it would not allow financial autonomy to offer sacrifices. To interfere in this way especially would defy Darius's interpretation of Cyrus's decree (6:3–4) and could potentially harm the king's own "well-being" (v. 10). It was not uncommon for Persian kings to look after the religious interests of their subjects. By so doing, they were attempting to secure both public and divine favor from the gods their subjects served.[2]

**Penalties (6:11–12).** Finally, Darius closes his response with the enforcement of a penalty to those who would "change" (that is, defy or disobey) the decree or attempt to destroy the Jerusalem temple (6:11–12). Such threats of punishment and curses for disobedient subjects were typical parts[3] of covenantal agreements in the ancient Near East. If Ezra 6:11, which states, "they are to be impaled on it," refers to impaling (the Aramaic is uncertain),[4] then the Persians join ranks with the Assyrians who were also known to impale rebellious subjects.[5] Thus, rebellious individuals will suffer a public disgrace. Ezra 6:12 also specifically counters any political power who might try to sack the temple again, "any king . . . who lifts a hand to . . . destroy this temple in Jerusalem." This is, perhaps, a not-so-veiled reference to the distasteful actions of the king of Babylon, as reported by the Judean elders (5:12). The language and imagery of one who "lifts a hand" implies opposition, an act of rebellion where one raises a hand in authority, control, or possession.[6]

---

2. So, too, the Cyrus Cylinder (cf. Pritchard, *The Ancient Near East,* 282–84).

3. For more on covenants see Meredith G. Kline, *The Treaty of the Great King: The Covenant Structure of Deuteronomy* (Eugene, OR: Wipf & Stock, 2012).

4. Because the phrase, "they are to be impaled on it" could also be translated "upright he shall be struck on it," verse 11 may not refer to being impaled. The latter translation suggests a milder punishment; one that entails a flogging with the use of a stake from one's house. Blenkinsopp, *Ezra-Nehemiah,* 126, supports this option. See also Kidner, *Ezra and Nehemiah,* 64–65.

5. For a helpful compilation of ancient Assyrian torture practices for rebellious subjects, see Erika Belibtreu, "Grisly Assyrian Record of Torture and Death." *BAR* 17:01 (1991). Fensham's description of impaling is worth repeating, "One side of a beam was sharpened and the other side planted in the ground. The sharp point was inserted under the chest of a person and pushed through his esophagus and lungs. He was then left to hang until he died" (*The Books of Ezra and Nehemiah,* 91).

6. This contrasts with lifting hands in an act of worship or act of submission (1 Tim 2:8). For more on the imagery see Leland Ryken, James C. Wilhoit, and Tremper Longman III, eds. *The Dictionary of Biblical Imagery* (Downer's Grove, IL: IVP Academic, 1998).

In short, opposition will be met with opposition. Thus, Darius not only sanctioned that the work continued, but he also guaranteed protection of God's people in the process of its completion. Ironically, this pagan king was opposing more opposition to God's people! Opposition does not last forever, because God eventually (on his timetable) intervenes in governments of the world. But divine intervention here is twofold. Not only does God intervene by raising up Haggai and Zechariah from within the covenantal community (5:1–5), but God also intervenes by raising up individuals, outside the covenantal community and from the government, to support and encourage his people and to achieve his broader purposes. It is fitting, therefore, that Ezra 6:1–12 concludes the narrator's discussion on temple building opposition with such a definitive statement.

ALTHOUGH THE JEWS WERE RECOMMISSIONED spiritually through Haggai's and Zechariah's ministries, a legal recommissioning, one in line with previous governmental leaders, was needed given the present inquiries (5:17). The narrator desires that his audience know that both the original act of commissioning (Ezra 1:1–4) and the act of recommissioning (6:8–12) the people to this task of temple building was politically legal. God's people were not venturing out on their own authority. This proves the claim of lack of submission unfounded (4:19). Indeed, secular channels sanctioned their continued work. But Ezra 6:1–12 also reveals that the results of the investigation were more than a secular government sanctioning a building project.

The result of the investigation and the nature of the recommissioning is remarkable, relative to favors it afforded the Jews. Interference with the Jews and their work is not just opposed, but it is radically opposed. Any interference with the king's orders has serious consequences with respect to one's person and property if violated. It also entails personal opposition from the God of the Jews! In the mind of an ancient, divine disfavor spelled disaster. After a time of suspicion and years of opposition imposed on God's people, this reversal of the norm is critical. From a biblical-theological perspective this reversal, favor, protection, and overall outcome for God's people in Ezra 6:1–12 are an outflow of Genesis 12:1–3. Through Darius's edict, the narrator is indirectly demonstrating to his audience that "whoever curses you [God] will curse" (Gen 12:3).

Along with Daniel and Esther, Ezra 4:1–6:12 unpacks how the rule of Gentile kingdoms over Jerusalem does bring opposition to individuals (Dan 1–6) but then expands and escalates to the covenantal community and their worship of Yahweh (Dan 8–12). The story of Esther, especially, highlights this fact with Haman, "the enemy of the Jews" (Esth 3:10), who plots to destroy all of God's people. Through the interworkings of Mordecai and Esther, what looked like an early Holocaust situation became a victory. The enemy was impaled (Esth 7:1–10) and Mordecai honored (Esth 6:1–14). God's people found favor and triumphed. It is an incredible portrait of triumph through opposition! Thus, a series of fits and starts emerges relative to moving toward God's goals for his people. Local enemies, political enemies, accusations, character defamation, government orders, and even benign investigations threaten God's people and purposes (Ezra 4:1–5:17). In the end, and with a surprising twist, God meets opposition with opposition (Ezra 6:11–12), because he promised Abram he would do so. God was doing his part, as were the people. What did these people do? They prayed, made their defense when necessary, and continued with their work.

Ezra ends this literary slice about opposition (4:1–6:12) on a high note: the restoration of Zion is a non-negotiable from God's perspective, because it rests on God's unchangeable word. Although opposition is real, it does have a definitive end—one in line with God's decreed purposes. This panoramic picture of opposition, painted by the narrator of Ezra, serves a key purpose.

The postexilic community's experience anticipates the early church as it struggled under Roman law and authority to advance the kingdom and build the church of God. The book of Acts underscores this. In the aftermath of Pentecost, Peter and John get arrested (4:3), the apostles are persecuted (5:18), Stephen gets stoned to death (7:59–60), and the church persecution gets underway (8:1–3). Both Judean and Roman rulers treat God's people unfairly as the church braves the Gospel in a hostile environment. Yet repeatedly in Acts, God meets opposition with opposition through displays of surprising power, including signs, wonders, healings (e.g., Acts 3:1–8; 6:8–10) and growth (e.g., Acts 5:14; 6:1; 9:31). In other words, the church triumphs through opposition. The fact that Acts ends with Paul under house arrest in Rome does not impede his ability to further the gospel. In fact, Luke's concluding statement about Paul in the book, "He proclaimed the kingdom of God and taught about the Lord Jesus Christ—with all boldness and without hindrance!" (Acts 28:31), indicates the triumph of the Gospel through opposition. Ultimately, Luke wanted his audience to apprehend that nothing can stop the word of God and the church's mission from advancing. In all of this, what did the early church do? The people prayed, made their defense when necessary, and continued with kingdom work.

The experiences of the postexilic Jews and the early church with opposition anticipates the church as it struggles under the authority of this world system called Babylon, the great harlot discussed in Revelation, who stands in opposition to God and God's people (Rev 17–19; see 19:2 specifically). This system has attempted to thwart God's purposes and to defeat God's people through a variety of means. Moreover, the church will face an escalation of opposition, a worldwide opposition, closer to the days of Christ's return (Mark 13:30; Rev 11:7–10; 19:19; 20:7–9a). The great battle, or "Armageddon" (Rev 16:16), is the final attack of forces upon the church.[7]

In Revelation, we also learn that this opposition does not last forever. God intervenes. We are told we *will* see the ultimate fulfillment of God's promise to Abraham, "I will curse those who curse you," become a reality (Gen 12:3). Revelation 18:8, in reference to the world system dubbed "Babylon," God promises that "in one day her plagues will overtake her: death, mourning and famine." She will be consumed by fire, because the Lord God whom she has opposed is strong. A trifold lament follows from those who enjoyed Babylon (18:9–19), but there is also an exhortation for the people of God to rejoice because Babylon's fall represents God's just retribution visited upon the world for persecuting his people. Babylon killed God's people, but God defeats Babylon. Satan, the beast, and the false prophet all go down together (20:7–10). Why? Because Christ's sudden return in judgment will oppose all opposition once and for all (2 Thess. 2:8). Even though they made war on the Lamb, Revelation reminds us that the Lamb conquered and opposed them (Rev 17:14) because he is Lord of lords and King of kings!

---

7. Ezekiel 38–39 and the forces of Gog against God's people anticipate what we read in Rev 16.

IF THE RESTORATION OF ZION IS A NON-NEGOTIABLE because it is tied to the very promises of God that "whoever curses you I will curse," then God's people can have a staunch assurance that opposition toward kingdom work will end. We can be assured that in the end, God will do something radical to oppose those who are opposed to him.

Yes, we are to expect delays, opposition, and even crippling effects on kingdom work. But we need to understand these delays in light of the end product. Nothing can ultimately stop God's covenantal promises from moving toward their fulfillment.

What must we as the church, locally, but especially abroad, do in this climate of opposition? What posture should we take? Yes, we must pray and keep on doing what we are doing. But Revelation also mentions that in this intense environment of opposition, we have a very specific call bound to the proclamation of the gospel. The call entails not just endurance, but a *patient* endurance; it entails faithfulness and wisdom for the people of God who keep his commands to *remain faithful* to Jesus (Rev. 13:10, 18; 14:12). As Daniel, Esther, Ezra, Nehemiah, and the returned exiles endured opposition, they attempted to exercise wisdom and a faithfulness toward keeping God's commands. Their stories make this clear.

What does faithfulness look like for us, then? What does it look like to remain faithful to Jesus and his commands? On the one hand, it is true that the church and Christianity do not look triumphant: "We need to understand how, very long ago, Christianity was introduced to many countries and regions—places that now seek to pull Christianity up by its ancient roots."[8] In the remaining communist countries, people die for declaring Caesar is not God.[9] In post-Communist countries, close scrutiny invites restrictions and ruin on many who profess faith.[10] In the Muslim world there sometimes exists the weight of repression, a policy of persecution, spreading repression, and war and terrorism against

8. Marshall, Gilbert, and Shea, *Persecuted*, 13.
9. Ibid., 21–62.
10. Ibid., 63–89.

Christian beliefs and practices.[11] In America, sociologists designate our times as post-Christian.[12] Churches are empty, and their doors are closing. These realities are a call for patient endurance, wisdom, and faithfulness to God's commands. These realities are a call to remain faithful to Jesus.

On the other hand, it is also true that "in some places in the final decades of the twentieth century, we saw the largest church growth in history, particularly in sub-Saharan Africa and China."[13] In fact, church historians note that Christianity in China in the twenty-first century is in its fourth great phase of expansion. Furthermore, "despite the fact that most Christian gatherings are illegal and can bring about arrest and lengthy sentences in labor camps, China might have the largest church attendance of any country in the world."[14] This reality reminds us, too, that nothing can ultimately stop or oppose God's word![15]

The book of Romans poses some pertinent questions. "What, then, shall we say in response to these things? . . . If God is for us, who can be against us? Who will bring any charge against those whom God has chosen? . . .Who shall separate us from the love of Christ? Shall trouble or hardship or persecution or famine or nakedness or danger or sword?" (Rom 8:31, 33; 35).

Not even the decrees of the king of China or Muslim kings can stop the advancement of the kingdom of God. Indeed, as the ensuing chapters of Ezra-Nehemiah reveal, no human agency, political or otherwise, can stop the advancement of God's kingdom and the promises of God to bring restoration! Nothing can oppose God.

---

11. Ibid., 90–256.
12. Ibid.
13. Ibid., 99.
14. Ibid., 100.
15. Ibid., 16.

# Ezra 6:13–22

13 Then, because of the decree King Darius had sent, Tattenai, governor of Trans-Euphrates, and Shethar-Bozenai and their associates carried it out with diligence. 14 So the elders of the Jews continued to build and prosper under the preaching of Haggai the prophet and Zechariah, a descendant of Iddo. They finished building the temple according to the command of the God of Israel and the decrees of Cyrus, Darius and Artaxerxes, kings of Persia. 15 The temple was completed on the third day of the month Adar, in the sixth year of the reign of King Darius.

16 Then the people of Israel—the priests, the Levites and the rest of the exiles—celebrated the dedication of the house of God with joy. 17 For the dedication of this house of God they offered a hundred bulls, two hundred rams, four hundred male lambs and, as a sin offering for all Israel, twelve male goats, one for each of the tribes of Israel. 18 And they installed the priests in their divisions and the Levites in their groups for the service of God at Jerusalem, according to what is written in the Book of Moses.

19 On the fourteenth day of the first month, the exiles celebrated the Passover. 20 The priests and Levites had purified themselves and were all ceremonially clean. The Levites slaughtered the Passover lamb for all the exiles, for their relatives the priests and for themselves. 21 So the Israelites who had returned from the exile ate it, together with all who had separated themselves from the unclean practices of their Gentile neighbors in order to seek the LORD, the God of Israel. 22 For seven days they celebrated with joy the Festival of Unleavened Bread, because the LORD had filled them with joy by changing the attitude of the king of Assyria so that he assisted them in the work on the house of God, the God of Israel.

## The Temple Rebuilt and Celebration (6:13–22)

IN THE FINAL SECTION OF CHAPTER 6 (EZRA 6:13–22), the narrator indicates that, in spite of the looming challenge that provoked the question of whether the Jews would be able to continue their work (5:3–4), the "Jews continued to build *and* prosper" under the influence of Haggai and Zechariah (6:14a; emphasis added). Moreover, they "finished building the temple," a project commanded by God and decreed by the government (6:14b–15), dedicated it (6:16–18), and then joyfully celebrated with the Passover (6:19–22).

From a literary perspective, the temple's completion in 6:13–22 forms an *inclusio* with Ezra 1:1–6, where temple building commenced. Together, Ezra 1:1–6:22 is framed by the topic of rebuilding the temple. Within this framework the narrator discusses opposition to the building project(s) at length (Ezra 4:1–6:12) and then devotes a mere two verses to mention the finished work (6:14–15). This literary arrangement makes a profound point. One must understand opposition in light of the completed task. As one sees the longevity and severity of the opposition, it makes the completion of the project even sweeter. Chief of all, it enables one to acknowledge God's faithful hand in the process, a point the narrator firmly established as he recounted the story.

From a theological perspective, Ezra 6:13–22 signals fulfilled prophecy (Ezra 1:1). The prophets, Isaiah and Jeremiah in particular, envisioned this moment, and Cyrus's decree triggered the restoration phase (see Ezra 1:1–3). Darius's decree brought completion to it in a temporal sense. Yet it took roughly sixteen years before a restored temple became a reality. Even in the context of restoration, God's people experienced opposition. But external opposition will not thwart God's unchangeable word relative to his promised restoration by the prophets. No matter how long or severe the opposition, no matter the delays, God's purposes will be accomplished. Threats always exist to the advancement of God's covenantal promises, but in the end God causes his own word to prevail. This is the viewpoint the narrator wishes to imbed in the mind of the reader as he brings the story of rebuilding the temple to a close.

**Temple completion (6:13–15).** Ezra 6:13–15 not only tells of the finished work (Ezra 1:1–6:22), but it also shows in a succinct summary statement how, why, and when the rebuilding was completed, as well as the results. These would be important facts for future generations. First, from a practical point of view, the lack of governmental interference enabled the Jews to continue to build (6:14). As a result of Darius's decree, the Persian officials got their questions answered about the building project in Judah (5:17). Cyrus commissioned the project, and Darius did not wish to interfere. The officials, therefore, carried out the king's decision as promised (5:17) and with diligence (6:13). Second, from a spiritual point of view, the "preaching" of the prophets motivated the Jews, enabling them "to build *and* prosper" (6:14; emphasis added). The impact of Haggai and Zechariah, mentioned now for the second time (5:1–2), carried significant weight.[1] "Prosper" (*tsalah*, v. 14), paraphrased, means getting the job done and doing what God commanded.

Ezra 6:13–14 communicates how and why the temple ultimately was rebuilt. The human side of the equation (work decreed by Persian kings) operated in tandem with the divine side (work commanded by God). Thus, the rebuilding took place "according to the command of the God of Israel and the decrees of Cyrus, Darius and Artaxerxes, kings of Persia" (6:14). The Aramaic word translated "command" is the same word translated "decree" (6:14b) but distinguished in the original with different vowels (*ta'am/te'em*). The "command of the God of Israel" likely refers to the prophetic words of Haggai and Zechariah that enabled the finished project, since finishing the completed work is in immediate view. It could include more, such as God's command to Cyrus from Isaiah.

The fact that the command originates from "the God of Israel" bears further comment. The designation appears several times in the book. It springs from the mouth of the narrator (3:2; 5:1; 6:14b), Persian officials (1:3; 7:15), and Zerubbabel (4:3) as a consistent reminder and claim that the postexilic community's religious identity has continuity with the preexilic community.[2] The God of Israel continues with the Israel of God in this new phrase.

Another important observation is that the Aramaic of Ezra 6:14 reads,

---

1. See commentary on Ezra 5:1–5.

2. The patriarch Jacob received the name Israel after his wrestling match with God (Gen 32:28). The name in Hebrew means "God contends." The designation speaks of his unique relationship with God. The name Israel was used of Jacob's spiritual descendants and refers to their religious heritage. The designation, therefore, expresses that unique relationship.

"the decree of Cyrus, Darius, and Artaxerxes king of Persia" (author's translation), not "the *decrees* of Cyrus, Darius and Artaxerxes, *kings* of Perisa (NIV, emphasis added). This reveals the theological perspective of the narrator. Through the decree of one king, Cyrus (as promised by Isaiah), God's command to rebuild is fulfilled. The mention of three separate Persian kings, however, reminds and shows the longevity of the project (6:14b). The inclusion of Artaxerxes is logical, though dischronological (as in 4:7–23), in so much as Ezra 6:14–15 offers a summary of how, with external help, the work got done. He could have in mind Artaxerxes's usefulness to Ezra (7:27) or Nehemiah (2:1–10), and perhaps both.

Lastly, in these verses the author has not only reviewed the how and why of the building project, but in Ezra 6:15 he also gives the answer to the when question. The date corresponds to March 12, 515 BC, some years after Haggai and Zechariah started preaching in Aug–Dec of 520 BC (Hag 1:1; Zech 1:1, second year of Darius).[3]

**Dedication, installation, and celebration of the building (6:16–18).** What results ensued with the completion of the project? This section, along with what follows in vv 19–22, answers that question. As was done in earlier building phases, with the altar and foundation respectively (3:3–5, 10–13), they celebrated and worshiped. The previous celebrations, however, were a mixed bag of fear (3:3), joy, and sadness (3:12–13). Joy alone characterizes this present celebration (6:16, 22 [2x]; see also Neh 12:43 for the theme of joy in the context of the dedication of the walls). Accordingly, they offer thanksgiving offerings as well as a sin offering because of the defilement acquired from being in exile (Ezek 4:13; Hos 9:3; Amos 7:17).

This moment recalls, too, the dedication of Solomon's temple, when the king, along with all Israel, offered sacrifices before the Lord (1 Kgs 8:62–63). Although only Judah, Benjamin, and Levi remained of the twelve tribes at this point in the nation's history, the narrator attempts to represent the past with the realities of the present. In fact, the present and the past are deeply connected. Although the exile changed the circumstances, it did not redefine them. The "Israel" designation appears three times in two verses (6:16–17) in an effort to underline this fact. The dedication, along with the installation of temple personnel (cf. Exod 29;

---

3. For a slightly different completion date see Williamson, *Ezra, Nehemiah*, 72; and Blekinsopp, *Ezra-Nehemiah*, 129.

Lev 8) that enables the new community ("the people of Israel," priests, Levites, and exiles) to worship God once again, retains a consistency with the standards of the preexilic community prescribed in the Book of Moses (so too Ezra 3:2, 4). This building dedication, installation, and celebration was just as valid as previous building dedications.

**Ultimate result: Passover worship (6:19–22).** The ultimate result flowing from these events pertains to restored worship. With all the cultic installations in place (a new temple and cultic personnel), the community resumes and conducts worship in the traditional way with the celebration of Passover in the first month of Nisan or March (Exod 12:6,14; Lev 23:5). God originally instituted the Passover celebration to commemorate Israel's deliverance from Egypt (Exod 12:14). The lamb's blood applied to their doors caused the "destroyer" to pass over each household (Exod 12:23); as a result, they were spared judgment. The instruction, therefore, was to mark their calendars yearly to observe and celebrate God's rescue mission on their behalf (Exod 12:14; 23:15). Finally, the day of Passover was followed by the week-long Feast of Unleavened Bread (Exod 12:15–20; Lev 23:6–8). These combined feasts were intended to bring the worshiper back to God, to remind the worshiper who was responsible for the joyous occasion. Together, these two feasts typify the sentiment of joy.

Beside the initial Passover and the one mentioned here in Ezra, the biblical writers only tell us of its celebration four other times: when Israel broke camp from Sinai (Num 9:5), after the nation crossed the Jordan (Josh 5:10), and under the revivals of two great kings, Josiah and Hezekiah (2 Kgs 23:21; 2 Chr 30:2, 2 Chr 35). In fact, 1 Kings mentions that before Josiah's time, "Neither in the days of the judges who led Israel nor in the days of the kings of Judah had any such Passover been observed" (2 Kgs 23:22). Given the profound meaning of Passover, it remains unthinkable that such neglect existed.

This celebration of Passover in Ezra not only connects them with their past, but it celebrates another rescue mission—Israel's deliverance from exile—and the motif of the second exodus resurfaces.[4] The temple completion marks a major turning point for the new community. God once again delivered his people, but from the bondage of exile. Now that opposition and the enemies of God's people have been put in their

4. See Introdution for a discussion of this motif.

place, the temple's completion is both a victory and a worship celebration signifying God's sovereign rule over his people. It was, therefore, appropriate to celebrate and worship Yahweh for his protection and favor in their lives.

Accordingly, measures were taken to ensure a proper celebration. The Levites do here what each family was required to do before the exile (Exod 12:6), slaughter the Passover lamb (Ezra 6:20). Likewise, those partaking in the meal had to demonstrate purity. Those that returned from exile were cleansed from exile due to the sin offering (6:17). Similarly, those who were living compromised lives by engaging in "unclean practices of their Gentile neighbors" (6:21) "separated themselves" from such practices in order to "seek the LORD, the God of Israel" in the worship of the Passover celebration. Such devotion to the God of Israel required cutting all other religious ties, allegiances, and ways of worship, something that "the enemies of Judah and Benjamin" mentioned in 4:1 were not willing to do thereby barring them from participation in temple building (4:2–3). Again, the exclusive rather than inclusive nature of those participating in worship is important because the identity and purity of God's people is at stake (see Neh 10:28). This exclusion points backward and forward, as the theme of exclusion/inclusion emerges in the rest of the book Ezra-Nehemiah.[5]

The appropriateness and timing of this Passover celebration cannot be overstated relative to the temple's completion. Although a powerful worship service accompanied the completion of the temple foundation earlier (3:12–13), the scale here differs due to Passover. In his concluding statement about the work on God's house (6:22), the narrator fully acknowledges that their source of joy in this worship service comes from a sovereign God who literally changed the heart of King Darius (6:6–12). Resistance turned into assistance. The Hebrew notes that the king "made strong their hands for the work" (author's translation 6:22). The NIV states, "he assisted them in the work." The wording is critical in the original. The paralysis noted in Ezra 4:4 is reversed where "the people of the land made weak the hands of the people of Judah," or as as the NIV states, the peoples around them, "set out to discourage" the people of Judah.[6]

---

5. See commentary on Ezra 4:1–3.
6. See commentary on Ezra 4:4–5.

The mention of the king of Assyria and not king of Persia, although unusual to the modern reader, would not be so to the ancient reader familiar with imperial ideology.[7] Since Assyrian territory now belongs to Persia, the conquering king becomes king of the people he conquered. The designation used for Darius is the author's way of acknowledging Persian hegemony over Assyria. The irony is that the Assyrians were responsible for the exile of Israel in 722 BC, and now, due to imperial ideology at play, they are responsible for aiding in restoration! Moreover, to have the prestigious king of Assyria "make strong the hands" (see above) of those working on the house of God speaks even more poignantly to the sovereignty of God.

Thus, in Ezra 6:13–22 the narrator summarizes how, why, and when the second temple was completed but zooms in on the ultimate result: the worship of Yahweh and their devotion to him, a reestablished relationship with their God who is mighty to protect and save. Although they were at the mercy of foreign kings, Ezra reveals that the results were in the hands of a sovereign God. Accordingly, they received assistance, not resistance! The narrative on the temple's completion ends in a joyful worship service celebrating God's assistance. The real victor over all obstacles and opposition is not Cyrus, not Darius, but Yahweh. God alone deserves their worship.

From a historical perspective, the temple's completion is the last of three building projects recorded in the Old Testament, along with the tabernacle in the wilderness (Exod 25–31; 40:34–38) and Solomon's temple in Jerusalem (1 Kgs 7:51; 8:62–66). Following ancient Near Eastern protocol, God commanded that architectural shrines be built as a visual aid of his victory and sovereignty over the enemy and all opposition; thus, the tabernacle in the wilderness showed his victory over Pharaoh and Egypt, and the temple in Jerusalem showed his victory over the Canaanites. God took his earthly seat as victor to be with his people, to guide and protect them by revealing his presence. Accordingly, the manifestation of God's presence via "the cloud" or the "glory of the LORD" was the crowning moment of each of

7. Cf. *ANET*, 566.

these building projects (Exod 40:34–38; 1 Kgs 8:6–11). All three projects shared in a dedication, installation, and joyous celebration.

Based on this historical precedent, the reader expects to hear of the glory cloud of God's presence filling this shrine, too. Clearly God is the victor over opposition as made clear in Ezra 4–6, and God should come and take his seat among his people in a visible way as before. Surprisingly, this does not appear to take place. The rebuilt temple in Ezra, therefore, differs—and even disappoints—in this respect. This pre-Ezra phase of temple rebuilding (1:1–6:22), although joyous and momentous, remains an incomplete restoration for two reasons.

The first reason this remains incomplete is simple: there is more to restoration than just a rebuilt temple. The attempts of Ezra to restore the community through the law (Ezra 7:1–10:44), and those of Nehemiah to restore the city's walls and sanctity of Zion (Neh 1:1–7:8), together with the pre-Ezra narrative (Ezra1:1–6:22), capture the restoration of Zion more fully. But even still this restoration falls short.

The second reason this part of the restoration remains incomplete concerns the missing ingredient of God's visible presence, "the glory of the LORD" represented by the appearance of "the cloud." Unless the divine presence shows up, full restoration is not possible for the people of God.[8] The expected visible manifestation of God's presence known as the "the glory of the LORD" represented by the cloud (Exod 40:34–35; 1 Kgs 8:10–11) does not fill the second temple as in the past because, as redemptive history unfolds, ultimately God "does not live in houses made by human hands" (Acts 7:48). Solomon's temple, and the subsequent divine glory manifested in the holy of holies, was a temporary measure

8. At this juncture in Israelite history, God's presence is still promised (Hag 1:13; 2:4) but is identified and experienced by the fact that "my Spirit remains among you" (Hag 2:5). Throughout both Testaments, the promise of the divine presence to individuals and communities involved in kingdom work dominates the narrative. However, the experience of the Spirit in the Old Testament was not on an individual level, "[i]t was a gift to the community in their covenant leaders" [Mark J. Boda, *Haggai, Zechariah*, NIVAC (Grand Rapids: Zondervan, 2004), 128–29]. Indeed, the leaders of the postexilic community experienced God's presence, without which they would not have been able to complete this kingdom project. For further discussion on God's glory relative to the second temple, see Joseph R. Greene, "Did God Dwell in the Second Temple? Clarifying the Relationship Between Theophany and Temple Building," *JETS* 61.4 (2018): 767–84 The theme of divine presence and its lexical background is picked up in more details in the commentary of Neh 13.

attempting to reflect God's intention of dwelling with his people. No dwelling made by human hands could ever contain the divine presence, because only God can create appropriate sacred space for his dwelling (Acts 7:49). As regards the rebuilt temple, God was no longer content to dwell in houses made with human hands. The anti-climactic ending to the second temple's dedication causes anticipation and expectation. This decrescendo prepares us for a crescendo! As we turn to the pages of the New Testament, we gain more understanding.

When the Word became flesh and "tabernacled" or "dwelt" (Gk. *skēnoō*) among us, John acknowledges that he and the disciples beheld God's glory (John 1:14), a revelation similar but far superior to that of the glory cloud seen and enshrined in both the tabernacle and temple. The radiant splendor of God's presence comes in a person, no longer shrouded by a cloud. Through Jesus and the incarnation, a "temple not built with human hands" (Acts 7:48; 17:24). God created his own sacred space where he dwells and reveals his presence. In Jesus, and through him, humankind could achieve and aspire to proper worship and a joyous devotion unto God. This is why the gospel writer notes that "something greater than the temple is here" (Matt 12:6).

But there is more. God appointed Jesus to do the final work of building him a dwelling with humankind. It was a work that would eventually cost him his life. God did not call upon enumerable masons, stonecutters or skilled workmen; God called upon one faithful and obedient carpenter from Galilee, namely, God's Son. Moreover, God asked this carpenter to pay the bill so God could dwell with his creation. As a result of Jesus's work on the cross, our debt is covered in full. We do not have to do the work to reach God ourselves; indeed, our labor and toil would be in vain. As a result of Jesus's work, God is free to build his house with humankind. The only way to pay him back is not with our work but our worship (Rev 22:3).

At the cross, Jesus vanquished the enemy and dealt with all opposition to his building plans (Col 2:15)! In the resurrection, God is victorious over sin and death. God is the real victor, because he delivered us from the bondage and exile of sin. As a result, we have an eternal rest from the enemy of our souls. In declaration of this victory and of his sovereign rule and authority over the devil, Christ erects the temple of his church (a temple not made with human hands) and the Holy Spirit fills the house of God (Acts 2:1–4). As believers, we are God's temple and his

Spirit dwells in us when we believe (1 Cor 3:16; 1 Cor 6:19; 2 Cor 6:16). This is the crescendo that arises from the decrescendo in Ezra 6:13–22. This is why God does not visibly show up in the rebuilt temple of Ezra's day. This is why the story of the completed temple breaks historical precedent with previous building projects.

In this New Testament building project, God has appointed a new place to attach his name and glory. It is a new place from which all spiritual life on earth will flow—temples not made with human hands. The book of Ephesians says it well: "In him the whole building is joined together and rises to become a holy temple in the Lord. And in him you, too, are being built together to become a dwelling in which God lives by his Spirit" (Eph. 2:21–22). God has made us individual places of worship. All of this should lead us to "For Christ, our Passover lamb has been sacrificed, Therefore let us keep the Festival . . ." (1 Cor. 5:7–8).

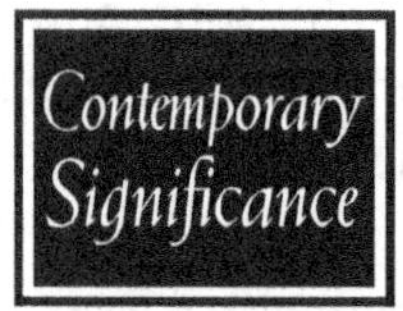


DEDICATION AND CELEBRATION! As temples of the living God, our lives should be marked by full service and dedication to God. Celebration leading to worship should naturally flow from our lives/temples as a result of what God has done; it should be our goal to "keep the Festival" as Paul exhorts (1 Cor. 5:7). Clearly Paul establishes a relationship between the prototypical Passover lamb and Jesus, the consummate Passover Lamb. Just as the Passover lamb's blood caused the destroyer to pass over each household (Exod 12:23), Christ's symbolically applied blood causes God's judgment to pass over sinners and give life to believers. We are rescued from eternal damnation and death (Rom 6:23). Just as the death of the lamb at the first Passover marked the Hebrews' rescue from Egyptian slavery, so the death of Christ marks our rescue and release from the slavery of sin (Rom 8:2). Just as the first Passover was to be held in remembrance as an annual feast, we are to remember the Lord's death by celebrating communion (1 Cor 11:26). Peter exhorts that the Old Testament Passover lamb, although a reality for the Israelites, merely foreshadowed the ultimate and final Passover Lamb, Jesus. Through His perfect life and sacrificial death, Jesus was our only option to rescue us from death to life (1 Pet 1:19–21).

Thus, both Easter Sunday, the height of our religious calendar where we celebrate Jesus as our Passover lamb, and communion Sundays, where we demonstrate these theological realities are moments that allow us to rededicate our lives afresh to God. But rededicating our lives to God is particularly necessary after a lapse in faith. Imagine the impact of going back to church on Easter Sunday after a serious lapse in your dedication and worship to God? Imagine your first communion service after a lapse in your dedication and worship to God? Our sentiments would not be unlike the deep joy and gratitude the Israelites expressed and experienced in the Passover after the second temple was built (Ezra 6:19–22). A life dedicated and/or rededicated to God does not mean attending worship only on Easter and Communion Sunday; it entails a lifestyle regulated by the reality of the cross. This means that there is no room to be a nominal follower of Jesus. Either one is dedicated or either rededicated to God. This means ongoing and daily acknowledgement of who God is, which then characterizes our actions. Worship will then be a natural outflow of our lives.

Indeed, there will be a time in the New Jerusalem when the anthem of God's people will resound with a continual outflow of praise. John sees the holy city, the New Jerusalem, coming down out of heaven from God, the true spiritual hub (Rev 21:2). Mourning has turned to joy and out of death comes life, for "He will wipe away every tear from their eyes and death shall be no more, neither shall there be mourning nor crying nor pain anymore, for the former things have passed away" (Rev 21:4, ESV). Revelation also tells us that "the dwelling place of God is with man. He will dwell with them, and they will be his people, and God himself will be with them as their God" (Rev 21:3, ESV). This is why John mentions, "I did not see a temple in the city, because the Lord God Almighty and the Lamb are its temple" (Rev 21:22). The New Jerusalem is the seat of the divine presence.

Is it any wonder, then, that the heavenly anthem that resounds in the book of Revelation, especially in 7:9–12, is all about granting God praise and worship? The four living creatures, the twenty-four elders, myriads upon myriads of angels, *and* people from every tongue and language are around the throne of God, his seat of sovereignty over the universe. It is a jammed packed worship service that goes on 24/7. Their declaration recognizes that God alone possesses salvation, and that salvation could come by no other means *except* by God: "Salvation belongs to our God, who sits on the throne, and to the lamb" (Rev 7:10). All of these are said to serve him day and night (7:15; 22:3). I would submit that they serve him by giving him loud, ceaseless praise—"Salvation belongs to our God" (7:10)! Their unending song serves God by giving him the name recognition he deserves. Worship is the only response. God's ceaseless dedication to us ends with all of creation's ceaseless dedication to God in worship.

In the meantime, before that worship service begins (!) and as we leave this section, it seems appropriate to ask yourself and your audience the following questions: Does your life song sing to him? Does your life bring worship to him, not just on Sunday mornings or in an isolated worship service, but as a life in a full surrender expressed in worship to him? May the chorus of our lives match the words of this beautiful song, "Let my lifesong sing to you."[9]

9. Casting Crowns, *Lifesong* (Beach Street/Reunion, 2005).

# Ezra 7:1–10

1 After these things, during the reign of Artaxerxes king of
Persia, Ezra son of Seraiah, the son of Azariah, the son of
Hilkiah, 2 the son of Shallum, the son of Zadok, the son of
Ahitub, 3 the son of Amariah, the son of Azariah, the son of
Meraioth, 4 the son of Zerahiah, the son of Uzzi, the son of
Bukki, 5 the son of Abishua, the son of Phinehas, the son of
Eleazar, the son of Aaron the chief priest—6 this Ezra came
up from Babylon. He was a teacher well versed in the Law of
Moses, which the LORD, the God of Israel, had given. The king
had granted him everything he asked, for the hand of the LORD
his God was on him. 7 Some of the Israelites, including priests,
Levites, musicians, gatekeepers and temple servants, also came
up to Jerusalem in the seventh year of King Artaxerxes.

8 Ezra arrived in Jerusalem in the fifth month of the seventh
year of the king. 9 He had begun his journey from Babylon on
the first day of the first month, and he arrived in Jerusalem on
the first day of the fifth month, for the gracious hand of his
God was on him. 10 For Ezra had devoted himself to the study
and observance of the Law of the LORD, and to teaching its
decrees and laws in Israel.

## The Second Return: Ezra Restores the Law (7:1–10:44)

## Ezra Comes to Jerusalem (7:1–28)

### Ezra's Background and Commission (7:1–10)

EZRA 7–10 OPENS WITH THE STATEMENT, "after these things, during the reign of Artaxerxes . . . Ezra came up from Babylon" (7:1, 6). In the chronology of the restoration phase of Israelite history, Ezra comes to Jerusalem after the temple is rebuilt (c. 516/515 BC) and after the story of Esther (483–471 BC) unfolds in Susa during the reign of Darius's son, Ahasuerus or Xerxes (486–465 BC). Ezra's trip to Jerusalem took place roughly in 458/457 BC, King Artaxerxes's (Artaxerxes I Longimanus; 465–425 BC) seventh year (7:8).[1] Thus, from a chronological point of view, about fifty-eight years pass between Ezra 6:22 and Ezra 7:1.

From a thematic perspective, Ezra 7–10 is the second of three returns in the book Ezra-Nehemiah that contribute to the restoration of Zion.[2] The first return focused on the physical rebuilding of the temple (Ezra 1–6), the second concerns a spiritual rebuilding (Ezra 7–10), and the third return (Neh 1–14) entails both physical and spiritual elements (restoration of Zion's walls and the sanctity of the community) The focus of the second return under Ezra concerns a spiritual rebuild through reviving the law in the new community (almost sixty years old). As a professional teacher for Israel in the Babylonian exile (7:6, 10), Ezra's profession informs his mission (7:25–26). Thus, the twin themes of a rebuilt temple, together with the teaching and administration of Mosaic law, reflect the restoration of Zion. The restoration of Zion will not be complete, however, until the walls are rebuilt in Nehemiah's time and sanctity restored.

From a narrative perspective, Ezra 7–10 is a mix of third- and first-person narration. It was common to mix third- and first-person narrative for ancient writers of history, as the engaging style of first-person narrative invites the reader into the storyline and gives depth to this historical narrative.[3] Other than actual quotes from official documentation, the pre-Ezra narrative (chs. 1–6) is told in third person. However, in this section, first-person narrative dominates, starting in 7:27–9:15. Because of this first-person narration, along with that in Nehemiah, many understand that Ezra, because of his teaching profession, may have compiled his memoir along with memoirs of Nehemiah to create the book Ezra-Nehemiah.

From a literary perspective, Ezra 7 serves as a summary prefacing the whole section of Ezra 7–10. It tells the reader when, how, and why Ezra ended up in Jerusalem. Chapters 8–10, therefore, unpack in more detail the event summarized and authorized in 7:1–28. 8:1–20 shows those who returned with Ezra in this "new exodus," their preparations for the

---

1. See Introduction. For a different perspective on Ezra's introduction into the storyline, see Williamson, *Ezra, Nehemiah*, 89–94. Consult Kidner, *Ezra-Nehemiah*, 146–58, for a more detailed discussion on the dating of the Persian kings.

2. Kidner, *Ezra-Nehemiah*, 146–58.

3. For understanding how an author might utilize third and first person to communicate point of view in narrative, see Michael Fishbane, *Biblical Interpretation in Ancient Israel* (Oxford: Clarendon Press, 1985).

journey (8:21–30), and their safe arrival in Jerusalem (8:31–36). Chapter 9 discloses Ezra's encounter with and response to mixed marriages in the camp (9:1–15). Chapter 10 closes this section with the people's response to Ezra's leadership on the matter of unholy alliances (10:1–44).

Structurally, Ezra 7 divides into three sections. Ezra 7:1–10 speaks of Ezra's ancestral and professional credentials authorizing him to make the trek back to Jerusalem, and Ezra 7:11–26 shows the official government credentials authorizing his return. A small section closes the chapter, however, with what was, for Ezra, the ultimate of credentials (7:27–28)—divine favor! For these three reasons Ezra ends up in Jerusalem.

Ezra 7:1–10 reveals much about the person of Ezra, and not without purpose. The narrator isolates four items purposefully highlighting Ezra's esteemed status. He draws attention to Ezra's family, standing in the community, his personal resolve, and favor with the government.

**Ezra's lineage: 7:1–6.** Ezra's lineage ties him to a great line-up of staunchly loyal and prestigious priests who served in powerful regimes: Hilkiah, during Josiah's reign (2 Kgs 22); Zadok, a prominent priest associated with David and Solomon's reign (2 Sam 20:25; 1 Kgs 4:4); and back to Aaron, the first high priest in the Mosaic era (Exod 28–29). Again, the author name-drops in order to underline Ezra's pedigree. "This Ezra" is not just any Ezra, but one with distinction (7:6). The use of the demonstrative adjective (the near demonstrative "this" and not the far demonstrative "that"), along with the genealogical record, also draws attention to Ezra the priest in a specific and definite way. Compare this to Ezra 2:59–63, where no legitimate records were found for the priests.

**Ezra's standing in the community: 7:6b.** Next, the author reveals Ezra's social and religious standing within the priesthood, a "teacher" well versed in the Law of Moses" (7:6b); another translation might be an "experienced," or "skilled teacher" with respect to the law (author's translation). The esteem of such a position derives from information about the law offered in the subsequent clause, "which the LORD, the God of Israel, had given" (v. 6b). The importance of the law is tied to the fact that Israel's God graciously gave them the law (Exod 24:12; Ezek 20:11). Moreover, the importance of the law is seen by the repetition of the term eight times in chapter 7.[4] Indeed, Ezra's role as teacher further

4. 7:6, 10, 11, 12, 14, 21. Observe in verse 25, "laws of your God", and in verse 26, "law of your God."

sets him apart socially and professionally. The author introduces Ezra as priest and teacher, a dual designation used throughout Ezra-Nehemiah for Ezra.[5] The designations show that Ezra fulfilled an important role in the postexile phase, a role further unpacked by the statement in 7:10.

**Ezra's personal resolve: 7:10.** Ezra had a strong resolve, "he devoted himself" to a task. A more helpful reading would be (*hekin levavo*) "he made firm his heart" or "had set his heart" (author's translation) to a task. This preferred reading gives proper attention to the Hebrew verbal form used (*hekin*) which indicates an internally causative action. The usage reveals that Ezra had a deliberate positioning of his heart (or entire being). In other words, the inward action of his heart tilted in a certain direction, one that caused him to take action. The action is indicated by the line up of three infinitive constructs that in Hebrew show a purposeful action, "for the purpose of studying (*lidrosh*) , for the purpose of doing [it] (*la'asot*), and for the purpose of teaching [it] (*lelammed*)." Accordingly, his deliberate heart posture was to study (*lidrosh* from "seek" or "inquire"), to practice (*la'asot*), and to teach (*lelammed*) the law of the Lord with all its requirements (*hoq*, statutes/decrees, and *mishpat*, ordinances/laws) in Israel. As it reads in Hebrew, we learn much of Ezra's resolve in 7:10.

What Ezra did in Babylon, he would *continue* to do in Israel. His entire life was given over to that purpose. His IOS (internal operating system) was oriented toward the word of God. This self-imposed firmness toward the study, practice, and teaching of the law speaks volumes about Ezra's character and his life's purposeful intentions. His firmness contrasts the priests of the past. One of the things that Israel's priests failed to do, according to Ezekiel and other Israelite historians, was to communicate properly the legal traditions of *torah* (Ezek 22:26). They failed with respect to teaching *torah* in Israel and were judged as a result (Ezek 22:26; Jer 2:8). Therefore, having such a role in the Babylonian exile would have been helpful, but as he goes back to Jerusalem, the need would be even greater with the renewed Israel assembled.

His study (time in the inquiry of God's instructions), which consisted mainly of the Pentateuch and perhaps some of the prophets, was not an end but a means toward an end, both personally and publicly. With respect to the personal, his study was to be accompanied by a virtuous

5. Note variation in usage, however, of the designations in Ezra 7:11, 12, 21; 10:16; Neh 8:1, 2, 4, 9, 13; 12:26, 36.

lifestyle. The fruit of his study was personal piety and application of the truths of God's law. In addition, his study would lead to a public platform of teaching others in the covenantal community to do the same.

Ezra's public platform of teaching and urging the community in the direction of Torah is showcased twice in the book. The first concerns the problem he faces with unholy alliances (Ezra 9:1–2) and how he deals with the situation as priest/scribe (9:3–10:17).[6] The second takes place a few years later when a third (very small) contingent comes to Jerusalem with Nehemiah (Neh 2:9).The people assemble themselves to celebrate the New Year, and Ezra leads the celebration by reading the law (Neh 8:1, 4, 5, 7–9, 13, 18).[7] In this way, content for his teaching and his lifestyle derived from God's word—a model for the people. Thus Ezra 7:10 highlights Ezra's critical role and his depth of character.

**Ezra's favor with the government.** Finally, the author reveals that Ezra had favor with the Persian king.[8] Artaxerxes gave Ezra what he asked for (7:6) and more, based on the content of that letter recorded in what follows (7:11–26).[9] However, the favor Ezra experienced was not because of his impressive credentials as priest and teacher but for one main reason: "the hand of the LORD his God was on him" (v. 6; causal clause in Hebrew), an active presence to provide. The author also attributes Ezra's safe arrival to Jerusalem because "the gracious (*hatobah*) hand of his God was on him," an active presence to protect (7:9). The success of his safe arrival derived from God's presence. The God Ezra claimed as "his," the God to whom he had uncompromising and wholehearted devotion, had his hand on Ezra. Thus, the favor he found with the king and the safe arrival to Jerusalem provides evidence of the active presence of God in his life.

In general, the hand imagery refers figuratively to God's blessing, and here the specific blessing pertains to provision and protection from the government.[10] It might also be comparable to the laying on of hands,

---

6. See commentary on Ezra 9.

7. See commentary on Nehemiah 8.

8. Contrast this with Ezra 4:7–22 where Artaxerxes did not act favorably towards God's people.

9. See the commentary below on 7:11–28.

10. God's power and strength are spoken of figuratively in Exodus as a "mighty hand" that will compel Pharaoh to release the Israelites (Exod 3:19–20; 6;1; 7:4–5; 13:9, 14, 16; Deut 9:26). Elsewhere "God's outstretched hand" judges and restores (Jer 21:5; Ezek 20:33–34).

mentioned elsewhere in the Old Testament, relative to the commissioning for a certain task or office (i.e., Num 27:18).

Either the "hand" of God or the "gracious hand" of God repeats itself seven times in Ezra-Nehemiah (7:9, 28; 8:18, 22, 31; Neh 2:8, 18). The phrase and its repetition signify that Ezra was acutely aware of God's involvement and presence in his life and that God had set him apart for the task of going to Jerusalem.[11] The favor he found with Artaxerxes, therefore, derived from being set apart by God or the active presence of God in his life. The fact that he had favor is also linked to a heart devoted to the Law of God (7:1–7).[12] In these ways, the author introduces Ezra to the reader: an important person for the next phase of restoration in Israelite history, a legitimate authority[13] to take them to the next level of restoration. He shows how and why Ezra ended up in Jerusalem—on account of divine favor for the divine purpose of reviving the law in the covenantal community after years of neglect and deficit.

ALONG WITH ZERUBABBEL MANY YEARS PRIOR,[14] and Nehemiah a few years later,[15] Ezra stands in the middle of one of three movements bringing restoration to Zion in this period. Although about one hundred years separate the beginning from the end of the restoration of the sanctity of Zion (from Cyrus's decree to Nehemiah's final reforms in Neh 13), the author wishes the reader to see a panoramic view of restoration by juxtaposing the various phases into one book. The spiritual restoration Ezra provides remains critical to this overarching picture. Without a revival of the word of God, without a tethering to *torah*, attempts at restoration remain impossible.

The importance of the law as demonstrated in Ezra's life and his specialized mission anchors the historic value of the law within the

11. This is not unlike Ezra 5:5 where the writer is aware and asserts that "the eye of their God was watching over the elders."

12. Psalm 1, among several, connects the blessing one receives in life directly to possessing a high view of Scripture.

13. This is not unlike what we saw in chapter 2 and the importance of lineage to legalize one's return to the land.

14. Zerubbabel was on the scene about eighty years prior.

15. Nehemiah was on the scene about fourteen years afterwards.

covenantal community both individually and corporately. As a marker of ancestral identity, the law was greatly revered at the time of its inception because it was understood as the very words of God to Israel since the time of Moses (Exod 19–20). In this way the law of Moses was established as canonical, authoritative, and an essential part of Israelite/Mosaic identity (cf. Deuteronomy 6; cf. Josh 1:1–9). Accordingly, in its original setting under Mosaic jurisdiction during the Late Bronze and early Iron Age, "the book of the Law" and the rest of the writings related to ancestral history (the Pentateuch) were deemed authoritative (see Josh 24). However, immediately following the death of Joshua, the process of Canaanization began in earnest (Judg 2:11–23) with its paradigmatic cycle of sin-judgment-repentance-salvation-sin (see Neh 9; cf. 2 Kgs 17; 21). Only intermittent returns to the law (notably under Hezekiah and Josiah, duly noted in the Chronicler's history, 2 Chr 29–32; 34–35) provide some light in a culture otherwise devoid of a Scripture-centered pure worship of Yahweh (see Isa 1 for a window into the problem).

The initial eagerness to follow *torah* in the pre-Ezra phase (chapters 1–6) further underscores this new atmosphere of receptivity to the law of Moses.[16] The value and esteem individuals placed on the law is readily seen in the Psalms. We read repeatedly of the importance of a life with wholehearted devotion to the law and the associated blessings and favor of God as a result. The entire Psalter opens (Ps 1:1–3) declaring a covenantal blessing on the one who, like Ezra, has a self-imposed firmness relative to the place of the word of God in one's life. The specific blessing of an individual with such a demeanor equates to fruitfulness, a type of prosperity that money cannot buy. In God's economy, true prosperity involves experiencing the riches of his word. Moreover, in God's economy, where we are considered a "kingdom of priests" (1 Pet 2:9; Rev 1:6)[17] one could argue there is a need to study and know the law of God/word of God even though we are not clergy in an official sense! Psalm 1 assigns a blessing to anyone who places a premium on the law of God.

Moreover, several psalms throughout the Psalter laud God's word. This is especially so of Psalm 119 with its correlation to the establishment

16. As the narrative unfolds in Ezra-Nehemiah, old habits are hard to break as the setbacks on Ezra 9–10 and Nehemiah 13 will reveal.

17. For example, Pss 1, 19, 119.

of the law as the focus of the postexilic community. The psalmist expresses that in hardships he held fast to (119:31), had hidden (119:11) and meditated (119:15) on God's law and testimonies. The psalmist was attached to, used his heart as a storeroom for, and was centered mentally on God's word. As a result, he had sustaining power (119:92) and learned obedience through hardships (119:67–71).

In addition, clinging to the word in times of hardship gave him affection for the word. Out of great affliction arose great affection and commitment to the word. Numerous times throughout Psalm 119 he expresses both a love for (i.e., 119:47, 97, 167) and a mouth-watering delight toward the word, similar to honey in the mouth (119:103; Ps 19:10; Prov 16:24). In this way, the psalmist reveals his personal sentiment toward the word and its importance in an individual's life. The psalmist provides a worldview refocused and re-centered on *torah*, the fruit of which is immeasurable. The Law's ability to restore and revive, both individually and corporately, was the experience of God's people in the Old Testament.

As we cling to the word or set our hearts on it, and as we embrace the teaching of the word through modern-day Ezras, we need to realize that we are clinging to the very voice of God. As Paul reminded Timothy, we are likewise reminded that, "All scripture is God breathed" or "inspired by God" (2 Tim 3:16), and as such it provides the needed navigation for life. John's gospel also reminds us that a disciple of Jesus is one who knows and continues in the word (John 8:31). In other words, we must not detach ourselves from caring about the truths of Scripture even though we may not all be called to be teachers of the law like Ezra (1 Cor 12:29). This is so especially because of the Scripture's life-giving power to restore.

An encounter with the written word causes us to encounter the incarnate Word of God, Jesus. Hebrews declares that God has spoken to us in these last days by his Son (Heb 1:2). That is, Jesus is the living Word of God with the profound message that he is our support, comfort, and spiritual support system, because he embodies the Word. The word (written oracles) became the flesh and blood Word (John 1:1–14). Hebrews further encourages us that, because the Son has spoken so profoundly, we are to fix our eyes on him (Heb 12:2). Fixing our eyes on Jesus (the incarnate Word) gives us supernatural power to sustain life and its hardships. Fixing our eyes on Jesus guarantees restoration in the life of the church both individually and corporately. Ezra 7:1–10 teaches, therefore, the interconnectedness between restoration and the reviving of the law, its importance, and one's demeanor toward it.

PLACING A PREMIUM ON GOD'S WORD HAS THE power to bring revival to individuals and churches. Church history testifies to this fact. One of the main issues of the Protestant Reformation pertained to the Scriptures, evidenced in the phrase *sola Scriptura*, a firm belief that the Scriptures matter. Indeed, another priest and scribe, Martin Luther,[18] changed the course of the church due to his scrutiny of the word and publication of commentaries on biblical books. Because of his discoveries in Greek and Hebrew he pursued a German translation of the Bible, an improvement from the Latin. His desire was for people from all walks of life to be able to read the Bible. His actions in the Reformation were motivated by his love for the word, especially in the original languages.

What place does the word hold in our churches and lives? While it is true that not everyone is called to be a reformer of the caliber of Luther or a scribe of the caliber of Ezra, the latter's specialized role does reveal the continued need to have experts like this in the church to help restore God's people. Institutions like Bible colleges and seminaries have a critical role to play as a result. In this regard professors with a heart for the word, teaching at a seminary, are critical to the church's mission.

The role of training pastors is akin to training people to become like Ezra, to become specialists in God's word. As his name suggests in Hebrew, Ezra was a "helper" (*'ezer*) to the covenantal community with his skills, a powerful assistance.[19] That is, having a staunch heart posture toward the word led to a serious inquiry, but that same heart posture

---

18. W. J. Kooiman, *Luther and the Bible*, trans. John Schmidt (Philadelphia: Muhlenberg, 1961). The discussion here follows Kooiman.

19. The term from which Ezra's name derives, *'ezer* or "helper" is not insignificant. The name *Eli'ezer* which means "My God is help" includes the same term. Eve was Adam's "help" (Gen 2:18, 20), *'ezer kenegdo*, a "suitable" or "powerful" help. The term also refers to the nations to whom Israel appealed for military help (Isa 30:5; Dan 11:34). Most usages pertain to God as Israel's helper (i.e., Exod 18:4; Deut 33:7, 26, 29; Pss 20:2; 33:20). As these verses suggest, *'ezer* is often used in a military context and implies more than the

gave him the desire to take the results of his study and live accordingly. Inquiry for the sake of inquiry was not what Ezra was about. He desired that his acquisition of knowledge dovetail into a lifestyle that mirrored his learning. In other words, to borrow James's illustration, he not only looked into the mirror of God's word, but he did what the mirror said and, as a result, walked away a changed person. He was what James would call one who "listens to the word" (Jas 1:22–25).

Imagine our churches being led by pastors with such training. We need to rely on seminaries that value the word of God and keep it front and center for those training for the ministry. What does it mean to be a specialist in the church? For a living, I train folks called by God to be specialists in the church. In other words, I train women and men going into the pastorate at a regional seminary in the Northeast. The training is a specialist training. As B. B. Warfield said, "specialists specialize";[20] to that end, those in the MDiv program where I teach are trained in the rigors of biblical studies. This means learning both Greek and Hebrew in order to read and interpret the Bible accurately. Our posture as a seminary, evidenced by both the mission statement and our articles of faith, place a premium on the value of the Scriptures, studying and interpreting in the original languages, for training women and men to do kingdom work.

One of my responsibilities is to teach Biblical Hebrew. I require students to read Psalm 119 in English as a meditation for the entire year. I do this because the psalm lauds God's word, and I want my students, who are already placing a premium on the word by studying Hebrew, to grasp further its power by reading Psalm 119 devotionally. Recently, as the school year commenced, one of my students told me she was memorizing Psalm 119 this past year! Not only was she encouraged by the requirement because it confirmed for her that God was in her decision to memorize it, but I was also encouraged, rather astounded, to hear that somebody so young was engaged in what I consider the lost art of Bible memorization.

---

English translation "help" or "helper" can convey. The meaning of Ezra's name suggests something of his role in the restored community.

20. Benjamin B. Warfield, "Our Seminary Curriculum," in *Benjamin B. Warfield: Selected Shorter Writings*, ed. John E. Meeter; 2 vols. (Phillipsburg, NJ: Presbyterian & Reformed, 2001), 1:369 (orig. published in *The Presbyterian* [September 15, 1909]: 7–8).

What was amazing, though, was why this student memorized Psalm 119. "Sally"[21] did not set out to memorize this psalm because she wanted to become more spiritual, but, in her words, "because I knew my condition." Although she grew up in a godly family, she fought temptation and strayed into sin. Sin programmed her mind, and it became destructive in every aspect of her life. She desperately wanted to be reprogrammed and see her life changed, so she turned to Psalm 119. God's word *did* reprogram her and, with a lot of desire and daily discipline, her mind has been renewed and she experienced firsthand the power of God's word to renew a person's life! Her experience was that of the psalmist! I asked her to share her "story" with the class and to recite all of Psalm 119 if she felt comfortable. She graciously accepted the challenge. When "Sally" shared with the class why she memorized this psalm, you could hear a pin drop in the room. However, when she started to recite the psalm, it was even more deafening. She was not merely reciting Psalm 119 from memory, although that would have been profound enough! The intonation of her voice indicated the depth of belief she had in the words spoken. From her voice we actually heard what it sounded like for a desperate soul to cling to the word. The day she shared goes down in the books as *the* most profound classroom experience shared with my students. We were all deeply moved and humbled.

Prior to teaching at a seminary, I served as a missionary in Youth With A Mission (YWAM). In addition to several short-term outreaches in various countries of southeast and east Asia, I also had the privilege of serving for five years as co-director (with my husband) in the School of Biblical Studies, an academic-year inductive study of the complete text of the Bible. To that end, each book of Scripture is read five times through a succession of steps that provide both an overview of each book as well as analytical observations, interpretations, and application of the content. The outcome results in hundreds of pages of commentary under supervision and guidance from trained staff.[22] The intensive nature of the process has a way to "upload" the text into the mind in a remarkable way. It is fair to say many students in this program have their

---

21. The student's real name will not be disclosed in this true story.

22. The genesis of the inductive Bible study method goes back to Dr. William Harper, professor of Hebrew and Old Testament at Yale Divinity School and first president of the University of Chicago. https://www.seedbed.com/inductive-bible-study-history/.

hearts set, much like Ezra did, to study, do, and teach his word. Such an intense study oftentimes will lead to life transformation and the shaping of a biblical worldview. I praise God for the founders of this school in YWAM, Ron and Judy Smith, not only because they trained me but because they understood the importance of the word of God. Today the program flourishes around the world in many different cultures and settings.

In fact, Ezra's example in Ezra-Nehemiah became a role model for an evangelistic organization in New Zealand back in the early 90's.[23] A project called Operation Ezra had as its goal to evangelize New Zealand. Teams of six people were recruited from around the world and then sent to key cities in New Zealand. Team members were to stand on the busy street corners of these cities and take turns reading the Bible out loud from Genesis to Revelation. The hope was that people would be restored to God through the reading of the word. One team member named Mary was reading from Leviticus 18 and the subsequent chapters. These chapters catalogue the terrible sins of the Egyptians and Canaanites such as idolatry, but especially repulsive and unclean sexuality.

As Mary read these specific chapters in Leviticus, a woman passing by heard and said to one of Mary's teammates, "As I hear this lady reading, I feel dirty. Is there anyone among you who can tell me how to get clean?" God's word impacted her, and as a result she gave her life to the Lord on a busy street in Auckland, New Zealand.[24] God's word revived this woman and gave her a worldview refocused and re-centered. This happened because a group of people actually believed that "The law of the LORD is perfect, refreshing the soul" (Ps 19:7)! This happened because a group of people had their hearts fixed on the importance of the word. All these examples show the value and premium people placed on the word of God to restore and change lives. The Scriptures matter!

---

23. This story comes from Ron Smith, *Hooked on the Word: Changing Your Life through Bible Meditation* (Lakeside, MT: West Shore Books, 1994), 23.

24. Ibid.

# Ezra 7:11–28

[11] This is a copy of the letter King Artaxerxes had given to
Ezra the priest, a teacher of the Law, a man learned in matters
concerning the commands and decrees of the LORD for Israel:

[12] Artaxerxes, king of kings,

To Ezra the priest, teacher of the Law of the God
of heaven:

Greetings.

[13] Now I decree that any of the Israelites in my kingdom,
including priests and Levites, who volunteer to go to
Jerusalem with you, may go. [14] You are sent by the
king and his seven advisers to inquire about Judah and
Jerusalem with regard to the Law of your God, which
is in your hand. [15] Moreover, you are to take with you
the silver and gold that the king and his advisers have
freely given to the God of Israel, whose dwelling is in
Jerusalem, [16] together with all the silver and gold you
may obtain from the province of Babylon, as well as the
freewill offerings of the people and priests for the temple
of their God in Jerusalem. [17] With this money be sure to
buy bulls, rams and male lambs, together with their grain
offerings and drink offerings, and sacrifice them on the
altar of the temple of your God in Jerusalem.

[18] You and your fellow Israelites may then do
whatever seems best with the rest of the silver and gold,
in accordance with the will of your God. [19] Deliver to
the God of Jerusalem all the articles entrusted to you
for worship in the temple of your God. [20] And anything
else needed for the temple of your God that you
are responsible to supply, you may provide from the
royal treasury.

[21] Now I, King Artaxerxes, decree that all the
treasurers of Trans-Euphrates are to provide with
diligence whatever Ezra the priest, the teacher of the Law
of the God of heaven, may ask of you—[22] up to a hundred
talents of silver, a hundred cors of wheat, a hundred baths
of wine, a hundred baths of olive oil, and salt without
limit. [23] Whatever the God of heaven has prescribed, let
it be done with diligence for the temple of the God of
heaven. Why should his wrath fall on the realm of the king
and of his sons? [24] You are also to know that you have no
authority to impose taxes, tribute or duty on any of the
priests, Levites, musicians, gatekeepers, temple servants or
other workers at this house of God.

[25] And you, Ezra, in accordance with the wisdom
of your God, which you possess, appoint magistrates
and judges to administer justice to all the people of
Trans-Euphrates—all who know the laws of your God.
And you are to teach any who do not know them.
[26] Whoever does not obey the law of your God and
the law of the king must surely be punished by death,
banishment, confiscation of property, or imprisonment.

[27] Praise be to the LORD, the God of our ancestors, who has
put it into the king's heart to bring honor to the house of the
LORD in Jerusalem in this way [28] and who has extended his
good favor to me before the king and his advisers and all the
king's powerful officials. Because the hand of the LORD my
God was on me, I took courage and gathered leaders from
Israel to go up with me.

### A Letter Legitimizing Ezra's Return (7:11–28)

THE SUMMARY IN 7:1–10 PURPOSEFULLY NOTED Ezra's ancestral and professional credentials authorizing him to go to Jerusalem. We now know how and why Ezra ended up there. The chapter continues in 7:11–26 by showing the official government credential authorizing his return, a personal letter to Ezra from the Persian King Artaxerxes. The text of Ezra 7:12–26 returns to the Aramaic script; this is not unexpected, since Aramaic was used in official work and correspondence in the Persian period. The letter offers important details concerning finances not mentioned in 7:1–10. The chapter concludes (7:27–28) with Ezra's own opinion on how and why he was able to go back to Jerusalem.

Although an important piece of evidence legitimizing his trip, the author did not have to include it. In other words, one could read Ezra 7:1–10, skip to Ezra 8:1, and fully understand the storyline. The inclusion of the letter, however, gives the reader a non-Israelite point of view. The letter's content largely concerns Ezra's acquisition of proper provisions enabling worship in Jerusalem. The emphasis on worship is readily observed by the repetition of terms for the deity's earthly living space, "dwelling" (v. 15 *mishkan*). In verses (vv. 16, 17, 19, 20, 23, 24, the Hebrew reads "house of God" (*beth 'elah* or *beth yhwh*, v. 27). To be sure, the letter further emphasizes the importance of the law, especially as it leads to worship and the exercising of justice in Israel. Remarkably, this emphasis comes from the perspective of King Artaxerxes himself.

Thus the purpose of Ezra's mission in 7:1–10 (which highlights the origin of the law) together with the letter in 7:12–26 (which highlights the proper function of the law in worship) packs a powerful one-two punch concerning the potential to revive a religious community through the marriage of law and worship.[1] From the time of Zerubbabel until now, a return to true worship of Yahweh has been the goal. Getting to that goal had many ups and downs along the way. But now they have Ezra and the backing of the government to do so. By including the correspondence, one sees how a non-Israelite valued law and order and its direct ties to religion.

### *The setting, tone, and structure of the letter*

This positive correspondence from Artaxerxes drastically differs in tone to that mentioned in Ezra 4:7–22 that generated a negative response from Artaxerxes but is similar to the experience Nehemiah had

1. Worship is carried out in 8:35. One also sees the marriage of law and worship in chapter 3 where worship is the outcome (Ezra 3:10–13) of following God's law relative to rebuilding the altar and temple foundation (Ezra 3:3–4).

years later with the same king. The following outlines those interactions in the order they appear in the text:

Ezra 4:7–22 = unknown year of Artaxerxes, negative correspondence
Ezra 7:6 = the seventh year of Artaxerxes (ca. 457 BC) positive correspondence
Neh 2:1 = the twentieth year of Artaxerxes (ca. 444 BC) positive interactions

In the undated letter (4:7–22), the king ordered all work on the walls and foundation to stop until he issued a counter decree (4:21). His resistance, although not stated as such in the text, could simply have been because there was no official paper trail authorizing such work in the first place, unlike what the investigation produced with respect to rebuilding the temple (6:1–12). Regardless of not knowing the rationale for resistance at that time, the author shows how God allowed for it. The counter decree, one that enabled work on the walls, does not happen until the time of Nehemiah's positive interactions with Artaxerxes beginning in Nehemiah 2:1.

Thus, the king's communication to Ezra, a response to an expressed need (7:6) which likely included people and worship provisions (7:13–20), conveys Artaxerxes's surprising generosity toward Ezra. Ezra interprets all of this through the lens of God's favor (7:27–28). The tone and content of the letter from this pagan king beautifully underscores that favor.

The structure of the letter is tripartite. After the standard greeting touting Artaxerxes's own sovereignty as "king of kings" (7:12), a typical declaration of sovereignty, Ezra 7:13–20 contains specific orders to Ezra and the Israelites in Babylon. Subsequently, Ezra 7:21–24 consists of specific orders to the treasurers of Trans-Euphrates, and the letter closes with personal orders to Ezra (7:25–26).

**Orders to Ezra and the Israelites (7:12–20).** In the first set of orders Artaxerxes entrusts Ezra with two main things, amassing a volunteer team of people (13–14) and the acquisition of financial aid (7:15–20). "I decree that any of the Israelites . . . who volunteer to go . . . may go" (7:13). These volunteers are to make an important inquiry in Jerusalem. The nature of the investigation concerns sizing up the well-being of "Judah and Jerusalem" in relationship to the "Law of your God, which is in your hand" (v. 14). As a man learned in such matters (7:6, 11), the investigation makes sense. Not only was the hand of God on Ezra (7:6, 9), but Ezra also possessed in his hand God's written law as he went to Jerusalem (7:14). In this Artaxerxes affirms that the standard of measure for the community was legal statutes tied to a religious system. In 7:14 the king grants him that privilege, and much more, as the letter informs.

The statement in 7:14 is revealing: "You are sent by the king . . . to inquire about Judah and Jerusalem with regard to the Law of your God, which is in your hand." Artaxerxes, without knowing it, portrays Ezra as a lawgiver and keeper akin to Moses (Exod 31:18) or one of the nation's great kings, such as Josiah (2 Kgs 22:1–23:32) and Hezekiah (2 Chr 31:21), who possessed the law and attempted to reform the nation before the exile. Thus Ezra 7:14, together with the statement already made about Ezra in 7:6 prior to Artaxerxes's letter, adds to the picture of portraying Ezra as a lawgiver. We are told, likely by Ezra himself—assuming he is the author—both the origin and designation of the law. "The God of Israel" (v. 15) along with the phrase, "the Law of your God," brings this point out further. Ezra, like Moses, was a lawgiver, another important tie to preexilic Israel.

The second item the king entrusts Ezra with concerns money. Artaxerxes entrusts Ezra with no small amount of finances deriving from three different sources to aid sacrifices for temple worship (7:15–17). In this context Artaxerxes also trusts that any financial surplus not used for temple services would be used by Ezra "in accordance with the will of your God" (7:18). The will of God is knowable because Ezra possesses God's will in his hand (7:14). The Law of God and God's will are one and the same. For this reason, the king has tremendous confidence in Ezra. This section of the letter concludes with a major statement of generosity ensuring that Ezra will not lack in resources for reestablishing proper worship at the Jerusalem temple. Thus, a team is assembled and provided with no little resources to execute worship in Jerusalem.

**Orders to the treasurers of Trans-Euphrates (7:21–24).** Another set of orders is directed toward the king's officials living in Judah and Jerusalem, or "Trans-Euphrates": "Now I . . . decree that all the treasurers" (v. 21). The king requires that government workers in his territories abroad trust Ezra, relative to matters of worship, upon his arrival. They are to provide Ezra with gifts in kind (7:22) and do "whatever the God of heaven has prescribed" (7:23). The rationale behind this concerns the religious paradigm of the day. Paying homage to another deity's territory through the enabling of worship to that god merits favor rather than wrath associated with neglect (7:23). Likewise, the treasurers may not collect any revenues (taxes) from the temple clergy (7:24).

**Orders personally to Ezra (7:25–26).** The last part of the letter is orders directed toward Ezra: "And you, Ezra" (7:25). Artaxerxes entrusts Ezra with governmental affairs! He asks him to dispense justice in the land by delegating people like himself to the task, people "who know the laws of your God" (7:25a). And those deemed as able for leadership but lack knowledge of God's laws, Ezra is to teach (7:25b). That doing justice derives from the Law drives the king's order to Ezra. The king allows for Ezra's involvement this way because of the awareness that divine wisdom derives from knowing the Law. The king recognizes that Ezra possesses godly wisdom, a wisdom directly connected to the Law of God. Deuteronomy promised that the fruit of following God's commands would be a display of wisdom and understanding to the nations, causing them to say, "Surely this great nation is a wise and understanding people" (Deut 4:6). When the nation and individuals are recognized as wise, it directly correlates to a life given over to God's commands. Artaxerxes recognizes Ezra's ability to regulate and reorder life in Trans-Euphrates because of a heart set on the law of God (Ezra 7:10).

Finally, this section closes with a strong word reminding Ezra of the consequences for those who break either God's or the king's laws (v. 26). Disobedience to the law would not be tolerated, and Ezra, along with those appointed by Ezra, were to hold lawbreakers accountable.[2] Thus the letter and its contents shows more specifically (from a non-Israelite perspective) how the law and proper worship are to function practically under Ezra's leadership. It indirectly lauds Ezra's character. The confidence and trust that Artaxerxes places in Ezra is based on knowledge of his esteemed position as priest/teacher (7:12, 21) in Babylon. Ezra's reputation precedes him, and the king perceives Ezra as an asset, not a threat, and one who will deliver. It affirms why it was critical for the king to have Ezra in Jerusalem. Artaxerxes's confidence in Ezra is directly related to and a testimony of Ezra's heart posture toward God's law and his godly lifestyle as noted in 7:10.[3]

---

2. Thus, the events that unfold in chapter 10 with mixed marriages. See commentary on Ezra 10.

3. See commentary on Ezra 7:10 above.

**Ezra's own understanding of how and why he got to Jerusalem (7:27–28).** The final section of this chapter returns to the use of the Hebrew language and brings Ezra's personal point of view back to the reader, describing how the letter from the king touched Ezra. It is Ezra's first-person interpretation of how and why he ended up taking the trek to Jerusalem and a preface to the list of people who volunteered to follow him in this new Exodus (8:1–14). Although Ezra and those who journeyed with him to Jerusalem were literally being sent by "Artaxerxes, king of kings" (7:12, 14), Ezra acknowledges something greater at play. As elsewhere in the book, these concluding two verses show the theological grid of the author and his basis for understanding restoration in Israel at this time. Given his role as priest/teacher, a theological grid was the main grid he possessed for interpreting these events!

Ezra 7:27 reads like a mini psalm of praise with the opening statement, "praise be to the LORD, the God of our ancestors." He worships God as a result of Artaxerxes's letter. As one steeped in the law of God, he presently blesses Yahweh in the same way his ancestors blessed the LORD for his previous workings in their history as evidenced in the specific psalms in the psalter.[4] Ezra lauds God specifically for three things.

First, God dealt with the king's heart. The idea for Ezra to go to Jerusalem originated with Ezra's request to go and teach the law in Israel (7:6). Ultimately, God honored Ezra's request by working on the king's heart to allow it (cf. 1:1). For Ezra, going to Jerusalem to teach the law of God, beyond the reasons articulated by Artaxerxes, had other merits. The result of his going was "to "bring honor to the house of the LORD" (7:27). The word "honor" (*pa'ar*) is better translated as "glory," "glorious," or "beauty." Outside of Ezra, only Isaiah uses this term with respect to God's house (Isa 60:7, 13). In the restoration of Zion that Isaiah envisions, Gentile peoples and lavish sacrifices are brought to God's house resulting in its beautification or glorification. The arrival of the law of God via Ezra's mission directly affects the aesthetics of the house of the LORD in Jerusalem. Ezra attributes beauty and glory to God's dwelling as a result of the revival of the Law.

Second, Ezra lauds God because God was more powerful than Persian kings and officials (Ezra 7:28). That is, God rolled out the red carpet and extended *hesed* to him with respect to the decision made by the king and

4. See for example, Book IV of the Psalter, Pss 90–106.

his powerful advisors. NIV translates *ḥesed* as "good favor" here, but in 9:9 NIV translates it as "kindness."[5] Ezra understood this as a manifestation of Yahweh's loyalty to him in the relationship. The extension of *ḥesed* is directed to Ezra ("to me," v. 28), but later God's extension of *ḥesed* will be "to us" (9:9). Here Ezra verbalizes a concept about God's interactions with his people with its roots deep in the nation's experience with the LORD.

Third, Ezra lauds God for enabling him to take action, again through divine intervention: "the hand the LORD my God was on me, I took courage and gathered leaders . . . to go up" (7:28). Again, this is due to an important result clause, "because the hand of the LORD my God was on me" (7:28b, already mentioned in 7:6, 9). Thus, the letter from Artaxerxes was a manifestation of this reality in Ezra's life. Through yet another Persian king, provision for worship of the LORD manifests itself. The Law that leads to true justice and worship in the land was going forth from Jerusalem, and God was restoring the beauty of his house. That which was lost was found.

THIS PASSAGE TEACHES ABOUT THE REINSTATEMENT of the law of God that leads to true justice and worship, and its potential to revive, restore, and give direction to a religious community—from the perspective of a gentile king. This foreign king affirms that the law is from God. God entrusts his law to people. It is the means of evaluation, the plumb line, the standard; it is the will of God; it regulates life's relationships; it makes one wise; and not following it entails consequences. The picture is a secular government not only enforcing (7:13–25) but also reinforcing biblical law and principles (7:26). In this there is recognition that God's law gives a society a blueprint for quality of life.

The irony is that with few exceptions (good kings in Israel and Judah),[6] the Israelite theocracy failed in its execution of *torah*. God relentlessly raised up the prophets to reinforce covenantal law and administration in Israelite society but with abysmal results (2 Chr 36:15–16). And now the people of God have been given another chance to get it right—ironically,

5. See Ezra 9:9 on this important term.

6. 2 Chronicles 14:1–35:27 records a total of eight good kings in Judah, none are noted in the northern kingdom.

through the agency of a foreign government, a backing from one of the most powerful empires the ancient Near East has ever seen.

Ezra is commissioned to revive the law in the new Israel of God. That which was lost on account of the exile is now, in a sense, found. The Mosaic law, God's gift of wisdom to the nation, has now been found, graciously hand delivered through Ezra, the postexilic law-giver's commission. The anticipation would be nothing less than a national transformation. The loss of the law of Moses (an identity marker to be sure) was great, and many of the psalms reflect the pain of such loss. That is why numerous exilic psalms speak so highly of God's law, particularly Book V (Pss 107–150).

In terms of this lost and found concept, Ezra attempts and is commissioned to do in the postexilic community what King Josiah did previously in the seventh century (2 Kgs 22:1–23:32), bring a national transformation. After the lawless and wicked reigns of both Manasseh (687–643 BC) and Amon (643–641 BC) in Judah, the young twenty-six-year-old Josiah (641–609 BC) brings restoration and repairs to the temple, damaged due to years of neglect through idolatry by these kings (2 Chr 34:8–33, particularly v. 11; see also 2 Kgs 22:3–10). With repairs to the temple underway, in the midst of the rubble Hilkiah the priest found something wrapped in hides. One can only imagine what he felt when he saw "the Book of the Law of the LORD that had been given through Moses" (2 Chr 34:14; see also 2 Kgs 22:8),the long-forgotten scrolls, the word of God—abandoned by the people, then lost entirely. Hilkiah runs to Shaphan the secretary with the manuscript in hand and exclaims, "I have found the Book of the Law in the temple of the LORD" (2 Kgs 22:8). Shaphan brought the parchments directly to King Josiah and began reading aloud the words (2 Kgs 22:10).

Upon hearing the words of the book of the law, the king's demeanor revealed his attitude toward the importance of the word. He grieved before the LORD over the lack of obedience to such instructions (2 Kgs 22:10–11, 13). God saw young Josiah's responsive heart, humbled before God in repentance and pierced with guilt over sin. Josiah rightly feared God's wrath, the promised covenantal curses for not obeying, and thus consulted the prophetess Huldah who confirmed his worst nightmare (2 Kgs 22:16–17). The nation would be destroyed, but he would not witness it in his lifetime and be spared (2 Kgs 22:19–20). He then read the words aloud to the people, who in turn promised to keep the words of the covenant (2 Kgs 23:2–3). The discovery of the lost law directly led to the subsequent reforms Josiah implemented (2 Kgs 23:4–25). At the command of the king they destroyed pagan shrines and stopped their vile practices. A great revival and transformation broke out, reshaping the nation as people learned to follow God's ways. Josiah turned his heart to obey the word and guided his people to do the same. Healing and restoration took place. Reviving the law in Israel was the king's attempt to provide a worldview refocused and re-centered on *torah* after years of neglect and decline.

Thus, Ezra's role and demeanor toward the word compares significantly to that of Josiah, an observation reinforced in what follows in Ezra 9–10 with Ezra's handling of unholy alliances. Both historical incidents demonstrate that a way to restore and revive the community is through acute awareness of the importance of the word of God. Finding what has been lost is critical to restoration for individuals and communities.

THE HOPE OF A NATIONAL TRANSFORMATION BY applying the truths and principles of God's word was the goal of Ezra and the Persian king. This teaches us how the Bible becomes critical as a source of wisdom, not just at the personal level but in the public sphere, as well.[7] The presence or absence of godly principles directly affects the well-being of a nation.

Quoting Pulitzer Prize-winning author Garry Wills, president of Biola, Barry Corey notes Wills's critique of evangelicals: "The problem with evangelical religion is not (so much) that it encroaches on politics, but that it has so carelessly neglected its own sources of wisdom. It cannot contribute what it no longer possesses."[8] To remain Christian and have an influence means we need to retain the Bible, "We cannot neglect the rich resources of the past in efforts to be relevant in the future. We dare not neglect the word of God as our anchoring source of wisdom. For if we do, we cannot contribute what we no longer possess."[9]

---

7. See Loren Cunningham, *The Book that Transform Nations: The Power of the Bible to Change any Country*, (Edmonds, WA: YWAM Publishing, 2007). This section depends heavily on his insights.

8. Barry H. Corey, "Anchored in the Word," *Biola* (Winter 2018): 6.

9. Ibid.

This is the challenge of the church, not to mention Bible colleges and seminaries. Losing the importance of the Bible is costly and not without serious consequences. As Loren Cunningham notes, "There are many ways to lose God's Word. The results are always tragic. Whenever a critical number of people abandon the Bible and stop applying it in their personal lives, that nation begins to destroy itself."[10] He recognizes that America and other Western nations threaten to spiral into decline by turning away from the Bible.[11]

Although we may not be aware of it, Western society as we know it relies heavily on the presence of such principles. In commenting about the historical reliability of the Exodus account, one author correctly notes:

> Not only does Christian faith rest squarely on the historicity of the Moses account. So does the foundation of law and order in Western society. Our traditions of common law and jurisprudence go back to Jewish notions of covenant. Without Moses, we lose divine sanction for limits on government and the power of human authorities. What is the goal of this constitutionalism rooted in *torah*? It seeks to prevent tyranny and to guarantee liberty and rights of individuals on which free society depends. Are we on the precipice of losing the blessings of liberty, security, creativity, and material prosperity—the very things these founding principles provide—because of turning away from the Scriptures?[12]

The opposite is also true; "Blessings always come when a nation finds God's Book again. Throughout history, the record is clear: when a critical mass of people have the Bible and apply what it teaches in their lives, a nation is transformed."[13] Could it be that China's growth and leadership in the world has to do with the rate of people following Jesus and basing their lives on the Scriptures?[14]

Transformation happens when we immerse ourselves in the word,

---

10. Cunningham, *The Book that Transformed Nations*, 22.
11. Ibid., 25.
12. Gregory Alan Thornbury, "Why it Matters that the Exodus Really Happened," *Christianity Today*, https://www.christianitytoday.com/ct/2015/february-web-only/why-it-matters-that-exodus-really-happened.html.
13. Cunningham, *The Book that Transformed Nations*, 22.
14. Ibid., 24–25.

asking God's help as we search for principles to order our lives, the process Paul called the renewal of the mind (Rom 12:2).[15] In fact, quoting Cunningham on J. Wesley Bready, "the revivals led by the Wesleys in England kicked off substantial societal changes, including political and economic. Many were lifted out of injustice and poverty and into a more robust middle class.[16] John Wesley did not live to see all the reforms, but they reached other European nations and America. It is hard to imagine our world today had it not been for thousands and thousands of people in small groups studying the Bible and applying it to their lives. It all began when one man had his heart strangely warmed and obeyed God and his Word, teaching his nation how to live God's way."[17]

As Cunningham rightly notes,[18] the Great Commission entails going and discipling nations, teaching them to obey—not just offering them head knowledge (Matt 28:18–20). This means it is possible for God's will to be done on earth and for the nations to learn from God's wise commandments. As we obey God and his word, we grow in character. God's word becomes a part of us, the standard for all our lives. This is what changes a nation. God transforms nations the way God transforms individual lives. A nation that has the word or is attempting to apply its principles (however those principles have come to that nation such as a pagan king, a missionary, a pastor/teacher) will be better off than without it.[19]

---

15. Ibid., 38.

16. Ibid., 42. J. Wesley Bready, *England before and after Wesley: The Evangelical Revival and Social Reform* (Russell & Russell, 1971).

17. Ibid., 42.

18. Ibid.

19. Ibid.

# Ezra 8:1–36

[1] These are the family heads and those registered with them
who came up with me from Babylon during the reign of King
Artaxerxes:

[2] of the descendants of Phinehas, Gershom;
of the descendants of Ithamar, Daniel;
of the descendants of David, Hattush [3] of the
descendants of Shekaniah;
of the descendants of Parosh, Zechariah, and
with him were registered 150 men;
[4] of the descendants of Pahath-Moab, Eliehoenai
son of Zerahiah, and with him 200 men;
[5] of the descendants of Zattu, Shekaniah son of
Jahaziel, and with him 300 men;
[6] of the descendants of Adin, Ebed son of
Jonathan, and with him 50 men;
[7] of the descendants of Elam, Jeshaiah son of
Athaliah, and with him 70 men;
[8] of the descendants of Shephatiah, Zebadiah son
of Michael, and with him 80 men;
[9] of the descendants of Joab, Obadiah son of
Jehiel, and with him 218 men;
[10] of the descendants of Bani, Shelomith son of
Josiphiah, and with him 160 men;
[11] of the descendants of Bebai, Zechariah son of
Bebai, and with him 28 men;
[12] of the descendants of Azgad, Johanan son of
Hakkatan, and with him 110 men;
[13] of the descendants of Adonikam, the last
ones, whose names were Eliphelet, Jeuel and
Shemaiah, and with them 60 men;
[14] of the descendants of Bigvai, Uthai and
Zakkur, and with them 70 men.

[15] I assembled them at the canal that flows toward Ahava,
and we camped there three days. When I checked among
the people and the priests, I found no Levites there. [16] So I
summoned Eliezer, Ariel, Shemaiah, Elnathan, Jarib, Elnathan,
Nathan, Zechariah and Meshullam, who were leaders, and
Joiarib and Elnathan, who were men of learning, [17] and I
ordered them to go to Iddo, the leader in Kasiphia. I told them
what to say to Iddo and his fellow Levites, the temple servants
in Kasiphia, so that they might bring attendants to us for the
house of our God. [18] Because the gracious hand of our God
was on us, they brought us Sherebiah, a capable man, from
the descendants of Mahli son of Levi, the son of Israel, and
Sherebiah's sons and brothers, 18 in all; [19] and Hashabiah,
together with Jeshaiah from the descendants of Merari, and his
brothers and nephews, 20 in all. [20] They also brought 220 of
the temple servants—a body that David and the officials had
established to assist the Levites. All were registered by name.

[21] There, by the Ahava Canal, I proclaimed a fast, so that
we might humble ourselves before our God and ask him for a
safe journey for us and our children, with all our possessions.
[22] I was ashamed to ask the king for soldiers and horsemen to
protect us from enemies on the road, because we had told the
king, "The gracious hand of our God is on everyone who looks
to him, but his great anger is against all who forsake him." [23] So
we fasted and petitioned our God about this, and he answered
our prayer.

[24] Then I set apart twelve of the leading priests, namely,
Sherebiah, Hashabiah and ten of their brothers, [25] and I
weighed out to them the offering of silver and gold and the
articles that the king, his advisers, his officials and all Israel
present there had donated for the house of our God. [26] I
weighed out to them 650 talents of silver, silver articles
weighing 100 talents, 100 talents of gold, [27] 20 bowls of
gold valued at 1,000 darics, and two fine articles of polished
bronze, as precious as gold.

[28] I said to them, "You as well as these articles are
consecrated to the LORD. The silver and gold are a freewill
offering to the LORD, the God of your ancestors. [29] Guard

them carefully until you weigh them out in the chambers of the
house of the LORD in Jerusalem before the leading priests and
the Levites and the family heads of Israel." 30 Then the priests
and Levites received the silver and gold and sacred articles that
had been weighed out to be taken to the house of our God
in Jerusalem.

31 On the twelfth day of the first month we set out from the
Ahava Canal to go to Jerusalem. The hand of our God was on
us, and he protected us from enemies and bandits along the
way. 32 So we arrived in Jerusalem, where we rested three days.

33 On the fourth day, in the house of our God, we weighed
out the silver and gold and the sacred articles into the hands
of Meremoth son of Uriah, the priest. Eleazar son of Phinehas
was with him, and so were the Levites Jozabad son of Jeshua
and Noadiah son of Binnui. 34 Everything was accounted for
by number and weight, and the entire weight was recorded
at that time.

35 Then the exiles who had returned from captivity
sacrificed burnt offerings to the God of Israel: twelve bulls for
all Israel, ninety-six rams, seventy-seven male lambs and, as a
sin offering, twelve male goats. All this was a burnt offering to
the LORD. 36 They also delivered the king's orders to the royal
satraps and to the governors of Trans-Euphrates, who then
gave assistance to the people and to the house of God.

CHAPTER 8 CONTINUES EZRA'S FIRST-PERSON narrative that commenced in 7:27–28. The chapter expresses in more detail what was only summarized in 7:1–10: Ezra's journey and safe arrival to Jerusalem. Due to the amount of space given to the topic, the author is less concerned that the reader knows that they made it from Ahava to Jerusalem, for this is recorded in two short verses (8:31–32). Instead, the author seems more concerned to communicate important preparatory elements, especially concerning the proper handling of the money they were given by the king (8:15–30, cf. 7:13–20). First, Ezra records the list of those families that volunteered to journey with him (8:1–14). Second, he mentions three other preparatory elements

needed before the journey got under way. He needed to secure Levites to attend to the work of God's house, because there were none among those making the trek (8:15–20). He desired to lead the people in a fast for protection (8:21–23). Finally, he gave responsibility of the purse as they journeyed to twelve leading priests (8:24–30). After these things were in place, the journey back to Jerusalem is recorded in two verses (8:31–32), followed by three days of rest and a note that all orders were executed and followed as previously directed (8:35–36).

## The People Returning with Ezra and the Journey (8:1–36)

### List of the Returning Families (8:1–14)

THE LIST IN EZRA 8:1–14 NUMBERS about one thousand five hundred Jews who returned with Ezra from fifteen different families, relatives of those who went to Jerusalem previously (Ezra 2; Neh 7). The list commences with the needed workers for temple services in Jerusalem, family heads associated with the priestly lines of Phinehas and Ithamar and descendants of David (Ezra 8:2–3), With regard to the former, the lineage of Aaron is followed. By this the author draws attention to the prestige of the preexilic priestly line. With the mention of David's descendants it lauds the preexilic royal line. As to the entire list Kidner notes, "these groups are joining, at long last, the descendants of the pioneers from their own family stock, who had been in the first party to return from Babylon eighty years ago."[1] Rebuilding the present community with its representative key members and their ties to the first generation of returnees paves the way for the new Israel of God to be realized.

The numbers on the list are not exhaustive, as they do not include the women and children associated with these male descendants. Accordingly, the number is likely larger, as a result. Even so, these statistics pale in comparison with those who accompanied Sheshbazzar and Zerubbabel on the first return (about 42,360 exiles, plus 7,337 servants; 2:64). Moreover, the narrator distinguishes the second group of returnees in that they are volunteers (7:13). The original returnees were stirred by God's Spirit, a point the author underlines (1:5). Both sets of returnees,

---

1. Kidner (*Ezra and Nehemiah*, 73) says this on the basis that in 8:4–13 all but one family name can be found in Ezra 2:3–15.

however, are very small in relationship to the estimated population of two to three million Jews living in Persia during this period (550–430 BC). Both sets of returnees are, nonetheless, viewed by the author as divine provision (7:27–28; 8:18, 31; see also 1:5). Although the list does not reveal much about these male descendants, Ezra deems them as "leaders from Israel" (7:28).

### The Journey: Problems and Preparations (8:15–20)

THOSE THAT EZRA GATHERED (7:28) were now assembled geographically at one location (8:15). Only a few Levites returned earlier (2:40), and now Ezra realizes the deficit in the present group (8:15). His goals for the Levites are mapped out in what follows. They were needed for temple duties (8:17) and to carry the holy things of God back to the temple (8:28).

The men Ezra chooses to send are described in an intentional way by the use of relative clauses in 8:16. They are "leaders" and "men of learning" who "go to Iddo, the leader in Kasiphia" to recruit attendants for the house of God (8:16–17).Of the thirty-eight recruits, Sherebiah heads up the list (8:18). The appositional statement about Shereibah, "a capable man," likely emphasizes his abilities as a Levite to do what is needed "for the house of our God" (8:17). He must have been an important leader as his name appears seven times in Ezra-Nehemiah (Ezra 8:24; Neh 8:7; 9:4–5; 10:12; 12:8, 24). Kasiphia was a place apparently populated by Levites, those given "to the service of the sanctuary" (author's translation) or, as the NIV translates, "temple servants in Kasiphia" (Ezra 8:17). The phrase does not necessarily imply that a temple existed in Kasiphia, but that temple personnel lived there. If evidence were to reveal that a worship structure existed in Kasiphia, it would likely[2] be an antecedent to the synagogue.

Among the recruits were also 220 temple servants to aid the Levites, an arrangement made previously by David and his court officials (8:20). The mention of David here recalls Ezra 3:10 and his mention there relative to the praise and worship he instituted with the first temple as the basis for the second temple worship. Once again, the author wishes to reestablish that what was normative for preexilic Israel remains so for the postexilic people of God.

---

2. Rachel Hachlili, *Ancient Synagogues: Archaelogy and Art: New Discoveries and Current Research* (Leiden: Brill, 2013).

The time spent at Ahava was more than three days (8:15). In fact, it was just over a two-week period, given the unexpected need to recruit Levites. The journey began on the first day of the first month (7:9), but they didn't set out until the twelfth day of the first month (8:31). They arrived about three and half months later (7:9). Ezra attributes the success in recruiting Levites to God's good hand on them corporately (8:18). This is now the fourth time (7:6, 9, 28) he mentions a correlation between their success with practical matters and divine activity and guidance. Ezra's own interpretive grid for daily life was God. He understood that the practical things that fall into place, such as obtaining Levites and traveling mercies, all stem from God. The reality of God's presence manifests itself in everyday occurrences, and Ezra was sharpened to this fact.

### The Solution about Safety and Finances and their Safe Arrival (8:21–36)

**EZRA 8:21–23 AND THE FAST.** Now that the Levite problem was solved, but before the journey could begin, Ezra put into place two more preparatory elements. The first concerned a fast for their physical safety, that God would give them a "straight way" (8:21; author's translation); the second was a delegation of the finances for safekeeping to the priests and Levites (8:28–29). By fasting,[3] Ezra wanted to procure spiritual assistance, since he hesitated to get physical assistance from the king. In verse 22, the NIV says "protect us, from enemies on the road," but it could be read as "help us" (author's translation). These "enemies on the road" represent another type of opposition, not a small theme in the book mentioned elsewhere. His hesitancy, however, not to ask for military assistance (and in contrast to Neh 2:7–9) was driven by a specific religious conviction.

Seekers of God (in this context Ezra and company, but ultimately anyone) experience God's favor. Those who do not seek God experience his disfavor. Seeking God means relying on divine assistance; abandoning him means relying on human assistance. This recalls the past failures of the people, something Ezra was not willing to relive. As one steeped in the law of God, together with enduring the exile, Ezra knows both

3. Fasting accompanied with prayer was usually done at critical junctures in the life of the nation or individuals. For example, before the exile: Judg 20:26; Jer 14:12. For special occasions (Jer 36:6; Ps 35:13). After exile, there seems to be more emphasis (Zech 7:2–7; Ezra 10:6; Neh 1:4; 9:1; Esth 4:3, 16).

cognitively and experientially God's favor and disfavor. Help in the face of potential enemies, therefore, is Ezra's hope. Accordingly, his statement does not assume a hassle-free journey, but it does assume divine assistance when problems arise. Such assistance is also evidence to the king that they are seekers of God. In this way, Ezra and those traveling with him testified to Artaxerxes something of the nature of their God and God's people. The outcome of fasting and praying was not just a safe journey to Jerusalem but a testimony of God's character to the king. Accordingly, in Ezra's mind there was more on the line than just a safe journey physically to Jerusalem. Yahweh was clearly different than the gods of the Persian pantheon. Thus, two of the three preparations have been completed.

**Ezra 8:24–30 and the stewardship of the money.** These verses record the final element of preparation, but not the least significant. Ezra's concern here is for the safe keeping of the finances that poured in from donors back in Babylon (8:25). These donations were to be handled by twelve priests (8:24). Both the donations and those bearing them were deemed "consecrated to the LORD." The sum total of these donations and their safe handling represented an act of worship, "a freewill offering, to the LORD, the God of your ancestors" (8:28), an act of celebration that would be realized not long after their safe arrival in Jerusalem (8:35). As in 7:27, Ezra's religious memory gives weight to their present responsibilities. All of this (the holiness, and purpose of finances) was an indirect charge to be faithful to the task. It reflects the importance Ezra placed on godly stewardship leading to worship of Yahweh. Now that the reader has been made aware of these important preparations (securing Levites, fasting, and proper stewardship of finances), the notification of their safe arrival is recorded.

**Ezra 8:31–36 and their arrival and worship at the intended destination.** Ezra 8:31–32 shows how God answered their plea for help through fasting and praying. On the journey, they were indeed "rescued" (*natsal*; author's translation) from opposition. NIV has "he protected us from enemies and bandits" (v. 31). They seem to have encountered opposition, but God took care of it. They escaped and were rescued. Likewise, all was carried out as planned with the finances (8:33–34). Then Ezra 8:35–36 returns to third-person narrative, and the chapter closes with a note of celebration. They were able to worship their God through the prescribed means, "burnt offerings to the God of Israel" (8:35). This section ends similarly to chapters three and six in a few ways.

When the temple foundation and temple were completed God's people celebrated and worshiped (3:10–13; 6:13–22),. At the same time there was recognition that all this was possible only because divine assistance was given to them (3:11; 6:14). Now with the lawgiver and his entourage back in Jerusalem, yet another celebration ensues, and Ezra has made it abundantly clear that divine assistance was given to the people of God every step of the way.

A TOTAL OF THREE TREKS ARE MADE BACK TO Jerusalem in Ezra-Nehemiah (Ezra 1; 8, Neh 1). The fact that people are returning to Zion was something promised in general terms by many of the prophets.[4] Two of the three pilgrimages mentioned in Ezra-Nehemiah contribute to the beginning of specific prophetic fulfillments.[5] The return in Ezra 1:1 and the list of those returning (Ezra 2) is possible because of Cyrus. It fulfills Jeremiah's prophetic utterances concerning the defeat of Babylon, completion of seventy years, and the rise of the king of the Medes (Jer 25:12; 50:9; 51:1, 11). But Ezra 1:1 also fulfills Isaiah's prophetic utterances relative to Jerusalem being inhabited again, and the temple being rebuilt under Cyrus (Isa 44:26–45:13). The author relays the events as prophesy fulfilled (see commentary on Ezra 1:1–11). The return in Ezra 8:1–36 is possible because of Artaxerxes. Although no mention is made that the journey is specifically fulfilling a prophetic word, Ezra's interpretive framework and knowledge of the word seem to suggest that he understands this return as partial fulfillment of Isaiah's previous utterances. This is so for several reasons.

This chapter, because of its emphases and language, makes clear that Ezra's interests are broader than merely providing a list of volunteers who went back to Jerusalem, like the lists in Ezra 2/Nehemiah 7. The list of names, in conjunction with preparations for the journey and their safe arrival or "straight way" (author's translation), speaks to this fact. He describes the journey as safe and holy because of divine protection and guidance.

---

4. Isa 35:10; 51:11; Jer 3:14; 31:6, 12; 50:5; Ezek 36:24; 39:27; Zech 2:7.

5. The (intentional) repetition of the return motif from Ezra 2 in Neh 7 will be discussed in the commentary on Neh 7 below.

First, Isaiah promised a pilgrimage for God's people that would be safe and holy. In fact, Ezra 8:21 reminds of Isaiah 40:3, whereby God promised an unhindered pathway to bring people back to the land. Second, in Ezra 8:24–28 the delegation of priests and the articles they are bearing for God's house are "consecrated to the LORD." Isaiah charges those who "carry the articles of the LORD's house" to leave Babylon "pure" and to "touch no unclean thing" (Isa 52:11). Third, four times Ezra 8 mentions God's good hand, something that made the pilgrimage possible (7:28; 8:18, 22, 31). Similarly, Isaiah promised that the holy departure would not be forced, but a journey prepared by God, and one marked by his presence to protect: "you will not leave in haste or go in flight; for the LORD will go before you, the God of Israel will be your rear guard" (Isa 52:12). This return marks the beginning of the new exodus, a motif used by Isaiah; as Ezra recounts and interprets the events, it seems Isaianic reflexes are implicit. Thus, prophetic fulfillments, specifically those of Jeremiah and Isaiah, provide a framework for understanding the restoration phase of Israelite history. God's people were being rerouted back to Him.

Along with Ezra's arrival in Jerusalem, the law of the LORD is, in a manner of speaking, likewise arriving given Ezra's mission (7:10). Jerusalem now has a temple and people repopulating the land; thus, the law is reintroduced in a formal way with Ezra. The intention is that God's people will be taught his law and thus walk accordingly. In this way the word will go forth from Jerusalem, the way it was originally intended.

These realities represent the first fruit of what Isaiah and Micah envision as the "last days" (Isa 2:2–3; Mic 4:1–2). Not only will Israelites be flocking back to their homeland, and specifically to the temple, but foreigners will also. Their purpose in making the pilgrimage concerns being taught by God so they will walk in his ways. As a result, the *torah* is magnified, as the "word of the LORD" goes forth from Zion/Jerusalem (Isa 2:2–4; Mic 4:1–2). Thus, the journey itself and what Ezra brings as the new lawgiver (Ezra 7:10, 25) represents the beginnings of the fulfillment of the prophetic word and, from a biblical-theological perspective, points us forward to the time ("latter days," i.e., Isa 2:2, 4; Jer 23:20; Dan 2:28) when it will be fully accomplished.

The spiritual reality for believers is that we are on our way to Zion, the house of our God (Heb 12:22–24) from the exile of this life (1 Pet 1:1). Jesus made straight the way toward redemption for us to be in relationship with our God (Isa 40:3; John 1:23). Safe passage is ours because of God's active presence via the Holy Spirit. Restoration from sin and exile through the new covenant, with the law written on our hearts, enables us to live out the gospel message (2 Cor 3:1–6). This, in turn, enables us to teach others about God and his ways in the hopes that they, too, will make the pilgrimage and take the paved road Jesus prepared for them. Thus, in the age of the Spirit there is greater fulfillment of this pilgrimage, because the way is paved for both Jews and Gentiles (Rom 1–3) to reach Zion, the house of our God. Indeed, the ultimate fulfillment of this manifests itself in the Age to Come, when people from every tribe and tongue have successfully made the pilgrimage and are before the throne, worshiping and celebrating the Lamb who made access to Zion possible (Rev 7:9–10).

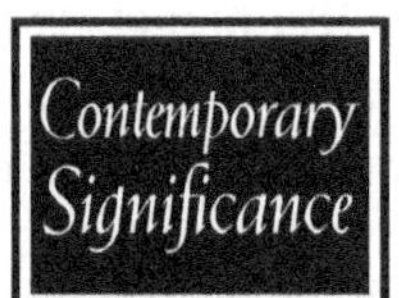


THIS EZRA PASSAGE INVITES US TO CONTEMPLATE our own perspectives about the journey we are on in life. Navigation in this world to do kingdom work is not easy nor without hassle, but God has graciously given us a system to navigate it with success. The text invites us to recall that we are on a journey with a *clear* destination—to arrive home safely at the house of our God, to be in relationship with him. It also reminds us that the journey *is not hassle free.* Needed help may not necessarily be available and at times it may be unsafe. Moreover, the journey requires a God-dependent mindset. That is, we must be aware and assured of divine assistance when problems arise.

In *The Pilgrim's Progress,*[6] the most renowned Christian allegory, translated into more languages than any other book except the Bible, John Bunyan depicts the life of a pilgrim named Christian. His purpose is to portray the life of someone seeking heaven (The Celestial City, known as Mt. Zion), what one does and does not do to get there, and the struggles that abound. He also portrays the lives of people who set out as if they intend to go toward the city, but who end up falling by the wayside. He encourages anyone who reads his book to become a seeker of God and arrive at their final destination. How much more will we end up at our destination if we rely on God's word and the Holy Spirit?

6. John Bunyan, *The Pilgrim's Progress* (New York: Penguin, 2008).

# Ezra 9:1–15

1 After these things had been done, the leaders came to me
and said, "The people of Israel, including the priests and
the Levites, have not kept themselves separate from the
neighboring peoples with their detestable practices, like those
of the Canaanites, Hittites, Perizzites, Jebusites, Ammonites,
Moabites, Egyptians and Amorites. 2 They have taken some
of their daughters as wives for themselves and their sons, and
have mingled the holy race with the peoples around them. And
the leaders and officials have led the way in this unfaithfulness."

3 When I heard this, I tore my tunic and cloak, pulled
hair from my head and beard and sat down appalled. 4 Then
everyone who trembled at the words of the God of Israel
gathered around me because of this unfaithfulness of the exiles.
And I sat there appalled until the evening sacrifice.

5 Then, at the evening sacrifice, I rose from my self-
abasement, with my tunic and cloak torn, and fell on my knees
with my hands spread out to the LORD my God 6 and prayed:

> "I am too ashamed and disgraced, my God, to lift up
> my face to you, because our sins are higher than our heads
> and our guilt has reached to the heavens. 7 From the
> days of our ancestors until now, our guilt has been great.
> Because of our sins, we and our kings and our priests have
> been subjected to the sword and captivity, to pillage and
> humiliation at the hand of foreign kings, as it is today.
>
> 8 "But now, for a brief moment, the LORD our God
> has been gracious in leaving us a remnant and giving us
> a firm place in his sanctuary, and so our God gives light
> to our eyes and a little relief in our bondage. 9 Though
> we are slaves, our God has not forsaken us in our
> bondage. He has shown us kindness in the sight of the
> kings of Persia: He has granted us new life to rebuild
> the house of our God and repair its ruins, and he has
> given us a wall of protection in Judah and Jerusalem.

[10] "But now, our God, what can we say after this?
For we have forsaken the commands [11] you gave
through your servants the prophets when you said:
'The land you are entering to possess is a land polluted
by the corruption of its peoples. By their detestable
practices they have filled it with their impurity from
one end to the other. [12] Therefore, do not give your
daughters in marriage to their sons or take their
daughters for your sons. Do not seek a treaty of
friendship with them at any time, that you may be
strong and eat the good things of the land and leave it
to your children as an everlasting inheritance.'

[13] "What has happened to us is a result of our evil
deeds and our great guilt, and yet, our God, you have
punished us less than our sins deserved and have given
us a remnant like this. [14] Shall we then break your
commands again and intermarry with the peoples who
commit such detestable practices? Would you not be
angry enough with us to destroy us, leaving us no
remnant or survivor? [15] LORD, the God of Israel, you
are righteous! We are left this day as a remnant. Here
we are before you in our guilt, though because of it not
one of us can stand in your presence."

## Marriage Problems and Ezra's Response (9:1–15)

### Ezra Mourns and Confesses Corporate Sin (9:1–15)

EZRA 9:1–15, TOGETHER WITH CHAPTER 10, forms a literary unit. The unit reveals internal opposition in the renewed covenantal community. In the pre-Ezra phase external opposition dominated the storyline. However, when Ezra comes on the scene, unlike the earlier phase of temple rebuilding, another type of opposition surfaces. We learn of a devastating internal opposition arising from within Israel's leadership, leaving Ezra to cry out for God's mercy. Ezra 9, therefore, is a report to Ezra of unfaithfulness in the community and the priest's prayerful response to it.

Ezra 9:1–15 can be divided into two sections, 9:1–2 reports unholy marriage alliances, and 9:3–15 shows Ezra's response to it in first person narrative. The underlying irony in this chapter seems to be that Ezra's reforms either took time or only worked in part. His orders by Artaxerxes were clear. He was to administer justice and teach the laws of God to any who did not know them (7:25). Lawbreakers were to suffer consequences, which could include death, banishment, confiscation of property, or imprisonment (v. 26). Ezra 9 exposes lawbreakers within the renewed covenantal community, and chapter 10 shows the ensuing consequences for lawbreaking (10:8). Thus, what unfolds in 9–10 is Ezra functioning in his delegated authority from the Persian king.

Here we learn what is on Ezra's heart, and we learn much more about him as a person. The content of his prayer highlights the people's undeniable sin through the repetition of the term for guilt (9:6, 7, 13, 15). More specifically, the people's unfaithfulness (9:4) surfaces in matters of marriage (9:1–2,14). Ezra interprets this as a blatant disregard for God's commands (vv. 10, 14) and responds with a heart-wrenching prayer acknowledging guilt and confessing their sin before God (vv. 6, 7, 13 [2x]). Accordingly, his confession characterizes their actions as "sin" or "evil deeds," an unfaithfulness making even those who survived God's first judgment of exile, the "remnant" (vv. 8, 13–15), "guilty" and vulnerable again to God's judgment because of mixed marriages (vv. 6–7, 13).

The context of his prayer should not go unnoticed. Given the fact that they are presently basking in God's mercy and grace, manifested in their restoration to the land (9:8–9), the people's guilt leaves Ezra literally speechless: "But now, our God, what can we say after this?" (9:10). Their present experience of God's renewed mercy and faithfulness make such unfaithfulness even more deplorable.

**Ezra approached (9:1–2).** When the leaders approached Ezra about the matter is unclear. The text indicates it was "after these things had been done" (v. 1), referring to some unidentified time after the arrival and celebration of Ezra and his team in Jerusalem (7:9; 8:1), likely within four to five months (10:6–9). It would be naïve to think that Ezra's mission fixed all the problems upon his arrival. But with the law and lawgiver in their midst, the people possessed the gold standard. This gave them a renewed awareness of sin and accountability toward God and each other. People's lifestyles were scrutinized as a result. Their lives were under the light of God's law, and it exposed poor lifestyle choices.

The fact that the list of "leaders" includes "priests" and "Levites" speaks to the extreme gravity of the situation (v. 1). The defiling of the priesthood through intermarriage with "neighboring peoples" (v. 1; i.e., those outside the covenantal community) evokes what preexilic Israel did with the Canaanites from the outset of the settlement process to the end.[1] These neighboring nations, itemized as Canaanites, Hittites, Perizzites, Jebusites, Ammonites, Moabites, Egyptians, and Amorites (9:1; Gen 15:16, see also vv. 19–20) is literally a "Who's Who" of Israel's enemies.[2] The rhetorical effect is not missed with the targeted language describing their present practices as "detestable practices" (9:1; *to'ebah*, "abominations,"). Those directly responsible for the restoration of worship (priests and Levites) have "not kept themselves separate from the neighboring peoples around them" (v. 1). This type of fellowship tampered with and polluted the purity of God's people in the most profound way. According to Levitical law, those who are held to the highest degree of holiness among the people of Yahweh are here listed as compromised. Levites and priests are indeed a set-apart lineage, a holy race or "holy seed" in Hebrew (*zera' haqodesh*, v. 2).[3] Thus, the specific designation holy race in Ezra 9:2 goes to the heart of Israelite ethnic identity, which consisted of the category of bloodlines ("seed" or NIV "race"; Gen 12:1–3) as well as the category of faith/loyalty to Yahweh (Gen 15:6). Especially for those in leadership, this amounts to a proper attitude toward holiness.[4]

---

1. See Judg 3:5–6; see also Judg 17:1–13; see commentary on Neh 13 for further discussion.

2. For similar lists see Exod 34:11; Deut 7:1; 20:17 for comparison. Ezra 9:1 adds Ammonites, Moabites, and Egyptians. The first two groups were not granted permission to worship with the Israelites (Deut 23:3–6), and only Egyptian grandchildren could worship (Deut 23:7–8).

3. See Isa 6:13 for the only other mention of the phrase but translated there as holy seed; see also "holy nation"/*goy qodesh*, Exod 19:6; cf. Lev 19:2; Deut 7:6.

4. In the earliest phase of Israelite identity in the land of Canaan, simply to claim ancestry was never enough. One needed to live out this ancestry with faith/loyalty to Yahweh. In the case of Achan, he defiled himself by stealing *herem* objects which, in turn, provoked the most radical form of separation from the group: *herem*-destruction, i.e., death (see Josh 7). However, perhaps an even better example for the context of Ezra 9–10 is that of Aaron's sons, Nadab and Abihu, who were found unholy before Yahweh and lost their lives as a result (Lev 10). For a detailed definition of "holy race" in the context of Ezra 9, see K. Southwood, *Ethnicity and the Mixed Marriage Crisis*, 125–32. See also K. Sparks, *Ethnicity and Identity in Ancient Israel* and T. Petter, *The Land Between Two Rivers*, 55–65.

In defining the community of worshipers as distinct from their non-Yahwist neighbors in Ezra-Nehemiah (e.g., Ezra 3:3), the practice of intermarriage represents a major setback. The direct mention of Israel's preexilic enemies singles out, in no uncertain terms, that a renewed process of Canaanization was underway (see commentary on Neh 13:23 for another installment of this process).

This news of intermarriage strikes particularly hard since outsiders had previously been excluded *with* a religious compromise in view (cf. Ezra 4:1–3; 6:21). The leadership seemed fully aware that the peoples of the land who wanted to be a part of the covenantal community could not join apart from "conversion" (Ezra 6:21; Deut 23:7–8).[5] What was at stake, in preexilic times as in the province of Judah in the fifth century, was steadfast loyalty to God. Intermarrying with foreigners/non-Yahwists would turn hearts away from the LORD and not keep them holy (Exod 34:11–16; Deut 7:1–6; Deut 20:10–18). As a result, God's anger would "burn" and threaten to destroy them (see Deut 7:1–7). Also, looming large in the narrative is the Deuteronomic background that no one of illicit marriages to Ammonites or Moabites may enter the LORD's assembly because of divided loyalties inherent in such a union (see Deut 23:2–4).

By placing the focus on priestly and Levitical compromise in the context of the significance of legitimate ancestral identities, what the leaders, priests, and Levites have done is no less than defiled themselves like Israel of old. Just as their ancestors entered the promised land and polluted themselves with the people of the land, so too the exiled remnant population reentered the land and are polluted in similar fashion, with devastating consequences.[6]

---

5. In this respect the inclusive language reflected in the resumption of the Passover in Ezra 6 reflects preexilic attitudes toward members of other "peoples" who joined Yahwism (e.g., Ruth's positive example). See D. Petter, "Ruth" in Gary M. Burge, and Andrew E. Hill, eds. *The Baker Illustrated Bible Commentary* (Grand Rapids: Baker Books), 2012.

6. One of the justifications for the conquest of Canaan includes what Eugene Merrill categorizes as "protection of Israel." Appealing to, among others, the foundational text of Deut 7:1–5, Merrill underscores that "alliance of any kind with the inhabitants of Canaan would result in Israel's falling away from Yahweh into idolatry and thus under his judgment," in C. S. Cowles, Eugene H. Merrill, Daniel L. Gard, and Tremper Longman, *Show Them No Mercy: Four Views on God and Canaanite Genocide*, ed. Stanley N. Gundry (Grand Rapids: Zondervan, 2003), 86–87.

Those holding the exiles to account before Ezra characterize such lifestyle choices as "unfaithfulness" (9:2, 4 *ma'al*). The term here refers to an individual or corporate act that brings guilt requiring confession and cleansing.[7] Ezra interprets this unfaithfulness as a disregard for God's commands given through the prophets (9:10–12, 14), who charted, generation after generation, how the worship of other gods would lead to the downfall and destruction of God's people.[8]

It should be no surprise, then, that Ezra's reaction to this news is deeply emotional and an outward demonstration of grief coupled with fasting and prayer. In what follows he mourns in silent shame and then cries out to God for mercy in a prayer of confession, the only rightful response to the sin-guilt problem. The mission to restore the sanctity of Zion has come to a screeching halt and faces an existential threat.

**Ezra mourns (9:3–5).** Ezra himself tells us that he assumes the role of a mourner by discarding his garments and pulling hair from his head (compare Neh 13:25). His use of first person makes it especially dramatic and gives the reader a window into how he was personally affected by the circumstances. His posture also informs us that he is in mourning. He "sat down appalled," or a more nuanced translation such as he "sat in stunned silence" for a lengthy time, meaning he chose not to speak out of grief.[9] His mourning represents a penitent act in response to the grievous news of sin in the community. His actions drew a crowd around him, those "who trembled at the words of the God of Israel" (9:4). Isaiah uses the same term to describe people with humility and contrite hearts who receive favor from God because they do not despise his word, but this also conjures up hatred on the part of their foes toward them (Isa 66:2, 5). Ezra draws a crowd of like-minded, courageous people around him, those that feared God and revered God's word.

---

7. For corporate unfaithfulness see for example Lev 26:40; for individual unfaithfulness see Num 5:6; Josh 7:1; 22:16. For Saul's unfaithfulness that did not lead to confession, see 1 Chr 10:13.

8. The term "unfaithfulness" usually speaks of infidelity to the word of God (e.g., Lev 6:2; Josh 7:1; Ezek 14:13).

9. This movement, earthward, in grief is similar to what Job and his friends do (Job 2:13). The same language is used of Ezekiel after eating the scroll containing lament and mourning and woe (Ezek 2:9). He sat down among the exiles "deeply distressed" (NIV) or appalled (3:14). Likewise, the mariners who mourn over Tyre's fall "sit on the ground appalled" (Ezek 26:16).

Ezra's mourning lasted until the "evening sacrifice" (Ezra 9:5) which was at twilight (Num 28:4), at which time his mourning silence is broken with a prayer of confession recorded in the verses that follow (Ezra 9:6–15). From mourning ("I tore my tunic and cloak . . . and sat down appalled," v. 3), he "rose" from "self-abasement" (9:5; root *'anah* in the sense of humbled) to a knee-bent position on the ground with hands spread out. This new posture symbolizes utter surrender and dependence on God for help (Exod 9:29; Isa 1:15). In this entire act of mourning, subduing his bodily desires and dying to self, he revealed a visceral reaction to sin. All he had to fall back on was his deep awareness of God's merciful and gracious character.

### *Ezra's Prayer (9:6–15)*

These verses record the prayer proper. In general terms, the prayer begins and ends with honest confession and acknowledgement of corporate guilt (9:6–7, 15). This sort of honesty and acknowledgement marks a break from the past, when many of Israel's leaders met a confrontation with God's word with strong resistance or disdain (e.g., Jer 36). Moreover, although clearly not among those who have "forsaken the commands" (Ezra 9:10), Ezra prays as one who himself had despised God's commands. In his mind, he stands in solidarity with and as a representative for the people; therefore, he too stands before God in guilt (see also Neh 1).

Of note is the repeated phrase utilized throughout his prayer, "our God" (Ezra 9:8, 9[2x], 10, 13). Four of the six times, the designation is clustered in the section of his prayer that highlights the LORD's graciousness to bring them restoration. The repeated use of the designation "our God" reflects how their sin, yet again, brought about a loss in the relationship. Although they stopped acting like God's people even after experiencing his grace, God never stopped acting like their God. Ezra's overemphasis highlights God's continual faithfulness in the covenantal relationship. It shows how Ezra wanted to close the distance in their relationship, created by their sin.

In this vulnerable and embarrassing position of guilt he admits there is nothing to say in light of God's inexhaustible grace (v. 10). He also admits that their lifestyle choices are not aligned with the word of God, the only basis for evaluation of human conduct (9:10–12; cf. Deut 7:1–4). God's word (not Ezra's) scrutinizes and evaluates the actions of God's people. Thus, Ezra's prayer unintentionally reveals his own interpretive framework! His prayer also reveals a deep understanding and awareness of both the human and divine natures and the tension the differences between them bring in the relationship. God is righteous. And God's people are guilty and "because of it not one of us can stand in your presence" (9:15).

**Awareness and confession of guilt (9:6–7).** The grief and guilt associated with lifestyle choices not aligned with God's word weighed Ezra down physically and spiritually. Both his prostrate posture (9:5) and inability to "lift up my face to you" (v. 6) visually demonstrate this reality. The level of their sin and guilt is metaphorically described as limitless, "higher than our heads," and "reach[ing] to the heavens" (9:6). Moreover, just as preexilic Israel was guilty, so is postexilic Israel, "from the days of our ancestors until now" (v. 7). And so the story goes: guilty in the garden (Gen 3:1–7), guilty in the wilderness (Exod 32:1–6), guilty in Egypt, guilty in the land of Canaan, and guilty after exile (Ezek 20:7–44)! Even after suffering the exile, the consequence of breaking God's law, and even after returning to the land, the consequence of God's grace and mercy, God's people were still guilty and not able to keep God's law. Thus, Ezra acknowledges expansive and ongoing guilt among the people of God. He also acknowledges the ongoing and long-term consequences for such behavior, "our kings . . . have been subjected to . . . humiliation at the hand of foreign kings, as it is today" (v. 7; Neh 9:32–37).

**Awareness and confession of God's mercy and grace (9:8–9).**[10] As Ezra's prayer continues, the awareness of God's grace takes center stage. Without his grace there would be no remnant, nor a "firm place in his sanctuary" or "foothold" (9:8; see NIV note). The Hebrew of 9:8 says that the two purposes of God's grace manifested itself in "leaving an escaped remnant" and "giving us a peg" (author's translation). The term for "peg" (*yated*) is rendered as "secure hold" or "firm place" in English translations (ESV, NIV). It is a term associated with the instrument that holds up a tent (Judges 4:21–22) and the tabernacle (Exodus 27:19; 35:18). The use of the metaphor in Ezra's prayer affirms that God has

---

10. Together with fulfilled prophecy (see Ezra 1:1–11), Ezra 9:8–9 gives the author's framework of theological interpretation for the restoration period and thus functions as key verses to Ezra-Nehemiah. As will be noted in the discussion, awareness of God's character shapes his understanding of the events.

given them something firm in the renewed sanctuary: a secure place where, indeed, one can tangibly see a manifestation of God's grace.[11] Indeed, God's grace inexplicably emerged in tangible ways in the midst of sin's consequences. It recalls God's action in Ezra 1:1 when he moved hearts to ignite the restoration process. Ezra's prayer recognizes that, in contrast to the long years of dependence both politically and economically on foreign powers (9:7), they are now granted "a brief moment" of independence through the restoration only because of God's grace and mercy (vv. 8–9). In so doing God has given a "light to our eyes" (v. 8) or, metaphorically speaking for those in spiritual darkness, has broken through with revival (Isaiah 9:2; 42:6–7; 60:1–3). His grace has also given them "a little relief" ("a little reviving," author's translation) while in "bondage" (while dependent upon the foreign Persian government, 9:8). This is so because a "remnant" (v. 8) remains, those who survived judgment and who now have full access to all of God's promises. The fact that a remnant remains and has begun to rebuild is tangible evidence of God's grace triumphing over judgment. God has, in fact, withheld the full measure of his punishment (9:8, 13; cf. Ezek 20:7–29).

Furthermore, regardless of their present servitude to the Persian Empire ("though we are slaves," [Ezra 9:9], not an unfamiliar reality for God's people; Exod 2:23–25; 3:7–9), Ezra's prayer underscores more concrete evidence of God's grace. Ezra 9:9 affirms that the LORD has remembered his people. This covenantal remembering, simply put, means he has not "forsaken us" (*'azab*), and this act of remembering translates to action on his part (Lev 26:40–45). Far from mere mental recall, when God remembers people or things, God acts (i.e., Exod 2:23–25). Often in the biblical narrative when God acts or causes things to happen, it corresponds to the fact that God is specifically remembering his covenant, usually with Abraham. The same is true with the use of the negative expression, "God has not forsaken us" (Ezra 9:9). This notion of not being forsaken (from *'azab*) is commonly used to describe Israel's own willful separation from Yahweh (e.g., Deut 31:6, 8; Jos 1:5; 1 Chr 28:20; Isa 1:4).

Although slaves (to a foreign regime because of sin), they have not

---

11. Based on the use of the same Hebrew term in Isaiah, Ezra's use in his current context of restoration represents a movement forward to the day where Zion will receive ultimate restoration in the age to come (Isa 33:20; 54:1–4).

been forsaken by God. God has acted on their behalf and the evidence is found in the positive interactions with the Persian kings that have brought restoration to God's people. Ezra admits in 9:9 that God has, as the NIV puts it, "shown us kindness" through the unexpected means of the Persian Empire. This translation of "kindness" for *hesed* misses some of the nuance of this rich Hebrew term. Although *hesed* as kindness is appropriate in some contexts, here it misses Ezra's point entirely. God was not merely offering a gesture equivalent to a job offer or the use of one's vehicle by commissioning restoration (the temple's reconstruction and building up Judah and Jerusalem) through the Persian kings (9:9). He was extending "covenantal loyalty" or "relational loyalty," such as the full weight of God's covenantal commitment, behind the entire venture. God was demonstrating loyalty in the relationship, an affection for and commitment to his people. Indeed, God reaffirmed his loyalty by forgiving rather than destroying Israel after the great failure with the golden calf (Exod 34:5–7) and did so repeatedly in the subsequent some eight hundred years of their blatant stiff-necked conduct.[12] For these many years, he was slow to anger and "abounding in covenantal loyalties" (Exod 34:6 author's translation). Thus, Ezra understood that both the remnant and political favor from the Persians represent tangible expressions and evidence of God's grace, expressions not unfamiliar to the people of God in the past. Once again, God is presently reaching out and extending such loyalty through Israel's restoration. In this way he is giving them "new life" (Ezra 9:9). The promise of new life was something the prophet Ezekiel envisioned, as well (Ezek 37:1–14).[13]

---

12. To name a few examples, this is first seen where the people disbelieve God's promises about the land of Canaan after hearing the report by the spies (Num 14:10–12). Per Moses's request (14:17–19), God forgives the people, but they suffer serious consequences even still (14:20–35). The book of Judges shows that in the face of blatant rebellion by the third generation of Israelites (Judg 3:10–15), God graciously raised up judges to save them "because of their groaning" (Judg 2:18). The purpose in raising up prophets was God's "pity" or compassion on his people (2 Chr 36:15–16). Israel's history indicts her according to Ezekiel (see especially Ezek 16, 20). These entire chapters are devoted to recalling the nation's poor behavior regardless of God's gracious care and provision.

13. See Steinmann, *Ezra and Nehemiah*, 333–38, who makes this connection. Evidently, the resurrection motif of this new life needs to be framed within its redemptive-historical setting. Ezra-Nehemiah and the restoration of worship in the postexilic period are the forerunners of the King and his own resurrection, as those who have faith in Christ await theirs.

Ezra's use of the term *hesed* is a reminder to God of his own character (paralleling Moses's strategy prior (Exod 32:13; 34:8–9; Num 14:17–19). Its use redirects God, Ezra, and the gathered crowd to reflect on previous moments where God displayed such loyalties, moments where God demonstrated his *hesed*. Ezra's present interpretive lens for dealing with sin, therefore, is God's relentless, gracious, and merciful character. Again, their guilt and shame seem even more deplorable and unfathomable given their present experience of God's mercy and grace to them in the covenantal relationship. The loyalty again, as so often in the past, seems to be one-sided.

Why would God bother to continue to show undeserved relational loyalties to a guilty people? Why would he be faithful to the unfaithful remnant (9:10–14a)? This is a people who already "paid" a heavy price for sin's consequences through exile but apparently learned little (Isa 40:2). This is a people who exist only because of God's grace (9:8)! This is a people who have been punished far less than their sins deserve (9:13).

God obligated himself to such loyalties with Abraham in the covenantal ritual highlighted in Genesis 15:12–21. Not only did the LORD promise Abraham a people and a place (Gen 12:1–3), but by a solemn oath he also guaranteed that those promises, particularly the land portion of the promise, was untouchable (Gen 15:12–21). That is, rather than allow his promises to lapse for *any* reason, God declared he would curse himself even unto death, if necessary, to avoid it. In Genesis 15:12–21 God took a self-maledictory oath obligating himself to unwavering loyalties for both parties in the relationship even at the cost of his own life.[14] Why does God bother? It is out of faithfulness to his own promises and the revelation of God's character. Therefore, Ezra's only recourse and hope to repair yet another breach in the relationship was reliance on God's character and God's unchangeable word, that solemn oath made to Abraham back in Genesis 15. Ultimately, Ezra asks God to act to advance his covenantal promises. Ezra's words powerfully demonstrate such reliance.

---

14. The oath that God takes in Gen 15:12–21 could be compared to the familiar childhood oath, "Cross my heart and hope to die, stick a needle in my eye." The oath is a child's way of saying I will stand by you through thick and thin. Through the good times and the bad times, even when you hurt me, I will still be your best friend for life. This deep bond of friendship was exemplified by the child's willingness to inflict pain upon her/himself so as not to break the bond of friendship. Meredith G. Kline, *By Oath Consigned: A Reinterpretation of the Covenant Signs of Circumcision and Baptism* (Grand Rapids: Eerdmans, 1968).

**Awareness of accountability (9:10–12).** "But now, our God, what can we say after this?" (Ezra 9:10). This rhetorical question captures the intensity of the moment. The answer, of course, is nothing! There is nothing to say about their lack of loyalty in light of his unflinching loyalty (9:8–9). The contrast could not be greater. These verses highlight their accountability through the prophets. Starting with the prophet Moses (Deut 7:1–4), God raised up his "servants the prophets" (Ezra 9:11) to warn about the dangers of such things—but to no avail (2 Kgs 17:23; 2 Chr 36:15–16).[15] In addition, the snippets of biblical inferences in verses 11–12 that provided a warning for God's people rely on a hodge-podge of pentateuchal phrases mostly found in Deuteronomy, but not exclusively (e.g., Lev 18:26–30; Deut 4:5; 11:10; 18:9; 23:2–8; Isa 1:19; Ezek 7:20). Accordingly, Ezra's use of "scripture" in his prayer not only reflects his knowledge of the law but also his ability to extract principles for proper contextualization, something that will be made clear in chapter 10.[16] Sadly, their neglectful behavior relative to the application of God's word is yet another connection to preexilic Israel. Their character flaw is great (lack of loyalty in the relationship), and they deserve his wrath, not mercy. The final section of Ezra's prayer soberly acknowledges such realities.

**Awareness of what is deserved (9:13–15).** As Ezra's prayer draws to a close, he asks in verse 14, "Would you not be angry enough with us to destroy us?" He concedes that their ongoing guilt deserves God's full wrath, particularly in light of his grace. In fact, as a priest and teacher, he knows that God's character ("You are righteous") legally demands that the unfaithful remnant's end should be, and very likely could be, destruction (9:15). In other words, the ruling of the divine court would be just if dishing out further consequences for sin were in view (Exod 9:27). The existence of God's people hangs in the balance, not unlike the threat that existed with the golden calf prior to Moses' intercession (Exod 32–34).

The theology that surfaces from this part of his prayer reveals how

---

15. See also Dan 9:6, 10 and Zech 1:6 for usage elsewhere of the prophets as servants of the Lord.

16. As a teacher and priest Ezra knows the importance of extracting principles from God's word for the purposes of contextualization. Not only is this fact observed in his prayer, a natural outflow of being immersed in the word, but it is also observed in how he handles the unfaithfulness in chapter 10.

the sin-guilt cycle endemic to God's people exposes a bigger problem. Guilty people cannot legally stand before a holy God. Guilty people cannot stand before a just judge without divine intervention in judgment (9:15). The exile and any looming threats of destruction currently perceived by Ezra are justified. Ezra's prayer does not call the people to action, but it calls God's mercy to action. God's mercy is what will eventually bring people to a place of action. Ezra knows that the future existence of the exiles is based solely on the fact that God is and always will be the God of Israel.

Thus, Ezra's prayer reflects an honest awareness of and tension between both the human and divine natures. Israel stands guilty once again when sized up against God's law, and God's law demands justice. Ezra's frank acknowledgement of these realities, demonstrated in his mournful prayer, paves the way for others to follow his lead. Indeed, Ezra 10 is a fitting conclusion to the problem exposed in chapter 9, giving the solution to the ongoing sin and guilt issue that Ezra faced. Corporate confession leads to admission of wrongdoing and an action plan to correct the wrongdoing.

EZRA 9 SHOWS A LEADER'S RESPONSE TO RECEIVING a report of unfaithfulness in the covenantal community. With respect to content, this prayer of confession by Ezra (9:6–15) has affinities to prayers and utterances of others, such as Moses (Exod 32:11–14, 30–32; Jeremiah (Jer 14:19–22), Ezekiel (Ezek 9:8), Daniel (Dan 9:4–19), and Nehemiah (Neh 1:5–11; 9:5–36; see commentary in Nehemiah on those passages), that were offered when God's people were unfaithful.[17] Like Ezra's, these prayers show deep awareness of the human condition. Guilt and shame cover Israel because of sin. Sin consists of not heeding God's Word via his servants (either Moses or the prophets). Sin brings devastating consequences to God's people and the place he selected for them to dwell. The covenant leaders and mediators

17. Ezra's prayer is not to be confused with, and is distinct from, the prayer offered in Neh 9:1–36. The latter is part of a literary unit consisting of Neh 8–10. Although Neh 9:1–36 mentions mixed marriages and divorce, this subject matter is not what drives the prayer nor its context in Neh 8–10 (see further discussion in Nehemiah below).

are acutely aware of the serious nature of the sin-guilt problem and react with deep emotion as a result.

The prayers also show a deep awareness of God's character. As the covenantal leader confesses the sin and guilt of the people, he does so with a sober realization of two aspects of God's nature. First, God is great and awesome because he guards Israel and shows loyalty despite their condition. Second, God is righteous (an affirmation of his justice to judge sin) in all interactions with his people. The latter is a legal declaration, a formula of confession that goes back to Exodus 9:27. The covenant leaders are sober to the fact that reliance on God's mercy is their only hope. Only God's character of *hesed* can reach higher than their sins that reach to the highest of heavens. Only God's *hesed* can cover sin's shame that covers them. Every covenant leader from Moses onward calls and depends upon God's *hesed* as their interpretive framework for understanding their relationship with the Lord.

The template for all such prayers, however, derives from Moses's experience with the newly-formed nation in the wilderness, particularly the revelation he had of God in response to the golden calf incident. In the wilderness, the golden calf continues to expose the sin-guilt problem for Israel.[18] The calf was an outward manifestation of the reality of an inward heart problem, the propensity to disobey God's law. On the heels of this incident, however, rather than destroy them, as was his right, the LORD reaffirms his commitment and affection for them. The LORD makes a pointed and powerful declaration concerning himself: "The LORD, the LORD, a God merciful [*rahum*] and gracious [*hannun*], slow to anger and *abounding in steadfast love* [*hesed*] *and faithfulness, keeping steadfast love* [*hesed*] for thousands, forgiving iniquity, transgression and sin and who will by no means clear the guilty" (Exod 34:6–7; author's translation, emphasis added). Embedded in this divine declaration is his twofold remedy for dealing with the sin-guilt problem exposed with the calf. On the one hand, he forgives; on the other hand, he does not clear guilty people.

With respect to "forgiving," in this divine self-disclosure Yahweh explains himself and defines his nature to Moses on the heels of this incident. God's slowness to judge or to anger flows out of the deep affection God has for his people (*rahum* and *hannun*). It flows out of God's

18. The sin-guilt problem is, of course, a primeval problem, according to the biblical arc of redemptive history (cf. Gen 3).

*hesed*, his unwavering loyalty in the relationship. As a result, God persists and forgives them *although* or *in spite* of the fact that they are stiff-necked (Exod 34:9). In short, the LORD's remedy for their sin-guilt problem is his forgiveness. God confronts Israel's problem with the abundance of his *hesed*. Divine forgiveness, as noted by one scholar suggests, it has a threefold foundational function in the declaration: it secures the community, it secures Yahweh's presence, and it secures a new way of relating to the sin-guilt problem.[19]

In the declaration to Moses, the LORD also says he would by no means clear the guilty (Exod 34:7). This is yet another remedy for dealing with the sin-guilt problem. The sin with the golden calf angered Yahweh. This is evidenced by the three thousand deaths at the Levites' hands and the later plague (Exod 32:28, 35). Embedded in the declaration is the important idea that Yahweh metes out the consequences for sin. The framework of *hesed*-based forgiveness allows for punishment to carry forward God's justice to the sin-guilty community.[20] Instead of venting his full wrath on these covenant breakers as he threatens to do, God's wrath is demonstrated in that he only lets out, as it were, a little puff of steam. Furthermore, God's wrath is stayed because of the covenant mediator. In this way, God describes himself to Moses as one who is slow to anger.

Thus, the declaration of Exodus 34:5–7 reveals two ways God deals with the sin-guilt problem: he forgives yet judges. In all this Yahweh earns himself a reputation, one that becomes paradigmatic not only for Israel's history, but also for all of redemptive history. Israel was guilty but forgiven on account of God's *hesed*, and the glory of the LORD in the tabernacle was there to prove it in Exodus. Mercy triumphed over judgment (Jas 2:13).

As redemptive history moves forward, after about eight hundred years of blatant stiff-necked conduct, the people of God have overdrawn on their *hesed* account. The prophet Ezekiel comes face to face with a God who "does not leave the guilty unpunished" (Exod 34:7). Ezekiel notes, in a stunning historical recollection, that God's people were guilty in Egypt, in the wilderness, in Canaan, and in exile (Ezek 20). In fact,

---

19. K. D. Sakenfeld, *The Meaning of Hesed in the Bible: A New Inquiry* (Eugene, OR: Wipf & Stock, 2002), 119–22.

20. Ibid., 74.

the topic of Jerusalem's guilt shapes several of Ezekiel's messages to those already in exile, especially chapters 16–23. From the covenantal perspective, guilt provides the legal rationale for the demise of the city. Ezekiel and his compatriots experience exile and divine abandonment as God's "cure" for stiff necks and the sin-guilt problem. The people of Israel remain guilty and will be judged, Yahweh's anger is unleashed, and the departure of the LORD from the Jerusalem temple is proof (Ezek 10:18–19). God's wrath is not stayed any longer by the covenant mediator. Indeed, the covenant mediator, Ezekiel, is muted. Here judgment triumphs over mercy.

Now, after experiencing sin's consequences, even after surviving exile, Ezra 9 exposes the ongoing sin-guilt problem of the postexilic people of God. Ezra, the covenant mediator, cries out to God, aware of the history of the interactions of his people with God. Even though God graciously restored their markers of identity and showed them mercy, they sin and still are guilty. The exile, with its devastating effects, did not remedy the situation. Essentially, neither the exile nor the return fixed the heart problem of unfaithfulness to God's commands. No postexilic reformer, not even Ezra the lawgiver, had the ability to cure the human heart's propensity toward sin and associated guilt. Even the so-called righteous remnant is guilty. Equally true is the fact that the exile, as painful as it was, did not fully exhaust God's wrath. The exile was merely a down payment of more to come, relative to a deeper expression of God's anger. The exile did not fully appease God's anger.

This tension in Ezra 9 points us forward, from a biblical-theological perspective, to the bigger picture of redemptive history. When we turn to the pages of the New Testament, it is crystal clear that the guilt of God's people continues! The condition of God's people is the same, something exposed by Jesus in all four of the gospels. Through Jesus, the true Lawgiver and incarnate Word, God gives a standard by which he evaluates human conduct. In this regard, the religious leaders of his day came up short. Luke's gospel highlights this in particular (i.e., Lk 5:27–32; 11:37–52; 14:1–24). In the book of Acts, Stephen received opposition in his ministry of signs and wonders from the religious leaders of his day and was unfairly charged with blasphemy (Acts 6:9, 11, 12–15). His riveting defense speech boldly targets the heart problem of these leaders. They are stiff-necked, or stubborn, *just* like their ancestors. Even though they have the law, they have not obeyed the law (7:51–53). The leadership was guilty in matters pertaining to God's law, and Stephen lowers the gavel and pronounces them guilty. His confrontation with stiff-necked people cost Stephen his life (7:57–59).

However, it is not just the religious leaders that are guilty and fall short of the standard of the incarnate Word. The New Testament also makes the guilt of all humankind clear from several angles. Unfortunately, humankind comes up short: "All have sinned and fall short of the glory of God," Paul reminds us (Rom 3:23). In this condition people lack the ability to live holy lives and to demonstrate God's holy character to the world. People rob God of glory, reputation, and character. This angers God, resulting in divine judgment—"for the wages of sin is death" (Rom 6:23).

The apostle John assumes our ongoing guilt-ridden nature is due to sin. He recognizes it is not *that* we sin, but the fact that we *keep on* sinning that prompts the need for an advocate with the Father (1 John 2:1). Paul describes his own struggle well in this regard (Rom 7:21–25). Furthermore, it is in this guilt-ridden condition that God reaches out and restores us: "while we were God's enemies, we were reconciled to him through the death of his Son" (Rom 5:10). As Peter plainly puts it to the Gentiles, "once you had not received mercy, but now you have received mercy" (1 Pet 2:10) and, as a result, can have a relationship with God and be a part of God's people. Even though God graciously restored us and showed us mercy, we continue to sin and stand guilty before a holy God. Ezra chapter 9 prepares us for this reality, a continually guilty people continually in need of receiving mercy.

IF YOU KNOW MERCY, YOU WILL SHOW MERCY. Although centuries stand between us and the ancient context, it seems no such barrier exists when it comes to unearthing the timeless truths and application of Ezra's experience as recorded in chapter 9. It will only be a matter of time before the church leader or pastor receives a report from trusted leaders about the unfaithfulness of other trusted leaders and members in a congregation. A report that both clergy and laity are involved in sin sadly remains a reality.

God's people blow it by engaging in a particular unfaithfulness resulting in sin's consequences, the equivalent of the exile. Because of God's merciful restoration, the equivalent of the return from exile, they experience his grace and joy. For a time, and out of deep, genuine gratitude, they do everything according to the word of God as it relates to regulating their worship of him (Ezra 1–6). With the passing of time, gratitude for his mercy and favor fade, and people can easily slip back into their old patterns of unfaithfulness. When it comes to the attention of our spiritual leaders that we have fallen back or backslidden, the hope is that they are grieved and cry out to God on our behalf. In this way, the contemporary significance of this text is perhaps closer to the surface for us than some other Old Testament texts.

There are two major things we can learn from observing Ezra's response. First, his reaction was mourning and grief, an outward display of despair. Do we as leaders have deep emotional responses to sin in the camp? Are we pained and grieved by sin as Ezra was, or do we judge and condemn? Are we willing to wear our emotions on our sleeves? Ezra's demonstration of grief, depending on one's church culture/affiliation, might by certain standards look unsophisticated, too staged or, dare I say, too charismatic and contrived. Ezra's response, however, flows out of exposure to God's character as merciful yet just, through experience and knowledge of the word of God. We might see more changes and correctives to wrong behaviors if, as leaders, we allow ourselves to be gripped by sin because of exposure to God through knowledge of his word.

Prior to becoming a professor, I proudly spent several years as a missionary in Youth With A Mission (YWAM), one of the largest short-term missionary organizations. When there was sin in the camp, the base leaders exposed it, not hid it. A meeting was called and often fasting was involved. These were designated "openness and brokenness" times. The leadership, grown men and women, would publicly weep and wail over the exposed sin. They would, like Ezra, respond as though they were the guilty ones and thus, they cried out for God's undeserved mercy on the base and mission. They were, like Ezra, conduits for conviction, and it didn't take long for others to join in the prayer of confession.

Although I was not aware of it at the time, they were deliberately trying to follow Ezra's example. Needless to say, their intentionality marked me for life even though I was only a part of the mission for eight years. Sadly, I have not seen or experienced this in the places I have ministered since. I have often wondered, though, what would happen if I (or other leaders), so touched and moved, responded like Ezra? I would submit that what Ezra does here (clearly not contrived but based on conviction) becomes the springboard for the needed change; something evidenced in the events that unfold in chapter 10.

The second thing we can learn from Ezra's response is that he prayed and did not confront people right away. He believed his trusted sources, but then he prayed. To be sure, there is a time for confrontation and investigation, but Ezra shows us the importance of going to God in prayer and agonizing over sin first. When confronted with sin, a thoughtful leader would do well to take example from Ezra. Although not prescriptive, his prayer teaches us a lot about Ezra's leadership style, beliefs, and theological framework. Their problem is his problem, even though he is not among the guilty. His incarnational leadership style allowed him to identify with the exiles. He believed in and knew God's word. God's word is the mirror reflecting and revealing the problem, not Ezra's opinions about their actions. Due to his knowledge of the word and "church history" (Israelite history), he swiftly acknowledges failure because of an understanding of the human condition. In this regard, Ezra reminds us of another great reformer, Martin Luther. As Luther acknowledged, "always righteous and always a sinner";[21] such a perspective grounds and enables us to deal with sin, not be surprised by it. It is imperative for a leader or pastor to be aware of the propensity toward sin that exists in those he/she shepherds. One's awareness of humanity's sinful nature will greatly affect how the problem of recurring sins in a congregation is approached. It is not *if*, but *when* sins surface and resurface that an appeal to God's mercy is all one has.

Ultimately, as a leader, if you know mercy you will show mercy! The cross shows us God's mercy. If the cross is always before us, then we will have a fresh understanding that when we could not reach mercy, mercy came running to us. If the cross is always before us, regardless of how we are otherwise wired, then we *can* show mercy and cry out to God for mercy on behalf of others. "Blessed are the merciful, for they will be shown mercy" (Matt 5:7). If you know mercy, you will show mercy.

---

21. *LW* 25:260.

# Ezra 10:1–44

1 While Ezra was praying and confessing, weeping and
throwing himself down before the house of God, a large crowd
of Israelites—men, women and children—gathered around
him. They too wept bitterly. 2 Then Shekaniah son of Jehiel,
one of the descendants of Elam, said to Ezra, "We have been
unfaithful to our God by marrying foreign women from the
peoples around us. But in spite of this, there is still hope for
Israel. 3 Now let us make a covenant before our God to send
away all these women and their children, in accordance with
the counsel of my lord and of those who fear the commands of
our God. Let it be done according to the Law. 4 Rise up; this
matter is in your hands. We will support you, so take courage
and do it."

5 So Ezra rose up and put the leading priests and Levites
and all Israel under oath to do what had been suggested.
And they took the oath. 6 Then Ezra withdrew from before
the house of God and went to the room of Jehohanan son of
Eliashib. While he was there, he ate no food and drank no
water, because he continued to mourn over the unfaithfulness
of the exiles.

7 A proclamation was then issued throughout Judah and
Jerusalem for all the exiles to assemble in Jerusalem. 8 Anyone who
failed to appear within three days would forfeit all his property,
in accordance with the decision of the officials and elders, and
would himself be expelled from the assembly of the exiles.

9 Within the three days, all the men of Judah and Benjamin
had gathered in Jerusalem. And on the twentieth day of the
ninth month, all the people were sitting in the square before
the house of God, greatly distressed by the occasion and
because of the rain. 10 Then Ezra the priest stood up and said
to them, "You have been unfaithful; you have married foreign
women, adding to Israel's guilt. 11 Now honor the LORD, the
God of your ancestors, and do his will. Separate yourselves
from the peoples around you and from your foreign wives."

12 The whole assembly responded with a loud voice: "You
are right! We must do as you say. 13 But there are many people
here and it is the rainy season; so we cannot stand outside.
Besides, this matter cannot be taken care of in a day or two,
because we have sinned greatly in this thing. 14 Let our officials
act for the whole assembly. Then let everyone in our towns
who has married a foreign woman come at a set time, along
with the elders and judges of each town, until the fierce anger
of our God in this matter is turned away from us." 15 Only
Jonathan son of Asahel and Jahzeiah son of Tikvah, supported
by Meshullam and Shabbethai the Levite, opposed this.

16 So the exiles did as was proposed. Ezra the priest
selected men who were family heads, one from each family
division, and all of them designated by name. On the first day
of the tenth month they sat down to investigate the cases,
17 and by the first day of the first month they finished dealing
with all the men who had married foreign women.

18 Among the descendants of the priests, the following had
married foreign women:
From the descendants of Joshua son of Jozadak, and his
brothers: Maaseiah, Eliezer, Jarib and Gedaliah. 19
(They all gave their hands in pledge to put away their
wives, and for their guilt they each presented a ram
from the flock as a guilt offering.)

20 From the descendants of Immer:
Hanani and Zebadiah.

21 From the descendants of Harim:
Maaseiah, Elijah, Shemaiah, Jehiel and Uzziah.

22 From the descendants of Pashhur:
Elioenai, Maaseiah, Ishmael, Nethanel, Jozabad and Elasah.

23 Among the Levites:
Jozabad, Shimei, Kelaiah (that is, Kelita),
Pethahiah, Judah and Eliezer.

24 From the musicians:
Eliashib.

From the gatekeepers:
Shallum, Telem and Uri.

25 And among the other Israelites:

From the descendants of Parosh:
Ramiah, Izziah, Malkijah, Mijamin, Eleazar,
Malkijah and Benaiah.

26 From the descendants of Elam:
Mattaniah, Zechariah, Jehiel, Abdi, Jeremoth and Elijah.

27 From the descendants of Zattu:
Elioenai, Eliashib, Mattaniah, Jeremoth, Zabad and Aziza.

28 From the descendants of Bebai:
Jehohanan, Hananiah, Zabbai and Athlai.

29 From the descendants of Bani:
Meshullam, Malluk, Adaiah, Jashub, Sheal and Jeremoth.

30 From the descendants of Pahath-Moab:
Adna, Kelal, Benaiah, Maaseiah, Mattaniah,
Bezalel, Binnui and Manasseh.

31 From the descendants of Harim:
Eliezer, Ishijah, Malkijah, Shemaiah, Shimeon,
32 Benjamin, Malluk and Shemariah.

33 From the descendants of Hashum:
Mattenai, Mattattah, Zabad, Eliphelet, Jeremai,
Manasseh and Shimei.

34 From the descendants of Bani:

Maadai, Amram, Uel, [35] Benaiah, Bedeiah,
Keluhi, [36] Vaniah, Meremoth, Eliashib,
[37] Mattaniah, Mattenai and Jaasu.

[38] From the descendants of Binnui:
Shimei, [39] Shelemiah, Nathan, Adaiah,
[40] Maknadebai, Shashai, Sharai, [41] Azarel,
Shelemiah, Shemariah, [42] Shallum, Amariah and Joseph.

[43] From the descendants of Nebo:
Jeiel, Mattithiah, Zabad, Zebina, Jaddai, Joel and Benaiah.

[44] All these had married foreign women, and some of them had children by these wives.

CHAPTER 10 BRINGS THE MATTER OF MIXED marriages, the unfaithfulness in the renewed covenant community (9:1–2), to a dramatic and decisive conclusion. Action is taken to fix the problem. It can be divided into two sections, 10:1–17 and 10:18–44. The first section records the confessions of unfaithfulness and the covenant or intended plan of reform in the community (10:1–17). Immediately following this, the chapter ends rather abruptly with documentary proof of the investigation, consisting of a list of approximately one hundred guilty offenders (10:18–44). The names of the guilty parties, those who came forward in confession, are then listed, bringing the chapter to an anti-climactic close (10:18–44; see outline). Thus chapter 10 provides a resolution to the problem exposed in 9:1–2.

There are four big-picture points important to note before we explore this chapter in more detail. First, chapter 10 consists mostly of third-person narrative. The change to third person from first (7:27–9:15) shifts attention away from Ezra to the people and deliberately affords the reader another viewpoint. This zoom lens redirects the reader to the response of the people to Ezra's display of emotion over sin.

The second item to consider before looking at the specifics of the chapter concerns its main theme. From a thematic point of view, the ongoing guilt of the people and associated anger of God drives the actions in chapter 10. With respect to the people, their guilty conduct is reported (9:1–2), is comparable to their ancestors (9:7,13), the exile is evidence of their great guilt (9:13), yet they stand guilty presently (9:15) and now we are told in chapter 10 they are, in fact, adding to Israel's guilt (10:10).

With respect to the anger of God, Ezra's ultimate goal was to avert God's wrath based on his knowledge of both their history and God's word (Deut 7:1–6, 23:2–7). Their ancestors' conduct provoked God to anger (Ezra 5:12), and God's anger awaits those who forsake him (8:22). God's anger ultimately led to the exile (9:12) and could now lead to the annihilation of the remnant (9:14). Now we are told they are hopeful that "the fierce anger of our God . . . [will turn] away" (10:14) should they take appropriate actions, that is, attempt to do his will.

Guilty people attempting to avert God's wrath are not uncommon in the biblical narrative,[1] and this hope informs the specific actions taken here. The context in which this unfolds, however, is critical. Encouraged by Ezra's own response, the desire to do something arises, not just to avoid more of sin's consequences (God's wrath) but as a realization that they themselves have been unfaithful to God (10:2). The desire also arises out of a fresh awareness that God has been good to them by leaving a remnant, allowing the return, and enabling to rebuild, and even now God has refrained from destroying them Ezra (Ezra 9:8–9, 14).

The third consideration before looking fully at chapter 10 pertains to the way this compromise of intermarriage was handled. Ezra, together with the council of others, appears to contexualize Scriptures (such as Lev 18; Deut 7:1–6; 23:4–9). In other words, the law did not give specific guidance regarding the handling of intermarriages with foreigners *after the fact*. To be sure, Nehemiah, some twenty-five years later, handles the same situation differently (Neh 13:23–31). Rather than demand separation, Nehemiah asks that the people take an oath and vow not to allow their children to get embroiled in the same sin (Neh 13:25).[2]

---

1. See also these other intertextual examples of those who took action to have God's wrath turned away: Exod 32:12, where Moses pleads with God to turn away from his fierce anger because of the golden calf; Josh 7:26, with the actions of Joshua relative to Achan and the LORD turning (*shub*) from his fierce anger, as God's anger subsides when Achan and his family are stoned; 1 Chr 21:3–14, the census of David.

2. It should not surprise the reader that the two leaders (Ezra and Nehemiah)

The actions taken by Ezra, therefore, are contextually driven coming on the heels of exile and require that principles be extracted from the biblical texts available (Leviticus and Deuteronomy) due to a lack of a one-to-one correspondence.[3]

The fourth item to consider before looking at the chapter in more depth pertains to the historical and theological grid of the author. The author's own historical and theological grid informs the specific actions taken in these circumstances. As has been noted previously, the author interprets the return from exile as a new exodus. If this is a new exodus, then the expulsion of the women and children could equate to a re-conquering of the promised land. As will be explained below, one must understand the immediate solution of separation not as a sanction for divorce but potentially as a cleansing of the land/a new conquest of the land akin to what God did with the Canaanites. This contextual reality might explain the differences between Ezra and Nehemiah in handling the situation. Thus, these four big picture points, the third-person narrative, the theme of averting God's anger, the contextualization of Scripture, and the historical/theological grid of the author must be kept in mind as one interprets Ezra 10.

## The People's Response to Ezra's Prayer of Confession (10:1–44)

### Confessions of Unfaithfulness in Community and Action Taken (10:1–17)

WHILE IN PRAYER (9:5–15), EZRA'S OPEN, honest, and heartfelt confession not only attracted attention from a large and diverse crowd of Israelites, but the prayer also produced a sense of remorse and grief in the group (10:1).[4] From this crowd arose a spokesperson moved to confess their corporate unfaithfulness. He not only made confession to Ezra but immediately proposed a "covenant" or decisive action plan "to send

---

tackle the problem differently. In other words, Nehemiah didn't get it wrong because he didn't follow Ezra's way previously. Nehemiah's slightly different context drives his own interpretation and application of the principles from God's word.

3. As a priest and teacher Ezra naturally extracts principles from Torah, something already demonstrated in his prayer (9:11–12).

4. This prayer of lamentation is similar to those found in the Psalter (Pss 44, 60, 74, 79, 80, 85, 90).

away" the foreigners in their midst (10:2–4). After hearing the plan, Ezra rallies staunch support from the leaders by a verbal commitment to do what was suggested. Once securing their allegiance through an oath, he leaves them to handle the matter and withdraws to a temple chamber room and continues to grieve and intercede (10:5–6).

A proclamation to assemble—with consequences for not attending—gets issued (10:7–8). The crowd then assembles, and Ezra confronts and assigns a guilty verdict to the people, informing them of the plan of action (10:9–11). In a jaw-dropping scene, the assembly accepts both the sentence of guilt and the difficult consequences with only four dissenters (10:15). They also propose that a systematic investigation be conducted over time in order to deal with the matter appropriately (10:12–15). This part of the chapter ends, in typical narrative style, with a report that the investigation was successfully carried out, and it took roughly three months to conduct (10:16–17).

**Community conviction (10:1).** The shift to third-person narrative (rather than Ezra's first-person perspective) gives specific attention to those in the community and their critical viewpoint on the event. Others—the common Israelites, including children—were not only curious but came under conviction, a recognition and admission of guilt. Those mentioned in 10:1 are likely the same folks who gathered around Ezra and are characterized there as "everyone who trembled at the words of God" (9:4). These are God-fearers, those who had a sober understanding of God's word.[5] Ezra was a conduit for conviction in the community. As a leader he set a tone of conviction, not condemnation, and others responded accordingly. Ezra's actions of praying, weeping, and especially "throwing himself down" (10:1) mirrors that of Moses's own response to the golden calf narrative (see Deut 9:18, 25 for Moses's interpretation of Exod 32:1–7). In contrast to the golden calf narrative, Ezra's corporate confession and expression of grief lead not only to an admission of wrongdoing but a commitment to practical actions to correct the wrongdoing out of a renewed fear of God. Thus, the covenantal community's conviction, highlighted by third-person narrative, shows the emotional effects of sin in the camp were deep and not confined just to Ezra.

**Unfaithfulness and hope (10:2–4).** The reported speech of Shecaniah moves the story forward to resolution. Based on 10:26 it seems his

---

5. See commentary on Ezra 9:3–5.

father and other family members were among those guilty. Perhaps this motivated him to speak up. Regardless, he confesses two things: their unfaithfulness and yet their hope, two seemingly contradictory points. With regard to their unfaithfulness, the NIV does not capture the force of the Hebrew. Through the use of a pronoun fronting the verb, the phrase in Hebrew emphasizes the confession and reads, "We, *we* have been unfaithful [*'anahnu ma'alnu*] to our God" or another way to put it: "We *ourselves* have been unfaithful to our God" (v. 2; author's translation). Remarkable ownership of their sin is witnessed by this confession. Moreover, their unfaithfulness is toward a person, "we, we have been unfaithful to our God" (v. 3, 2x author's translation). Again, we see the repeated possessive pronoun, "our God," as a demonstration of trying to reclaim their identity as God's people.

Moreover, their unfaithfulness manifested itself by "marrying foreign women from the peoples around us" (v. 2). A more literal translation might be "by *dwelling* [root *yashab*] with foreign women from the peoples around us" (author's translation). The Hebrew does not use the typical words for giving and taking in marriage, as one expects (root *natan*; see 9:12). So, it is odd to have such a term used here in 10:2 and in 10:10 for marriage. More literally, it reads "we have caused foreign women to reside" or "establish households," an idiom used only in Ezra-Nehemiah (thus Ezra 10:10, 14, 17, 18; Neh 13:23, 27). Likewise, it should also be kept in mind that these same people had polluted the land from one end to the other on account of their detestable practices (9:11). In fact, the land's defilement seems to be the focal point in 9:10–14, as one of the reasons Israel was to avoid any ties to the land through foreign marriages. To be sure, the land was their possession in preexilic times, but it was polluted fully and completely by its people. At the same time, the land and its bounty was a provision and inheritance for their children. For these reasons they were not to team up with, nor further the welfare of, the unbelieving Canaanites. The confession of "dwelling" with foreign women, combined with this emphasis on contamination of the land, suggests that Israel is re-polluting the land in similar fashion to the Canaanites who once dwelled there.[6]

The second thing that Shecaniah confesses in 10:2 is hope for the nation. Hope is obviously needed because the threat of destruction or

---

6. For further discussion see commentary on Ezra 10:9–11 below.

another exile looms large yet again (9:14–15). His hopefulness derives from knowing God's character. His hope concerns an idea that he proposes to Ezra and the leaders as an attempt to make things right and to avert further exposure to God's wrath. His hope is directly connected to making things right with God through a covenant before "our God" (v. 3), the nature of which is divorce or separation. Shecaniah seems to be contextualizing concerns of the law as Ezra has done.

The notion "to go out" which is applied to all these women and their children comes from the verb "to cause to go out" (from *yatsa'* "to go out" in the *hiphil* [causative]; NIV, "send away"). The verb "to send off" (from *shalah*) is used in the context of a divorce in Deut 24:1 which, in the broader context of this particular case law, also results in adverse consequences to the land itself (Deut 24:4). Thus, while the typical noun for divorce[7] is avoided, clearly divorce is in view in the Deuteronomic context. Although not exclusive to this meaning, *yatsa'* (*hiphil* construct, *lehotsi'*) often refers to bringing forth people out of a place of pollution and bondage, usually Egypt (Exod 6:13, 27; 12:42; 14:11; Jer 31:32; Ezek 20:9; Hos 9:13). Because of the language used, the proposed action of Shecaniah seems to warrant the suggestion that the land was also polluted, so their going forth was necessary.

This covenant, however, was to be agreed upon by Ezra and other leaders who feared God's commands, a gesture showing compliance "according to the Law" (Ezra 10:3). How could the specific arrangement of this covenant—sending away the women and their children—be done according to the law? Again, there is no specific covenantal legislation from the law that sanctions Shecaniah's solution. In the pre-Ezra phrase of restoration, rebuilding the altar was said to be done in "accordance with what is written in the Law of Moses" (3:2). In that case they possessed Mosaic legislation from Exodus 29:38–42 and Numbers 28:1–8 that prescribed how to rebuild the altar, and the first returnees attempted to follow it. Such is not the case in Ezra 10:3. In the statement "Let it be done according to the Law," the *it* because of context likely refers to the terms of the covenant and the legal requirement of the oath associated with covenant making (such as the oath which Ezra immediately calls for in 10:5–6),[8] but certainly not a specific law for

7. The typical term for divorce is *kerytut* (Deut 24:1, 3; Isa 50:1; Jer 3:8).
8. See, for example, Deut 29:14; Josh 9:15.

sending away women. Those who accept the terms of the covenant are designated as ones who "fear the commands of our God" (v. 3). In this regard they are covenanting afresh to keep all of God's law in general, but more specifically and in this context, not to have any other gods besides Yahweh, since marrying foreigners equates to idolatry (Deut 20:18; Jer 16:18; Ezek 7:20) and involves detestable practices (Ezra 9:1, 11, 14).[9] Thus, those who fear the commands of God return to true and exclusive worship of the LORD.

For this reason, *and* because of the radical nature of the suggestion, obtaining unanimity and an oath sealing the deal from all the leaders was imperative (10:5–6). Just as imperative was the fact that Ezra led the way in announcing the solution. As the lead teacher of the Law, ultimate authority rested with him as to the appropriateness of the solution proposed (7:10, 11, 12). Shecaniah, then, comes alongside Ezra and strongly urges him to take immediate action.

**A pledge and prayer (10:5–6).** Ezra acts in two specific ways. First, he secures the group's consensus by calling for an oath or pledge of allegiance to follow through with the arrangements of the covenant. This was typical of making covenants in the ancient world.[10] The nature of the oath was such that lack of follow through could ensure a curse (see 7:26; also Ruth 1:17; 2 Sam 3:35). But an oath garnering group consensus was not enough for Ezra. His subsequent action was quite revealing about his own spiritual stature.

The second way Ezra acts concerns a return to prayer. Ezra returns to prayer and fasting, but this time in private. His previous group fast (8:21) was to secure God's safety and protection for the trip to Jerusalem. Now his personal fast is not unlike that of Nehemiah's, before a difficult course of action that may not turn out to be favorable (Neh 1:4). He needed to garner God's grace and mercy, through mournful prayer and petition most of all. The confession of Shecaniah and the assembly (10:2; 12), along with the oath of the leaders to take appropriate steps to fix the problem, was not a guarantee that the covenantal community not present would respond favorably or that God would have mercy (10:2–5), but it

---

9. See Steinmann, *Ezra-Nehemiah*, 94–98, who suggests that the real issue behind the marriage to foreign women pertains to breaking the first commandment.

10. Although many examples could be referenced for the connection between covenant and oath, consider Gen 21:31–32; Deut 4:31; Judg 2:1; Ezek 16:8.

was a necessary action. Ezra thus returns to praying and fasting, the kind done only under severe circumstances (Exod 34:28; Esth 4:15–16; Jonah 3:7), in hopes to avert God's wrath (10:6). Accordingly, he continues to mourn. Likewise, the group assembled recognizes the urgent need to avert God's fierce anger. Their swift confession along with agreement by oath to take responsibility and suffer the consequences of separation or divorce, "exiling loved ones, was their only hope (10:2–4). Ezra acts in these two ways based on Shekaniah's encouragement.

**A proclamation (10:7–8).** A communication was then put out for "all the exiles" (10:7). The stern nature of the communication was expressed in the need for timeliness in getting to Jerusalem. They were to assemble within a three-day period, a time that would allow those farther away to participate. The stern nature of the communication, however, was expressed by a two-part ultimatum that had its genesis and authority in Artaxerxes's letter to Ezra (7:26). The first part of the ultimatum might be summarized as "assemble or forfeit your property." This means their property, possessions, or goods would "be proscribed by destruction" or "be put under the ban." The Hebrew word translated as "forfeit" is *herem*. That which is *herem* was devoted to the LORD in one of two ways, either by destruction or being set apart (e.g., Lev 7:21).[11] Their property would be confiscated and set apart for Yahweh. The second part of the ultimatum could be summarized as "assemble" or be an "exile" among the exiles. The irony in this cannot be understated! To be without possessions nor a place in the community implies an excommunication and banishment from the land. They would become like the ones they have married: non-Yahwist foreigners! Thus, the serious nature of the communication brings heaviness to a situation already packed with drama and emotion.

**Call to confession and reform (10:9–11).** The location and date of their gathering is not insignificant. It takes place in Jerusalem, but more specifically "in the square before the house of God" (v. 9). This is the same place used later when Ezra together with Nehemiah gather to read the law (Neh 8:1). It occurs just four months after Ezra arrived in Jerusalem (7:8–9), so a short time after his arrival. The gathering is in the month of December (*Chislev* = ninth month), a cold and rainy season. The sentiment of the people matches the situation, both physically and spiritually.

---

11. See discussions in *Show Them No Mercy*, 98–100; 116–17.

Ezra cuts to the chase and does what a faithful priest in the covenant community ought to have done. As their spiritual leader he holds them accountable for their actions and calls them to reform their ways. As noted above in 10:2, the NIV translation of 10:10 does not fully do justice to the emphasis of the original. The Hebrew reads, "*You, you* have been unfaithful" or "You *yourselves* have been unfaithful" rather than, "you have been unfaithful." The statement by Ezra reinforces the accountability of God's people for their actions expressed in Shekaniah's confession (10:2). Ezra's confrontation calls for their confession but also for articulation of the agreed-upon covenant of the leaders. He sums up the problem and repeats to them what he verbalized in prayer concerning their unfaithful conduct (9:6–15): they have been untrue and violated their legal obligations to God. Their act of treachery manifested itself by the fact that they are dwelling with foreign women (10:2, 10). This unfaithfulness not only makes them guilty, but it has added guilt to the nation. Not only was preexilic Israel guilty, but now postexilic Israel is guilty.

Ezra commands them accordingly to "honor the LORD, the God of your ancestors" (v. 11). The NIV note suggests "Now make confession to the LORD, the God of your ancestors" as a translation option for the Hebrew based on Joshua 7:19.[12] The notion of giving praise, however, comes as a result of their immediate actions, fearing the commands of God (10:3), and seems appropriate. Accordingly, Ezra also commands "and do his will" (v. 11). Doing God's will entails both praise *and* reform. This leads to the third command, "separate yourselves." He reminds them of the previous agreed-upon action of sending away what appears to be the defilement in the land, their foreign wives and children (10:3).

The separation in 10:11 is twofold here, too. Separate first from "the peoples around you" (*'am ha'arets*) and "from your foreign wives." The preposition "from" (*min*) is used twice for each separate object. Separation from the people of the land was the real issue according to God's law mapped out in the Pentateuch. One way a clear separation could be achieved would be by not intermarrying with foreign women in the first place. These foreign wives cannot be in the assembly of the LORD because they simply have not become followers of Yahweh. Ironically,

12. Some commentators such as Breneman, *Ezra, Nehemiah, Esther*, 160, and Williamson, *Ezra, Nehemiah*, 155, follow this rendering.

they are re-defiling the land by their affiliation to women who worship other gods, a defilement that God warned about previously (9:11–12, cf. Deut 13). The pollution of the land seems to be in view,[13] something caused by the first inhabitants (Canaanites), then perpetuated by (pre-exilic) Israel, and now carried on by the returned (postexilic) inhabitants of it (Ezra 9:11–12).

Thus, the forced departure is not unlike the forced removal that God imposed on the inhabitants of Canaan through Joshua's conquests. God warned that the land was polluted by the corruption of its people and their detestable practices. God had to bring a cleansing to the land; hence, the destruction of the Canaanites was necessary to fulfill God's promises and to establish God's holy presence in the land. Even still, the warning remained because the land was not entirely cleansed of such inhabitants (Judg 2–3 as the paradigm). Those remaining inhabitants became a snare for God's people, and they defiled themselves *and* the land, with the exile as the outcome.

Now it seems that God's people are re-defiling themselves (9:2) and the land (9:11–12). Something radical needs to be done about it. The "holy race" (9:2) reminiscent of the royal priesthood and holy nation in Exodus 19:4–6 and a people holy to the LORD in Deuteronomy 7:6, is polluted, and so is the land. Thus, after the return from exile, a second exodus of sorts (Isa 40; 60:10; 61:4), a new conquest emerges. The expulsion of the women and children represents a re-conquering of the promised land. The forced departure was necessary in the hope of assuaging God's anger. It was a cleansing of the land that would enable them to stay alive there and for the promises of God to be furthered in the life of the community.

Within the broader setting of the restoration of the sanctity of Zion, this mandated solution leading to exclusion is not unlike other situations of exclusion already encountered and understood as acceptable in the book of Ezra.[14] Some descendants without family records were excluded from the priesthood as unclean (2:62). Zerubbabel excludes the enemies of Judah who wanted to help build the temple (4:1–3) because they were not true worshipers of the Lord. And those who had not separated themselves from the unclean practices of their Gentile neighbors were

---

13. There is an interrelationship of holiness, pollution, and removal (see Lev. 18:28).

14. We are not told, however, that these situations involved a covenant and oath.

excluded from celebrating Passover (6:20–21). When Ezra eventually comes on the scene, even the King of Persia counsels him to banish people if they do not obey the law of God and the law of the king (7:26). Thus, the theme of exclusion for the sake of purity and adherence to God's law is not a new theme in the narrative (see Ezra 4:1–3). Separation from that which is unholy was a value from the beginning because of their status as the people of God. In fact, *purity* is becoming a strong marker of identity for the *'am Yahweh* in the postexilic context, along with the givens of land (Zion), traditions (*torah*), and the authority of elders (Moses and David) as mediated by the current leadership. This last point makes the situation all the more poignant, since the leadership itself is compromised through intermarriage alliances. Without these drastic measures the very restoration promised by the prophets is in serious danger.

The proposal at hand in 10:11, then, represents another way one achieves separation. It reflects damage control. Conviction, admission of guilt, and confession lead to action, a changed lifestyle. To be sure, this demonstrates a change in heart. In other words, confession alone was not enough. Ezra delivered the difficult message agreed upon by the leadership. In what follows we learn how the people responded to Ezra's difficult word, one that was bathed in prayer.

**Assembly's response (10:12–15).** The author wastes no time; he breaks the tension and shows that the people responded swiftly to Ezra's command and solution. Their swift response shows awareness, not denial, of their transgression and guilt, and a healthy fear of God's just anger with respect to it (vv. 13–14). They actually believe their reforms will avert God's wrath and more consequences for sin, not an unhealthy motivation for change. With the exception of four people who stood against the idea for unknown reasons (v. 15; the final statement of opposition in this storyline), Ezra gets the surprising but hoped for cooperation evidenced in the unified *and* loud voice of the assembly, "You are right! We must do as you say" (v. 12; see Exod 24:3, 7 for the desire to do what God says). This loud, unified voice should not be glossed over. Rarely does one see such quick admission of wrongdoing in the biblical text. They express admission and confession of guilt and their intention to reform. They are wholeheartedly agreeing to do God's will. Moreover, they are re-identifying God as their God. Probably due to the logistics involved, they ask for the leaders to act for the whole, "until the fierce anger of our God . . . is turned away from us" (10:14).

One cannot help but see their favorable response as an answer to Ezra's continued petitions to God (10:6). This is a visual aid of repentance. Although the people agree to do what was proposed, they offer a procedure that will ensure the best results. The scope of the problem meant the matter would take time.

**Summary (10:16–17).** The final section of chapter 10 closes with another summary or narrative report that the parties involved did what was legislated and that it took them several months

## The Guilty Parties (10:18–44)

THE CHAPTER CONCLUDES RATHER ABRUPTLY with documentary proof of the investigation which consists of a list of approximately one hundred guilty offenders (10:18–44). The names of the guilty parties, those that came forward in confession, are documented, bringing the chapter to an anti-climatic close. The list of names here is not unlike lists elsewhere in Ezra (chs. 2 and 8). The offenders include both clergy and laity: priests (v. 18), Levites (v. 23), musicians and gatekeepers (v. 24), and other Israelites (v. 25).

**Guilty priests (10:18–22).** Sixteen offending priests are noted. At the top of the list was Joshua, the son of Jozadak, the high priest at the time (Haggai 1:1, 12; 2:1). As the representative of God's people, the high priest offered sacrifices on his behalf and on behalf of the entire community. As a spiritual leader, the high priest was held to high standards according to the law. Those following Joshua in the priestly lineup derive from the family of the high priest. Their poor example is now made right. As worship leaders in the community, these priests do two things in particular. We are told they "gave their hands in pledge" and "presented a ram from the flock as a guilt offering" (10:19). To give one's hand in pledge represents a visual demonstration (2 Kgs 10:15; Ezek 17:18) backing up the verbal oath offered earlier (10:5). From the perspective of Old Testament law, God's anger is not appeased and poses a continual threat until a sacrifice is made. Thus, the offending priests confessed their own sins, and, by offering a guilt offering, they were ministering as appropriate in the community for unfaithfulness (Lev 5:14–19). From a narrative perspective, the tension and threat of divine anger is alleviated once a guilt offering for sin takes place by the priests.

**Guilty laity (10:25–43).** The list of offending laity comes next. From the general population of Israelites, noteworthy is the mention of the descendants of Elam who include Mattaniah, Zechariah, Jehiel, Abdi, Jeremoth, and Elijah (10:26). The man who stood up and confessed sin in 10:2 is "Shekaniah son of Jehiel," one of Elam's descendants. He is apparently related, and perhaps the relationship motivated his leadership in the event.

**Summary of the event (10:44).** This verse represents a final summary statement by the author with respect to the events that unfolded beginning in chapter 9: "All these had married foreign women, and some of them had children by these wives."

**Conclusions.** Chapter 10 resolves the tension by providing a solution to the problem articulated in 9:1–2. Ultimately, knowing and doing God's will, based on and discovered in the law, was Ezra's goal for his life and the community, his *raison d'être* (7:10). Getting to that goal demanded appropriate teaching. But given the breech, getting back to adherence of torah required a two-step process, confession and reform. Reform, therefore, entailed a plan of action, realized in this case by the forced departure of foreign wives and their children—a plan conceived by the council of elders in conjunction with a contextualization of the principles of torah. The belief and hope was that this call to repentance, along with the guilt offering for sin, would turn aside God's anger and spare guilty people of further consequences.

The repentance arises as a result of experiencing God's goodness in allowing them to return to the land, rebuild the temple, and restore the law under Persian rule (9:8–9). Their shameful conduct is not acceptable at any time, but especially not in light of the LORD's gracious restoration afforded them. They deserved death and destruction, but God withholds it. The restoration they received is a visual aid of Yahweh's kindness as a restraint from destruction, a kindness that actually led guilty people to repentance. In this way, the picture painted of restoration in Ezra is not only a series of events (i.e., a return to the land, temple rebuilt, law restored). Restoration reflects a change of heart. Restoration is ongoing and achieved through conviction or mourning for sin and a confession of wrongdoing, followed by radical, visible reforms in the life of an individual or community because of one's continual awareness of God's just and gracious character. This was the nature of Shekaniah's hope, a change of heart to make things right with God. One could argue that chapters 9–10 together paint a picture of "God's kindness [leading people] to repentance" (Rom 2:4).

THE CONFESSIONS LEADING TO ACTION OFFERED by Ezra and the people in chapters 9–10 encapsulate ideas of repentance and restoration expressed previously in the book of Ezekiel. Ezekiel the priest, like Ezra the priest, understood that knowing and doing God's will based on Torah was the goal. A breach of unfaithfulness that required the exile also required that Ezekiel's exilic community living in Babylon get back to Torah. This demanded a process of confession and reform.

In that context the exiles were exhorted on three occasions to turn (Ezek 14:6; 18:23, 30, 32; 33:11), to repent even though the judgment of 586 BC was inevitable. But how was Ezekiel's audience to understand this? Indeed, the scroll that Ezekiel ingested promised nothing but lamentation, mourning, and woe (Ezek 2:10; 3:2). The scroll guaranteed, along with all of Ezekiel's prophecies and dramatic acts, that the judgment of God could not be reversed nor deferred any longer. In other words, the people could not alter their future. What effect would the repeated messages of inevitable judgment, together with calls to repent, have on his audience? It would affect the hearers by giving *them* the possibility to change. God wanted changed hearts even though a change of consequences was not possible.

Moreover, this irreversible and irrevocable judgment would render repentance impossible *if*, indeed, repentance was a precondition for the restoration afforded to Israel. Repentance, however, was a consequence of the restoration afforded to Israel. By means of the calls to repentance, what is primarily emphasized is the exiles' guilt, an acknowledgement of wrongdoing that was meant to produce a godly shame. Being ashamed was not the precursor to the restorative acts of Yahweh but the consequences of it (Ezek 16:54, 66; 36:31–32; 43:10–11; see also Jer 31:8–9). In other words, God shows Ezekiel's audience a vision of restoration in the hope that knowing God's future goodness would lead them to have a present change in heart, to mourn and weep over their misconduct in advance of restoration. But hard-hearted people were incapable of mourning and coming under conviction. Ezekiel becomes a mourner in their midst (Ezek 3:2, 14–15).

In the fuller description of restoration predicted in Ezekiel 34–39, the stress falls on the efforts and acts of Yahweh, who will give his people the power to do what he commands (Ezek 34:11–16, 25–31). Restoration extends from the LORD, not the people. In Ezekiel, Yahweh will take the initiative to cleanse those who belong to him (Ezek 36:24–38). God will restore the people because they are made in his image. Ezekiel makes it clear that, although human activity caused the exile, only divine activity could cause the return and restoration (Ezek 37:1–14). Yahweh alone will do it (Ezek 37:18–28). It is a picture of God's future kindness leading people to repentance. In other words, although 586 BC was inevitable, the visions of restoration show that God will not wipe them out as they deserve. The heart of true spiritual transformation is repentance from past conduct (Ezek 36:31). Repentance, as articulated by Ezekiel, was a part of restoration.[15] Ezekiel anticipates, in part, what we see unfolding in Ezra's generation.

Therefore, the confession and subsequent repentance and reform that unfolds in Ezra 10 comes from their current context of experiencing God's goodness to restore. It also stems from the hope that God will withhold more of his just judgment. God graciously restored their markers of identity, and the fact they are alive as a remnant testifies to it (Ezra 9:8–9). Ezra's prayer in chapter 9 emphasizes their guilt against the backdrop of God's mercy to restore. That prayer is an acknowledgement of wrongdoing that produced in Ezra and the people a godly shame (9:6, 10; 10:1–2, 12). Their lived-out experience of restoration brought Ezra's audience to a realization about their conduct and the need to reform in light of God's mercy. Likewise, their lived-out experience of judgment via exile brought Ezra's audience to a realization about their conduct and the need to reform in light of God's justice.

How could they not weep and be ashamed? Ezra and the community do come under conviction of sin, recognize guilt, and mourn their sin! Ezra's audience does what Ezekiel's audience was not capable of doing. Although their repentance was a consequence of Israel's restoration and an awareness of God's mercy, they were acutely aware of God's justice and their potential demise because God by no means clears the guilty

15. As noticed by other commentators on Ezekiel, there are several similarities between the transformation described in Ezekiel (34:25–31; 36:8–11; 37:26–27) and Lev 26:4–13. The difference is that the conditional introduction (Lev 26:3) to the blessings described in Lev 26:4–13 is not found in Ezekiel. See D. I. Block, *The Book of Ezekiel Chapters 25–48*. NICOT (Grand Rapids, Eerdmans, 1998); Iain M. Duguid, *Ezekiel*, NIVAC (Grand Rapids: Zondervan, 1999).

(Exod 34:7). God's people continued to be covenant breakers and have not changed their behavior from former days; God's kindness was leading guilty people to repentance, to have a change in heart and to amend their ways (Rom 2:4). Thus, not only do the events and the outcome that unfold in chapters 9–10 cause us to look back to the prophet Ezekiel, but they also prepare us for the hope that lies ahead in redemptive history.

On the one hand, Ezra 10 ends, albeit anticlimactically, with a list of the guilty parties acquitted with an appropriate guilt offering. On the other hand, it leaves the reader hanging. How does God deal with ongoing unfaithfulness to his word? People continued to break God's law regardless of having the law in their midst, such as Nehemiah will have to deal with (Neh 13:23–31). Are people to hold their breath wondering if or when God's anger will consume them? Are human efforts and plans enough to avert God's wrath? The exile, as God's judgment, did not fix or exhaust God's angers; likewise, neither the exile nor the return, showing God's mercy, fix the people's unfaithfulness. The answer to the ongoing sin-guilt cycle, therefore, needed a more permanent solution.

The book of Ezra keeps the reader hanging because it does not fulfill the grandiose restoration as promised by Ezekiel (chs. 34–38) and other prophets such as Isaiah (40–66). Restoration in Ezra concerns the return of God's people to the land, the rebuilt temple, and the reestablishment of the law. Restoration in Ezra also concerns conviction and confession of sin followed by a reformed life—and *even* a guilt offering to atone for sin! In the absence of a godly leader like Ezra, how does conviction and confession of sin, followed by reform, come to individuals and the community? As good as all this was, Ezra's reforms could not deliver; indeed, they did not deliver (see Nehemiah 13:23–31). Even the prophet Malachi, whose message follows Nehemiah chronologically, deals with unfaithfulness to God on account of marriages to foreign women (Mal 2:10–11). Malachi affirms and upholds the necessity of separation between the holy and unholy based on legislation in the Pentateuch (Deut 7:2–4, 6). As with Ezra-Nehemiah, threats to the sanctity of Zion must be handled, so the prophet warns accordingly. In addition, Malachi rebukes some who were divorcing their true covenantal partners (Mal 2:13–16), a sanctified union. Such an act God will not tolerate. Ezra, therefore, points the reader forward to the New Testament, where restoration reaches its zenith. Ezra prepares us for the reality of God's kindness that Jesus demonstrated at the cross, that leads people to conviction, confession, and a reformed life (Rom 2:4; 2 Cor. 7:9–10). In this manner "there is still *hope* for Israel" (Ezra 10:2, emphasis added).

THERE IS STILL HOPE FOR GOD'S GUILTY PEOPLE. The wrongdoing in our lives clearly makes us guilty, but how do we handle both the ongoing wrongdoings and the feelings of deep guilt associated with it? Perhaps we handle it by harsh judgment and condemnation of ourselves and of others? Some of us prefer our own rigid works righteousness to appease a guilty conscious. If you find yourself working, it might suggest a self-reliance and not a God-reliance.

Ultimately, we must look to the cross where *our true hope is found*. Guilty people anger God, to be sure. But we do not have to fear God's wrath, anger or punishment. We certainly do not need to be gripped by guilt. Why? The cross definitively confronts our situation. It deals with the rift in the relationship. The cross is the great image of God's justice that deals with the sin-guilt cycle. Our guilt leads God to intervene, venting his wrath as he pours it out on Jesus, not us. Jesus bears the penalty by experiencing divine abandonment from the Father, an exile of sorts and the ultimate covenantal curse. God's wrath is satisfied once and for all. At the cross, a permanent guilt offering was made on our behalf. The great exchange takes place, our guilt for Jesus's righteousness. Guilty people are now pronounced righteous!

Furthermore, continually guilty people can stand before a holy God. John assures us that we now "have an advocate with the Father" (1 John 2:1). And "If we confess our sins, he is faithful and just and will forgive us our sins and purify us from all unrighteousness" (1 John 1:9). All human attempts to deal with guilt and the associated uncleanness fall short in light of the cross. Because God's goodness and kindness are demonstrated to us in that God withholds the wrath we deserve (Rom 2:2–4), it propels people to have a change of heart. This is how God's kindness leads people to amend their ways repeatedly; it melts our hearts, making us want to reform for the *right* reasons. This is how the cross is an optic of God's kindness leading people to repentance. Imagine guilt-free living—this is God's goal for you and me.

The cross is the greatest image of God's *hesed*-based forgiveness remedying our inability to obey God's law, our refusal of the living Word.

Jesus's blood cleanses us from all sin and unrighteousness (1 John 1:9); in so doing, he saves us by performing heart surgery. He fills us with the new life of his Spirit, who empowers us for holy living, so that we might enjoy his promises forever in a *renewed relationship*. At the cross the problem is fixed permanently, and guilty people can stand as righteous before a holy God because of his justice, mercy, and grace. There is *still* hope for God's guilty people.

In practical terms we must listen to counsel and take seriously the encouragement to confess our sins and make changes in our lives, to turn around in accordance with wise counsel but especially with God's will revealed in his word. What we essentially are wanting to do is confess and repent in order to avoid further difficult consequences, but explicitly to get our relationship with God back on track. Although the passage sanctions divorce, it really is a sanction to do the will of God. And getting back to the will of God will likely require confession and serious reform in one's life; in this case it means separation, such as divorce. The passage teaches us how to address sin not directly found in the Bible. This requires human counsel and the ability to extract principles from God's word, so that we enable others to return to the will of God and restore their relationship with him. It requires an agreed upon plan of action by all parties to move in the direction of doing God's will.

Two questions naturally emerge from this hard passage in Ezra. First, should Christians with unbelieving spouses and unbelieving children follow the example of Ezra's contemporaries? The New Testament provides a guardrail against such conduct, particularly Paul's advice to the Corinthians (1 Cor 7:1–24). For those in Corinth who thought it was more spiritual to be single, Paul warns married people *not* to divorce an unbelieving spouse. His rationale pertains to a sanctification attributed to unbelieving spouses and children by virtue of marriage with a believer. Rather than contaminate the believer as in the Old Testament administration, the reverse is true here in the New Testament.[16]

---

16. In the Gospels uncleanness comes from *within* and that which is in a person's own heart (e.g., Matt 15:18) rather than external manifestations of ritual uncleanness (e.g., Lev 15; cf. Matt 9:20–22; Mark 5:25–34; Luke 8:43–48). The holy makes the unclean holy, by faith in the one who makes us holy through his perfect sacrifice. See David Garland, "Mishnah Zabim and Mark 5:21–6:6a: The Rules on Purity," in *Reading Mark in Context: Jesus and Second Temple Judaism*, ed. B. C. Blackwell, J.K. Goodrich, and J. Maston (Grand Rapids: Zondervan 2018).

The believer makes the unbelieving spouse holy or set apart. Paul does not fully explain how such a sanctification takes place in the union nor in the life of the unbelieving spouse. What he does, though, is offer hope that the union is not unholy and that divorce need not be an option (1 Cor 7:14). He also offers hope that the believer could potentially influence the unbeliever toward a relationship with God. Paul highlights the positive of such circumstances. Thus, to do God's will means not to exile oneself from an unbelieving partner. Perhaps it also means to pray for the salvation of your loved one (1 Cor 7:16).

Popular materials such as the Bible Project video series on Ezra-Nehemiah rush to condemn the action of Ezra. In doing so, they entirely miss the requirement of holiness for worship. In Ezra's context, the requirements of holiness pertaining to worship demanded immediate action and separation from any contact with pagan worship. It was clearly a contextually-driven (and exceptional) interpretation of torah in order to protect the newly-restored sanctity of Zion. The precedent occurs with the destruction of life by the Levites at Horeb (Exod 32:25–29) and the action of Phinheas at Baal Peor (see Neh 13:1–3). Pauline ethics in 1 Corinthians 7 evidently discourage this course of action. Nevertheless, the warning against being willfully in fellowship with unbelievers, including marriage, remains in effect for the new covenant. Paul warns strongly not to be yoked intentionally with a non-believer and highlights the negative of such circumstances (2 Cor 6:14; see further discussion in the commentary on Nehemiah 13:23–31). Put simply: do not willfully marry an unbeliever in the first place, but if you have, do not divorce them since God is able to sanctify this union through the believer's faith.

The second question that arises from this hard passage in Ezra pertains to those who were sent away. The text in Ezra remains silent about their welfare. In trying to answer this question, we first need to remember that the people of Yahweh are very much a minority in a Persian province. The wives and children would be returned to the majority culture and would not necessarily be left without care. In this regard, the precedent can be found on two occasions, with the implied promise of provision for those sent off. The first example is evidently general, but still speaks to the situation. When Hagar and Ishmael are "sent away" (Gen 21:14), the child stayed with his mother after a divorce and they were provided for. The second example seems perhaps more contextually helpful regarding the prospect of provision for those estranged. In the book of Ruth, after

Naomi loses her husband and two sons, she urges her daughters-in-law to return home to Moab, to their "mother's home" with the intent of finding other husbands (Ruth 1:8). Although death, rather than divorce, caused the separation of the wives with their husbands, Naomi's words indicate deep and natural ties to their homeland. Orpah and Ruth still had a future and should hope in God's kindness to provide for them (see also Exod 21:2–4). Orpah remains in Moab. Perhaps Ruth allows us to imagine that something similar could have unfolded during Ezra's time with the non-Yahwist spouses and children after their forced separation.

Finally, human attempts at averting God's wrath and further consequences for sin are natural and needed and can derive from a healthy fear of the LORD. Confession, consultation, praying and fasting, and actions to fix things are the right things to do. When such actions are guided and informed by God's Word, they are honorable. While we need an action plan that realigns us relationally with God and his will, one must have a correct and deep understanding of the cross first and foremost, otherwise our efforts become works righteousness. Therefore, the cross must always be before us as Jesus' work of righteousness on our behalf. Restoring our relationship with God means receiving, not rejecting, *his* merciful offer to fix the problem, to realign the relationship. He puts us right with him and this, in turn, changes our hearts. There is *still* hope for God's guilty people.

### A Personal Story

THERE I WAS, AT THE TENDER AGE OF SIXTEEN, in the back seat of a police car with my best friend Lisa! We told our parents we were going all-night bowling and that we would be locked in from midnight to 6:00 a.m., hours not acceptable to be on the road with a junior permit. They had nothing to worry about. However, we had no intentions of going all-night bowling. Instead, we had a plan in place to go to a local disco and dance the night away with some school friends. Armed with our fake IDs and our parents' trust, off we went.

We made it past the bouncer successfully; our fake IDs worked! Now we could settle in and have some good, clean fun and dance. Lisa and I danced and then sat down together. We sheepishly decided to order a drink: our first-ever adult beverage. This was quite a daring move for two teenage girls not prone to such mischief! Our drinks came, and no sooner had my lips tasted the forbidden liquid than I had a tap on the shoulder. "Finally, somebody wanted to dance with me," I thought! I turned in acknowledgement of the tap and, to my puzzlement and surprise, it was an older, unattractive gentleman wearing a suit who, as it turned out, clearly did not want to escort me to the dance floor. Instead, he wanted to escort me swiftly and quietly out of the building and into a police car for underage drinking! With my eyes wide, I turned to Lisa, and the same thing was happening to her.

The establishment—notorious for allowing under-aged folks in, not just to dance, but to drink—was raided the evening Lisa and I chose for a girls' night out! The policeman at the entrance of the building got our names and then required that we sit in his car. There we were, my best friend and I, my partner in crime, caught and guilty as charged.

The policeman entered the car and, at that moment, Lisa burst into tears, worried about what our trusting parents would say and do. I, on the other hand, not a crier by nature, kept my cool. I boldly knocked on the window separating us "criminals" in the back from the policeman in the front, waiting for him to open it so I could ask, "Sir, what are you going to do with us?" Seeing that Lisa was very emotional, he was kind but firm: we are going to the station, writing up a report, and then calling your parents. Lisa's cries turned into shouts, "No, no, please don't call our parents, I beg you!" I quickly jumped in with my own plea for mercy, "We told our parents that we were going all-night bowling, my dad just had an operation, sir please, please don't call our parents! We will sit up all night at the local diner and go home in the morning after 6:00 a.m." By this time, we had arrived at the station. The report was written up, all things checked out, and, by some strange turn of events, he agreed not to call our parents.

The policeman drove us back to the establishment to get our car and followed us to the 24-hour diner, and there we sat in utter disbelief about the turn of events that evening. Although the police officer was merciful to us, he did warn that *justice* would be administered in the form of a fine forthcoming in the mail. We sat up all night drinking coffee, plotting further how to continue to hide the evidence from our parents. As soon as 6:00 a.m. rolled around, we left the restaurant and returned to our homes, exhausted physically and mentally because of the ordeal. We were thankful that although we imposed a rift in our relationship with our parents by breaking the law, lying, and covering it up, it seemed we were able to repair the problem on our own. Essentially, we were happy that we could keep our solid relationship with our parents intact, but especially thankful that we were able to spare our loving, trusting, and committed parents the heartache of knowing about our mischief . . . or so we thought.

I was guilty and quite ashamed of my conduct with Lisa. Clearly, my goal was to hide, lie, and deny, to spare my father the heartache of my misconduct and myself of his wrath. I was unaware, however, of what still lay ahead with the passing of a few weeks. The phone rang, and it was Lisa. I could barely understand her words as she was sobbing! "It is all over," she cried, "it is all over! You have to tell your dad. My mom found out!" Although the police officer was *merciful* to us the night we got caught by not giving us what we deserved in calling our parents, he warned us that *justice/consequences* would be administered as we would get what we deserved in the form of a fine, forthcoming in the mail. Lisa and I had a perfect plan in place to deal with this inevitability. We could easily retrieve the mail before our parents because it was delivered to our homes, like clockwork, not long after school let out. However, the mail came early this particular day while we were still at school. Lisa's mom retrieved the mail before Lisa was able to. In it was the notice of a nice, juicy fine: clear, undeniable evidence of our guilt. We were found out.

My hand was now forced, by the weight of the evidence stacked against me, to tell my dad. Surely, I couldn't have Lisa's parents tell my dad, nor could I let my partner in crime go it alone. That would be even worse. I mustered up courage and strength and sat down with my dad for a "little talk." I can remember his response as if it were yesterday, instead of 36 years ago! He lay on the couch, still recovering from surgery, while I sat beside him. He just listened to the report of my misconduct without any show of emotions. Not even the amount of the fine, $250, revealed his sentiments. I finished my forced confession and, as I did, he lifted his big, rough, construction hand and gently stroked my face. "Honey," he said, "I wish you would have come to me sooner." "That's it," I thought to myself. "These things can happen," he continued. "But honey, I would never reject you even if you came home pregnant! I will always love you no matter what you do. Now go and get the checkbook for me and let's take care of this thing once and for all!" He withheld wrath and instead wrote a check. This is mercy and grace!

I feared rejection and punishment from my father. I just knew it would be a barrier in our relationship. How could he possibly respond this way?

He fixed the rift in the relationship that I caused. He didn't require one penny of me for the fine. He offered not one ounce of condemnation. I clearly didn't deserve to be treated this way: my confession was forced, my guilt and shame undeniable, and I didn't really feel contrite because of my stubborn nature. I was just bummed that I got caught and had to tell him. Yet I got what I didn't deserve! He extended mercy and grace to me, an undeserved extension to be sure. That's when my own emotions kicked in. His kindness (and lack of anger) warmed my heart. His unconditional love and unwavering, staunch loyalty to me in the father-daughter relationship assured my heart that everything was going to be all right. He reached out and rescued me *even* in my guilt! I got what I didn't deserve. He restored the relationship. In the end it is all about relationships. This *is* mercy and grace!

Looking back on this incident, it never occurred to me to question, much less reject, my dad's love and kind offer. It would have been crazy, even arrogant for me to have said, "Oh, no thank you, Daddy, you don't have to do this for me." The fact of the matter is that, although I had some money, I didn't have enough to cover the fine. It would, however, have been reasonable for me to have said, let me work some and then pay you back; it would have eased the guilt! In fact, he put me in such a position that I couldn't resist his warm, generous, no-strings-attached, gracious invitation!

Although some still do, out of arrogance and self-sufficiency or stiffed-neckness, it is just as crazy for us to resist God's warm, generous, no-strings-attached invitation to know him and experience him through Jesus! When we blow it before God, we want to ease the guilt. We think it is reasonable to offer him a little assistance, so we often turn to works righteousness. But this doesn't work! The only thing that works to alleviate the guilt is allowing ourselves to be embraced by his warm, generous, no-strings-attached mercy and grace. The only thing that works is knowing that his grace and mercy are chasing us even today, that God relentlessly pursues us for relationship! In the end it is *all* about relationships.

# Nehemiah 1:1–11

[1] The words of Nehemiah son of Hakaliah:

In the month of Kislev in the twentieth year, while I was in
the citadel of Susa, [2] Hanani, one of my brothers, came from
Judah with some other men, and I questioned them about the
Jewish remnant that had survived the exile, and also about
Jerusalem.

[3] They said to me, "Those who survived the exile and are
back in the province are in great trouble and disgrace. The
wall of Jerusalem is broken down, and its gates have been
burned with fire."

[4] When I heard these things, I sat down and wept. For
some days I mourned and fasted and prayed before the God
of heaven. [5] Then I said:

> "Lord, the God of heaven, the great and awesome
> God, who keeps his covenant of love with those who
> love him and keep his commandments, [6] let your ear
> be attentive and your eyes open to hear the prayer
> your servant is praying before you day and night for
> your servants, the people of Israel. I confess the sins we
> Israelites, including myself and my father's family, have
> committed against you. [7] We have acted very wickedly
> toward you. We have not obeyed the commands,
> decrees and laws you gave your servant Moses.
>
> [8] "Remember the instruction you gave your servant
> Moses, saying, 'If you are unfaithful, I will scatter you
> among the nations, [9] but if you return to me and obey
> my commands, then even if your exiled people are at
> the farthest horizon, I will gather them from there and
> bring them to the place I have chosen as a dwelling for
> my Name.'
>
> [10] "They are your servants and your people, whom
> you redeemed by your great strength and your mighty
> hand. [11] Lord, let your ear be attentive to the prayer

of this your servant and to the prayer of your servants who delight in revering your name. Give your servant success today by granting him favor in the presence of this man."

I was cupbearer to the king.

## The Third Return: Nehemiah Restores the Walls and Sanctity of Zion (Neh 1:1–13:31)

### Nehemiah's Prayer (1:1–11)

**THE SETTING (1:1–4).** Nehemiah, the person responsible for this account ("word," v. 1; cf. 1 Chr 29:29),[1] is designated in the shortest possible patronymic, "son of Hakaliah."[2] Unlike Ezra, who receives full tribal and patronymic credentials (Ezra 7:1–6), Nehemiah's are surprisingly terse, but no less potent, since this identifies him as Jewish (i.e., non-Persian) from the outset. Beyond the patrimonial designation, we do not know what Hakaliah's specific affiliation is, though a priestly or, more likely, Judean background can be surmised on account of his ancestors' burial grounds in Jerusalem (Neh 2:3). The designation "brother" in 1:2 may be in the sense of brethren (RSV), but on the basis of Nehemiah 7:2 where Nehemiah singles out Hanani as "my brother," the most reasonable assumption appears to view Hanani as part of Nehemiah's immediate family,[3] which has the advantage to bolster further his Jewish identity.[4]

The text also signals Nehemiah's high-ranking status at the Persian court (made explicit in verse 11, "cupbearer to the king") by the way Nehemiah emphasizes (*'ani hayiti*, "I myself") his location in Susa and, more specifically, in the "citadel" (v. 1), a technical term (Aramaic loanword *birah*) referring to the royal enclosure at Susa, which included the Apadana (Old Persian loanword, cf. Dan 11:45, ESV "palatial") and the

1. For questions of authorship and genre, see Introduction.

2. Nehemiah seems to be a common name among the exiles, e.g., Neh 3:16.

3. Pierre Briant, *From Cyrus to Alexander: A History of the Persian Empire* (Winona Lake, IN: Eisenbrauns, 2002), 585.

4. See also the reference to the sin of his "father's house" in 1:7, which could be an oblique reference to his brother.

Acropolis to the south. These two areas together represented a platform some twenty meters high and thirteen hectares in surface (= 2.25 American football fields), built during the reign of Darius I and in use during the reigns of subsequent Achaemenid rulers, including Xerxes[5] and now Artaxerxes I. Because of his presence at the center of Persian political power, Nehemiah sees fit to establish the chronology of events on the basis of the reigning king, Artaxerxes I (444 BC; see 2:1 where it is still the "twentieth year" of Artaxerxes).[6] Nevertheless, in keeping with Nehemiah's own desire to identify this historical account as Jewish (written in Hebrew), the account still preserves the Jewish names for the months ("Kislev,"1:1; "Nisan," 2:1).

The text generalizes the setting in what we know to be the cold season ("Kislev" = November-December; see Ezra 10:9) without specifying any day.[7] However, as the narrative unfolds, the noted chronology of events bears special significance. The waiting period represents a longer period (from Kislev to Nisan = as much as a five-month period)[8] than the actual rebuilding of the wall (less than two months, Neh 6:15). Thus, the process appears slow at first (with time spent waiting and praying), but once the decree of the king comes (Neh 2:8), events take place at a fast rate of speed in real time. In narrative time, apart from the indication that Nehemiah prayed for "some days" (1:4), details preceding the meeting with the king in chapter 2 are scant, which further emphasizes the significance of Nehemiah's prayer in chapter 1.

The plot of the book is wrapped in the report from "Judah," that is, the province of *Yehud* (Aramaic for "Judah"), provided by Hanani, "one of my brothers," and "some other men" (v. 2). We do not know who initiated the meeting since the text omits these background details. On the basis of

---

5. The phrase "Susa, the Citadel" occurs no less than eight times in the intrigue of Esther. Attesting to the scope of the structure (in addition to the archaeological context both at Susa and at Persepolis), Esther details that a larger number of her people's enemies (500) were eliminated within the *birah* (9:6, 12). For a brief summary of the settlement history of Susa, see Holly Pittman, "Susa," in *The Oxford Encyclopedia of Archeology in the Near East*, ed. Eric M. Meyers (New York: Oxford University Press, 1997), 106–10.

6. See Williamson, *Ezra, Nehemiah*, 169–70.

7. Susa is located in Khuzistan, where summer temperatures were extreme in antiquity, as they are today (e.g., August 19, 2015 at 6pm, the temperatures were 115F/46C). See also W. C. Kaiser and P. D. Wegner's discussion on the chronology of Nehemiah in *A History of Israel*, rev. ed. (Nashville: Broadman and Holman, 2016): 604–6.

8. Kislev, Tebeth, Shebat, Adar, Nisan.

Hanani's role as a landowner (Neh 5) and principal official in Jerusalem (Neh 7:2), he may have taken the initiative and sought an audience (they "came from Judah," 1:2) with what was probably the highest ranking Jewish official in the Persian court at the time. Or perhaps Nehemiah commissioned his blood brother Hanani for a fact-finding mission.[9]

Nehemiah asks a pointed two-part question: first, regarding the "Jewish remnant that had survived the exile" (v. 2), which could refer to the community that has lived in Yehud since the Babylonian exiles (605 BC, 597 BC, 586 BC), the group that returned under Zerubbabel and Joshua in 539 BC, or the group led by Ezra who recently returned (458 BC). A straightforward and reasonable answer to this issue is that perhaps Nehemiah has all groups in view, that is, all surviving Jews in Yehud.[10] Second, the query focuses on the actual city of "Jerusalem" (v. 2). The response on the part of these emissaries from Zion directly answers these specific questions: the survivors of the exile in the "province" (Aramaic loanword, *medinah* of Yehud) are "in great trouble and disgrace" (v. 3). The language of "trouble and disgrace" conjures up the Deuteronomic background of curses (see Deut 28:15–68). In Yahwistic jurisprudence, no one gets into this kind of trouble apart from covenantal disobedience and rebellion. The devastating news that the city of Jerusalem is in ruins ("broken down") and, worse yet, "its gates have been burned with fire" (v. 3) recalls the sinister images of burning cities typically at home in the preexilic period (Isa 1:7) and fits squarely within the Sinaitic covenant equation of judgment-destruction (Deut 28:52). Disloyalty to Yahweh results in foreign invasion and exile.

Questions remain on the chronology of events with respect to this report. It could refer to the destruction of the city at the hands of the Babylonians in 586 BC.[11] This idea can be countered on the basis that Nehemiah must have known the city had been destroyed in 586 BC and, more importantly, that the temple had been rebuilt during the first return (515 BC). Williamson places the description of the city in flames to a time that is contemporary to Nehemiah but which precedes

---

9. While Hanani does not reach the fame of the like of Mordechai in the storyline of Esther, the report he provides is nevertheless the catalyst that precipitates the crisis.

10. Williamson, *Ezra-Nehemiah*, 171.

11. Karl F. Keil and Sophia Taylor, *The Books of Ezra, Nehemiah, and Esther* (Sydney, Australia: Wentworth, 2016), 156–59.

the twentieth year of Artaxerxes.[12] The time that is specifically in view relates to the account in Ezra 4:12, which describes that the city's reconstruction of its walls had been forcefully interrupted and cancelled until further notice by King Artaxerxes himself (see Ezra 4:21, 23 and *commentary* on Ezra 4 above). Accordingly, it would explain the extraordinary reaction by Nehemiah: He "wept," "mourned," "fasted and prayed" (Neh 10:4). Both options appear possible a priori. However, attempts to single out a specific moment seems to be missing the larger point as revealed by the content of Nehemiah's prayer: he is petitioning Yahweh to complete the restoration of Zion, begun in 539 BC as announced by the prophets, that is now under serious threat. Therefore, this regress report (breached walls and burnt gates) could very well encompass the tragedy of 586 BC *as well as* more recent setbacks, which are clearly documented in the summary of opposition to the rebuilding of Zion in Ezra 4.[13] Viewed in this light, the cause of Nehemiah's deep despair stems principally from the fact that the restoration had not been *completed*. This, in turn, highlights the profound significance of Nehemiah's prayer. He is pleading with the God of "heaven" (e.g., Ezra 7:23) not only to complete the restoration of Zion (begun 539–515) but also to reverse the action of "this man" (Neh 1:11) that stopped the rebuilding of the walls of Jerusalem in more recent times. Without divine intervention, Yahweh's program of redemption remains on life support, as it were.

Verse 4 breaks down Nehemiah's reaction to the report into three parts. As soon as he heard the news ("these things"), he "sat down." This immediate reaction is then followed by the sequence of the two verbs, weeping and mourning,[14] that are temporally modified by "days" (NIV "some days"). The context suggests the idea of many days, since the next chronological marker is found in 2:1: "in the month of Nisan," some four months later. Significantly, Nehemiah continues to be in some emotional discomfort in the presence of the king (2:2), which is clearly connected to his disposition described in 1:4. Thus, Nehemiah's formal time of mourning lasted for an extended period. The third dimension to the

---

12. Williamson, *Ezra, Nehemiah*, 169–70.

13. See Lisbeth S. Fried, "The Artaxerxes Correspondence of Ezra 4, Nehemiah's Wall, and Persian Provincial Administration," in *Go Out and Study the Land (Judges 18:2)*, ed. A. M. Maeir, J. Magness, and L. Schiffman (Leiden: Brill, 2011), 35–57.

14. Examples of mourning: Gen. 37:34; Ezra 10:6; Neh 8:9; Isa 66:10; Ezek 7:9, 27; Dan 10:2.

bad news is framed as an ongoing action in the Hebrew, "I was fasting and praying" (NIV "fasted and prayed," v. 4), that signals Nehemiah retained a posture of fasting and praying during his self-imposed season of mourning. In this request, he is not unlike Ezekiel, who was called by Yahweh to mourn for the destruction of Jerusalem (Ezek 7:9; 27). Thus, we should view Nehemiah's prayer as a formal and brief synopsis of his prayer journal during this intensive and lengthy time of seeking the "God of heaven" (Neh 1:5) rather than a more detailed and comprehensive account, as in the case of other postexilic prayers (Ezra 9, Dan 9, Neh 9). A noted similarity with other postexilic prayers includes the disposition of contrite repentance with the sometimes-added garb of a mourner—sackcloth and ashes (Dan 9:3) or torn clothing (Ezra 9:3, 5)—which Nehemiah probably could not emulate given his responsibilities at the court. In addition to its brevity, Nehemiah's petition (that also includes confession, as in the case of Ezra 9 and Dan 9) contains no substantial historical dimension (as in Neh 9). Instead, Nehemiah focuses on interceding with Yahweh to act upon his promises, which would result in Nehemiah obtaining "success" and "favor in the presence of" (Neh 1:11) Artaxerxes in light of his recent call to stop the rebuilding of the walls and Jerusalem. What Nehemiah is asking is nothing short of a supernatural intervention to sway the heart and change the mind of his boss, for the resumption of the restoration of Zion begun under Cyrus, continued by Darius, and now under serious threat.

**The prayer (1:5–11).** The prayer's brevity should not be construed as theologically shallow. The theological background to the prayer is anchored in the covenant at Sinai and the Deuteronomic promises of blessings and curses premised upon loyalty/disloyalty of the members of the covenant community. The composition itself borrows vocabulary from the prayer of Daniel 9, Deuteronomy (chs. 7, 9, and 30), the prayer of Solomon in 1 Kings 8:23–53, and the redemption story of the exodus with elements of Moses's intercessory prayer in Exodus 32.

By attaching the familiar "God of Heaven" to Yahweh (NIV "Lord"; Neh 1:5), Nehemiah's invocation anchors the prayer to the Sinaitic revelation of God to Moses (Exod 6:2–3)[15] and thereby sets the theological context for the rest of the prayer. The emphatic vocative "O" in

---

15. See the classic essay by J. Alec Motyer, *The Revelation of the Divine Name* (London: Tyndale, 1959).

the original draws further attention to the fact that the covenantal God of the Hebrews is being addressed. When Nehemiah closes the prayer and returns to the vocative "O Lord" (NIV "Lord") in verse 11, he has switched to the designation *Adonai* (Lord), which further signals how important the appeal to Yahweh is at the outset of the prayer.

Modifying "LORD" (v. 5) the compound adverbial sentence "great and awesome God, who keeps his covenant of love with those who love him and obey his commandments" is borrowed from Daniel's own prayer in a previous generation (Dan 9:4), which is itself drawn from the Sinaitic context (Deut 7:21; see also Exod 20:6 and, especially, Exod 34:5–7). As such, the designation forms the backbone of the relationship Yahweh forged with his people, from the days of Israel's creation as the people of Yahweh in the Exodus narrative. "Love" is linked to the idea of *hesed* (see Exod 34:5–7), one of the most meaningful terms to describe Yahweh's character in the Old Testament. "Covenant of love" (Neh 1:5, NIV) should be read as "Yahweh who keeps the covenant *and hesed*" (author's translation; emphasis added). By singling out *hesed*, Nehemiah wishes to appeal to Yahweh's divine favor and forgiveness as revealed within the context of the golden calf narrative (Exod 32–34) and follows in the footsteps of many preexilic prophets (e.g., Jonah 4:2). This appeal to *hesed* gives Nehemiah the boldness to petition Yahweh for the matters that are on his heart and mind.

Verse 6a, "Let your ears be attentive," provides a neat structural bracket and serves as introduction and conclusion to the petition as a whole (see v. 11). The anthropomorphic imagery of "ears" and "eyes" evokes the Exodus context where Yahweh "saw" and "heard" the cry of the Israelites when they were slaves in Egypt (Exod 2:24–25), but it particularly evokes the Solomonic prayer of dedication to the temple in 1 Kings 8:22–53.[16] The repeated language of "servant" (vv. 6 [2x], 7, 8, 10, 11 [2x]) bears some significance as it helps us understand the way Nehemiah perceives his own intercessory ministry in a lineage of prophetic mediators that can be traced back to no other than Moses himself, Yahweh's servant (Josh 1:1). Furthermore, by designating the postexilic escapees Yahweh's "servants," Nehemiah's rhetoric also mirrors

16. Klaus Baltzer, "Moses Servant of God and the Servants: Text and Tradition in the Prayer of Nehemiah (Neh 1:5–11)," in *The Future of Early Christianity*, ed. Birger A. Pearson (Philadelphia: Fortress, 1991), 125–29.

Moses by calling upon the LORD to remember the identity of the people (Exod 32:11, "your people") which will, in turn, cause Yahweh to act according to his steadfast love/*hesed*.

Nehemiah also invokes the reality that the exiles are in fact "the people of Israel" (1:6), even though there are really only two tribes left, along with the Levites. By appealing to the unity of Israel, Nehemiah taps into a common theme in postexilic literature that seeks to restore the image of the covenant people of God (e.g., the genealogies of 1 Chronicles and Neh 8 below). The theme of identity as the "people of Israel" defines them as apart from the Persian Empire: these are people who belong to another Great King, Yahweh, who will remember his promise to his people and restore them. In this prayer, again, not unlike Moses in Exodus 32 (and Solomon in 1 Kgs 8), Nehemiah reminds Yahweh of his promises (see commentary on 1:8 below). The adverbial merism "day and night" is a common language in the Psalms (e.g., Ps 1:2) and reinforces the persistent nature of his prayers from the time of hearing the news to the time of his next meeting with Artaxerxes in chapter 2.

Verse 6b's "I confess" begins the actual content of Nehemiah's confession of sins for the nation, for himself, and for his "father's family" (*bet 'ab*). While it does not develop the specific nature of the sin, Nehemiah assumes that the bad report from Hanani means the people have sinned and incurred God's wrath with the resulting catastrophic results. To bring about restoration, confession is essential in the Mosaic economy (see Solomon's confession in 1 Kgs 8:33). Nehemiah's prayer reflects a conviction that, without a confession of sin, no promises of God can be fulfilled for the exiles. In this respect, Nehemiah provides a neat balance to the sovereign tone of Ezra 1, where the decree of Cyrus rests solely upon Yahweh's initiative. In Deuteronomic terms, participation via covenant loyalty is essential for Yahweh to act upon his promise of restoration.

Verse 7 continues the confession of sin, but now with emphatic language: "we have acted very wickedly toward you." In specific terms, "we have not obeyed the stipulations, decrees and laws," which is the typical preexilic tripartite designation for Deuteronomic law (Deut 4:44–45). This assumption of uncompromising obedience to the law sets the tone for the restoration of Zion, not only here but also throughout the corpus of Ezra-Nehemiah. The repeated ascription of the law to Moses ("you gave your servant Moses"; also v. 8) reinforces the legitimacy and reliability of the promise upon which Yahweh needs to act. Nehemiah essentially defers to the covenant mediator *par excellence* and appeals to truths that Nehemiah himself did not create, but that Yahweh originated and gave to his servant Moses.

Verses 8–10 mark the shift in the prayer from confession to petition by appealing directly to the Deuteronomic promise of return from exile following the repentance of the people (Deut 30:1–5) to "the place the LORD your God will choose from among all your tribes to put his Name there for his dwelling" (Deut 12:5). This rich and textured theological phrase emphasizes the significance of Jerusalem in the Deuteronomic theology of the divine presence. In a most remarkable way, Nehemiah's intercessory strategy mirrors Moses's by calling Yahweh to "remember" his promises (Neh 1:8; Exod 32:13) in order to reverse the effects of the people's disobedience. Nehemiah assumes that since Yahweh did remember then, he would also remember his people now and be faithful to them to restore the divine presence in their midst by establishing them in Zion. The climactic conclusion further anchors the petition within its Exodus/Deuteronomic context by appealing to Yahweh's mighty act of redemption, signaled by yet another archetypical phrase: "your people, whom you redeemed by your great strength and your mighty hand" (Neh 1:10; Exod 32:11; Deut 9:29).

The return to the vocative "O" in the original in verse 11a brings the whole prayer to a close and returns to the appeal for the Lord to listen to the prayer of Nehemiah ("your servant"), and, significantly, also to "the prayer of your servants who delight in revering your name." By adding others, Nehemiah does not see himself as a lone individual but as member of a covenant community that is, just as he is, deeply vested into the fulfillment of the restoration of Zion.[17]

While it would be appropriate to include verse 11b ("Give your servant success today . . . in the presence of this man") as part of the whole prayer (NIV and most other translations), it perhaps fits the context better to single out the last part of the prayer as a hinge that introduces the next chapter of Nehemiah's memoir and the encounter with "this man" (v 11b) who is also "the king" (v 11c): "Artaxerxes" (2:1). By adding the adverbial "today" and the resulting temporal specificity, Nehemiah

17. Leslie C. Allen and Timothy S. Laniak, *Ezra, Nehemiah, Esther*, UBCS (Grand Rapids: Baker Books, 2003), 90.

reinforces this sense of a temporal shift from the preceding confession and petition which went on for "many days" (1:4). Now the prayer has a focus: the encounter with the king in chapter 2 and the reality that this meeting was, to use a popular phrase, "bathed in prayer" (see Neh 2:4 and commentary below). In this context, the placement of Nehemiah's function as a "cupbearer" (v. 11) following the prayer reinforces the material and secondary function of his professional status in the narrative: he is first and foremost a Jew, and, more importantly, a servant of Yahweh who possesses an exceptional command of the traditions of his fathers, along with an equally impressive appreciation for the moment in which he finds himself within the broader history of redemption.

WITH NEHEMIAH THE MAN WE ARE ENCOUNTERING a familiar pattern in postexilic Scripture, with antecedents harking back to the time of Joseph in the second millennium BC at the court of Egypt: the faithful God-fearer, who happens to be a high-ranking official, that becomes a special instrument in God's redemptive purposes in salvation history. The postexilic era is not the time of the theocracy anymore. The prophets cannot speak into the affairs of the court from the standpoint of legitimacy and authority (even when their authority was denied; e.g., Micaiah, son of Imlah in 1 Kgs 22:6–28). Nevertheless, those appointed at the Persian court and under foreign rule (Daniel and Esther provide the best parallel to Nehemiah's situation) did not disengage from the context in which they found themselves. On the contrary, those who "walked the halls of power" (quite literally as in the case of Nehemiah and Esther; the Apadana was a columned hall) redoubled their effort to pray on behalf of God's people so that his will (meaning his redemptive purposes according to covenantal promises) might be accomplished. In the New Testament, this clarion call to pray for the state so that the kingdom might be furthered unhindered is explicitly commanded in a well-known text: "I urge, then, first of all, that petitions, prayers, intercession and thanksgiving be made for all people—for kings and all those in authority, that we may live peaceful and quiet lives in all godliness and holiness" (1 Tim 2:1–2).

In Nehemiah's context, to pray for the authorities takes on a bold dimension, that the Lord would jumpstart the restoration of Zion by allowing Nehemiah to persuade Artaxerxes to rebuild Jerusalem. By appealing to the paradigmatic prayers of Moses and Solomon, Nehemiah anchors the moment within a much larger context, which is no less than the restoration of the divine presence in their midst. In particular, Solomon's own prayer at the temple dedication provides Nehemiah's impetus to invoke the intervention of Yahweh, the God of heaven, for the (re)building of Zion:

> When your people Israel have been defeated by an enemy because they have sinned against you, and when they turn back to you and give praise to your name, praying and making supplication to you in this temple, then hear from heaven and forgive the sin of your people Israel and bring them back to the land you gave to their ancestors. (1 Kgs 8:33–34)

Nehemiah's context of setback, opposition, and the necessity of prayer remain in place within the context of the new covenant. Paul experiences great delays in reaching Rome (two-year imprisonment in Caesarea, Acts 21:10–14; 24:27), and he is candid about the setbacks caused by Satan's opposition (1 Thess 2:18). In light of Christ's work on the cross, the Deuteronomic curses Nehemiah's generation experienced have been taken up by Christ's life of perfect obedience to the law and his death on the cross; nevertheless, the sometimes devastating consequences for sins remain until Christ's return, which are a constant reminder that the New Testament context also assumes fervent prayers will be offered "night and day" (1 Thess 3:10), involving confession of sins (1 John 1:8–10) which can so easily hinder the work of God (Heb 12:1).

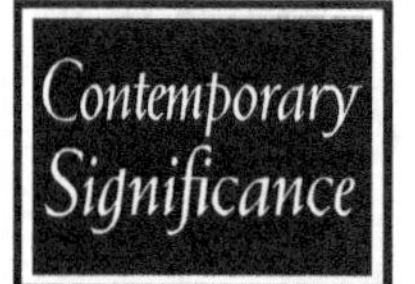


NEHEMIAH'S OPENING PRAYER UNDERSCORES THE significance of confession of sin for our own lives, for those of our family, and for the sins of others. This identification with the sin of others is the best antidote to smugness and aloofness, and it goes beyond mere rhetoric. Nehemiah meant what he prayed: "I and my father's house have sinned" (Neh 1:6–7; author's translation). All too often we maintain a posture of rightfulness when, in fact, we should assume a posture of openness and brokenness before the LORD because of the grievousness of sin and its consequences. The prayer of confession in a church service is not simply a quiet moment in the liturgy but should be considered one of the highlights of corporate worship, along with the reading of the Word. This prayer of identification, however, should not be misconstrued as shared guilt. As Ezekiel reminded the exiles, the "one who sins is the one who will die" (Ezek 18:20), himself quoting the law: "Parents are not to be put to death for their children, nor children put to death for their parents; each will die for their own sins" (Deut 24:16).

In a universe subjected to the power of sin (Rom 8:20), every culture, nation, and organization carries a measure of guilt for wrongs done to others in the past (here we fill in the blank for our own nation or culture). What Nehemiah offers us in his prayer is a posture of humility and contrition in the realization of the *consequences* that the sins of his forebearers has brought to his own present, even though Nehemiah himself did not participate in the idolatry of preexilic Israel and the resulting consequence of exile. We as Christians have a responsibility in our own particular cultural contexts to identify and weep with the aftermaths of the sins of our ancestors. A posture of humility will prevent us, in turn, from smugness, arrogance, and defensiveness when confronted with our own corporate past.

The prayer also highlights the significance of relying on God's promises when we pray. "Thy kingdom come, thy will be done in earth as it is in Heaven" (Matt 6:10 KJV) forms the theological underpinning of Nehemiah's plea, which allows Nehemiah to petition in specific and extraordinary terms; "Go big or go home" seems to be his motto. He is asking big things because his confidence rests in the past record of the LORD's faithfulness and based on the LORD's character: God is always faithful to his promises. Paul invites us to participate in this sort of grand vision for prayer in his letter to the Ephesians. The nature and scope of God's promises and responses to our prayers according to his will[18] are undoubtedly far greater than anything we could think or imagine (Eph 3).

First John 5:14–15 puts it this way: "This is the confidence we have in approaching God: that if we ask anything according to his will, he hears us. And if we know that he hears us—whatever we ask—we know that we have what we asked of him." However, a successful prayer life

18. That which pertains to the furthering of his kingdom on earth as it is in heaven.

and a lifestyle of sin do not mix. The caveat to this promise of answered prayer rests on the presumption that we can live in blatant sin and violation of his commandments and at the same time expect God to answer our prayers.

Nehemiah, as a secular official at the Persian court, feels confident enough to call himself a servant of the LORD in the prophetic lineage harking back to Moses himself. What gave him such confidence? The content of his prayer (a masterful synthesis of biblical-theological themes) betrays a profound knowledge of God's word and an exceptional ability to apply Scripture to the specific situation at hand. The fact that Nehemiah is able to draw from a rich variety of textual traditions and to apply these theological truths to the situation he faces reveals credentials that are just as potent as Ezra's formal resume in Ezra 7. The application is clear: knowledge of the word of God, coupled with the wisdom to apply specific truths to specific situations, represents essential characteristics for all of us who aspire and feel called to serve him, whether ordained through formal means (Levitical bloodlines as Ezra was) or through ad hoc responsive leadership tasks, as Nehemiah was. Today we receive our credentials to serve the Lord Jesus according to the same principle (see 2 Tim 1:7–9).

Finally, how do we respond to delays and setbacks in our own calling to further God's kingdom? Nehemiah teaches us that we do not belong to those who shrink back in fear, but we boldly approach the throne of grace (Heb 4:16), petitioning the "Our father who is in heaven" (Matt 6:9) to provide according to the riches of his promises in Christ Jesus (Eph 1:3–14). This is the confidence we have as we seek God and probe our own hearts in confession, repentance, and intercession. As we look ahead at the rest of the book of Nehemiah, we will find that our unlikely candidate's confidence in his God was not misplaced; neither will ours be.

# Nehemiah 2:1–8

1 In the month of Nisan in the twentieth year of King
Artaxerxes, when wine was brought for him, I took the wine
and gave it to the king. I had not been sad in his presence
before, 2 so the king asked me, "Why does your face look so
sad when you are not ill? This can be nothing but sadness
of heart."

I was very much afraid, 3 but I said to the king, "May the
king live forever! Why should my face not look sad when the
city where my ancestors are buried lies in ruins, and its gates
have been destroyed by fire?"

4 The king said to me, "What is it you want?"

Then I prayed to the God of heaven, 5 and I answered the
king, "If it pleases the king and if your servant has found favor
in his sight, let him send me to the city in Judah where my
ancestors are buried so that I can rebuild it."

6 Then the king, with the queen sitting beside him, asked
me, "How long will your journey take, and when will you
get back?" It pleased the king to send me; so I set a time.

7 I also said to him, "If it pleases the king, may I have letters
to the governors of Trans-Euphrates, so that they will provide
me safe conduct until I arrive in Judah? 8 And may I have a
letter to Asaph, keeper of the royal park, so he will give me
timber to make beams for the gates of the citadel by the temple
and for the city wall and for the residence I will occupy?" And
because the gracious hand of my God was on me, the king
granted my requests.

## Nehemiah's Commission (2:1–8)

**Setting.** The intense time of prayer has passed and now is the time for action. Nehemiah is about to receive his commission to go back to Jerusalem to shore up the restoration of Zion that was begun under Zerubbabel and now continued by Ezra. The relatively brief interchange between King Artaxerxes and Nehemiah reflects the language of the court and provides a record of legitimacy to the Jewish community. Nehemiah was, in fact, called to the task of restoration of Zion in the same way Ezra had been commissioned by the LORD some eight years earlier (458 BC; see commentary on Ezra 7:1–6). However, Nehemiah also goes to Yehud with much-needed credentials, which Ezra as a priest did not and could not obtain from the Persian authorities: a king's commission (Neh 2:7, "letters") to rebuild the city and its walls, thereby guaranteeing the resumption of the stalled efforts to restore Zion (per Hanani's report in 1:3). Significantly, Nehemiah leaves out the fact that he goes back not just as a private citizen but invested by the king as "governor" of Yehud. This revelation of his full credentials will need to wait until Nehemiah 5, and we will discuss its significance at that time.

**Carpe Diem (2:1–2).** In crafting his account (cf. 1:1), in 2:1, the chronological marker ("month of Nisan in the twentieth year of King Artaxerxes") forms the next natural break in his memoir and sets the stage for a unique encounter in what otherwise would have been a routine scene between the "king" (vv. 2 [2x], 2, 3, 4, 5 [2x], 6 [2x], 7 [2x], 8 [2x]) and his cupbearer ("I took [habitual tense in Heb.] the wine and gave it to the king"). The next sentence, however—"I had not been sad . . . before"—provides a unique background that sets the context for the ensuing conversation and will change Nehemiah's destiny forever. As a result of a brief exchange, he will pack up his bags and find himself in Yehud, placed in charge of the restoration of Zion! As already noted in the commentary on Nehemiah 1, the rapidity with which these events take place must be contrasted to the slow process of praying and preparing for this moment since he heard the fateful news a few months earlier. The phrase "had not been" (v. 1), conveyed in the pluperfect, or prior time, indicates that Nehemiah had somehow always managed to compose himself in the presence of the king during his extended period of mourning and fasting. Today, however, would be different. The text leaves open the question of whether this display of emotion was staged or unintentional. The language of fervent prayer to change "this man" at the end of chapter 1 (v. 11) perhaps suggests that on this particular day Nehemiah might have let his emotional guards down.

"So the king asked me" (2:2) typically frames reported speeches in the Old Testament, and the nuance of "so" in NIV is implied rather than explicit in the original text. Nevertheless, the question of verse 2 naturally flows from the added detail by Nehemiah about his own disposition before the king as "sad" at the end of verse 1 (*ra'*; "evil" in the sense of unwell). The king's observation that Nehemiah's "sad" (*ra'im*) "face" is connected to a "sadness [*ra'*] of the heart" is critical in the development of the narrative. The king has noticed there is something wrong with Nehemiah on this particular occasion. Commentators mention the background from Herodotus regarding court attendants facing great danger should they appear before the king with an inappropriate appearance.[1] However, without necessarily detracting from this idea, a more realistic explanation for the emphatic information provided ("I was very much [emphatic adverb "very"] afraid"; v. 2c)[2] is that structurally it represents a separate line in the narrative sequence and should not be considered background but essential to the unfolding of the conversation. Thus, Nehemiah carefully structures his narrative by strategically inserting three observations regarding his own emotions[3] that serve as catalysts to propel the entire narrative story forward. As soon as the king notices Nehemiah's incongruous mood, Nehemiah becomes convinced he has reached the point of no return. Now is the time for action and for the request to be presented. Will he find favor with the king as he has been praying for several weeks now?

**The bait (2:3–5).** Verse 3 structurally launches the next line ("But I said to the king") without any other background information, which perhaps suggests that Nehemiah was prepared to face the king with his request. Nehemiah's recorded response, "May the king live forever," which, paraphrased, would be "long live the king" or "God save the Queen" (for those from Commonwealth countries), projects the obvious deferential tone of the language of the court and pronounces a blessing of dynastic continuity.[4] Nehemiah's rhetorical response, "why should

---

1. Kidner, *Ezra and Nehemiah*, 87.

2. This is the only time Nehemiah is shown to display the emotion of fear in the narrative (not that he is afraid to display emotions throughout the narrative).

3. "I had not been sad in his presence before" in verse 1, followed by the observation of his uncertain emotional state by the king in verse 2a, b; and in verse 2c "I was very much afraid."

4. "May the king live forever" should not be construed to mean more than a formal address required in the protocol of the court. However, the aspiration of ancient Near Eastern cultures was that kingship was eternal and considerable effort and energy was

my face not look sad" (fourth time the root *ra'* comes up, but now as a modal verbal form), deftly omits the political designation of the "city" as Jerusalem (see Ezra 4 and the context of the previous decree by Artaxerxes which cancelled the progress of restoration) and places the emphasis on Nehemiah's ancestral roots. The NIV translation, "the city where my fathers are buried" (v. 3), does not quite capture the sense of patrimonial ancestral identity reflected in the Hebrew, "the house of the graves of my fathers" (author's translation). This designation, repeated in verse 5, would resonate deeply in an ancient context where the place of burial carried particular weight in terms of ethnic identity and origins.[5] This would be especially the case for non-indigenous members of the population like Nehemiah; burial grounds were sacred and should not be disturbed.

While Nehemiah personalizes the plight of Jerusalem, he does not withhold the facts of Hanani's report but adapts it to the context. The broken-down wall of 1:3 (a preeminent part of the mission!) becomes a generic "lies in ruins" (Heb. "is [verbless] desolate") that gives the sense that the city lies in a state of abandonment. The added phrase "gates . . . destroyed by fire"[6] stands closer to the original report by Hanani, with the implication that Nehemiah's ancestral burial grounds are in great danger of being desecrated and looted. The second question framed by the formulaic "the king said to me" suggests Nehemiah's rhetorical strategy seems to work: "What is it you want?" (v. 4; "what are you

---

spend in promoting and instilling this sense via documentary (the Sumerian King List), iconographic (the Narmer Palette), and archaeological monumental structures, such as the Achaemenid rock-hewn tomb in the Susiana plains (see A. Khurt, *The Ancient Near East c. 3000–330 BC*. Vols 1–2 [London: Routledge, 1997]). This aspiration, part of general revelation, evokes the deep-seated human dream for rulership by a benevolent, protecting kingly Father who dispenses his blessings in a merciful and just way, thereby protecting the people from harm and providing them fullness of blessing. In the case of Nehemiah, however, as a faithful Yahwist well versed in the traditions, including the Zion promise of restoration (which included a king that would live forever, e.g., Isa 9), he could not possibly mean that he wishes his ruler actually to "live forever."

5. Petter, *The Land Between Two Rivers*, 93–94.

6. Nehemiah opts to use a different verb ("destroyed") than in the original report of 1:3 ("burned"). These two verbs (both in the passive voice) carry the same meaning, but *yatsat* of 1:3 ("to set on fire," e.g., in the passive, Jer 2:15; in active form, Josh 8:8) is far more frequent in usage than "destroyed" here (passive participle with a root derived from "eaten," e.g., Neh 2:13; Nah. 1:10).

looking for right now," as it were). What appears so forthright to the modern reader seems to be echoed by the ancient context as well.

Nehemiah himself might have been taken aback at how effective his own scheme panned out, since the text interjects a new line in the narrative sequence. We expect the framing formula of "and I answered the king" (v. 5), but instead we hear that Nehemiah prayed to the God of heaven (v. 4). This phrase, syntactically highlighted, is also unique in the Bible semantically. One would expect such a framing device ("and I prayed," v. 4) to be followed by an actual prayer, but here the prayer is omitted from the record. We assume Nehemiah must have prayed a silent prayer to the God of heaven before answering the king, but why this unusual detail is added into the memoir remains an open question. Perhaps the reference to the God of heaven represents a nod to his extended time of prayer of the past few months, which, in the overall thrust of his memoir, serves a fundamental purpose. In any case, whatever Nehemiah will say next reflects his sudden readiness for the moment. In this heightened tension, he draws closer to the God of heaven (much like David in his greatest times of need; see 1 Sam 30:1–6), in spite of his declared state of unrest in which he finds himself before the king ("sad"; "very much afraid"; Neh 2:2).

Nehemiah responds in the continued reverential language of the court in verse 5 with "[i]f it pleases the king" (lit., "if it is good [*tob*] for the king," author's translation) but also adds "if your servant has found favor (verbal form of *tob*, "good," in the sense of blessing) in his sight." The lexical connector *tob* (see v. 8, "good") puts the emphasis on the mutually beneficial nature of the request. The role of "servant," an emphasized designation in Nehemiah's prayer of chapter 1, underscores Nehemiah's functions as both servant of Yahweh, the God of heaven, and of Artaxerxes, the "Great King" (v. 5).

In presenting his formal request for a commission, Nehemiah carefully avoids the mention of Jerusalem and the temple and continues his focus on the ancestral nature of the city, but with a noted addition: the city is in "Judah" (v. 5; i.e., the province of Yehud).[7] The goal is plainly stated: "so that I can rebuild it" (v. 5). The original text does not differentiate

---

7. Rainer Albertz reminds us that in the Hebrew text there is no difference between preexilic Judah and postexilic Judah. Both terms are spelled in the same way. See Rainer Albertz, *Israel in Exile: The History and Literature of the Sixth Century B.C.E.* (Atlanta: Society

between "build" or "rebuild." In the context, the language suggests a rebuilding project, which carries considerable prestige in the ancient world, since a lot of resources would be needed. The text is remarkably silent as to the process through which Nehemiah transformed himself from an intercessor to putting himself forward as the main character of the narrative. He could have asked for a detachment to shore up Ezra's efforts or requested an emissary to the local satrap to intervene for the rebuilding of the city. But that is not what he asked. Instead, he enters the arena and hopes to become the lead character in this process of rebuilding Zion. While the text significantly omits the title of "governor" (see commentary on chapter 5 below), clearly, with such a prestigious request and lofty goal, a title commensurate with the task would be needed from the king.

Verse 6 leaves no suspense in narrative time as to what the king's answer will be (unlike Esther's request, which spans several meetings with the king). Artaxerxes's decisiveness, which previously had worked against the interest of the exiles (Ezra 4), now works in their favor. The nature of the king's response—"How long will your journey take, and when will you get back?"—speaks of the concerns for Nehemiah's safety en route and his desire for Nehemiah to return to service at the court with a status report. In other words, the answer to Nehemiah's request is a "yes, but," since the king makes it clear this is not going to be a permanent return to Zion for Nehemiah—unlike Ezra and the other returnees. The desire of the king for Nehemiah to return to his post perhaps also serves as a nod to Nehemiah's valuable service to the king in his newly found role as the Persian king's troubleshooter in Yehud. *This* also sets the stage for the sense of urgency that permeates the denouement of the rebuilding narrative (chs. 3–5).[8] A significant and much-discussed addition that is syntactically dependent on the main clause, "with the queen sitting beside him," enriches the regal nature of the setting.[9] Since no further mention of her role is provided, any role or influence she might have played in the king's decision remains an

---

of Biblical Liturature, 2004), 1. *Yehud* is an Aramaism used in contemporary scholarship to differentiate between preexilic Judah and postexilic Judah.

8. Here the text confirms the high standing Nehemiah holds in the eyes of Artaxerxes.

9. Hebrew "*shegal*" is a rare usage for "queen" (Neh 2:6; Ps 45:9)—normally queen is *malkah* (cf. Esth 1:9)—and probably reflects a technical term of the Persian court. For further discussion, see Williamson, *Ezra, Nehemiah*, 179–80.

exercise in speculation, in sharp contrast to the influential role of Esther at Xerxes's court (e.g., Esth 4:14). Nehemiah's response is broken down into three distinct sentences in the narrative memoir:

1. "It was good before the king" (author's translation; NIV, "It pleased the king")
2. "He sent [or commissioned] me" (author's translslation; NIV, "to send me"
3. "I gave him a time frame" (author's translation; NIV, "I set a time.")[10]

The next and final section of the formal exchange at the court (vv. 7–8) represents a literary unit that we might call the *Let's put this in writing* part and reveals just how well-prepared Nehemiah was for the meeting as there is no indicator that the events described at the court happened over an extended period of time (as in the case of Esther).

Once Nehemiah receives the go-ahead from the king, he also secures crucial documents that will give him the legal and material means to finish the task of restoring Zion. While the text signals no angst on his part, as in the first exchange, the ensuing request is no less significant and important. For the third time now, Nehemiah's response is framed in the formulaic, "I said to the king" (v. 3 and v. 5), and for the second time he addresses his monarch with "if it pleases the king" (v. 5) but now adds a request for "letters" for the "governors of Trans-Euphrates" for "safe conduct" on his way to "Judah" (v. 7). The request relates to diplomatic immunity, so that the governors of the satrapy west of the Euphrates would not misunderstand Nehemiah's intentions as seditious and would allow his delegation to continue past Damascus and other main cities in the satrapy without any undue delays.

The second "letter" (v. 8) relates directly to the heart of the problem and Hanani's report (1:3). Accessing lumber supplies from "Asaph, keeper of the king's forest," must be authorized at the highest levels since wood was a prized commodity in the ancient Near East.[11] This is indeed a bold request on Nehemiah's part and continues to reflect his careful research

---

10. Hebrew *zeman* is best translated as appointed time or timeframe.

11. The region of Byblos and the Lebanon Mountain range in general served as supplier of lumber to Mesopotamian and Egyptian rulers. See Peter I. Kuniholm,

prior to meeting with the king for this interchange (e.g., knowledge of "Asaph," the name of the official in charge of timber). The request for supplies in verse 8 concerns three specific projects: the "gates," "the city walls" and Nehemiah's "residence" (original "house"). The first two projects are expected, while the third one suggests Nehemiah's identification as governor of the province (5:14) and assumes some sort of tenure ("time"; 2:6) in Judah. The targeted language of "citadel" (Heb. *birah*; see commentary on 1:1) for the temple" unequivocally identifies Nehemiah's ancestral city as Jerusalem, with its rebuilt temple (completed in 515 BC; see Ezra 6:14). The final narrative framing sentence of this fateful meeting in Susa's royal enclosure bypasses the king's actual response and links the success of the meeting to the answered prayer of Nehemiah 1:11, in the familiar language of favor ("the good hand of my God"; 2:8). In Hebrew, the clause-initial "and the king gave to me" (2:8) underscores that Nehemiah got everything he wanted out of this meeting, which prompts him to recognize the good hand of Providence. This sentence stands in obvious parallel to Ezra's request from the king to go to Jerusalem in 458 BC, "the king had granted him everything he asked, for the hand of the LORD his God was on him" (Ezra 7:6).

**Boldness before the king.** The boldness displayed before the King of kings in prayer in chapter 1 is matched by the same boldness in the presence of the king of Persia in chapter 2. Such a boldness before temporal authorities recalls Esther, Daniel, and in a much earlier generation, Joseph (Gen 41:15–16). This confidence is grounded in the fact that God holds the will of kings and authorities in his hands (Ps 2; Isa 40). There is nothing that falls outside of God's control, particularly as it pertains to the destiny of Zion. The theme of witness before kings and authorities is picked up in the Gospels, as well (e.g., Matt 10:18; Mark 13:11). The apostle Paul will dutifully follow in his Lord's footsteps. He testifies before Felix and Festus (Acts 24–25) and ultimately in Rome (Acts 28).

Nehemiah's favor in the eyes of the king (as his "servant," 2:5) comes

---

"Wood" in *The Oxford Encyclopedia of Archaeology in the Near East*, ed. Eric Meyers (New York: Oxford University Press, 1997), 347–49.

in no small part due to his trustworthiness. Since the king is concerned about his length of stay in Judah, presumably because he did not want him gone for long. This favor is also reflected in Artaxerxes's trust in Nehemiah not to become a seditious king in Judah, since he agrees to give him everything he wanted, including the potential to build up Jerusalem as a competing polity to Persia's interests. From Artaxerxes's viewpoint, he is sending a loyal and trusted collaborator (right-hand man) to fix a potential problem in the province of Yehud. The idea that Nehemiah would be a fomenter of rebellion is obviously far from his mind, otherwise he would never have sent him to an area that historically has been a hotbed of sedition. Nehemiah is sent back as Artaxerxes's problem solver, as far as he is concerned.

However, Nehemiah is first and foremost the servant of Yahweh in this narrative. Nehemiah sees no contradiction in his dual role as both servant of the state and as servant the LORD. He will seek to fulfill this dual calling with equal fervor and diligence, as the narrative will show, especially in chapter 5. Nehemiah demonstrates that spiritual leadership is not limited to being a member of a professional religious class. Instead, Nehemiah is commissioned to both the ministry of the king as well as to the ministry of the LORD. In biblical history, Esther, the queen of Persia, and Joseph, the ruler of Egypt, find themselves in similar circumstances.

## Contemporary Significance

*"The prayer of a Righteous man availeth much."*
*(Jas 5:16 KJV)*

FROM NEHEMIAH'S PRAYERS (SEE CHAPTER 1), WE are now introduced to the wonderful outcome of answered prayer in chapter 2. Yahweh's character anchors the prayer of chapter 1, which in turns sets up the expectation that Yahweh will be faithful to his promise and purposes in chapter 2. Nehemiah's conviction stems from the fact that he was interceding on behalf of Zion and the people of Israel, rather than for his own purposes or agenda. He was "seek[ing] first his kingdom" (Matt 6:33). Likewise, our own prayer life has to be governed by the priorities of the kingdom and the restoration and expansion of God's people, rather than our own self-aggrandizing agendas and self-preservation. Nehemiah also serves as a guardrail against false dichotomies between sacred and secular service. One is equally and worthily called to the ministry of word and sacrament as to the biotechnology industry, custodial services, or plumbing.

There are numerous examples in church history for when the people of God pray to see the will of the Lord accomplished. Examples include George Müller in his work among orphans,[12] George Verwer, the founder of Operation Mobilization,[13] or Hudson Taylor (China Inland Mission).[14] The SIM headquarters for the US in Charlotte, North Carolina, has a statement at the entrance of the campus: "By prayer since 1893."[15] The story of Youth With A Mission and the Mercy Ship *MV Anastasis* recounts how the *Anastasis*, an Italian ocean liner (originally christened *Victoria*) built in the 1950s, was purchased and recommissioned as a vessel to bring health care to nations in need in Africa.[16] The work of God in building the spiritual building of the church continues to this day. The vision of the restoration of Zion, the city of God, continues until Christ's return, and the foundation of intercession established by Nehemiah (and others before and after) remains the foundation of any venture intending to restore Zion, the people of God (Heb 12:22). Paul's magnificent vision in Ephesians compares the church to a body, but also to a building:

> In him the whole building is joined together and rises to become a holy temple in the Lord. And in him you too are being built together to become a dwelling in which God lives by his Spirit. (Eph 2:21–22)

This is the ministry to which you and I have been called as intercessors. We should not think that this kind of success is restricted to the covenant people in the history of redemption. As God's people we, too, are writing the history of redemption of the people the LORD has placed on our path, and we, too, are called to see the rebuilding of the

---

12. A. T. Pierson, *George Muller of Bristol: His Life of Prayer and Faith* (Grand Rapids: Kregel, 1999).

13. https://www.thegospelcoalition.org/blogs/justin-taylor/george-verwers-conversion-60-years-ago-today-god-created-a-global-evangelist/.

14. https://www.christianitytoday.com/history/people/missionaries/hudson-taylor.html.

15. https://www.sim.org/home.

16. As captured in Loren Cunningham with Janice Rogers, *Is That Really You, God? Hearing the Voice of God* (Grand Rapids: Chosen, 1984), 132–50.

church take place. Within the context of the global church, while the church is building up foundations in South America, Africa, and many parts of Asia, Old Europe is working on a new wave of renewal of God's work—especially among immigrant churches. In North America, we are also witnessing a great move of the LORD in urban and suburban settings. In other words, the Holy Spirit is a Spirit of restoration. We, as believers filled with the Holy Spirit, are equal to the task that was placed before Nehemiah. We, too, are called to create opportunities out of seemingly impossible situations—not for ourselves and our development or career but for the expansion of God's kingdom and the preparation for his return in glory. In this in-between time, we, too, labor in prayer to see the church, Zion, the heavenly Jerusalem being prepared for the return of the King within its walls. What a great adventure! Nehemiah should serve as a great encouragement to all of us, whether new in the faith or old and battle-weary. God is the one who changes times and seasons and who changes the heart of the king to conform to his good, perfect and pleasing will.

**Boldness in our testimony.** The other application is the theme of a witness before kings. Again, the history of the expansion of Christianity is replete with witnesses before kings. Billy Graham always sought the favor of local authorities to conduct his evangelistic rallies.[17] We, too, may have to testify before high authorities and request favors pertaining to the kingdom of God: building permits, accreditation, favor with the town officials or our neighbors, to name a few. Nehemiah teaches us to take courage, even if we are "very much afraid" (Neh 2:2) to face what can sometimes be very intimidating audiences. The divine presence is with Nehemiah: "I will be with you always" (Matt 28:20) echoes behind the text, as well.

We are, likewise, thrown into situations that put us on high alert and cause stress. Nehemiah provides us an example, as David did before him at Ziklag (1 Sam 30:1–6), that in our moment of greatest need, we should pray and reach out to the God of heaven for assistance. Yet, too often we resort to our own devices and find independent means of support. The life of faith demands complete surrender to the God of heaven so that we learn to pray "night and day" (e.g., 2 Tim 1:3) by sending quick

---

17. Billy Graham, *Just as I am: The Autobiography of Billy Graham* (New York: Harper Collins, 2018).

interjections to heaven throughout our days, rather than living our lives in virtual ignorance of the one who is with us always. Nehemiah could find the presence of the LORD even in the fortress of Susa, in the presence of the "king," the Achaemenid ruler of the known world, on whose shoulders rested the fate of Nehemiah's people. He sets the tone for our lives as well, by refusing to create a false sense of what is *sacred* and what is *secular.* As John Wesley said, "I look upon the world as my parish."[18]

18. *John Wesley: Journal*, June 11, 1739. https://www.ccel.org/ccel/wesley/journal.vi.iii.v.html.

# Nehemiah 2:9–20

9 So I went to the governors of Trans-Euphrates and gave them
the king's letters. The king had also sent army officers and
cavalry with me.

10 When Sanballat the Horonite and Tobiah the Ammonite
official heard about this, they were very much disturbed that
someone had come to promote the welfare of the Israelites.

11 I went to Jerusalem, and after staying there three days
12 I set out during the night with a few others. I had not told
anyone what my God had put in my heart to do for Jerusalem.
There were no mounts with me except the one I was riding on.

13 By night I went out through the Valley Gate toward the
Jackal Well and the Dung Gate, examining the walls of Jerusalem,
which had been broken down, and its gates, which had been
destroyed by fire. 14 Then I moved on toward the Fountain Gate
and the King's Pool, but there was not enough room for my mount
to get through; 15 so I went up the valley by night, examining
the wall. Finally, I turned back and reentered through the Valley
Gate. 16 The officials did not know where I had gone or what I was
doing, because as yet I had said nothing to the Jews or the priests
or nobles or officials or any others who would be doing the work.

17 Then I said to them, "You see the trouble we are in:
Jerusalem lies in ruins, and its gates have been burned with
fire. Come, let us rebuild the wall of Jerusalem, and we will no
longer be in disgrace." 18 I also told them about the gracious
hand of my God on me and what the king had said to me.

They replied, "Let us start rebuilding." So they began this
good work.

19 But when Sanballat the Horonite, Tobiah the Ammonite
official and Geshem the Arab heard about it, they mocked and
ridiculed us. "What is this you are doing?" they asked. "Are
you rebelling against the king?"

20 I answered them by saying, "The God of heaven will give us
success. We his servants will start rebuilding, but as for you, you
have no share in Jerusalem or any claim or historic right to it."

Original Meaning

## Initial Impressions in Jerusalem (2:9–20)

**The new conquest (2:9–10).** Verse 9 could just as easily be incorporated with the preceding section, since it functions as a concluding summary to Nehemiah's audience with the king. Nehemiah acts upon the instructions of the "king" (mentioned twice in verse 9) regarding the "letters" for the "governors of Trans-Euphrates." However, the mention of the governors also provides background to Nehemiah's anticipated opposition from the governors (v. 10) that forms the framing backdrop to the rest of the chapter, since the theme of opposition returns in 2:19–20. In addition, the mention of an imperial escort further stresses Nehemiah's role as a new political force to be reckoned with in the eyes of the regional establishment, unlike Ezra, who concerned himself with strictly religious concerns without a royal escort (Ezra 7:21–23).[1]

Verse 10 launches a major theme of Nehemiah's memoirs and provides a neat literary connection with the documenting of oppositions chronicled in Ezra 4. We know from the Elephantine papyri (*AP* 30) that Sanballat was the governor of the Persian province of Samaria in 407 BC, and by then had delegated his duties to his two sons (Neh 4:2 situates Sanballat's base of operations in Samaria).[2] His Babylonian name (Sin-uballit, "The god Sin has provided life")[3] fits in well with the history of the region (see 2 Kgs 17:24). The adjective "Horonite" refers to the geography of Samaria, but the specific location

---

1. Thus, the absence and presence of escort should not be construed to mean Nehemiah was more *practical* than the *pseudo-pious* Ezra (so Williamson, *Ezra, Nehemiah*, 184). Nehemiah, as the king's special envoy and formal representative of the Persian crown, did not have a choice in the matter and could not have traveled on his own. Ezra, however, wanted the reforms to stay religious and chose not to implicate Persian officials beyond the letter provided by Artaxerxes in 458 BC.

2. Kidner (*Ezra and Nehemiah*, 88–89) raises the possibility Sanballat was not yet a governor at the time of Nehemiah; however, the influential role he wields throughout the narrative suggests a position of regional authority.

3. Paul-Alain Beaulieu, "Yahwistic Names in Light of Late Babylonian Onomastics," in *Judah and the Judeans in the Achaemenid Period: Negotiating Identity in an International Context*, ed. Oded Lipschits, Gary N. Knoppers, and Manfred Oeming (Winona Lake, IN: Eisenbrauns, 2011), 247.

remains unknown.[4] His colleague is "Tobiah" ("Yahweh is good") "the Ammonite."[5] Thus, Nehemiah intentionally identifies his enemies and seeks to put a historical and tribal context to the ensuing struggle (see Ezra 4:2): "Sanballat, the Horonite" inevitably evokes the capital city of the preexilic northern kingdom Samaria and sets the stage for the well-known struggles between the Jews and the Samaritans during the intertestamental and New Testament periods (cf. John 4).[6] Tobiah the "Ammonite" reminds the reader of the long and troubled history of Israel with its Transjordanian neighbor (e.g., Judg 11; 2 Sam 10; see commentary on Neh 13:1). He is also called a "servant" (NIV "official"), most likely a high-ranking official alongside Sanballat, perhaps over the region of "Ammon" during the Persian period.[7] Finally, by choosing to refer to Judah/Yehud with the preexilic designation "Israelites" (*beney yisra'el* / "sons of Israel"), Nehemiah confirms the intentionality of these historic designations and paves the way for what will be a theme in the book: the new conquest of the land (see Neh 4 and related context in Ezra 10:8 see Commentary on Ezra 10).

Sanballat and Tobiah's displeasure, strongly worded in the narrative voice ("they were very much disturbed," v. 10) emphasizes how "evil" (*ra'* used twice) Nehemiah's intentions were to them: a man had come specifically to "promote the welfare" (*tobah*, "good") of the Israelites! Thus, by fronting the identity and the intent of Nehemiah's enemies even before he sets foot in Jerusalem, the text captures the prevailing theme of opposition throughout the memoir.

**Surveying the extent of the damage (2:11–15).** Literarily, the description of the night survey introduces us to the actual building project

---

4. In Hebrew, a Gentilic adjective can speak either of specific tribal ("Ephraimite") or general geographical origins ("Gileadite"). See E. J. Revell, *The Designation of the Individual: Expressive Usage in Biblical Narrative* (Kampen: Kok Pharos, 1997), 175–76.

5. Theophoric names do not always signal a corresponding religious adherence, as is clearly the case with the Yahwistic name Tobiah (cf. Neh 13:1). See Beaulieu, "Yahwistic Names," 247.

6. According to Josephus, the Samaritans built a competing sacred space on Mount Gerizim in the fourth c. BC, which would be destroyed by the Hasmonean John Hyrcanus in the second c. BC. See Gary N. Knoppers, *Jews and Samaritans: The Origins and History of Their Early Relations* (Oxford: Oxford University Press, 2013), 173.

7. L. S. Fried, "Something There is That Doesn't Love a Wall: The Crisis Created by the Wall Around Jerusalem," *Transeuphratène* 39 (2010): 83–84.

described in both chapters 3 and 4 of Nehemiah.[8] Its immediate function, however, is to prepare us for the main event of the rest of chapter 2: the meeting with the leaders of the community of Yehud (vv. 17–18). This high-stake meeting parallels in significance the meeting with the king in chapter 1. We know in no uncertain terms (v. 10) Nehemiah will not be able to solicit the help of the local political authorities to the north and west of Yehud (or, as it turns out, its southern neighbors; see v. 19 and discussion below). Without local Jewish support, Nehemiah's commission will fail. The background details of the account reveal Nehemiah's characteristic deftness and discretion in negotiating the restoration of Zion with authorities, whether through the stealth of a concerted time of prayer before meeting the king of Persia in chapter 1 or the stealth of a pedestrian night survey before addressing the people of Yehud.

While Nehemiah doesn't say what he did for three days in Jerusalem or who were the "few others" with him (v. 11), we can imagine an intense time of preparation to survey the scope of the project and to vet trusted associates to conduct this secret night survey (engineers?).[9] This lack of details[10] is contrasted with other features that underscore the secret nature of the survey: "night" is mentioned twice (vv. 12, 13), plus the "few others" along with only one "mount" (v. 12; to avoid unnecessary noise). Nehemiah's intention for this secrecy (conveyed via prior time, i.e., background information, "I had not told anyone"; v. 12) is understandable in light of the frontal opposition prior to his arrival in Jerusalem (v. 10). To show off letters from the Persian king may not have been the most effective way to solicit the help of the local Jewish leaders, which is also

---

8. Due to the specific landmarks described in the text, commentators spend considerable time and effort to discuss matters of geography pertaining to Jerusalem during the Persian period. However, the incomplete and at times ambiguous nature of the material-cultural data cautions us in relying too heavily upon these data for our interpretation of the text. The documentary sources (Neh 2–3; 12:27–39) remain the primary window into the historical context of fifth c. BC Jerusalem. See Nadav Na'aman, "Text and Archaeology in a Period of Great Decline: The Contribution of the Amarna Letters to the Debate on the Historicity of Nehemiah's Wall," in *The Historian and the Bible: Essays in Honour of Lester L. Grabbe*, ed. Philip R. Davies and Diana V. Edelman (New York: Bloomsbury, 2010), 20–29.

9. This omission is significant since Nehemiah meticulously names the people involved in the project in chapter 3 and elsewhere.

10. NIV "mounts" could refer either to a horse or a donkey. It seems to be the latter since a donkey would be more sure-footed in the rubble and quieter, as well.

probably why his identity as governor is not divulged until later on in the narrative (5:14). The wisdom of this approach is further confirmed later on when we realize how compromised some of the Jewish leadership is (see commentary on Neh 6:17–19). The rest of the sentence, "what my God had put in my heart to do for Jerusalem" (2:12), underscores Nehemiah's selfless motivation, revealed earlier via the prayer summary of chapter 1. Nehemiah's concerns do not rest with his own credentials but with getting the job done and accomplishing the mission to which he felt called by his God. His approach emphasized his primary loyalty to Yahweh rather than to the Persian king, a motif picked up also in his address to leaders in v. 18).

Nehemiah's laconic description of the pedestrian survey[11] does not mask the level of devastation that results in an aborted operation before its completion. The first sign of trouble on this circuitous route around "the walls of Jerusalem" (v. 13) to survey the "broken down" wall and the "gates. . . destroyed by fire."[12] As the small party attempts to cross over to the "Fountain Gate," (Heb. "Gate of the Spring"), Nehemiah has to dismount since no passage through the rubble could be found (v. 14). The shift in verse 15, literally, "I was going up *in* the valley" (NIV "I went up the valley) puts the focus on where he is finding himself ("*in* the valley"). This change of plan is said to take place "by night" (v. 15), a redundant repetition underscoring perhaps the precariousness of his situation: He is now on foot in the dark (whereas donkeys are incredibly sure-footed). The next part, "examining the wall" conveys the sense of a close inspection , as much as a nighttime operation allowed. This examination perhaps suggests most of the work would be needed there.

The next sequence of events in verse 15c (NIV "Finally, I turned back and reentered through the Valley Gate") also deserves further analysis, since the NIV misses the significance of the verbal sequence in Hebrew. There a built-in redundancy reflected through the following chiasm:

---

11. The itinerary, laid out in precise terms—"through the Valley Gate toward the Jackal Well and the Dung Gate (v. 13)" toward the "Fountain Gate and the King's Pool" (v. 14)—indicates a departure point on the western side of the enclosure wall toward the southern end of the city (along the Tyropoean/central Valley toward the Hinnom Valley) and up around the southeastern corner in a northward direction along the Kidron Valley toward the temple. [The map provided in Kidner (*Ezra and Nehemiah*, 93) reflects as a good a guess as any.]

12. This language intentionally connects the narrative to the report of chapter 1.

(A) I returned
(B) I entered in the gate of the Valley
(A') I returned

Nehemiah appears to describe an intentional turnaround rather than the sense that he completed the circular route and simply ended up back at the Valley Gate. Instead, we should view the first "I returned" (A) as an interruption signaling Nehemiah did not, in fact, go around the city to inspect the walls.[13] Following the completion of the night survey of the wall in the valley (Kidron), he retraced his steps back to the "Valley Gate." The description highlights the magnitude of the devastation on the eastern side of Jerusalem and south of the Temple Mount.

**Addressing the local Jewish leadership (2:16–18).** Before addressing the leadership and the delicate question of task allocation (v. 16), Nehemiah sees fit to emphasize, by way of background information, the secrecy of not only this initial survey but also the nature of the gathering of a literal *who's who* in Yehud. The "officials" (mentioned twice in v. 16) refer to the local Jewish officials that would answer to Nehemiah as the newly-minted governor of Yehud. The rest represents every major stakeholder among the "Jews," including religious authorities ("priests" which, most likely would have included Ezra; v. 16). The mention of "nobles" does not suggest royalty but free persons in the sense of landowners (see commentary on Neh 5:7).

Nehemiah's succinct address (v. 17) intentionally repeats the familiar vocabulary of both chapter 1 and his address to the king in chapter 2: "the trouble we are in" (root *ra'*; cf. 1:3); "Jerusalem lies in ruins" (Heb. "desolate;" cf. 2:3); and, for the fourth time, the "gates have been burned with fire."[14] The pitch comes right away in an emphatic imperative voice: "come, let us rebuild (or "build" since *banah* "to build" doesn't differentiate between rebuilding or building) the wall of Jerusalem" (v. 17). The removal of "disgrace" (v. 17) as a result of the building project recalls the cause-and-effect Deuteronomic relationship between the restoration of Zion and the absence of disgrace.

Nehemiah in verse 18 describes another foundational theme of

---

13. So Williamson, *Ezra, Nehemiah*, 190–91, and other commentators.

14. The language of "burned" alternates between two verbs in Hebrew: *'uklu* (2:3; 2:13) and *nitstu* (1:3; 2:17).

answered prayer, which resulted both in the "the gracious (*tobah*) hand of my God on me" and a favorable response with the king of Persia. Thus, in a remarkably short account, the time for secrecy has passed, and Nehemiah shows his hand: He is first a Yahwist on a successful (so far!) mission from God ("my God," v. 18); and second, he is a servant of the king on an official and diplomatic mission to rebuild the walls of Jerusalem. Without any interruption or delay, a consensus emerges so that the response from his audience comes without any qualifications: "Let us start rebuilding" (or "build"; v. 18). The account of the meeting with the people concludes with an added note of optimism. The NIV's "so they began this good work" (v. 18) is "they strengthened their hand for good (*tobah*)" in the Hebrew. Yahweh has answered Nehemiah's prayers beyond what he could have imagined. The miracle of *favor* with the king is now matched with the miracle of *favor* with the local authorities, which, in light of the constant internecine struggles between competing parties and factions in Yehud (see Neh 6) and the long history of disunity between God's people in the Old Testament, represents a momentous event in the history of redemption.

**Responding to his enemies (2:19–20).** Not everyone, however, is persuaded by Nehemiah's official task. His counterparts' strong reaction in verse 10 (especially in light of the letters to the governors) is developed in verses 19–20 and underscores the epic political struggle Nehemiah faces with the local governors of the Trans-Euphrates. We are, after all, a long way from Susa and Artaxerxes! To the list from verse 10 (verbatim designations for both Sanballat and Tobiah), "Geshem the Arab" is added (v. 19), underscoring how Jerusalem is surrounded by hostiles to the north, west, and south. Thus, the restoration of Zion is no *fait accompli* yet (per the events described in Ezra 4). The trio's brash dismissal of Nehemiah's commission by Artaxerxes ("they mocked and ridiculed us"; v. 19, and below) is reflected by two questions about the legitimacy of the task ("What is this you are doing?") and their motives ("Are you rebelling against the king?").[15] This time, however, the familiar charge

15. If Yehud had been under Samaritan jurisdiction, this would then explain the deep threat Nehemiah represented to Sanballat and Tobiah (Ralph W. Klein, "Ezra-Nehemiah, Book of," *ABD* 2:735). However, we do know that Yehud had its own governors in prior generations (see Neh 5:15); nevertheless, the text certainly reflects the idea that a leadership vacuum existed prior to Nehemiah's return and puts a political context to the epic struggle Nehemiah will chronicle in the ensuing phases of his tenure.

of sedition (Ezra 4) sounds hollow in light of Nehemiah's special envoy from the Persian court. Under Nehemiah's leadership, the enemies of Zion will not have the legal ground to prevent the restoration of the holy city. However, Nehemiah is equally forceful in his reply. He relies on his commission from "the God of heaven" who will grant "success" to his "servants" (v. 20; cf. Nehemiah's prayer in Neh 1:11). These three antagonists have no historical claim to Zion, in the past, present, and its future. Thus, as the first shot across the bow, this brief but vivid encounter prepares us for the struggles to come and also for the personal animus directed at Nehemiah himself and at the Jews.

**QUALIFYING THE NOTION OF FAVOR WITH GOD AND HUMANKIND.** The promise of Zion and its restoration remains first and foremost an act of the sovereign God (see the background of creation in Yahweh's redemptive act of restoration in Isa 40). Human participation is essential, but the impetus can only come from Yahweh himself. Nehemiah continues to acknowledge this reality in his report to the elders and spiritual leadership in Jerusalem as to why he has come to Jerusalem. The theme of "favor" from earlier in chapter 2 (v. 5; connected to the root word "good") continues to express itself here at the end of chapter 2. Nehemiah's favor with the king in Susa has now translated into favor with the people in Jerusalem. The people are unified in their desire to accomplish the task. In the same way, "the boy Samuel continued to grow in stature and in favor with the LORD and with people" (1 Sam 2:26). Likewise, "Jesus grew in wisdom and stature, and in favor with God and man" (Luke 2:52).

Answered prayer and favor does not translate into an absence of opposition. Favor is clearly not what is on Sanballat's mind when he thinks of Nehemiah! Thus, the theme of favor with others needs some qualifying. Nehemiah may have experienced favor with the Persian king and local Judean officials, but this was clearly not the case with his gubernatorial counterparts. Israel's neighbors, with some exceptions, were sworn enemies of Israel during the time of the conquest and settlement in Canaan all the way to the end of the monarchy in the early seventh century BC. We recall what Edom thought of the destruction of Jerusalem in 586 BC from Psalm 137:7: "'Tear it down,' they cried, 'tear it down to its foundations!'" (see the message of Obadiah the prophet against Edom's gloating as a "brother" of Israel; Obad 8–14). This theme of strife between brothers has deep roots in the Genesis narrative (Cain vs. Abel, Gen 4:8; Esau vs. Jacob, Gen 27:41; and Joseph vs. his brothers, Gen 37–40) and is expressed again here in this narrative. We are reminded that the *beney 'ammon* (aka the Ammonites) are part of the broader Abrahamic family (as is Moab, even if the details of both Ammon and Moab's origins are unsavory; Gen 19:30–38). Also, but to a lesser degree, the Samaritans do have some ties in the land, as well (see 2 Kgs 17:24–40). So here, the sad reality expresses itself that brother, neighbor, and enemy can easily become one and the same.

**Loving without becoming the enemy.** Nehemiah takes a strong posture toward these neighbors/brothers/enemies. From here on in the book, Governor Nehemiah will be unflinching in not allowing Sanballat et al. to participate in the rebuilding of Zion. In this regard he follows in the footsteps of the previous generation of returnees, Zerubabbel and the authorities who shut down any hope of collaboration with "the enemies of Judah and Benjamin" when they asserted: "You have no part with us in building a temple to our God; we alone will build it for the LORD, the God of Israel" (Ezra 4:1–3; see commentary above). This determination is also reflected in Jeremiah's posture toward false prophets of Yahweh (Jer 28) and Paul's toward the false brothers who are seeking to take away his freedom in the gospel of Christ (Gal 2:4; 2 Tim 3:8). Revelation 22 serves as a stark reminder that not everyone will belong to Zion and inside its walls in the end (Rev 22:14–15). The sense of tension between Jews and Samaritans comes to a head also in the gospel of John with the woman at the well in John 4. Jesus does not hide the fact that Samaritans do not worship "in the Spirit and in truth" (John 4:23) and that "salvation is from the Jews" (4:21–22). A clear line is drawn. The waters of eternal life will not be drawn from Jacob's (aka Israel!) well. Nehemiah confronts us with this stark reality, that not everyone necessarily has our best intention in view and is on our side.

ON THE BASIS THAT WE, TOO, ARE BUILDING Zion (the image in Ephesians and Hebrews 12:22–23), the range of application of chapter 2 appears mind-boggling, but there are limits to its applicability as well. Chapter 2 and the success that

Nehemiah encounters is no promise of success in our own ministries. Nevertheless, there are points of connection with the realities we face in our contemporary context in the body of Christ worldwide that are relevant and powerful. Just as the early church faced the reality of opposition from false brothers (the evidence from the New Testament abounds: Titus 1:10–11, 2 Peter; Jude; 1 Thess 2:2, etc.), we will face some level of opposition in the building of Zion, the people of God in the new covenant. False brothers will seek alliances with us (those who do not confess Jesus as Lord and deny his deity and his resurrection, 1 John 2:22–23; 4:1–3), and we should not participate in building up the kingdom of God with them. To those of us ministering in the West, Nehemiah's approach may sound separatist and intolerant in an age of pluralism, tolerance, and inclusivity. However, in the eyes of the majority church elsewhere in the world, especially in areas facing persecutions, this no-compromise approach makes sense since it is a matter of physical survival of the community of believers in parts of the Global South.[16] This image of "circling the wagon" usually elicits negative images of stubborn resistance to cooperation and coexistence, but we forget that without spiritual protection the community of faith runs the risk of being overrun by opponents.

How do we translate this uncompromising stance in light of the second commandment to love your neighbor as yourself (Lev 19:18; Mark 12:30–31), who also happens to be your enemies in the context of Nehemiah? From the bigger picture of redemptive history and in light of what Christ has done, the love of neighbor-turned-enemy finds an illustration also involving a Samaritan. As Fee and Stuart so well explain in their classic *How to Read the Bible for All Its Worth*, the neighbor to be loved becomes the one toward whom we have prejudice and hostility, who also happens to be a Samaritan![17] So the merging of love of neighbor/love of enemy comes to a head for those who claim the mantle of Christ follower. This love for enemies in the new covenant is only possible through the eye of the cross. Jesus did not die for the "good folks," but he died for his enemies (all of us, since all have fallen short of his glory; Rom 3:23; Rom 5:10; e.g., Saul of Tarsus!, 1 Tim 1:12–15). Thus, the posture

---

16. https://www.persecution.com/globalprayerguide.

17. Gordon D. Fee and Douglas Stuart, *How to Read the Bible for All Its Worth*, 3rd ed. (Grand Rapids: Zondervan, 2003), 155–56.

of smug self-righteousness and any "us versus them" ideology evaporates in light of the great equalizer for all of mankind: sin and guilt before a holy God. At the same time, Nehemiah tells us we are not to roll over and embark into partnerships with those who clearly oppose the welfare of Zion/God's people. Not everyone has pure intentions toward the building of God's kingdom! Proverbs warns us against entering into any partnership without careful consideration from a practical (economic) standpoint (Prov 11:15). How much more discernment is required when it comes to the welfare of God's people. The element of separation from evil is a prevailing theme from beginning to the end in Scripture. The motto, instead, should be: Love your neighbor turned enemy, but do not become like them!

**Answered prayer begets opposition.** Answered prayers beget boldness, which, in turn, begets opposition. This cause and effect relationship is reflected in our own lives and throughout the history of the church. Any success and forward movement in the expansion of the kingdom of God is first and foremost generated by the gracious initiative of the LORD and is bathed in the prayers of God's people. This, in turn, triggers the demonstrable activity of God in his answered prayers, but this success is also the trigger for the devil's backlash and pushback. It would be naïve to expect our engagement with the task of preparing the city for the coming of the king would not draw powerful opposition and setbacks throughout. However, in this respect, we are also like Nehemiah and countless others who have dared to commit their lives to the building of Zion, the city of God: We persevere in prayer, wait for the opportune time to act, and are not intimidated by the devil and his tactics (2 Cor 2:11).

In this regard, the call to be wise as serpents and innocent as doves (Matt 10:16) is also reflected in the way Nehemiah conducts his night survey. The way prayers are answered also involves practical wisdom on the part of Nehemiah. He is wise as a serpent in the way he examines the wall by night. He perhaps senses the danger of the situation (see Neh 6!) and does not know who can be trusted. There is wisdom in not divulging our plans until the opportune time: Mary "cherished these things in her heart" in the Lukan birth narrative (2:19). Jesus concealed his identity in the first half of the Markan narrative (see Mark 8:31 as the turning point).

# Nehemiah 3:1–32

1 Eliashib the high priest and his fellow priests went to work
and rebuilt the Sheep Gate. They dedicated it and set its doors
in place, building as far as the Tower of the Hundred, which
they dedicated, and as far as the Tower of Hananel. 2 The men
of Jericho built the adjoining section, and Zakkur son of Imri
built next to them.

3 The Fish Gate was rebuilt by the sons of Hassenaah. They
laid its beams and put its doors and bolts and bars in place.
4 Meremoth son of Uriah, the son of Hakkoz, repaired the next
section. Next to him Meshullam son of Berekiah, the son of
Meshezabel, made repairs, and next to him Zadok son of Baana
also made repairs. 5 The next section was repaired by the men
of Tekoa, but their nobles would not put their shoulders to the
work under their supervisors.

6 The Jeshanah Gate was repaired by Joiada son of Paseah
and Meshullam son of Besodeiah. They laid its beams and put its
doors with their bolts and bars in place. 7 Next to them, repairs
were made by men from Gibeon and Mizpah—Melatiah of
Gibeon and Jadon of Meronoth—places under the authority of
the governor of Trans-Euphrates. 8 Uzziel son of Harhaiah, one
of the goldsmiths, repaired the next section; and Hananiah, one
of the perfume-makers, made repairs next to that. They restored
Jerusalem as far as the Broad Wall. 9 Rephaiah son of Hur,
ruler of a half-district of Jerusalem, repaired the next section.
10 Adjoining this, Jedaiah son of Harumaph made repairs opposite
his house, and Hattush son of Hashabneiah made repairs next to
him. 11 Malkijah son of Harim and Hasshub son of Pahath-Moab
repaired another section and the Tower of the Ovens. 12 Shallum
son of Hallohesh, ruler of a half-district of Jerusalem, repaired the
next section with the help of his daughters.

13 The Valley Gate was repaired by Hanun and the
residents of Zanoah. They rebuilt it and put its doors with
their bolts and bars in place. They also repaired a thousand
cubits of the wall as far as the Dung Gate.

14 The Dung Gate was repaired by Malkijah son of Rekab,
ruler of the district of Beth Hakkerem. He rebuilt it and put its
doors with their bolts and bars in place.

15 The Fountain Gate was repaired by Shallun son of Kol-
Hozeh, ruler of the district of Mizpah. He rebuilt it, roofing
it over and putting its doors and bolts and bars in place. He
also repaired the wall of the Pool of Siloam, by the King's
Garden, as far as the steps going down from the City of David.
16 Beyond him, Nehemiah son of Azbuk, ruler of a half-district
of Beth Zur, made repairs up to a point opposite the tombs of
David, as far as the artificial pool and the House of the Heroes.

17 Next to him, the repairs were made by the Levites under
Rehum son of Bani. Beside him, Hashabiah, ruler of half the
district of Keilah, carried out repairs for his district. 18 Next
to him, the repairs were made by their fellow Levites under
Binnui son of Henadad, ruler of the other half-district of
Keilah. 19 Next to him, Ezer son of Jeshua, ruler of Mizpah,
repaired another section, from a point facing the ascent to the
armory as far as the angle of the wall. 20 Next to him, Baruch
son of Zabbai zealously repaired another section, from the
angle to the entrance of the house of Eliashib the high priest.
21 Next to him, Meremoth son of Uriah, the son of Hakkoz,
repaired another section, from the entrance of Eliashib's house
to the end of it.

22 The repairs next to him were made by the priests
from the surrounding region. 23 Beyond them, Benjamin and
Hasshub made repairs in front of their house; and next to
them, Azariah son of Maaseiah, the son of Ananiah, made
repairs beside his house. 24 Next to him, Binnui son of
Henadad repaired another section, from Azariah's house to the
angle and the corner, 25 and Palal son of Uzai worked opposite
the angle and the tower projecting from the upper palace near
the court of the guard. Next to him, Pedaiah son of Parosh
26 and the temple servants living on the hill of Ophel made
repairs up to a point opposite the Water Gate toward the east
and the projecting tower. 27 Next to them, the men of Tekoa
repaired another section, from the great projecting tower to
the wall of Ophel.

[28] Above the Horse Gate, the priests made repairs, each in
front of his own house. [29] Next to them, Zadok son of Immer
made repairs opposite his house. Next to him, Shemaiah son of
Shekaniah, the guard at the East Gate, made repairs. [30] Next
to him, Hananiah son of Shelemiah, and Hanun, the sixth son
of Zalaph, repaired another section. Next to them, Meshullam
son of Berekiah made repairs opposite his living quarters.
[31] Next to him, Malkijah, one of the goldsmiths, made repairs
as far as the house of the temple servants and the merchants,
opposite the Inspection Gate, and as far as the room above
the corner; [32] and between the room above the corner and the
Sheep Gate the goldsmiths and merchants made repairs.

*Original Meaning*

## The Rebuilding of the Gates and Repairing the Walls (3:1–32)

**Setting.** Following the planning phases (Neh 1–2), chapter 3 lists those who contributed to the restoration of the gates and wall of the "holy city" (cf. 11:18). It functions as an introductory summary of the building narrative (Neh 4–6) and offers parallels to the list of those who resettled Jerusalem in Nehemiah 11, but especially the dedication of the sacred enclosure in chapter 12. Literarily, connections between these sections of the book are rich: those who are involved in the restoration of Zion are specifically singled out by name along with topographical and architectural landmarks (both monumental and domestic) that relate to the restoration project. Each of these sections follows a highly-formulaic genre which, in the case of chapter 3, is reminiscent of an ancient Near Eastern building inscription (e.g., the ninth c. BC Mesha Inscription)[1] with the marked difference that rather than having a first-person account that lauds the achievements of the king (e.g., "I built this"), we now have an official record of the participation of the people by name. The shift to the third-person narrative voice and Nehemiah's noticeable absence from this list underscores the involvement of the community as a whole. The people are acting upon the

1. A. Dearman, *Studies in the Mesha Inscription and Moab* (Atlanta: Scholars Press, 1989).

verbal agreement of Nehemiah 2:18, "Let us start rebuilding."[2] Chapter 3 becomes part of the official summary of their contributions from beginning to end of the project.[3] The amazing degree of consensus reflected in chapter 3 also anticipates a similar unity when the covenant is renewed in chapter 8, in contrast to other moments of disunity in the book (chs. 5, 13). Chapter 3 builds upon the string of Nehemiah's successes following his extended time of prayer and mourning: both the king and the people wholeheartedly embrace Nehemiah's project of restoration, and now the diverse community of Yehud gets involved. The summary of opposition at the end of the building narrative (Heb 3:33–38; English translation 4:1–6) provides an additional connection to Nehemiah's meeting with the local officials in chapter 2. The "letters" (2:9), the successful enrollment of the community (2:18), and the widespread participation of the people in chapter 3 all serve as triggers for fierce verbal opposition from Nehemiah's enemies. These, in turn, prepare us for the physical threats encountered in chapter 4.

**Formulaic emphasis.**[4] Nehemiah skillfully structures his onomasticon (name list) with formulaic language that includes patronymics, place of residence, rank, occupation, and tasks (physical location and specific repair assignments). Beyond the identification of the participants, the chapter recounts the restoration of the enclosure wall with a particular emphasis on the rebuilding and restoration of some gates in the first half of the account (vv.1–15), and the wall in relationship to individuals' houses and other landmarks in the second half (vv. 16–32). The description alternates between topographical and architectural features. From a historical standpoint, chapter 3 is a treasure trove of historical-geographical information, and we ought to capitalize on this ancient "Bible atlas" of fifth century BC Yehud (e.g., Eusebius's *Onomasticon*). Nehemiah, the highest ranking Persian official in the province of Yehud

---

2. This includes the intentional shared vocabulary between the people's intent (2:18) and their action (3:1): *qum* "to rise" and *banah* "to build." This lexical connection is not apparent in the NIV translation: "Let us start rebuilding" (2:18); "went to work and rebuilt" (3:1).

3. Smith aptly describes the chapter as Nehemiah's "thank you" to the community. Gary V. Smith, *Ezra, Nehemiah, Esther*, CBC, ed. Philip W. Comfort (Carol Stream, IL: Tyndale House, 2010), 12.

4. NIV has smoothed out the formulaic language of chapter 3. However, the Hebrew is considerably more repetitive in its vocabulary (hence formulaic) and reads like an official administrative report.

at the time, provides us with a fascinating eyewitness perspective and an invaluable witness from a historical standpoint (the Madaba Map in the Early Byzantine Period offers a similar appeal).[5] As tempting as it is for us to delve into the historical-archaeological details of the narrative, from the standpoint of the literary and theological context of the book, the chapter proleptically announces that the purpose of rebuilding Zion is to sanctify it ("to dedicate" [lit., "to make holy"] in 3: 1), so that worship in the "holy city" might be restored.

**Building and repairing.** As a building project, the language of "repaired" (*hazaq* in the causative, "cause to strengthen," i.e., "to shore up") and "rebuilt" (*banah*, either "to build" or "to rebuild") dominates the account. A case could be made that the terms are synonymous.[6] However, it appears the verbs do have different technical meanings in the particular context of chapter 3: "to re/build" is no longer used in a generic sense as in chapters 2 and 4, but seems to be describing activities that are distinct from the verb "to repair" (used only here in chapter 3). In the formulaic language pertaining to the building of the gates, attention is drawn to the work on the "doors" (3:3). These needed to be rebuilt from scratch since the Babylonian and subsequent attacks on Jerusalem destroyed them (see 1:3). Thus, when it says gates were rebuilt, we should probably understand this to mean new doors were installed. After all, a gate without doors loses all usefulness as a line of demarcation and protection. The gate structure itself may have stood largely intact (with some notable exceptions, e.g., the "roof" of the "Fountain Gate"; v. 15) and needed only to be repaired in the majority of cases (Jeshanah Gate, v. 6; Valley Gate, v. 13; Dung Gate, v. 14; and Fountain Gate, v. 15).[7] However, the Sheep Gate (v.1, including the adjacent walls connected to two "towers") and the Fish Gate (v. 3) perhaps needed to be rebuilt in a substantial way, since they stood closest to the temple precinct and might have suffered

---

5. Nehemiah as the king's envoy was mandated to repair Jerusalem. The formal nature of the report likely represents the governor's report to the king (our modern day "quarterly report").

6. So Williamson, *Ezra, Nehemiah*, 203–4.

7. In the archaeological record, the greatest threat (besides destruction and erosion) to monumental features like gates and walls is the recycling of the building materials by subsequent communities. The Roman period, for instance, wreaked havoc on ancient settlements (e.g., Byblos). The Roman Coliseum suffered the same fate during the Renaissance.

the most damage, considering the Babylonians burned the temple to the ground in 586 BC. For these two gates, the language of "repair" is therefore absent. This new construction (undoubtedly using existing materials from the rubble, as for the whole project; see chapter 4) would also provide further explanation as to why in the case of the Sheep Gate the high priest himself became involved and the priestly class felt the need to "dedicate" the Sheep Gate (in the sense of making it holy, v. 1).

For building activities pertaining to walls, the verb "to repair" dominates the account (with one notable exception in v. 2 "built"). This emphasis on strengthening or shoring up an existing feature bears significance. First, it might explain why no building supplies from quarries are mentioned in the account (contrast lumber in the previous chapter). The needed stonework would be recycled from the existing building materials found in the debris caused by the damage of the 586 BC destruction (see *commentary* on chapter 4 below for supporting evidence). This would also explain the rapidity with which the community restored the sanctity and (relative) safety of Zion. Finally, in light of the stated demographics of the account (a few hundred people at the most) and what we know of the demographics of Yehud at the time, we should not imagine large public works of the magnitude of the Solomonic era (1 Kgs 9:10–19).[8] As a result, tracing Nehemiah's wall in the archaeological record may prove quite the elusive task, and any conclusions should be held with some caution.[9]

**Identification of individuals.** Next to the actual parts of the walls that were affected, the identification of individuals dominates the chapter, and significant elements for interpretation are embedded into the names, occupation, and tasks.

1. Patrimonial heads of the community carried out the majority of the work (signaled by their patronymics [e.g., "son of"]; mostly one, never beyond two generations).[10] In tribal societies then and now, nothing gets done without the consent and participation of the tribal leaders.

---

8. For demographics see Charles E. Carter, *The Emergence of Yehud in the Persian Period: A Social and Demographic Study*, JSOT 294 (Sheffield: Sheffield Academic, 1999), 79–80.

9. Eilat Mazar, "The Wall that Nehemiah Built," *Biblical Archaeology Review* 35/2 (2009).

10. There are thirty-two names with patronymics, three of which list two ancestors ("Meremoth" [twice: vv. 4; 21]"; Meshullam," v. 4; "Azariah," v. 23).

2. Several tribal heads also function as "ruler" (v. 9, 12, 14, 15, 16, 17, 18, 19) of a " half-district" (v. 9, 12, 16, 17,18) or "district" (v. 14, 15).[11] As Persian officials in Yehud and according to Artaxerxes's commission to Nehemiah, they lead no less than six building projects (vv. 9, 12, 14, 15, 16, 19), thereby validating the legitimacy and legality of the enterprise and, conversely, underscoring the illegal nature of the opposition by Nehemiah's opponents (see chapter 4).
3. Including members of outlying communities (e.g., "men of Jericho"; v. 2), including patrimonial heads and rulers, points to a geographical distribution of the effort that encompassed the Jordan Valley ("Jericho") and the highlands surrounding Jerusalem to the north, east, and south. The effort was not a phenomenon limited to the community in Jerusalem but reflect a widespread geographical participation throughout the province of Yehud.
4. "Priests" (vv. 1, 22), including Eliashib "the high priest," feature prominently at the beginning of the list (v. 1) and also toward the end (vv. 20, 28). Other members of the religious class also include "Levites" (v. 17) and "Temple servants (v. 26)." These three groups play a central role later in the account (see chs. 8–12).
5. Specialized craftsmen, "goldsmiths" (vv. 8, 31 lit., "refiners"), "perfumers" (v.8) and "merchants" (v. 32) are involved as well. Further pointing to socio-organizational diversity, the "daughters" of "Shallum," "ruler of a half-district of Jerusalem" also participated in repairing a section of the wall (v. 12).

## The Rebuilding of the Gates and Repairing the Walls (3:1–32)

DETAILS ON THE GATES' CONSTRUCTION (3:1–15) are covered by the recurring phrase "[they] put its doors and bolts and bars in place." The phrase emphasizes the sanctity of the site has been restored (see ch. 13:19) and also confirms the gates as the focal point of the Babylonian and subsequent destructions (e.g., 1:3).

*Details pertaining to wall restoration abutting the Gates* are signaled by the formula that includes the following elements: Participant(s) + "repaired"[12]

11. Hebrew *pelek,* which is a technical term with Mesopotamian (Akkadian) origins.
12. Both *banah* "to rebuild" *and hazaq* "to strengthen" are used.

+ "next to him/them"[13] (e.g., v. 10 "Hattush son of Hashabneiah made repairs next to him").

*Supplementary details occur for every gate* except for the Sheep Gate and the Dung Gate. These details offer us a window into the extent of the damage and where most of the work needed to take place. We may assume other gates mentioned in the second part of the report required no work (e.g., "Water Gate," v. 26; see Neh 8:1) since they are not mentioned as a repair project.

After the gate repair list (vv. 1–15), the structural emphasis shifts to strictly wall repairs (vv.16–32), also with the formulaic language "next to him" (slightly different in the original than the previous occurrences in vv. 1–15). Walls that needed to be repaired are geographically situated according to:

1. Preeminent architecture (e.g., "house of Eliashib the high priest" vv. 21–22)
2. Topographical landmarks (e.g., "hill of Ophel" v. 26)
3. Individuals' houses (v. 23)
4. Towers (e.g., "the great projecting tower"; v. 27)
5. Gates ("Water," [v. 26] "Horse," [v.28] "East," [v. 29] "Inspection," [v.31]).

The commentary below highlights some of the departures from the expected formulae.

**Sheep Gate (3:1–2).** In the Sheep Gate[14] building account (vv. 1–2), "Eliashib the High Priest," along with his "fellow priests" (lit., "brothers," v. 1; see also vv. 20, 21), leads the effort, which is part of the larger theme of the book. Priests act as the principal roles in the restoration of worship in Zion. This introduction also prepares us for a less favorable interaction between Nehemiah and the high priest, most notably in 13:4–5. The text emphasizes the priests' direct involvement (lit., "they by themselves made it holy"; v. 1). In addition, they "dedicated" the wall sections "as far as the Tower of the Hundred" and "as far as the Tower

13. NIV also uses the variation "adjoining section" (e.g., v. 2), but in Hebrew the language remains the same throughout.

14. A gate near the temple precinct.

of Hananel."[15] The unique focus on the sanctification process of both the Sheep Gate and abutting walls signals the spiritual nature of the venture and its endorsement by the priestly class in Jerusalem. They are saying: "we endorse this project; we think God is in it." This is why from the beginning of the project to its dedication in chapter 12, akin to a modern-day "opening ceremony," priestly involvement is emphasized.[16] Complementing the work of the priests (with the formulaic "next to them" or "adjoining" as NIV), the "men of Jericho" in the Jordan Valley highlight a broad geographical distribution eastward, but which does not include members of the Transjordanian community.[17]

**Fish Gate (3:3–5).** An oft-noted feature of the Fish Gate building account (its precise location is unknown) relates to the "nobles"[18] from "Tekoa"[19]) who "would not put their shoulders to the work under their supervisors" (*'adon* v. 5).[20] This contrarian stance, unique in the account of chapter 3, on the part of the tribal heads stands in sharp contrast to the overall spirit of collaboration exhibited by other leaders involved in the project (the priests and the governors), *including* the "men of Tekoa" themselves, along with three other groups who completed a total of four sections of the wall connected to the Fish Gate.

**Jeshanah Gate (3:6–12).** The Jeshanah Gate account, repaired by "Joiada" and "Meshullam" (v. 6), involves the most groups who participated in the wall repairs—10 project supervisors are mentioned by name. This suggests the work covered an extensive area from the upper western part of the wall to the "Valley Gate" (v. 13; lower western part of the wall). Nehemiah seems to highlight the following individuals in particular:

1. "Men from Gibeon and Mizpah" (v. 7), whose leaders are mentioned by name: Melatiah and Jadon. These communities are noted to fall under oversight of the "governor of Trans-Euphrates."

---

15. The actual location of these towers is unknown.

16. Unlike in this account, individual priests are mentioned by name in 12:41.

17. A seat of opposition to the work, represented by Tobiah the Ammonite, see ch. 2:19; 4:3.

18. *'adir* in the sense of a "tribal chief"; cf. Judg 5:13, 25; 2 Chr 23:20; Neh 10:29.

19. South of Bethlehem; 2 Sam 14:2; 23:26; Amos 1:1.

20. Work overseers rather than political officers ("governors").

This detail serves as a legal record that not everyone in Trans-Euphrates followed Sanballat's opposition to the work.[21]

2. "Uzziel" and "Hananiah" (v. 8)[22] "restored Jerusalem as far as the Broad Wall." There is some debate concerning the meaning of "restored" (*'azab*, "abandon") either as "discontinued" or "extended." Kidner makes a compelling case on the basis of usage elsewhere (principally, Neh 4:2) that the verb should be understood in the sense of *extended* to the "broad wall."[23] Thus, even though the text does not specify, this extension might have represented a substantial amount of work, which is all the more remarkable considering the two leaders' tradecraft.
3. Attesting further to the significance of this section of the project, the two half-rulers of Jerusalem are involved, Rephaiah (v. 9) and Shallum (v. 12). The latter solicited the help of "his daughters" who, while not mentioned by name represent yet another illustration of the degree of motivation and support this work elicited among the people of Yehud. Hard labor was no deterrent for Shallum's daughters.

**Valley, Dung, and Fountain Gates (3:13–15).** The accounts for these three gates stick close to the formulaic script, and the added details pertain to physical elements of the work. Hanum (without patronymics) and the "residents of Zanoah" (v. 13) were responsible for both the repair of the Valley Gate and the wall to the Dung Gate, which is the equivalent of five hundred yards/450 meters (NIV "1000 cubits"). This considerable distance speaks either to the substantial amount of work they produced or that a large section of the wall needed relatively little attention—probably the latter. The Dung Gate was repaired by Malkijah, a ruler of the district of Beth Hakkerem (south of Jerusalem), which was too small to be subdivided. Shallun, like Hanum above, is credited with both the repairing of the Fountain Gate and a section of the wall,

---

21. Nehemiah's own title for the province of Yehud, Neh 5:14.

22. "Goldsmiths" (root *tsaraf*, "refiners") i.e., metallurgical craftsmen; "perfumers" (root *raqah*) i.e., merchants involved in trading these goods.

23. Kidner, *Ezra and Nehemiah*, 95. The "broad wall" is the western perimeter wall added to the city in the eighth century BC after the fall of Samaria in 722 BC. See Amihai Mazar, *Archeology of the Land of the Bible: 10,000–586 B.C.E.* (New York: Doubleday, 1992), 420.

which in this case is a specific feature: "the wall of the pool of Siloam," situated "by the King's Garden," for a distance obviously well known to Nehemiah's audience—"as far as the steps going down from the city of David" (v. 15). Thus, these three gate accounts may be shorter than the previous three, but the work produced under the supervision of these leaders was significant.

**Wall repairs (3:16–32).** The second half of the account focuses exclusively on wall repairs, with the impression that no section of the wall was left unattended. The account here is packed with fascinating details pertaining to the layout of Jerusalem during the Persian period. Distances are measured on the basis of landmarks and individual houses. The language of *repair* continues (no mentioning of *building* the wall), which suggests that the work perhaps consisted mostly of restoring a previously-existing structure in the circuitous route that Nehemiah surveyed by night, and extending further north following the Kidron Valley (see ch. 2) back up to the Sheep Gate. As in the first half of the account, the identification of individual project leaders predominates:

**3:16–21.** In addition to four rulers of Yehud singled out, which again underscores the widespread provincial support,[24] Levites are mentioned for the first time, under Rehum's supervision. The "house of Eliashib the high priest" becomes a reconstruction landmark (v. 20) for both Baruch[25] and Meremoth (vv. 20–21).

**3:22–32.** The final tally reflects an emphasis on the priests' involvement (vv. 22, 28) and forms an *inclusio* of sorts with the opening paragraph (vv. 1–2), since we are nearing the temple precinct on the east side and northeastern side of the wall. "Temple servants" join in the work (v. 26); however, none of the priests and temple servants is mentioned by name. Since it was their expected duty, perhaps Nehemiah did not see the need to single them out. Volunteers, however, continue to be highlighted by name, including now "merchants," (v. 32) "Shemaiah, . . . the guard at the East Gate" (v. 29), and more "goldsmiths" (vv. 31–32). The contribution of Jerusalemites is emphasized by the formula "in front

---

24. "Nehemiah, ruler of the half-district of Beth Zur"; "Hashabiah" and "Binnui" (Heb. *bavvai*) both rulers of half districts at "Keilah"; and "Ezer, ruler of Mizpah."

25. The meaning of the term "zealously" is debated, and Williamson suggests eliding it (*Ezra, Nehemiah*, 198). However, the notion of zeal seems to fit well with the rest of the account.

of/beside his house" (e.g., v. 23). Of note, the "men of Tekoa" reappear (v. 27) to shore up the work, along with "Meremoth" (v. 21; cf. v. 4) and "Meshullam" (v. 30; cf. v. 4).

**BACKGROUND TO WALL BUILDING AND REPAIRS IN JERUSALEM.** In the ancient world, the responsibility to secure the capital city and the temples fell on the executive branch (the king). This pattern is reflected in ancient Israel. However, the focal point of physical descriptions of construction available in Scripture usually focuses on the temple itself. Nevertheless, the few mentions of wall building and repair point to the strategic and spiritual significance of maintaining a strong perimeter wall in the "city of the Great King" (Ps 48:2–3).

When David takes Jerusalem from the Jebusites (2 Sam 5) and renames it "the City of David" (2 Sam 5:7, 9), there is no discussion of building up the wall except for the general statement that "he restored the city" (1 Chr 11:7–8). There are comparatively few descriptions of wall construction in Solomon's otherwise substantial building projects in Jerusalem (1 Kgs 5–7). In the building of the temple, walls are mentioned, but only in relationship to the sacred precinct itself: "the great courtyard was surrounded by a wall of three courses of dressed stone and one course of trimmed cedar beams" (1 Kgs 7:12). However, this does not suggest the defensive wall was unattended. The biblical record states that Solomon also "built the terraces[26] and had filled in the gap in the wall of the city of David his father" (1 Kgs 11:27). Subsequent repairs and new constructions in Jerusalem are mentioned during the reigns of three Judean kings in the eighth century BC, the period of Neo-Assyrian imposition on Israel and Judah. Uzziah heavily fortified Jerusalem's Corner and Valley Gates by building towers on them (2 Chr 26:9; NIV "at them"); he also built a tower above the "angle of the wall" (2 Chr 26:9–10, the western side of the wall; cf. Neh 2:13). Jotham "rebuilt the Upper Gate of the temple" and undertook "extensive work on the wall at the

26. The NIV has "*the Millo*" (*millo'* for "terraces") as a footnote. Archaeologists have used this designation to describe the retaining wall excavated in the city of David by the Kidron Valley. See map in Mazar, *Archeology of the Land of the Bible*, 418.

hill of Ophel" (2 Chr 27:3,which is identified as the eastern section of the wall, south of the temple precinct; cf. Neh 3:26).[27] Hezekiah is famous for commissioning the construction of his eponymous underground aqueduct (2 Chr 32:30), with a commemorative building inscription to boot ("Hezekiah's Tunnel").[28] He also conducted extensive work on the enclosure wall, more than any other preexilic king, according to the biblical record: "He strengthened himself and he rebuilt all the broken sections of the wall. He also raised up towers on it" (2 Chr 32:5 author's translation). In addition, he built a westward expansion wall (probably following the influx of refugees from the north following the collapse of Samaria in 722 BC) in the area of Jerusalem named the *mishneh* (2 Chr 34:22; 2 Kgs 22:14, NIV "New Quarter"). This expansion wall is identified as the "Broad Wall" of Nehemiah 3:8 and 12:38, a section of which was excavated during the 1970 excavations in Jerusalem and is still visible today.[29] During the seventh century, Manasseh, upon his return to Jerusalem following his brief exile in Babylon, also conducted extensive work in the eastern section of the wall overlooking the Kidron Valley: "He rebuilt (*banah*) the outer wall of the City of David, west of the Gihon spring in the valley" (2 Chr 33:14). The wall extended all the way up to the Fish Gate (cf. Neh 3:3), "encircling the Hill of Ophel" (2 Chr 33:14). Adding to the significance of the work, the record states he raised the height of the wall greatly (2 Chr 33:14).

Finally, mention of the fortifications' damage is noted on two occasions. First, during the reign of Amaziah in the ninth century BC, within the context of the protracted civil war with the northern kingdom, "Jehoash [king of Israel] went to Jerusalem and broke down the wall of Jerusalem from the Ephraim Gate to the Corner Gate" (2 Kgs 14:13). These gates are not mentioned in the book of Nehemiah, but they probably should be located in the northern section of the city, since Ephraim was north of the city. The scope of the devastation is made clear since the length of the breach is mentioned ("four hundred cubits" is 180 m/600 ft; 2 Kgs 14:13). The second mention reflects the systematic and intentional breaking down (Heb. *natats*) of the perimeter wall by the

---

27. Currid and Barrett, *Crossway ESV Bible Atlas*, 184.

28. Ibid., 483–84.

29. See Williamson, *Ezra, Nehemiah*, 205–6, 375, and Mazar, *Archeology of the Land of the Bible*, 421.

Babylonians in 586 BC (2 Kgs 25:10; 2 Chr 36:19; Jer 52:14). Nebuchadnezzar's imperial guard was singled out to fulfill this task which, along with the burning down of the temple and all the houses in Jerusalem, underscores the desire to permanently erase Jerusalem from historical memory (Ps 137:7 speaks of the Edomites' desire for Jerusalem to be leveled down to bedrock). This context of complete devastation (Jer 52:14, "all the walls"), as opposed to breaches, forms the background to the rebuilding during Nehemiah's time.[30] It also provides an explanation as to why chapter 3 carefully plots the course of the repairs from the Sheep Gate and back: every area of the wall needed some work.

**Functions of walls and gates as protectors and delineators of sacred space.** Besides the obvious function of protecting the city itself, chapter 3 underscores the spiritual significance of the enclosure delineating Yahweh's sacred space in the midst of his people. A high degree of specificity regarding materials and measurements typically accompanies physical descriptions of Yahweh's sacred enclosure (the tabernacle's inner and outer court, Exod 25–31). This perhaps helps us understand the opening statement in chapter 3, that functions in both a political and spiritual sense. Without the political support of the priestly class, and the high priest Eliashib in particular, Nehemiah could not have completed the task he was commissioned to fulfill by Artaxerxes. However, the fact that the priests "dedicated" the space they rebuilt also speaks to the spiritual nature of the work. Later in the account, Levites and "temple servants" also actively participate. Thus, they understand that this is not a mere public work project but the restoration of the sacred nature of Zion and the preparation for its repopulation in fulfillment of the promise of Zion (see Introduction). Nevertheless, the emphasis in these texts regarding the establishment of Yahweh's sacred space, be it the tabernacle or the temple, lies with the temple and its implements, not the enclosure itself. In Israelite historical texts, the fortification system of Jerusalem are mentioned a priori in a military context (cf. Uzziah [2 Chr 26:9]), not necessarily as a demarcation line between sacred space and the outside. This is certainly reflected in ancient Israel's archetypical

---

30. L.-H. Vincent's caution is well taken regarding modern vs. ancient warfare and the varying scope of devastation one can expect. In other words, we can't expect a complete razing of the walls. Cited in "L'étendue de Jerusalem" in *La Palestine à L'Epoque Perse*, ed. E.-M. Laperrousaz and A. Lemaire (Paris: Editions du Cerf, 1994), 121.

sacred space, the tabernacle and its ark, which was surrounded by Israel's tribal military units (Num 2:1–2; 10:35). However, as in the case of the tabernacle, to limit the function of defensive structures around Yahweh's sacred space only to military purposes fails to do justice to the symbolism also reflected in Scripture: defensive features are meant to safeguard Yahweh's holiness. The tabernacle represents an exercise in "graded holiness."[31] The spiritual dimension of Zion's walls is captured particularly in the Psalms. In Psalm 51, the great psalm of confession, David concludes his confession (vv. 18–19) with the idea that the walls of Jerusalem function as a protective barrier so that righteous sacrifices might be offered within its walls:

> May it please you to prosper Zion,
> to build up the walls of Jerusalem.
> Then you will delight in the sacrifices of the righteous,
> in burnt offerings offered whole;
> then bulls will be offered on your altar.

In the context of David's confession, the relationship between the restoration of personal righteousness (see also Ps 32; Rom 4) and national security is profound and becomes a guiding light for subsequent generations, including Nehemiah's. The theological significance of Zion's enclosure is perhaps best reflected in Psalm 48, one of the great Zion psalms:

> Great is the LORD, and most worthy of praise,
> in the city of our God, his holy mountain.
>
> Beautiful in its loftiness,
> the joy of the whole earth,
> like the heights of Zaphon is Mount Zion,
> the city of the Great King.
> God is in her citadels;
> he has shown himself to be her fortress. (vv. 1–3)

---

31. Some areas of the precinct are more holy than others (e.g., holy of holies vs. the court). See Philip P. Jenson, *Graded Holiness: A Key to the Priestly Conception of the World*, JSOTSup 106 (Sheffield: JSOT Press, 1992), 89–96.

The "Great King" is said to dwell in her "citadels" (Heb. lexeme speaks of a royal building complex) and speaks of *Yahweh* as Zion's "fortress" (v. 3; in the sense of stronghold or refuge cf. Ps 94:22). Thus, any breakdown in the defensive integrity of the complex reflects poorly on the deity. If Zion's walls are broken down, the perception is that Yahweh is diminished.[32] Not only do walls and the complex as a whole uphold Yahweh's reputation, but they protect it from hostile kings:

> When the kings joined forces,
> when they advanced together,
> they saw her and were astounded;
> they fled in terror. (Ps 48:4–5)

The presence of the Great King within Zion makes the city secure and impregnable (see Jer 7:12–15 for qualifications on this theology). Conversely, if the walls are broken, this would make Yahweh vulnerable to attacks from his enemies and rob Yahweh of his glory and fame among the nations.

At the end of the poem, the psalm brings to the fore another crucial dimension to the walls' function:

> Walk about Zion, go around her,
> count her towers,
> consider well her ramparts,
> view her citadels,
> that you may tell of them
> to the next generation.
>
> For this God is our God for ever and ever;
> he will be our guide even to the end. (Ps 48:12–14)

Here the emphasis is placed on the enduring value of the walls of Zion, which should be passed on to the "next generation." Without its walls, Zion is incomplete and cannot fulfill its purpose as the "city of

32. A crucial theme in the book of Ezekiel. By restoring the people from exile, Yahweh vindicates his name, i.e., his reputation, in the eyes of the nations, e.g., Ezek 37:15–28.

the Great King," which points to the eternal value of Zion in God's plan of redemption.

In Isaiah the righteous person is compared to a jeweled and fortified city (Isa 49:16): "your walls are ever before me." A fascinating dimension to the wall restoration as part of the eschatological restoration, which may bear great significance for our context in Nehemiah, is the promise of a coming "Repairer of Broken Walls" (Isa 58:12), which may or may not be directly connected to Nehemiah. The specificity with which Isaiah can sometimes speak in his prophecy may not de facto rule out the possibility.

WE ARE ZION. THE LANGUAGE OF WALLS AND gates takes on special significance in the Christian life and builds upon the symbolism established in the Old Testament. The church is characterized as "bulwark of truth" (1 Tim 3:15 RSV), and the "Gates of Hell shall not prevail against it" (Matt 16:18 ESV). Likewise, from an individual standpoint, the "living stones" of 1 Peter 2:5 also allude to the temple enclosure. The author of Hebrews reminds his audience they belong to a heavenly Zion, with their names registered (as in a census) there (12:22–24):

> But you have come to Mount Zion, to the city of the living God, the heavenly Jerusalem. You have come to thousands upon thousands of angels in joyful assembly, to the church of the firstborn, whose names are written in heaven. You have come to God, the Judge of all, to the spirits of the righteous made perfect, to Jesus the mediator of a new covenant, and to the sprinkled blood that speaks a better word than the blood of Abel.

Revelation 21:9–27 offers the most detailed description of the eschatological City of God with great walls and twelve gates, which is the fulfillment of Isaiah's vision of the heavenly Jerusalem: a jeweled royal enclosure that is impregnable because righteousness reigns in its midst (Isa 54:11–17).

One aspect of the wall imagery is the personification of fortress Zion as Yahweh himself. Yahweh is said to be a "stronghold," and "a fortress" (see Ps 18/2 Sam 24 as a paradigm). We remember Martin Luther's hymn, "Ein Feste Burg," "A Mighty Fortress Is Our God," that captures the psalm's notion that God *is* the stronghold: "A mighty fortress is our God, a bulwark never failing!" In the second stanza, Luther characteristically (and rightly) equates "Lord Sabaoth" (the Lord of Hosts) with Jesus himself, "from age to age the same, and He must win the battle." This is precisely where the author of Hebrews takes us: "you have come to Mount Zion, . . . to Jesus the mediator of a new covenant (Heb 12:22, 24)."

**We are all in this together.** The people coming together to rebuild Zion also parallels the situation during the time of the first restoration under Zerubabbel and Joshua, where the people agreed (after some prodding from Haggai [1:4] and Zechariah [4:6–10]) to rebuild the temple. What is clearly intentional in this account is the remarkable diversity of representation for the building project. People of all walks of life participated. The expected ones, such as the priests, Levites, and temple servants, are present, since the restoration of the sanctity of Zion is the primary mission. Nehemiah also underscores the widespread support from the officials in Yehud (six "rulers"; see discussion above). Qualification for participation does not relate to one's particular skillsets but is based on the desire to rebuild Zion (e.g., perfumers, merchants and daughters, see discussion above) which for us means the edification and sanctification of the body of Christ. This image painted by Nehemiah 3 prepares us for the unity of the body of Christ reflected in the list of Romans 12:1–8, which allows a diversity of role and functions so that the whole body/temple (1 Cor 3:16; Eph 2:22) is built together. In our work of service in the church, we, too, as it were, shore up Zion and sanctify it as members of the priesthood of God (1 Pet 2:9). Everybody gets a part in the building up of Zion: tribal heads, and established leaders actively participate along with those whose gifts are not directly connected to the work of the ministry (i.e., the "perfumers" of Nehemiah's time; see discussion above). It is community work! Every pastor and church staff know how hard it is to get volunteers for ministry work in the local church, on the mission field, and in other areas of Christian service. However, once people grab hold of the fact that their involvement is far greater than themselves, being the edification and building up of Zion/people of God, Nehemiah 3 gives us the encouragement that unity of purpose and the raising up of volunteers can in fact be achieved. How? Nehemiah sets the context in chapter 1 that the restoration of the sanctity of Zion needs to be bathed in prayer, but without the sovereign intervention of Yahweh, in the hearts of the king of Persia, the rulers, and all the people in Yehud, the work could not have begun and this sense of community (which reminds us of Paul's notion of *koinonia*/partnership in Phil 1:6) would have had very little traction. As Zechariah had claimed (Zech 4:6), the building up of God's work is "not by might nor by power, but by my Spirit." To this day, we must remember that every venture needs to be Spirit-led and Spirit-infused if we hope to see any measure of success.

Some look at the book of Nehemiah as a leadership manual and admire Nehemiah as the entrepreneurial leader who takes the initiative and "gets things done" (via high productivity, the mighty idol of our time). Chapter 3 omits Nehemiah's name, as if he had nothing to do with this important first phase of the project. We need to be careful not to read too much into this absence of his name; however, it should cause the reader to reflect upon it at some level. Perhaps the omission was Nehemiah's way to underscore that without the people the project could not have been completed. If this is the case, it directs the credit away from himself and seems in line with his passion for the city of the Great King (Ps 48:2) as reflected in chapter 1. What we can say with great assurance is that the theme of continued answers to prayer continues in earnest. Nehemiah has capitalized on the initial momentum, and we should read the success reflected in chapter 3 as Yahweh's continued "good hand" to be upon the people. The following chapter provides a stark reminder that spiritual successes in building up Zion breeds fierce opposition.

# Nehemiah 4:1–23

1 When Sanballat heard that we were rebuilding the wall, he
became angry and was greatly incensed. He ridiculed the Jews,
2 and in the presence of his associates and the army of Samaria,
he said, "What are those feeble Jews doing? Will they restore
their wall? Will they offer sacrifices? Will they finish in a day?
Can they bring the stones back to life from those heaps of
rubble—burned as they are?"

3 Tobiah the Ammonite, who was at his side, said, "What
they are building—even a fox climbing up on it would break
down their wall of stones!"

4 Hear us, our God, for we are despised. Turn their insults
back on their own heads. Give them over as plunder in a land
of captivity. 5 Do not cover up their guilt or blot out their sins
from your sight, for they have thrown insults in the face of
the builders.

6 So we rebuilt the wall till all of it reached half its height,
for the people worked with all their heart.

7 But when Sanballat, Tobiah, the Arabs, the Ammonites
and the people of Ashdod heard that the repairs to Jerusalem's
walls had gone ahead and that the gaps were being closed,
they were very angry. 8 They all plotted together to come and
fight against Jerusalem and stir up trouble against it. 9 But we
prayed to our God and posted a guard day and night to meet
this threat.

10 Meanwhile, the people in Judah said, "The strength of
the laborers is giving out, and there is so much rubble that we
cannot rebuild the wall."

11 Also our enemies said, "Before they know it or see us, we
will be right there among them and will kill them and put an
end to the work."

12 Then the Jews who lived near them came and told us ten
times over, "Wherever you turn, they will attack us."

13 Therefore I stationed some of the people behind the
lowest points of the wall at the exposed places, posting them by

families, with their swords, spears and bows. 14 After I looked
things over, I stood up and said to the nobles, the officials and
the rest of the people, "Don't be afraid of them. Remember the
Lord, who is great and awesome, and fight for your families,
your sons and your daughters, your wives and your homes."

15 When our enemies heard that we were aware of their
plot and that God had frustrated it, we all returned to the wall,
each to our own work.

16 From that day on, half of my men did the work, while
the other half were equipped with spears, shields, bows and
armor. The officers posted themselves behind all the people
of Judah 17 who were building the wall. Those who carried
materials did their work with one hand and held a weapon in
the other, 18 and each of the builders wore his sword at his side
as he worked. But the man who sounded the trumpet stayed
with me.

19 Then I said to the nobles, the officials and the rest of
the people, "The work is extensive and spread out, and we are
widely separated from each other along the wall. 20 Wherever
you hear the sound of the trumpet, join us there. Our God will
fight for us!"

21 So we continued the work with half the men holding
spears, from the first light of dawn till the stars came out. 22 At
that time I also said to the people, "Have every man and his
helper stay inside Jerusalem at night, so they can serve us as
guards by night and as workers by day." 23 Neither I nor my
brothers nor my men nor the guards with me took off our
clothes; each had his weapon, even when he went for water.

## Physical Threat (4:1–23)

**Setting.** Within the wall construction account of Nehemiah's memoir (chs. 3–6), Nehemiah 4 represents the greatest danger to the rebuilding of the wall, following the verbal threats introduced in Nehemiah 2:10, 19. The account could be dubbed "Zion strikes back" since the last time the community tried to restore "the walls" (Ezra 4:13), they were forcibly stopped (Ezra 4:23). This time however, the attempt to prevent the rebuilding of "fortress" Zion will fail, due in no small part to Nehemiah's crucial interventions. The language common to preexilic conquest and warfare narratives (e.g., "our God will fight for us"; 4:20) undergirds the report. The chapter alternates between reported speeches by the enemies of Yehud (vv. 2–3, 11), the people's concerns (vv. 10, 12), and Nehemiah's strategic addresses (vv. 4–5; 14; 19–20; 22–23). Structurally, the repeated temporal phrase, "when Sanballat [and others] heard" introduces each section of the chapter (vv. 1, 7, 15). Nehemiah's third-person narration reads like eyewitness accounts of the typical high stress found at times of conflicts. Not surprisingly (from chs. 1–2), Nehemiah underscores the centrality and effectiveness of prayer, either in reported speech (cf. 4–5) or in the narrative voice (v. 9).

The central idea of chapter 4 is perhaps best summed up in Nehemiah's critical address to the community in verse 14 (see commentary below) with three pointed imperatives: "Don't be afraid; remember the Lord; fight for your own." Thus, whereas Nehemiah removes himself from the building account in Nehemiah 3, chapter 4 propels him to the forefront of the action and gives him a central role in the rebuilding of the wall. This is not surprising since the project essentially becomes a power play between varying political factions jockeying for the control of Yehud. We do not know who was governor at the time of the first stoppage of the work (as recorded in Ezra 4), but on Nehemiah's watch, his spiritual stamina and determination (as reflected by several months of prayer and fasting; see Neh 1) is now matched by his courage to confront this immediate and serious physical threat against the welfare of Zion.

**Sanballat's Brinkmanship (4:1–3).**[1] The opposition's strong opposition to the building of the walls has a straightforward reason: ". . . Sanballat heard that we were rebuilding the wall."[2] Evidently, Sanballat was *predisposed* to undermine the galvanizing effect of the newly-appointed governor of Yehud, but what took him by surprise was the scope of involvement. Chapter 3, of course, underscores that the effort was the

---

1. 3:33–38 in the Hebrew Text.

2. As a temporal dependent clause, the syntactical construction "we" + "were rebuilding" (as ongoing action) directly links the events of Neh 3 to Sanballat's and Tobiah's comments found in 4:2–3. In addition, it signals that Nehemiah was fully involved in organizing the work in chapter 3, even though his name is not mentioned (see commentary on Neh 3).

work of a large portion of the population, which is itself the fruit of God's "good hand" upon Nehemiah and the community ("for the people worked with all their heart," 4:6). Thus, the narrative's building blocks create a coherent whole so far, and the threat of violence to come in this chapter is reflected by the selection of three key verbs to express Sanballat's sentiments: "He became angry."[3] That Sanballat was "greatly incensed" recalls images of intense vexation and pain, such as how Peninah harangued Hannah (1 Sam 1:6) or Yahweh's intense displeasure at Israel's prostitution with idols (Ezek 16:42). The third verb, "[h]e ridiculed the Jews" is also familiar lexical territory in the Old Testament, particularly when it is paired with the language of "despising" (Neh 2:19, NIV "mocked and ridiculed us"; see also Ps 22:7).

Offering a further parallel to the initial threat of 2:19, the taunting is accentuated by a reported speech framed as a series of rhetorical questions (v. 2). The otherwise typical introduction of reported speech, "he said," includes "in the presence of his associates" but contains an ominous addition: "and the army of Samaria." Thus, Sanballat gives a counterpart speech to motivate *his* troops as Nehemiah did to the leaders of Yehud in 2:17–18, with equal success. Sanballat is prepared to escalate the conflict to armed confrontation in order to prevent the Jews from achieving their goal. This strategy worked in the past (Ezra 4); there is no reason to think that it will not work this time. This, in part, explains the boldness and the forcefulness of the rhetorical questions (five of them) that are organized in a clear sequence in the text. His address reflects propagandist brinkmanship typical of this genre of jingoistic speeches: first, the deliberate demeaning of the enemy ("those feeble Jews") and their action ("what are [they] doing?"); second, the assurance of their failure ("will they restore[4] their wall?" ["wall" is absent in the original text]); third, knowledge and thwarting of their ultimate purpose ("will they offer sacrifices?").[5] The fourth taunt betrays the urgency for this call to arms (*casus belli*)—"will they finish in a day?"—and uncovers Sanballat's thinly-veiled anxiety in the face of the Jews' initial success.

---

3. "To be angry" is typically used to describe Yahweh's anger at Israel's sin in preexilic documents, e.g., Judg 2:14.

4. See 3:8.

5. Akin to, "We know what you're up to; don't you think you're going to get away with it."

The final question focuses on the physical impossibility of the undertaking, indirectly providing a window into the scope of the walls' devastation and the magnitude of the work, undoubtedly with a touch of hyperbole: calcified ("burned") limestone building materials are no better than dust (NIV "rubble").

"Tobiah the Ammonite" (v. 3) is re-introduced without his title of "servant," but the echo-chamber effect of his rhetorical question supports the idea of his role as Sanballat's junior partner. His colorful image of a light canid causing the collapse of the "wall of stones" adds nothing to the substance of Sanballat's rhetoric but does speak to the undoubtedly hurried and flimsy nature of the work. The reference to ruins populated only by jackals/foxes (the original can mean both) does conjure up image of the devastation of ruined cities (Lam 5:18; Ezek 13:4).

This intentional use of repeated language to characterize the posture of Nehemiah's enemies paves the way for the corporate imprecatory prayer of the community in verses 4–5. Sanballat and his allies are considered enemies of Yahweh in this narrative in the same way preexilic historical texts frame Yahweh's enemies. As the narrative unfolds elsewhere in the book, however, Nehemiah's sentiment toward them is not always shared by key members of the community of Yehud.

**Nehemiah's corporate prayer (4:4–6).** The third prayer in the book is cast as a community prayer ("O our God," author's translation), but the rest of the chapter, in light of Nehemiah's direct involvement, leaves little doubt Nehemiah himself led this prayer, rather than the religious authorities (e.g., Eliashib, cf. 3:1). The prayer fits the genre of imprecation, common in the psalms, where the Yahwist prays down Deuteronomic curses upon his enemies' head. The imprecation is subdivided into three distinct curses:

1. Following the ancient rule of *lex talionis* ("eye for eye," cf. Exod 21:24): "Turn their insults back on their own head" (Neh 4:4).
2. Much more severe is the second imprecation, which clearly evokes the worst of Deuteronomic curses (apart from death) in Deuteronomy 28:41: "give them over as plunder in a land of captivity" (author's translation) which, according to Nehemiah's rank and legal authorization, it would be well within his rights to call upon "Persian power" to squash their attempt from stopping what Artaxerxes authorized. However, considering the urgency

of the situation and the imminent threat, by the time the appeal reached Artaxerxes and his ruling, the community of Zion could be long disabled. Sanballat knows time is on his side in this matter, and he adopts a "strike while the iron is hot" approach. This is why Nehemiah wastes no time and makes his appeal to a higher authority directly concerning this matter.

3. The third appeal falls squarely in the spiritual realm, since it deals with the Deuteronomic categories of "guilt" and "sins" (4:5). The community is calling upon Yahweh as judge to adjudicate. There is no doubt as to who the guilty party is in this matter, and the prayer is framed accordingly: "for they have thrown insults (the same root used in 4:1, "he ridiculed them") in the face of the builders." Thus, the last imprecation circles back to an appeal for vindication by Yahweh upon those who have sinned against Zion. Nehemiah is calling upon Yahweh to take sides.

Verse 6 summarizes the situation at the halfway point and functions as a bridge statement, serving both as an explanation for the strongly, worded opposition and looming threat of the "army of Samaria" of the preceding paragraph (vv. 1–5). It also prepares us for the impending struggle of the rest of the chapter. The initial progress report will now be met with fierce opposition. The explanatory "for the people worked with all their heart" (v. 6) exemplifies the turnaround among the people from "disgrace" (1:3) to motivation, following Nehemiah's arrival in Yehud (2:18). This summary also underscores the continuing theme of Yahweh's favor upon Nehemiah, the project, and its participants.

**Escalation of the crisis (4:7–9).** This summary paragraph is structurally a mirror image of the sequence of verses 1–5. The temporal phrase "but when Sanballat . . . heard" (vv. 1, 7), coupled with the enemies' violent reaction, "they were very angry" (v. 7; "he became angry," v. 1) are intentionally repeated to reflect the persistence of the opposition. As in verses 4–5, this escalating threat is met by the prayers of the community (v. 9), which points to the determination of the community to face this threat with keen spiritual awareness. To counter this physical threat will require spiritual means. The obvious parallels thus draw attention to the two crucial new facts emerging out of the second summary, which signals a clear escalation in the dispute. First, new opponents are added to the known lists (cf. 2:10, 19; 4:1, 3). The naming of "the Arabs" and "the

Ammonites" (v. 7) suggest Geshem and Tobiah are more than isolated underlings on the political scenes but are in fact tribal leaders in alliance with Sanballat against the Jews. "The people of Ashdod" (v. 7) are new enemies on Nehemiah's left flank, and this reinforces the impression of an all-azimuth threat, with enemies in front, to the right, the left, and behind Jerusalem (Sanballat, Tobiah, Ashdod and Geshem, respectively). The picture recalls the sinister days of the preexilic era when Jerusalem was encircled by enemies (e.g., 2 Kgs 25). The reason for Sanballat's reinforcements is neatly signaled structurally by the doublet of the particle "that" in v. 7 (which itself repeats the information from v. 6):

- "That the repairs of Jerusalem's walls had gone ahead"
- "and that the gaps[6] were being closed"

The repeat of the progress report on the wall is echoed by another repeated and now familiar reaction by Yehud's rapidly-growing enemies: "they were very angry" (cf. 4:1; 2:10).

The second added element in the second paragraph builds upon the first one: the coalition of tribal groups are ready to take Sanballat's war of words to the next level (v.8).

"They all plotted together" matches the unity of purpose demonstrated by Yehud in rebuilding the wall in Nehemiah 3. This consensus has a dual purpose:

- "to come and fight[7] against Jerusalem"
- "and stir up trouble[8] against it"

The spiritual reaction to this physical threat continues to mirror the structure of the previous paragraph (v. 9, "we prayed to our God" // "our God," v. 4) but is now conveyed in the narrative voice. Its brevity recalls Nehemiah's own prayer to the king in 2:4, with significant supplementary detail: "[we] posted a guard day and night to meet this threat"

---

6. A technical term to describe the breach in the wall of a city (usually caused by invading armies, cf. 2 Chr. 32:5).

7. A verb unmistakably linked to armed conflict in conquests and war texts of the OT (e.g., Josh 9:2).

8. In the sense of spreading confusion (see Isa 19:14).

(v. 8). Proleptically, this statement sets the tone for the rest of the chapter: the community answers Sanballat's brinkmanship via both spiritual and physical means. This existential threat will remain constant, "day and night" (cf. 4:22, "by night" and "by day").

**Nehemiah's address to community: Remember and fight! (4:10–15).** In quick succession, three reported speeches (framed by the typical introduction "and he said/and they said") expose the depth of the threat at the half-way mark and sets the stage for the events narrated in the rest of the chapter. The speeches also provide the background to Nehemiah's second major address to the community in verse 14 (see his first address in 2:17). The first speech by "the people in Judah" (v. 10) reflects the sentiment of the community at large (cf. Neh 3): the extent of the devastation, principally at the hands of the Babylonians in 586 BC,[9] seriously hampers the debris-clearing process. Workers cannot go about their task of wall restoration, and they are faltering. Nehemiah's own struggles during his night survey (2:14) provide legitimacy to the people's complaint. The emphasis in the people's concern lies in the last sentence of v.10: "we[10] cannot rebuild the wall," which underscores the gravity of the moment. The workers are hitting the proverbial wall and provide an eerie reversal to Nehemiah's call to action in 2:17: "Let us rebuild the wall of Jerusalem."

The second speech (v. 11) shifts the focus to an impending threat from the "enemies." The coalition's (see 4:9) covert special operation ("before they know it or see us") and objective ("we . . . will kill them and put an end to the work"; v. 11) represents a marked escalation in the conflict. Attesting to the strategic value of this ancient city even during the Persian period, a determined enemy is ready to terminate the workers in order to prevent the rebuilding of the wall. However, the element of surprise is lost. In addition to God's providential oversight (v. 15), what appears to be Nehemiah's effective human intelligence network (see verse 12; also 6:19) prepares the people for this impending attack and sets the stage for the prevailing theme of military readiness in the chapter. What began as a civilian public works building project

---

9. In 52:14, Jeremiah specifies that "all" the walls around Jerusalem were broken down by "the whole Babylonian army."

10. This emphasis is conveyed in the original via the redundant use of the personal pronoun, "we, we are not able to build/rebuild the wall."

could become a full-blown asymmetric insurgency in Yehud, all within the first days of Nehemiah's governorship!

The third speech (v. 12) shifts to a reported quotation from "Jews who lived near them [the "enemies" of v. 11)" and continues the movement toward an escalation of the conflict, now outside the bounds of Jerusalem proper. The repeated nature of their report ("ten times over") underscores the determination of the hostile coalition to expand the conflict beyond the wall project in Jerusalem. The meaning of the quote "Wherever you turn, they will attack us" is somewhat obscure, and conflicting translations reflect this sense of ambiguity.[11] However, the overall meaning of the statement remains quite clear: Jews in outlying communities are feeling the imposition from Sanballat's tribal alliance. It appears the enemy has seized the opportunity created by the fluid situation in Jerusalem to assert a more robust regional stance over Jewish settlements outside the city. This, in turn, places intense pressure on Nehemiah at the outset of his governorship to provide protection for the Jewish communities living outside Jerusalem. He is potentially facing a regional conflict between the varying populations in Yehud. As governor of Yehud, any report of sedition making its way back to Persia would reflect quite poorly upon Nehemiah's skills to maintain the peace. Evidently Sanballat knows that, and he is putting a full-court press on Nehemiah to back down from rebuilding Jerusalem.

This backdrop of three speeches emphasizes the significance of Nehemiah's first address since his arrival (4:14). The initial enthusiasm has waned; people are tired and feel, with good reasons, that the project cannot be completed. Reliable intelligence suggests an imminent surprise attack is expected. The Jewish inhabitants living in the province fear reprisal from their northern, southern, eastern, and western neighbors

---

11. A more literal translation would be, "And it happened when the Jews came—those who dwell near them—they said to us ten times, from all places, that 'you must return (masculine plural) to us.'" Thus, the language of "attack" (NIV) is absent from the original text. Structurally, it seems preferable to view "you must return to us" alone as the reported speech from the Jews to the builders in Jerusalem. Therefore, "ten times, from all places" are adverbials of time and space modifying the speech itself. The hyperbolic nature of the adverbs points to the tremendous pressure placed on the outlying communities, which in turn puts equal pressure on Nehemiah to respond to their call for help. ESV seems to capture the sense best: "At that time the Jews who lived near them came from all directions and said to us ten times, 'You must return to us'" (so Williamson, *Ezra, Nehemiah*, 220).

if the work goes on in Jerusalem. They are putting constant pressure on Nehemiah on this front. It is not an understatement to describe the situation as dire. However, Nehemiah rises to the moment and addresses the leadership, but not before taking two practical steps to protect Zion (v. 13). These practical measures are signaled by the use of the main verb "I stationed" repeated twice in v. 13 ("I stationed" and "posting them" in NIV). The first action seeks to establish a presence at a particularly vulnerable spot in the wall. The verse is not without its difficulties in Hebrew, but the general idea is clear: Nehemiah himself sets up a military presence in a vulnerable spot (NIV "exposed places"), facing out at its "lowest point" (i.e., most easily penetrated by an enemy force).[12] The second immediate action taken is directly dependent upon the first, since it describes those assigned to this area of the wall: "posting" the people according to "families (*mishpahot*), with their swords, their spears, and their bows" (v. 13). The significance of "families" lies in the tribal ancestral ties binding the people together, which assumes loyalty and solidarity, should there be an armed confrontation with the enemy. The triplicate description of their weapon systems suggests heavily armed guards were stationed in this most vulnerable spot of the wall.

With these stop-gap measures in place, he is ready to address the community ("I saw, I arose and I said"; v. 14, author's translation) as a whole as he did when he first arrived in Jerusalem ("the nobles, the officials, and the rest of the people," v. 14) with a sequence of three imperatives that point to the urgency of the matter:

- "Don't be afraid"
- "Remember"
- "Fight"

The structural arrangement of this call for solidarity intentionally juxtaposes the two verbs—"remember" and "fight"—in the Hebrew and emphasizes remembrance of the Lord's (*'adonai*) past faithfulness in battle. The description of the Lord as "great and awesome" (v. 14) evokes Yahweh's revelation of his might in Israel's past (e.g., Exod 15:11; Deut 10:17), along with the inevitable martial connotations. The initial exhortation "Don't be afraid of them" is also an enshrined exhortation in

12. See Williamson's (*Ezra, Nehemiah*, 220–22) lucid explanation.

Israelite lore, since Joshua and Caleb exhorted the *beney yisra'el* ("the sons of Israel" e.g., Num 1:2) to stand their ground against the giants of the land: "Do not be afraid of them" (Num 14:9). This call to remembrance of the past is bonded to the call to fight *in the present.* The chief rationale for this fight does not reach for lofty theological and eschatological ideals concerning the restoration of Zion (as Nehemiah's prayer in ch. 1 implies). Nehemiah does not lean on his own credentials as Persian official, either. He instead reaches for the people's own sense of tribal identity: "families" speaks of solidarity and togetherness (amply demonstrated in the list of ch. 3); "wives" and "homes" (*battim* "houses") speak of the very personal nature of the threat. "Your sons and your daughters," while also very personal, addresses more directly the future of the community. Thus, in a terse address, Nehemiah motivates a discouraged community to stand up and fight. The rest of the chapter chronicles the success of Nehemiah's approach and speaks to his deftness as a motivator in the community. By calling them to remember and fight, Nehemiah accomplished the dual purpose of not only averting a serious physical threat to the work but also motivating the community to return to their work, in spite the logistical difficulties.

Verse 15 represents a significant marker in Nehemiah's narrative and provides the theological summary of why the community went from a high state of military readiness to the resumption of the work. To the end of the chapter, and in the rest of the account, the community will not face a similar sense of physical danger. Rather, the themes become vigilance and collaboration in the rest of chapter 4. Subsequent problems will relate to other matters. For the governor himself, however, physical threats will return later in his tenure in the province (see chapter 6). Two significant factors contributed to the reduced threat level in Jerusalem and Yehud: "when our enemies heard that we were aware of their plot" and "that God had frustrated (Heb. is a causative verb) it" (v. 15). From an operational standpoint, the success of a covert operation is proportional to the degree of surprise achieved.[13] The second factor relates to the main theological undercurrent governing the Ezra-Nehemiah narrative: God's providential intervention to restore his people and worship in Jerusalem. Nehemiah typically credits God, as does Ezra, as the prime mover to

13. William H. McRaven, *Spec Ops Case Studies in Special Operations Warfare: Theory and Practice* (New York: Random House, 1995), 16–19.

establish God's covenantal plan of restoration and to level the obstacles in front of the returnees (Isa 40; cf. Ezra 8). Thus, here in this moment of great threat, Nehemiah credits God as the deliverer of his people.

Success is conveyed through a summary statement that underscores that the crucial element of unity has also been restored: "we all[14] returned to the wall, each to our own work" (Neh 4:15). Unity of purpose has been restored; no one has abandoned his or her station. The tiresomeness of the work and the concerns of the outlying communities are not directly addressed, which underscores the strategic focus was and remains the building of the walls. To address the crisis, Nehemiah chose not to get distracted with the events happening outside Jerusalem proper. So far, his strategy seems to be working.

**Total commitment (4:16–23).** From verse 16 to the end of the chapter, the tide has turned. The builders have regained the initiative. Preparedness, solidarity, and unity of purpose, along with the inevitable sacrifices, dominate the account. To rebuild this wall demands total commitment.

As a result of the successful dismantling of the enemy's plan, Nehemiah makes a significant shift to the strategy of rebuilding. In order to make sure workers stay on the job, he puts half the labor force (he calls them "my men") on security duty (v. 16). These are heavily armed, but defensive "shields" and "armor" (v. 16) are added to the kit (cf. v. 13). To complete the picture, "officers" (for the first time Nehemiah uses this common term to describe tribal leaders) are said to be "behind all the people of Judah (v. 16) who were building the wall" (v. 17), underscoring again that unity has been restored, since the province as a whole has come back together for the project of rebuilding the walls. Sanballat's plan to weaken the force present in Jerusalem by putting pressure on the outlying community has failed. Nehemiah did not take the bait.

However, as a precautionary measure, exposed workers, who found themselves frequently outside the wall because of their assignment, carried a "weapon" (v. 17) as they moved the building materials.[15] The third

14. "We all" confirms Nehemiah's own direct involvement in the building project, even though his name is not mentioned on the list of chapter 3. He is willing to work without taking credit.

15. The term for "materials" (*sebel* v. 17, "burden") refers to the building materials from the debris, found outside the wall, that put the workers in a vulnerable position.

group, "each of the builders" (v. 18), those assigned to the building of the wall proper, also carried a weapon on them. In contrast to the carriers (who probably were moving the stones on their head), both hands were needed, hence the added detail of "his sword at his side as he worked." The final element of this sophisticated defense strategy includes communication to the various parties via a "trumpet" at Nehemiah's side ("stayed with me"; v. 18). The assumption here is that Nehemiah himself moved frequently on the site and functioned as the overall supervisor of both the work and the defense of the city.

Verse 19 introduces us to Nehemiah's next major speech in his memoirs, which relates to the logistical role of the trumpet and the call to readiness, should Sanballat attempt to ambush them again. The address is as formal as the previous two (2:16–17; 4:14) since it addresses "the nobles, the officials and the rest of the people." The mention of the work as "extensive and spread out" recognizes the concerns of the people in 4:10. To rebuild the wall is a massive undertaking in light of the record of a perimeter-wide disabling of the city's defense capabilities by the Babylonian army in 586 BC. The address also recognized how the project is understaffed and vulnerable. However, in a pep talk echoing the words of Joshua in the conquest of Canaan, Nehemiah again looks beyond the adverse circumstances, as he did during his time of prayer and fasting, and looks up to "our God" who "will fight for us" (v. 20), but not without addressing the question of preparedness in the case of an attack: "whenever you hear the sound of the trumpet, join us there." The "there" presupposes the expected point of attack would be the place that represented the most vulnerable place of the enclosure. Thus, with remarkable economy of words, Nehemiah describes in specific ways how the defense of the city could be pursued without interfering with the pace or reassigning workers to the security details. Everyone contributed in that dual role, including those most exposed to a potential ambush. The mention of the "trumpet man" (v. 18) next to Nehemiah underscores the sense of solidarity, so that the whole group effectively functioned as a rapid-response unit, should Sanballat attempt to attack them again.

Verse 21 provides another summary that functions as a framing device with the summary of verse 21, "so we continued the work with half the men holding spears." This state of heightened security lasted until the completion of the wall in 6:15. The language now focuses on the revised working hours in light of Sanballat's threat. Nehemiah is under no illusion that Sanballat has given up on trying to prevent the rebuilding of the wall. As a result, he imposes on the workers and himself a new operational tempo that essentially becomes a 24-hours-a-day operation. Since the building project has now become a military operation, regular work hours have been expanded and are "from the first light of dawn till the stars came out" (v. 21). Additionally, leaves have been cancelled since workers now function as night guards "inside Jerusalem" (v. 22); there are no exceptions ("every man"). We are also given another indicator to Nehemiah's strategy that had been left unclear in the narrative. Every worker (with his sidearm) also enjoyed the added security of an armed guard by his side ("his helper"; v. 21). This final detail speaks to Nehemiah's own determination to guard the community (v. 23): "neither I nor my brothers nor my men nor the guards with me" let down their guard since no one removed his garments at night for personal hygiene. Instead, he kept his weapon, "even when he went for water" (v. 23).

Thus, the account of Jerusalem's greatest physical threat ends on this personal detail regarding Nehemiah's own commitment to the restoration. They bathed with their clothes on and with their side arms at the ready. While other accounts will end with a prayer for God to remember Nehemiah's faithfulness (ch. 5 and, especially, ch. 13), this account focuses on a very personal detail regarding Nehemiah and his men's hygiene. Nevertheless, the theme of testifying to his diligence to restore the worship of Zion remains intact. Nehemiah "walked the walk" and made tremendous sacrifices, like everyone else during this time of crisis. Chapter 5 will continue this theme in a much more direct way, since it affects Nehemiah's willingness to forego the perks associated with his rank as the Persian-appointed governor.

**Intimidation.** To all the rhetorical questions posed by Sanballat and the one by Tobiah, the truthful answers would be in the affirmative (4:1–3). The central plank of their strategy is to undermine the work and create discouragement by highlighting some realities the community faces (see Ezra 3–4). Previous failure, an unproven record, an unrealistic outcome both in terms of quality and timeframe, and the apparent hopelessness of the task all suggest that, based on their demonstrated weakness and inexperience, the task is doomed to fail and should, therefore, be permanently cancelled. The truth, however, is otherwise.

1. What the community is doing is not insignificant; in fact, it's the opposite, since they are restoring Zion in preparation for the coming of the King; Isaiah's prophecy and its promise of success based on Yahweh's sovereignty (Isa 40) looms large as the theological rationale for the rebuilding.
2. The community is not weak and feeble but is, in fact, strong "in the strength of the Lord." This message was made clear to the first returnees and especially as a personal prophetic word to Zerubbabel in Zechariah 4:6: "This is the word of the LORD to Zerubbabel: 'Not by might nor by power, but by my Spirit,' says the LORD Almighty."
3. Yes, they will restore the wall.
4. Yes, they will sacrifice at the temple again (by restoring the sanctity of Zion via its sacred enclosure wall).
5. Granted, they will not finish in a day, but fifty-two days might as well as be the equivalent of a symbolic day, since the restoration project is proceeding at a record pace.
6. Yes, the Jews will, in fact, revert the Deuteronomic curse of the destruction of the temple site (2 Kgs 25:9) and the Babylonian intentional cancelling of worship in Zion. Sanballat has enough perception and discernment to know what is at stake, hence the gathering of the "army of Samaria" (4:2).
7. Tobiah's comment functions as a footnote to Sanballat's and reiterates the principal charge that the task is essentially worthless, and the actual work amounts to nothing more than a hack job. In fact, it is so shoddy, no military intervention will be necessary, since wild animals will cause the downfall of the wall. The mention of the jackal as an enduring symbol of the desolation of a cursed city adds to this atmosphere of intimidation. Lamentations especially capture the mood following the Babylonian destruction of 586 BC:

Joy is gone from our hearts;
   our dancing has turned to mourning.
The crown has fallen from our head.
   Woe to us, for we have sinned!

Because of this our hearts are faint,
  Because of these things our eyes grow dim
for Mount Zion, which lies desolate,
  with jackals prowling over it. (Lam. 5:15–18)

The imagery of Lamentations taps into a broader literary context of the city lament in ancient Near Eastern literature.[16] In this particular genre, animals have replaced humans as population of the cursed cities. In the prophetic corpus, Isaiah envisions the future of Babylon in this way:

She will never be inhabited
  or lived in through all generations;
there no nomads will pitch their tents,
  there no shepherds will rest their flocks.
But desert creatures will lie there,
  jackals will fill her houses;
there the owls will dwell,
  and there the wild goats will leap about.
Hyenas will inhabit her strongholds,
  jackals her luxurious palaces.
Her time is at hand,
  and her days will not be prolonged. (Isa 13:20–22)

Tobiah's taunt alludes to the permanence and irreversible nature of the curse upon Jerusalem. History seems to be on his side as well, since the city has laid in ruins since 586 BC, and previous attempts at restoration have failed thus far (Ezra 4). However, what is missing from his understanding is that the curse has indeed been reversed. Starting with the first return, continued under the second return, and now under Nehemiah's leadership, the community is convinced that Yahweh is indeed restoring his promise as announced by Jeremiah in his letter to the exiles (Jer 29; see Ezra 1).

Thus, the accusations of Sanballat and Tobiah strike a raw nerve since they are based on partial or half-truths. The enemy of Zion tries to intimidate the people by reinforcing the idea that nothing has been

16. On city laments, see F. W. Dobbs-Allsopp, *Weep O Daughter of Zion: A Study of the City-Lament Genre in the Hebrew Bible* (Rome: Biblical Institute Press, 1993).

changed, and the curses upon Zion are irreversible. The truth, however, lies completely elsewhere and serves as a powerful reminder that half-truths are mere disguise for outright lies.

**Imprecation.** The question of imprecation as an enduring principle beyond Old Testament times and theological context (Deuteronomic blessings and curses) is difficult to understand in light of Jesus's strong injunction to pray for our enemies and to love them (Matt 5:44). However, the appeal here is for *vindication* based upon the justice of Yahweh and his law and reliance upon the Lord to adjudicate on their behalf. A remarkable dimension of the prayer (4:4) is the sense of confidence Nehemiah and the community exude in the face of very strongly disparaging words (see 1 Sam 25:39 for a lexical parallel and Ezek 21:28 related to retributive justice upon the Ammonites).

**Motivation.** The heart constitutes a major theme in Old Testament theology. Deuteronomy constantly refers to the heart as the seat of moral decision making as well as action: "Love the LORD your God with all your heart and with all your soul and with all your strength" (Deut 6:5). However, even a cursory glance at Israelite history reveals, in a cyclical and persistent way, that the heart of the people was not in step with Yahweh's will and law (e.g., Judg 3). In the books of Kings and Chronicles, the heart of kings is under particular scrutiny as Yahweh's regents on earth. Very late in Judean history and as we approach Zion's imminent downfall, Jeremiah, the principal architect of Judah's demise, offers a devastating diagnosis for the human heart: incurable and terminal in the same way David's first son by Bathsheba was (Jer 17:9; see 2 Sam 12:15). This hopeless situation sets up the contrast that in a "new" covenant yet to come, the human heart will be equally new (Jer 31:31–34). Wisdom literature and the Psalms also put the human heart in the balance by way of contrasts: wickedness versus righteousness, even as righteousness ("upright in heart" is the recurring phrase) can never be obtained apart from Yahweh's forgiveness (Ps 32). In this light of the documented unfavorable disposition of Yahweh's people throughout its history, moments in time when the hearts of the people are favorable toward Yahweh and his purposes are relatively rare. This particular moment of history in the fifth century BC underscores the glimmer of hope represented by the rebuilding of Zion following the destruction of Jerusalem and the cancelling out of the old Covenant when the Israelites were taken into exile. While we should not imagine the hearts of the people have turned to Yahweh in a permanent way (see chapter 13), nevertheless, the language does suggest something new is happening, as the Deuteronomic promise of restoration itself declares in Deuteronomy 30:6, "The LORD will circumcise your hearts."

**Solidarity, vigilance, and sacrifices.** Perhaps the most obvious element of general application in chapter 4 relates to the idea of solidarity and vigilance, building upon the spirit of the preceding chapter, where everyone contributes to the building of the wall. Solidarity, togetherness, and unity are evidenced in the way Nehemiah constructs the chapter. While the reported speeches function as linchpins (see Setting in Original Meaning above), the narrative descriptions of work and weaponry, the call for help by some, the significance of the trumpet call, and the determination reflected by the day and night nature of the vigil all lead the same direction: solidarity among the people. A united front against the opposition continues to represent a crucial dimension to the reestablishment and restoration of Zion in the fifth century BC. In contrast, subsequent threat to that hard-earned unity will only illustrate how important maintaining the concept of unity is among the people for the rebuilding of Zion.

Nehemiah also fully participates in the rebuilding and makes the necessary sacrifices. Here is truly a David figure in the Old Testament. David spent time with the troops and elicited loyalty from them. This is why people loved David. And this is why the people would listen to Nehemiah in chapter 5. Thus, Nehemiah stands in contrast to Solomon, who put a heavy burden on the people but did not participate himself in the sufferings and the cost involved (since David had paid for the temple building; 1 Chr 29:2–5). Nehemiah is also like Joshua, since he rallies the troops to recall that Yahweh fights the battle of Israel in its past. He will do the same now as they are rebuilding Zion together.

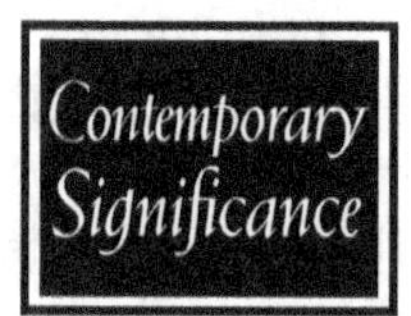


DO WE BELIEVE AND LIVE AS IF THE CURSE HAS BEEN *reversed, or as if we are still under the curse? Do we listen to the voice of intimidation as we seek to build the kingdom of God (i.e., prepare the way for the King of Zion's Return)?*

While Satan is not mentioned in the account, and without resorting to forced typological connections, we are able to understand his activities behind the scene. His tactics of intimidation remain the same today. The principal lie is that we cannot change the consequence of the past, that what we have done is irreversible. The role of the enemy is to remind us of our past and the failures of the past, but the restoring power of the Holy Spirit breaks through this lie and changes the circumstances accordingly. This is why this chapter is pivotal in the book of Nehemiah. It is the proof that the curse of 586 BC has been reversed and that Zion will, in fact, be rebuilt, preparing the way for the King to return (Jesus in the New Testament).

**Solidarity among a common enemy.** In the business of preparing the people of God for the return of the king and in facing the opposition in expanding the kingdom of God, the notion of maintaining unity is primary in Paul's mind in the book of Ephesians: "make every effort to keep the unity of the Spirit through the bond of peace" (Eph 4:3). While some may object to extrapolating this spiritual unity out of Nehemiah 4, the New Testament does suggest this is a crucial theme that needs to be applied in the life of the church today. How often have we witnessed setbacks in the advancement of God's kingdom that were the result of disunity among believers? Without maintaining unity, it allows Satan to attack us and overrun us in the work of the kingdom. This solidarity goes back to the concept of the priesthood of all believers (1 Pet 2:9). Without one another, we cannot build the kingdom. Peter tells us we are "living stones" (1 Pet 2:5), and the context also includes the enemy which seeks to devour us (1 Pet 5:8).

**Remember and fight.** In our struggles and spiritual warfare, we, too, are called to remember and fight, and also to remember what we fight for: our brothers and sisters, our wives, our children, and our home. We cannot extrapolate physical application to the modern context in the Middle East (as the Crusaders did), but the application remains powerful. We are called to solidarity with one another, called to protect that which is precious (the building up of the kingdom of God), and to invest in its future with our children, whether physical or spiritual. The motivation to fight the enemy has to be based on a personal "buy in" on our parts, rather than lofty theological ideals (although these are crucial foundations, as the corpus of Ezra-Nehemiah makes abundantly clear). We need to grow in appropriating the personal nature of the fight in which we find ourselves. The confidence that the battle is the Lord's, not our own, even if the threat is considerable.

**Spiritual leadership is sacrificial and hands-on.** Nehemiah enters into the suffering and the dedication that is needed in order to finish the task. This theme will be developed in chapter 5, but already here, we are given a powerful example of leadership through participatory suffering. Nehemiah is not asking them to do something he is not willing to do. For him to have solidarity with his own men (by not bathing, Neh 4:23) shows a remarkable commitment to the task and how he did not really trust the leadership to carry this task through. There is a limit to delegation. Ultimately you have to be responsible for the vision the Lord has entrusted to you, and you need to be willing to do the "dirty work" (in the case of Nehemiah, this turned out to be literal) in order to make sure the task gets done. You cannot expect to wash your hands (another bad pun) of a project and delegate without any further involvement if you want the task to be completed in a timely fashion. You own your call, and you need to accept the cost and that no one else will look at this call with the same diligence (i.e., "pride of ownership"). As we will find out (see ch. 6), some of the leaders were thoroughly compromised with Sanballat and Tobiah, so we see the wisdom of Nehemiah's hands-on approach in chapter 4.

**Productivity and heart change.** The change of heart and spiritual productivity go hand in hand in the new covenant (Paul's prayers of encouragement to be/do "more and more," e.g., Phil 1:9). We cannot underestimate the level of opposition we will face when we try to do new things. Disparaging words will come our way, and we will need to stand up to them as Nehemiah did, without heaping words of judgment upon our opponents, allowing God to act on our behalf in order to vindicate our cause. The narrative laconically suggests so: In spite of their words of death to them, the community "rebuilt [*banah*] the wall till all of it reached half its height" (v. 6).

# Nehemiah 5:1–19

[1] Now the men and their wives raised a great outcry against their fellow Jews. [2] Some were saying, "We and our sons and daughters are numerous; in order for us to eat and stay alive, we must get grain."

[3] Others were saying, "We are mortgaging our fields, our vineyards and our homes to get grain during the famine."

[4] Still others were saying, "We have had to borrow money to pay the king's tax on our fields and vineyards. [5] Although we are of the same flesh and blood as our fellow Jews and though our children are as good as theirs, yet we have to subject our sons and daughters to slavery. Some of our daughters have already been enslaved, but we are powerless, because our fields and our vineyards belong to others."

[6] When I heard their outcry and these charges, I was very angry. [7] I pondered them in my mind and then accused the nobles and officials. I told them, "You are charging your own people interest!" So I called together a large meeting to deal with them [8] and said: "As far as possible, we have bought back our fellow Jews who were sold to the Gentiles. Now you are selling your own people, only for them to be sold back to us!" They kept quiet, because they could find nothing to say.

[9] So I continued, "What you are doing is not right. Shouldn't you walk in the fear of our God to avoid the reproach of our Gentile enemies? [10] I and my brothers and my men are also lending the people money and grain. But let us stop charging interest! [11] Give back to them immediately their fields, vineyards, olive groves and houses, and also the interest you are charging them—one percent of the money, grain, new wine and olive oil."

[12] "We will give it back," they said. "And we will not demand anything more from them. We will do as you say."

Then I summoned the priests and made the nobles and officials take an oath to do what they had promised. [13] I also shook out the folds of my robe and said, "In this way may God shake out of their house and possessions anyone who does not keep this promise. So may such a person be shaken out and emptied!"

At this the whole assembly said, "Amen," and praised the LORD. And the people did as they had promised.

[14] Moreover, from the twentieth year of King Artaxerxes, when I was appointed to be their governor in the land of Judah, until his thirty-second year—twelve years—neither I nor my brothers ate the food allotted to the governor. [15] But the earlier governors—those preceding me—placed a heavy burden on the people and took forty shekels of silver from them in addition to food and wine. Their assistants also lorded it over the people. But out of reverence for God I did not act like that. [16] Instead, I devoted myself to the work on this wall. All my men were assembled there for the work; we did not acquire any land.

[17] Furthermore, a hundred and fifty Jews and officials ate at my table, as well as those who came to us from the surrounding nations. [18] Each day one ox, six choice sheep and some poultry were prepared for me, and every ten days an abundant supply of wine of all kinds. In spite of all this, I never demanded the food allotted to the governor, because the demands were heavy on these people.

[19] Remember me with favor, my God, for all I have done for these people.

## Internal Threat (5:1–19)

**SETTING.** Chapter 5 continues the theme of impending existential threats to the community rebuilding the wall of Jerusalem.[1] Following the thwarting of a clear

1. Commentators debate whether the placement of this chapter coincides with a chronological sequence of events (Williamson, *Ezra, Nehemiah*, 235). The last section of the account was written from a perspective following the completion of the wall (5:14–19), but nothing suggests in the narrative that we should view this outcry by the people any other way than occurring during the phase of rebuilding. However, as Kidner (*Ezra and Nehemiah*, 103) astutely suggests, the problems discussed are deep-seated and

and present physical danger in the previous installment of Nehemiah's report (chapter 4) and the subsequent all-out effort produced by the community to continue the work, this chapter outlines a related problem to the work: depleted stocks of food supplies because of a "famine" (v. 3). Without food supplies and funding for the workers at the wall and their families at home (the "wives" join in the "outcry" v. 1), the work comes to a screeching halt. Evidently some of the problems preceded the rebuilding of the wall since some "daughters" have already been sold into sex slavery (v. 5), but the sudden demand upon the community only served to exacerbate the situation. Thus, after functioning as a military commander in the previous chapter, Nehemiah now dons his "governor" (v. 14) hat to address complex political and economic matters of taxes, land ownership, and food shortages in the province. As in the previous chapter, Nehemiah diffuses the crisis through a strategically-worded address to the whole community and a pointed challenge to his fellow wealthy landowners who have placed a heavy (and unfair, Nehemiah argues) burden upon the community as a whole. Unless these concerns for equity are addressed, the fragile coalition Nehemiah has managed to create since his arrival in Jerusalem will collapse. The good will and solidarity reflected in chapters 3–4 seems like a distant memory in the heat of the opening arguments by the people, the whole community (v. 1; NIV "men" inadvertently misses the scope of the problem; see commentary below). As in the previous chapter, Nehemiah's skills as a coordinator of the effort and as a problem-solver are intentionally highlighted. The chapter also serves as a legal document before the king of Persia (5:14–18), but more importantly before the King of kings (5:19), that as a Persian governor and servant of the LORD, he used the crisis heaped upon himself to carry out successful political and fiscal reforms, in faithful observance to the spirit of God's law. This success, however, does not come without a personal economic sacrifice on his part.

**Three famine-related problems (5:1–5).** The structure of the first paragraph breaks down the problem into three distinct concerns voiced by what could be taken as three different constituencies ("some," "others," "still others" vv. 2, 3, 4) that all point to voicing concerns that threaten the physical well-being of the community. These specific immediate

---

reflect an ongoing issue in Yehud. The rebuilding effort serves as a lightning rod to these long-term problems of inequity during the postexilic era.

complaints also uncover deeper-seated problems within the community in Yehud and highlights long-standing practices that needed addressing by the new governor, as well.

The brief introductory statement (v. 1) succinctly exposes the seriousness of the matter since it is a widespread sentiment shared among the "people" (*ʿam*, contra NIV "men"), which, significantly, also include "their wives." The cause of this second existential threat no longer comes from a common external enemy (and the cause of the unity of purpose reflected in the previous chapter). Instead, the opponent is now identified as "their fellow Jews" (v. 1). The problem is characterized as substantial (a "great outcry"). For the first time since Nehemiah's arrival, discord among the community is present and clearly outside of Nehemiah's control, since the problem preceded his tenure as governor. The rebuilding project only serves to exacerbate and expose the deep economic disparity present within the community of Yehud at the time.

The first concern (v. 2) focuses on the immediate and urgent need for food: "we [including the "wives"] must get grain" in order to survive ("to eat and to live," author's translation). "Sons and daughters" in large numbers are deemed immediately at risk. Thus, the newly-appointed governor is confronted with an unforeseen effect of his call for an all-out effort on the building of Zion. How to feed all these people?

The second complaint and the reference to a "famine" (v. 3) provides crucial background and underscores how this food shortage quickly escalates into a full-blown crisis that threatens to tear apart the community. Not only are the people running out of "grain," but they are liquidating[2] (ongoing present action in the Hebrew) all their commercial and real estate assets ("our fields, our vineyards and our homes"[3]) in order to procure foodstuff for their day-to-day subsistence in the midst of this big push on the wall construction. What we are witnessing is essentially a "fire sale" of ancestral properties and vital resources for future livelihood. The final round of complaints (vv. 4–5) reflects a situation that has gone quickly from bad to worse: the selling of human

2. Hebrew *ʿarab* (ongoing present action) is rendered accurately by NIV as "mortgaging." In other contexts, the term reflects the same general meaning of a pledge, cf. Gen. 43:9; 44:32 (pledge for surety); Prov. 6:1 (to put up security); Ezek 27:9 (to barter).

3. The three direct objects are fronted in the syntax, which suggests emphasis on what is being lost to them, namely, every piece of private and commercial real estate they own.

property (slavery) for cash ("money") in order to pay property taxes[4] to Persian authorities ("the king," v. 4). The culprit is identified again as "our fellow Jews" (v. 5; as in v. 1) who have failed to uphold a fundamental principal of equal value between their "children" who are free and "our sons and daughters" who are running the risk of being enslaved. The reality that "some of our daughters have already been enslaved" brings home the fact the community is "powerless" (v. 5), losing control of its ancestral property rights and its progeny. Williamson rightly suggests on the basis of the parallel with Esther 7:8 that the "subduing" (Heb. *kabash*) of the daughters implies a sexual context, as well.[5] The threat that tribal identity could be erased is real here and needs to be addressed before the work on the wall can be completed.

**Nehemiah resolves the dispute with the tribal leadership (5:6–13).** Nehemiah's reaction to the "outcry" and the "charges" matches his opponents' strong emotional reactions in previous encounters ("I was very angry," v. 6; see 4:1, 7)[6] and anticipates similar sentiments on Nehemiah's part during his second gubernatorial term in Yehud (13:8 Heb. *ra'a*). Rather than reacting on the spot (never a good idea when one is angry!), he "pondered" in his "mind" what the proper course of action should be (v. 7). The following verb ("accused") reflects a distinct and separate phase in the verbal sequence of actions, which implies that some (unknown) amount of time has elapsed. The meaning of the verb "accused" has a long history in Deuteronomic writings, reflecting the lawsuits Yahweh brought against his people in Deuteronomy 32 and carried out by his prophets in preexilic history (e.g., Isa 1), when the people stand liable before God's law. The recipients of this legal contention are "the nobles and officials," the people without whose support he could not have started the project in the first place (see 2:16 for an identical designation). It also explains why Nehemiah needed to regain his composure and mount a proper strategy to address the problem. He cannot afford to alienate the tribal leadership. "I told them" continues the same verbal sequence and is directly related to the judicial setting provided by the

---

4. Hebrew *midah* is unique and probably refers to a technical Akkadian loanword best described as "tax" or "tribute" (see discussions in Williamson, *Ezra, Nehemiah*, 233, 55).

5. Williamson, *Ezra, Nehemiah*, 238.

6. The language of the enemies' anger varies in Neh 2:10, lit. "it was very evil to them." In 13:8, Nehemiah's anger is also expressed with the same language, "it was very evil to me."

verb "to accuse." Nehemiah here acts as formal arbitrator and governor with considerable authority over the rulers. The actual economic issue at hand has elicited varying interpretations. The NIV renders the Hebrew word *masa'* as "interest" (so ESV); however, it is preferable to translate the term as "pledge" since the subsequent exchange (when the leaders return property to their owners) suggests the problem was not interest but that landowners traded their assets for food.[7] Pledging itself is not condemned in biblical jurisprudence (Exod 22:25; Deut 24:10).[8]

Underlining the grave situation the community is facing, Nehemiah calls for a "large meeting to deal with them" (v. 7b). Nehemiah's address to the group (v. 8) convincingly argues that at stake is not simply an economic issue but one of solidarity and identity. For Nehemiah, the problem boils down to a fundamental value that family members do not sell one another into slavery. The point is especially poignant since they live under Persian rule rather than as free citizens. As slaves to Persian rule (see Neh 9:36), and sometimes even slaves to local competing powers ("Gentiles"), why should we then enslave ourselves to one another, Nehemiah contends. The people "kept quiet" since Nehemiah was obviously right. Nehemiah's appeal to the unity of the community is part and parcel of his overall strategy. The wall would be built as a community; this problem of injustice also would be resolved through the community coming together as one.

In light of the people's silence, Nehemiah is emboldened to continue (v. 9) and state in plain terms: "What you are doing in not right." This rebuke not only rests on the spiritual need for covenantal loyalty to Yahweh ("fear of our God") but also on the practical reality of the existential threat posed by Sanballat et al. ("to avoid the reproach of our Gentile enemies," v. 9). The community cannot afford to leave things as they stand, since its enemies will undoubtedly find a way to leverage this crisis to their advantage. Nehemiah is keenly aware that this problem could quickly escalate.

The next part of his address takes a surprising turn, since he recognizes his own involvement in the practice of "lending the people money and grain," along with his "brothers" and "men" (v. 10). To identify

---

7. Williamson (*Ezra, Nehemiah*, 233) defines it as "pledge on loan."

8. Ibid.

himself as part of the problem gives him the authority to reiterate that the practice of pledge on loan during these exceptionally trying times must stop.[9] The imperative that includes himself ("let us" in v. 10) now shifts to a command directed at the community leaders in v. 11: "Give back to them immediately" all land and property. The specific terms of restitution ("fields, vineyards, olive groves and houses") allow for no loopholes. In addition, as reparation, Nehemiah is requiring them to return whatever percentage[10] was exacted on money and commodities ("money, grain, new wine and oil," v. 11).

The people's silence of the first part of the address is now broken with a stunningly unequivocal response broken down in three promises (v. 12a):

- We will give it back
- We will not demand anything more from them
- We will do as you say

Capitalizing on this verbal commitment, Nehemiah immediately seeks to ratify the promise by a formal oath ceremony (v. 12b) with "priests" officiating. Nehemiah leaves no doubt the financial commitment by the "nobles and officials" is made under the watchful eyes of the deity. To underline the point, Nehemiah himself enacts an imprecatory curse formula by shaking the fold of his garment (v. 13a). The symbolism digs deep into Israelite history (Gen 15; Ruth 1:16–17): whoever would break this verbal commitment of restitution and reparation would meet the same fate as those wronged—loss of property and livelihood. The results of Nehemiah's deft and bold words, his own identification with the problem, and appeal to Yahweh in the dispute could not have occasioned a more successful outcome: the "whole assembly" said "amen" (see Neh 8:6) and acted accordingly. Nehemiah has averted the biggest crisis yet, and restored unity that allows for the rebuilding of the wall to resume (see ch. 6).

---

9. In verse 10, the NIV misleadingly implies that lending is contrasted to "usury." The text, instead, reads "in addition, I, my brothers and my servants are lending them money and grain; let us abandon this *massa'*, i.e., pledge on loan" (author's translation).

10. NIV "percentage" is literally "hundred," which commentators and some translations have connected to our modern idea of "percentage."

**Two examples from Nehemiah's integrity as governor (5:14–19).** As post scriptum ("moreover"), Nehemiah sees fit to testify to a remarkable dimension to his twelve-year tenure as "governor" of the province ("land of Judah," v. 14a). Of note, this is the first mention that Nehemiah was governor, though his actions in the previous chapters betray his delegated authority from the king (see chapter 2). He refers to two practices that pertain specifically to food procurement and allowances. First, Nehemiah sets himself in sharp contrast to his predecessors (v. 15) in that neither he nor his "brothers" took advantage of the perk due his rank: free food (v. 14b). In sharp contrast, his predecessors and their associates used the office to enrich themselves ("heavy burden," v. 15). The specific itemization of the previous governors' reprehensible practices (a levy of "forty shekels of silver" and "food and wine," v. 15) reminds us that Nehemiah ultimately answers not to his Persian boss but to God. The Hebrew of v. 15b is emphatic, as if Nehemiah was under oath: "I myself, I never did it, because of the presence of the fear of God" (author's translation). The theme of the fear of God literarily links this part of the chapter to the preceding one. Nehemiah's Persian governorship is under the authority of Yahweh himself, since Nehemiah rules over Yahweh's people in Yehud. For Nehemiah, the focal point of his governorship was the task for which he was commissioned in the first place: "I devoted myself to the work on this wall" (v. 16a). By fronting "work on this wall" before "I devoted myself" in the original text, it underscores this emphasis on the task at hand. A similar syntactical construction follows v. 16b: word order in the orginal puts "we did not acquire any land" before "all my men were assembled there for the work." The single-minded focus on the task at hand kept Nehemiah from falling into the greedy practices of his predecessors.

Nehemiah as a character in the story line of the book bearing his name perhaps shines brightest in the second part of his post-scriptum (vv. 17–19). As such, it serves as an elaboration and itemization of the foods allocated to the governor, which Nehemiah chose to forgo during his twelve-year term in Yehud (v. 14b). Instead he provided out of his own pocket for 150 people (plus guests from "surrounding nations," v. 17) at the governor's house (see ch. 2:8): a daily supply of one ox, six choice sheep and unnumbered poultry and large supplies of different wines in a ten-day delivery rotation (v. 18). The delivery of supplies went on for about 4680 days. Nehemiah adds that he did it "because the demands were heavy on these people" (v. 18b).

As a closing statement, Nehemiah appeals not to human rewards (most probably from the Persian king, who sent him on this mission), but to God's "favor" (Heb. *tobah*; see Neh 2:8) with respect to his single-minded dedication to the task, and, more importantly, to the "people."

**GENEROSITY BY EXAMPLE LEADS TO SOLIDARITY.** The language of food supplies evokes a perennial problem for agro-pastoral societies in the Levant. From the beginning of the story in Genesis 12, food supplies are directly connected to regular cycles of climate change in the transitional zone that represents the southern Levant as a whole. The hinterland can easily sustain dry farming (200 mm isohyet/annual rainfall),[11] but the situation on the fringe was always more precarious, which, in turn, put pressure on the highland population itself. Droughts are a constant and serious existential threat in the ancient world, as they are today in many parts of the world. According to the principles enunciated in biblical law, the response to a drought in the community should never be the taking away of properties by richer neighbors, since it infringes upon sacred inheritance property as Yahweh's sacred space which Canaan represented (see 1 Kgs 21:3). To do so incurs Yahweh's Deuteronomic curses associated with unlawful land grabs, as Isaiah 5:8–10 describes:

> Woe to you who add house to house
> and join field to field
> till no space is left
> and you live alone in the land.
>
> The LORD Almighty has declared in my hearing:
>
> "Surely the great houses will become desolate,
> the fine mansions left without occupants.
> A ten-acre vineyard will produce only a bath of wine;
> a homer of seed will yield only an ephah of grain."

11. Currid and Barrett, *Crossway ESV Bible Atlas*, 30.

Instead, in the spirit of solidarity and care for one another, the richer neighbor is called upon to perform acts of mercy toward his less fortunate neighbor and provide in his time of need; this is best exemplified in preexilic history in the story of Ruth. Nehemiah reenacts this spirit of generosity on a larger scale in this account and thus represents an act of leadership akin to David's when he provides for the building of the temple out of his own sacrificial giving (1 Chr 29:1–5). Both accounts, therefore, exemplify the spirit of the law and the need to lead by example in generosity.

**Economically-based slavery.** In biblical law, the system allows for redemption of slaves and also regular emancipation (Exod 21:2; Deut 15:13–14). The letter of the law is clear regarding exacting interests within the covenant community (Exod 22:25; Lev 25:35–37; Deut 23:19–20). It is not so clear on pledges. To be sure, Proverbs condemns surety for others (Prov 6:1; 22:26), but surety itself is not a problem (e.g., Joseph and his brothers in Gen 43–44). As explained in the Original Meaning section of the commentary above, the problem does not seem to be based on exacting heavy interest on the borrowers (the word for interest in Hebrew is not used in this passage) but rather on the spirit of the law, which speaks of compassion and solidarity with one another. Thus, Nehemiah's appeal is not strictly based on a particular law but a broader appeal of compassion and concern for others during this time of need. Proverbs calls upon us to have compassion for those in need, and it seems Nehemiah is applying this principle in his own life as a person in power and of great wealth. Nehemiah sets a powerful and persuasive example for those who are in power and of certain means. He was not afraid to forego the privilege due his rank for the sake of others. Paul sets a similar tone in his passion for the poor in Jerusalem. He is relentless in pursuing the Achaian churches to give for their brothers in need in Jerusalem (2 Cor 9). He maintains a similar posture and attitude during his time of ministry in Thessalonica (1 Thess 2).

**Applying the spirit of the law in disputes.** Anger per se is not condemned in Scripture as we recount the famous words of Paul, "in your anger do not sin" (Eph. 4:26). However, uncontrolled and impulsive reaction to anger never brings out good fruit. In the case of Nehemiah, the text deliberately creates a pause so that Nehemiah could think through how he would respond to this new crisis. The risk of alienating the leaders of the community was too great for him to react immediately upon hearing what was going on. The sordid detail concerning the "daughters" (Neh 5:5) must have struck a particularly nasty cord for him, as well. The matter is also especially delicate since under the law, the nobles and officials had done nothing wrong. In fact, Nehemiah himself acknowledges that, coming from a wealthy family of landowners, he also accepted pledge from his compatriots. Pledging one's property is not condemned in Scripture per se, but in this particular *context*, it clearly was a violation of a higher law: compassion for those less fortunate and the need to look after them in their time of need. Thus, Nehemiah functions like a preexilic prophet in this context of dispute. In contrast to the preexilic setting, however, the people respond favorably and change course, making restitutions so that the work can resume.

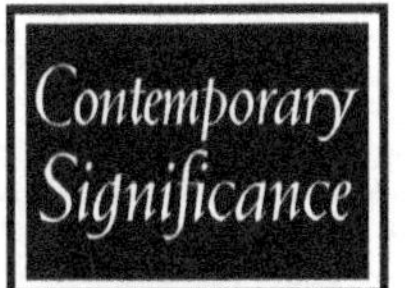


SINCE THE MAJORITY WORLD'S ECONOMY HINGES on agro-pastoral output, droughts and famines still represent an existential threat to many communities today. While it is difficult to extrapolate specific principles out of Old Testament texts for the contemporary situation, the principles of justice outlined through Nehemiah's sacrificial giving represent a powerful example for today's contexts. The plight of families pressured to sell their own children to others (with malevolent intent in most cases) is very real to this day.[12]

Modern day indenture is also caused by financial debt. Students who come to our seminary leave with a staggering debt and are enslaved, as well. What are we doing to help them? In my case I felt convicted to help my fellow students at the seminary by setting up a scholarship fund. I could not simply continue living comfortably while watching my students struggle financially. Nehemiah calls us to have compassion for those in need within the body of Christ. Churches should always be on the lookout for those in need within their midst, and leaders should keep a particularly keen eye on these matters instead of growing complacent and ensconced in the material blessings they enjoy.

Inequity among the people of God tears a community apart and represents a bad witness to the Lord. We are supposed to be known

12. https://www.cnn.com/interactive/2013/12/world/cambodia-child-sex-trade/.

for our acts of compassion toward one another and to take care of our own within the community. Economic slavery of the day is debt and economic oppression.

*Leading by example* is perhaps the most obvious (and emphasized by Nehemiah himself) dimension of application in the text. Leadership has its privileges and elders/leaders in the church are worthy of double honor (Gal 6:6; 1 Tim 5:17). However, Nehemiah provides a powerful example of selflessness that led him to forgo the perks of his position to help the people under his care. Such altruistic behavior, and great leadership, will always manifest itself through sacrifices rather than authority, manipulation, or winning power struggles.

# Nehemiah 6:1–19

When word came to Sanballat, Tobiah, Geshem the Arab and the rest of our enemies that I had rebuilt the wall and not a gap was left in it—though up to that time I had not set the doors in the gates—[2] Sanballat and Geshem sent me this message: "Come, let us meet together in one of the villages on the plain of Ono."

But they were scheming to harm me; [3] so I sent messengers to them with this reply: "I am carrying on a great project and cannot go down. Why should the work stop while I leave it and go down to you?" [4] Four times they sent me the same message, and each time I gave them the same answer.

[5] Then, the fifth time, Sanballat sent his aide to me with the same message, and in his hand was an unsealed letter [6] in which was written:

> "It is reported among the nations—and Geshem says it is true—that you and the Jews are plotting to revolt, and therefore you are building the wall. Moreover, according to these reports you are about to become their king [7] and have even appointed prophets to make this proclamation about you in Jerusalem: 'There is a king in Judah!' Now this report will get back to the king; so come, let us meet together."

[8] I sent him this reply: "Nothing like what you are saying is happening; you are just making it up out of your head."

[9] They were all trying to frighten us, thinking, "Their hands will get too weak for the work, and it will not be completed."

But I prayed, "Now strengthen my hands."

[10] One day I went to the house of Shemaiah son of Delaiah, the son of Mehetabel, who was shut in at his home. He said, "Let us meet in the house of God, inside the temple, and let us close the temple doors, because men are coming to kill you—by night they are coming to kill you."

[11] But I said, "Should a man like me run away? Or should
someone like me go into the temple to save his life? I will
not go!" [12] I realized that God had not sent him, but that he
had prophesied against me because Tobiah and Sanballat had
hired him. [13] He had been hired to intimidate me so that I
would commit a sin by doing this, and then they would give
me a bad name to discredit me.

[14] Remember Tobiah and Sanballat, my God, because of
what they have done; remember also the prophet Noadiah
and how she and the rest of the prophets have been trying to
intimidate me. [15] So the wall was completed on the twenty-fifth
of Elul, in fifty-two days.

[16] When all our enemies heard about this, all the
surrounding nations were afraid and lost their self-confidence,
because they realized that this work had been done with the
help of our God.

[17] Also, in those days the nobles of Judah were sending
many letters to Tobiah, and replies from Tobiah kept coming
to them. [18] For many in Judah were under oath to him, since
he was son-in-law to Shekaniah son of Arah, and his son
Jehohanan had married the daughter of Meshullam son of
Berekiah. [19] Moreover, they kept reporting to me his good
deeds and then telling him what I said. And Tobiah sent letters
to intimidate me.

## Personal Threat (6:1–19)

**Setting.** The final round of opposition from Sanballat, Tobiah, and Geshem represents the most comprehensive and personal attack on Nehemiah yet. The subtext of the chapter is "trust no-one and be intimidated by no-one." As the drama unfolds, Nehemiah uncovers conspirational layers of entanglement that have penetrated even the inner circle of Jewish leadership in Yehud. The chapter marks a low point in Nehemiah's tenure as a governor since he finds himself isolated even from those he thought he could trust. However, the deceptive tactics of his enemies are matched by his resolve and discernment in uncovering their stratagems. An escalation is clearly present since now the opposition takes on a personal and existential nature. Beginning with the usual suspects (Sanballat and Geshem), the account ends with opponents counted among the Jewish priesthood, the prophetic guild, and high-ranking officials who are complicit in their effort to thwart the project. Not unlike Jeremiah in a previous generation (see Jer 20; Ps 35), Nehemiah stands quite isolated. Nevertheless, as in past attempts, his enemies' efforts fail to intimidate him (we will not hear of them again until chapter 13), since "the wall was completed" (Neh 6:15) in a remarkably short period of time. Nehemiah's introductory prayer for favor (chapter 1) has been answered. Moving past this chapter, the book shifts to the process of preparation and dedication for the restoration of the cult in Zion, "the holy city" (11:1). This is in keeping with restoring the sanctity of Zion, which constitutes the central mission of Nehemiah.

**Intimidation and distraction tactics from Sanballat and Geshem (6:1–4).** The opposition is listed in the usual order, except now "the rest of our enemies" (v. 1) are added to the list, indicating an all-hands-on deck approach to their attempts to stop the work. They must have felt motivated to act since, by Nehemiah's own admission, the "doors in the gates" (v. 1) had yet to be installed. Without the wooden doors, the city remains vulnerable to unwanted intrusion. The moment seems opportune for the opponents to apply a different tactic: neutralizing Nehemiah's direct influence in this reconstruction project ("*I* had rebuilt the wall"; "*I* had not set the doors to the gates"; v. 1 [emphasis added]). This is sound reasoning on the part of the opponents and represents an oblique statement regarding Nehemiah's own effectiveness in the project. "Cut the head off the snake" has routinely been a favored strategy during times of military confrontation. At first, one wonders whether a change in leadership so close to completion would have slowed down the process at all. However, as we read about Sanballat's overall strategy to accuse Nehemiah of sedition in Yehud, it becomes clear that to eliminate Nehemiah would have allowed Sanballat's version of the events to stand before the king in Persia, with the resulting stoppage as in the previous time (see Ezra 4). Verse 2 calls for a meeting between equals (Sanballat as official over Samaria; Nehemiah as official over Judah) and seems innocuous enough. The location of the rendezvous in the "plain of Ono" (thirty miles northwest of Jerusalem where Benjaminites resettled; cf. Ezra 2:33; Neh 11:35) places the meeting at the border between the provinces of Samaria and Judah, away from any protection for Nehemiah.[1] The vague allusion to "one of the villages" (NIV, following the Vulgate and Septuagint) should be read instead as "Hakkephirim," a geographical name unknown to us but evidently situated in the Ono area (6:2). Though the text remains silent, the invitation may also suggest that a sort of backroom deal involving bribery might have been on Sanballat's mind, as well. At the very least, it would have stopped the hard-earned momentum created in chapter 4 (see especially 4:23, "neither I nor my brothers . . . took off our clothes").

The abrupt "but they were scheming to harm me" (v. 2, ongoing action in the Hebrew) cuts short any hope that Nehemiah would fall for their trap. Since Nehemiah did not answer the plea by *Judeans* to divert efforts from Jerusalem in 4:12, he would not be inclined to oblige a similar request from his opponents. He knows the momentum has shifted in his favor, and he is not about to fall for their trap to distract him from completing the task. This stands in contrast to the imminent danger in Jerusalem that is reflected in the previous existential threat of chapter 4. Now the danger (NIV "harm" in the sense of "evil" in verse 2) lies away from Jerusalem, further underscoring the sense of desperation on the part of Sanballat, since he cannot go on the offensive anymore and has to resort to other tactics to draw Nehemiah away from the work.

In keeping with the official nature of the relationship between two Persian officials, Nehemiah is obligated to respond via courier. The plural "messengers" in v. 3 represents Nehemiah's insurance policy since one messenger might have been easy to eliminate (thereby incriminating Nehemiah to the Persian court). Since Nehemiah "is carrying on" (ongoing action) such a "great project,"[2] he has to politely decline. The final part of the brief dispatch confirms the crucial connection between Nehemiah's presence and the successful completion of the project: "Why should the work stop?" (v. 3; the same language is used by Nehemiah's enemies in ch. 4:11). The emphasis on the project itself ("work" is repeated twice) also puts the pressure on Sanballat to explain why Nehemiah would leave the very task that he was commissioned by Artaxerxes to complete (ch. 2). As an official document, it allows Nehemiah to stay focused on this "great" work. In Nehemiah's mind,

1. Williamson, *Ezra, Nehemiah*; 255.
2. "Great project" is fronted and emphasized in the Hebrew word order.

Sanballat and Geshem provide no compelling reason for Nehemiah to stop the work to meet them. The mention that the diplomatic exchange occurred "four times" with the "same message," along with the same "answer" speaks to both the determination of Sanballat and Nehemiah (v. 4). In the absence of new information (it was, after all, the "same message"), Nehemiah felt no need to alter his response.

**Accusation of sedition (6:5–9).** Since this initial plan to neutralize Nehemiah has failed, the conflict escalates according to a tested and proven approach (vv. 5–9): the accusation of sedition against Persian rule (see Neh 2:19, "Are you rebelling against the king?"). It proved effective prior to Nehemiah's arrival in the province (Ezra 4:23), and now, since the work has progressed significantly, the scenario provided by Sanballat and Geshem would no longer ring hollow in the ears of Artaxerxes as it did when Nehemiah first arrived in Jerusalem (Neh 2:19). Nehemiah chooses the approach of full disclosure in the ensuing diplomatic exchange, which in turn allows him to mount a forceful denial of the allegations.

Underscoring the high stakes, Sanballat's *aide de camp* (NIV "aide") personally hand delivers "an unsealed letter" with, for the "fifth time," the "same message" as the preceding letters (6:5). This open document was meant to carry maximum impact, since the content was intentionally made public; its explosive nature would spread quickly throughout the province Beyond the River. Imperial authorities do not take rebellion too kindly, whether in the distant or more recent past (e.g., the *Raj* at the time of the British Empire). In his response, Nehemiah feels no need to hide the exact content of the allegations as part of his "memoir." The open letter (the equivalent to a "send to all" email today) uncovers nothing short of a *coup d'état* on a large scale. According to this narrative, the building of the wall was never about restoring and protecting the dignity of Nehemiah's ancestral city (see Neh 2:5). Instead, the rebuilding was always about starting a political "revolt" (the same language is used in Neh 2:19 and Ezra 4) in order to reestablish the kingship in Judah. The letter also alleges corroborating evidence, since Geshem confirms the testimony of Sanballat, along with other multiple reports. Thus, the fabricated evidence has an aura of truthfulness, since it comes from multiple witnesses. The finger is pointed directly at Nehemiah himself, who is the center of this imminent conspiracy: he is seeking a promotion from Persian governor to king in Yehud (v. 6).

To add (emphatic "moreover") to this false veneer of authenticity, the claim is made that "prophets" have been "appointed" by Nehemiah "in Jerusalem" to prophesy the restoration of kingship in Zion: "There is a king in Judah!" (v. 7). Sanballat appears to have enough knowledge of regional history that he is convinced the charge will stick with the king of Persia. It is also quite clear that he will do his level best for this report to get back to Artaxerxes. So, as a gesture, Sanballat reiterates the request for a get-together on the plain of Ono so they might "meet together" (v. 7).

This last point is especially noteworthy and must have struck a chord, since many prophetic texts, including postexilic ones (Haggai and Zechariah), do promise the restoration of Zion along with the restoration of kingship (e.g., Hag 2:23; Zech 9:9).

Nehemiah's reply remains terse (v. 8), unflinching, and amounts to a flat denial of all the charges: "Nothing like what you are saying is happening." From the vantage point of being in Jerusalem himself, he would be the first to know if any monarchist movement was in the making among the political factions present in Jerusalem. His denial is a powerful reminder that Nehemiah knows full well the boundaries of his commission, to both the king of Persia and the King of kings. He is here to rebuild the city, and that is all; he is not the Davidic king that is yet to come (e,g, Jer 23:5). In this respect, it is his "John the Baptist" moment, when he, too, declares that he is the forerunner rather than the King of Zion himself. At times, it is difficult to grasp the ancients' use of irony; however, in this case, Nehemiah's ironic tone lies just under the surface: "you are just making it up out of your head." We might say, "you are dreaming." Or, when presented with terms of surrender by the Nazi army at Bastogne, Belgium, in December 1944 during World War II, the commander of the encircled American division 101st simply responded: "Nuts."[3]

Verse 9 reverts to a familiar literary device in the book, Nehemiah's own assessment of the situation, and exposes the heart of the enemies of Zion's strategy, *intimidation* and the accusation of inability to complete the task (ch. 4). Nehemiah is able to read between the lines of these letters to see yet another attempt by Sanballat to get into Nehemiah's head. The intent is that he would get discouraged and quit, even as they are near the completion of the task ("the work . . . will not be completed,"

---

3. https://www.archivesfoundation.org/documents/surrender-nuts-gen-anthony-mcauliffes-1944-christmas-message-troops/.

v. 9). His response to these blatant lies that stand in contradiction to the Deuteronomic promises, which launched the project in chapter 1, is a familiar one in the form of a "Twitter prayer": "Strengthen my hands" (v. 9). The theme of the personal dimension to the attack in this chapter thus continues with the first-person pronoun: "*my* hands."

**Tobiah the Godfather (6:10–15).** The high-stake drama of deception and intimidation heats up exponentially in the concluding section of this part of Nehemiah's memoir. "One day" (NIV; absent in the Hebrew text) projects the false sense of a random house call on the part of Nehemiah to Shemaiah. Instead, the emphatic nature of the original text projects the idea that Nehemiah personally went to Shemaiah's house ("I myself went" [*wa'ani ba'ti*] author's translation). In spite of his patronymic credentials ("son of Delaiah, the son of Mehetabel"; v. 10), the identity of Shemaiah remains a mystery beyond this incident. From the context of verse 12 ("he prophesied"), we can safely surmise he belonged to the guild, along with a female prophet "Noadiah."[4] Assuming, his house was near the temple precinct, it is possible he could also have belonged to the priestly class. Another unanswered question relates to the reason as to why he is "shut in at his home" (v. 10). Nehemiah feels no obligation to fill in these details, since his main point is to project the image that Shemaiah is an insider whom Nehemiah would consider friend rather than foe (the opposite of Sanballat et al.). Nevertheless, Nehemiah is not one to be duped, and the vocabulary used by Shemaiah (v. 10, "let us meet" is identical to 6:2) takes the reader back to the entrapment offer of 6:2, especially since the meeting is to be held in a place just as unlikely as the "plains of Ono": "in the house of God, inside the temple" (v. 10). The first designation might be construed to mean a non-restricted area of the temple precinct (as in, "let's meet by the Jaffa Gate in Jerusalem"), but the specificity of the designation "temple" and the call to "close the temple doors" (v. 10) raises red flags in Nehemiah's mind. We know from his prayer in chapter 1 that Nehemiah is well versed in the sacred traditions. He would know that no one is allowed in this sacred space, let alone be confined inside the temple with its doors closed. The interior of the temple is sacred space. It belongs to the priestly class for sacrificial rituals, for which a person like Nehemiah would have no part. It appears, however, that Shemaiah's ploy reaches deeper than a trap to which anyone remotely aware of

4. Huldah was also a female prophet (2 Kgs 22:14–20) along with Deborah (Judg 4–5).

priestly laws would have flagged. By evoking a sudden existential threat to Nehemiah's life (repeated for emphasis: "because men are coming to kill you—by night they are coming to kill you"; v. 10), Nehemiah might have been tempted to apply what David did when he and his men were hungry and ate the "bread of the presence" (1 Sam 21:6). God's law of life overrides the holiness requirements connected to ritual ("obedience is better than sacrifice" 1 Sam 15:22). In this case, Nehemiah might have been justified to seek protection inside the temple.

However, Nehemiah faces this existential threat in his typical courageous demeanor: the first question, "Should a man *like me* (emphasis added) run away?" has a follow up, "Should someone *like me* (*kamoni*, same word in Hebrew) go into the temple to save his life?"

The text makes it clear Nehemiah is not afraid to lose his life. His greatest concern is not his own personal safety as a sitting governor of the province, but the sanctity of Yahweh's sacred space. He would rather die than desecrate the temple (v. 13, "I would commit a sin by doing this"). The call to enter into this space to find protection seems highly suspicious to him, which immediately causes him to call into question the credibility of the threat: "I realized (v. 13, in the sense of "perceived") that God had not sent him." Nehemiah is faced with a textbook example of a false prophet. The law states explicitly that whoever prophesies rebellion against God's law is never to be taken as a true prophet of Yahweh (Deut 13:1–5). Furthermore, in light of the relentless attempts by his enemies, Nehemiah takes little time to figure out the origins of this machination goes back to the usual suspects. Only this time, and for the first time here in this chapter, the blame is laid at the feet of Tobiah first, rather than Sanballat. Subsequent events in chapter 13 will make amply evident that Tobiah had infiltrated the religious establishment in the most profound of ways.

By entering the temple's sacred space, Nehemiah would have been discredited in the eyes of the faithful community of Yahwists and would have seriously compromised his larger plan to restore the sanctity of Zion: "They would give me a bad name to discredit (in the sense of "reproach") me" (v. 13). So, his foes' tactic remains the same: intimidation, so that the work of the restoration of the sanctity of Zion would be compromised. This newest threat is especially vicious because Nehemiah entering the temple would have been quite grievous in the eyes of Ezra and other faithful Levites. They would have most certainly disapproved of Nehemiah entering the sacred space. The subsequent reform and covenant renewal (chapter 8), without the moral support and leadership of the governor, might have been compromised beyond repair. Here the true plot is uncovered: Let's try to discredit Nehemiah in the eyes of his Yahwist friends. This is, in effect, a direct attack on Nehemiah's own *integrity.* This interpretation seems to be reflected in Nehemiah's own words, when he summarizes the effort of his enemy in the second "remember me" prayer of the chapter: the prophetic guild as a whole, apparently led by one prophetess "Noadiah," "have been trying to intimidate me" (v. 14; repeated phrase "to cause me to fear"), specifically by demoralizing the people involved in the rebuilding of the wall in order to stop the work, now so close to completion. To hear that Nehemiah had fled inside the temple would have had a demoralizing effect on the whole project. "Why should we continue to work on making Zion sacred again, if our leader goes around desecrating the temple?" might have been their response.

The existential threat, therefore, does not seem to relate to the holiness of the space that might have killed Nehemiah but rather the ruined reputation of Nehemiah in the eyes of the faithful Yahwists in Yehud.[5] Nehemiah displays his courage by saying, in effect, that he would rather die than sin against God's purity laws for his sacred space in order to save his life. He'd rather confront those who are seeking his life directly in a face to face confrontation than cut and run. We are getting, yet again, a measure of the personality of the governor during this crucial time that is so close to the project's completion.

This episode marks the conclusion of the attempts on Nehemiah's life. The text quickly pivots to a summary that the task of building the wall was completed in "52 days" (v. 15). The rapidity with which the task was completed underscores the reality that the true purpose was to restore the sanctity of the site rather than to rebuild Zion as a military fortress worthy of a king.

**Victory (6:16).** Verse 16 is a hinge verse and functions in the manner of an official bulletin announcing the cessation of hostilities. The synonymous relationship between "our enemies" and "all the surrounding nations" underscores the scope of the external opposition to the restoration of Zion (see chapter 4). Nehemiah and the community were literally under siege, but now the threat has been removed. Ironically, the tables have been turned, because now it is the nations that are "afraid"

---

5. Williamson, *Ezra, Nehemiah,* 259–60.

(*wayir'u*, same language applied to Nehemiah) and intimidated: they have "lost their self-confidence" ("they fell *greatly* [*me'od* in their [own] eyes" [author's emphasis and translation]).

The siege motif reminds us of a familiar preexilic sequence of events and keeps the theme of divine warfare going in Nehemiah's mind.

- Zion is besieged by overwhelming forces (Isa 36)
- God intervenes ("this work had been done with the help of our God"; v. 16)
- Fear enters the hearts of the enemies ("afraid")
- The threat is removed ("lost their self-confidence")

By placing the emphasis on "our God" (v. 16), Nehemiah circles back to the very beginning of his time of prayer and fasting. He knew from the outset the project needed to be a God-centered idea, or else it would fail.

**Post scriptum: Letters of intimidation by the nobles of Judah (6:17–19).** As a post scriptum, Nehemiah injects a conspiratorial dimension to the opposition against him and the project. Concurrent to the events described ("in those days"), correspondence was not limited to Sanballat and Nehemiah but also involved regular correspondence ("many letters") between "Tobiah" and "the nobles of Judah" (v. 17). This development comes as a surprise, since the "nobles" supported Nehemiah in the effort from the beginning (see Neh 2:16; 4:14). The text does not elaborate on the content of the letters; unlike the correspondence between Sanballat and Nehemiah, their mail remains unopened to us. However, verse 18 explicitly states why open channels of communication existed between Tobiah and the nobles: "many in Judah were under oath to him," because of marriage alliances that span two generations. Tobiah himself is "son-in-law to Shekaniah," who is the "son of Arah" (Arah is mentioned in Ezra 2:5). In addition, Tobiah's own son Jehohanan was given into marriage to the unnamed "daughter of Meshullam" (v. 18). While we do not know much about Arah, Meshullam is significant since he was involved in the rebuilding of the wall (see Neh 3:4, 30). This long list of patronymics speaks to the extent of the alliance and circles back to the reasons why Ezra and Nehemiah both speak so strongly against intermarriage within the context of the sanctity of Zion. The extent of the relationship with Tobiah also perhaps reflects a "wait and see" attitude on the nobles' part. Meshullam fully participated in the rebuilding of the wall, while at the same keeping himself close to Tobiah. In the case Nehemiah failed in this venture, Meshullam and the other members of the "Tobiad party," as Williamson dubs them, would not have completely severed relationships with the regional powerbrokers.[6] This sort of political grandstanding is clearly not approved by Nehemiah, who expected a lot more loyalty from the provincial leadership.

Verse 19 adds an additional layer of correspondence and now divulges on which side these nobles really were. In addition, it helps us understand how well informed Nehemiah's enemies were: "they kept reporting to me his good deeds, and then telling him what I said." Clearly these nobles were not on the side of Zion. Tobiah, in turn, tried also to "intimidate" (see v. 14) Nehemiah in his work. Verse 19, therefore, holds interpretive significance for the whole of Nehemiah's opposition and qualifies the sense of unity that existed at the outset of his mission in chapters 1–3 ("let us start rebuilding," Neh 2:18). His situation remained precarious throughout, since some remained very much in the camp of the local authorities. It also explains the sense of discretion that existed in his approach to the task in the early goings, including the survey by night (2:11–16). However, the fact that this important dimension to the struggle is placed *after* the completion of the wall indicates that their intimidation tactics failed in the same way Sanballat's did. This last statement magnifies the courage Nehemiah displays throughout the account. Sadly, it seems we are a long way from the tremendous unity reflected at the outset of the project along with the unity reflected in chapters 3 and 4. The mention of an illicit marriage alliance is a fresh reminder that these unlawful (or unwise) partnerships hold a powerful sway over human affairs, then and now.

**DECEPTIVE TACTICS.** Regardless of how one interprets the book of Revelation and the two beasts of chapters 13, the theme of deception is hard to miss, especially regarding the second beast (Rev 13:11–14):

> Then I saw a second beast, coming out of the earth. It had two horns like a lamb, but it spoke like a dragon. It exercised all

6. Ibid., 261.

> the authority of the first beast on its behalf, and made the earth and its inhabitants worship the first beast, whose fatal wound had been healed. And it performed great signs, even causing fire to come down from heaven to the earth in full view of the people. Because of the signs it was given power to perform on behalf of the first beast, it deceived the inhabitants of the earth. It ordered them to set up an image in honor of the beast who was wounded by the sword and yet lived.

The theme of deception lies at the heart of the activities of Satan on earth through the guise of the established structures (see Rev 2:13). While the text of Nehemiah never mentions the adversary (see the work of Satan emphasized in other postexilic literature, Zech 3:2; 1 Chr 21:1), the tactics employed by Tobiah and Sanballat leave little doubt that the father of lies is fully involved in this next round of attacks against the welfare of Zion. Without resorting to overdrawn typological interpretations, the theme of spiritual warfare is not absent in other postexilic documents, and with the overarching theme of deceptive tactics permeating the final round of attacks against Zion and Nehemiah personally, we, too, heed the call of Paul that we should not be unaware of the devil's schemes (2 Cor 2:11).

**Deception through false charges of sedition.** In the escalating nature of the attacks, Nehemiah remains steadfast through the onslaught. He flatly denies that he is fomenting sedition against the Persian rule (a well-known accusation; see Neh 2:19), except now the false charge goes public. This sort of escalating false charge of sedition find parallels in the life of Jeremiah, in his dealing with the false prophets and the charge of treason against the interests of the state (see Jer 38:4–5). In the life of Jesus, the charge of sedition against the state culminates with the crucifixion (Matt 27:37). The first followers of Christ also faced the constant charges of sedition and disturbing the peace: in Jerusalem (Acts 4:1–2) and through the missionary journeys, such as at Philippi (Acts 16:19–21):

> When her owners realized that their hope of making money was gone, they seized Paul and Silas and dragged them into the marketplace to face the authorities. They brought them before the magistrates and said, "These men are Jews, and are throwing our city into an uproar by advocating customs unlawful for us Romans to accept or practice."

During the first organized persecution in the early church, in Rome during the reign of Nero (July AD 64), the Christians became the scapegoat for the fire that decimated Rome. Tacitus records the events as follows:

> But all human efforts, all the lavish gifts of the emperor, and the propitiations of the gods, did not banish the sinister belief that the conflagration was the result of an order. Consequently, to get rid of the report, Nero fastened the guilt and inflicted the most exquisite tortures on a class hated for their abominations, called "Chrestians" by the populace.
>
> Christus, from whom the name had its origin, suffered the extreme penalty during the reign of Tiberius at the hands of one of our procurators, Pontius Pilate, and a most mischievous superstition, thus checked for the moment, again broke out not only in Judaea, the first source of the evil, but even in Rome, where all things hideous and shameful from every part of the world find their center and become popular.
>
> Accordingly, an arrest was first made of all who pleaded guilty; then, upon their information, an immense multitude was convicted, not so much of the crime of firing the city, as of hatred against mankind. Mockery of every sort was added to their deaths. Covered with the skins of beasts, they were torn by dogs and perished, or were nailed to crosses, or were doomed to the flames and burnt, to serve as a nightly illumination, when daylight had expired.[7]

Depending on the setting today, persecution through false charges may result in open warfare and physical death or it may be through the action of town committees opposing the building of a new church in the neighborhood. Maligning the motives of Christians and impugning guilt as non-team players in a community is part of the territory in our efforts to build up the kingdom of God. The coalition of organized religious majority comes alongside the temporal powers to wield its heavy stick in opposition to the work of the kingdom.

**Deception through false prophets.** Directly tied to the theme of deception, conflict with false prophets was a prevailing theme during

7. https://www.livius.org/sources/content/tacitus/tacitus-on-the-christians/.

the time of the monarchy, and it carried over into the familiar New Testament warning against false teaching (e.g., 2 Pet 2; Jude). At the time of the Omrides (ninth century BC; 1 Kgs 16–22; Mic 6:16), the compromised Northern Kingdom trafficked in falsity on a routine basis,[8] but it also entailed deception among the prophetic guild at the court of the king. The account of Micaiah (1 Kgs 22) provides a textbook description of the deception related to court prophets. In the particular case of Micaiah, the deception also implicates Jehoshaphat, king of Judah, who stands shoulder to shoulder with Ahab, of the house of Omri (1 Kgs 22:4; "I am as you are, my people as your people, my horses as your horses"). In seeking the counsel of the LORD, four hundred prophets advise Ahab to go into battle with the promise of assured victory (22:6). However, Jehoshaphat, as a Yahwistic king, also would like to consult with a prophet of Yahweh to make sure the LORD is really behind this campaign. Micaiah, summoned to the court, is loathed by Ahab for "he never prophesies anything good about me, but always bad" (22:8). When pressed to speak what is really on his mind, Micaiah finally lets out that the people are "sheep without a shepherd" (22:17) and that everyone should just go home. Next comes one of the most fascinating displays of how deception takes place behind the scenes in the presence of the heavenly council (see also Job 1):

> The king of Israel said to Jehoshaphat, "Didn't I tell you that he never prophesies anything good about me, but only bad?"
>
> Micaiah continued, "Therefore, hear the word of the LORD: I saw the LORD sitting on his throne with all the multitudes of heaven standing around him on his right and on his left. And the LORD said, 'Who will entice Ahab into attacking Ramoth Gilead and going to his death there?'
>
> "One suggested this, and another that. Finally, a spirit came forward, stood before the LORD and said, 'I will entice him.'
>
> "'By what means?' the LORD asked."
>
> 'I will go out and be a deceiving spirit in the mouths of all his prophets,' he said.
>
> "'You will succeed in enticing him,' said the LORD. 'Go and do it.'

---

8. E.g., Naboth's vineyard (1 Kgs 21) and the conflict with the Baal prophets at Mount Carmel (1 Kgs 18).

"So now the LORD has put a deceiving spirit in the mouths of all these prophets of yours. The LORD has decreed disaster for you." (1 Kgs 22:18–23)

God will not be the cause of evil, but he does allow it to occur to accomplish his purposes; in this case, to carry out judgment against Ahab (and Jezebel, see 2 Kgs 9:30–37). Other high moments in deceptive prophetic activities include the Late Judean period and the time of Jeremiah (Jer 28), which resulted in his temporary imprisonment. Turning to the New Testament, the theme of deceptive prophets and false teachers amplifies and is evidently a well-rehearsed phenomenon encountered routinely by the early church (e.g., Gal 1:7; Phil 3:2; Titus 1:10–11; 2 Pet 2:1–4). The characteristics of heretical teachings, nonbiblical ethics pertaining to sexuality, rejection of God's authority, and greedy financial dealings become the prevailing traits of false teachers (2 Pet 2:3). NT writers are not shy about discerning who is behind the deception either (Rev 12:9).

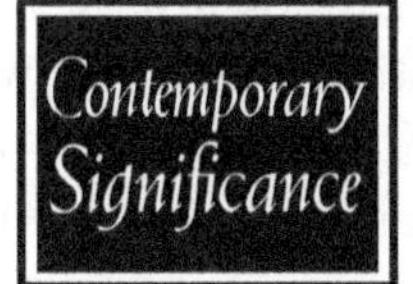


**DEALING WITH BULLIES.** Nehemiah's experience of betrayal by those he thought he could trust is not an unfamiliar one in the ministry. It would be naïve to think that everyone has our best interests at heart as we focus on the building up and edification of God's people in our respective callings. We should not be surprised how entangled the ministry of the gospel can be with folks with ulterior motives such as greed and power. Opposition to the building up of Zion comes in all sorts of ways, and Nehemiah offers some solid advice on how to conduct ourselves, especially among those friends-turned-foes, whether through bullying, intimidation, or the uncovering of hidden ungodly alliances.

From the outset of the book, Nehemiah's singlemindedness kept him from engaging his known enemies and able to stay focused on the task at hand. He is fleshing out for us the commandment to turn the other cheek by simply not responding in kind to his detractors. In his stubborn refusal to engage the nagging and deceptive offers to meet on the plain of Ono, he essentially refuses to allow his enemies to set the context and engage them on the (literally) same playing field. As archetype of spiritual warfare, the confrontation with Pharaoh gives away the secret to success: "The LORD will fight for you; you only need to be still" (Exod 14:14). To ignore the bully and not take the bait is sometimes the best approach.

The intensity to which the conflict escalates, with the open letter accusing Nehemiah of sedition, would not be a surprise to Nehemiah. Oftentimes the tactics of the enemy are, in fact, repetitive ("we have seen this before"). We do get a sense of the mettle of Nehemiah the person by his forceful response. The direct response on his part underscores that there is a time to stay quiet but also times when speaking up is necessary. Nehemiah summarily dismisses the charge as nonsense but without engaging the argument in specific terms. "Don't argue with a fool" is always sound advice, and Nehemiah is giving us a good example here. Even as we are tempted to answer point by point the accusations of our detractors, we are in fact playing into their game in seeking to justify ourselves to them. Just as Nehemiah answered both to the king of Persia and to God, we answer to higher powers than merely engaging in petty tit-for-tat arguments. In the case of Tobiah, Sanballat, and this final attempt to accuse Nehemiah of sedition, it is worth remembering: they are spending their last shells. The intensity of the attacks increases in proportion to the opponents' level of desperation. After that, we really do not hear from them again, as the threat to the restoration of Zion now shifts to within Zion. Nehemiah's steadfastness to hold steady is commendable as an example recorded for posterity.

**Intimidation.** The next level of attack that rings all too familiar in the ministry is when the attacks come from within Zion, from among those that supposedly belong to the community, including the establishment and the prophetic guild. The motivation of power and greed seems to fuel much of the opposition to the restoration of the sanctity of Zion. The establishment does not like the way this reformer Nehemiah is shaping the community. Whenever reformers face entrenched power structures, the pushback can be overwhelming, as in the case of Martin Luther confronting the indulgence scam in the early 1500s in Germany. The cash-for-souls scheme to fund the building of Saint Peter Cathedral by Leo X was too much to take for Martin.[9] He would face tremendous

9. See Eric Metaxas's recent biography for a colorful but accurate description of the intrigues of the times, *Martin Luther: The Man who Rediscovered God and Changed the World* (New York: Viking, 2017).

forces of intimidation not to speak and continue to challenge the religious establishment of his time. Ironically, he would himself resort to bully tactics and intimidation in some of his tractates, as well (against the peasants).[10] From the early church (Gal 2:4) to today, it is always painful to realize that those we thought were on our side end up being opponents of the Gospel. The key to Nehemiah's resolve is also ours in Christ, not to fear those who seek to cause us to fear and intimidate us.

**Vindication in the end.** By standing firm, however, the book of Nehemiah's greatest lesson may be the *vindication* that always comes at the end. It may be the literal *end* when Christ returns (2 Thess 2), or it may be in our lifetime when the rightness of the mission to restore Zion (defined as the people of God; see Heb 12:22–23) prevails over the loud voice of our detractors. As Isaiah prophesied (Isa 54:17):

> "[N]o weapon forged against you will prevail,
> and you will refute every tongue that accuses you.
> This is the heritage of the servants of the LORD,
> and this is their vindication from me,"
> declares the LORD.

This was the heritage of the fledgling community of Yehud, who by faith were led to restore the sanctity of Zion and literally shut down the voice of their detractors so that they, in turn, were in fear of the community, as they perceived that God was in their midst. Perhaps here lies the wisdom of the book for the ages, as well. Allowing the LORD to reveal himself through the success of the mission may be the believers' best response to the tactics of Zion's opponents.

10. E.g., E. G. Rupp and B. Drewery, *Martin Luther, Documents of Modern History* (London: Edward Arnold, 1970), 121–26.

# Nehemiah 7:1–73a

After the wall had been rebuilt and I had set the doors in place,
the gatekeepers, the musicians and the Levites were appointed.
2 I put in charge of Jerusalem my brother Hanani, along with
Hananiah the commander of the citadel, because he was a man
of integrity and feared God more than most people do. 3 I said
to them, "The gates of Jerusalem are not to be opened until
the sun is hot. While the gatekeepers are still on duty, have
them shut the doors and bar them. Also appoint residents of
Jerusalem as guards, some at their posts and some near their
own houses."

4 Now the city was large and spacious, but there were few
people in it, and the houses had not yet been rebuilt. 5 So my
God put it into my heart to assemble the nobles, the officials
and the common people for registration by families. I found the
genealogical record of those who had been the first to return.
This is what I found written there:

> 6 These are the people of the province who came up
> from the captivity of the exiles whom Nebuchadnezzar
> king of Babylon had taken captive (they returned
> to Jerusalem and Judah, each to his own town, 7 in
> company with Zerubbabel, Joshua, Nehemiah, Azariah,
> Raamiah, Nahamani, Mordecai, Bilshan, Mispereth,
> Bigvai, Nehum and Baanah):

The list of the men of Israel:

| | |
|---|---|
| 8 the descendants of Parosh | 2,172 |
| 9 of Shephatiah | 372 |
| 10 of Arah | 652 |
| 11 of Pahath-Moab (through the line of Jeshua and Joab) | 2,818 |
| 12 of Elam | 1,254 |
| 13 of Zattu | 845 |
| 14 of Zakkai | 760 |

| | |
|---|---|
| 15 of Binnui | 648 |
| 16 of Bebai | 628 |
| 17 of Azgad | 2,322 |
| 18 of Adonikam | 667 |
| 19 of Bigvai | 2,067 |
| 20 of Adin | 655 |
| 21 of Ater (through Hezekiah) | 98 |
| 22 of Hashum | 328 |
| 23 of Bezai | 324 |
| 24 of Hariph | 112 |
| 25 of Gibeon | 95 |
| 26 the men of Bethlehem and Netophah | 188 |
| 27 of Anathoth | 128 |
| 28 of Beth Azmaveth | 42 |
| 29 of Kiriath Jearim, Kephirah and Beeroth | 743 |
| 30 of Ramah and Geba | 621 |
| 31 of Mikmash | 122 |
| 32 of Bethel and Ai | 123 |
| 33 of the other Nebo | 52 |
| 34 of the other Elam | 1,254 |
| 35 of Harim | 320 |
| 36 of Jericho | 345 |
| 37 of Lod, Hadid and Ono | 721 |
| 38 of Senaah | 3,930 |

39 The priests:

| | |
|---|---|
| the descendants of Jedaiah (through the family of Jeshua) | 973 |
| 40 of Immer | 1,052 |
| 41 of Pashhur | 1,247 |
| 42 of Harim | 1,017 |

43 The Levites:

| | |
|---|---|
| the descendants of Jeshua (through Kadmiel through the line of Hodaviah) | 74 |

44 The musicians:

the descendants of Asaph 148

45 The gatekeepers:
the descendants of
Shallum, Ater, Talmon, Akkub, Hatita and Shobai 138

46 The temple servants:
the descendants of
Ziha, Hasupha, Tabbaoth,
47 Keros, Sia, Padon,
48 Lebana, Hagaba, Shalmai,
49 Hanan, Giddel, Gahar,
50 Reaiah, Rezin, Nekoda,
51 Gazzam, Uzza, Paseah,
52 Besai, Meunim, Nephusim,
53 Bakbuk, Hakupha, Harhur,
54 Bazluth, Mehida, Harsha,
55 Barkos, Sisera, Temah,
56 Neziah and Hatipha

57 The descendants of the servants of Solomon:
the descendants of
Sotai, Sophereth, Perida,
58 Jaala, Darkon, Giddel,
59 Shephatiah, Hattil,
Pokereth-Hazzebaim and Amon
60 The temple servants and the descendants of
the servants of Solomon 392

61 The following came up from the towns of Tel
Melah, Tel Harsha, Kerub, Addon and Immer, but they
could not show that their families were descended from
Israel:
62 the descendants of
Delaiah, Tobiah and Nekoda 642

63 And from among the priests:
the descendants of

Hobaiah, Hakkoz and Barzillai (a man who
had married a daughter of Barzillai the
Gileadite and was called by that name).

64 These searched for their family records, but they
could not find them and so were excluded from the
priesthood as unclean. 65 The governor, therefore,
ordered them not to eat any of the most sacred food
until there should be a priest ministering with the Urim
and Thummim.

66 The whole company numbered 42,360, 67 besides
their 7,337 male and female slaves; and they also had
245 male and female singers. 68 There were 736 horses,
245 mules, 69 435 camels and 6,720 donkeys.

70 Some of the heads of the families contributed to
the work. The governor gave to the treasury 1,000
darics of gold, 50 bowls and 530 garments for priests.
71 Some of the heads of the families gave to the treasury
for the work 20,000 darics of gold and 2,200 minas
of silver. 72 The total given by the rest of the people
was 20,000 darics of gold, 2,000 minas of silver and
67 garments for priests.

73 The priests, the Levites, the gatekeepers, the
musicians and the temple servants, along with certain of
the people and the rest of the Israelites, settled in their
own towns.

## Genealogical Record (7:1–73a)

**Setting.** The chapter consists mostly of genealogies extracted from existing archives and plays an important role in the enterprise to which Nehemiah has been commissioned by both Yahweh and the king of Persia:[1] to restore and protect the sanctity of Zion. For this dual purpose, the acropolis needs to be repopulated with reliable "men of Israel" (7:7) and especially

1. Kidner, *Ezra and Nehemiah*, 111.

with those responsible for the worship of Yahweh: priests, Levites, musicians, gatekeepers, and temple servants. Thus, following the list of people involved in the rebuilding process in chapter 3, the extensive list of names in chapter 7 frames the restoration within a broader framework that harks back to the beginning of the return under Zerubbabel and Joshua (see Commentary on Ezra 2:1–70). In this context, the genealogy gives due attention to proper origins, so that those who could not prove their ancestry were excluded (see Ezra 2:59–63).

Discussions concerning chapter 7 inevitably turn to the fact that Nehemiah includes the genealogy found in Ezra 2.[2] With differences mostly dealing with discrepancies in the computation, grammatical (absence/presence of connective "and" [Neh 7:11; Ezra 2:6]), and lexical variations spelling of a few names,[3] the list of Ezra 2 is re-introduced for the purpose of historical, legal validation of the repopulating of Zion with "men of Israel." Nehemiah chooses to include the names, harking back to a previous generation, to underscore that if Zion could not be populated with non-Israelites then it should not be now, either. This is especially the case since now the wall has been rebuilt and the city needs to be repopulated.[4] To include the genealogy also adds texture to the context of unity of purpose and historical continuity when the people come together to renew the covenant in 7:73b–8:1.

**Completing the task of securing Zion (7:1–3).** "After the wall had been rebuilt and I had set the doors in place" (NIV, v. 1) captures the

---

2. For a summary of the discussion, see Williamson (*Ezra, Nehemiah*, 268–69).

3. Williamson lists the textual variants in some detail (*Ezra, Nehemiah*, 24–28). A pattern emerges between the lists in Ezra 2 and Neh 7 that revolves around scribal errors in the transmission of numbers, in particular (of the forty-three [forty-five in Ezra] specific numbers listed, only nineteen match). These discrepancies do not represent wild departures from each other (Ibid.) and can easily be attributed to scribal errors (our typos). Other discrepancies relate to the spelling of certain names and the use of *beney* instead of *'anshey* ("men of Bethlehem" in Neh 7:26; Ezra 2:21). While Nehemiah also uses *beney*, he favors *'anshey*; Ezra also uses *'anshey* in 2:27, "men of Anatoth." Other minor variations include the presence/absence of the particle "and" to link names (7:11 "and Joab") and digits (7:11/Ezra 2:6). Of some significance, the list of priests (Neh 7:39–42; Ezra 2:36–39), albeit shorter than others (five names and four digits), is exact in both Neh 7 and Ezra 2, as is the final tally of the people: 42360. Evidently, the scribes were more concerned with copying the manuscripts than adding numbers, since neither list comes up to 42360. As Kidner aptly puts it: "numbers were the bane of copyists" (Kidner, *Ezra and Nehemiah*, 42).

4. Williamson, *Ezra, Nehemiah*, 270–71.

chronological emphasis of the text. However, adding "and" between the tasks of wall and gate building suggests a false sense of simultaneity. In the original, the main verb is "I set up the gates," following the dependent temporal clause "after the wall had been rebuilt." Nehemiah wishes to focus the attention on the gates.[5] In Nehemiah's mind, the gates and their security—through the appointment of a strong security detail in Zion—becomes his top priority (see 2 Samuel 5:6–8 and how David took Zion from the Jebusites).

In verse 2, Nehemiah is not about to lose the momentum. In light of the motto of "trust no one," based on the compromised nature of part of the Jewish and religious leadership in Yehud in the preceding chapter, he will only entrust the guarding of the *birah* (v. 2, NIV "citadel" aka "fortress Zion," see chapter 1) to his own trusted blood brother "Hanani, along with Hananiah commander of the citadel" (v. 2). Hananiah's credentials are then listed: "he was a man of integrity" (in the sense of "truthful/trustworthy") and "he feared God" (like Nehemiah himself, see chapter 5:9, 15) "more than most people do." In light of the sense of betrayal captured with the last verse of the preceding chapter, Nehemiah cannot afford to set up a compromised security protocol at the gates, the most vulnerable points in an enclosure; they must be absolutely loyal to the cause of Zion and therefore to Yahweh himself. Nehemiah knows to focus first on the character of a person in relationship to God, as this becomes the basis for trustworthiness in human affairs. This, in turn, provides a strong firewall for the security of Zion. The added "more than most" perhaps suggests that Nehemiah has done a bit of growing up in the rough and tumble politics of Persian Yehud.

Verse 3 speaks of three sets of specific instructions given to both Hanani and Hananiah ("I said to them"). The first directive is not without difficulty in understanding the exact meaning in the original. The NIV represents the idea that gates should stay closed well into the morning ("until the sun is hot," v. 3), perhaps even noontime. Second, the "gatekeepers" are specifically commanded to "shut the doors and bar them" "while they are still on duty" (v. 3). Could it mean the gates stay permanently closed, and only open on demand during daytime? Or that

5. The use of the first-person singular also confirms that this section is part of his memoir (ibid., 266).

the guards' duty is to make sure they close and shut the gates as part of their duties? The latter seems a more likely scenario. Finally, Hanani and Hananiah should also commission the help of "residents of Jerusalem as guards," both "at their posts" and also "near their houses" (v. 3). This militia will thus serve double duty: both living in houses near or on the wall (see chapter 3) and serving as sentinels.

**Divine initiative to register people (7:4–5).** Verse 4 frames the context for his intentional reuse of the Ezra 2 genealogy.[6] Nehemiah is now setting his sight on the next task: rebuilding the city itself and setting up a relocation program so that people of the province of Yehud actually move back in permanently.

We know by now that Nehemiah has a well-established *modus operandi*. He is not one who will act without consulting Yahweh, even when it comes to seemingly mundane tasks, such as summoning the people together and conducting administrative tasks. The phrase "my God put it into my heart" (v. 5) rings familiar and provides further authentication that this section of the book belongs to his memoir. More importantly, this recalls the days when the prophet heard from God and passed on the information to the people (e.g., Moses, e.g., Exod 20:22). The summoning of the "nobles, the officials, and the common[7] people" recalls a similar situation in 2:16, 4:14, and 4:19 (see also 5:7 where mention of the "nobles and officials" is also found). Thus, the phrase is expected, when it comes to Nehemiah's role as governor, to summon the leaders of Yehud. In addition, the "nobles" were also the ones singled out as part of the intimidation campaign against him in 6:17–19. This context heightens the need for divine guidance as he tries to take his task to the next phase of repopulation.

Nehemiah plainly and clearly explains why he is summoning the people "for registration" (v. 5): he needs legal evidence that the people he is gathering actually belong to Israel, a noted designation that symbolizes the beginning of the restoration promised by the prophets. The way to prove it is that if people can be traced back to this original list at the time of Zerubabbel and Joshua's return in 539 BC, they, in turn, will be able to re-occupy Jerusalem and, more importantly, serve in the worship in the temple.

---

6. See Kidner's lucid discussion (*Ezra and Nehemiah*, 111–15).
7. NIV "common" is actually not in the original, which simply says "people."

**List of returnees (7:6–73a).** The literary, social, and theological significance of the list is discussed in the commentary of Ezra 2. For our purpose here in Nehemiah, we are focused on the role of the list for Nehemiah's goal to repopulate Zion after the rebuilding of the wall and gates. The variations in content between the Ezra and Nehemiah lists amount to editorial touches that fit in with Nehemiah's own purposes in using the list of names.[8] For example, Nehemiah (7:6) provides a shorter introduction to the names than Ezra's list, which directly fits in with the chronology of chapter 2. One noted variation occurs in the first list headed by Zerubbabel and Joshua (Ezra 2:2; Neh 7:7), where Ezra has eleven names but Nehemiah has twelve.[9] The lists of the "men" in Nehemiah 7:21–26 has slight differences in order from Ezra 2:16–21, as does the list in Nehemiah 7:33–37 (Ezra 2:29–34). The most name discrepancies occur in the list of the "temple servants," in terms of names listed and the order of presentation (Neh 7:46–56; Ezra 2:43–54). In contrast, the list of priests is exactly the same in both Ezra and Nehemiah (Neh 7:39–42; Ezra 2:36–39). Finally, where financial contributions to the rebuilding of the temple are listed (Neh 7:70–72), Ezra elaborates on some details, which do not serve Nehemiah's purpose (e.g., the giving was toward the "rebuilding of the house of God on its site," Ezra 2:68–69).[10]

Verse 73 deserves particular comment, as it provides the transition from the official record (v. 73a), which mentions that the "priests, the Levites, the gatekeepers, the musicians (Ezra puts the "musicians" before the "gatekeepers," 2:70), and the temple servants, along with certain of

---

8. NIV "the list of the men of Israel" in Neh 7:7 erroneously provides a different reading from Ezra 2:2 (NIV "the list of the men of the people of Israel"). Both texts are identical in the original: "the number [NIV "list"] of the men of the people of Israel."

9. Ezra's list of eleven: Zerubbabel, Jeshua, Nehemiah, Seraiah, Reelaiah, Mordecai, Bilshan, Mispar, Bigvai, Rehum and Baanah. Nehemiah's list of twelve: Zerubbabel, Jeshua, Nehemiah, *Azariah, Raamiah, Nahamni,* Mordecai, Bilshan, Mispereth, Bigvai, Nehum, Baanah (emphasis added). These variations do not significantly violate the integrity of the account. Nehemiah probably reflects the more original reading with twelve names on the basis of 1 Esd 5:8 (scribal error would be in the Ezra ms.; Steinmann, *Ezra-Nehemiah,* 154. Some commentators have taken this number as a nod to the twelve tribes).

10. The amounts of gold and silver donated are not identical in the two lists, but this can be explained on the basis of Nehemiah's own purposes, as well. He breaks down the giving by including the "governor's" own contribution (perhaps in light of his successor's dishonesty until Nehemiah's tenure? See commentary on Neh 5:15).

the people and the rest of the Israelites, settled in their towns," to the resumption of the narrative at the time of Nehemiah and Ezra in chapter 8. A fuller discussion of the issue is presented in the commentary on chapter 8, but suffice it to say that verse 73b belongs to the next chapter in the saga of Zion's restoration during the Persian period: "When the seventh month came and the Israelites had settled in their towns."

CAREFUL RECORD KEEPING VIA GENEALOGIES AND lists belong to a long-standing practice in Scripture that harks back to the book of generations *par excellence*: Genesis.[11] This may look tedious to the modern mindset, but in the record of the restoration of Zion during the Persian period and in light of the fierce opposition and the constant threat of legal action against Nehemiah and the community, Nehemiah wants to make sure legitimacy is maintained. Chapter 7 affirms the population about to repopulate Zion has the legitimate rights to be there on the basis of what was established by the first generation of returnees in 539 BC. To reinsert the list from Ezra 2 is, therefore, no mere administrative *duplicata* on the part of Nehemiah. He is establishing precedent so that the current generation of priests, Levites, and other temple attendants have every right to relocate there. The sense of supernatural guidance in this process of data collection has strong parallels elsewhere in Scripture, where material and physical tasks are conducted under direct spiritual supervision. The manufacturing processes for the tabernacle came under the supervision of artisans "filled . . . with the Spirit" (Exod 31:1–6). Likewise, waiting table in the early church was entrusted to wise men filled with the Spirit (Acts 6:1–6). The apparently menial task of record-finding and documenting the names of the first generation falls under the same category of divine guidance. Nehemiah knows the stakes are high if and when Zion's enemies come to question the legitimacy of the venture of repopulation and restoration of Zion. Yet Nehemiah entrusts the process to "my God" (Neh 7:5), anticipating the famous Pauline words that "if God is for us, who can be against us"

11. *Toledoth*/generation structure, e.g., Gen 2:4; 5:1; 6:9; 10:1; 11:10, 27; 25:12, 19; 36:1, 9; 37:2; see Gordon J. Wenham, *Genesis 1–15*, WBC 1 (Waco, TX: Word, 1987), xxi–xxii, for a good discussion.

(Rom 8:31; in Nehemiah's own words, it sounded more like, "our God will fight for us."). In the same vein, Nehemiah is sure to note the *trustworthiness* and spirituality of those in charge of protecting the newly-established sanctity of Zion. Without resorting to overdrawn typologies, the role of gatekeepers in the Psalms is highly exalted and prized, since they are evoking the guardians of God's presence in primeval times (and in other cultures as well, e.g., the Assyrian *lamassu*).

> Better is one day in your courts
> than a thousand elsewhere;
> I would rather be a doorkeeper in the house of my God
> than dwell in the tents of the wicked. (Ps 84:10)

The significance of the sanctity of the priesthood is reaffirmed and picked up in earnest from the narrative of the first return under Zerubbabel and Joshua. Significantly, this effort to confirm that everyone about to get involved in the covenant renewal was, in fact, qualified to be a servant of the LORD in the temple is a major theme in Ezra-Nehemiah. That the first round of vetting is repeated virtually word for word speaks of the high degree of importance attributed to the marker of ancestral purity. In the mind of the editor of Nehemiah, the vetting of the first generation merits a full duplication. The list of chapter 7, in effect, serves as an anchor text for the ensuing reform (Neh 8–10) and the subsequent dedication of the "holy city" (Neh 11:1). The list connects the beginning of the return (539 BC) with the current and final phase of the process of the restoration of the sanctity of Zion under Nehemiah. Nehemiah is a careful recordkeeper, so it makes sense that the list in Ezra 2 would reappear in its entirety as an integral part of the Nehemiah corpus.

This sort of duplication is a common literary device in Hebrew narrative (Gen 1 and 2). In the priestly materials, the description of the tabernacle occurs twice (Exod 25–31; 35–39). The details of the apparatus for the worship of Yahweh, as instructed by Yahweh to his servant Moses, was in fact implemented by the book and to the letter. This sort of duplication serves as an enhancer to the reality of Yahweh's strictest holiness standard and shows that these standards need to be applied with the utmost precision. Perhaps more tellingly in the context of the postexilic ferment, the entire history of preexilic Judean kings is duplicated from the account in the Book of Kings and becomes 1–2 Chronicles in the Christian canon. Literarily within Ezra-Nehemiah, this sort of stringent approach to identity (as discussed in the commentary on Ezra 2), with its primordial emphases on descent, land, history and the traditions from Moses and subsequent leaders, is not a thing of the past for Nehemiah. On the contrary, re-including the ancestral list of qualified temple personnel (down to the name and the number of them) speaks of his own conviction that the connection between what Zerubabbel and Joshua started will be continued in detail under Nehemiah. Nehemiah in this chapter asserts himself as a religious leader in the footsteps of Zerubabbel, and this gives him a spiritual and personal connection with a key leader of the first return. Of course, that one of the names in the first generation of returnees included his namesake "Nehemiah" serves only to enhance this sense and ideal of continuity (Ezra 2:2/Neh 7:7). Haggai had already enhanced Zerubbabel's cachet when he framed the eschatological coming of the king in the direct lineage of the first governor in the province (Hag 2:23):

> "On that day," declares the LORD Almighty, "I will take you, my servant Zerubbabel son of Shealtiel," declares the LORD, "and I will make you like my signet ring, for I have chosen you," declares the LORD Almighty.

In this respect and as a governor of Yehud like Zerubabbel was before him, Nehemiah finds himself, if not formally included, at least connected historically as a governor to the lineage from which the Son of David will come. The genealogy in Matthew 1:12–16 makes it clear Nehemiah is not related to the lineage of David in the same way as Zerubabbel was, but the instrumental/circumstantial connection nevertheless remains:

> After the exile to Babylon:
> Jeconiah was the father of Shealtiel,
> Shealtiel the father of Zerubbabel,
> Zerubbabel the father of Abihud,
> Abihud the father of Eliakim,
> Eliakim the father of Azor,
> Azor the father of Zadok,
> Zadok the father of Akim,
> Akim the father of Elihud,

Elihud the father of Eleazar,
Eleazar the father of Matthan,
Matthan the father of Jacob,
and Jacob the father of Joseph, the husband of Mary, and
Mary was the mother of Jesus who is called the Messiah.
(Matt 1:12–16)

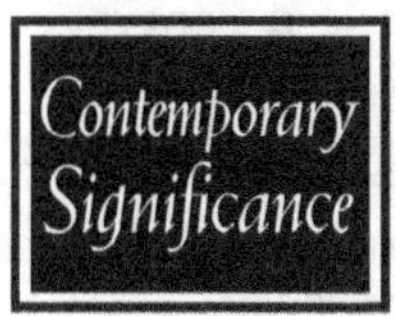


TO INTERJECT SUCH RELIGIOUS SENTIMENT IN AN official memoir may seem strange to modern western mindsets, but in many parts of the world, appeal to divine intervention and guidance is routine and actually expected. In a world that constantly seeks to create false dichotomies, this chapter reminds us of the importance of trustworthiness in carrying out administrative tasks. Nehemiah's divine prompting to find lists of names is equally valid to the divine promptings to go preach the gospel to a land/place/city/people the Lord puts on the hearts of his people. Divine guidance is not only for tasks pertaining to spiritual activities alone. In the comprehensive call to restore the sanctity of Zion and to prepare the city of God for the return of the King, we should take the so-called menial tasks of data entry, compiling directories, or schedules seriously. Legitimate membership in the community of faith is especially important, since we, too, face strong opponents in the proclamation of the gospel. We need to know who is who—or perhaps, who is whose!

Chapter 7 also reminds us that membership has its privileges and responsibilities to contribute financially for the welfare of Zion. More will be said when this generation actually contributes in chapter 10, but chapter 7 prepares the way on the basis of the example of the first generation. Zerubbabel and Joshua's returnees *did provide,* and Nehemiah is using their example and recording it for posterity. His expectation is also ours. We remember the generous deeds of the past. The application for us is to recall church budgets or missionary organizations' spreadsheets to see how the saints contributed in the past so that we might be inspired to follow in their footsteps. The same can be said for our personal budgets. We remember the times of our giving in the past (or lack thereof!), so that we might be encouraged again to contribute. Paul used the same approach in his letter to the Philippians (4:14–20) and in his appeal to the churches in Achaia (see 2 Cor 9:1–15 to make good on their words to contribute to the Jerusalem collection).

The duplication of the list speaks of spiritual continuity. We do remember the traditions, and we pass them on faithfully. Paul exhorts Timothy (2 Tim 5:7) to remember the faith of his mother and grandmother, a nod both to the deep respect Paul maintains for these women's spiritual stature and how important it is to remember those who have gone before us. Without resorting to the cult and veneration of the deceased (a practice also of some Protestant traditions, including evangelicals; e.g., endowed chairs, names on buildings, etc.), this second list in Ezra-Nehemiah reminds us that directories and memberships matter immensely in the eyes of the one who not only knows his sheep but who also keeps a detailed capillary inventory for every one of his own children. What the duplication means is that the agenda of holiness and purity of worship remains central in Nehemiah's time, as it was in Zerubabbel's times. In a century that has already witnessed incredibly rapid changes (Amazon was created in 1994; Facebook in 2004), the consistent standard of holiness ("Be holy because I am holy," 1 Pet 1:16) remains in effect, from one generation to the next. In the Gospel, however, we now know any holiness we might have in our lives derives from the one who makes us holy "in Him" (1 Cor 1:30).

# Nehemiah 7:73b–8:18

When the seventh month came and the Israelites had settled in
their towns,

[1] all the people came together as one in the square before
the Water Gate. They told Ezra the teacher of the Law to
bring out the Book of the Law of Moses, which the LORD had
commanded for Israel.

[2] So on the first day of the seventh month Ezra the priest
brought the Law before the assembly, which was made up of
men and women and all who were able to understand. [3] He
read it aloud from daybreak till noon as he faced the square
before the Water Gate in the presence of the men, women
and others who could understand. And all the people listened
attentively to the Book of the Law.

[4] Ezra the teacher of the Law stood on a high wooden
platform built for the occasion. Beside him on his right stood
Mattithiah, Shema, Anaiah, Uriah, Hilkiah and Maaseiah;
and on his left were Pedaiah, Mishael, Malkijah, Hashum,
Hashbaddanah, Zechariah and Meshullam.

[5] Ezra opened the book. All the people could see him because
he was standing above them; and as he opened it, the people all
stood up. [6] Ezra praised the LORD, the great God; and all the people
lifted their hands and responded, "Amen! Amen!" Then they bowed
down and worshiped the LORD with their faces to the ground.

[7] The Levites—Jeshua, Bani, Sherebiah, Jamin, Akkub,
Shabbethai, Hodiah, Maaseiah, Kelita, Azariah, Jozabad,
Hanan and Pelaiah—instructed the people in the Law while
the people were standing there. [8] They read from the Book of
the Law of God, making it clear and giving the meaning so that
the people understood what was being read.

[9] Then Nehemiah the governor, Ezra the priest and teacher
of the Law, and the Levites who were instructing the people
said to them all, "This day is holy to the LORD your God.
Do not mourn or weep." For all the people had been weeping
as they listened to the words of the Law.

10 Nehemiah said, "Go and enjoy choice food and sweet
drinks, and send some to those who have nothing prepared.
This day is holy to our Lord. Do not grieve, for the joy of the
LORD is your strength."
11 The Levites calmed all the people, saying, "Be still, for
this is a holy day. Do not grieve."
12 Then all the people went away to eat and drink, to send
portions of food and to celebrate with great joy, because they
now understood the words that had been made known to them.
13 On the second day of the month, the heads of all the
families, along with the priests and the Levites, gathered around
Ezra the teacher to give attention to the words of the Law. 14 They
found written in the Law, which the LORD had commanded
through Moses, that the Israelites were to live in temporary
shelters during the festival of the seventh month 15 and that they
should proclaim this word and spread it throughout their towns
and in Jerusalem: "Go out into the hill country and bring back
branches from olive and wild olive trees, and from myrtles, palms
and shade trees, to make temporary shelters"—as it is written.
16 So the people went out and brought back branches and
built themselves temporary shelters on their own roofs, in their
courtyards, in the courts of the house of God and in the square by
the Water Gate and the one by the Gate of Ephraim. 17 The whole
company that had returned from exile built temporary shelters and
lived in them. From the days of Joshua son of Nun until that day, the
Israelites had not celebrated it like this. And their joy was very great.
18 Day after day, from the first day to the last, Ezra read
from the Book of the Law of God. They celebrated the festival
for seven days, and on the eighth day, in accordance with the
regulation, there was an assembly.

## Covenant Renewal (7:73b–8:18)

**SETTING.** Beginning in chapter 8, Nehemiah's account (1:1 or "memoir") pauses, only to be resumed from chapter 12:27 to the end of the account. Literarily, the format takes on the familiar elements of preexilic covenant documents:

public reading of the law of Moses, (chapters 8 and 9), a historical retrospective (in the form of penitential psalm, chapter 9) and a formal oath ceremony (chapter 10).[1] In continuity with the covenantal dimensions of the account, chapter 11 evokes the land apportioning of the book of Joshua with official lists of people populating the land. Finally, the list of the priests in chapter 12 serves as the climactic finale of the mission: the restoration of proper worship of Yahweh in Zion with a celebration ceremony of dedication on the newly-restored walls.

Due to the presence of Ezra in the text for the first time in the book of Nehemiah, critical scholars typically remove Nehemiah 8–9 from this historical setting and link the events to Ezra's reforms recorded in Ezra 9–10 (and by eliding "Nehemiah" in Neh 8:9).[2] The text, however, makes a point to underscore the presence of Ezra *and* Nehemiah ("Nehemiah, *he [was]* governor") as part of Nehemiah's work in 445–444 BC. The reading of the law, the reestablishment of the religious calendar (a sort of new Exodus, cf. Isa 1:1; 40), the celebration, the prayer, and the oath ("We will not neglect the house of our God" Neh 10:39) all naturally follow the completion of the wall and the securing of fortress Zion. Theologically, Nehemiah's primary emphasis (see chapter 1), following the successful demarcation of Yahweh's sacred space, is that "the holy city" (Neh 11:1) is restored based on the promises concerning Zion by the prophets. Therefore, the list of priests and Levites, including Ezra, takes on an essential role, as the restoration of worship can begin in earnest now that the sanctity of Zion has been restored through the rebuilding of the wall. This is indeed a fresh start in Zion!

Specifically, chapter 8 focuses on the restoration of the sanctity of the law in the community, the beginning of a new start (Lev 23:23–25), without which there can be no commitment to the restoration of worship in Zion. The role of the Levites is preeminent, but the person at center stage for this part of the reform is the scribe/"teacher" and priest, Ezra. It would seem strange if the governor and the architect of the physical restoration of Zion did not have a direct role in the proceedings. Chapter 8 thus captures the moment when the two reformers are working hand in hand for the restoration of Zion (v. 9).[3]

---

1. Kline, *Treaty of the Great King*.
2. See Williamson (*Ezra, Nehemiah*, 291) for a summary of the issues.
3. Written some fifty years ago, Kidner's argument in support of the chapter's

**Reading of the Law (7:73b–8:8).** The historical-theological significance of the moment is established with the indication of the setting in "the seventh month" (7:73b). The seventh month represents, along with the first month and the Passover in the spring (Lev 23:6), the high point in the calendar year (Lev 23:23, 26, 33) with the Feast of Trumpets on the first day (today's *Rosh Hashanah*), the Day of Atonement (today's *Yom Kippur*) on the tenth, and the Feast of Booths on the fifteenth (kept for one week). As the narrative unfolds, however, it is the third feast that receives special attention.

"All the people came together as one" (8:1) captures the same unity of purpose as at crucial moments in Nehemiah's mission. This event should not be dislodged chronologically from the momentum established both in chapter 6 and chapter 7. Nehemiah is riding the wave, as it were. This is a sharp contrast to the sense of intimidation in chapter 6 and the loneliness he will feel some twelve years from now (Neh 13). The sense of unity is signaled by the syntax of the passage: the fact that "all the people"—men, women, young, and old—are participating is repeated several times. The reader is taken back to the solemn assemblies in the nation's glorious past when "all Israel came together" (Ezra 3:1; 2 Kgs 22–23; Deut 26–28; Josh 24).

The unnamed "they" in 8:1 refers to those involved in the gathering (Nehemiah and the Levites, see below) but also, in keeping with the unity of the people, to the assembly as a whole. They specifically request "Ezra the teacher (scribe/*sopher*)," prominent among the scribes (see Ezra 7:6), "to bring out" a specific scroll that is given its full title, along with subtitle: "the book [*sepher*] of the Law of Moses which the LORD had commanded for Israel" (v. 1). Not surprisingly, scholars have had various responses to the question of the identity of the book of the law of Moses (*torah*), but in light of the specific nature of the designation, it is likely referring to either sections of the Pentateuch as we know it today (e.g., Lev 23; see below) or, equally possible, the one book that actually carries this designation in the canon: the book of Deuteronomy (Deut 30:10; 31:9). The full designation suggests the ancients in the fifth century BC bear witness to both the antiquity and the sacred origins of the "Law."

---

historicity remains unparalleled in its lucidity (*Ezra and Nehemiah,* appendix 4). Any effort to dislodge the historical figures of Ezra and Nehemiah from each other stumbles upon 8:9. Both figures fulfilled an equally valid function in the program of restoration.

It ultimately emanated from Yahweh through Moses and commanded to Israel. One cannot but pause at the awesomeness of the moment, since the law and other sacred writings had been neglected, ignored, hidden, and even burned in ages past (2 Kgs 22:8–10; Jer 36:23)! In this context it is given the honor due to its value as the words of Yahweh. The preexilic designation "Israel" is not insignificant, since the events related to the postexilic restoration seek to reestablish the bond between the covenantal past and the present context. Of course, Israel no longer exists as a polity in the province of Yehud, but the theological ties to the past identity are unbroken. The words of Yahweh to ancient Israel remain the words of Yahweh throughout the generations, including now. The word of promise stands forever (Isa 40:8; 1 Pet 1:24–25).

The sequence of events is carefully organized chronologically: "on the first day of the seventh month" (v. 2). Ezra dons two hats. He is curator of the law when asked to bring out the book of the law in verse 1. But as he is about to read from it, he is now designated "priest," (*kohen*) as he "brought the Law before the assembly" (v. 2). The account will specify several times throughout who constituted the assembly. It was not only "men and women" but also "all who were able to understand" (twice in verse 2).[4] This is indeed an extraordinary moment, and it also explains the specificity of the location: "the square ("broad place," author's translation) before the Water Gate" (vv. 1, 3), which is east of the city near the Gihon Spring (see chapter 3). This was the area where everyone could gather and hydrate easily through the day (the site did not have many houses at the time, Neh 7:4). Its proximity to the temple area must also be noted.[5]

Verse 3 provides a summary of the whole event on this first day: Ezra "read aloud" to a captive audience from dawn to noon, which at this time of year represents about six hours.[6] In short order, the text pivots back

---

4. Syntactically, the phrase "men and women" (lit. "from man to woman" [*me'ish we'ad 'ishah*] in a collective sense) is supplemented by "and everyone who could understand." The question relates to the relationship between the two clauses. One option is to view the second sentence (connected by Heb. *waw*) as a clarification of the first: Men and women were gathered, that is, all those who could understand. But more likely in the overall context of the event, those who could understand represent yet another group, including the children of the age of understanding and also the Levites who explained the Law to those who couldn't understand it in verse 7–8 (see below).

5. Smith, *Ezra, Nehemiah, Esther*, 162–64.

6. The public reading of the law was mandated in Deuteronomy for both the whole

to the audience itself, defined a second time as "men, women and others who could understand" (v. 3). In addition, a note is made of how attentive everyone was to the reading of "the Book of the Law." The original (NIV "listened attentively," v. 3) has the poetic "and the ears of all the people (*kol ha'am*) [were] toward the Book of the Law" (author's translation). The imagery is that everyone was leaning forward to pay attention. Their ears are opened, and they have become active listeners. The fact that "all the people" is repeated from verse 1 and picked up in the subsequent verses represents a substantial rhetorical strategy of the account and points toward the solidarity of the people toward the word of God (see especially v. 5 below). This is all the more remarkable since, in ages past, prophets routinely lamented the people's poor listening skills for all things pertained to the word of God (Hos 4:6; Isa 1:2). On this day, however, things are different: they are paying careful attention. This comes perhaps as a result of the extraordinary way the wall has been rebuilt and how the people themselves have had a firsthand experience of God's activity since the arrival of both Ezra and Nehemiah.

Verses 4–5 provide further background to the morning scene of the reading of the law by Ezra that was described whole in verses 2–3. Prior to the assembling, a "high wooden platform" (lit., a "tower of wood," *migdal 'ets*) had been "built for the occasion. (v. 4). Kidner astutely sees the hand of Nehemiah behind this organized gathering, but the text does not specify, since the focus has now shifted from Nehemiah's direct intervention to Ezra's, as both priest and teacher/scribe.[7] Another remarkable detail is added: next to him on both his right and left stood no less than thirteen men. Whether these were priests, Levites,[8] or officials,[9] the text does not elaborate. In favor of the latter, the three other lists in the context of the gathering in the seventh month (chapters 8–9) signal they were Levites (8:7; 9:4, 5).[10] These men are mentioned by name (six on his right and seven on his left), which attests to their importance. Whether the men stand with Ezra on the elevated platform

---

assembly and for individuals (the Psalter attests to this reality), especially the king in Israel (Deut 17:18–20).

7. Kidner, *Ezra and Nehemiah*, 115.

8. Ibid.

9. Smith, *Ezra, Nehemiah, Esther*, 164.

10. "Meshullam" (v. 4) could be "Meshullam, son of Berekiah," a prominent rebuilder in the list of ch. 3 (vv. 4, 30).

or are on the ground on both sides is not clear, but the overall picture only adds to the exceptional nature of the moment, akin to Israel's great addresses in the past: "the Plains of Moab" (Deut 29), Mount Ebal (Josh 8:30–35), and the covenant renewals during the late Judean period.

Verse 5 highlights a time prior to the actual reading of the word and captures the mood of the moment. It is structured in three distinct parts, each signaled by the phrase *all the people*. Before the start of the reading at first light, when Ezra "opened the book," "*all the people* could see him" (see vv. 1 and 3) on the elevated platform. The fact that everyone could see him is explained next: "because he was above *all the people*" (NIV "because he was standing above them," v. 5). The third part actively involves the audience: As he "opened" the book, "*all the people* stood up" (NIV "the people all stood up," v. 5).[11] Here the text conveys the solemnity of the moment and further underscores the full and wholesale participation of the entire community.

Verse 6 resumes the narrative flow with a series of main verbs and provides yet more crucial details associated with this memorable morning: "Ezra blessed (NIV "praised") the LORD, the great God."[12] The peoples' response comes in quick succession (author's translation):

- *all the people* answered: amen amen, with their hands above[13]
- they bowed
- they worshiped the LORD, faces to the ground (lit., "earthward")

That "*all the people* lifted their hands" was a clear sign of worship, adoration, and honor to God. For the first time in the narrative of the

11. This raises the question whether everyone stood at attention for six hours non-stop. The subsequent description provides the nuance that there were other activities connected to the time of reading the word, including interaction and interpretation by those who understood the reading with those who could not. What verse 5 highlights is the sense of great attentiveness and reverence toward the Law as Ezra begins the reading.

12. This particular designation, "Yahweh the Great God" occurs only here in the OT but is a clear echo of Nehemiah's introductory prayer in Neh 1:5, "Then I said: "'LORD, the God of heaven, the great and awesome God, who keeps his covenant of love with those who love him and keep his commandments'" (see commentary on Neh 1 and the exact parallel designation in Dan 9:4). The need to appeal to God's greatness is self-evident to the exile community and for this context here. Only God's greatness could have turned their desperate and hopeless state of affairs around. To be able to read the words of the law in Jerusalem on this first day of the seventh month is fittingly attributed to his greatness.

13. NIV "and all the people lifted their hands and responded, 'Amen! Amen!'"

event, we now hear voices via reported speech. We will never know what specific sections were read of the law for these six hours; we will never know what specific words Ezra used to bless the LORD, but we do know what *all the people* said in response: "amen! amen!," which is a transliteration for the interjection *'amen* in Hebrew[14] and is connected to believing and trusting (e.g., famously, Gen 15:6; cf. Jer. 11:5). Here in this context, we might say, "how true!" The doublet, whether in apposition (see Num 5:22 for the only appositional parallel) or with connective "and" (*waw*, e.g., Pss 41:13; 72:19; 89:52), underscores the emphatic nature of the interjection.[15]

The assembly at the time of Nehemiah had already indicated their "amen" to Nehemiah's solution to resolve the problems of social injustice in chapter 5 (v. 13, see commentary). Perhaps the best context of proclaiming an "amen" with praise and worship is captured in Psalm 106:48:

> Praise be to the LORD, the God of Israel,
> from everlasting to everlasting.
>
> Let all the people say, "Amen!"
>
> Praise the LORD.

Following this acclamation, the people participate in the typical physical manifestation of worship in the Old Testament and New Testament: "They bowed down and worshiped the LORD with their faces to the ground." The extraordinary nature of the moment is thus continued with this vivid image etched in our minds: a whole group of people galvanized and united in time and space to focus their attention to the listening and understanding of the word in worshipful adoration.

Verses 7 and 8 offer additional information to the events of the day, with emphasis on the critical role of thirteen Levites (also listed by individual name, as the men connected to the platform; we will find some of them involved again in 9:4, 5). These were dispatched into the crowds

---

14. See the curses of Deut 27 for a concentration of the thirty occurrences of the lexeme in the Old Testament.

15. Doublets are typical feature of Hebrew syntax for emphasis; triplets are extremely rare and symbolize *ad infinitum*, "holy, holy, holy" in Isa 6:3.

and "instructed the people in the Law" as the law was being read by Ezra. Their specific task was "making it clear" (*parash* is an Aramaism) and "giving the meaning" (*bin* "insight"; same root as "understand" of verses 2 and 3), with the purpose that the "people understood (*sekel*, "discern"; e.g., 1 Sam 25:3 [NIV "intelligent"; Ps 111:10) what was being read." Thus, the Levites functioned as simultaneous interpreters, probably providing quick words of clarification, all without disrupting the actual reading of the Law by Ezra.[16]

**Holy day of celebration (8:9–12).** For the first time (v. 9) the record provides an excerpt of the content of the actual speeches on that day. This time it's a joint statement from the leadership speaking with one voice, including, notably, "Nehemiah the governor" (see Neh 5:14), Ezra in his dual role of "priest and teacher/scribe," and the second group of Levites, "who were instructing the people." The adjective "all" continues the theme of wholesale participation in the community.

The content of the reported speech focuses on the people's reaction to the morning address. To listen for several hours, along with interpretation from the Levites, caused great dismay among the crowds: "*For all the people* had been weeping as they listened to the words of the Law" (v. 9). In response, the leadership does not join in the mourning as in ages past (Josiah's response upon hearing the word of the law, 2 Kgs 22:11), but instead exhort the people to embrace the day as one set apart (*kadosh* "holy," NIV "sacred") "to the LORD your God." The pronominal "your God" bears significance as well, since it signals ownership of their identity as the *'am Yahweh* (people of Yahweh of preexilic times). The imperative to the assembly, "do not mourn or weep," goes at the heart of the mood of the day. There will be time for repentance and confession (see chapter 9)—but not today.[17]

In verse 10, the speech is further broken down with an individual address by Nehemiah, which succinctly reminds us of his targeted

16. Smith summarizes well the question of whether the language of "translation" should be used in this context (*Ezra, Nehemiah, Esther*, 168–69). If some in Yehud only understood Aramaic, the Levites might have served as translators from Hebrew to Aramaic. We cannot know for certain. However, ironically, our own lack of understanding of the specific nature of the process cannot distract us as readers of this ancient text from the main point of the narrative: everyone *that was there* understood what was being read to them!

17. Kidner, *Ezra and Nehemiah*, 117–18.

speeches during the height of the physical threat upon Zion (chapter 4): instead of mourning (and, though not mentioned, fasting), Nehemiah commissions a celebration banquet, filled with "choice food and sweet drinks" (v. 10, lit., "eat the fat and drink the best wine"). In words recalling his own largesse (ch. 5), Nehemiah encourages sharing with those "who have nothing prepared." He then repeats the initial injunction, "This day is sacred (*qadosh*/holy) to *our* Lord [Adonai, as opposed to Yahweh; emphasis added]."[18] The designation *our* Lord further underscores the tone of solidarity that permeates the account from beginning to end. The third element of his speech further emphasizes the injunction, "do not grieve," but adds a reason: "for the joy of the LORD [now Yahweh] is your strength." The focus on a banquet instead of mourning recalls the eschatological promise that when Yahweh restores Zion, he will turn "our mourning into joy" (author's translation) to be celebrated with a great feast (Isa 25:6). The appeal to "strength" also belongs to the characteristics of the restoration of Zion, since the strength to wait for the restoration would originate with God himself (Isa 40:31).

The third speech in verse 11 is there for continued emphasis and allows the Levites to weigh in. Again, the whole group is in view: they "calmed all the people (again, *kol ha'am*, as in v. 3), and stayed perfectly on message:

- "Be still (lit., "hush!" [*has*] e.g., Judg 3:19)"
- "For this is a sacred [*qadosh*/holy] day"
- "Do not grieve" (repeated from Nehemiah's speech in v. 10)

The congregation's reaction pivots to the desired outcome: "all the people (*kol ha'am*) went away to eat and drink, to send portions of food" and, to the point, "to celebrate with great joy" (v. 12). As a fitting conclusion to the momentous day, the report circles back to the main point: "they now understood (*bin*) the words" as they had been

18. Some modern languages carry within themselves the different nuances reflecting the different Hebrew designation: "Lord/Yahweh" and Lord/Adonai." For instance, in French, *Seigneur* connects with Adonai while *l'Eternel* relates to Yahweh who is forever (see Exod 3:12). Psalm 110 (the most quoted OT text in the NT) in French provides the illustration: "Oracle de l'Eternel à mon Seigneur: Assieds-toi à ma droite" ("the oracle of the Lord/Yahweh to my Lord/Adonai: sit at my right hand," 110:1, from *La Colombe* edition).

interpreted to them. One of the great promises of the restoration of Zion would be *understanding and delight in God's word and commands* (Jer 31:33) and the promise of new hearts toward the law. After the first day, the community is led to understand and apply the word properly. They are dismissed and went on their way.

**The Feast of Booths is observed (8:13–18).** Under Ezra's leadership, the tribal leaders ("the heads of all the families" ["fathers," *ha'abot*]) and the "priests and the Levites" reconvened by themselves the following day "to give attention ("to make wise" from the word-group *sakal* as in v. 8) to the words of the Law" (v. 13). They "found written in the Law" (v. 14) that the whole assembly should immediately regather to Jerusalem and celebrate the Festival of Booths (NIV "temporary shelters"). The attention given to the Festival of Booths (on the fifteenth of the month) rather than on the Day of Atonement (on the tenth of the month) suggests a Deuteronomic tripartite breakdown of the yearly festivals in ancient Israel: Passover/Unleavened Bread, Weeks, and Booths (Deut 16). Ezra is well aware of the Levitical Day of Atonement (Lev 23). This decision is in keeping with the celebratory nature of the gathering, into which the Feast of Booths fits in from both the Levitical and Deuteronomic account (see Lev 23:39; Deut 16:14, 16). The time for contrition will come later in the month, on the twenty-fourth (9:1). The specific commandments regarding the gathering of "branches" including olive, wild olive, myrtles, palms, and shade trees to "make temporary shelters" points to the broad interpretation (but no less accurate, "as it is written"; v. 15) taken to the application of God's law for this momentous occasion.[19]

As on the first day, the people respond right away and return (v. 16) and build booths within the city of Jerusalem at specific locations, "their own roofs" and "courtyards" (for those who live inside the walls), "in the courts of the house of God," the locus of the original gathering in the "square at the Water Gate," and also at the northern "Gate of Ephraim." Evoking the broader theological context of return from exile, "the whole company that had returned from exile" participated in the celebration (v. 17). The unparalleled nature of the celebration since the "days of Joshua, the son of Nun" does not mean the festival had not been

---

19. See Leviticus 23:40 which has a less detailed list, see Smith (*Ezra, Nehemiah, Esther*, 166).

celebrated before (see Ezra 4 for another celebration). However, the exceptional nature of this particular edition ("like this") cannot be overstated, since now Zion stands again as a protected sacred site. Indeed, "their joy was very great" (v. 17), which is pursuant to the injunction by Nehemiah for the people to rejoice.

This reminds us that the promise that the "ransomed of the Lord shall return with gladness and joy" is beginning to be fulfilled in Zion (Isa 35:10; 51:11, ESV and Introduction). We are now beginning the "already-not-yet" phase of the restoration of Zion.

In conclusion (v. 18), the account fittingly summarizes the role of Ezra in the daily attending to the reading of the "Book of the Law of God" and the atmosphere of celebration for the duration of the "feast." The last sentence serves as an intentional literary and chronological link to the events described in 9:1 (see commentary below): On the "eighth day" (= 23th of the month), "in accordance to the regulation, there was an assembly" (Lev 23:36). The account intentionally provides a seamless transition in the chronology of events between the reading of the Law on the first day of the month, the feast of weeks observed from the fifteenth to the twenty-second, and a gathering a day after, to which chapters 9–10 are devoted.

**The new exodus motif.** As foreseen by the prophet Isaiah, son of Amoz, the future restoration and return from exile would be a reenactment of the exodus (see also Isa 12// Exod 15): a new wilderness journey to the place where the glory of the Lord will be revealed: "In the wilderness prepare the way of the Lord. . . . [t]he rough ground shall become level. . . . [a]nd the glory of the Lord will be revealed" (Isa 40:3,4,5). The centrality of the word cannot be understated, since it will endure forever (Isa 40:8). Only this journey would not be a departure from the slavery of a mighty polity, but from a far more powerful enemy, the bondage of sin ("her hard service has been completed, . . . her sin has been paid for," Isa 40:2). The precise time when the events foreseen by Isaiah are fulfilled is a matter of debate, but in the mind of the postexilic community as reflected in Nehemiah 8, the sense of *joy* signals that the ceremony represents a renewed covenantal commitment. The reality is that a page has turned since they have returned from exile: "Those the LORD has rescued will return. They will enter Zion with singing; everlasting joy will crown their heads. Gladness and joy will overtake them, and sorrow and sighing will flee away" (Isa 51:11; Isa 35:10).

Whether sin has been fully dealt with in the manner conceptualized by Isaiah (Isa 52:13–53:12), Zechariah (3:1–5), and others (Jer 31:34; Ezek 37:23) is another matter. If the enthusiasm of the Levitical leadership prevails in chapter 8, it is cut down to size by the sad reality they are still in bondage "to this day" in Nehemiah 9:36. Nehemiah 13 and the harsh reality that the power of sin remains firmly embedded in the law (see commentary on ch 13 and 1 Cor 15:56) squelch any hope that the new exodus is fully realized in the Persian period. Nehemiah leaves no room for over-realized eschatology in Zion. We will need to wait for Elijah/John the Baptist to fulfill that role of forerunner in the Markan prologue (Mal 4:5–6; Luke 1:17) and its eschatological fulfillment: "He will wipe every tear from their eyes. There will be no more death or mourning or crying or pain, for the old order of things has passed away" (Rev 21:4).

In summary, the postexilic period represents a prototypical now-and-not-yet phase in redemptive history with a strong tilt toward the not-yet: Things are definitely not as they were, but we have a long way to go before we will see the beginning of the end of the reign of sin, death, and the devil. In light of these realities, chapter 8 does point to the hope that is yet to come.

### The Centrality of the Public Reading of the Law in Old Testament and New Testament

THE SHIFT FROM A SACRIFICIAL SYSTEM to the *torah* taking a central role heralds the announcement in Jeremiah that the law will take a preponderant space in the community life of God's people (Jer 31:33–34; see Ezra 7 commentary for a parallel emphasis):

> "This is the covenant I will make with the people of Israel
> after that time," declares the LORD.
> "I will put my law in their minds
> and write it on their hearts.
> I will be their God,
> and they will be my people.
> No longer will they teach their neighbor,

> or say to one another, 'Know the LORD,'
> because they will all know me,
> from the least of them to the greatest,"
> declares the LORD.
> "For I will forgive their wickedness
> and will remember their sins no more." (Jer 31:33–34)

Isaiah himself envisions a similar centripetal force, but for him the vision entails "many" nations (Isa 2:1–4). Here also the not-yet is emphasized, since we are not in the "last days." Commentators (e.g., Blenkinsopp) have long noted the reading of *torah* prepares us for the Second Temple Judaism tradition of the centrality of the written word. This impetus accelerates after the destruction of the temple in AD 70 and has continued unabated to this day. This is an extraordinary tribute to the resilience of the written word and of a persecuted minority who took it upon itself to preserve "the book of the Law of Moses." A community that has known full well the intrinsic value of the documents, both as a cultural heritage preserving its collective memory and more importantly (albeit with different interpretations of their value in everyday life) as *sacred texts* that needed to be transcribed and passed on to the next generation with the utmost care and precision. The very nature of the transmission process attests to how the community viewed these texts. For the ancient and for most of its tumultuous history, *torah* was sacred, to be preserved and not to be tampered with.

The dedicated public reading of the sacred texts continues throughout the New Testament and is well documented. Jesus famously stands up and reads from the scroll of Isaiah (Luke 4:17); the Reformation's *Sola Scriptura* asserts the centrality of the word of God in worship. This correlation between revival and renewal and the faithful reading of the Law finds evidence throughout history. The corollary is that whenever God's people forsake this practice, now measured in millennia, the loss in the transfer is incalculable and invites an understanding of worship that is human-centered rather than God-centered.

### The Role of Ezra and the Levites as Interpreters

THE CENTRALITY OF UNDERSTANDING the word and the unity of the body also represent a significant departure from the ordinary attitudes toward God's law in ancient Israel. The fact that *everyone* is on the same page connects to the past only in the fact that there was unanimity—only this time, this unanimous vote is in favor of God's word, rather than against it. A cursory study of the history of the book of the law of Moses in the Old Testament reveals a sad reality that it was seldom cared for or read, let alone followed. During the Late Judean period, the situation changed drastically with significant periods of renewed interests in the public reading of the law (short-lived, as it turned out) during the reigns of Hezekiah and Josiah (2 Kgs 18–19; 22–23). In contrast to that "top-down" approach to renewal from the royal court and the religious establishment, the community is now getting it, with the emphasis on understanding (word-group *sakal*)[20] on the part of everyone involved. The days of Jeremiah (read Jer 1–20) when the people were far from the LORD, even as Josiah enacts his religious reforms, seem to be left far behind, at least here in chapters 8–9 and in the dedication of the walls and the restoration of worship. However, old habits are hard to break, as chapter 13 will remind Nehemiah and the reader. Turning toward the New Testament, God is raising up "the apostles, the prophets, the evangelists, the pastors and teachers" (Eph 4:11) to bring God's people into maturity and deeper knowledge of Christ. The priesthood of all believers, a celebrated Reformation value, is thus anticipated here in chapter 8. Paul will claim with great confidence that the word of God can be (and should be) "correctly handl[ed]" (2 Tim 2:15) and is suitable for instruction (2 Tim 3:16). The standards remain high in terms of accountability, since not everyone is called to teach the word (Jas 3:1).

## Turning from Mourning into Joy

THE FULFILLMENT OF THE PROMISE OF ZION is a return to joy (Isa 3). Isaiah envisions a return from exile that would be filled with joy (Isa 55:12). The intentional dischronologized observance of the sacred days of the seventh month attests to the desire to imprint upon the community and for posterity that this return from exile and the completion of the task of restoring the sanctity of Zion should be marked first and foremost by celebration and joy. The theme of joy in the now and the not-yet receives a fuller treatment in the book of Philippians with Paul's constant exhortation to "rejoice" (3:1; 4:4). However, this joy should not be viewed

---

20. E.g., Gen 3:8; Deut 29:9; Josh 1:7; 1 Sam 18:5, 14; 1 Kgs 2:3; 2 Kgs 18:7; Pss 2:10; 14:2; 32:8; 36:3; Prov 1:3; Isa 41:20; 52:13; Jer 3:15; 9:24; 10:21; 20:11; 23:5.

as an emotion anchored in favorable circumstances, as reflected, for instance, in the celebration of the father upon the return of the prodigal son (Luke 15:20–24). Instead, it should be understood as a conviction anchored in the hope of a future eschatological restoration (see Zeph 3:14–17). The prepositional phrase "in the LORD" provides the line of demarcation between emotion and conviction. When the Levites exhort the people to rejoice in Nehemiah 8, this call is anchored in the LORD himself, which, in turn, will give them "strength" to face the future: "the joy of the LORD is your strength" (Neh 8:10). This posture is also reflected in Habakkuk's attitude of joy and praise even if/when faced with catastrophic crop failure (which, in an agro-pastoral society, would have dire consequences):

> Though the fig tree does not bud
> and there are no grapes on the vines,
> though the olive crop fails
> and the fields produce no food,
> though there are no sheep in the pen
> and no cattle in the stalls,
> yet I will rejoice in the LORD,
> I will be joyful in God my Savior.
>
> The Sovereign LORD is my strength;
> he makes my feet like the feet of a deer,
> he enables me to tread on the heights. (Hab. 3:17–19)

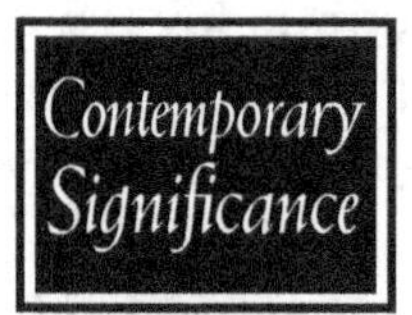


**CENTRALITY OF GOD'S WORD IN CHRISTIAN MINISTRY.** The obvious application of this text across cultural and ethnic fault-lines centers around the centrality of God's word in Christian ministry, regardless of our diversity. The history of Christian mission attests to the amazing adaptability of the word of God to different cultures. The common denominator will be a high view of Scripture and its authority. Every culture (per the vision of Rev 7) contains the ability to understand the word and apply it. The role of Christian ministers is to make sure we explain it so that people can understand it. Students of homiletics may argue whether certain techniques, delivery systems, or technologies may be superior to others, but regardless of strategies of persuasion, the reading of Scripture and its interpretation forms a central function in public worship. Jesus enters the synagogue in Capernaum and reads from Isaiah (Luke 4:17–19). Peter stands up and interprets the prophets and the Psalms to his audience in Acts 2:14–21. Stephen recapitulates Israelite history (see commentary on chapter 9:6–37). Martin Lloyd-Jones proclaimed the word in London as Charles Haddon Spurgeon did before him and as Nicky Gumbel and others are doing now. Chinese house churches are gathering around the word; persecuted believers who gather clandestinely cling to the precious few and worn out Bibles they possess. Bible studies continue to be formed in so-called closed-access Muslim countries. The model of the centrality of God's word adapts itself to different circumstances and in different time periods and cultures. Nehemiah 8 anchors the centrality of God's word in the restoration of worship in Zion and challenges us through the ages until Christ's return to continue in this trajectory into the presence of the "Word of God" himself (John 1:1; Rev 19:13).

The centrality of the word must be coupled with intelligibility. The great missiologist Lamin Sanneh (along with another famous African missiologist David Bosch) has left a great legacy of the importance of Bible translation for cultures to develop their own expression of the faith.[21] The role of the folks who explain the word in the assembly in Nehemiah 8 serves as a vivid and early witness to the importance not only of hearing the word, but of understanding it. Thus, the task is upon the modern Ezras among us, not only to know the Scripture but also to explain it so that people who hear it can understand it.

**Choosing joy as an eschatological declaration of restoration.** As we rejoice in the LORD, his joy is our strength. Like our spiritual forefathers in the province of Yehud, our joy is not dictated by the circumstances in our lives. Paul in prison exhorts his beloved audience at Philippi to rejoice (Phil 4:4). Isaiah anchors the joy of the LORD to the realm of eschatological end-time prophecy (Isa 51:11). When God's people "consider it pure joy" (Jas 1:2) in the midst of adverse circumstances, we also declare that the present trouble/tribulation is seen as a sign that the end is coming (Rom 8:18). The imagery of feasting is tied to

21. Lamin Sanneh, *Translating the Message*, 2nd ed. (Maryknoll, NY: Orbis, 2009). David Bosch, *Transforming Mission* (Maryknoll, NY: Orbis, 1991).

this theme of joy, as well. Paul assures the Philippians that "my God will meet all your needs according to the riches of his glory in Christ Jesus" (Phil 4:19). Isaiah's invitation is ongoing: "Come, buy and eat," he says (55:1–2), because the great banquet is being prepared (Luke 14:15–24). In Revelation, the "wedding supper of the Lamb" marks the fulfillment of this motif of feasting and rejoicing in the Lord (Rev 19:6–9):

> Then I heard what sounded like a great multitude, like the roar of rushing waters and like loud peals of thunder, shouting:
>
> "Hallelujah!
> For our Lord God Almighty reigns.
> Let us rejoice and be glad
> and give him glory!
> For the wedding of the Lamb has come,
> and his bride has made herself ready.
> Fine linen, bright and clean,
> was given her to wear."
> (Fine linen stands for the righteous acts of God's holy people.)
>
> Then the angel said to me, "Write this: Blessed are those who are invited to the wedding supper of the Lamb!" And he added, "These are the true words of God."

**Worshiping together.** Models of worship in contemporary churches throughout the world abound. I remember being in a church service where the worship emulated the format in Nehemiah 8 and extended to several hours. Other monochronic approaches manage the clock as it were a rocket-launch countdown. As the palmist says, "Better is one day in your court than a thousand elsewhere" (Ps 84:10). Taking extended times together in the reading of the word and the presence of the LORD is a sound biblical model that is lost on some cultures. Those of us enslaved to the clock need to reconsider the value of a polychronic approach to the reading and interpretation of the word.

Some experts in children's education advocate separating parents from children based on age-appropriate education. Others advocate the incorporation of school-age children in worship with parents. Yet still others seek some *via media* that allows some measure of both/and, so that different age-groups worship together for part of the service and then leave for their own educational classes. Whatever conclusion one draws on these matters, Nehemiah 8 does offer some guidelines in its insistence on a strong sense of solidarity and common experience in worship. Worship tilts toward inclusivity with *understanding* as the single-most important criterium. The experience of the reading of the word and its interpretation seems to cross generational lines, perhaps more readily than we might realize. This, in turn, anticipates the priesthood of all believers (1 Pet 2:9) and the promise of the Holy Spirit, when all age groups and genders will be filled with the Holy Spirit and be able to prophesy (which assumes understanding of the word, Acts 2; Joel 2:28–32). The application of the text seems to indicate that we should not underestimate the power of the word of God in the ears of the attentive hearer, regardless of age or gender. Here also, Nehemiah points toward an eschatological future, already anticipated by Joel (2:28–32) and beginning to be fulfilled in Acts 2:17–21:

> In the last days, God says,
> I will pour out my Spirit on all people.
> Your sons and daughters will prophesy,
> your young men will see visions,
> your old men will dream dreams.
> Even on my servants, both men and women,
> I will pour out my Spirit in those days,
> and they will prophesy.
> I will show wonders in the heavens above
> and signs on the earth below,
> blood and fire and billows of smoke.
> The sun will be turned to darkness
> and the moon to blood
> before the coming of the great and glorious day of
> the LORD.
> And everyone who calls
> on the name of the Lord will be saved.

# Nehemiah 9:1–37

1 On the twenty-fourth day of the same month, the Israelites
gathered together, fasting and wearing sackcloth and putting
dust on their heads. 2 Those of Israelite descent had separated
themselves from all foreigners. They stood in their places and
confessed their sins and the sins of their ancestors. 3 They
stood where they were and read from the Book of the Law
of the LORD their God for a quarter of the day, and spent
another quarter in confession and in worshiping the LORD
their God. 4 Standing on the stairs of the Levites were Jeshua,
Bani, Kadmiel, Shebaniah, Bunni, Sherebiah, Bani and Kenani.
They cried out with loud voices to the LORD their God. 5 And
the Levites—Jeshua, Kadmiel, Bani, Hashabneiah, Sherebiah,
Hodiah, Shebaniah and Pethahiah—said: "Stand up and praise
the LORD your God, who is from everlasting to everlasting."

"Blessed be your glorious name, and may it be
exalted above all blessing and praise. 6 You alone are
the LORD. You made the heavens, even the highest
heavens, and all their starry host, the earth and all that
is on it, the seas and all that is in them. You give life to
everything, and the multitudes of heaven worship you.

7 "You are the LORD God, who chose Abram and
brought him out of Ur of the Chaldeans and named him
Abraham. 8 You found his heart faithful to you, and you
made a covenant with him to give to his descendants the
land of the Canaanites, Hittites, Amorites, Perizzites,
Jebusites and Girgashites. You have kept your promise
because you are righteous.

9 "You saw the suffering of our ancestors in Egypt;
you heard their cry at the Red Sea. 10 You sent signs and
wonders against Pharaoh, against all his officials and all
the people of his land, for you knew how arrogantly the
Egyptians treated them. You made a name for yourself,
which remains to this day. 11 You divided the sea before

them, so that they passed through it on dry ground, but
you hurled their pursuers into the depths, like a stone
into mighty waters. 12 By day you led them with a pillar
of cloud, and by night with a pillar of fire to give them
light on the way they were to take.

13 "You came down on Mount Sinai; you spoke to them
from heaven. You gave them regulations and laws that are
just and right, and decrees and commands that are good.
14 You made known to them your holy Sabbath and gave
them commands, decrees and laws through your servant
Moses. 15 In their hunger you gave them bread from
heaven and in their thirst you brought them water from
the rock; you told them to go in and take possession of the
land you had sworn with uplifted hand to give them.

16 "But they, our ancestors, became arrogant and
stiff-necked, and they did not obey your commands.
17 They refused to listen and failed to remember the
miracles you performed among them. They became
stiff-necked and in their rebellion appointed a leader in
order to return to their slavery. But you are a forgiving
God, gracious and compassionate, slow to anger and
abounding in love. Therefore you did not desert them,
18 even when they cast for themselves an image of a calf
and said, 'This is your god, who brought you up out of
Egypt,' or when they committed awful blasphemies.

19 "Because of your great compassion you did not
abandon them in the wilderness. By day the pillar of
cloud did not fail to guide them on their path, nor the
pillar of fire by night to shine on the way they were to
take. 20 You gave your good Spirit to instruct them.
You did not withhold your manna from their mouths,
and you gave them water for their thirst. 21 For forty
years you sustained them in the wilderness; they lacked
nothing, their clothes did not wear out nor did their
feet become swollen.

22 "You gave them kingdoms and nations, allotting
to them even the remotest frontiers. They took over
the country of Sihon king of Heshbon and the country

of Og king of Bashan. [23] You made their children as
numerous as the stars in the sky, and you brought them
into the land that you told their parents to enter and
possess. [24] Their children went in and took possession
of the land. You subdued before them the Canaanites,
who lived in the land; you gave the Canaanites into
their hands, along with their kings and the peoples of
the land, to deal with them as they pleased. [25] They
captured fortified cities and fertile land; they took
possession of houses filled with all kinds of good things,
wells already dug, vineyards, olive groves and fruit
trees in abundance. They ate to the full and were well-
nourished; they reveled in your great goodness.

[26] "But they were disobedient and rebelled against
you; they turned their backs on your law. They killed
your prophets, who had warned them in order to turn
them back to you; they committed awful blasphemies.
[27] So you delivered them into the hands of their enemies,
who oppressed them. But when they were oppressed
they cried out to you. From heaven you heard them, and
in your great compassion you gave them deliverers, who
rescued them from the hand of their enemies.

[28] "But as soon as they were at rest, they again did
what was evil in your sight. Then you abandoned them
to the hand of their enemies so that they ruled over
them. And when they cried out to you again, you heard
from heaven, and in your compassion you delivered
them time after time.

[29] "You warned them in order to turn them back
to your law, but they became arrogant and disobeyed
your commands. They sinned against your ordinances,
of which you said, 'The person who obeys them will
live by them.' Stubbornly they turned their backs on
you, became stiff-necked and refused to listen. [30] For
many years you were patient with them. By your Spirit
you warned them through your prophets. Yet they paid
no attention, so you gave them into the hands of the
neighboring peoples. [31] But in your great mercy you did

not put an end to them or abandon them, for you are a
gracious and merciful God.

32 "Now therefore, our God, the great God, mighty and
awesome, who keeps his covenant of love, do not let all
this hardship seem trifling in your eyes—the hardship that
has come on us, on our kings and leaders, on our priests
and prophets, on our ancestors and all your people, from
the days of the kings of Assyria until today. 33 In all that has
happened to us, you have remained righteous; you have
acted faithfully, while we acted wickedly. 34 Our kings,
our leaders, our priests and our ancestors did not follow
your law; they did not pay attention to your commands
or the statutes you warned them to keep. 35 Even while
they were in their kingdom, enjoying your great goodness
to them in the spacious and fertile land you gave them,
they did not serve you or turn from their evil ways.

36 "But see, we are slaves today, slaves in the land
you gave our ancestors so they could eat its fruit and
the other good things it produces. 37 Because of our
sins, its abundant harvest goes to the kings you have
placed over us. They rule over our bodies and our
cattle as they please. We are in great distress.

*Original Meaning*

## Historical Retrospective (9:1–37)

**SETTING:** According to the account, chapters 8 through 10 provide an intentionally connected narrative of reforms during Nehemiah's first term as governor of Yehud. At the end of chapter 8, we are leaving the community gathered in an "assembly" on the twenty-third of the seventh month (8:18). The narrative sequence resumes in 9:1 and makes a point to tell us that the events should be viewed in sequence with what precedes rather than in a different time period[1]: "on the twenty-fourth day of the *same* month" (emphasis mine,

1. See in contrast Ezra 4, where the account makes it clear the events are dis-chronologized.

"this [*hazeh*] month"). The author leaves little doubt that Ezra and Nehemiah's reforms occurred at different times, including the vexed question of mixed marriages:

- During the time of Ezra's reforms (Ezra 9–10)
- During the first governorship of Nehemiah (Neh 9:1–2), but now with the active participation of Ezra
- During Nehemiah's second term in office (Neh 13:6–7)

To allow the record to stand as is represents the least problematic historical reconstruction. Critical efforts since the ninteenth century, including Williamson's,[2] have provided some extraordinarily sophisticated ways to reconstruct the times of Nehemiah and Ezra apart from the received chronology.[3] The purpose of this commentary, while not seeking to brush off the critical debates, seeks to frame the account from a narrative-historical perspective, which gives the ancient text room to speak with all the nuances and diversities embedded in it. For instance, the absence of Ezra the priest and scribe (NIV "teacher") in chapter 9, who is featured so prominently in Nehemiah 8, does not de facto disqualify chapter 9 from being in sequence with the events of chapter 8. Such variations can have equally valid and intelligent explanations other than the default critical instinct to dislodge a text from the milieu to which it is said to belong (see 9:1). In summary, we side with the notion that "many commentators have . . . assumed that no new setting is presupposed."[4]

The time of mandated rejoicing during the reading and understanding of the law by Ezra and the Levites (chapter 8), along with the observance of the celebration of the Feast of Booths *in situ* in the now reconstituted Zion, all constitute signs of the beginning of a new era. Indeed, this is the new exodus promised by the prophet Isaiah (see Isa 40:3–5): mourning will be turned into joy, and the LORD will appear in Zion (see Isa 35:10). However, before any of these events can unfold,

---

2. Williamson, *Ezra, Nehemiah*, 308–9.

3. Recently this includes Jacob Wright's complex and magisterial reworking of the editorial process. Jacob Wright, *Rebuilding Identity: the Nehemiah-Memoir and Its Earliest Readers* (Berlin: de Gruyter, 2005).

4. Williamson (*Ezra, Nehemiah*, 308) himself disputes the received chronology.

the breach in the relationship must be repaired through confession. This theme of confession of sin during the postexilic era is fundamental, since repentance is *associated* with the return from exile in Deuteronomic law (see Deut 30:1–3). Daniel 9, Ezra 9, and Nehemiah 9 take their place beside Israel's Book of Prayer—the Psalter—among the greatest prayers of confession in the canon. Nehemiah 9 represents a fitting corporate response to Nehemiah's own penitential prayer at the outset of his epic commission to restore Zion (1:4, see commentary on Neh 1:5–11). The communal prayer of chapter 9 here is not triumphalistic and lacks a sense of over-realized eschatology on the part of the community. They recognize they are at the very initial phase of the restoration, since they are still "slaves" in a Persian province (9:36). However, for the restoration wheels to begin moving again, the covenant (formal relationship) must be renewed. The observation of the Feast of Booths was a start, and it needed to be celebratory. However, for the covenantal relationship to take root, a time of repentance was equally required. Following this time of corporate repentance (vv. 1–5), the prayer by the Levites[5] functions as a historical retrospective that catalogues the twin themes of Yahweh's faithfulness and the people's unfaithfulness. It is only toward the end that an actual confession is found (9:33–35), followed by an oblique petition (e.g., Exod 2:23): "we are in great distress" (9:37). This sweeping overview of Israelite history captures a familiar theme of the Old Testament: a repeated catalogue of Yahweh's *hesed*, answered by the unfaithfulness of the people. In the end, as the prayer powerfully states, the exiles are utterly dependent on Yahweh's mercy and intervention for the restoration of Zion to proceed. They are, in fact, in no position to dictate terms, since they are "slaves in the land you gave our ancestors" (9:36). The prayer and the account end with a formal request for the covenant to be renewed (9:38), along with the list of signatories (chapter 10). Those who have agreed to affix their names in effect commit to obeying the terms of the covenant, much in the same way as the preexilic community did on the plains of Moab (cf. Deut 29:1), at Shechem with Joshua (Josh 24:1), with Josiah in Jerusalem (2 Chr 34:29–31), and now again in the newly-reestablished fortress Zion. This is indeed a solemn assembly that exalts Yahweh's character and places the people in a less than savory light, following the pattern indictment in Deuteronomy 32.

---

5. The Hebrew text does not follow the lead of the LXX to assign the prayer to Ezra.

The next time we will have such retrospectives will be Jesus's condemnation of the Pharisees in Matthew 23 and Stephen before the Sanhedrin in Acts 7.

**Call to worship (9:1–6).** The time of corporate mourning and repentance ("fasting and wearing sackcloth and putting dust on their heads," v. 1) recalls Ezra's gathering of the assembly in Ezra 10 but with positive evidence these two accounts should not be conflated into one event. The two gatherings are set apart from each other, one taking place "on the twentieth day of the ninth month" (Ezra 10:9, see commentary) and the other "on the twenty-fourth day of the same month" (Neh 9:1), in different years (Neh 1:1).[6] The posture of willing repentance regarding intermarriage is especially noted in the account. The act of separating from "all foreigners" ("sons of foreigners" [*mikol beney nekar*]) is framed in clear ethnic primordial terms: "sons of Israel" (v.1 *beney yisr'ael*) and "seed of Israel" (author's translation [v.2 *zer'a yisra'el* ] NIV "Israelites" and "Israelite descent"). In quick succession, "they stood" and "confessed" (as an ongoing action) "their sins and the sins ("iniquity") of their ancestors" (v. 2). The time of confession[7] is set in the broader context of a public reading of the "Book of the Law of the LORD their God" (v. 3) that alternated between times of confession and repentance, and the reading of the word (a "quarter of the day" is approximately 4 hours). Thus, the people immersed themselves into a time of deep introspection rooted in a responsive reading of the word and prayer. The sense of personal commitment pervades the account (the word is from the LORD *their* God; see also v. 4 "*their* God" and v. 5 "*your* God"; emphasis added), and the commitment recalls the first day of the seventh month and should not be dislodged from this contextual mooring. This is indeed an extraordinary three-week period in the history of Israel! To add to the parallel with that fateful first day, Levites by name are strategically inserted into the drama, some of whom were part of the original group of "interpreters" in ch. 8.[8] Presumably following the time of responsive reading, a group of eight Levites stood "on the stairs" (of the platform

6. Methodology of critical scholarship allows for various degrees (some more so than others) of intentional and unintentional errors in ancient historical recordings. However, the presence of parallel accounts by themselves should not be used as sole criterion, as is the case here.

7. For the definition of confession, see commentary on Ezra 10:10.

8. Jeshua, Bani, and Sherebiah.

in 8:4, or other stairs?) to lead in loud acclamations of praise ("with loud voices") "to the LORD *their* God" (v. 4, emphasis added).[9] A second group of eight joins the chorus, including Jeshua, Bani,[10] Kadmiel, Shebaniah and Sherebiah from the first group (v. 4–5). This time, they are exhorting the congregation to "stand up and praise the LORD *your* God, who is from everlasting to everlasting" (1 Chr 29:10; Pss 41:13; 106:48).[11] Thus, the time of confession remains anchored in the context of celebration of the past week (Feast of Booths). The connection between the reading of the word, confession of sin, and celebration will be taken up under Bridging Contexts below.

The "invocation" continues in vv. 5b and 6 with an exaltation of the divine name ("Blessed be your glorious name"), which is fitting since the declaration of the glory (*kabod*) of the divine name from Exodus 34:5–6 is a major theme of the prayer. "You alone are the LORD" (NIV, v. 6) captures only a fraction of the redundant and emphatic nature of the syntax in the original pertaining to the uniqueness of Yahweh as sole Creator of the created realms. To be sure, it makes for an awkward sequence in English but it certainly gets the point across:

> You are He[12] Yahweh, you alone, you, you made[13] the heavens . . .
> [and] the earth (v.6)

This exclusive claim to the rights of the work of creation is unrivaled and extensive. There are no collaborating entities since every realm ("the heavens," "the earth," and "the seas") is modified by "and all that is in it/them" (v. 6). The last concluding thought is carried in the original as an ongoing action, attesting to Yahweh's sustaining power to hold the universe together: you are giving "life to everything" and the hosts of heavens are worshiping you (*mishtahevim*, author's translation cf. NIV "the multitudes of heaven worship you"). This permanent worship service

9. See Kidner, *Ezra and Nehemiah*, 121.

10. There are two "Bani" in 9:4. Factoring in possibly an unintentional copyist error in transmission, one of them could be Binnui (see 10:9; Williamson, *Ezra, Nehemiah*, 303).

11. See Williamson (ibid., 303).

12. Repeated as a framing device in v. 7 to launch the retrospective of the promise of Abraham and his name change.

13. *'asah* as in manufacturing, rather than the typical *bar'a* of creation (itself a verb of material production as well, see Gen 1:1).

("from everlasting to everlasting," Neh 9:5) anticipates the great temple visions of Revelation 4–5, where the entire created realm participates in the worship of the Creator "day and night" (cf. Rev 4:8; 5:13).

*Main features of the prayer.* Students of the prayer have noted parallels with Psalms 78, 105, 106, 135, and 136.[14] The prayer gives us valuable clues regarding the materials the Levites[15] worked with in composing this prayer. Elements of the Old Testament canon as we know it today permeate the prayer: the Abrahamic covenant in Genesis 12 and 15; the exodus event; the giving of the law at Sinai (Exod 20); the wilderness wanderings (in the book of Numbers); the first fruit of conquest of Numbers 21; the conquest narratives in both Joshua and Judges. In this regard, the Deuteronomic cyclical model of sin-judgment-repentance-salvation-sin in Judges 2 provides the foundation for the history of the monarchy as a whole. While the ministry of the prophets is recognized, there is *no* mention of the Davidic dynasty in the retrospective proper (only once "kings" are mentioned in the confession, Neh 9:34). From a covenantal framework, the Sinaitic covenant expectedly supplies the theological underpinnings of the prayer, along with the land-people promissory covenant made to Abraham as a foundation. The tone of the prayer is both somber and worshipful, since it underscores the people's persistent unfaithfulness while at the same time exalting Yahweh's persistent faithfulness toward the undeserving Israelites. In the end, it is Yahweh alone who gets all the glory, since it is his character as revealed in Exodus 34:5–6 that is shown to have sustained the people.

**The covenant with Abraham (9:7–8).** The recalling of the promise of the land made to Abraham (Gen 12:1–2; 15:18–21; 17:8; 22:17) puts the emphasis on the name change and his response of faith to Yahweh: "you found his heart faithful" (root *ʾaman* "believing" or "trusting"; Neh 9:8; same root as "believed" in Gen 15:6). This is a unique phrase in the

---

14. See Charles Fensham, *The Books of Ezra and Nehemiah,* NICOT (Grand Rapids: Eerdmans, 1982), 228; Williamson, *Ezra, Nehemiah,* 306; and Smith, *Ezra, Nehemiah, Esther,* 177.

15. LXX singles out "Ezra" as the one who prayed. While no mention of his name is notable in the best Hebrew manuscript available (Leningrad Codex), there is no reason to assume he was not present on the twenty-fourth day as he was during the first three weeks. The emphasis placed on the role of other Levites underscores the corporate nature of the reform: all participated (see commentary on chapter 8; see also Smith [*Ezra, Nehemiah, Esther,* 177] for similar conclusions).

canon, but clearly the author wishes to connect Abram's response to his "amening" Yahweh's promise in Genesis 15:6: "Abram believed [*wehe'emin*] the LORD, and he credited it to him as righteousness."[16] Yahweh "cut" (*karat*; author's translation; NIV "made a covenant with him") a covenant with Abram to give "his descendants the land" (v. 8). As an interpretive summary,[17] it anticipates the reliability of Yahweh's character in his dealing with his wayward people. As a result of being "righteous" (*tsadiq*), "You have kept your promise" (v. 8). Thus, his faithfulness to the promise to Abraham reveals that Yahweh is righteous (i.e., he does the right thing). However, it would be too reductive to limit Yahweh's righteous acts to his faithfulness to Abram, as the prayer will demonstrate.[18]

**Exodus (9:9–11).** The next installment of Israelite recapitulative history is anchored on the exodus event, particularly the salvation of Yahweh at the "Red Sea" ("sea of reeds," [*yam suph*] v. 9). "Pharaoh" and "the Egyptians" could not encroach on Yahweh's plans with "our ancestors," for "you knew how arrogantly the Egyptians treated them" (v. 10). Details drawn from the Song of the Sea—"you divided the sea before them," "you hurled their pursuers into the depths, like a stone in the mighty waters" (v. 11)—all recall the vivid images enshrined in Israelite memory in Exodus 15 (and Exod 14:9, "pursuers"). This decisive victory was the crowning moment of Yahweh's revelation as the uncontested one God over all the gods of Egypt ("Who among the gods is like you?" Exod 15:11); "you made a name for yourself" (Neh 9:10).

**Sinai (9:12–15).** The guidance of cloud and fire serves as prolepsis (v. 12) and as a connecting verse to the next main event: "Mount Sinai" and the giving of the law, with an emphasis on its divine origin: "you came down" and "you spoke to them from heaven" (v. 13). The law is spoken in the most positive way: upright, true, and good regulations and commands (v. 13). The "holy Sabbath" is singled out, as is the role of Moses in the reception of the laws ("through your servant Moses," v. 14). The Sinai account circles back to the wilderness journey by highlighting God's provision of "bread from heaven" and "water from the rock" (again,

---

16. See J. Bergman Kline in Gary D. Pratico and Miles V. Van Pelt, *Basics of Biblical Hebrew* (Grand Rapids: Zondervan, 2001), 364–66.

17. This is also unique to this prayer in the canon.

18. See the excellent discussion by Charles Lee Irons, *The Righteousness of God* (Tübingen: Mohr Siebeck, 2015) on the *tsedeq* word group.

the wilderness wanderings is used proleptically) "to go in and take possession of the land" (v. 15).

**The people's arrogance and Yahweh's *hesed* (9:16–18).** One cannot help but think the history so far serves as an introduction to the main point of the prayer, which is to highlight the people's disobedience in the midst of Yahweh's mighty acts of salvation, protection, and provision. Indeed, seen in this light, Israelite history underscored Yahweh's righteous dealings with Israel: he is the promise keeper.

In response to this perfect record of faithfulness, "they, our ancestors" (v. 16) "became arrogant," see v. 10 also for the use of the same Hebrew verb *zyd*). The text adds the one word coined in the crucible of the Israelites' disobedience: "stiff-necked" (see Exod 32:9), an animal husbandry term that characterizes a stubborn beast of burden. The damning catalogue of their failure continues (v. 17a):

- "they refused to listen"
- "failed to remember the miracles (in the sense of wonders) you performed among them"
- "they became stiff-necked" ("they hardened [root *qashah*] their necks")
- "in their rebellion, they appointed a leader . . . to return to slavery"

The last count directly points to the building of the golden calf in Exodus 32:1–6. Nehemiah 9:18, "an image of a calf" makes the connection to this event in a similar way Psalm 106:19–20 does. Nehemiah reminds the reader that the forefathers did in fact substitute Yahweh for this image: "This is your [singular] god, who brought you up out of Egypt" (v. 18). The moment is etched in Israelite memory and becomes the paradigm to describe Israel's idolatrous ways throughout its tormented relationship with Yahweh (Ps 106:19–22; Jer 2:11; Rom 1:23).[19]

However, in response to this paradigm of inflexibility and rebellion, the prayer pivots to Yahweh's revelation of his character, first revealed in the same context of the golden calf incident (Exod 34:5–6), which serves as a point by point response to their rebellion (v. 17b).

---

19. Richard Lints, *Identity and Idolatry: The Image of God and its Inversion* (Downers Grove, IL: IVP Academic, 2015).

- you are a forgiving God ("a God of forgiveness" [*selyhoth* is plural])
- gracious and compassionate (*hannun werahum*)
- slow to anger (*'ereh 'apaim*)
- abounding in love (*hesed*)
- you did not desert (*'azab*, "abandon") them.

**Wilderness (9:19–21).** The recalling of wilderness years (see Deut 8:1–4) concludes the whole first part of the history of Israel. The appeal is to the character of Yahweh as revealed in the declaration of the divine name at Sinai: "Because of your great compassion, you did not abandon (*'azab*) them in the wilderness" (v. 19). The themes of divine guidance and provision throughout the forty years (v. 21), all under the superintendence of the Spirit,[20] lead to one conclusion: "they lacked [*hasar*] nothing" (v. 21). The phrase itself alludes to the promise of the good Shepherd (Ps 23:1).

Yahweh is indeed righteous and cannot be faulted despite rampant disobedience on the part of the people. This marks the conclusion of the first part of the historical retrospective. The second part deals with Israelite history in the land all the way up to the exile.

**Summary.** The next installment of the sweeping historical recapitulation takes the congregation through the conquest and settlement in the land. The prevailing interpretive paradigm remains the same: History is viewed as a testament to Yahweh's *hesed* toward his people. Notably, a *longue durée* approach based on Deuteronomic law provides a powerful explanatory model to account for the ebb and flow operating through the exile until the time of the Persian period. Times of rebellion invariably result in times of political decline and unrest, which can only be reversed if the people of the theocracy return to Yahweh in repentance (2 Chr 7:14). Relapse into disobedience to God's law resumes the cycle.

**Conquest and settlement (9:22–25).** Verse 22 returns to a well-rehearsed dimension to the conquest of Canaan in Israelite lore: the conquest of the Transjordanian tribal kingships of Sihon in Heshbon in the highlands of central Transjordan and of Og in the northern Transjordan region of Bashan (Num 21:23–35; Deut 2:24–27; 3:1–11). These two

---

20. A notable theme in postexilic context, Zech 6:8 with its foundations in the Isaianic promise of the restoration of Zion; Isa 11:1–3; 61:1–3).

initial defeats of Canaanite/Amorite polities (Num 21:21–35) function as a harbinger of the future conquest of the land west of the Jordan. The contested nature of the area throughout Israelite history (see 2 Kgs 3:1–27) serves as a continued reminder of God's faithfulness in the past.[21] Even Israel's sworn enemies acknowledged Israelite dominance over the area (Mesha Inscription, line 10: "Men of Gad has been there from time immemorial").[22] The prayer pointedly recalls that the land promise is not complete without the presence of "children as numerous as the stars in the sky" (v. 23), along with the accompanying subduing of the Canaanites and numerous material blessings as fruit of conquest: "fortified cities and fertile lands" (v. 25). The catalog of blessings is itemized (see Deut 6:11; Josh 24:13):

- houses ("filled with all kinds of good things")
- wells ("already dug")
- vineyards
- olive groves
- fruit trees ("in abundance")

In summary, as they took hold of the land promised to them,[23] the prayer employs four main verbs in uninterrupted sequence to underscore the extent of Yahweh's "great goodness" toward them (v. 25; NIV reduces the four narrative summary verbs to three and thus misses the impact of the original text):

---

21. We also remember that Tobiah is an Ammonite, a Transjordan tribal group.

22. See Petter, *The Land Between the Two Rivers*, 72.

23. Scholars with a high view of the biblical record for historical reconstruction of the region during the Late Bronze Age and early Iron Age (approx. 1400–1000 BC) recognize that the Israelite settlement in Canaan should be viewed as a process rather than an event, spanning several generations. While Joshua records initial successes and the apportioning of territories indicates that Yahweh was faithful to give them the land (Josh 21:43), the period of the Judges and early monarchy catalogues persistent imposition by local factions (either indigenous, e.g., Moab, Ammon, Midian, or non-indigenous, e.g., the *Peleshet*/Philistines). 2 Samuel 5 does provide a certain sense of closure to the process when King David finally takes the "prize" of Jerusalem from the Jebusites (see Exod 15:17; Zion = "the mountain of your inheritance"). Thus, from a strictly historical perspective, the land was never fully conquered, which of course anticipates a "better" land promised in the new covenant: a Jerusalem "above" that is "free" (Gal 4:26).

- They ate (*'akal*)
- They were satiated (*saba'*; NIV "ate to the full," see Deut 8:10–12)
- They grew fat (*shaman*; NIV "well-nourished," see Deut 32:15)
- They "reveled" (*'adan* is a unique verb connected to the term "Eden," i.e., "luxuriate").

**The time of the judges as paradigm of Israelite history (9:26–31).** The people's response to Yahweh's *hesed* at the time of the exodus (v. 17a) is matched at the time of the settlement in Canaan and throughout the time of the monarchy. Syntactically, the verbs of abundance of verse 25 are matched by three verbs of open rebellion in verse 26, along with some orthographic symmetry:

- They were disobedient (*marah*, "they rebelled")
- and [they] rebelled against you (Hebrew root is *mrd*)
- They put your law behind their backs ("threw")

As an illustration of these blatant acts of rebellion, "they killed your prophets" (v. 25b, lit., "your prophets, they had killed"). The reference to the prophets confirms that the entire Israelite history is in view rather than a specific timeframe. That they "had warned them in order to turn them back to you" will be repeated at the end of the indictment in *inclusio* (see v. 30 and commentary below). The lack of responsiveness is answered by Yahweh's predictable action based on Deuteronomic law (with phraseology [italicized] borrowed from Judg 2:10–19, see also Ps 106:41), both in terms of judgment and compassion (v. 27; see Judg 2:14, 16, 18 especially):

> you *delivered them* into the hands of their *enemies*, who *oppressed* them. But when they were *oppressed* they *cried out* to you. From heaven you heard them, and in your great *compassion* you gave them *deliverers*, who rescued them from the hand of their enemies.

Reflecting the tormented history of the east Mediterranean corridor between the great powers, any notion of "rest" in the land was always short lived (v. 28, see Judg 3:30).

In quick succession, two additional full cycles of sin-judgment-deliverance are added. But there were many times (NIV "time after time") that Yahweh continued to display his "compassion" by delivering them (v. 28).

The dramatic conclusion of this summary of Israelite history is marked by a relentless lexical repetition of themes parallel to Israel's response with the golden calf incident (see vv. 16–17a):

- "they became arrogant" (v. 29; cf. v. 16; same word is applied to the Egyptians' treatment of the Israelites in Egypt, v. 10)
- "they disobeyed your commands" (v. 29; cf. v. 16)
- "became stiff-necked" (v. 29; cf. v. 16)
- "refused to listen" (v. 29; cf. v. 17)

In addition, the list returns to the theme of the warning of the prophets, now clearly associated with the activity of the Spirit (v. 30, cf. v. 20; see Bridging Contexts below), along with a modified version to the vivid imagery of v. 26: they "stubbornly . . . turned their back on you" (v. 29). The goodness of God's law is also repeated (v. 29, cf. v. 13; cf. Deut 30). With this kind of behavior, the inescapable outcome is exile, removal from the land: "you gave them into the hand of the neighboring peoples" (v. 30, [*'ame ha'aratsot*] "peoples of the lands").[24]

Yet, in spite of this tremendous list of catastrophic failure on the part of Israel, Yahweh's "great mercy" (v. 31) prevails in the end. Yahweh has the last word in this recapitulation of Israelite history up to the mid fifth century BC. As witnessed by the postexilic community gathered in Jerusalem on the twenty-fourth day of the seventh month: "you have not abandoned them (*'azab*) *because* a God of grace and compassion you are" (*ki e'l hannun werahum a'tah*).[25]

**Confession: We have acted unfaithfully while you have been righteous (9:32–35).** The only real petition is extraordinarily terse and oblique—"do not let all this hardship ("burden" [*tela'ah*]) seem trifling in your eyes" (v. 32)—and is embedded in the inevitable implication ("now therefore," v. 32) of the preceding account of Israelite history.

---

24. A clear allusion to the language of the curse of exile by foreign nations is taken from Deut 28:64. NIV "neighboring peoples" creates a false impression. The exile of 586 BC is clearly in view, rather than invasion by neighboring polities.

25. NIV "for you are a gracious and merciful God."

Yahweh has been fully justified in his actions to judge Israel and the verdict is in: Yahweh is righteous (NIV "just"), while the people "acted wickedly" (v. 33). But this verdict is not without a formal recognition by this current generation that they belong to this indictment, as well, since their ancestors were "*our* kings,[26] *our* leaders ("princes" *sarenu*), *our* priests and *our* ancestors" (v. 34; emphasis added). The postexilic community recognizes the universal and pervasive guilt shared by every sphere of society. In this regard, they stand in agreement with the prophetic indictments that catalog a complete societal breakdown (Isa 1:17), who consistently isolated the same core problem: They "did not follow your law" (v. 34), "pay attention to your commands," or heed the "warnings you gave to them."

By invoking the divine name ("our God" as "the great God, mighty and awesome," v. 32), the appeal is to both Yahweh's covenant-keeping actions and his *hesed* (the phrase "covenant of love" in the NIV is not supported by the syntax). As elsewhere (see Ps 51:1–2), Yahweh's character of faithfulness to the covenant and of *hesed* is not only the centerpiece of their appeal, it is the only one. Thus, they echo the great confessions of Scripture (e.g., Ps 51:1–2).

**Petition: We are slaves! (9:36–37).** If there is a formal petition, it is intentionally oblique ("we are slaves today," v. 36) and remains permeated with a deep sense that their lot is fully deserved ("because of our sins"; v. 37) and of the undeserved favor of God toward them (the squandered gift of the land). In a clear allusion to the slavery of Egypt, "kings" are reaping the benefit of their labor and "rule over our bodies and our cattle as they please" (v. 37). The community is fully aware that in order to see the promise of Zion fulfilled as articulated by the prophets, they first need to witness a new exodus from their new Egypt in the province of Yehud. Thus, their cry—"we are in great distress" (v. 37)—resembles the cry of their fathers in Exodus 2:23 who "groaned in their slavery" under Egyptian domination. We are essentially taken back to square one in this magisterial and sweeping overview of the history of Israel, which parallels Ezra's own prayer in Ezra 9:9.

26. It is the only time the kings of Israel, some of the worst violators of God's law, are mentioned in this history.

**God said "zig" and they zagged.** The paradigm of the history of Israel outlined in Nehemiah 9 can be summarized in God's gracious response time after time despite the people's repeated unfaithfulness. In this respect, the prayers of Nehemiah 9 and Ezra 9 have strong parallels in their understanding of God's character. The history of the Hebrew kings enshrined in Kings and Chronicles offers the same consistent picture, along with the long lists of indictment in the prophetic corpus. This sense catastrophic and systemic failure on the part of the people becomes the bedrock of Paul's recapitulative history in Romans. The conclusion remains the same: "There is no one righteous, not even one" (Rom 3:10). The sin, guilt, and shame of the people is incontrovertible. Conversely, Yahweh is shown to be entirely above reproach in meting out his justice. Hence the realization: We are guilty, and you are righteous in executing your judgment of exile upon us (Neh 9:3, 32–35). Long gone are the days of Israel's blindness to her own sin: "Woe to those who are wise in their own eyes and clever in their own sight" (Isa 5:21). Even the tepid and terse petition at the end of the account, to remove slavery from them, sounds more like an admission that they got what they deserved and that Yahweh has been entirely justified. His judgment against their waywardness cannot be questioned. This admission, "we are slaves to this day" (v. 36), is crucial, because it is also a realization that *more restoration is yet to come*. The restoration of Zion is underway to be sure, but perhaps, as in the words attributed to Winston Churchill at the end of the Battle of Britain: "Now, this is not the end. It is not even the beginning of the end. But it is, perhaps, the end of the beginning."[27]

What is particularly indicting in Nehemiah 9 is Israel's pattern of inability to reciprocate and respond favorably to God's extraordinary goodness, favor, mercy, and provision. It appears as if the modus operandi of the people—every time Yahweh saves, hears their cry, and provides for them ("'they lacked nothing" Neh 9:21)—is to respond in blatant disregard for the very provision and goodness of the Lord exhibited toward them. Ungratefulness and entitlement do not even begin to characterize the people's stiff-necked attitudes in light of God's character! If the postexilic community was looking for idealized lore

27. http://www.churchill-society-london.org.uk/EndoBegn.html.

injected with romantic views of the forefathers, they were sorely disappointed. Instead, what we have here, recorded for posterity, is a version of the past that reminds us of 2 Kings 17, 21, and especially the cyclical paradigm of the book of Judges 2: rest-sin-judgment-crying-out to God-deliverance-sin. This is the unvarnished reality of an epic fail, where the fault lies with one party one hundred percent. The dark ages of the time of the Judges becomes the paradigm for Israel's history as a whole (e.g., Ezek 16:3, "Your father was an Amorite and your mother a Hittite.") In any conflict with Yahweh, when it comes to the deeper questions of sin, unfaithfulness, and unholiness, there is never a share of any blame. The people find themselves guilty and Yahweh righteous. He is not complicit in any way to their plight.

But Yahweh has the last word and his name is exalted. As the prophets fall back (e.g., Jon 4:2; Nah 1:2–3) on the declaration of the divine name in Exodus 34:6–7, the recapitulative history of Nehemiah 9 also falls back on the prevailing attributes of God from a *longue durée* perspective: he is indeed patient and slow to anger, and forgiving in light of Israel's perpetual addiction to rebellion and sin. So, on the one hand, his justice is magnified, but on the other, his mercy is exalted even above his justice, since Israel finds itself restored to the land according to the promise. Yahweh never abandoned (*'azab*, a key verb in the narrative) them, in spite of Israel's best efforts to turn their back on him. This will be Stephen's testimony to the Sanhedrin: God's gracious hand of guidance, provision, and protection is consistently rejected because the people remain "stiff-necked," with "hearts and ears still uncircumcised" who "resist the Holy Spirit" (Acts 7:51); yet Yahweh continues to reach out to them in the revelation of Jesus Christ.

**Reading of the word as prelude to confession of sin and praise.** The prayer of penitence of Nehemiah 9 underscores a well-known relationship in Scripture: The reading and hearing of the word leads to conviction and confession of sin. Psalm 119, the *torah* Psalm par excellence, makes clear the relationship between the reading/study of the word and an awareness of sin: "I have hidden your word in my heart that I might not sin against you" (Ps 119:11); "How can a young person stay on the path of purity? By living according to your word" (Ps 119:9). In the history of the Hebrew kings, the starting point of Josiah's reforms (a key dimension to both Kings's and Chronicles's account of Josiah's reign; 2 Kgs 22–23; 2 Chr 34–35) is directly attributed to both the reading by

Shaphan (2 Chr 34:18) and the interpretation of the word from Huldah (34:23–28). Upon hearing the law and understanding its implications (curses upon the theocracy as a result of disobedience), Josiah breaks down in repentance and confession of sin. The excerpt of the law read to Josiah (which included Deuteronomic curses for disobedience, 2 Chr 34:24) has left the theocracy exposed to God's judgment. Without the reading of the law, Josiah would have remained woefully unaware of the impending threat of judgment upon Judah. The discrepancy between lived religion and the religion of the word is exposed and leads to conviction of sin. Josiah "tore his robes" when he heard the book of the law of Moses (2 Chr 34:19). He is thinking in terms of the consequences of not obeying the terms of the covenant as expressed at Sinai via blessings and curses. The religious landscape of Judah is littered with idols, from one end of the land to the other. Evidently the reforms of Hezekiah were not sufficient to eradicate the problem (2 Kgs 18:3–4).

It is tempting to surmise the reading of the law in Nehemiah 8–9 included preexilic historical books as well as the Pentateuch, since the retrospective of Nehemiah 9 covers the history in a comprehensive manner. Regardless of the exact content of what was read (select passages to be sure), the effect is not left to ambiguity or speculation. In the New Testament, "the curse of the law" due to disobedience has been removed through Christ's death on a cross (Gal 3:10); nevertheless, the convicting power of biblical law (which for New Testament writers means the Old Testament, along with the New Testament text; see 2 Tim 3:16; 2 Pet 3:16) continues unabated. The Scriptures (Old and New Testaments) teach us examples (see 1 Cor 10:1) and are "sharper than any double-edged sword" (Heb 4:12–23). Galatians also warns against the deception of ignoring the principle of sowing and reaping (Gal 6:7). The consequences of sin and the warnings associated with the apostasy of unbelief remain as real as in the old covenant ("Let us, therefore, make every effort to enter that rest, so that no one will perish by following their example of disobedience," Heb 4:11).

**The theme of conviction of sin and confession of sin is not divorced from praise.** The weight of sin creates tremendous sadness and despair, but in confession, joy and praise are released, since the heaviness and weight of sin lifted—hence the exhortation to "[s]tand up and praise the LORD your God" (Neh 9:5). David says, "restore to me the joy of your salvation" (Ps 51:12); "let me hear joy and gladness" (Ps 51:8).

The praise and joy described is not rooted in changed circumstances. For instance, they remain slaves in Yehud; David suffered the consequences of his sin against Bathsheba for the rest of his life. However, the confession changes one's own perspective on the situation, and praise returns: "Open my lips, Lord, and my mouth will declare your praise (Ps 51:15). Psalm 32, a great penitential psalm, drives the point home where it concludes, after the sinner has received righteousness from the Lord, "Rejoice in the LORD and be glad, you righteous; sing, all you who are upright in heart! (Ps 32:11).

**WITHOUT SPENDING TIME IN THE WORD, WE ARE FLYING BLIND.** The biblical narrative is our narrative. It is our story. One of the great themes of the story of God's people is that once they lost the narrative of Scripture, they lost the narrative of their lives. Without spending time in the Scripture, we are flying blind and remain woefully unaware of our sinful condition. The Scripture provides a diagnostic, a sort of health report of where we stand and what adjustment we need to make to stay close to God. Without these regular checkups, we do not know how healthy or unhealthy we are. Just as with our own health, to avoid doctor checkups and regular diagnostics (what to eat or not eat, etc.) is akin to flying blind. We do not have a sense of what is ahead on the journey. We should not wait until we crash and burn spiritually to get our lives with God back on track. The Scripture is our guide. Nehemiah 9 is a bitter realization that without his word, the Israelites grew cold and stiff-necked with God—with the consequences that they have essentially returned to Egypt in the province of Yehud. We need to heed the wise words of the psalmist: "I have hidden your word in my heart that I might not sin against you" (Ps 119:11). By embracing the narrative of Scripture and the big picture of the cycles of creation-sin-judgment-deliverance-redemption in our lives, we grow in our dependence upon God's *hesed* as revealed in the person of Jesus Christ. We are rooted in him, the one who is the perfect Israelite and who has fulfilled all righteousness.

**The significance and importance of confession in our lives.** The reading of the word will convict us, but without confession of our sins, we will not experience again the joy of his presence. The contemporary church in the West in the past twenty years, ever since the advent of the missional movement, has moved away from public prayers of confession of sin as well as the public reading of the word. However, this chapter serves as a fresh reminder that this ancient tradition carries tremendous weight and should not be easily discarded except in special circumstances. As in everything in Christian worship, rote repetition of a ritual can never substitute for the habits of the heart ("a broken and contrite heart" Ps 51:17) that God will always receive. However, it seems artificial simply to jump into praise and worship without a clear moment for pause for confession of sin in our corporate lives.

**God provides in our wilderness.** The wilderness wanderings carry a paradigmatic imprint upon the Christian life (1 Cor 10:11; Rev 12:6). The wilderness was a testing ground, and it remains so in the Christian journey. One of the chief ways we are tested is to question God's provision in our wilderness wanderings. How often do we murmur like the children of Israel, "we detest this miserable food!" (Num 21:5). In an age when God is routinely placed on trial with respect to his justice and ways, Nehemiah 9 serves as a corrective to our warped sense of justice. The guilt of a stiff-necked heart also expresses itself in assigning blame for our woes to our loving heavenly parent. All of us, if we dig deeper in our lives, will find areas where we feel God has left and abandoned us, or has not provided according to our needs (Ps 22:2). We, too, question God, like the rebellious generation in the wilderness: "Can God really spread a table in the wilderness?" (Ps 78:19). The sense of divine abandonment is real, since it was a human experience Jesus himself lived through in his death-ordeal on the cross (Ps 22:2; Matt 27:46; Mark 15:34). Nevertheless, in the rythms of life in a fallen world, where injustice seems to go unanswered, both at the individual and corporate level, we also cling to God's character and we will not be disappointed (Ps 22:24). In the end, the Lord has the last word. His mercy has the last word. In spite of our waywardness, he manifests his presence through his guidance, provision, and protection. The statement that they "lacked nothing" (Neh 9:21) echoes the twenty-third Psalm and serves as a reminder that the Lord provides for his people. Jesus is the "bread of heaven" who becomes our provision in the wilderness (John 6:48–58):

> "I am the bread of life. Your ancestors ate the manna in the wilderness, yet they died. But here is the bread that comes down

from heaven, which anyone may eat and not die. I am the living bread that came down from heaven. Whoever eats this bread will live forever. This bread is my flesh, which I will give for the life of the world."

Then the Jews began to argue sharply among themselves, "How can this man give us his flesh to eat?"

Jesus said to them, "Very truly I tell you, unless you eat the flesh of the Son of Man and drink his blood, you have no life in you. Whoever eats my flesh and drinks my blood has eternal life, and I will raise them up at the last day. For my flesh is real food and my blood is real drink. Whoever eats my flesh and drinks my blood remains in me, and I in them. Just as the living Father sent me and I live because of the Father, so the one who feeds on me will live because of me. This is the bread that came down from heaven. Your ancestors ate manna and died, but whoever feeds on this bread will live forever."

Even in times of perceived "lack" in our lives (Phil 4:12–13; NIV "need," Gk. *hustereo,* "lack" in LXX Ps 22:1 [23 ET]), we are provided for. But the real provision comes through our contentment in the manner and way through which the LORD provides in our lives, whether it is quantified according to our own system of weight and measure or his.

# Nehemiah 9:38–10:39

38 "In view of all this, we are making a binding agreement, putting it in writing, and our leaders, our Levites and our priests are affixing their seals to it."

Those who sealed it were:
1 Nehemiah the governor, the son of Hakaliah.
Zedekiah, 2 Seraiah, Azariah, Jeremiah,
3 Pashhur, Amariah, Malkijah,
4 Hattush, Shebaniah, Malluk,
5 Harim, Meremoth, Obadiah,
6 Daniel, Ginnethon, Baruch,
7 Meshullam, Abijah, Mijamin,
8 Maaziah, Bilgai and Shemaiah.
These were the priests.

9 The Levites:
Jeshua son of Azaniah, Binnui of the sons of Henadad, Kadmiel,
10 and their associates: Shebaniah,
Hodiah, Kelita, Pelaiah, Hanan,
11 Mika, Rehob, Hashabiah,
12 Zakkur, Sherebiah, Shebaniah,
13 Hodiah, Bani and Beninu.

14 The leaders of the people:
Parosh, Pahath-Moab, Elam, Zattu, Bani,
15 Bunni, Azgad, Bebai,
16 Adonijah, Bigvai, Adin,
17 Ater, Hezekiah, Azzur,
18 Hodiah, Hashum, Bezai,
19 Hariph, Anathoth, Nebai,
20 Magpiash, Meshullam, Hezir,
21 Meshezabel, Zadok, Jaddua,

22 Pelatiah, Hanan, Anaiah,
23 Hoshea, Hananiah, Hasshub,
24 Hallohesh, Pilha, Shobek,
25 Rehum, Hashabnah, Maaseiah,
26 Ahiah, Hanan, Anan,
27 Malluk, Harim and Baanah.

28 "The rest of the people—priests, Levites,
gatekeepers, musicians, temple servants and all who
separated themselves from the neighboring peoples
for the sake of the Law of God, together with their
wives and all their sons and daughters who are able to
understand—29 all these now join their fellow Israelites
the nobles, and bind themselves with a curse and an
oath to follow the Law of God given through Moses the
servant of God and to obey carefully all the commands,
regulations and decrees of the LORD our Lord.

30 "We promise not to give our daughters in marriage
to the peoples around us or take their daughters for
our sons.

31 "When the neighboring peoples bring merchandise
or grain to sell on the Sabbath, we will not buy from them
on the Sabbath or on any holy day. Every seventh year we
will forgo working the land and will cancel all debts.

32 "We assume the responsibility for carrying out the
commands to give a third of a shekel each year for the
service of the house of our God: 33 for the bread set out
on the table; for the regular grain offerings and burnt
offerings; for the offerings on the Sabbaths, at the New
Moon feasts and at the appointed festivals; for the holy
offerings; for sin offerings to make atonement for Israel;
and for all the duties of the house of our God.

34 "We—the priests, the Levites and the people—
have cast lots to determine when each of our families is
to bring to the house of our God at set times each year
a contribution of wood to burn on the altar of the LORD
our God, as it is written in the Law.

[35] "We also assume responsibility for bringing to the
house of the LORD each year the firstfruits of our crops
and of every fruit tree.

[36] "As it is also written in the Law, we will bring the
firstborn of our sons and of our cattle, of our herds and
of our flocks to the house of our God, to the priests
ministering there.

[37] "Moreover, we will bring to the storerooms of the
house of our God, to the priests, the first of our ground
meal, of our grain offerings, of the fruit of all our trees
and of our new wine and olive oil. And we will bring
a tithe of our crops to the Levites, for it is the Levites
who collect the tithes in all the towns where we work.
[38] A priest descended from Aaron is to accompany the
Levites when they receive the tithes, and the Levites
are to bring a tenth of the tithes up to the house of
our God, to the storerooms of the treasury. [39] The
people of Israel, including the Levites, are to bring
their contributions of grain, new wine and olive oil to
the storerooms, where the articles for the sanctuary
and for the ministering priests, the gatekeepers and the
musicians are also kept.

"We will not neglect the house of our God."

*Original Meaning*

## Covenant Ratification (9:38–10:39)

CHAPTER 10 PROVIDES A FITTING RESPONSE TO THE public prayer of Nehemiah 9. As a formal document ("binding agreement," 9:38, which is 10:1 in the MT), chapter 10 recalls the covenant-making practices of the preexilic era. In familiar fashion for Nehemiah, an exhaustive list of those who agreed to the terms of the covenant is provided (10:1–27), along with "the rest of the people" (10:28). The document includes a "curse and an oath" along with promises made by the vassals to the suzerain Yahweh (10:30–39), "to obey carefully all the commands . . . of the LORD our Lord" (10:29).

In view of this covenant backdrop, the public prayer of chapter 9 resembles the historical prologue of the covenant-making ceremony and paves the way for the actual stipulations of the covenant (10:28–38), along with the oath-taking: "We will not neglect the house of God" (10:39; see Exod 24).

**The binding agreement (9:38).** The prayer of chapter 9 seamlessly morphs into the basis of a "binding agreement" the community makes (Neh 9:38). While the word "covenant"' is not actually present in verse 38, the verb (NIV "we are making") is the idiomatic "cutting" (*karat*), which is always used in the context of covenant making (Gen 15:18). Thus it says, "we are cutting a binding agreement" (author's translation). The actual word for "binding agreement" is the noun *'amanah*, which occurs only here and in Nehemiah 11:23. The root *'aman* from which the word *'amanah* derives is well known, however. When the root occurs in a covenantal context, especially the Abrahamic covenant, the word is connected to the verb as an act of believing in the sense of trusting (Gen 15:6). The adjective carries the same denotation (Neh 9:8; Abraham's heart was "believing" [NIV "faithful" see comment above]). For the specific meaning of *'amanah*, Nehemiah 11:23 sheds further light, since the idea of "regulation" seems to fit the context well there (see commentary on 11:23). In effect, the community is "cutting" a sure (firm) regulation in a covenantal sense.

The sense of immediacy and urgency is captured by the ongoing aspect of "we are making." Adding to this sense of temporal emphasis—we might say, "strike the iron while it's hot"—the act of "putting it in writing" (9:38) stands in a concurrent relationship in the syntax: "we are cutting a binding agreement, *and writing*" (author's translation, emphasis added). The third and final act, which prepares for the actual detail of the names, has "our leaders, our Levites and our priests . . . affixing their seals on it" (9:38) and further speaks to the expeditious manner with which the events of the day are codified and become a matter of public record.

**The list of signatories (10:1–27).** The organization of the names follows the pattern anticipated from 9:38. Expectedly heading the list of leaders is "Nehemiah, the son of Hakaliah" (10:1).[1] The NIV puts him

1. We know nothing of Zedekiah. His name does not belong to the three lists of priests in the book of Nehemiah (Chapters 7, 11, 12). However, the name strongly evokes preexilic history since, coincidentally, his eponym was the last king of Judah.

with the list of priests, but the conjunction "and" in the original intentionally connects him with Nehemiah, not the ensuing list of priests.[2] Nehemiah affixes his name on the list of signatories and fulfills his role as servant of the king ("the governor" is an Aramaic term which was the *langue diplomatique* of the Persian period). He is also a servant of the "king of kings" and fully complies with this theological confession of faith (see commentary on chapter 2). By affixing his name as governor, Nehemiah provides assurance to the crown that this *'amanah* should not be confused with some formal unilateral declaration of independence (UDI), especially in light of the cry to Yahweh for freedom from foreign oppression at the end of the prayer (9:37). The list of priests actually refers to the patrimonial social organization rather than individuals proper (vv. 2–8), which explains why Ezra is omitted from the list.[3] However, as "the son of Seraiah" (Ezra 7:1), Ezra's family fittingly heads the list of priests, which confirms the solemn occasion and the historical continuity with the events begun at the beginning of the seventh month (Neh 7:73; 8:1). The list of the Levites (vv. 9–13), along with families harking back to the original returnees (Ezra 2:40; see Neh 12:8a), now also singles out individuals that are quite familiar to the narrative.[4] Several of the signatories are involved in explaining the law to the community in Nehemiah 8. Others returned with Ezra, including perhaps one mentioned on the list of those who rebuilt the wall in Nehemiah 3.[5]

The "leaders ("heads" [*r'oshe ha'am*]) of the people" (vv. 14–27) continue the pattern of patrimonial heads typical of the tribal lists in Nehemiah. Commentators point out that the list overlaps with the list of Ezra 2 and Nehemiah 7, thus underscoring the historical continuity of the signatories of this binding agreement. Kidner points out that the new names in the list are also tied to the original list of returnees in some way.[6] To weave in names that hark back to the past, along with names from the context of the present, thus reflects the expected sensitivity of tribal characteristics of belonging in a past, present, and future sense

---

2. Kidner, *Ezra and Nehemiah*, 125.

3. Ibid.

4. Ibid.

5. Ibid. This sense of historical continuity between the lists in Nehemiah and the events narrated in the book represents a formidable firewall to any theory that would challenge the historical integrity of the text.

6. Ibid., 126.

(as the promises of the people will indicate presently). Thus, to flow in and out of the present in this list should not be viewed as anomalous but expected, and it adds to the authenticity reflected both in the list itself and in the way the account has come down to us. The author and compiler of these documents certainly does not leave any doubt that readers of this document, including the Persian authorities, would view it no other way than as a historically-rooted account of one gathering in Jerusalem in the seventh month. This moment in Israelite history was formally codified into a binding agreement to restore the worship of the house of Yahweh in Jerusalem. Any other scenario relegates the account to a fabricated and fraudulent account the Persian authorities (and especially the enemies of Zion) would have been sure to note and decry.[7] It is a good reminder these ancient legal documents do not belong to the academic setting of an age long removed from the fifth century BC (e.g., the study halls of modern universities and seminaries), but, in fact, belong to the people of God in the fifth century BC and throughout the ages.

**The rest of the people join in (10:28–29).** The official nature of the document becomes clear, since the restoration of worship of local temples was at the heart of the original decree of Cyrus in 539 BC. Here also, therefore, the dual nature of the task is emphasized. This spiritual restoration fits in with the governor's role to make sure order is maintained in the province Beyond the River, including the temple economy and resulting revenues for the crown—even if here, the only crown that is ultimately in view is the King of kings': "We will not neglect the house of our God" (v. 39).

Verse 28 adds "the rest of the people" (v. 28) to the list of those who are also committing themselves to what is now unmistakably couched in preexilic Sinaitic covenantal terms: they "are entering" (author's translation; NIV "bind themselves") into a "curse and an oath" (v. 29) in a ceremony strongly reminiscent of the one in the plains of Moab (Deut 30:11–19) and at Mount Ebal (Josh 8:30–35; cf. Deut 27). The theme of solidarity established in chapter 8 (see Commentary above) continues with the detailed list of those who also signed up alongside "their fellow Israelites the nobles" (v. 29). In addition to the spiritual leadership

7. See the original De Wette thesis concerning Josiah's reforms in the seventh century BC. Wilhelm Martin Leberecht De Wette, *Beitrage zur Einleitung in das Alte Testament*, 2 vols. (Halle: Schimmelpfennig, 1806, 1807).

("priests, Levites, gatekeepers, musicians, temple servants"; v. 28), the list singles out "all who separated themselves" from the "peoples of the land" (author's translation; NIV "neighboring peoples"). The separation from the peoples of the land in the original specifies *their* "wives," *their* "sons," and *their* "daughters" (emphasis added; lost in the NIV translation). As a concluding summary, and returning to a familiar theme from chapter 8, the list summarizes the entire group as "*all*[8] who know [and have] understanding" (author's translation; v. 28). The motivation for this commitment is "for the sake of the Law of God" (v. 28), which is described further in terms recalling the first day of their gathering three weeks earlier: "The Law of God given through Moses the servant of God" (v. 29). In strongly-evocative Abrahamic and Deuteronomic terms, their "oath"[9] is to "follow" and "to obey carefully"[10] the Deuteronomic Law, "all commands (plural *mitzvoth*), regulations (plural *mishpatim*), and decrees (plural *huqoth*) of the LORD our Lord."[11] Once Deuteronomic law is appealed to, the warning of the consequences of breaking such an oath inevitably ensues. The consequence of not following the "Law of God," by upholding this "oath" (which is a legal obligation; see Bridging Context below) is put in plain terms: it is a "curse" (v. 29; *'alah*). Since the agreement is not between human parties, as is sometimes the case with the use of "oath/*shebu'ah* (e.g., Joshua 2:20), but directly to God and his Law, retribution for not upholding the terms of the agreement will not come from a human authority but from divine authority.[12]

We observe also that no one is coercing them to join in this covenant. The people are willingly signing up, in large part because the God of the spiritual leadership is also "*our* God" (emphasis added). Thus, the themes we have encountered throughout this amazing three weeks in Israelite history are neatly grouped together in this signed deposition: Together, they belong to God, to his word, which is expressed through the commitment to obey and serve him, even at the cost of tearing

---

8. NIV "all" incorrectly modifies "sons."

9. *Shebu'ah*, a term connected to the Abrahamic promise; cf. Gen 26:3; Deut 7:8; 1 Chr 16:16; Ps 105:9.

10. = "to keep and to do" in the original, which is a typical pairing, e.g., Deut 4.

11. Cf. Deut 4–5; see also "stipulations" *'edoth* Deut 4:45.

12. See also Num 5:21 (the ritual of the "law of jealousy," Num. 5:29) and Daniel 9:11 for the two instances in the OT where "oath"/*shebu'ah* and "curse"/*'alah* are used in the same context. Both contexts confirm severe consequences for the guilty party.

apart the existing social norms of intermarriage with non-Yahwists (see commentary on Ezra 10).

**Promise to maintain their own sanctity (10:30–31).** The first set of three promises (vv. 30–31) are carefully delineated by the use of three modal (ie., imperative force) verbs, strongly reminiscent of a form found in Old Testament laws such as the Ten Commandments (e.g., "you shall not . . ." Deut 5:7).

The first "we shall not" (v. 30, *l'o niten* [Hebrew text is v. 31] NIV "we promise") fittingly relates to the practice of intermarriage (cf. v. 28) with words borrowed from the language of Judges 3:6, "they took their daughters in marriage and gave their own daughters to their sons." In light of the Judges paradigm of apostasy and Canaanization applied to Israelite history in Nehemiah 9 (see commentary above), the promise carries tremendous importance. In effect, the people are making a promise not to repeat the mistakes of the past: we will not get entangled with the "peoples of the land" (author's translation; *'ame ha'arets*, NIV "peoples around us") and will maintain our own sanctity. The second "we shall not" (author's translation; "we will not buy," v. 31) keeps the focus on the peoples of the land (NIV now has switched the designation to "neighboring peoples") but now extends to economic partnerships, particularly in the context of buying and selling "merchandise or grain" on the "Sabbath . . . or on any holy day" (31). While the original Sabbath law says nothing about buying and selling on the Sabbath, the connection with the work prohibition is not hard to find and keeps the focus on maintaining holiness standards in partnerships with non-Yahwists.[13] The promise, therefore, does not call for a complete trade embargo any other day of the week, but keeps the focus on the theological dimension of the relationship with their neighbors. The third promise (v. 31b "we shall," author's translation) is a positive one, with the main verb "forgo" modifying two practices: "Every seventh year, we will forgo working the land and the exaction of all debt" (author's translation; NIV "will cancel all debts"). The law of the Sabbath year is wellknown across the legal Old Testament corpus (Exod 23:11; Lev 25:4–7, 20–22; Deut 15:1–11). In this context, the specific reference to "debts" (*mash'a*) directly connects to the commitment not to repeat the problems of injustice described in

13. Smith, *Ezra, Nehemiah, Esther,* 189–90.

chapter 5 (Neh 5:10–11, see commentary above), thereby falling short of holiness standards within the community itself.

**Promises to maintain the sanctity of Zion (10:32–39).** The rest of the promises (vv. 32–39) are specifically tied to the worship of Yahweh and "the service of the house of our God" (v. 32). The phrase "house of *our* God" (emphasis added) occurs no less than seven times, along with the "altar of the LORD *our* God" (emphasis added) once in verse 34 and "house of the LORD" once in verse 35. The climactic statement, "we will not neglect the house of our God" contains the key verb *'azab* (to abandon), used in key moments of the historical retrospective of Nehemiah 9 (see commentary above). This seems a fitting promissory response on the part of the community. Since Yahweh did not *'azab* us, we will not *'azab* him, either.

Thus, the emphasis established from the beginning of the seventh month, that Yahweh is indeed *their* God, now translates into a commitment to look after the house of *their* God in the most practical of ways: collecting financial and material resources for the maintaining of sacrifices and the worship of Yahweh. For the sanctity of Zion to be restored, the worship in the temple must continue uninterrupted, and this must involve "each of our families," from the "priests, the Levites, and the people" (v. 34), standing in *solidarity* together (a central theme to the entire account in the book of Nehemiah).

Heading off the list of promises ("we assume the responsibility," v. 32–33) is the collection of a temple tax ("a third of a shekel each year")[14] for the maintenance of the *raison d'être* of the temple: "offerings," including "grain," "burnt," and "sin offerings to make atonement for Israel" (v. 33). Without a steady flow of income, quite apart from Persian financial aid

---

14. Williamson and Smith detail the application and contextualization of Biblical Law pertaining to the maintenance of the worship in ancient Israel from Exodus, Leviticus, and Numbers, in particular. The general principle to retain is that the "Law" is applied in the context of the needs of the province of Yehud. For instance, there is no such thing as a yearly half-shekel tax in the Law (see Williamson, *Ezra, Nehemiah*, 335). However, as Smith (*Ezra, Nehemiah, Esther*, 186) has noted, citing Exod 30:11–16 and 38:25–26, there is evidence of a "half-shekel payment to the Temple by all males over 20 years old." Thus, the community is applying the principles of the law (mentioned twice specifically in 10:34, 36, e.g., "as it is written in the law") to their particular context and prepares us for the context of the New Testament interpretations of the Law and the age of the Mishnah (see David J. A. Clines, "Nehemiah 10 as an Example of Early Jewish Biblical Exegesis." *JSOT* 21 [1981]: 111–17, cited in Williamson, 334).

(Ezra 6, see commentary above), the maintenance of the sanctity of Zion will not go on. Other itemized offerings include "Sabbaths, New Moon feasts and at appointed festivals" (v. 33). In effect, the tax will support "all the duties of the house of our God" (v. 33).

Following the temple tax (see Matt 17:24), the entire community—including, "we the priests" and "Levites" along with "the people" (v. 34)—is involved through the casting of lots in what Kidner describes[15] as "in kind" offerings: the very practical task of collecting of firewood "at set times each year." The text is almost disarming in its practicality: without wood supplies, there can be no sacrifice.

Another essential dimension to the worship of Israel in the "Law" (mentioned directly in v. 34 and v. 36) was the bringing of "firstfruits" (v. 35) to Yahweh and the "storerooms" of the temple (v. 37).[16] Here, the list is also itemized and includes typical commodities associated with agriculture and horticulture: crop, every fruit tree, ground meal, grain offerings, fruit of all trees, and new wines and oil. Significantly in the law, the firstfruits also included the "firstborn" (sons, cattle, herds, flocks; v. 36), which could according to biblical law could be bought back via sacrifices (cf. Exod 13:12–13; 34:19–20; Num 18:15–17).[17] The recipients are specifically stated as the "priests ministering there" (v. 36). Without the active support of the people, the ministers cannot continue to serve in the temple.

The "tithe" (v. 37), another well-known revenue stream in the law,[18] must be collected through the Levites "in all the towns" that belong to Yehud ("where we work"; v. 37). Perhaps for supervisory purposes, a "priest descended from Aaron" is to accompany the Levites in their collecting duties (v. 38). In turn, from this tithe a tenth must go to the "house of our God" to be stored in the "storerooms of the treasury" (v. 38, cf. Num 18:26).

As a final note, all "the people of Israel" (no exemption for the Levites, v. 39) are responsible to bring in "contributions of grain, new wine and olive oil" to the storerooms "for the ministering priests, the gatekeepers and the musicians." This last point underscores that, without the people's

---

15. Kidner, *Ezra and Nehemiah*, 127.
16. See Exod 34:26; Num 18:12; Deut 26:1–11; Smith (*Ezra, Nehemiah, Esther*), 187.
17. Ibid.
18. Num 18:21–24; Deut 14:22–29; ibid.

active involvement in supplying foods to the temple personnel, worship will not be sustainable.

The official promissory note, signed by all concerned parties, including all the principals, ends as a direct speech quotation: "We will not neglect the house of our God" (v. 39). The next step in the process of the restoration of the sanctity of Zion will be the formal settlement of the land, along with the people who will inhabit "Jerusalem, the holy city" (Neh 11:1) again, the subject of the following official account in Nehemiah's mission (chapter 11).

**Self-imprecation.** The covenantal context of the ceremony of Nehemiah 10 (especially 10:29 [Heb 10:30]) takes us back to Deuteronomic covenant renewal ceremonies, when curses are invoked should the involved parties break the terms of the promise. Prior to the Deuteronomic context, Yahweh invokes a curse upon himself, when he walks between the parted animals in the ritual of Genesis 15.[19] The Mount Ebal ceremony, announced in Deuteronomy 27 and fulfilled in Joshua 8:30–35, also forms a powerful backdrop in terms of the dire consequences of not keeping true to the law of God (see Nehemiah 13 commentary below).[20] Perhaps, in this particular moment in the narrative of Nehemiah's program of restoration, a relevant parallel is found in the reign of King Asa, following a program of reform (2 Chr 15:10–15):

> They assembled at Jerusalem in the third month of the fifteenth year of Asa's reign. At that time they sacrificed to the Lord seven hundred head of cattle and seven thousand sheep and goats from the plunder they had brought back. They entered into a

19. Meredith G. Kline, *Genesis: A New Commentary* (Peabody: Hendricksen, 2016).

20. A noticeable contrast to the Mount Ebal enactment is that it includes "the whole assembly of Israel, including the women and children, and the foreigners who lived among them" (Josh 8:35). This inclusion motif underscores the fact that biblical law does not preclude the inclusion of foreigners in the worship of Yahweh (e.g., Rahab and Ruth as paradigm in the time of Judges). Instead, the prohibition focuses on the consequences of intermarriage with non-Yahwists, both in the time of the Judges (Judg 3:5–6) and here during the postexilic period.

> covenant to seek the LORD, the God of their ancestors, with all their heart and soul. All who would not seek the LORD, the God of Israel, were to be put to death, whether small or great, man or woman. They took an oath to the LORD with loud acclamation, with shouting and with trumpets and horns. All Judah rejoiced about the oath because they had sworn it wholeheartedly. They sought God eagerly, and he was found by them. So the LORD gave them rest on every side. (2 Chr 15:10–15)

Common traits between the postexilic oath ceremony of Nehemiah 10 and the Chronicler's account of Asa's reign (death ca. 870 BC) include the following: general participation, common mindset, joy, heightened sense of the gravity of breaking Deuteronomic Law, resulting awareness of the consequences of disobedience (curse/death), and the radical way with which they wish to eradicate evil among themselves. In short, the community in the province, as at the time of Asa, realizes that disobedience will bring disaster upon themselves, hence the urgency and need to remove evil elements among themselves; "whatever it takes" is the posture (see Neh 13 commentary below).

Thus, in Nehemiah 10, the self-imprecatory appeal puts *everyone* on notice: "Nehemiah" (10:1), "priests" (10:8), "Levites" (10:9), "the leaders of the people" (10:14), and "the rest of the people" (10:28, e.g., "priests, Levites, gatekeepers, musicians, temple servants, and all who separated themselves from the neighboring peoples"). The detailed itemization of the people speaks to the corporate solidarity that is a major theme of the book of Nehemiah as a whole. Everyone is in this together for better (blessing) or for worse (curse).

**Operational commitment to worship.** In this context, worship is defined as "atonement" and attending to "all the duties of the house of our God," v. 33. A practical dimension is to maintain the worship of the Lord through material means. As backdrop, the paradigm to giving for the worship in the temple (apart from Egyptian wealth[21] to supply the material goods to build the tabernacle in Exodus) is found in the postexilic Chroniclers' account of Judean history. The postexilic setting of both Nehemiah and Chronicles becomes significant, since the historical dimension of giving to the work of the temple in preexilic times

21. Nubia, to the south of Egypt proper, means "gold." See Exod 3:22.

is reactualized in the postexilic era (see Neh 12 commentary below). Appeal to the order established by David, the architect of temple building, and his son Solomon, the actual builder, forms the bedrock of the restoration of worship by Ezra and Nehemiah. They are restoring the worship literally by the book (Neh 12:24, 36, 46).

The backdrop to giving is found in the Chronicler's account, which details the considerable contribution of David and the leaders toward the building of the temple (1 Chr 29:1–9). David leads the way in giving from his official account, "with all my resources I have provided for the temple of my God . . . all of these in large quantities" (1 Chr 29:2). In addition, he gives from his "personal treasures of gold and silver for the temple of my God" (1 Chr 29:3). This extravagant giving is motivated by his "devotion to the temple of *my God*" (emphasis added, 1 Chr 29:3). It is no surprise, then, that others quickly followed suit: "the leaders of families, the officers of the tribes of Israel, the commanders of thousands and commanders of hundreds, and the officials in charge of the king's work gave willingly" (1 Chr 29:6). This sort of commitment to the worship of the house of the LORD caused the people to rejoice "at the willing response of their leaders" (1 Chr 29:9). The rejoicing is expressly connected to the voluntary nature of the leaders' giving: "for they had given freely and wholeheartedly to the LORD" (1 Chr 29:9). Of course, David himself was ecstatic: "David the king also rejoiced greatly" (1 Chr 29:9). This theme of joy will be picked up and developed later when the wall is dedicated (see Neh 12). The apostle Paul capitalizes on the relationship between giving and joy in both Philippians (4:2, 10) and 2 Corinthians, where giving becomes an "indescribable gift" (2 Cor 9:15).

**Securing continuity in worship.** The purpose of chapter 10 is to secure continuity in worship. The sanctity of Zion via the restoration of the perimeter and public repentance would mean nothing unless the system of sacrifice is restored on a permanent basis. The written promise to provide guarantees the permanence of the work of securing the city and the previous generation of returnees' effort to rebuild the temple. In addition, we should not forget that Nehemiah also answers to the king of Persia's mandate to restore the city of his fathers' graves (see Neh 2:5). The restoration of the worship of the temple and to Yahweh assures that the mandate set by Cyrus in 539 BC has staying power in Yehud. Without the financial commitment of the people, Nehemiah's official mission as a Persian official is guaranteed to be short-lived.

The commitment not to neglect the house of the LORD needs to be firmed up, especially in light of the sketchy record of the people in the province to do so (from 539 BC to 444 BC). The moment captured in chapter 10 is indeed a solemn occasion to renew vows to make sure the worship of Yahweh continues uninterrupted following the rebuilding of the sacred perimeter. People are fickle, hence the urgency to put things in writing.

The same sort of pressing urgency is reflected in the New Testament. The call of Paul to urge giving from the churches in Achaia to their brothers in Jerusalem is a well-known undercurrent to the Corinthian correspondence. Indeed, churches in Greece are notorious foot-draggers and can at times be unwilling to part with their hard-earned money to supply the needs of the church in Jerusalem (2 Cor 9). Paul's persistence in trying to secure a commitment finds a distant, though no less poignant, parallel to the unresponsive citizens of Yehud for the things pertaining to the worship of God. It seems that commitment to the worship without a practical dimension, a price tag, as it were, hollows out the very idea of worship. In other words, contributions to the worship of Zion need to become a considerable line-item in the budget, both in terms of operations and payroll (see Contemporary Significance below.)

**Commitment to holiness/keeping the Law.** Directly connected to giving in chapter 10 is the careful attention to obedience to the law as a means of preserving the holiness of the site and its people, all preexilic fundamentals of worship (Lev 11:44) and Israelite identity (Exod 19:6). We are reminded that the sanctity of marriage is upheld (Gen 2:24), as is that of the Sabbath (Gen 2:3). Due attention to details and to the law pertaining to Sabbath-keeping are emphasized in this chapter (see also Neh 13). The commitment is to the sanctity of Zion and its worship, now that the walls are restored. The promissory nature of the commitment is seeking to avoid the mistakes of the past.

**HOLINESS AS WORSHIP.** The conditional dimension of the relationship between holiness, blessing and protection of Zion *is a given* in the Old Testament. Jeremiah, in his temple sermon, makes it plain: "Reform your ways and your actions, and I will let you live in this place" (Jer 7:3). Without holiness and a clear delineation between that which is profane and that which is holy, the LORD's presence cannot be experienced by the worshiper. Eventually, the LORD removes himself from the temple and expels the profane from his sacred space on earth (the destruction of the temple in 586 BC by the Babylonians). In the New Testament, the holiness of God is upheld on earth through the presence of the "Holy One of God" (Mark 1:24), who himself never departed from the standards of holiness established in God's Law. Through our union with Christ ("in Christ"), we become saints (holy) in a positional sense (1 Cor 1:2, 30). However, in continuity with the Old Testament, we also pursue holiness in emulation to the one who is holy. First Peter 1:16 explicitly ties the Old and the New covenants when he proclaims, "Be holy, because I am holy," as does 1 Thessalonians 4:3, "It is God's will that you should be sanctified," in the context of sexual immorality. Any departure from Old Testament sexual ethics and holiness standards is also prohibited in the new covenant (see 1 Cor 6:18–20). To claim sexual ethical standards for the Christian life other than those grounded in the Old Testament leads to precisely the kind of immorality condemned by both prophets and apostles.

**Worship costs money.** Making a commitment to support the work and worship of God is not optional if we desire a continuous worship among God's people. It is hard to imagine proper worship without sacrifices and consistent contributions to the house of the LORD and the work of God. In other words, supporting the material needs of worship on a permanent basis is an essential part of worship! It is not enough to build programs, read the Bible, and confess sins; worship always involves giving. The imagery of supplying firewood evokes the mundane and unappealing. However, appeals for these supplies in a modern context are equally important (building maintenance and payroll come to mind in today's context).

In this process of giving, everyone contributes to the work of God, including the Levites! No one is exempted. And everyone makes a promise. Second Corinthians 9:7 provides the wisdom that we need to have in supporting the worship of the living God: God loves a cheerful giver. The moment giving becomes legalistic, we have lost the spirit of giving, which flows out of contentment (Phil 4:18–19).

Finally, giving becomes personal. Without understanding that Yahweh is *our* God, giving will fall short. Paul puts this under the rubric of cheerful giving, but the idea remains the same. Financial giving and material contributions without the undercurrent of a personal relationship with the living Christ will only result in rote ritual, devoid of true sacrifice and acceptable worship. We do not give to the work of Zion in the same way we pay membership dues or subscriptions to Netflix. It is not a mere item in our budget (whether 10 percent, 2 percent, 30 percent, or whatever). Giving is an act of worship we perform as regularly as we expect the worship of the LORD to be regular. It is hard to imagine a model of worship that is occasional in the pages of the Psalms, God's people's main prayer book. The psalmists long to be in God's presence *permanently*: "Better is one day in your courts than a thousand elsewhere" (Ps 84:10). If the history of the postexilic period teaches us anything, it is a warning of the consequences of an occasional and episodic commitment to the building of the house of the LORD. It took them quite a long time to get to this place in Nehemiah. Nothing will slow down God's work and progress in the expansion of the kingdom more than an irregular commitment to financial giving.

# Nehemiah 11:1–36

[1] Now the leaders of the people settled in Jerusalem. The rest
of the people cast lots to bring one out of every ten of them to
live in Jerusalem, the holy city, while the remaining nine were
to stay in their own towns. [2] The people commended all who
volunteered to live in Jerusalem.

[3] These are the provincial leaders who settled in Jerusalem
(now some Israelites, priests, Levites, temple servants and
descendants of Solomon's servants lived in the towns of Judah,
each on their own property in the various towns, [4] while other
people from both Judah and Benjamin lived in Jerusalem):
From the descendants of Judah:

> Athaiah son of Uzziah, the son of Zechariah, the son of
> Amariah, the son of Shephatiah, the son of Mahalalel,
> a descendant of Perez; [5] and Maaseiah son of Baruch,
> the son of Kol-Hozeh, the son of Hazaiah, the son
> of Adaiah, the son of Joiarib, the son of Zechariah, a
> descendant of Shelah. [6] The descendants of Perez who
> lived in Jerusalem totaled 468 men of standing.

[7] From the descendants of Benjamin:

> Sallu son of Meshullam, the son of Joed, the son of
> Pedaiah, the son of Kolaiah, the son of Maaseiah, the
> son of Ithiel, the son of Jeshaiah, [8] and his followers,
> Gabbai and Sallai—928 men. [9] Joel son of Zikri was
> their chief officer, and Judah son of Hassenuah was over
> the New Quarter of the city.

[10] From the priests:

> Jedaiah; the son of Joiarib; Jakin; [11] Seraiah son of Hilkiah,
> the son of Meshullam, the son of Zadok, the son of
> Meraioth, the son of Ahitub, the official in charge of the

house of God, [12] and their associates, who carried on work
for the temple—822 men; Adaiah son of Jeroham, the son
of Pelaliah, the son of Amzi, the son of Zechariah, the son
of Pashhur, the son of Malkijah, [13] and his associates, who
were heads of families—242 men; Amashsai son of Azarel,
the son of Ahzai, the son of Meshillemoth, the son of Immer,
[14] and his associates, who were men of standing—128.
Their chief officer was Zabdiel son of Haggedolim.

[15] From the Levites:

Shemaiah son of Hasshub, the son of Azrikam, the
son of Hashabiah, the son of Bunni; [16] Shabbethai
and Jozabad, two of the heads of the Levites, who
had charge of the outside work of the house of God;
[17] Mattaniah son of Mika, the son of Zabdi, the son of
Asaph, the director who led in thanksgiving and prayer;
Bakbukiah, second among his associates; and Abda son
of Shammua, the son of Galal, the son of Jeduthun.
[18] The Levites in the holy city totaled 284.

[19] The gatekeepers:

Akkub, Talmon and their associates, who kept watch at
the gates—172 men.

[20] The rest of the Israelites, with the priests and Levites,
were in all the towns of Judah, each on their ancestral property.
[21] The temple servants lived on the hill of Ophel, and Ziha
and Gishpa were in charge of them.
[22] The chief officer of the Levites in Jerusalem was Uzzi son of
Bani, the son of Hashabiah, the son of Mattaniah, the son of Mika.
Uzzi was one of Asaph's descendants, who were the musicians
responsible for the service of the house of God. [23] The musicians
were under the king's orders, which regulated their daily activity.
[24] Pethahiah son of Meshezabel, one of the descendants of
Zerah son of Judah, was the king's agent in all affairs relating
to the people.

[25] As for the villages with their fields, some of the people
of Judah lived in Kiriath Arba and its surrounding settlements,
in Dibon and its settlements, in Jekabzeel and its villages,
[26] in Jeshua, in Moladah, in Beth Pelet, [27] in Hazar Shual, in
Beersheba and its settlements, [28] in Ziklag, in Mekonah and its
settlements, [29] in En Rimmon, in Zorah, in Jarmuth, [30] Zanoah,
Adullam and their villages, in Lachish and its fields, and in
Azekah and its settlements. So they were living all the way
from Beersheba to the Valley of Hinnom.

[31] The descendants of the Benjamites from Geba lived in
Mikmash, Aija, Bethel and its settlements, [32] in Anathoth, Nob
and Ananiah, [33] in Hazor, Ramah and Gittaim, [34] in Hadid,
Zeboim and Neballat, [35] in Lod and Ono, and in Ge Harashim.

[36] Some of the divisions of the Levites of Judah settled in
Benjamin.

## Resettling the Land (11:1–26)

THE CHAPTER REPRESENTS THE FOURTH LIST OF names (one remains in Neh 12) in the book of Nehemiah, in line with the official nature of the record from the governor of the Province of Yehud in the empire of Persia. The "account" (author's translation; NIV "words" [*debarim*]; Neh 1:1) turns now to the administrative task of population resettlement in both "Jerusalem, the holy city" (11:1), and in the land.[1] The tribal allocation dimension of the chapter evokes the settlement allocation in the book of Joshua 12–18 (by casting "lots," Neh 11:1, cf. Josh 14:2), although the geographical details are far less detailed and comprehensive than in the original land apportionment, since now the tribes are left to three (Judah, Benjamin, and Levi) within a territory that is considerably smaller than in preexilic times (Josh 1:1).[2] While the parallels exists with the preexilic settlement

1. "The holy city," *'ir haqodesh*, is attested four times in the OT and twice in Neh 11 (vv. 1, 18). See Isa 52:1 for the same designation with a vocative "O Jerusalem, the holy city" (*yerushalaim 'ir haqodesh*). See also Isa 48:2.

2. Scholars have long noted the list of names in Neh 11 is a shorter adaptation to the one in 1 Chr 9, which also deals with the resettlement of Jerusalem after the exile. The Nehemiah account lists a total of "men of standing" of 468 (Neh 11:6) vs. a total of

process, the small community in Zion very much remains "slaves" under the rule of others (see Neh 9:36). This is still a far cry from the promise for Zion of multiplication, absolute territorial autonomy, and the establishment of the rule of Yahweh over the nations. Thus, we are some ways from the ideal expressed by Zechariah, who envisions that "the city streets will be filled with boys and girls playing there" (Zech 8:5) "and many peoples and powerful nations will come to Jerusalem to seek the LORD Almighty and to entreat him" (Zech 8:22; see Isa 2:1–4). The limited territory of Yehud cannot compare to the expansive territorial hegemony and idealism of Ezekiel's vision of land allotment when Yahweh restores Zion in the fullness of time (Ezek 40:2). Nevertheless, and following the exhortation of both Haggai and Zechariah to the previous generation of returnees in 515 BC, the task remains to establish the worship and the people in the land, in anticipation of the "glory" that is yet to come (Hag 2:9) and the coming of the king (Hag 2:23).

In addition to the "tribal allotment" motif, the list returns to a familiar emphasis in Nehemiah's method of record keeping: he carefully provides a record of the "priests" (v. 10), "Levites" (v. 15), and "gatekeepers" (v. 19) who relocated into the city. The list complements the initial group of trusted people who secured Zion immediately following the completion of the wall (see commentary on Neh 7). It would not be enough to have a small contingent living inside the walls, but, for the worship to be restored, some needed to relocate permanently into an essentially deserted settlement. The list thus also mirrors the thank-you-note aspect of Nehemiah 3 (see commentary above) and highlights the personal commitment and sacrifices the community is willing to make to live in Zion, which during the fifth century BC was a far less glamorous site than during the monarchy.

**Summary of the resettlement of the holy city and the land (11:1–3).** In this introductory and formal record of who repopulated the "holy city" (v. 1), the theme of contribution to the work of the house of the LORD continues in earnest from the preceding chapter. In addition to the "leaders of the people," the "rest of the people" in effect tithed

---

690 in 1 Chronicles 9:6, (See Kidner, *Ezra and Nehemiah*, 129; Williamson [*Ezra, Nehemiah*, 350–351] notes other differences as well.) The Chronicles' list is more inclusive, since it mentions "Ephraim and Manasseh" as a nod to Yahweh's faithfulness to the Northern Kingdom (1 Chr 9:3).

themselves ("one out of every ten") by "lots" to determine who should "live in Jerusalem, the holy city" (v. 1). The rest would be allowed to "stay in their own towns." In corporate solidarity, so typical of the time, the community "blessed" (author's translation; *barak*, NIV "commended," v. 2) "all the men" who participated (*nadab*, NIV "volunteered")[3] in the relocation program.

Verse 3 provides an important detail to the relocation process and points out that in addition to the "provincial leaders" (v. 3, Aramaic *medinah*) who had settled the city (mentioned in v. 1), a broad swath of the population of Israel (NIV "Israelites"), including "priests, Levites, temple servants and descendants of Solomon's servants," also "lived" outside Jerusalem, in the "towns of Judah" (v. 3). The summary thus provides equal legitimacy to those who lived in the city and those who lived in the province.

**Judah and Benjamin[4] (11:4–9).** The list begins appropriately with the one surviving eponymous tribe, "Judah," with a list of "men of standing" (v. 6) that further underscores the courage and the honor given to them for living in Jerusalem. The language of "standing" is a frequent term associated with courage in the corpus (Gideon is "valiant" [Judg 6:12] and so is the "wife of valor" of Prov 31:10).

Of note, the list of "descendants of Benjamin" outnumbers the list of Judah (v. 8 "928"). However, lest a wedge is created between the two entities, the heading of verse 4 serves as a reminder of the close relationship between the two tribes in the postexilic era. This stands in contrast to the well-recorded ebb and flow between Judah, aka the tribe of David, and Benjamin, the tribe of Saul, in Israelite history (see also

---

3. The language of "volunteered" evokes images of those who put themselves forward in an act of courage (see Judg 5:9; 2 Chr 17:16). Perhaps those chosen by lots could be different from those who volunteer. However, it seems more likely that those chosen by lots "offered themselves willingly" in the task. In other words, they willingly embraced the decision initially made by lot to relocate (Kidner, *Ezra and Nehemiah*, 128).

4. NIV wrongly links verse 4a as part of verse 3 by adding an unsubstantiated syntactical connection between the last phrase of verse 3 ("the sons of the servants of Solomon") and the first phrase of verse 4 (NIV "while other people from both Judah and Benjamin lived in Jerusalem"). In the original syntax, verse 3 marks the end of a sentence. Verse 4a begins a new sentence (NIV "while other" is not in the original) and provides the heading for the list of both "descendants" of Judah and Benjamin that lived in Jerusalem: "In Jerusalem lived some of the sons of Judah and some of the sons of Benjamin." This heading is then further broken down into two subheadings: "sons of Judah" (v. 4b) and "the sons of Benjamin" (v. 7).

Judges 20–21). Of note is "Judah son of Hassenuah" (v. 9) who was part of the oversight of the city (alongside Hanani and Hananiah; see 7:2): "over the New Quarter of the city."[5]

**The priests (11:10–14).** As with the list in the previous chapter, the names (connected to the list of Ezra 2/Neh 7) could refer to individuals or families.[6] In addition to rooting the priests in genealogies that hark back to preexilic times,[7] the list also focuses on the particular tasks of those who relocated in the temple area: Seraiah was "in charge of the house of God," which is another way to describe the role of the high priest (v. 11; cf. 2 Chr 31:10, 13).[8] Along with the high priest are unnamed "associates, who carried on the work for the temple" for a total of "822 men" (v. 12). Adaiah (six patronymics) "and his associates, who were heads of families" with "242" men listed, have no particular tasks (v. 13). The Amashsai family is said to consist of "men of standing" (*giborey hayil* v. 14, see vv. 5–6), but here the language also evokes the preexilic warrior class of mighty men of valor (e.g., Josh 6:2; Judg 6:12; 1 Sam 16:18). This designation serves as a reminder that to be a priest in these precarious times involved a bivocational element of protective detail, as well. Their "chief officer was Zabdiel son of Haggedolim" (v. 14), further reinforcing the idea that a security role was assigned to this particular group of priests. The term "Haggedolim" probably was an epithet, "the great one" (root *gadal*), rather than a proper name *per se*, and reflects the warriors of ages past in Israel, as well.[9]

**The Levites and the gatekeepers (11:15–19).** The mixing of religious duties and protective duties continues with the list of Levites. Their formal work in the "holy city" (v. 18) consisted of tasks on the precinct of the "house of God" (v. 16). Leading the worship ("director"), the family of Mattaniah led in "thanksgiving and prayer" (v. 17). In addition, a special detachment of 172, "the gatekeepers," were in charge of security and "kept watch at the gates" (v. 19). The *ad hoc* security in place in chapter 7 now becomes formalized and assumes a permanent role.

---

5. The *mishneh* is a well-known quarter in preexilic Jerusalem (see 2 Kgs 22:14 [2 Chr 34:22]; 2 Kgs 23:4; Zeph 1:10).

6. See Williamson, *Ezra, Nehemiah*, 351, and Kidner, *Ezra and Nehemiah*, 129–30.

7. "Seraiah" has five patronymics (see 10:2 and especially Ezra 7:1–5 for Ezra's own ties to the priesthood).

8. Smith, *Ezra, Nehemiah, Esther*, 192.

9. Kidner, *Ezra, Nehemiah*, 130.

**Other temple attendants (11:20–24).** In addition to "the rest of the Israelites . . . in all the towns of Judah, each on his ancestral property" (v. 20),[10] the list now extends to others who are also closely related to the temple and the worship, including the "temple servants who lived on the hill of Ophel" (v. 21; see 3:26). Uzzi was the chief officer (like an overseer, see v. 14 for the same word) of the Levites in Jerusalem. He traces his lineage to Asaph, and thus brings the psalmodic tradition of the "musicians responsible for the service of the house of God" (v. 22). Finally, Pethahiah (Ezra 10:23) fulfills a formal observer role as "king's agent." In the same way, the musicians come under Persian supervisory rule (v. 23). The crown will allow the worship of Yahweh to proceed, but not entirely without supervision.

**Allotments in the province (11:25–36).** In the form of an onomasticon (i.e, a list of place names), the historical geography reveals a map that is a mere fraction of the original Israel-Judah territory. The first section (vv. 25–29) concerns Judah and extends to settlements in Transjordan (Dibon, the capital of Moab during the monarchy), the Negeb (Beersheba and Ziklag), and the Shephelah (Jarmuth, Lachish, Azekah, and Adullam). The northern boundary marker is the Valley of Hinnom (v. 30) in the Judean highlands of Jerusalem. Thus, the map overlaps with the southern Persian province of Idumea and highlights, in a poignant way, Israel's precarious situation in their coexistence with their neighbors. The second half of the list (Benjaminites vv. 31–36) focuses on the Benjaminite territory north of Jerusalem (Anathoth and Ramah) but also extends into adjoining areas historically connected to Ephraim (Bethel).

As a *post scriptum*, "some of the divisions of the Levites of Judah" also lived in Benjamin (v. 36).

The settlement patterns in fifth century Yehud strongly suggest that designations such as "Judah" and "Benjamin" should not be taken at face value and in a literal territorial sense. Instead, Israel consisted of individual settlements in a region occupied by many ethnic groups in the provinces comprising the province of Yehud. In other words, "x marks the spot" only indicates that Israelite presence was in a particular settlement, which may or may not have overlapped sites historically

---

10. This insertion related to the "towns of Judah" serves a proleptic function when the settlement of Judah proper is recorded below (vv. 25–36).

connected to preexilic territories. This composite map serves as further indication of the level of opposition the community faced in claiming Jerusalem as their own territory, in claiming to rebuild the walls, and now in claiming that the worship of Yahweh can resume there. In addition, it also gives a stark visual as to the challenge not to intermarry and interact with the peoples of the land who were all around them. It also provides context as to why establishing identities through genealogies was so important to the community at the time, and why Nehemiah (and Ezra before him) was adamant about not entering into partnership in anyway with the peoples of the land. Again, we end this part of the report with our eyes wide open as to the precariousness and fragile nature of the restoration of Zion at this particular time in redemptive history. Nevertheless, the protection of Yahweh's sacred space continues to take precedence over the reality that the people of Yahweh continue to be very much a minority in the land.

**A DIFFERENT KIND OF CONQUEST AND SETTLEMENT.** The task of making the land holy is no longer associated with military conquest, which would violate Nehemiah's official mission (see Neh 2) and the eschatological purposes of Zion, when swords will be turned into plowshares (Isa 2:1–4). Long gone are the days of territorial expansion in the holy land as mandated by Yahweh to establish his presence on earth (the Deuteronomic program). However, the task to set apart a sacred space, a place of his own choosing, is emphasized:

> You must not worship the LORD your God in their way. But you are to seek the place the LORD your God will choose from among all your tribes to put his Name there for his dwelling. To that place you must go; there bring your burnt offerings and sacrifices, your tithes and special gifts, what you have vowed to give and your freewill offerings, and the firstborn of your herds and flocks. There, in the presence of the LORD your God, you and your families shall eat and shall rejoice in everything you have put your hand to, because the LORD your God has blessed you. (Deut 12:4–7; see also Exod 15:17)

Consequently, the focus is on the resettlement of the holy city in this chapter. Without the presence of temple officials, including the leaders inside the sacred precinct, it would be hard to imagine a stable restoration of worship in Zion. However, emphasis is also placed on temple attendants who live in the surrounding areas (Neh 11:20–35), which serves as a reminder of the concept of the "holy land," albeit in a much more diminutive way. In fact, the settlement landscape looks more like a reverse to the original conquest/settlement days of Joshua and Judges. Then, Israel occupied portions of the land (though never all), with pockets of unconquered territories (see Judg 1 in particular). Now, the people of Yahweh are spread out in pockets of settlements within the larger province of Yehud occupied by non-Yahwists. The settlement geography thus creates both an image of promise being fulfilled (they are, in fact, back in the land), and a promise that is yet to see its larger eschatological fulfillment, when "the knowledge of the glory of Yahweh will cover the earth as the waters cover the sea" (Hab 2:14, author's translation).

This chapter puts into sharp focus and concrete terms the reality that the land promised to Abraham was lost in 586 BC. The postexilic recovery should not be compared to the preexilic context of conquest and settlement. A return to the theocratic ideals is not what is in view here, but rather the reestablishment of holiness in Jerusalem. We are, therefore, moving the needle toward a concept of holiness that is separated from geo-political categories, as it was in the *ancient régime*. When Jesus comes, the personification of holiness in the land, the concept takes a much fuller meaning, especially in the sharp contrast Jesus will draw between his "kingdom" and the turbulent politics of the Roman province of Judea (John 18:36). Territorial expansion takes on a brand-new meaning in New Testament times, as well (Acts 1:8), so that the Isaianic vision of the good news/glory of the Lord expanding into all directions (Isa 40; 54:2–3) begins to be fulfilled. In the Persian province, we are a long way from the promise of territorial expansion, but it is a start, since the holy city is back in business.

**Personal commitment and sacrifice**. No one really wants to live in this landfill anymore, in contrast to the preexilic period, so that those who do are blessed and considered noble. What a contrast with what happened during the time of David and Solomon! So, the repopulation of the land takes on a reversed form, where to live in the towns is more appealing than to live in the city of the great King. As in the rebuilding of the walls (Neh 3), the leadership leads the way in resettling the city.

Outside the city walls and the settlement patterns in the province, the image is telling: the faithful are surrounded and remain in a precarious situation, the constant reminder that any political ambitions have to give way to their primary purpose, which is the worship of Yahweh. Psalm 137:4 wonders, "How can we sing the songs of the LORD while in a foreign land?" With the current map configuration in the homeland, one wonders whether anyone would have felt at home anywhere in Yehud which, in its own way, heightened the sense of importance of the spiritual significance of Jerusalem and the temple. In the old administration, Levites had to forgo a territorial inheritance (apart from the Levitical cities), but now the remaining tribes are joined together in that the LORD has become their inheritance, as well. From a strictly territorial standpoint, everything now rides on the sanctity of the holy city and the permanent presence of a worship detail—both to attend to the sacrifices and to the protection of the holiness of God on earth. Temporal priorities are giving way to spiritual ones and thus prepare us further for the definition of the temple and worship in the new covenant: mortar and brick emphases are transformed into spiritual categories. The people of God become the temple of the Holy Spirit, and territorial hegemony gives way to the presence of the LORD through the presence of his people of earth (Matt 18:20; 28:18–20; John 2:19; Eph 2:19–22).

All these images point to the reality of the postexilic period in redemptive historical terms: The returnees live in a now-and-not-yet, as anticipated by Isaiah the prophet during the period between the coming of Cyrus (Isaiah 44:28; 45:1; see Ezra 1:1) and the coming of the Suffering Servant in Isaiah 52:13–53:12 and illustrated with the following chart:

**Isaiah's Inaugurated Restoration:**

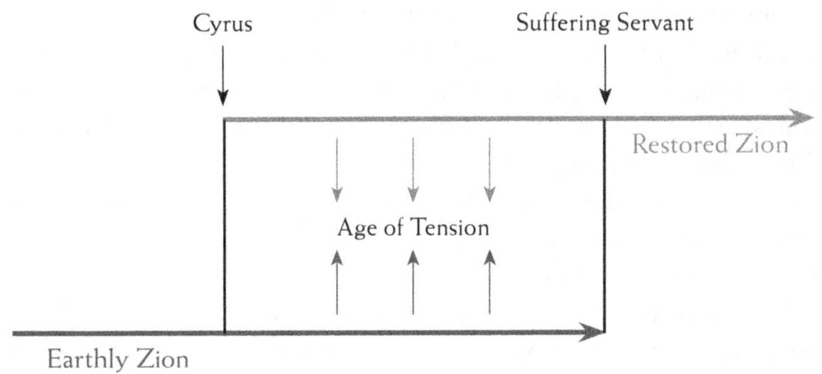

**PRESERVING THE SANCTITY OF ZION.** Through the ages of Christian history, believers have not always applied the principles outlined above. Temporal aspirations and ambitions for territorial expansion have to give way to the focal point of maintaining the sanctity of Zion, which now is defined as the people of God. Paul compares the church to a foundation of truth in 1 Timothy 3:15, and thus Scripture continues to challenge us by giving us marching orders away from unhealthy attachments to temporal categories (buildings, rituals, and theocratic aspirations) and toward spiritual ones. We need to realize we will never be a majority voice in the present evil age, from which Jesus came to save us (Gal 1:3–5). Even in the age of megachurches in the West and parts of Asia and Africa, from a standpoint of demographics, what is, for example, a 20,000-member church in a city of five million people? The Christian patterns of settlement in the present evil age will never be swayed in our favor. This radical redistribution will only occur when Christ establishes his kingdom on earth, in the new heaven and new earth (Isa 65:17; 66:22; 2 Pet 3:13; Rev 21). Our global map will always resemble the postexilic patterns of settlement in Yehud rather than the settlement patterns of the time of Joshua and Judges. Suddenly, we realize that the song of Psalm 137:1–6 becomes our song as well, until Christ finally establishes his kingdom and eradicates evil forever.

Thus, our task remains the same as those of the temple attendants in Yehud. We, as Levites (a royal priesthood, 1 Pet 2:9), are called to populate the holy city with God's people from the Jerusalem "above" (Gal 4:26) and making sure that we remain holy as he is holy (1 Pet 1:16). Temple attendants today work to make sure Zion remains set apart and distinct from the surrounding culture, while at the same time living in the culture. In the 1970s, Youth With A Mission, an organization known for its strong emphasis on personal piety, holiness, and obedience to the Lord, set up shop in the Red Light district of Amsterdam and managed refugee camps in Hong Kong, among other less-than-glamorous destinations. To this day, YWAMers routinely conduct outreach in areas frequented by very unholy people. The sanctity of Zion can, in fact, be preserved in very unholy surroundings.

The opposite emphasis, from the desert fathers during the Byzantine period to the fundamentalist movement in the twentieth century

Protestant movement worldwide, seeks separation rather than being embedded in the geographical fabric of our surroundings. According to this thinking, any sense of contamination with the surrounding communities should be avoided at all cost (see Ezra 10 commentary). As minority voices in the modern context of the body of Christ worldwide, it is tempting to yield to withdrawing rather than living in the midst of the culture, while at the same time preserving and promoting the sanctity of Zion. As John articulates, we are to live in the world but not be of the world (1 John 2:15–17).

**A call dictated by the worship of the LORD rather than convenience.** The corollary to this image of settlement pattern in Nehemiah 11 is that our call is never dictated by convenience and geography. Leaders decided to settle inside the wasteland that had become Jerusalem. Someone needed to lead the way, to stand up for the holiness of God, as it were. To minister to the LORD and his people will always encompass a measure of inconvenience and change. The apostle Paul, in his zeal to follow in the Lord's footsteps and desire to witness for Christ in Rome, took great risks and defied conventional wisdom to pursue this aim. We are called to do no less, all for the sake of the holy city. This is why the Christian faith is always dynamic and never static. People come and go. The church of the Lord Jesus Christ is always a sending church, and those of us privileged to serve as pastors are fully aware that people will leave according to his will and purposes; we should rejoice in seeing people movement in our congregations. However, as a wise pastor I know says, there are three reasons why people should leave a church: their own death, a new job/calling, or the church they attend has ceased to center its ministry and message on the Scripture and the gospel. These sort of restrictions, of course, do not fit the *à la carte* mentality of Western Christianity, especially with the endless proliferations of church plants in areas with already heavy concentrations of churches. However, in many parts of the world, now including western Europe, where church life is perhaps less convenient and more akin to the hostile environment reflected in Ezra-Nehemiah, the sense of deep commitment to Zion and the need of weekly regular worship are a given, a joy, and a privilege.

# Nehemiah 12:1–13:3

1 These were the priests and Levites who returned with
Zerubbabel son of Shealtiel and with Joshua:

Seraiah, Jeremiah, Ezra,
2 Amariah, Malluk, Hattush,
3 Shekaniah, Rehum, Meremoth,
4 Iddo, Ginnethon, Abijah,
5 Mijamin, Moadiah, Bilgah,
6 Shemaiah, Joiarib, Jedaiah,
7 Sallu, Amok, Hilkiah and Jedaiah.

These were the leaders of the priests and their associates in the days of Joshua.

8 The Levites were Jeshua, Binnui, Kadmiel, Sherebiah,
Judah, and also Mattaniah, who, together with his associates,
was in charge of the songs of thanksgiving. 9 Bakbukiah and
Unni, their associates, stood opposite them in the services.

10 Joshua was the father of Joiakim, Joiakim the father of
Eliashib, Eliashib the father of Joiada, 11 Joiada the father of
Jonathan, and Jonathan the father of Jaddua.

12 In the days of Joiakim, these were the heads of the
priestly families:

of Seraiah's family, Meraiah;
of Jeremiah's, Hananiah;
13 of Ezra's, Meshullam;
of Amariah's, Jehohanan;
14 of Malluk's, Jonathan;
of Shekaniah's, Joseph;
15 of Harim's, Adna;
of Meremoth's, Helkai;
16 of Iddo's, Zechariah;
of Ginnethon's, Meshullam;
17 of Abijah's, Zikri;

of Miniamin's and of Moadiah's, Piltai;
18 of Bilgah's, Shammua;
of Shemaiah's, Jehonathan;
19 of Joiarib's, Mattenai;
of Jedaiah's, Uzzi;
20 of Sallu's, Kallai;
of Amok's, Eber;
21 of Hilkiah's, Hashabiah;
of Jedaiah's, Nethanel.

22 The family heads of the Levites in the days of Eliashib,
Joiada, Johanan and Jaddua, as well as those of the priests,
were recorded in the reign of Darius the Persian.
23 The family
heads among the descendants of Levi up to the time of Johanan
son of Eliashib were recorded in the book of the annals.
24 And
the leaders of the Levites were Hashabiah, Sherebiah, Jeshua
son of Kadmiel, and their associates, who stood opposite them
to give praise and thanksgiving, one section responding to the
other, as prescribed by David the man of God.

25 Mattaniah, Bakbukiah, Obadiah, Meshullam, Talmon and
Akkub were gatekeepers who guarded the storerooms at the
gates.
26 They served in the days of Joiakim son of Joshua, the
son of Jozadak, and in the days of Nehemiah the governor and
of Ezra the priest, the teacher of the Law.

27 At the dedication of the wall of Jerusalem, the Levites
were sought out from where they lived and were brought to
Jerusalem to celebrate joyfully the dedication with songs of
thanksgiving and with the music of cymbals, harps and lyres.
28 The musicians also were brought together from the region
around Jerusalem—from the villages of the Netophathites,
29 from Beth Gilgal, and from the area of Geba and Azmaveth,
for the musicians had built villages for themselves around
Jerusalem.
30 When the priests and Levites had purified
themselves ceremonially, they purified the people, the gates
and the wall.

31 I had the leaders of Judah go up on top of the wall.
I also assigned two large choirs to give thanks. One was to
proceed on top of the wall to the right, toward the Dung

Gate. [32] Hoshaiah and half the leaders of Judah followed them,
[33] along with Azariah, Ezra, Meshullam, [34] Judah, Benjamin,
Shemaiah, Jeremiah, [35] as well as some priests with trumpets,
and also Zechariah son of Jonathan, the son of Shemaiah, the
son of Mattaniah, the son of Micaiah, the son of Zakkur, the
son of Asaph, [36] and his associates—Shemaiah, Azarel, Milalai,
Gilalai, Maai, Nethanel, Judah and Hanani—with musical
instruments prescribed by David the man of God. Ezra the
teacher of the Law led the procession. [37] At the Fountain Gate
they continued directly up the steps of the City of David on
the ascent to the wall and passed above the site of David's
palace to the Water Gate on the east.

[38] The second choir proceeded in the opposite direction.
I followed them on top of the wall, together with half the
people—past the Tower of the Ovens to the Broad Wall,
[39] over the Gate of Ephraim, the Jeshanah Gate, the Fish Gate,
the Tower of Hananel and the Tower of the Hundred, as far as
the Sheep Gate. At the Gate of the Guard they stopped.

[40] The two choirs that gave thanks then took their places in
the house of God; so did I, together with half the officials, [41] as
well as the priests—Eliakim, Maaseiah, Miniamin, Micaiah,
Elioenai, Zechariah and Hananiah with their trumpets—
[42] and also Maaseiah, Shemaiah, Eleazar, Uzzi, Jehohanan,
Malkijah, Elam and Ezer. The choirs sang under the direction
of Jezrahiah. [43] And on that day they offered great sacrifices,
rejoicing because God had given them great joy. The women
and children also rejoiced. The sound of rejoicing in Jerusalem
could be heard far away.

[44] At that time men were appointed to be in charge of
the storerooms for the contributions, firstfruits and tithes.
From the fields around the towns they were to bring into the
storerooms the portions required by the Law for the priests
and the Levites, for Judah was pleased with the ministering
priests and Levites. [45] They performed the service of their
God and the service of purification, as did also the musicians
and gatekeepers, according to the commands of David and
his son Solomon. [46] For long ago, in the days of David and
Asaph, there had been directors for the musicians and for the

songs of praise and thanksgiving to God. [47] So in the days of
Zerubbabel and of Nehemiah, all Israel contributed the daily
portions for the musicians and the gatekeepers. They also set
aside the portion for the other Levites, and the Levites set
aside the portion for the descendants of Aaron.

[1] On that day the Book of Moses was read aloud in the
hearing of the people and there it was found written that
no Ammonite or Moabite should ever be admitted into the
assembly of God, [2] because they had not met the Israelites with
food and water but had hired Balaam to call a curse down on
them. (Our God, however, turned the curse into a blessing.)
[3] When the people heard this law, they excluded from Israel all
who were of foreign descent.

## Lineage of Priests and Levites (12:1–26)

## Dedication of the Wall and Restoration of Worship (12:27–13:3)

CHAPTER 12 CONCLUDES NEHEMIAH'S stated mission with a formal dedication ceremony of the resumption of worship within the restored sanctity of Zion. The genealogical account in the first part of the chapter (vv. 1–26) establishes the legitimacy of the priesthood during the time of Nehemiah and Ezra (as "recorded in the book of the annals," v. 23) and its worship practices ("praise and thanksgiving" v. 24). The spiritual leaders' identity is grounded in priestly generations harking back to the return of Zerubbabel and Joshua (12:1, 7).

The genealogical list of verses 1–26 serves as a formal preface including the priests who ministered during the time of "Nehemiah the governor and of Ezra the priest, the teacher of the Law" (12:26). In turn, the second part of the chapter (vv. 27–47) describes a procession along the walls (perhaps in the tradition of the song of ascents in the Psalms?) with a final time of celebration at the temple, complete with sacrifices.

This finalizes Nehemiah's mission of rebuilding the wall in the city of his fathers (2:5). It is, therefore, fitting that he takes a leading role in the celebration, along with Ezra "the priest" (12:26) and "teacher of the Law"

(12:36). To celebrate this new era in Zion, Nehemiah ("I," v. 31) splits the congregation into two choirs that walked alongside the perimeter wall starting from opposite (v. 38) directions from each other in order to meet at the temple (v. 40). The two groups gather together at the "house of God" (v. 40) in a time of loud praise and worship and the offering of "great sacrifices" (v. 43). The account of dedication ends with an official report of the resumption of contributions for the "storerooms . . . for the priests and Levites" (v. 44), but especially for the "musicians and gatekeepers" (v. 47), as the community had promised via their binding agreement (10:38): "We will not neglect the house of our God" (10:39). As a post scriptum, Nehemiah records a final public reading of the law before the assembly "on that day," along with the (repeated) warning against assimilation with foreigners (no marriage is mentioned but it could be implied in light of the context), which underscores the theme of identity at the dedication ceremony and throughout the account (13:1–3). To end his mission on the topic of the "Book of Moses" (*sepher moshe*, a designation particular to Nehemiah) seems fitting, since it was this book that deeply influenced him to go on this journey in the first place (see Nehemiah 1 commentary).

**Unbroken lineage of priests and Levites to the present (12:1–26).** While a return to priestly genealogical records in Nehemiah may appear unnecessary (Neh 7:39–44; see Ezra 2 commentary), the genealogy in this context targets the priests and Levites ("gatekeepers" are added at the end, vv. 25–26) in a more comprehensive way than the list of Nehemiah 7, along with a practical rationale: The resumption of the worship can begin in earnest since everything and everyone is in place.[1] That priests and Levites "in the days of Nehemiah . . . and of Ezra" (v. 26) are ready to worship is specifically expressed through sanctioned singing ("as prescribed by David the man of God," v. 24). The priests and Levites can now officiate in the same way that their predecessors did. The genealogy emphasizes the legitimacy of the high priesthood (vv. 22–23) and singing in the temple (v. 24), all to legitimate the wall-dedication ceremony that follows in the account. In keeping with the holiness and security motif throughout Nehemiah's mission, the service of "gatekeepers" is also recognized (vv. 25–26; see also v. 45 below).

Commentators note that the list of the leadership who "returned with

---

1. Smith, *Ezra, Nehemiah, Esther*, 196.

Zerubbabel . . . and with Joshua" (see Ezra 1–2) is more comprehensive here than in Nehemiah 7:39–43.[2] Below is an adaptation of Kidner's presentation of the genealogical lay out:

- 12:1–7 = twenty-two names of those who returned in the days of Joshua the high priest (12:7). This list is more extensive than the one in Ezra 2/Nehemiah 7 and provides the historical background to the high priesthood in place at the time of Nehemiah.
- 12:8–9 = Levitical families who returned with Joshua. In this context, the names are associated with those "in charge of the songs of thanksgiving" (v. 8) and thus created continuity in the worship at the temple.
- 12:10–11 = The anchor genealogy of the chapter. It lists the names of the high priests from Joshua to the time of Nehemiah and thus stands in continuity with the formal high priestly genealogy of "1 Chronicles 6:3–15 . . . from Aaron to the Babylonian Exile."[3] The worship in Zion is legitimate and can resume based on the tradition harking back to Aaron himself (see Ezra 7:1–5).
- 12:12–21 = The priests of the generation following Joshua ("the days of Joiakim," v. 12). It attaches these names to the family names of verses 1–7.[4] A comparison with the list of the priests who signed the document in Nehemiah 10:2–8 shows that no less than 15 names of the signers are part of the list of 12:1–7/12–21.[5] This overlap fits with the "name as family" principle of recording.[6] The signers wanted to subsume their own individual names to their family name (e.g., our first name vs. last name).
- 12:22–23 = the anchor of the formal chronology/genealogy of the high priests of verses 10–11 in official Persian records ("in the reign

---

2. Ibid.

3. Kidner *Ezra, Nehemiah,* 135. Kidner (157) makes a good case that we should not place the last high priest on the list to a time far removed from Nehemiah's own lifetime. Thus, the "reign of Darius the Persian" (12:22) should be understood as Darius II (423–404), Artaxerxes I's successor.

4. Smith (*Ezra, Nehemiah, Esther,* 196) details the minor variations between the two lists that can be explained through unintentional scribal error that occurred in the transmission of manuscripts.

5. See Kidner's table, *Ezra, Nehemiah,* 134.

6. Ibid., 133.

of Darius," v. 22; "in the books of the annals," v. 23). In the absence of kings during the postexilic era, anchors to the relative chronology of Israel shifted to the tenure of high priests.[7] The restoration of the worship in Zion stands in historical continuity with Israel's historical tradition of worship during the Solomonic Temple era.

- 12:24–25 = Levitical list that partially finds its way into the list of chapter 10. Here, however, in keeping with the emphasis on the legitimacy of service, the Levites's official role as "prescribed" (*mitsvat david*) by David the man of God" specifies responsive "praise and thanksgiving" (v. 24), which fits into the broader context of responsive praise attached to the celebration of the completion of the wall.
- 12:25 = The "gatekeepers" mentioned in the list are assigned the specific role of guarding "the storerooms at the gates." The complementarity task of preserving the security and sanctity of the site also fits the context of the dedication ceremony. "Gatekeepers" will close the account (v. 47).

**Celebration and dedication of the walls (12:27–43).** No temporal framework is provided to situate the "dedication" (twice in v. 27, lit. *hanukkah*). The text leaves no indication that we should view the event any other way than in a chronological sequence (see 12:44; 13:1; see Ezra 4 for an example of an intentionally-dischronologized sequence). The intentional gathering of the Levites from "where they lived" (v. 27) does not preclude in any way a gathering following the repopulation of the city (see 11:3). The atmosphere surrounding the performance of this priestly ritual of dedication is established at the outset—they are gathered "joyfully" with thanksgiving and with singing, accompanied by the typical musical instruments associated with worship in the psalms: "cymbals, harps and lyres" (v. 27). "Musicians" are also summoned to converge from "around Jerusalem" for this momentous occasion (south, Netophah; east, "Gilgal;" and north, "Geba and Azmaveth;" v. 29). Recalling the songs of ascent and other psalms (see Pss 147; 148), the Levites

---

7. Ibid., 136. "Eliashib" is the high priest presiding over the events of the rebuilding of the walls (Neh 3:1). "Johanan" (v. 22, from which "John" derives) is probably the priest mentioned in Aramaic documents from Egypt at Elephantine (ibid.; see also Kidner's Appendix 4 for a masterful summary of the extrabiblical data).

unexpectedly take center stage (see above) in this gathering that recalls other summons in the brief time since Nehemiah came to Jerusalem (5:7), but especially the assembly on the first day of the seventh month (7:73–8:1). Before the celebration can begin, in keeping with the larger theological purpose of the entire project, the priests and Levites "purified themselves" (root *tahar* in a reflexive sense) and "purified the people, the gates and the wall" (v. 30). The restoration project thus has come full circle from chapter 3, where "Eliashib the high priest" began the work by "making holy" (author's translation; NIV "dedicated") the "Sheep Gate" as well as the "Tower of the Hundred" (3:1). This time, however, and in the context of the people's own dedication to Yahweh as reflected in chapters 8–10, all the people are making themselves pure for service to the LORD and for worship (see Levitical laws on priestly dedication; Lev 8–10).

Nehemiah's intervention resumes in verse 31 (he could be quite direct; see 5:12) with the appointment "on top of the wall" of "two large choirs" (two great *todoth* = thanking groups) that included "the leaders of Judah." In a way recalling Nehemiah's own journey on the wall a few months prior (2:13–14), one of the processions went up on the wall going to the "right" (or south) toward the Dung Gate (v. 31). Heading off the list is "Hoshaiah and half the leaders of Judah" (v. 32). "Ezra," the teacher/scribe is listed last, but he was the one who would actually go before the whole company ("led them," v. 36). The other members of the group consisted of names encountered before (e.g., Meshullam, 8:4); one "Zechariah" (descendant of Asaph v. 35) and his eight "associates" with musical instruments prescribed by "David the man of God" (v. 36) underscores the impeccable credentials of the first "thanking procession." The list also includes the strongly evocative "priests with trumpets" (v. 35), which allows the motif of conquest to resurface (see Bridging Context below). The final details go back to the actual route "on top of the wall" (v. 37), which suggests a movement down on the west side of the wall and back up past the "house of David" toward the "Water Gate on the east." Their final destination is clear: "the house of God" (v. 40).

"The second choir" ("the second *todah*," v. 38) went "the opposite direction." The group that Nehemiah followed, though equal in size ("half the people," v. 38), lists no one by name. The itinerary of the procession is more detailed, however, which shows the group started at the same place as the first group but went north on the western side of the wall (the Broad Wall is well-known feature in the ancient city of Jerusalem to this day), past several gates all on the northern end of the enclosure wall (Ephraim, Jeshanah, and Fish), along with the towers of Hanalel and Hundred and the Sheep Gate—all nearby the temple precinct. The last stop was right at the entrance of the temple: "the Gate of the Guard" (v. 39).

The two *todoth* (NIV "the choirs that gave thanks," v. 40) "took their places" in the temple area proper, including Nehemiah himself with half of the officials (see 2:16; 4:14, 19; 5:7; 7:5), who remain anonymous. In contrast, Nehemiah lists a total of fifteen priests by name, including seven "with their trumpets" (v. 41). The second action verb after "took their place" is the first of several mainline verbs in the original which creates a dynamic picture ("on that day," v. 43) and serves as the fitting and dramatic conclusion to an extraordinary past few months for Nehemiah and the rest of the people:

- The "choirs *sang*" (*wayashmi'u*, "caused to hear" [author's translation])
- "under the direction of Jezrahiah" (who is "the overseer," [author's translation] *paqid* in the original; v. 42)
- They *offered* (*wayyizbehu*) "great sacrifices" (v. 43, which then explained why so many of them are mentioned by name)
- They **rejoiced** (*wayyismahu*, v. 43)

This act of rejoicing echoes the "joy of the LORD" of 8:10 and is directly attributed to "God" himself who has "caused them to *rejoice* (same verbal root *samah*) with great *joy*" (*simhah*; author's translation; NIV "God had given them great joy," v. 43). To add to the picture and further recall the events of chapter 8, "the women and the children also *rejoiced*" (root *samah*). As in a crescendo, the atmosphere of rejoicing receives one last main verb describing a mood of extraordinary joy:

- the *joy* of Jerusalem (*simhat yerushalaim*) could be heard far away (v. 43)

Thus, in quick succession, the root for "joy" occurs five times in the original. The projected and public nature of the joy serves as a fitting conclusion that the enemies of Zion could not prevail and take away the joy of a community who put their faith in Yahweh.

**Securing the ongoing support for the house of the Lord (12:44–47).** Nehemiah wants to make sure the worship and service to the temple take on a permanent format beyond the events of the day and the past few months. He knows that unless people willingly contribute to the service of the house of the LORD, as promised in chapter 10, his efforts and success in restoring Zion could be reversed, especially since Jerusalem remains surrounded by hostile neighbors. As the current governor of Judah and successor of Zerubbabel (v. 47), he is also accountable to the crown to make sure that everyone involved in the service of the temple ("musicians and gatekeepers" along with Levites and the "descendants of Aaron," v. 47) are supported to fulfill their respective duties, including temple security and the protection of the sanctity of the site.

The identical temporal connectives of 12:44 and 13:1 make it clear the wall dedication and subsequent celebration did not mark the end of Nehemiah's project. Characteristic of Nehemiah's *modus operandi* to preserve momentum, "on that day" (author's translation; v. 44, NIV "at that time") "men were appointed" for the specific task of managing the storerooms so that the priests and Levites could receive their "portions" as mandated "by the Law" (v. 44). These priestly and levitical duties are summarized as both the "service of their God" proper and "the service of purification" (root *tarah* v. 45). As evident throughout this part of Nehemiah's report (see 12:24, 36), the "musicians" are singled out as recipients of credentials that hark back to the very beginning of formal worship (*todoth*) in the monarchy (time of "David and Asaph," v. 46). "Gatekeepers" are not left out either, since they also perform their duties alongside the singers "according to the commands of David and his son Solomon" (v. 45).

In one more effort to underscore the atmosphere associated with the day, the commitment to support the priesthood and temple service in general returns to a familiar mood: "the *joy* (*simhah*) of Judah was over the priests and the Levites who ministered" (author's translation; NIV "Judah was pleased," v. 44).

As a *a concluding thought* (v. 47), "all Israel" (a telling designation that recalls preexilic and Davidic/Solomonic tribal unity) were true to the promise to provide for the affairs of the temple attendants (musicians, gatekeepers, Levites, and descendants of Aaron). The obvious parallel between the "days of Zerubabbel" in the first return and those "of Nehemiah" (v. 47) underscores a return to normalcy and strongly hints at the success of Nehemiah's mission. His success is measured against the benchmark of the governor in Yehud: Zerubbabel. Nehemiah not only has been able to restore the physical aspects of worship, but he has also secured the needed supplies to support the continued worship in the temple. The people are beginning to fulfill their terms of the covenant made in chapter 10: "We will not neglect the house of our God" (10:39).

**One final warning about their hostile neighbors (13:1–3).** The final act of "that day" (13:1) is the public reading of "the Book of Moses," which underscores its newly-gained importance and forms a literary *inclusio* to the sequence of events launched at the beginning of the seventh month, only a few weeks ago (for chronological debates, see chapter 8 commentary). The community has gathered around the hearing of the law ("in the hearing of the people") one more time. On this occasion, however, the reading appears brief and targeted to an essentially-direct quotation from Deuteronomy 23:3–5: "No Ammonite and Moabite should ever be admitted in the assembly of God, because they had not met the Israelites with food and water but had hired Balaam to a curse down on them" (13:1–2). The added interpretation "Our God, however, turned the curse into a blessing" (v. 2), recalls the work of the Levites among the people in chapter 8 to clarify the law. However, the phrase also recalls Nehemiah's familiar prayerful interjections into the narrative ("our God," 4:4, 20), particularly in the struggle with his enemies Sanballat, Tobiah (the Ammonite), and Geshem. Just as these enemies sought to curse the work of Nehemiah and the community without success, so in the days of Balaam, Israel's chief designation was "blessed" (Num 23–24).[8]

Upon hearing this injunction ("law"), "they excluded from Israel all who were of foreign descent" (v. 3), which is a further connection with Israel's distant past. The theme of ethnic and theological purity is fused in Israel (which remains an intentional designation in Nehemiah) during the postexilic era in the same way that it was fused during the earliest phase of settlement in Canaan (and Transjordan). This last act marks the end of the mission of Nehemiah, since 13:4 takes place during a different time period, according to the preserved narrative-history tradition of the book of Nehemiah.

---

8. Petter, *The Land Beyond the Two Rivers.*

**Primacy of priesthood in worship.** We may wonder why there is yet another list of priests in Ezra-Nehemiah (vv. 1–26). What is the intent of this intentional duplication? In terms of its placement and function within the larger narrative, the list fits with the dedicatory tone of the whole chapter. The theme is well worn by now in Nehemiah: the restoration of the sanctity of Zion cannot happen apart from a restoration of sacrifices, which themselves cannot take place apart from temple personnel and their support by the rest of the community. The list here functions as a rhetorical exclamation point with respect to the significance of the priesthood, which has been emphasized repeatedly (Neh 3:1, etc.). By using, yet again, the tool of legitimacy established by descent (very much standard procedure in tribal societies), the text here connects to the primary role of the priesthood in the past (Moses and Aaron, Exod 2:1; 6:16–27) and highlights Yahweh's faithfulness to keep the priesthood lineage alive in spite of Israel's past unfaithfulness (Neh 7 commentary). At the risk of stating the obvious, without the Levitical priesthood there can be no legitimate purification and dedication with the resulting praise to Yahweh. Without proper personnel to dedicate the wall, the holiness of Yahweh in the restored place of worship will be short-lived. All the work accomplished in the past few weeks would mean nothing unless the site is made pure (Neh 12:30). Even a cursory exploration in preexilic literature reveals how devastating priestly failure becomes in the maintenance of proper worship. Isaiah, among others, vividly chronicled the failures of the preexilic priesthood to offer acceptable sacrifices (e.g., "the multitude of your sacrifices—what are they to me?" Isa 1:11). The gathered community does not want to go back to the ways of the past. From a broad redemptive-historical perspective, the genealogy continues to underscore the primacy of the priesthood and Christ's sacerdotal role. Christ is the "Lamb of God who takes away the sin of the world" (John 1:29 ESV). Without proper purification through Christ's atoning sacrifice, any hope of dedication for service and holiness will remain vain (Titus 2:11–15). Of course, the author of Hebrews makes the case that Christ comes from a different priesthood than Levi/Abraham (Heb 7:23–28; 9:11–14; 10:10–14), but he does fulfill the role of the Levitical high priest all the same. In short, the list here provides continuity and prepares the way for Jesus to come to fulfill his mission as the Suffering Servant, an atoning substitutionary sacrifice (Isa 53:6; Mark 10:45).

**Dedication ceremony.** The genealogical list of chapter 12:1–26 only functions as a prelude to the main event of this chapter (12:27–47), which itself marks the final phase of Nehemiah's mission: "When the priests and the Levites had purified themselves ceremonially, they purified the people, the gates and the wall" (12:30). We have now come full circle from chapter 3:1 and the sanctification (NIV "dedicated") of the work at the outset by Eliashib the high priest. In this respect, the event takes its place alongside other hallowed ceremonies when the task of establishing holiness on earth is completed: all of creation as the sanctuary of Yahweh (e.g., Isa 66:1 and Acts 7:49), the tabernacle in Exodus (Exod 40:1–38), the Solomonic temple (1 Kgs 8:62–66), and the foundations of the postexilic temple (Ezra 3:10–11).

There are even more specific parallels as it relates to wall dedication and musical procession. Joshua's march around the wall of Jericho served a dedicatory role led by the priests, also accompanied by musical instruments (Josh 6). Yahweh, in judgment against unrighteousness and unbelief (see Heb 11:31; Jas 2:25) manifested his holiness in the land of Canaan. The site itself becomes both set apart and devoted to destruction (*herem*; Josh 6:21).[9]

The theme of joy finds its way also in the entering of the ark into Jerusalem by King David (2 Sam 6). In the Chronicler's account, emphasis is given to priests and the Levites when the ark is brought into Jerusalem (1 Chr 15:3–10). The themes of consecration (vv. 12, 14), singing and musical instruments (vv. 16, 19–22), emphasis of joy (vv. 16, 25, 29), and processional celebration are integral to the ceremony (v. 28):

> So all Israel brought up the ark of the covenant of the LORD with shouts, with the sounding of rams' horns and trumpets, and of cymbals, and the playing of lyres and harps.

---

9. See Tremper Longman, III, "Eschatological Continuity" in *Show Them No Mercy; Four Views on God and Canaanite Genocide*, ed. Stanley Gundry (Grand Rapids: Zondervan, 2003). Thomas Petter, "Tribes and Nomads in the Iron Age Levant," in *Behind the Scenes of the Old Testament*, ed. Jonathan S. Greer, John W. Hilber, and John H. Walton (Grand Rapids: Baker, 2018), 391–95.

Thus, the backdrop of the Chronicler's history looms large in this account of the dedication of the wall in Nehemiah. Everything was accomplished according to precedent set by David, "the man of God" (Neh 12:24, 36), with the leading role attributed to the priesthood and Levites.

As an added connection to the theme of dedication in the Old Testament, but of a more macabre nature, is the account of King Mesha[10] of Moab in 2 Kings 3. As the battle with an Israelite-Judean coalition turned against him, Mesha sacrificed his son on a city wall (2 Kgs 3:27).

Turning to the New Testament, dedication/purification/holiness becomes the person of Christ and his work, both on the cross and through his life. He is the one who purifies us (e.g., Luke 8:43–48). Through our union with Christ, we are set apart and made pure (1 Cor 1:30) both at the individual level and corporate level ("to purify for himself a people that are his very own, eager to do what is good," Titus 2:14). Furthermore, the walls and gates of the heavenly Jerusalem, the eschatological Zion, which is, figuratively speaking, God's own people are now the scene of a joyful gathering:

> But you have come to Mount Zion, to the city of the living God, the heavenly Jerusalem. You have come to thousands upon thousands of angels in joyful assembly, to the church of the firstborn, whose names are written in heaven. You have come to God, the Judge of all, to the spirits of the righteous made perfect, to Jesus the mediator of a new covenant, and to the sprinkled blood that speaks a better word than the blood of Abel. (Heb 12:22–24)

In the eschatological fulfillment of this dedication ceremony (Rev 21–22), the sanctity of the site is permanently sealed. In figurative imagery far surpassing the rich adornment of the first tabernacle/temple

10. The Mesha Inscription/Stele (Moabite Stone) provides an immensely useful window into the world of the Iron Age II polities of the time (Israel, Judah, Moab, and by analogy, other polities of the southern Levant). For the text of the Mesha Inscription, see the Louvre Museum website (https://www.louvre.fr/en/oeuvre-notices/mesha-stele). A brief synopsis of the text and historical background is provided at the following website: Ancient History Encyclopedia, "Moabite Stone [Mesha Stele]", https://www.ancient.eu/Moabite_Stone_[Mesha_Stele]/. The classic treatment of the text and its context remains: Andrew Dearman, *Studies in the Mesha Inscription and Moab* (Atlanta: Scholars Press, 1989).

(e.g., 1 Pet 2:5),[11] "the wall was made of jasper" (Rev 21:18) and its twelve "foundations . . . were decorated with every kind of precious stone" (Rev 21:19–20). The twelve gates themselves are made of pearl (v. 21), and they will be permanently open (v. 25; see commentary on Neh 13 for the open gates imagery). "Nothing impure will even enter it" (Rev 21:27). Thus, the gates and walls are set apart as well as those "who have washed their robes" ("a great multitude" who have "washed their robes and made them white in the blood of the Lamb," Rev 7:9, 14).[12] They may now "go through the gates into the city" unencumbered by sin (Rev 22:14). The substitutionary sacrifice of Christ holds center stage in this eschatological picture, in fulfillment of the central Levitical dedicatory role exercised in the province of Yehud under the guidance of both "Nehemiah the governor and of Ezra the priest and teacher" (Neh 12:26).

**More of the exclusion motif (Nehemiah 13:1–3).** Upon yet another public reading of the law, further action is taken to separate themselves from all those of non-Israelite background. The topic of separation of foreign wives has been covered prior in Ezra 9:1–5; 10:1–44, but more discussion is needed, since the subject of exclusion returns twice in the final chapter of the book of Nehemiah. It would be tempting to create a wedge in the postexilic corpus between the historic theme of inclusivity in the Judean genealogy of the Chronicler and the hard line adopted in Ezra-Nehemiah.[13] However, lest we create a false sense of either harmony or dichotomy, the historical context as presented to us in the available materials suggests a both/and rather than an either/or when it comes to the question of mixed marriages. The time of the judges and its recorded Deuteronomic history suggest that the cultural fault lines did not simply line up along bloodlines but rather upon the all-important question of allegiance to Yahwism. Thus, a Canaanite prostitute (a sort of unclean of uncleans, according to Levitical law) could find herself integrated into the community, she and her household (Josh 2; 6), while a Judean could find himself declared unclean and *herem* and destroyed, he and his household (Josh 7). The same could be said regarding Ruth, a Transjordanian Moabite,

11. G. K. Beale, *Revelation: A Shorter Commentary* (Grand Rapids: Eerdmans, 2015), 486–89.

12. Ibid., 518.

13. Gary N. Knoppers, "Intermarriage, Social Complexity, and Ethnic Diversity in the Genealogy of Judah," *JBL* 120.1 (2001): 15–20. We thank our colleague and friend Carol Kaminski for bringing this study to our attention.

who essentially becomes a Yahwist,[14] which then allows her to stand in the lineage of the Judean dynastic line of David. The Chronicler picks up on this undercurrent of tribal ethnic identity, which always contains many nuances connected to Israelite identities in the earliest phases of settlement.[15] However, the lines are drawn equally clearly when it comes to allegiance to Yahweh. In the case of the vast majority of Canaanites, they did not follow Yahweh. In the case of the Moabites, 99.9 percent did not know Yahweh, as with all the other nations around them. However, Yahweh welcomes the .1 percent who did welcome him, regardless of their ethnic background: Rahab, Ruth, and, at a later time, Uriah the Hittite (2 Sam 11:11). In the corpus of Ezra-Nehemiah, there is no discernable evidence that any of the "foreigners" (including foreign wives) in their midst were Yahwists. Furthermore, in light of the compromised stance exhibited by some members of the community itself, the urgency to separate must have been even more pressing in the minds of both Ezra and Nehemiah (see commentary on Ezra 9–10 and below in Neh 13).

Likewise, Paul, the apostle to the Gentiles, did not seem to consider it a problem to proclaim the inclusion of the Gentiles into God's family by faith while at the same time establishing very strict boundaries on the question of relating to unbelievers. Paul cites Levitical law, among other Old Testament texts (Lev 26:12), to make the point in the strongest possible terms that to be yoked with unbelievers should never happen: "therefore come out from them and be separate" (2 Cor 6:14–18; v. 17 in particular). As in the case of Ezra-Nehemiah, holiness is the *leitmotiv*: "Let us purify ourselves from everything that contaminates body and spirit, perfecting holiness out of reverence for God" (2 Cor 7:1; see Ezra 10 commentary for the New Testament context of marriage).

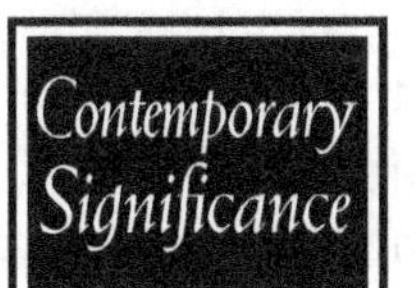


**Purity and dedication means service.** The application of the dedication of the wall and the procession of thanksgiving is profound. As the new priesthood, we offer up songs of thanksgiving not simply on special occasions but as a way of life

14. Donna Petter, "Ruth," in *Baker Illustrated Bible Commentary*, ed. Gary M. Burge, Andrew E. Hill (Grand Rapids: Baker, 2012), 242–53.

15. See Thomas Petter, *The Land Between the Two Rivers*, 56–62.

(Eph 5:19). This posture anticipates the eschatological worship envisioned by John on the Island of Patmos (Rev 7:9–12), which takes place forever by those who have been made pure and perfected through Christ's atoning sacrifice (Heb 10:14). So, as the city of God personified, God's people are set apart for worship, praise, and celebration in joy. We offer ourselves as "living sacrifices" as "spiritual worship" (Rom 12:1–2 ESV). We have been purified and have become "zealous for good works" (Titus 2:11–15 ESV). Just as the people of Yehud made a stand as a minority, to praise the LORD in anticipation of the return of the King to Zion (per the promise of the prophets), we do the same as an eschatological declaration that the kingdom of God is both here and yet to come.

**Processional praise.** Several Christian traditions are known for festival and public processions. I remember vividly Armenian Christmas 2017 on January 18 in Jerusalem and Bethlehem.[16] There was a procession of teenagers entering the Old City of Jerusalem by the Jaffa Gate, who were beating their drums as loud as possible in celebration of Christmas, under the watching eye of the police. They were returning to the Armenian Quarter in the midst of normal life with rabbis and tourists walking about. They were undeterred in celebrating loudly the birth of the Savior. Another personal and equally vivid recollection of another type of procession was in Aného, Togo. While missionaries in the heartland of Voodooism, we became accustomed to periodic manifestations of the presence of this powerful religion through loud processions in town. On one of these occasions, as we heard the drums in the distance, Donna was in the middle of lecturing on the historical background of the letter to the Ephesians and how the city was a religious Disneyland. The sense of chronological and cultural detachment from the context of Asia Minor quickly evaporated as we watched the procession go by.

In the West, Christian short-term outreach teams do prayer walks routinely (on one occasion we walked around the main plaza in Mexico City several times), as do church staff in their neighborhoods. What is the significance of all these processions? The proclamation of God's faithfulness in a very public way is an act of worship to him. We are declaring to the world around us that God is at work and that he is

16. The Patriarchate in Jerusalem uniquely observes Christmas about two weeks later than other Armenian churches around the world (Epiphany, January 6, according to the Julian Calendar). Western churches follow the Gregorian Calendar.

faithful to carry out his purposes. It took courage for the fledgling minority in Yehud to have such a public display on the walls of the city, but they (men, women, and children) did it with their whole heart, so much so that their joy was heard from afar (Neh 12:43).

**We owe everything to him**. In all these points of application, we remember that Jesus is the focal point of our purification, holiness, and dedication. As the psalmist said with respect to temple-building (Ps 127:1):

> Unless the LORD builds the house,
> the builders labor in vain.
> Unless the LORD watches over the city,
> the guards stand watch in vain.

As we know from the community in Yehud, temple building is a long and protracted process. But now they have completed the rebuilding of the walls and the restoring of the gates. The promise of Zechariah 4:6 is beginning to be fulfilled ("not by might, nor by power, but by my Spirit"). So, we do the same knowing that the Lord is building up his house (his people). It is his work, and we give him all the glory and the praise for the ways in which he causes his church to grow, many times in spite of ourselves. We also recognize that the process includes a lot of fits and starts, as Paul warns us (1 Thess 2:18). But the promise of the minority in Yehud also stands—they did complete the task eventually, as Paul assures us that "he who began a good work in you will carry it on to completion until the day of Christ Jesus" (Phil 1:6). Anyone who has spent any measure of time in the temple-building business that is Christian ministry knows all too well that the process contains many delays, setbacks, and opposition, all in the midst of a climate of isolation and loneliness. The book of Nehemiah stands as a witness that, indeed, "Our God will fight for us" (Neh 4:20).

**Inclusion and exclusion.** Outsiders versus insiders continues as an important theme in Ezra-Nehemiah. We will take up the significance of this motif at the end of chapter 13.

# Nehemiah 13:4–31

4 Before this, Eliashib the priest had been put in charge of the
storerooms of the house of our God. He was closely associated
with Tobiah, 5 and he had provided him with a large room
formerly used to store the grain offerings and incense and
temple articles, and also the tithes of grain, new wine and olive
oil prescribed for the Levites, musicians and gatekeepers, as
well as the contributions for the priests.

6 But while all this was going on, I was not in Jerusalem, for
in the thirty-second year of Artaxerxes king of Babylon I had
returned to the king. Some time later I asked his permission
7 and came back to Jerusalem. Here I learned about the evil
thing Eliashib had done in providing Tobiah a room in the
courts of the house of God. 8 I was greatly displeased and threw
all Tobiah's household goods out of the room. 9 I gave orders to
purify the rooms, and then I put back into them the equipment
of the house of God, with the grain offerings and the incense.

10 I also learned that the portions assigned to the Levites
had not been given to them, and that all the Levites and
musicians responsible for the service had gone back to their
own fields. 11 So I rebuked the officials and asked them, "Why
is the house of God neglected?" Then I called them together
and stationed them at their posts.

12 All Judah brought the tithes of grain, new wine and
olive oil into the storerooms. 13 I put Shelemiah the priest,
Zadok the scribe, and a Levite named Pedaiah in charge of
the storerooms and made Hanan son of Zakkur, the son of
Mattaniah, their assistant, because they were considered
trustworthy. They were made responsible for distributing the
supplies to their fellow Levites.

14 Remember me for this, my God, and do not blot out what I
have so faithfully done for the house of my God and its services.

15 In those days I saw people in Judah treading winepresses
on the Sabbath and bringing in grain and loading it on
donkeys, together with wine, grapes, figs and all other kinds

of loads. And they were bringing all this into Jerusalem on
the Sabbath. Therefore I warned them against selling food
on that day. 16 People from Tyre who lived in Jerusalem were
bringing in fish and all kinds of merchandise and selling them in
Jerusalem on the Sabbath to the people of Judah. 17 I rebuked
the nobles of Judah and said to them, "What is this wicked
thing you are doing—desecrating the Sabbath day? 18 Didn't
your ancestors do the same things, so that our God brought all
this calamity on us and on this city? Now you are stirring up
more wrath against Israel by desecrating the Sabbath."

19 When evening shadows fell on the gates of Jerusalem before
the Sabbath, I ordered the doors to be shut and not opened until
the Sabbath was over. I stationed some of my own men at the
gates so that no load could be brought in on the Sabbath day.
20 Once or twice the merchants and sellers of all kinds of goods
spent the night outside Jerusalem. 21 But I warned them and said,
"Why do you spend the night by the wall? If you do this again,
I will arrest you." From that time on they no longer came on the
Sabbath. 22 Then I commanded the Levites to purify themselves
and go and guard the gates in order to keep the Sabbath day holy.

Remember me for this also, my God, and show mercy to me
according to your great love.

23 Moreover, in those days I saw men of Judah who had
married women from Ashdod, Ammon and Moab. 24 Half of their
children spoke the language of Ashdod or the language of one of
the other peoples, and did not know how to speak the language
of Judah. 25 I rebuked them and called curses down on them.
I beat some of the men and pulled out their hair. I made them
take an oath in God's name and said: "You are not to give your
daughters in marriage to their sons, nor are you to take their
daughters in marriage for your sons or for yourselves. 26 Was it
not because of marriages like these that Solomon king of Israel
sinned? Among the many nations there was no king like him. He
was loved by his God, and God made him king over all Israel,
but even he was led into sin by foreign women. 27 Must we hear
now that you too are doing all this terrible wickedness and are
being unfaithful to our God by marrying foreign women?"

28 One of the sons of Joiada son of Eliashib the high priest

was son-in-law to Sanballat the Horonite. And I drove him
away from me.

[29] Remember them, my God, because they defiled the priestly
office and the covenant of the priesthood and of the Levites.

[30] So I purified the priests and the Levites of everything
foreign, and assigned them duties, each to his own task. [31] I
also made provision for contributions of wood at designated
times, and for the firstfruits.

Remember me with favor, my God.

## Nehemiah's Final Attempts at Reform (13:4–31)

THE DETAILED LISTS AND COMMITMENTS COMPRISING Nehemiah 10, 11, and 12 all serve as an intentional strategy on the part of Nehemiah to make sure the worship of Yahweh can carry on now that the walls and gates are restored. The promissory declaration of Nehemiah 10, including the signatures and details regarding the proper functioning of the worship, casts an especially long shadow in this regard, with the commitment: "We will not neglect the house of our God" (10:39). Nehemiah's final chapter of his scramblings amongst Yehud documents the methodical and point by point unravelling of his work of restoration of "the house of my God and its services" (13:14):

- A compromised priesthood (13:4–9/10:30)
- Disrupted worship in the temple since the Levites and the singers are no longer supported in their work (13:10–13/10:37–39)
- Sabbath-day transactions with the "peoples of the land" (13:15–22/10:31)
- Compromised sanctity of the temple (13:22/12:30)
- Intermarriage (13:23–29/10:30; 13:3)
- Defiled priesthood and dereliction of duties (13:30/12:30, 44–47)
- Shortage of firewood and contributions (13:30–31/10:30–39; 12:44–47)

The scope of Nehemiah's final reforms is extensive, since the problems affect virtually every aspect and everyone (including the senior leadership,

"Eliashib the priest" and the "officials," 13:4, 11) related to the proper worship of Yahweh in Zion. Nehemiah finds himself looking again for individuals "considered trustworthy" (v. 13). The sense of distance (twelve years, v. 6) is the only explanation provided as to why the other faithful architects of the reforms have simply vanished from the scene (e.g., Ezra along with the other priests and Levites, Nehemiah's brother Hanani, and Hananiah; cf. Neh 7:1–2). The "remember" prayers (5:19; 6:14) resurface more frequently and with a more insistent tone (13:14, 22, 29, 31) and actually conclude his account: "Remember me with favor, my God."

The final chapter in the book underscores Nehemiah's own faithfulness to the health of Zion, which continued unabated beyond his first commission as a governor. While many soon forgot the extraordinary encounter with the "joy of the LORD" in Zion (Neh 8:10), Nehemiah did not forget that his own name headed the list of names affixed to the promise (10:1). His passion for compliance to the law and the preservation of the sanctity of Zion was not dictated by duty but by his love for God and proper worship.

Second, the account mirrors the atmosphere of neglect to the house of the LORD encountered at other times during the postexilic era (the time of Haggai, Zechariah, and Malachi). However, none provides such a swift and precipitous fall from the genuine sense of corporate and unified commitment reflected throughout the community (see Neh 8 commentary). The repeated (and perhaps redundant) warning against apostasy and Canaanization interspersed throughout the narrative history (see Neh 9 commentary) now appears completely justified, even as it evidently fell on deaf ears. It is no surprise, therefore, that the related themes of exclusion and separation are prioritized again (see discussion in Ezra 2). The people of Yahweh have reentered the cycle described in the book of Judges and are liable to "curses" (Neh 13:25) as the first generation did, including the great King Solomon (v. 26).

**Dealing with Eliashib (13:4–9).** It is the irony of a narrative history that begins with "Eliashib the high priest" (3:1), who took the lead in making holy (NIV "dedicate") the work of restoration at the Sheep Gate, now concludes with one "Eliashib the priest" as well (see also 13:28).[1] At the heart of what Eliashib had done was an illicit partnership

---

1. Opinions are divided as to whether Eliashib of v. 4 is in fact the high priest of 3:1 and 12:28, since he is invariably designated the "high" priest. Whether they are

with Tobiah ("related" e.g., Lev 21:1; NIV "closely associated"). Tobiah needs no introduction in his twin role as joint-chief protagonist and double agent by marriage alliance (6:18). In light of the significance of the "storerooms" for proper worship in the temple (see 12:44), the securing of a large room "in the courts of the house of God" (v. 7) originally assigned for the storage of supplies essential to worship[2] seriously disrupted temple personnel (priests, Levites, singers, gatekeepers; v. 5) and essentially forced them out of the temple precincts (see v. 10). In light of how significant the genealogies pertaining to these people are in chapters 11 and 12, a catastrophe does not even begin to describe what is going on, and it thrusts us back to the dark ages of the preexilic systemic neglect of the worship in Judah.

The official record provides crucial temporal details about Nehemiah's return to the service of "Artaxerxes king of Babylon"[3] (v. 6; see 2:6) for what amounted to twelve years away from the province, so that Nehemiah did not superintend this development. The syntactical structure of mainline verbs formats Nehemiah's response in expectedly swift and decisive terms (vv. 7–9):

- "I came back"
- "I learned about the evil thing (*ra'ah*) Eliashib had done"
- "It was very (*me'od*) evil (*ra'*) to me" (author's translation; NIV "I was greatly displeased")
- "I threw all Tobiah's household goods out of the room"
- "I said" (*'amar*; NIV "I gave orders")
- "'they purified (root *tahar*, see 12:30) the chambers" (author's

---

one and the same certainly does not shield Eliashib the "high priest" from his own complicity in the practice of alliances with the enemy via intermarriage (Eliashib of v. 4 with Tobiah; the high priest of v. 28 with Sanballat). If they are one and the same person, then Eliashib the high priest compromised himself with two out of the three main enemies of Nehemiah's mission. The theme of internal betrayal, adumbrated in chapter 6, has resurfaced here, as well.

2. "grain offerings, incense, temple articles . . . tithes of grains, new wine and oil" (v. 5).

3. As the chief holy city of the ancient Near East, every conqueror of the Mesopotamian lowlands claimed the title King of Babylon, whether Amorite (Hammurabi), Assyrian (Sennacherib), or from the highlands of the western Zagros such as the Median and Persians tribal groups that made up the Achaemenid dynasty from which Artaxerxes I belonged.

translation; NIV merges the two sentences into one: "I gave orders to purify the rooms")

- "I put back the equipment ("vessels") of the house of God"

**Restoring the support of the house (13:10–14).** The next round of reforms is given no chronological marker and must be assumed to have occurred within the same context, in light of Eliashib's failure and Tobiah's disruptive presence within the sacred space of Zion. The confrontation with the "officials" shares the legal language of 5:6 (see commentary), "I contended" (author's translation; NIV "rebuked"), with the pointed question: "Why is the house of God neglected (*'azab*)?" (v. 11) in precise contradiction to the terms the leadership had agreed to uphold—"We will not abandon (*'azab*) the house of our God" (Neh 10:39). Nehemiah's response mirrors his decisiveness in dealing with Tobiah.

Upon summoning the community, "all Judah" returned their contributions ("tithes of grain, new wine and oil") to the storerooms (v. 12). Nehemiah promptly transitions Eliashib out of his position and replaces him with three individuals all mentioned by name. Headed by "Shelemiah the priest," all were "considered believing" (author's translation; NIV "trustworthy").[4] Nehemiah is hoping these appointments will create more accountability and prevent future problems. This is, in fact, the motivation of the first of four "remember" (*zakar*) prayers from Nehemiah in this final chapter. He is entrusting the continuity of the worship in Zion to "my God" and hoping his own work of *hesed* (lovingkindness; NIV "faithfully") will not be in vain (v. 14). The "blotting out" (*machah*) language is rich and harks back to the flood narrative and subsequent instances of great judgment in redemptive history (Gen 6:7; Exod 32:32; etc.) The usage in 2 Kings 21:13 is especially relevant is the context of the threat of yet another exile due to neglect (*'azab*). In this intercessory prayer, Nehemiah realizes all too well that the work accomplished to

---

4. The juxtaposition of the verb "to consider/credit" (Heb. *hashab*) paired with the adjective "believing" (from the root *'aman*) has a close parallel in Gen 15:6, "he believed (*'aman*) and it was credited (*hashab*) as righteousness." See commentary on Neh 9:8 and Neh 9:38. In the context of the failure of the officials to uphold their *'amanah* (Neh 9:38), Nehemiah is now looking for men who will have this kind of "reliability," in the sense that they will care enough to maintain the worship of Yahweh through careful oversight of the support for temple personnel.

restore Zion could quickly be wiped out as a result of Eliashib's grievous failure. The uncompromising standards of holiness in the worship of Yahweh continue to loom large in this narrative.

**Restoring the sanctity of Zion and of the Sabbath (13:15–22).** The reforms continue at a rapid pace ("in those days," v. 15), organized by three pointed addresses. Nehemiah speaks like a *bona fide* prophet and testifies in the first person: "I warned" (as a prophet would, see Neh 9:29) those who are violating both the Sabbath ("treading winepresses"; v. 15) and the terms of the agreement regarding "selling food on that day" in Jerusalem (v. 15; see 10:31). The details of "wine, grapes, figs" (v. 15) being carried into Jerusalem underscores that commerce did not go unabated at the time, which puts the neglect of the house of the LORD in a more somber light. The people had stopped caring for the house of Yahweh and conducted business as if the worship of Yahweh was unimportant.

The second address, "I rebuked the nobles of Judah" ("contended," author's translation, v. 17; see v. 11; 5:6), elicits a second question: "What is this wicked thing you are doing, desecrating ("defiling," author's translation) the Sabbath day?" (v. 17). The focus of Nehemiah's ire, the fish trade from Tyre (v. 16), combines the violation of the Sabbath law along with trading with the peoples of the land—non-Israelites (NIV "neighboring peoples"; see 10:31).

In light of the compromised spiritual security of the site, Nehemiah appropriately turns his attention to re-securing the sanctity of Zion by guarding who is allowed to come in on the Sabbath (v. 19). In a similar protocol to the measures related to the storerooms (v. 13), Nehemiah focuses on the prevention of violations. For this task, specific steps are taken, all marked by action verbs in the first person.

- "I ordered the doors to be shut" before dusk on the day before the Sabbath (v. 19).
- "I stationed some of my own men" (v. 19).
- "I warned" (see v. 15) traders who loitered around the gates on the Sabbath with physical threat. As a high-ranking Persian official, the verbal reprimand evidently stuck: "they no longer came on the Sabbath" (v. 21).
- "I commanded the Levites to purify (see 10:30) themselves" and to "guard the gates" (v. 22).

In conclusion, the purpose of the Sabbath reform is made explicitly clear: "in order to keep the Sabbath day holy" (*qadesh*, v. 22), which then prompts Nehemiah to invoke the second "remember me" prayer. He again appeals to *hesed*, only this time, it is Yahweh's own *hesed* (v. 22), which, combined with "mercy," recalls a similar appeal in the great prayer of confession of Neh 9 (see commentary). Nehemiah knows his premonarchical history, and he knows that Yahweh will not tolerate the defiling of his sacred space. The appeal to his mercy is a last resort, especially in light of the solemn agreement of the community (Neh 10). The individual dimension to the appeal must be noted, as well. As one whose name is first on the list of signatories (10:1), he is aware that by solidarity (see his prayer in chapter 1), he is complicit in the guilt of the community and is thereby liable to facing the consequences of others' disobedience, as well (e.g., Jeremiah the prophet who follows the people to Egypt).

**Restoring the sanctity of marriage (13:23–27).** The temporal tempo, marked by another "in those days" (vv. 15, 23) continues unabated ("moreover") and returns to a well-worn theme, both in the historical retrospective of Nehemiah 9 and in the context of Ezra's reforms (see commentary on Ezra 9–10). By couching the designations in clearly preexilic Philistine ("Ashdod"), Ammonite, and Moabite terms, the violation of the "men of Judah" finds no excuse (v. 23). The reference to the loss of the "language of Judah" (v. 24) simply compounds the extent of the dilution of their identity as the people of Yahweh. The structural format of a sequence of main verbs characterizing the report of reforms continues, as well. In quick succession (v. 25):

- "I rebuked them" (*rib* "contended")
- "I cursed them" (author's translation; *qalal*, NIV "and called curses down on them")
- "I beat[5] (*nakah*) some of the men"
- "I polished them" (root *marat*; NIV "pulled their hair")[6]
- "I caused them to swear by God" (NIV "made them take an oath")

---

5. In preexilic contexts, the verb is common in the context of warfare in conquest narratives ("struck"). While here it evidently cannot be translated as deadly force, nevertheless, the force of the action captured by this verb needs to be noted.

6. Hair removal was linked to shame and judgment in the available biblical tradition (e.g., Isa 7:20; 2 Sam 10:4), though natural baldness was not (Lev 13:40).

The oath itself focuses on the exchange of "daughters" and "sons" (v. 25) and essentially repeats the one that had already been taken in Nehemiah 10:30. However, the illustration from Israelite history is drawn from the most spectacular downfall in the royal annals—no other than David's own son, Solomon (v. 26). Solomon's superlative credentials ("there was no king like him"; "loved by his God," v. 26; see 12:45) did not prevent him from being "led into sin by foreign women" (v. 26). Thus, postexilic history also remembers Solomon's downfall as recorded in 1 Kings 11 (see 2 Chronicles 9 in contrast) whenever it is deemed important. Nehemiah's final question to them underscores the "terrible wickedness" (*hara'ah hagedolah*) and the unfaithfulness (*ma'al*) "to our God by marrying foreign women" (v. 27).

**Restoring the sanctity of the priesthood (13:28–31).** The final round of reform focuses on the priestly leadership, starting at the highest echelon, since the grandson of "Eliashib the high priest" was married to a daughter of "Sanballat the Horonite" (v. 28).The action taken by Nehemiah is as terse as it is effective: "I drove (*barah* e.g., to flee, Exod 14:5, etc.) him away from me" (v. 28). The third "remember" departs from the three others (one yet to follow in v. 31), since it returns to an imprecatory "remember them" (6:14) for their defilement of the priesthood through intermarriage. Nehemiah holds both the high priest and the culprit in equal contempt of God's Law (see 10:28, 30; cf. Lev 21:13–15).[7] The reference to the "covenant of the priesthood" (v. 29)[8] is unique but may very well deal with the covenantal obligations pertaining to them within the broader covenant of Sinai. Yahweh holds the ministers to his standards of holiness, and they are held accountable (Lev 10:1–3).

Nehemiah concludes his account with the focus on what ultimately mattered most to him (apart from the restoration of the wall): the preservation of the sanctity of Zion, including its leadership. The summary (see 10:34–35 and 12:30, 44–45) itself fronts and thereby emphasizes the purification process from "everything foreign" (v. 30). Attesting to a deep sense of commitment to the worship of Yahweh, Nehemiah singles himself out in assigning the spiritual leadership "duties, each to his own task" (v. 30). He took it upon himself to supervise the provision

---

7. Williamson, *Ezra, Nehemiah*, 401.

8. Forged through ordeal of the golden calf (Exod 32:28–29) and the sin of Baal Peor (Num 25:12–13).

of firewood (see 10:34) and "firstfruits" (v. 31; see 10:35). All these tasks were, of course, supposed to be overseen by the priests and Levites themselves. However, in light of the catastrophic failure witnessed upon his return, he, as a governor and non-Levite, took it upon himself to carry out the maintenance of the worship in Jerusalem, the holy city.

In the context of this tremendous (and lonely) responsibility comes the final "remember" prayer (v. 31): "Remember me, O my God, for good" (*tobah* NIV "favor"; author's translation). The shortest "remember" prayer of the chapter returns to his time of prayer in chapter 1 ("remember," 1:8) and recalls the "good" he received from the king (*tob*; 2:5, 6, 7, 8, 18 [2x]). Nehemiah thus ends his account on a wonderfully hopeful note. Just as he receives *tobah* at the outset of his ministry, he is asking his God to remember him for *tobah* at the very end of his ministry in Zion. Based on the existing record, and in light of subsequent history, we know that Nehemiah's prayer has been answered in ways far greater than he could have ever imagined.

**Zeal for the Lord.** Nehemiah confirms his place among the great Yahwists in this final chapter. He reminds us of another great Yahwist in ancient Israel, whose zeal for the house of the LORD was unquestioned. When King David entered the city of Jerusalem with the ark, he danced before the LORD (2 Sam 6:12–16). When he realized that the ark was sacred and cannot be handled like a mere object (2 Sam 6:6–11), he kept it away from Jerusalem and from himself, for fear that it would be defiled with the resulting deadly consequences. When it was time to bring the ark into Jerusalem, the Chronicler emphasizes the care with which the ark should be handled by the Levites, upon careful inquiry of the LORD and according to priestly regulations (cf. Num 4:15):

> Then David summoned Zadok and Abiathar the priests, and Uriel, Asaiah, Joel, Shemaiah, Eliel and Amminadab the Levites. He said to them, "You are the heads of the Levitical families; you and your fellow Levites are to consecrate yourselves and bring up the ark of the LORD, the God of Israel, to the place I have prepared for it. It was because you, the Levites, did not bring it up the first

> time that the LORD our God broke out in anger against us. We did not inquire of him about how to do it in the prescribed way." So the priests and Levites consecrated themselves in order to bring up the ark of the LORD, the God of Israel. And the Levites carried the ark of God with the poles on their shoulders, as Moses had commanded in accordance with the word of the LORD. (1 Chr 15:11–15)

Nehemiah also joins the long list of Yahwists who were not afraid to stand up to the spiritual leadership of Zion to challenge their wayward attitudes toward the cult and Yahweh's holiness.

However, perhaps the best precedent might be the earliest Levites who protected the sanctity of Yahweh's sacred space. Two events anchor the Levites into their ministry: at the time of the golden calf incident and its aftermath (Exod 32–34), but especially at the time of the Baal Peor deception (Num 25; Ps 106:28–31). Phinehas, Aaron's grandson (Num 25:7), is remembered "for endless generations to come" (Ps 106:31) in the specific context of illicit relationships with non-Yahwist Moabites and Midianites. When the New Testament recalls Baal Peor (the area of Khirbat al-Mukhayyat/Mount Nebo),[9] the sexual dimension of the idolatry of the people is made explicit (1 Cor 10:8; Rev 2:14). Phinehas's action against Zimri, a Simeonite tribal leader, and Cozbi, a Midianite princess, is particularly violent and graphic (Num 25:8). At the rate which the plague against Israel's sin spread in the camp, Phinehas's intervention recalls earlier confrontations between Yahweh's holiness and the people's sinfulness (Exod 32; Num 21). The sobering reality of the fundamental incompatibility of sin in the presence of the LORD jars us to this day and impresses upon readers through the ages the necessity of atoning measures to prevent the complete annihilation of the people (Num 25:13). This extreme-measure-for-an-extreme-situation approach points toward realities in the Old Covenant that can easily be lost upon those who live in the new covenantal administration (though dimensions of the implacability of Yahweh's holiness remain, e.g., Ananias

---

9. See Burton MacDonald, *East of the Jordan: Territories and Sites of the Hebrew Scriptures* (Alexandria, VA: American Schools of Oriental Research), 2001 for the best current historical geography of the Transjordan.

and Sapphira, Acts 5:1–11). To encounter the holy is a fearsome thing, whether you are a mighty prophet before the Lord (Isa 6:3–4), a devoted Yahwistic King (David; see above), or a priest, as in the case of Phinehas. That Phinehas's radical action is "credited to him as righteousness" (Ps 106:31) speaks much more of the fact that he essentially saved Israel from total destruction in the way "he stood up and intervened" (Ps 106:30, root *palal* often used also in the meaning to "pray") in what is shown to be a planned and intentional ploy to destroy Israel on the part of Balaam, Moab, and Midian (Num 25:18). In short, since the plan to use Balaam to curse Israel failed, Balaam, Moab, and Midian (e.g., the triumvirate of villains in Yehud) shifted tactics and pretended to turn Yahweh's standards of holiness against his own people. The enticement into idolatry (Ps 106:28) and sexual immorality (left out of the psalmist' account; implied in Num 25; explicit in the NT) *almost* worked, were it not for Phinehas's *in extremis* intervention. It is, in fact, Phinehas's zeal for Yahweh that is celebrated in Israel's communal memory of that sad day, rather than the gruesome act itself. In the recollected words of Yahweh (Num 25:10–13):

> The LORD said to Moses, "Phinehas son of Eleazar, the son of Aaron, the priest, has turned my anger away from the Israelites. Since he was as zealous for my honor among them as I am, I did not put an end to them in my zeal. Therefore tell him I am making my covenant of peace with him. He and his descendants will have a covenant of a lasting priesthood, because he was zealous for the honor of his God and made atonement for the Israelites."

Neither Nehemiah's nor Ezra's measures to protect the sanctity of Zion escalated to the crisis of Baal Peor, but his zeal and dedication do remind us that he stands upon the shoulders of others before him who stood and intervened with great courage. His own action of cleaning the chambers of the sacred space create an obvious bridge to Jesus's own housecleaning when it came to the priesthood (Luke 19:45–48). In this regard, he (and Ezra) is truly a forerunner who prepared the way for the return of the king to Zion, even if the rebuilt temple and the most spectacular aspect of the presence of Yahweh (the investiture of the Spirit of Exod 40:34 and 1 Kgs 8:10–11 / 2 Chr 5:13 is notably absent).

### Keeping the Sabbath

IN LIGHT OF THE SIGNIFICANCE of the gate system as a firewall to maintain the sanctity of the site, it is no wonder that Sabbath keeping and who can go in and out through the gates takes on such importance in the narrative (and the resulting consternation on Nehemiah's part). By way of a brief reminder, the fourth commandment is the most elaborate of the ten (Deut 5:6–21). Evidently, each of the Ten Commandments carries equal weight in its own way, but the fourth holds a particular significance since it regulates daily and weekly schedules. Embedded in the Deuteronomic version (see Exod 20 for the other complete version) is actually a total of four commandments:

1. Keep the day of Sabbath, "to keep it holy" (*qadash* word group, cf. Neh 3:1).
2. You shall labor and work the other six days.
3. You shall not work on the Sabbath.
4. You shall remember your redemption from slavery in Egypt.

The Sabbath regulated the cycle of life (along with the yearly feasts) in Israel. It was meant to give purpose to their week of work (what David Gill in his book *Doing Right*[10] calls "creation work"). The commandment puts the focus on the day of rest as an integral part of the week. In contrast, the work in Egypt was forced labor. To keep the Sabbath was a way to say, "We're done with slave work, now we do creation work unto the LORD."

The Old Testament talks about the Sabbath as physical rest, but it also takes on a spiritual sense. Whenever Israel returned to the LORD in repentance, the land would have "peace" in the sense of being at rest (root *shaqat*, e.g., Judg 3:11). Nehemiah 9:28 speaks of people resting from doing evil. So when Jesus announces his new Sabbath rest in the new covenant, he lives out the meaning of the original Sabbath: He fulfills the law by obeying the Great Commandment to love God with all your heart, soul, and strength (Deut 6:5–6) and to love your neighbor as yourself (Mark 12:30–31). He obeys Sabbath law when he heals people on the Sabbath and declares himself "Lord of the Sabbath." Paul will follow in Jesus's footsteps when he says the fulfillment of the law is to love our neighbor

---

10. D. Gill, *Doing Right: Practicing Ethical Principles* (Downers Grove, IL: InterVarsity Press, 2004).

as ourselves (Gal 5:14). Of course, this does not mean Paul unhitches himself from the law. Paul in Romans (3:31) will be careful to say "we uphold the law," but now the fulfillment of it is in Christ. The punishment of disobedience to the law has now been taken up by Jesus on the cross. He died for our sins so that we might live by faith in him (Gal 2:20). Nevertheless, the ethics of the kingdom of God are grounded in God's law as fulfilled in Christ, not apart from it. We obey the Sabbath law by keeping it holy just the same as Nehemiah, but now the definition of what the Sabbath means has been expanded. Paul explains in Romans 14:

> One person considers one day more sacred than another; another considers every day alike. Each of them should be fully convinced in their own mind. Whoever regards one day as special does so to the Lord. Whoever eats meat does so to the Lord, for they give thanks to God; and whoever abstains does so to the Lord and gives thanks to God. For none of us lives for ourselves alone, and none of us dies for ourselves alone. If we live, we live for the Lord; and if we die, we die for the Lord. So, whether we live or die, we belong to the Lord. For this very reason, Christ died and returned to life so that he might be the Lord of both the dead and the living. (Rom 14:5–9)

The context of this expanded definition remains firmly grounded in the Old Testament conception of holiness and rest. But now, we have already entered into the Sabbath rest (*sabbatismos*, Heb 4:8–10):

> For if Joshua had given them rest, God would not have spoken later about another day. There remains, then, a Sabbath-rest for the people of God; for anyone who enters God's rest also rests from their works, just as God did from his.

We will pick up the contemporary significance of the Sabbath rest and the theme of protecting the sanctity of Zion below.

**Qualifying the presence of Yahweh in the Second Temple.** The zeal of Nehemiah motif, indeed, the whole enterprise to restore the sanctity of Zion, raises the question as to how much of the glory of God dwelt in the newly-reestablished temple (see Ezra 6:13–18 and Commentary). The absence of an explicit description of the glory/Spirit filling the postexilic temple has been interpreted in different ways.[11] One outlook presumes the Spirit inhabited the new house in the same way as the Solomonic Temple. The other (favored in this commentary) views the presence of God in the Second Temple in qualified terms.

Any argument will need to deal with Matthew 23:21, which implies God dwells in the Second Temple. However, some qualification needs to be applied before we can use Jesus's words as inconvertible evidence the glory/Spirit filled the Second Temple. The larger context of the Matthean account is the famous seven woes of Jesus against the scribes and Pharisees (Matt 23:1–39) who have transformed the prescribed worship into ritualistic minutia at the expense of the "more important matters of the law" (Matt 23:23). Jesus condemns their worship outright and shows them what is actually "sacred" ("sanctified" root *hagiazo* Matt 23:17, 19; see Contemporary Significance). Jesus concludes: "your house is left to you desolate (*eremos*)," also with the meaning of wilderness (Matt 23:38). This stunning declaration regarding the Second Temple worship system prepares the way for the Olivet Discourse and the impending destruction of the physical temple (Matthew 24:1–2). A new way to worship God has come.

Yet, in this condemnation Jesus upholds (and affirms Ezra-Nehemiah's effort) the established biblical tradition that deems the temple "sacred." He also affirms that God dwells in the temple (root *katoikeo* "to live"; see discussion below) in the same way that God sits on his throne in heaven:

> Woe to you, blind guides! You say, "If anyone swears by the temple, it means nothing; but anyone who swears by the gold of the temple is bound by that oath." You blind fools! Which is greater: the gold, or the temple that makes the gold sacred? You also say, "If anyone swears by the altar, it means nothing; but anyone who swears by the gift on the altar is bound by that oath." You blind men! Which is greater: the gift, or the altar that makes the gift sacred? Therefore, anyone who swears by the altar swears by it and by everything on it. And anyone who swears by the temple swears by it and by the one who dwells in it. And anyone who swears by heaven swears by God's throne and by the one who sits on it. (Matt 23:16–22)

11. J. Greene, "Did God Dwell in the Second Temple? Clarifying the Relationship Between Theophany and Temple Dwelling," *JETS* 61.4 (2018): 767–84.

Thus, we could a priori construe that the divine presence "dwells" in the temple in continuity with the preexilic tradition of the glory/presence in the tabernacle and the Solomonic temple.

However, a more cautious stance acknowledges that whatever activity of the Spirit remained (see Haggai and Zechariah, who both assume the rebuilding process in the postexilic period is Spirit led), it could in no way be compared to what happened in the preexilic era when the glory presence of Yahweh filled both the tabernacle and the Solomonic temple. Such a momentous event is not recorded in Ezra-Nehemiah. If it had happened, the writers would have surely made note of it (the view espoused in this commentary).

Without entering into a protracted discussion here, it is worth noting the variety of vocabulary used in the LXX (Greek Old Testament), in contrast with a consistent usage in the Hebrew Old Testament, to describe the glory/presence (Heb. root *shakan*) of Yahweh. A few examples of how *shakan* is translated in the LXX are listed here:

- Exodus 24:16 [*katabaino*]
- Exodus 40:35 [*episkiazo*]
- Deuteronomy 12:5 [*eiserchomai*]
- Deuteronomy 33:12 [*skiazo*]
- 1 Kings 8:12 [LXX v. 10, 11 *pimplami*]
- Ezekiel 43:7 [*kataskanoo*]

In contrast, LXX is much more consistent in its translation of Heb. *yashab*[12] with the usage of Greek *katoikeo*. In the instances where Yahweh dwells/*yashab* (LXX *katoikeo*) somewhere, it is usually referring to his home in heaven (e.g., Ps 2:4), rather than a specific sense of the presence of the Spirit in the tabernacle or temple, as is the case with *shakan*. First Kings 8:27 / 2 Chronicles 6:18 is telling in this respect:

> But will God really dwell [Heb. *yashab*; Gk. *katoikeo*] on earth with humans? The heavens, even the highest heavens, cannot contain you. How much less this temple I have built!

---

12. Dwelling, as in living somewhere, e.g., Gen 13:7; 1 Kgs 8:27; 2 Chr 6:18 (in the case of Yahweh).

The (few) occasions in the LXX where the vocabulary of Matthew 23:21 is used (*katoikeo*) to describe Yahweh's presence (root *shakan*)[13] provide a parallel to Jesus's usage with the designation "the one who dwells in it" (*katoikounti*) and serves as a generic and formulaic designation for God (per the context of Matt 23 and his condemnation of the scribes and Pharisees' practices). *However,* when the language specifically speaks of the Spirit/presence of the Lord in the temple/tabernacle, in the LXX the language of *skēnoō* to describe the *shakan* glory of Yahweh is used instead.

In this regard, the contrast in the corpus is quite apparent on two occasions:

- Numbers 35:34, "Do not defile the land where you live and where I dwell, for I, the LORD, dwell among the Israelites.'"

This verse differentiates where the people live (= *katoikeo*/Heb. *yashab*) with where Yahweh dwells/*shakan* in the midst of Israel = *kataskanoo.*

In Jeremiah's temple sermon, Jeremiah 7:3, 7, and 12 also contrast usage pertaining to Yahweh versus the people along the same lines:

- Jeremiah 7:3 (cf. v. 7) "This is what the LORD Almighty, the God of Israel, says: Reform your ways and your actions, and I will let you live [Heb. *shakan*/Gk. *katoikeo*] in this place."

But when Yahweh's dwelling is mentioned in the same context in Jeremiah 7:12, *shakan* becomes *kataskanoo*:

- "'Go now to the place in Shiloh where I first made a dwelling for my Name [verb *shakan*], and see what I did to it because of the wickedness of my people Israel."

Thus, Hebrew *shakan*—Greek *kataskanoo* seems the more consistent pairing in LXX to characterize Yahweh's glory/presence specifically, not *katoikeo.* This observation is consistent with the usage in John 1:14 *skenoo*/to dwell to describe the personified glory/Spirit in the incarnation

13. E.g., Isa 8:18 (lit., "The Lord of Hosts who dwells on Mount Zion"); 33:5 (lit. "he who dwells on high"); 57:15 (lit. "the one dwelling forever").

(from the language which we get our English word for the tabernacle).[14] In other words, there is a material difference between the generic and formulaic phrase "he who dwells [*katoikeo*] in it" used by Jesus (and no doubt used by the scribes and Pharisees in their appeal to the sacredness of the Second Temple) and the technical description [*kataskanoo*, among others] of the filling of the temple with the glory of God. Further, this material difference carries considerable weight in the context of Jesus's condemnation of the temple as a wasteland in his city lament and prophecy against Jerusalem (Matt 23:38; 24). Jesus was careful to use a more generic/formulaic terminology to appeal to God's presence in the temple, especially since he is about to characterize the temple/house as a wasteland! Instead, in true prophetic terms, Jesus equates their misguided view of worship and God's dwelling on earth to an abandoned field and vain pursuits (e.g., Mic 3:12; Isa 1:11–15) which, within a few decades, will be realized (AD 70). Nevertheless, Jesus's words carry enough nuance to recognize the sanctity of the temple as restored by Ezra-Nehemiah so that the temple remains ground zero to meet God on earth, even if the glory/Spirit never returned to fill the space in the second temple.

These observations also match the view of Old Testament eschatological prophets (with Isaiah leading the charge; Isa 2:1–4) who recognize a glory/Spirit vacuum since the Spirit would only return in the eschatological temple in its full manifestation (Hag 2). Ezekiel looks forward to the return of the glory/Spirit via the East Gate (Ezek 43:4–5):[15]

> The glory of the Lord entered the temple through the gate facing east. Then the Spirit lifted me up and brought me into the inner court, and the glory of the Lord filled the temple.

Thus, the promise of the glory/presence to fill the temple is yet to come (Ezekiel 43:7), and it would be quite the strain on the redemptive-historical process to attach this glorious prophetic vision to what happened in Yehud, as wonderful and as Spirit-filled as the work of Joshua/Zerubabbel/Ezra/Nehemiah was. Ezekiel continues,

---

14. D. A. Carson, *The Gospel According to John*, PNTC (Leicester: Apollos, 1991), 126–27.

15. D. L. Petter, *Ezekiel*. Forthcoming.

> He said: "Son of man, this is the place of my throne and the place for the soles of my feet. This is where I will live [Heb. *shakan*; Gk. *kataskanoo*] among the Israelites forever. The people of Israel will never again defile my holy name—neither they nor their kings—by their prostitution and the funeral offerings for their kings at their death." (Ezek 43:7)

Of course, Nehemiah's reforms precisely seek to remove, yet again, the threat of defiling Yahweh's name. In contrast, in the eschatological temple and his presence, this threat is forever removed.

Turning to the New Testament, the evidence casts the return of the Spirit to the temple in eschatological terms in Acts 2, adumbrated by Jesus who is the manifestation of the glory of God (John 1). The intersection of God's glory/Spirit with the Herodian Temple only occurs when Jesus actually walks through it. He makes it quite clear to those so impressed with mortar and bricks that his "temple" is no longer the Herodian structure (John 2:19), as impressive as it might have been (e.g., Josephus Flavius's description).[16] Thus, there is a deliberate effort in the Gospels to create a separation between the glory made manifest through the incarnation and the Herodian Temple. It appears the nuance of vocabulary in Matthew 23:21 actually bolsters the claim that something (or rather Someone) is missing from the First Temple to the Second Temple. Rhetorically speaking, we might paraphrase the words of Jesus's condemnation in Matthew 23:21 in the following way: Yes, indeed, God is the one who lives in the temple, according to tradition, but you have defiled his temple and presence so that the temple is now no more than a wasteland! This, of course, came true until the Romans built a pagan city upon Mount Zion (Aelia Capitolina by Hadrian, AD 130). So in the end, Jesus would say to the scribes and Pharisees the same thing Jeremiah said to the deceived brokers of God's presence in Jerusalem: you say "the Temple of the LORD, the Temple of the LORD, the Temple of the LORD;" that is, "Are you sure God is with you in this?" (Jer 7:4).

Returning now to the context of Nehemiah's radical reforms in chapter 13, it is crucial to emphasize that in spite of these qualifications

---

16. G. K. Beale, *The Temple and the Church's Mission: A Biblical Theology of the Dwelling Place of God* (Downers Grove, IL: IVP Academic, 2014).

and the notable absence of a moment such as Exodus 40 or 1 Kings 8/2 Chronicles 6 in the Second Temple, Nehemiah also knows that without the sanctity of Zion preserved, the wrath of God and a repeat of exile is only a few Deuteronomic cycles away, as in the first generation. His fury at the people's sins will be no match for Yahweh's own, once his patience runs out. The determination to deal aggressively with the people's sin comes from a deep realization that they are in serious danger of being cast away one more time (see Ezra 9–10).

It is, therefore, in this context of eschatological expectation and the promise of a glorious house yet to come (Hag 2:9) that the ongoing theme of the sanctity of marriage (intermarriage with non-Yahwists viewed as "terrible wickedness," Neh 13:27), along with the sanctity of the Sabbath and the priesthood, are presented as Nehemiah's final actions.

This theme of *be holy as you wait* carries into the New Testament, as well (1 Pet 1:16; 1 Thess 4:3, etc.), including some of the very last words of the canon: "Blessed are those who wash their robes, that they may have the right to the tree of life and may go through the gates into the city. Outside are the dogs, those who practice magic arts, the sexually immoral, the murderers, the idolaters and everyone who loves and practices falsehood" (Rev 22:14–15). Thus, holiness matters from the beginning to the end of redemptive history. Adam and Eve were expelled out of the gates of the primeval sacred precinct. Unbelievers will be kept out of the eschatological Zion, since without "holiness no one will see the Lord" (Hebrews 12:14). The wrath of God against all sin, idolatry, and spiritual uncleanness is yet to be fully realized (Col 3:5–6), hence Paul's sense of certainty and urgency in Ephesians 5:5–7.

> For of this you can be sure: No immoral, impure or greedy person—such a person is an idolater—has any inheritance in the kingdom of Christ and of God. Let no one deceive you with empty words, for because of such things God's wrath comes on those who are disobedient. Therefore do not be partners with them.

The simple yet profound and stubborn fact is the Lord, in turn, expects his people to live in holiness (1 Thess 4:3), a holiness firmly grounded on Old Testament precedent.

**What does holiness look like today?** The call to remember the zeal of Nehemiah is also our call. We want to be remembered for what we have accomplished for the Lord, just as Phinehas was (though now we look to Christ for substitutionary salvation with his death and resurrection). We, too, uphold the sanctity of Zion as the will of God for our lives (1 Thess 4:3). Now, however, Christ is the one who makes us holy by faith in him (Acts 26:18). The Corinthians are declared "holy" by Paul (1 Cor 1:2) in spite of the temple's need for serious reforms:

> Or do you not know that wrongdoers will not inherit the kingdom of God? Do not be deceived: Neither the sexually immoral nor idolaters nor adulterers nor men who have sex with men nor thieves nor the greedy nor drunkards nor slanderers nor swindlers will inherit the kingdom of God. And that is what some of you were. But you were washed, you were sanctified, you were justified in the name of the Lord Jesus Christ and by the Spirit of our God. (1 Cor 6:9–11)
>
> Flee from sexual immorality. All other sins a person commits are outside the body, but whoever sins sexually, sins against their own body. Do you not know that your bodies are temples of the Holy Spirit, who is in you, whom you have received from God? You are not your own; you were bought at a price. Therefore, honor God with your bodies. (1 Cor 6:18–20)

Thus, the life of the Christian holds parallels to the situation Nehemiah faces. We, too, are waiting for the return of the King and find ourselves in this eschatological tension. We also know the fragility and brokenness of our lives (a "tent" Paul calls it, 2 Cor 5:1). These temples, filled with some but not the full measure of his glory, are only a preparation for the glory that is yet to come. It would be so easy to get discouraged and falter, but the "blessed hope" (Titus 2:13) is the driver for our motivation not to give up on the "temple" and the worship of the living God. We cry out with Paul, "Who will deliver me from this body of death?" (Rom 7:24 ESV).

A cursory look at Israelite and church history, in general, provides a sobering assessment as to the people of Zion's ability to keep their promise. The oath, "We will not neglect the house of our God" (Neh 10:39), seems to be broken repeatedly. Who has not faltered or procrastinated on a promise, whether financial or professional? Who has been always consistent in providing for the financial needs of the church, both at the local and the global level? Who has kept the temple from being defiled in light of Jesus's amplified version of the commandment against adultery, Sabbath keeping, and so on? The reality is that none of us have kept all our promises, all the time. If anything, the application of Nehemiah 13 should be a guard against judging the members of the community of Yehud too harshly, for we, too, can easily fall into the same patterns. It is tempting for us to quit at times (e.g., Paul, who at the end in 2 Tim was left alone, but "the Lord stood by my side," 4:17), but, just like Nehemiah, we call upon the Lord to remember us in his favor and as Paul reassures Timothy, the Lord "gave me strength" (2 Tim 4:17). Paul took solace in the divine presence. He knew that Jesus would never leave Him nor abandon Him. We do the same, knowing that "we are more than conquerors" in Christ Jesus (cf. Rom 8:37). We are filled with his Spirit and he helps us in our weakness (including this frail body that still carries the judgment of death upon itself) until we receive the redemption of our bodies and eternal life, finally free from the oppression of sin, death, and the devil. Romans 8 in its entirety anchors our hope in this promise of holiness and a freedom from sin that has begun now but also has yet to be fully experienced.

### Entering the Sabbath Rest

*CHARIOTS OF FIRE* IS A BELOVED MOVIE WITH PROFOUND MEANING. Made on a shoe-string budget, the movie took Hollywood by surprise when it garnered four Academy Awards, including Best Picture for 1982. The movie has a sort of *Downton Abbey* feel and contains the classic ingredients that make for a compelling story: pride and honor, conscience, victory, self-denial, and prejudice. Eric Liddell has a dual calling: he is to become a missionary to China, and he is a fast, Olympic-level runner. In his conversation with his sister Jennie, he explains it very well. Eric learned not to compartmentalize his life. He could run for God and he could be a missionary all at once (tragically, he would later die in China during WWII).

But this conviction was tested by his calendar. At the Paris Olympics in 1924, Eric could not bring himself to run a heat on the Sabbath

(Sunday), so he decided, against enormous pressure from the British Olympic Committee—and the Prince of Wales, no less—to forgo his strongest distance (100-meter dash). However, through the self-sacrifice of one of his team members who gave up his place in 400-meter final, Eric was able to win his gold medal after all. We may question his strict attitude toward sports on the Lord's Day (Rev 1:10); in fact, even John Calvin felt it could be ok to play some sports on Sunday. However, no one will ever question his admirable stance to let God be Lord of his calendar of events. In fact, while in a prison camp in China, Eric did relax his stance and started coaching sports on Sundays. He knew the true meaning of the Sabbath reached beyond the letter of the law into helping the kids have fun in their sufferings. Randy Alcorn has compiled a powerful collage of witnesses about Eric's life as a prisoner in China:

> Margaret shared with us a story that illustrated this man's Christ-like character. In the camp, the children played basketball, rounders, and hockey, and Eric Liddell was their referee. Not surprisingly, he refused to referee on Sundays. But in his absence, the children fought. Liddell struggled over this. He believed he shouldn't stop the children from playing because they needed the diversion.
>
> Finally, Liddell decided to referee on Sundays. This made a deep impression on Margaret—she saw that the athlete world famous for sacrificing success for principle was not a legalist. When it came to his own glory, Liddell would surrender it all rather than run on Sunday. But when it came to the good of children in a prison camp, he would referee on Sunday.
>
> Liddell would sacrifice a gold medal for himself (though he ultimately won the gold in a different race) in the name of truth but would bend over backward for others in the name of grace.[17]

When Jesus sends his universal call to find rest for our souls in him (Matthew 11:28–30), he is telling us to enter into his perpetual ongoing Sabbath rest (see Hebrews 4:8–10). We no longer work so that we can rest (a sort of TGIF mentality of work hard and play hard). Instead, we rest in

---

17. Randy Alcorn, "The Little Known Story of Olympian Eric Liddell's Final Years," *Eternal Perspectives Ministries*, February 12, 2018, https://www.epm.org/blog/2018/Feb/12/olympian-eric-liddell

Jesus so that we can work. To enter the Sabbath rest of the Lord also has a focal point of one day when we recalibrate our lives and remind ourselves why we are here. In God, we are not machines in need of a pause on the assembly line of life. We have a far greater purpose. Some are made to be missionaries to China and athletes; others are made for the purpose of working at a grocery store, being a good mother, husband, and so on. We all have our holy calling, and the Sabbath rest that Jesus is calling us into is the weekly reminder of that. Thus, the Sabbath will look different for all of us, but it achieves the same outcome from compartmentalization to integration in our lives. In fact, this goal for integration in our lives is another way to get at the application of holiness in a contemporary setting.

Finally, the call to Sabbath rest in Matthew 11:28–30 contrasts the yoke and burden of slave work with the yoke and burden that is the gentleness of Jesus himself (John 15:5). We shed the burden of our unrealistic expectations and the tyranny of the busyness of our lives, and we embrace his rest with a light burden and an easy yoke (actually the word is kind/good; cf. Rom 2:4; 1 Pet 2:3). Paul puts it in starker terms in Galatians 5:1, "for freedom Christ has set us free; stand firm therefore, and do not submit again to a yoke of slavery" (ESV, see Matt 23:4). We may not struggle with the legalism of Paul's day and our attitude to Old Testament law, as is the context of Galatians, but we have our own brand of heavy yoke and burden. We get tangled up with the same root problem: the restlessness of self-achievement and performance. We are doing slave work "in Egypt" more often than we care to admit!

But as we choose to rest and abide in him, an extraordinary (and counterintuitive) thing happens: our productivity goes up (John 15:5). It is rooted in him that we will bear much fruit (and we will let him define as to what that fruitfulness means for each of us). This is precisely what happened to Eric Liddell. He gave up the almost-certain victory for the 100-meter dash and instead ran a distance he was not supposed to win. But as his American rival Jackson Scholz wrote on a note for Eric in *Chariots of Fire*: "It says in the old Book: He who honors me, I will honor." This will be true for us as well.

### Nehemiah as a Leadership Manual?

NEHEMIAH IS OFTEN PROPPED AS A LEADERSHIP MANUAL, but I am not convinced at all that the book provides some sort of formula and guarantee for success in the modern context. Each one of us has to carry our own cross in ministry. Nevertheless, Nehemiah's knowledge of Scripture; his ability to apply that knowledge to the particular context; his courage to make highly unpopular decisions; and his skills to mobilize a highly fragmented, conflicted, and disengaged group of people are the dream of many pastors and leaders. His care and attention not to fleece the sheep stands as a rebuke to all health-and-wealth preachers who prey on the poor congregants with promises of financial breakthrough. Nehemiah's loyalty to both the Persian king and the King of kings is nothing short of exemplary. He truly fulfills the injunction to "honor the emperor," as the apostle Peter puts it (1 Pet 2:17). In the modern world, where even democracies are shown to be highly dysfunctional with corrupt leaders, immoral laws, and rampant injustice, Nehemiah puts the challenge before us both to challenge the established leadership when needed (keeping in mind that no one in the modern world lives in a theocracy where we can enforce God's laws upon our culture) while at the same time honoring the established pagan authorities in place.

Apart from the above qualities, Nehemiah's love for Zion caused him to answer the call. He was moved by the plight of Jerusalem (which for us translates as God's people). He showed up in Yehud and intervened at critical junctures in the process. He was there when he needed to be. In my four decades of experience watching folks in positions of responsibilities, there is a common thread. Once a person checks out and simply fills in the hours (or not, as the case may be), the whole system unravels. Conversely, if the person stays present and in contact with the process and the people, things tend to run a lot more smoothly. Even if the person is not the most highly skilled or experienced (Nehemiah had no prior gubernatorial experience before becoming the governor of Yehud), he or she can expect benefits that far outweigh an attitude of an Eliashib, always ready to make deals to compromise and to pursue his own gain (as some the governors prior to Nehemiah's tenure did). While the narrative is silent as to the long absence of Nehemiah from Yehud (though the commission required him to return to the court of the king), the absence of Nehemiah subsequent to the dedication of the wall created a great vacuum in Zion, which he himself had to fill again.

**Cross-centered hermeneutics.**[18] The zeal of Nehemiah ultimately

18. This historic orthodox model (per the Apostle's Creed; e.g., Leon Morris, *The Apostolic Preaching of the Cross* [Grand Rapids: Eerdmans, 1955]) is not to be confused with

falls short, as did Saul of Tarsus (Gal 1:14) and everyone else who thinks building the kingdom of God is accomplished through our own will power, aptitudes, or an unhealthy focus on ritual (see Matt 23). The sanctifying process of Zion finds its fulfillment, as our zeal for God's people and the establishment of his kingdom, in Christ alone. He alone is our sanctification (1 Cor 1:30), and he is the one at work in us to do and will according to his good and perfect will. We offer ourselves as "living sacrifices," which is our "spiritual worship" (Rom 12:1–2). At the cross, Jesus reveals for us the "weightier matters of the law": self-sacrifice, love of our enemies, and self-emptying (Phil 2) rather than the pursuit of vainglorious ambition.

Christ's work on the cross was not a senseless act of violence but was a self-sacrifice by God the Son who chose to offer himself up as an atoning sacrifice for the despondency of the people of Zion in Yehud, in our days, and in the future—until he returns to establish his kingdom. Thus, apart from Christ's work on the cross, we will not understand the implacability of God's holiness and his complete intolerance for the presence of sin in his presence (including Ezra's actions to break up marriages and Nehemiah's advocacy to separate). However complex these ethical questions get, we do know that at the cross, Christ experienced the injustice of a violent death as an innocent party. Christ tasted injustice. We put our trust in him and in the vindication against all injustice. The resurrection is the beginning of the restoration of justice that will be fulfilled when he returns. He will judge everyone according to what he or she has done (Rom 14:10). Those who have placed their faith in him will be found justified (whose justified state will be justified by their just actions) and those who continued to reject his gracious offer of salvation will find themselves permanently outside the gates of the holy city (Rev 22:15). Thus as we, too, are the guardians of Zion, we continue to make the gates of the city open at day time, as it were, so that whosoever believes in him would not perish but have eternal life (John 3:16).

---

some other recent approaches also focused on the cross and resurrection as central to the history of redemption (Gregory Boyd, *The Crucifixion of the Warrior God* [Philadelphia: Fortress, 2017]). In our case, the cross provides a solution to the reality of the wrath of God, satisfied at the cross, yet to come in the final judgment, but still with us in our body of death until the resurrection. Boyd's approach flatly denies that God would and could be capable of wrath. See Trevor Laurence, "Review of *The Crucifixion of the Warrior God: Interpreting the Old Testament's Violent Portraits of God in Light of the Cross*," Themelios 42.3 (2017).

# Scripture Index


**Genesis**

book of . . . . . 364
1 . . . . . 365
1:1 . . . . . 395
2 . . . . . 365
2:3 . . . . . 423
2:4 . . . . . 364
2:18, 20 . . . . . 181
2:24 . . . . . 423
3 . . . . . 220
3:1–7 . . . . . 214
3:8 . . . . . 383
3:15 . . . . . 65, 137
4:8 . . . . . 285
5:1 . . . . . 364
6:7 . . . . . 461
6:9 . . . . . 364
10:1 . . . . . 364
11:10, 27 . . . . . 364
12 . . . . . 64, 335, 396
12:1–2 . . . . . 396
12:1–3 . . . . . 33, 64, 87, 139, 156, 210, 217
12:3 . . . . . 135, 156, 158
12:7 . . . . . 87
13:7 . . . . . 471
15 . . 64, 217, 333, 396, 420
15:6 . . . 89, 210, 376, 396, 397, 413, 461
15:12–21 . . . . . 217
15:16 . . . . . 210
15:18 . . . . . 413
15:18–21 . . . . . 396
15:19–20 . . . . . 210
17:8 . . . . . 87, 396
19:30–38 . . . . . 285
21:14 . . . . . 247
21:31–32 . . . . . 235
22:17 . . . . . 396
24:3, 7 . . . . . 55
25:12, 19 . . . . . 364
26:3 . . . . . 57, 416
27:41 . . . . . 285
29:34 . . . . . 79
31:3 . . . . . 57
32:28 . . . . . 163
36:1, 9 . . . . . 364
37–40 . . . . . 285
37:2 . . . . . 364
37:34 . . . . . 256
41:15–16 . . . . . 272
43–44 . . . . . 336
43:9 . . . . . 330
44:32 . . . . . 330
49:5 . . . . . 79
50:3 . . . . . 53

**Exodus**

book of . . . . . 89, 113
1 . . . . . 177
1:10 . . . . . 135
1:15–16, 22 . . . . . 135
2:1 . . . . . 449
2:23 . . . . . 393, 403
2:23–25 . . . . . 215
2:24–25 . . . . . 258
3:7–9 . . . . . 215
3:12 . . . . . 29, 57, 378
3:13–15 . . . . . 113
3:18 . . . . . 29
3:19–20 . . . . . 177
3:22 . . . . . 421
4:23 . . . . . 29
5:3 . . . . . 29
6 . . . . . 177
6:2–3 . . . . . 257
6:2–8 . . . . . 113
6:7 . . . . . 87, 116
6:7–9 . . . . . 77
6:8 . . . . . 88
6:12–24 . . . . . 77
6:13 . . . . . 234
6:16–27 . . . . . 449
6:27 . . . . . 234
7:4–5 . . . . . 177
9:27 . . . . . 218, 220
9:29 . . . . . 213
12:6 . . . . . 165, 166
12:14 . . . . . 165
12:15–20 . . . . . 165
12:23 . . . . . 165, 170
12:35 . . . . . 58
12:38 . . . . . 29, 90
12:42 . . . . . 234
13:9 . . . . . 177
13:12–13 . . . . . 419
13:14, 16 . . . . . 177
14:5 . . . . . 464
14:9 . . . . . 397
14:11 . . . . . 234
14:14 . . . . . 354
15 . . . . . 380, 397
15:1–21 . . . . . 29, 125
15:11 . . . . . 316, 397
15:17 . . . . . 400, 433
18:4 . . . . . 181
19–20 . . . . . 179
19:4–6 . . . . . 238
19:6 . . . . . 116, 210, 423
20 . . . . . 396, 468
20:1–2 . . . . . 113
20:6 . . . . . 258
20:22 . . . . . 362
21:2 . . . . . 336
21:2–4 . . . . . 248
21:24 . . . . . 311
22:25 . . . . . 332, 336
23:11 . . . . . 417
23:14–17 . . . . . 107
23:15 . . . . . 165
24 . . . . . 413
24–40 . . . . . 79
24:3, 7 . . . . . 239
24:12 . . . . . 175
24:16 . . . . . 471
25–31 . . . . . 167, 301, 365
25:1–7 . . . . . 84
25:2–9 . . . . . 84
27:1–8 . . . . . 100, 101
27:19 . . . . . 214
28–29 . . . . . 175
28:1 . . . . . 79

28:29 . . . 99
28:30 . . . 83
29 . . . 164
29:38–42 . . . 105, 234
30:1–10 . . . 100
30:11–16 . . . 418
31:1–6 . . . 364
31:18 . . . 189
32 . . . 257, 259, 466
32–34 . . . 218, 258, 466
32:1–6 . . . 214, 398
32:1–7 . . . 232
32:9 . . . 398
32:11 . . . 259, 260
32:11–14 . . . 219
32:12 . . . 230
32:13 . . . 217, 260
32:25–29 . . . 247
32:28 . . . 221
32:28–29 . . . 464
32:29 . . . 79
32:30–32 . . . 219
32:32 . . . 461
32:35 . . . 221
33:13 . . . 120
33:18 . . . 117
33:19 . . . 117, 120
34:1–7 . . . 113
34:5–6 . . . 395, 396, 398
34:5–7 . . 117, 216, 221, 258
34:6 . . . 216
34:6–7 . . 113, 120, 220, 405
34:7 . . . 221, 244
34:8–9 . . . 217
34:9 . . . 221
34:11 . . . 210
34:11–16 . . . 211
34:19–20 . . . 419
34:22–23 . . . 107
34:26 . . . 419
34:28 . . . 236
35–39 . . . 365
35:18 . . . 214
35:21–29 . . . 84
35:29 . . . 58
36:3 . . . 58
38:1–7 . . . 100
38:25–26 . . . 418
40 . . . 475
40:1–38 . . . 450
40:34–35 . . . 168
40:34–38 . . . 167, 168
40:35 . . . 471

**Leviticus**

book of . . . 231
1:3–17 . . . 101
2 . . . 101
2:13 . . . 133
5:14–19 . . . 240
6:2 . . . 212
6:8–13 . . . 101
6:14–23 . . . 101
7:21 . . . 236
8 . . . 165
8–10 . . . 445
8:8 . . . 83
10 . . . 210
10:1–3 . . . 464
11:44 . . . 423
13:40 . . . 463
15 . . . 246
16:1–34 . . . 99
18 . . . 184, 230
18:26–30 . . . 218
18:28 . . . 238
19:2 . . . 210
19:18 . . . 286
21:1 . . . 460
21:13–15 . . . 464
23 . . . 372, 379
23:1–32 . . . 108
23:5 . . . 165
23:6 . . . 372
23:6–8 . . . 165
23:23 . . . 372
23:23–25 . . . 98, 371
23:26 . . . 372
23:26–32 . . . 98
23:32 . . . 98
23:33 . . . 372
23:33–43 . . . 98, 107
23:36 . . . 380
23:39 . . . 379
23:40 . . . 379
25:4–7, 20–22 . . . 417
25:23 . . . 88
25:35–37 . . . 336
26:3 . . . 243
26:4–13 . . . 243
26:12 . . . 453
26:40 . . . 212
26:40–45 . . . 215
26:41–45 . . . 64
26:42 . . . 64
26:43–44 . . . 64
26:45 . . . 64

**Numbers**

book of . . . 396
1:2 . . . 317
2:1–2 . . . 302
3–4 . . . 79
3:5–6 . . . 79
4:3 . . . 111
4:15 . . . 465
5:6 . . . 212
5:21 . . . 416
5:22 . . . 376
5:29 . . . 416
8:11, 15 . . . 79
8:19 . . . 79
8:24 . . . 111
9:5 . . . 165
10:10 . . . 108
10:35 . . . 302
14:9 . . . 317
14:10–12 . . . 216
14:17–19 . . . 216, 217
14:20–35 . . . 216
15:1–10 . . . 101
16:40 . . . 79
18:12 . . . 419
18:15–17 . . . 419
18:19 . . . 133
18:21–24 . . . 419
18:26 . . . 419
21 . . . 396, 466
21:5 . . . 408
21:21–35 . . . 400
21:23–35 . . . 399
22:1–6 . . . 135
23–24 . . . 448
25 . . . 466
25:7 . . . 466
25:8 . . . 466
25:10–13 . . . 467
25:12–13 . . . 464
25:13 . . . 466
25:18 . . . 467
27:18 . . . 178
27:21 . . . 83
28:1–8 . . . 105, 234

28:1–29:11 . . . . . . . . . 108
28:4. . . . . . . . . . . . . . . 213
28:11–15 . . . . . . . . . . . 108
29:1. . . . . . . . . . . . . . . .98
29:1–11 . . . . . . . . . . . . 107
29:12–38. . . . . . . . . . . 107
35:34. . . . . . . . . . . . . . 472

Deuteronomy

book of. . . . . . . . . . . . 231
2:24–27 . . . . . . . . . . . 399
3:1–11 . . . . . . . . . . . . . 399
4 . . . . . . . . . . . . . . . . . 416
4–5 . . . . . . . . . . . . . . . 416
4:5 . . . . . . . . . . . . . . . 218
4:6 . . . . . . . . . . . . . . . 190
4:31. . . . . . . . . . . . . . . 235
4:44–45 . . . . . . . . . . . 259
4:45 . . . . . . . . . . . . . . 416
5:6–21 . . . . . . . . . . . . 468
5:7. . . . . . . . . . . . . . . . 417
6 . . . . . . . . . . . . . . . . . 179
6:5 . . . . . . . . . . . . . . . 323
6:5–6 . . . . . . . . . . . . . 468
6:11. . . . . . . . . . . . . . . 400
7 . . . . . . . . . . . . . . . . . 257
7:1 . . . . . . . . . . . . . . . 210
7:1–4. . . . . . . . . . 213, 218
7:1–5. . . . . . . . . . . . . . 211
7:1–6. . . . . . . . . . 211, 230
7:1–7. . . . . . . . . . . . . . 211
7:1–11 . . . . . . . . . . . . . 31
7:2–4. . . . . . . . . . . . . . 244
7:6. . . . . . . 210, 238, 244
7:8. . . . . . . . . . . . . . . . 416
7:21 . . . . . . . . . . . . . . . 258
8:1–4. . . . . . . . . . . . . . 399
8:1—12. . . . . . . . . . . . 401
9 . . . . . . . . . . . . . . . . . 257
9:18, 25. . . . . . . . . . . . 232
9:26. . . . . . . . . . . . . . . 177
9:27. . . . . . . . . . . . . . . 148
9:29. . . . . . . . . . . . . . . 260
10:17. . . . . . . . . . . . . . 316
11:10 . . . . . . . . . . . . . . 218
12:4–7 . . . . . . . . 101, 433
12:5. . . . . . . . . . . 260, 471
13 . . . . . . . . . . . . . . . . 238
13:1–5. . . . . . . . . . . . . 346
14:22–29. . . . . . . . . . . 419
15:1–11 . . . . . . . . . . . . 417
15:13–14. . . . . . . . . . . 336
16 . . . . . . . . . . . . . . . . 379
16:13–16. . . . . . . . . . . 107
16:14. . . . . . . . . . . . . . 379
16:16. . . . . . . . . 107, 379
17:18–20. . . . . . . . . . . 374
18:9. . . . . . . . . . . . . . . 218
18:15. . . . . . . . . . . . . . 104
20:10–18. . . . . . . . . . . 211
20:17. . . . . . . . . . . . . . 210
20:18. . . . . . . . . . . . . . 235
23:2–4 . . . . . . . . . . . . 211
23:2–7 . . . . . . . . . . . . 230
23:2–8 . . . . . . . . . . . . 218
23:3–5 . . . . . . . . . . . . 448
23:3–6 . . . . . . . . . . . . 210
23:4–9 . . . . . . . . . . . . 230
23:7–8. . . . . . . . . 210, 211
23:19–20. . . . . . . . . . . 336
24:1. . . . . . . . . . . . . . . 234
24:3. . . . . . . . . . . . . . . 234
24:4. . . . . . . . . . . . . . . 234
24:10. . . . . . . . . . . . . . 332
24:16. . . . . . . . . . . . . . 263
26–28 . . . . . . . . . . . . . 372
26:1–11 . . . . . . . . . . . . 419
27 . . . . . . . 376, 415, 420
28:15–68 . . . . . . . . . . 255
28:41. . . . . . . . . . . . . . 311
28:52. . . . . . . . . . . . . . 255
28:63. . . . . . . . . . . . . . .88
28:64 . . . . . . . . . . . . . 402
29 . . . . . . . . . . . . . . . . 375
29:1. . . . . . . . . . . . . . . 393
29:9. . . . . . . . . . . . . . . 383
29:14. . . . . . . . . . . . . . 234
30 . . . . . . . . . 31, 257, 402
30:1–3. . . . . . . . . . . . . 393
30:1–5. . . . . . . . . .64, 260
30:10. . . . . . . . . . . . . . 372
30:11–19. . . . . . . . . . . 415
31:6, 8. . . . . . . . . . . . . 215
31:9. . . . . . . . . . . . . . . 372
32 . . . . . . . . . . . 331, 393
32:15. . . . . . . . . . . . . . 401
33:1 . . . . . . . . . . . . . . . 104
33:7. . . . . . . . . . . . . . . 181
33:8. . . . . . . . . . . . . . . .83
33:12. . . . . . . . . . . . . . 471
33:26, 29. . . . . . . . . . . 181
34:11–16. . . . . . . . . . . 211

Joshua

book of. . . . . . . . . . . . 396
1 . . . . . . . . . . . . . . . . . .86
1:1 . . . . . . . . . . . . 258, 428
1:1–9. . . . . . . . . . . . . . 179
1:2–6 . . . . . . . . . . . . . .88
1:5. . . . . . . . . . . . . 57, 215
1:7. . . . . . . . . . . . . . . . 383
2 . . . . . . . . . . . . . . 86, 452
2:20. . . . . . . . . . . . . . . 416
5:10. . . . . . . . . . . . . . . 165
6 . . . . . . . 10, 86, 450, 452
6:2. . . . . . . . . . . . . . . . 431
6:21. . . . . . . . . . . . . . . 450
6:24. . . . . . . . . . . . . . . .90
7 . . . . . . . . . . . . . 210, 452
7:1 . . . . . . . . . . . . . . . 212
7:19. . . . . . . . . . . . . . . 237
7:26. . . . . . . . . . . . . . . 230
8:8. . . . . . . . . . . . . . . . 268
8:30–35 . . . 375, 415, 420
8:31. . . . . . . . . . . 102, 103
8:35. . . . . . . . . . . . . . . 420
9:2. . . . . . . . . . . . . . . . 313
9:15. . . . . . . . . . . . . . . 234
12–18 . . . . . . . . . . . . . 428
13:1–19:51 . . . . . . . . . .88
14:2. . . . . . . . . . . . . . . 428
14:6. . . . . . . . . . . . . . . 104
21:43. . . . . . . 88, 90, 400
22:16. . . . . . . . . . . . . . 212
24 . . . . . . . . . . . 179, 372
24:1. . . . . . . . . . . . . . . 393
24:2. . . . . . . . . . . . . . . .90
24:13. . . . . . . . . . . . . . 400

Judges

book of. . . . . . . . . . . . 396
1 . . . . . . . . . . . . . . 86, 434
2 . . . . . . . . . . . . . 396, 405
2–3 . . . . . . . . . . . . . 28, 238
2:1 . . . . . . . . . . . . . . . 235
2:8. . . . . . . . . . . . . . . . 148
2:10–19. . . . . . . . . . . . 401
2:11–13 . . . . . . . . . . . . .88
2:11–23 . . . . . . . . . . . . 179
2:14. . . . . . . . . . . 310, 401
2:16. . . . . . . . . . . . . . . 401
2:18. . . . . . . . . . . 216, 401
3 . . . . . . . . . . . . . . . . . 323
3:5–6 . . . . . . . . . 210, 420

3:6 . . . . . . . . . . . . . . . 417
3:10–15 . . . . . . . . . . . . 216
3:11 . . . . . . . . . . . . . . . 468
3:19 . . . . . . . . . . . . . . . 378
3:30 . . . . . . . . . . . . . . . 401
4–5 . . . . . . . . . . . . . . . 345
4:21–22 . . . . . . . . . . . . 214
5 . . . . . . . . . . . . . . . . . 86
5:9 . . . . . . . . . . . . . . . 430
5:13 . . . . . . . . . . . . 91, 296
5:25 . . . . . . . . . . . . . . . 296
6:12 . . . . . . . . . . . 430, 431
11 . . . . . . . . . . . . . . . . 279
17:1–13 . . . . . . . . . . . . 210
20–21 . . . . . . . . . . . . . 431
20:1, 8, 11 . . . . . . . . . . . 99
20:26 . . . . . . . . . . . . . 202

**Ruth**

1:8 . . . . . . . . . . . . . . . . 248
1:16–17 . . . . . . . . . . . . 333
1:17 . . . . . . . . . . . . . . . 235

**1 Samuel**

1:6 . . . . . . . . . . . . . . . . 310
2:26 . . . . . . . . . . . . . . . 284
9:9 . . . . . . . . . . . . . . . . 104
14:41 . . . . . . . . . . . . . . . 83
15:22 . . . . . . . . . . . . . . 346
16:18 . . . . . . . . . . . . . . 431
18:5, 14 . . . . . . . . . . . . 383
21:6 . . . . . . . . . . . . . . . 346
23:9–12 . . . . . . . . . . . . . 83
25:3 . . . . . . . . . . . . . . . 377
25:39 . . . . . . . . . . . . . . 323
30:1–6 . . . . . . . . . 269, 275
30:7–8 . . . . . . . . . . . . . . 83

**2 Samuel**

3:35 . . . . . . . . . . . . . . . 235
4:1 . . . . . . . . . . . . . . . . 125
5 . . . . . . . . . . . . . 299, 400
5:6–8 . . . . . . . . . . . . . . 361
5:7, 9 . . . . . . . . . . . . . . 299
5:11 . . . . . . . . . . . . . . . 110
6 . . . . . . . . . . . . . . . . . 450
6:3–16 . . . . . . . . . . . . . 117
6:6–11 . . . . . . . . . . . . . 465
6:12–16 . . . . . . . . . . . . 465
8:16 . . . . . . . . . . . . . . . . 78
10 . . . . . . . . . . . . . . . . 279
10:4 . . . . . . . . . . . . . . . 463
11:6 . . . . . . . . . . . . . . . . 91
11:11 . . . . . . . . . . . . 91, 453
12:15 . . . . . . . . . . . . . . 323
14:2 . . . . . . . . . . . . . . . 296
17:27–29 . . . . . . . . . . . . 82
19:31–39 . . . . . . . . . . . . 82
20:23 . . . . . . . . . . . . . . . 78
20:25 . . . . . . . . . . . . . . 175
23:1 . . . . . . . . . . . . . . . 112
23:26 . . . . . . . . . . . . . . 296
24 . . . . . . . . . . . . . . . . 304

**1 Kings**

2:3 . . . . . . . . . . . . 102, 383
2:7 . . . . . . . . . . . . . . . . . 82
4:4 . . . . . . . . . . . . . . . . 175
5–7 . . . . . . . . . . . . . . . 299
5–8 . . . . . . . . . . . . . . . 145
5:7–10 . . . . . . . . . . . . . 110
5:20 . . . . . . . . . . . . . . . 110
6:1 . . . . . . . . . . . . . . . . 110
7:12 . . . . . . . . . . . . . . . 299
7:51 . . . . . . . . . . . . . . . 167
8 . . . . . . . . . . . . . 259, 475
8:6–11 . . . . . . . . . . . . . 168
8:10–11 . . . . . . . . 168, 467
8:12 . . . . . . . . . . . . . . . 471
8:22–53 . . . . . . . . . . . . 258
8:23–53 . . . . . . . . . . . . 257
8:27 . . . . . . . . . . . . . . . 471
8:33 . . . . . . . . . . . . . . . 259
8:33–34 . . . . . . . . . . . . 262
8:62–63 . . . . . . . . . . . . 164
8:62–66 . . . . . . . . 167, 450
9:10–19 . . . . . . . . . . . . 293
9:11 . . . . . . . . . . . . . . . . 58
11 . . . . . . . . . . . . . . . . 464
11:27 . . . . . . . . . . . . . . 299
12 . . . . . . . . . . . . . . . . . 84
16–22 . . . . . . . . . . . . . 352
17:18 . . . . . . . . . . . . . . 104
18 . . . . . . . . . . . . . . . . 352
21 . . . . . . . . . . . . . . . . 352
21:3 . . . . . . . . . . . . . . . 335
22 . . . . . . . . . . . . . . . . 352
22:4 . . . . . . . . . . . . . . . 352
22:6 . . . . . . . . . . . . . . . 352
22:6–28 . . . . . . . . . . . . 261
22:8 . . . . . . . . . . . . . . . 352
22:17 . . . . . . . . . . . . . . 352
22:18–23 . . . . . . . . . . . 353

**2 Kings**

3 . . . . . . . . . . . . . . . . . 451
3:1–27 . . . . . . . . . . . . . 400
3:27 . . . . . . . . . . . . . . . 451
4:7 . . . . . . . . . . . . . . . . 104
9:30–37 . . . . . . . . . . . . 353
10:15 . . . . . . . . . . . . . . 240
14:6 . . . . . . . . . . . 102, 103
14:13 . . . . . . . . . . . . . . 300
17 . . . . . . . . . . . . 179, 405
17:1–4 . . . . . . . . . . . . . 133
17:13–14 . . . . . . . . . . . 147
17:23 . . . . . . . . . . . 88, 218
17:24 . . . . . . . . . . 124, 278
17:24–40 . . . . . . . . . . . 285
17:24ff. . . . . . . . . . . . . 124
17:24–41 . . . . . . . . . . . 124
17:27–28 . . . . . . . . . . . 124
17:33 . . . . . . . . . . . . . . 105
17:34 . . . . . . . . . . . . . . 124
18–19 . . . . . . . . . . . . . 383
18–20 . . . . . . . . . . . . . . 78
18:3–4 . . . . . . . . . . . . . 406
18:7 . . . . . . . . . . . . . . . 383
21 . . . . . . . . . . . . 179, 405
21:13 . . . . . . . . . . . . . . 461
22 . . . . . . . . . . . . . . . . 175
22–23 . . . . . 372, 383, 405
22:1–23:32 . . . . . 189, 193
22:3–10 . . . . . . . . . . . . 193
22:4–14 . . . . . . . . . . . . . 76
22:8 . . . . . . . . . . . . . . . 193
22:8–10 . . . . . . . . . . . . 373
22:10 . . . . . . . . . . . . . . 193
22:10–11, 13 . . . . . . . . 193
22:11 . . . . . . . . . . . . . . 377
22:14 . . . . . . . . . . 300, 431
22:14–20 . . . . . . . . . . . 345
22:16–17 . . . . . . . . . . . 193
22:19–20 . . . . . . . . . . . 193
23:2 . . . . . . . . . . . . . . . 103
23:2–3 . . . . . . . . . . . . . 194
23:4 . . . . . . . . . . . . 76, 431
23:4–25 . . . . . . . . . . . . 194
23:21 . . . . . . . . . . . . . . 164
24–26 . . . . . . . . . . . . . 134
24:1 . . . . . . . . . . . . . . . 133
24:1–7 . . . . . . . . . . . . . . 54
24:8–17 . . . . . . . . . . . . . 54

24:20 . . . 88
25 . . . 313
25:1–21 . . . 54
25:9 . . . 321
25:10 . . . 301
25:13–14 . . . 63

**1 Chronicles**

book of . . . 259, 365
1–9 . . . 77
1:1–9:44 . . . 73
1:5 . . . 77
3:18 . . . 62
3:19 . . . 76
5:24 . . . 79
6:3–15 . . . 443
6:13 . . . 76
6:39 . . . 79, 80
6:49 . . . 100
7:1–6 . . . 77
8:1–14 . . . 77
9 . . . 428
9:2 . . . 80
9:3 . . . 429
9:6 . . . 429
9:23–25 . . . 80
9:26–27 . . . 80
10:13 . . . 212
11:6 . . . 78
11:7–8 . . . 299
12:25 . . . 80
15:3–10 . . . 450
15:11–15 . . . 466
15:12, 14 . . . 450
15:16 . . . 450
15:16–17 . . . 80
15:19–22 . . . 450
15:25 . . . 450
15:28 . . . 459
15:29 . . . 450
16:1–7 . . . 117
16:5–6 . . . 80
16:16 . . . 416
16:34 . . . 114
16:40 . . . 100, 104
21:1 . . . 350
21:3–14 . . . 230
21:29 . . . 100
22:4 . . . 110
23–25 . . . 112
23:4–32 . . . 111
23:5 . . . 79
23:14 . . . 104
23:24–32 . . . 79
23:32 . . . 79
24:5 . . . 79
24:11 . . . 78
25:1–8 . . . 80
25:8 . . . 80
26:12–13 . . . 80
28:20 . . . 215
29:1–5 . . . 336
29:1–9 . . . 84, 422
29:2 . . . 422
29:2–5 . . . 324
29:3 . . . 422
29:6 . . . 422
29:9 . . . 422
29:10 . . . 395
29:29 . . . 253

**2 Chronicles**

book of . . . 365
1:5–6 . . . 100
2:3 . . . 110
2:3–8 . . . 110
2:7 . . . 110
4:1 . . . 100, 101
5:2–14 . . . 114, 117
5:3 . . . 107
5:12 . . . 80
5:13 . . . 118, 467
6 . . . 475
6:18 . . . 471
6:20 . . . 143
7:3 . . . 114, 117, 118
7:6 . . . 118
7:8–10 . . . 107
7:14 . . . 399
9 . . . 464
13:5 . . . 133
14–32 . . . 126
14:1–35:27 . . . 192
15:10–15 . . . 420, 421
16:19 . . . 143
17:16 . . . 430
20:14 . . . 80
23:18 . . . 102, 104
23:19 . . . 80
23:20 . . . 296
23:22 . . . 165
25:4 . . . 102, 104
26:9 . . . 299, 301
26:9–10 . . . 299
27:3 . . . 300
29–32 . . . 179
30:2 . . . 165
30:5 . . . 102
30:16 . . . 104
30:18 . . . 102, 103
31:3 . . . 103, 104
31:4 . . . 104
31:10 . . . 431
31:13 . . . 78, 431
31:21 . . . 104, 189
32:5 . . . 300, 313
32:30 . . . 300
33:14 . . . 300
34–35 . . . 179, 405
34:8–33 . . . 193
34:9–22 . . . 76
34:11 . . . 193
34:14 . . . 193
34:18 . . . 406
34:19 . . . 406
34:22 . . . 300, 431
34:23–28 . . . 406
34:24 . . . 406
34:29–31 . . . 393
35 . . . 165
35:12 . . . 103
35:26 . . . 103, 104
36:15–16 . . . 147, 192, 216, 218
36:15–19 . . . 134
36:16 . . . 147
36:19 . . . 301
36:21 . . . 53
36:22–23 . . . 26, 50, 51

**Ezra**

1 . . . 50, 51, 61, 73, 85, 97, 115, 204, 259, 322
1–2 . . . 443
1–3 . . . 119
1–4 . . . 144
1–6 . . . 27, 32, 50, 123, 174, 179, 224
1:1 . . . 13, 31, 33, 51, 52, 53, 55, 58, 59, 63, 116, 123, 145, 162, 191, 204, 215, 435
1:1–3 . . . 26, 50, 144, 162

## Scripture Index


1:1–4 . . . . . . 25, 39, 51, 63, 75, 88, 156
1:1–5 . . . . . . . . . . . . . 153
1:1–6 . . . . . . 116, 147, 162
1:1–11 . . . 39, 49, 50, 142, 153, 204, 214
1:1–3:13 . . . . . . . . . . . 123
1:1–6:22 . . 39, 51, 162, 168
1:1a . . . . . . . . . . . . . 52, 59
1:2 . . . . . . 56, 57, 124, 144
1:2–4 . . 51, 52, 59, 109, 1 45, 154
1:2a . . . . . . . . . . . . . 55, 56
1:2b . . . . . . . . . . . . . . . 55
1:2b–3 . . . . . . . . . . . . . 55
1:3 . . 29, 56, 57, 58, 63, 163
1:3–4 . . . . . . . . . . . 56, 58
1:4 . . . . . . . . . . . 57, 58, 60
1:4–6 . . . . . . . . . . . . . . 84
1:4a . . . . . . . . . . . . . . . 57
1:4b . . . . . . . . . . . . . . . 58
1:5 . . . . . 31, 56, 57, 59, 73, 200, 201
1:5–6 . . . . . . . . . . . . . . 60
1:5–8 . . . . . . . . . . . . . . 62
1:5–11 . . . . . 39, 51, 59, 63
1:5a . . . . . . . . . . . . . . . 59
1:6 . . . . . . . 29, 58, 60, 62
1:6–7 . . . . . . . . . . . . . . 59
1:7 . . . . . . . . . . . 57, 61, 62
1:7–8 . . . . . . . . . . . . . . 60
1:7–11 . . . . . . . . . . . . 145
1:8 . . . . . . . . . . . 61, 75, 76
1:8–9 . . . . . . . . . . . . . . 58
1:9–10 . . . . . . . . . . . . . 73
1:9–11 . . . . . . . . . . . 61, 62
1:11 . 38, 61, 62, 63, 74, 75
2 . . . 55, 73, 76, 81, 89, 97, 105, 115, 125, 200, 204, 240, 360, 362, 363, 364, 365, 366, 414, 431, 442, 443, 459
2–3 . . . . . . . . . . . . . . 153
2:1 . . 73, 74, 75, 81, 84, 85
2:1–2 . . . . . . . . . . . . . . 74
2:1–2a . . . . . . . . . . . . . 76
2:1–58 . . . . . . . . . . . 39, 74
2:1–70 . . 39, 70, 74, 75, 360
2:2 . . . 75, 84, 99, 363, 366
2:2b . . . . . . . . . . . . 76, 81
2:2b–20 . . . . . . . . . . . . 77
2:2b–35 . . . . . . . . . . . . 77
2:2b–58 . . . . . . . . . . . . 73
2:2b–70 . . . . . . . . . . . . 77
2:3–15 . . . . . . . . . . . . 200
2:3–20 . . . . . . . . . . . . . 77
2:3–34 . . . . . . . . . . . . . 80
2:3–35 . . . . . . . . . . . . . 78
2:5 . . . . . . . . . . . . . . . 348
2:6 . . . . . . 77, 78, 81, 360
2:16 . . . . . . . . . . 77, 78, 81
2:16–21 . . . . . . . . . . . 363
2:21 . . . . . . . . . . . . . . 360
2:21–35 . . . . . . . . . . . . 78
2:27 . . . . . . . . . . . . . . 360
2:29–34 . . . . . . . . . . . 363
2:33 . . . . . . . . . . . . . . 341
2:36 . . . . . . . . . . . . . 78, 81
2:36–39 . . . 78, 360, 363
2:36–58 . . . . . . . . . . 77, 78
2:40 . . . . . . . 79, 201, 414
2:42 . . . . . . . . . . . . . . . 80
2:43–54 . . . . . . . . . . . 363
2:43–58 . . . . . . . . . . . . 80
2:55 . . . . . . . . . . . . . . . 80
2:58 . . . . . . . . . . . . . . . 80
2:59 . . . . . . . 74, 76, 81, 82
2:59–60 . . . . . . . . . . . . 82
2:59–63 . . . . . 73, 74, 83, 175, 360
2:59–70 . . . . . . . . . . 39, 81
2:60 . . . . . . . . . . . . . . . 81
2:61 . . . . . . . . . . . . . . . 81
2:62 . . . . . . . . 81, 82, 238
2:62–63 . . . . . . . . . . . . 82
2:63 . . . . . . . . . . . . . . . 83
2:64 . . . . . . . . . . . 83, 200
2:64–66 . . . . . . . . . . . . 73
2:64–70 . . . . . . . . . . 74, 83
2:65–66 . . . . . . . . . . . . 84
2:68–69 . . . . . . . . . . . 363
2:70 . . . . 75, 76, 77, 81, 84, 89, 98, 363
3 . . . . 28, 29, 84, 87, 106, 119, 125, 145, 187
3–4 . . . . . . . . . . . . . . 320
3:1 . 98, 108, 110, 111, 372
3:1–2 . . . . . . . . . . . . 97, 98
3:1–6 . . . 39, 98, 99, 101, 110, 112
3:1–13 . . . . . . . . . . . 39, 96
3:1–6:22 . . . . . . . . . . . . 97
3:1b . . . . . . . . . . . . . . . 98
3:2 . . . . 30, 38, 75, 76, 99, 100, 101, 102, 104, 153, 163, 165, 234
3:2–4 . . . . . . 27, 106, 107
3:3 . . . 101, 104, 105, 106, 107, 115, 124, 164, 211
3:3–4 . . . . . . . . . . . . . 187
3:3–5 . . . . . . . . . . . . . 164
3:3–6 . . . . . . . . . . . 97, 105
3:4 . . . . . 29, 30, 101, 103, 107, 153, 165
3:4–5 . . . . . . . . . . . . . 107
3:5 . . . . . . . . . . . . 101, 108
3:6 . . . . . . . . 98, 101, 108
3:7 . . . . . . . . . 27, 109, 112
3:7–9 . . . . . . . . . . . . . . 97
3:7–13 . . . . . . . . . . 39, 109
3:8 . . . 38, 75, 99, 110, 111
3:8–9 . . . . . . . . . . 110, 111
3:8–10 . . . . . . . . . 110, 145
3:8–13 . . . . . . . . . . . . . 110
3:9 . . . . . . . . . . . . 111, 112
3:10 . . . . . 30, 80, 112, 201
3:10–11 . . . . . . . . . . . . 450
3:10–13 . . 29, 97, 111, 164, 187, 204
3:11 29, 113, 114, 117, 204
3:12 . . . . . . . . . . . . . . 114
3:12–13 . . . . 108, 164, 166
3:13 . . . . . . . . . . . . . . 114
3:14 . . . . . . . . . . . . . . . 29
4 . . . . . . . 23, 28, 33, 122, 123, 124, 134, 141, 256, 268, 270, 278, 283, 284, 309, 310, 322, 341, 343, 380, 391, 444
4–6 . . . . . . . . . . 24, 32, 168
4:1 105, 115, 124, 154, 166
4:1–3 . . . . . . 101, 166, 211, 238, 239, 285
4:1–5 . . . . 27, 39, 122, 123, 124, 131, 134, 154
4:1–24 . . . . . . 39, 114, 122
4:1–5:17 . . . . . . . . . . . 157
4:1–6:12 . . . 123, 157, 162
4:2 . . . . . . . . 105, 124, 279
4:2–3 . . . . . . . . . . 106, 166
4:3 . . . . . 75, 124, 126, 163
4:4 . . . 38, 105, 106, 124, 125, 141, 148, 166

4:4–5 . . . . . 38, 104, 106, 125, 134, 166
4:4–23 . . . . . . . . . . . . 106
4:5 . . . . . . . . . . . . . . . 106
4:6 . . . . . 25, 38, 123, 132
4:6–23 . . . . 123, 131, 134
4:6–24 . . . . . 39, 130, 132
4:7. . . . . . . . 123, 132, 133
4:7–10. . . . . . . . . . . . . 132
4:7–22. . . . . 177, 187, 188
4:7–23. . . . . . . . . . 38, 164
4:8 . . . . . . . . . . . 122, 132
4:8–23 . . . . . . . . . . . . 123
4:8–24 . . . . . . . . . . . . . 26
4:9. . . . . . . . . . . . . . . . 132
4:9–10 . . . . . . . . . . . . 132
4:10. . . . . . . . . . . . . . . 124
4:11 . . . . . . . . . . . . . . . 133
4:11–22. . . . . . . . . . . . 132
4:12. . . . . . . . . . . 133, 256
4:12–16. . . . . . . . . . . . 143
4:12–23. . . . . . . . . . . . 132
4:13. . . . . . . . . . . . . . . 308
4:14. . . . . . . . . . . . . . . 133
4:14–16. . . . . . . . . . . . 133
4:15. . . . . . . . . . . 133, 134
4:16. . . . . . . . . . . . . . . 133
4:17–23. . . . . . . . . . . . 134
4:18. . . . . . . . . . . . . . . 133
4:19. . . . . . . . . . . . . . . 156
4:19–22. . . . . . . . . . . . 133
4:21. . . . . . . 133, 188, 256
4:23. . . 134, 256, 309, 343
4:24. . . .39, 122, 123, 124, 125, 131, 134, 141
5 . . . . . 141, 142, 143, 146
5:1 38, 100, 106, 142, 163
5:1–2. . .75, 123, 142, 146, 147, 148, 153, 163
5:1–5. . . 39, 142, 156, 163
5:1–17. . . . . . . . . . . . . 140
5:1–6:12 . . . . . . . 123, 143
5:1–6:18 . . . . . . . . . . . . 26
5:1–6:22 . . 39, 134, 141, 142
5:2. . . . . . . . . . 38, 75, 142
5:3. . . . . . . . . . . . . 38, 143
5:3–4 . . . . . . . . . . . . . 162
5:3–5 . . . . . . . . . 123, 142
5:5. . . . . 31, 143, 148, 178
5:6. . . . . . . . . . . . . . . . 143
5:6–10 . . . . . . . . . . . . 143
5:6–17. . . . . . 39, 142, 143
5:8. . . . . . . . . . . . . . . . 144
5:8–10. . . . . . . . . 143, 154
5:9. . . . . . . . . . . . . . . . 143
5:11 . . . . . . . . 55, 144, 148
5:11–17 . . . . . . . . . . . . 144
5:12. . . . . . . . 55, 144, 145, 155, 230
5:13–16. . . . . . . . . . 75, 145
5:14. . . . . . 38, 61, 76, 145
5:14–15. . . . . . . . . . . . 154
5:14–16. . . . . . . . . . . . . 61
5:15. . . . . . . . . . . . . . . . 62
5:16. . . . . 38, 62, 145, 146
5:17. . . . . . 146, 153, 154, 156, 163
6 . . .28, 141, 162, 211, 419
6:1. . . . . . . . . . . . . . . . 154
6:1–2. . . . . . . . . . . . . . 153
6:1–5. . . . . . . 38, 153, 154
6:1–12. . 39, 142, 152, 153, 154, 156, 188
6:2–4 . . . . . . . . . . . . . . 58
6:3. . . . . . . . . . . . . . . . 154
6:3–4 . . . . . . . . . 101, 155
6:3–5 . . . . . . 51, 145, 153
6:3b–4a . . . . . . . . . . . 154
6:4 . . . . . . . . . . . . 84, 154
6:5 . . . . . . . . . . . . . . . 154
6:6–7 . . . . . . . . . . . . . 154
6:6–10 . . . . . . . . . . . . 154
6:6–12 . . 25, 38, 153, 166
6:6b . . . . . . . . . . . . . . 154
6:7. . . . . . . . . . . . . . . . 123
6:7a. . . . . . . . . . . . . . . 154
6:7b . . . . . . . . . . . . . . 154
6:8 . . . . . . . . . . . . . . . 154
6:8–12 . . . . . . . . 153, 156
6:9, 10. . . . . . . . . . . . . . 55
6:10. . . . . . . . . . . . . . . 155
6:11 . . . . . . . . . . . . . . . 155
6:11–12 . . . . . . . . 155, 157
6:12. . . . . . . . . . . . . . . 155
6:13. . . . . . . . . . . . . . . 163
6:13–14. . . . . . . . . . . . 163
6:13–15. . . . . . . . . 134, 162
6:13–18. . . . . . . . . . . . 469
6:13–22 . . 39, 124, 142, 161, 162, 167, 170, 204
6:14. . 31, 38, 75, 100, 163, 204, 272
6:14ff. . . . . . . . . . . . . . 116
6:14–15. . 32, 123, 162, 164
6:14a. . . . . . . . . . . . . . 162
6:14b. . . . . . . . . . 163, 164
6:14b–15. . . . . . . . . . . 162
6:15. . . . . . . . . . . . . . . 164
6:16. . . . . . . . . . . 123, 164
6:16–17. . . . . . . . . . 38, 164
6:16–18. . . . . . . . 162, 164
6:17. . . . . . . . . . . . . . . 166
6:18. . . . . . . . . . . . . . . 122
6:19–22. . 29, 38, 64, 162, 164, 165, 171
6:20 . . . . . . . . . . . . . . 166
6:20–21 . . . . . . . . . . . 239
6:21. . . . . . . . . . . 166, 211
6:22 . . 123, 164, 166, 174
7 . . . . . . .87, 90, 174, 175, 264, 381
7–10 28, 50, 154, 173, 174
7:1 . . . . 132, 173, 174, 414
7:1–5. . . . . . . . . . 431, 443
7:1–6. . . . . . 175, 253, 266
7:1–7. . . . . . . . . . . . . . 178
7:1–10. . 39, 173, 175, 181, 186, 187, 199
7:1–26. . . . . . . . . . . . . . 26
7:1–28. . . . . . 39, 173, 174
7:1–10:44 . . . 39, 168, 173
7:6. . . .103, 104, 173, 174, 175, 177, 188, 189, 192, 202, 272, 372
7:6b. . . . . . . . . . . . . . . 175
7:8. . . . . . . . . . . . . . . . 174
7:8–9. . . . . . . . . . . . . . 236
7:9. . . . . . . .177, 178, 189, 192, 202, 209
7:10. . . . 38, 174, 175, 176, 177, 190, 205, 235, 241
7:11 . . . 175, 176, 188, 235
7:11–26 . . . . 175, 177, 186
7:11–28 . 39, 177, 185, 186
7:12. . . . 55, 175, 176, 188, 190, 191, 235
7:12–20. . . . . . . . . . . . 188
7:12–26. . . . . . . . . 26, 122
7:13 . . . . . . . . . . . 188, 200
7:13–14 . . . . . . . . . . . . 188
7:13–20. . . . . . . . 188, 199
7:13–25. . . . . . . . . . . . 192
7:14. . 38, 175, 188, 189, 191

7:15 . . . . . . . 163, 187, 189
7:15–17 . . . . . . . . . . . . 189
7:15–20 . . . . . . . . . . . . 188
7:16, 17 . . . . . . . . . . . . 187
7:18 . . . . . . . . . . . . . . . 189
7:19, 20 . . . . . . . . . . . . 187
7:21 . . . . . . . . 55, 175, 176, 189, 190
7:21–23 . . . . . . . . . . . . 278
7:21–24 . . . . . . . . 188, 189
7:22 . . . . . . . . . . . . . . . 189
7:23 . . . . . . . . 55, 187, 189, 190, 256
7:24 . . . . . . . . . . . 187, 190
7:25 . . . . . . . 38, 175, 190, 205, 209
7:25–26 . . . . . . . 103, 174, 188, 190
7:25a . . . . . . . . . . . . . . 190
7:25b . . . . . . . . . . . . . . 190
7:26 . . 175, 190, 192, 209, 235, 236, 239
7:27 . . . . . . . . 31, 164, 187, 191, 203
7:27–28 . . . . 175, 187, 188, 191, 199, 201
7:27–9:15 . . . . . . 174, 229
7:28 . . . 178, 191, 192, 201, 202, 205
7:28b . . . . . . . . . . . . . . 192
7:28–9:15 . . . . . . . . . . . 26
8 . 199, 201, 205, 240, 318
8–10 . . . . . . . . . . . . . . 174
8:1 . . . . . . . . . . . . 187, 201
8:1–14 . . 39, 191, 199, 200
8:1–20 . . . . . . . . . . . . . 174
8:1–36 . . . . . . 39, 197, 204
8:2–3 . . . . . . . . . . . . . 200
8:4–13 . . . . . . . . . . . . . 200
8:15 . . . . . . . . . . . 201, 202
8:15–20 . . 39, 79, 200, 201
8:15–30 . . . . . . . . . . . . 199
8:16 . . . . . . . . . . . . . . . 201
8:16–17 . . . . . . . . . . . . 201
8:17 . . . . . . . . . . . . . . . 201
8:18 . . . . . . . 178, 201, 205
8:20 . . . . . . . . . . . . 80, 201
8:21 . . . . . . . 202, 205, 235
8:21–23 . . . . . . . . 200, 202
8:21–30 . . . . . . . . . . . . 175
8:21–36 . . . . . . . . . 39, 202
8:22 . . . . . . 154, 178, 202, 205, 230
8:24 . . . . . . . . . . . 201, 203
8:24–28 . . . . . . . . . . . 205
8:24–30 . . . . . . . 200, 203
8:25 . . . . . . . . . . . . . . . 203
8:28 . . . . . . . . . . . 201, 203
8:28–29 . . . . . . . . . . . 202
8:31 . . . . . . 178, 201, 202, 203, 205
8:31–32 . . . . 199, 200, 203
8:31–36 . . . . . . . . 175, 203
8:33–34 . . . . . . . . . . . 203
8:35 . . . . . . . . . . . 187, 203
8:35–36 . . . . . . . 200, 203
9 . . . . 23, 86, 90, 113, 177, 209, 210, 219, 222, 223, 241, 243, 257, 393, 404
9–10 . . . . . 28, 82, 87, 90, 179, 194, 209, 210, 241, 242, 244, 371, 392, 453, 463, 475
9:1 . . 90, 105, 209, 210, 235
9:1–2 . . 32, 177, 208, 209, 229, 230, 241
9:1–5 . . . . . . . . . . . . . . 452
9:1–15 . . 40, 175, 207, 208
9:2 . . . . . 89, 210, 212, 238
9:3 . . . . . . . . . . . . 213, 257
9:3–5 . . . . . . . . . 212, 232
9:3–15 . . . . . . . . . . . . . 209
9:3–10:17 . . . . . . . . . . 177
9:4 . . . . . . . . 209, 212, 232
9:5 . . . . . . . . 213, 214, 257
9:5–15 . . . . . . . . . . 30, 231
9:6 . . . . . . . 209, 214, 243
9:6–7 . . . . . 209, 213, 214
9:6–15 . . . . 213, 219, 237
9:7 . . . . 209, 214, 215, 230
9:8 . . . . . . . . 209, 213, 214, 215, 217
9:8–9 . . . . . 214, 215, 218, 230, 241, 243
9:8–10 . . . . . . . . . . . . 209
9:9 . . . . . 29, 108, 192, 213, 216, 403
9:10 . . . 209, 213, 218, 243
9:10–12 . . . . 212, 213, 218
9:10–14 . . . . . . . . . . . . 233
9:10–14a . . . . . . . . . . . 217
9:11 . . . . . . . 218, 233, 235
9:11–12 . . . . 218, 231, 238
9:12 . . . . . . . 105, 230, 233
9:13 . . . . . . . 209, 213, 215, 217, 230
9:13–15 . . . . . 32, 209, 218
9:14 . . . . . . . 209, 212, 218, 230, 235
9:14–15 . . . . . . . . . . . . 234
9:15 . . . 209, 213, 214, 218, 219, 230
9:32–37 . . . . . . . . . . . . 214
10 . . . . . . 26, 31, 38, 190, 208, 209, 218, 219, 225, 229, 230, 231, 240, 241, 243, 244, 279, 394, 417, 437, 453
10:1 . . . . . . . . . 30, 231, 232
10:1–2 . . . . . . . . . . 30, 243
10:1–17 . . . . . 40, 229, 231
10:1–44 . . . 40, 175, 226, 231, 452
10:2 . . . 105, 230, 233, 235, 237, 241, 245
10:2–4 . . . . . . . . . 232, 236
10:2–5 . . . . . . . . . . . . . 235
10:3 . . . 233, 234, 235, 237
10:5 . . . . . . . . . . . . . . . 240
10:5–6 . . . . 232, 234, 235
10:6 . . . . . 202, 232, 236, 240, 256
10:6–9 . . . . . . . . . . . . . 209
10:7 . . . . . . . . . . . . . . . 236
10:7–8 . . . . . . . . . . 232, 236
10:8 . . . . . . . . . . . . 209, 279
10:9 . . . . . . . 236, 254, 394
10:9–11 . . . . 232, 233, 236
10:10 . . 230, 233, 237, 394
10:11 . . . . . . 105, 237, 239
10:12 . . . . . . 235, 239, 243
10:12–15 . . . . . . . 232, 239
10:13–14 . . . . . . . . . . . 239
10:14 . . . 32, 230, 233, 239
10:15 . . . . . . . . . . 232, 239
10:16 . . . . . . . . . . . . . . 176
10:16–17 . . . . . . . 232, 240
10:17 . . . . . . . . . . . . . . 233
10:18 . . . . . . . . . . 233, 240
10:18–22 . . . . . . . . . . . 240
10:18–44 . . 40, 73, 229, 240
10:19 . . . . . . . . . . . . . . 240
10:23 . . . . . . . . . . . . . . 240

10:24. . . . . . . . . . . . . . .240
10:25. . . . . . . . . . . . . . .240
10:25–43 . . . . . . . . . . .240
10:26. . . . . . . . . . . . . . .241
10:44 . . . . . . . . . . . . . .241

**Nehemiah**

book of. . . . . . . . . . . . . .28
1 . .90, 133, 134, 204, 213, 254, 266, 269, 272, 273, 280, 281, 282, 305, 306, 309, 317, 345, 361, 371, 375, 442, 463, 465
1–2 . . . . . . . . .87, 290, 309
1–3 . . . . . . . . . . . . . . . .349
1–14 . . . . . . . . . . . .50, 174
1:1. . . . 23, 253, 254, 266, 272, 284, 370, 394, 428
1:1–3. . . . . . . . . . . . . . . .38
1:1–4. . . . . . . . . . . .40, 253
1:1–11 . . . . . .40, 252, 253
1:1–7:8 . . . . . . . . . . . . .168
1:1–13:31. . . . . . . . .40, 253
1:2. . . . . . . . .253, 254, 255
1:3. . . 255, 266, 268, 271, 282, 292, 294, 312
1:4. . . . 55, 202, 235, 254, 256, 257, 261, 393
1:5. . . . . 55, 257, 258, 375
1:5–11 . . 40, 219, 257, 393
1:6. . . . . . . . 143, 258, 259
1:6–7 . . . . . . . . . . . . . .262
1:6a. . . . . . . . . . . . . . . .258
1:6b . . . . . . . . . . . . . . .259
1:7. . . . . . . . .253, 258, 259
1:8. . . .258, 259, 260, 465
1:8–10. . . . . . . . . . . . . .260
1:10. . . . . . . . . . . .258, 260
1:11 . . . 76, 253, 256, 257, 258, 261, 266, 272, 284
1:11b . . . . . . . . . . . . . .260
1:11c . . . . . . . . . . . . . .260
2 . . . . 259, 261, 272, 273, 282, 284, 285, 291, 292, 298, 334, 363, 414, 433
2–3 . . . . . . . . . . . .280, 374
2:1. . . 132, 188, 254, 256, 260, 266, 267
2:1–2. . . . . . . . . . . . . . .266
2:1–8. . . . . . . . . . . .40, 265
2:1–10. . . . . . . . . . . . . .164
2:2. . . . . . . 256, 266, 267, 269, 275
2:2a. . . . . . . . . . . . . . . .267
2:2b. . . . . . . . . . . . . . . .267
2:2c. . . . . . . . . . . . . . . .267
2:3. . . . . . . 253, 266, 267, 269, 271, 282
2:3–5 . . . . . . . . . .267, 270
2:4. . . . 55, 261, 266, 268, 269, 313
2:5. . . . . . . 266, 268, 269, 271, 272, 284, 343, 422, 441, 465
2:6 . . . . . . 266, 270, 272, 460, 465
2:7. . . . . . . . .266, 271, 465
2:7–8. . . . . . . . . . . . . . .271
2:7–9. . . . . . . . . . . . . . .202
2:8 . .31, 178, 254, 266, 269, 271, 272, 334, 335, 465
2:9. . . . . . . . 177, 278, 291
2:9–10. . . . . . . . . . . . . .278
2:9–20 . . . . .40, 277, 278
2:10. . 278, 279, 280, 283, 308, 312, 313, 331
2:11 . . . . . . . . . . . . . . .280
2:11–15 . . . . . . . . . . . .279
2:11–16 . . . . . . . . . . . .349
2:12. . . . . . . . . . . .280, 281
2:13. . . . . . 268, 280, 281, 282, 299
2:13–14 . . . . . . . . . . . .445
2:14. . . . . . . . . . . 281, 314
2:15. . . . . . . . . . . . . . . .281
2:15c. . . . . . . . . . . . . . .281
2:16. . . . . 282, 331, 348, 362, 446
2:16–17. . . . . . . . . . . . .319
2:16–18. . . . . . . . . . . . .282
2:17. . . . . . . . . . . 282, 314
2:17–18 . . . . . . . .280, 310
2:18. . .178, 281, 282, 283, 291, 312, 349, 465
2:19. . . 33, 280, 283, 296, 308, 310, 312, 343, 350
2:19–20. . . . . . . . .278, 283
2:20. . . . . . . . . . 31, 55, 284
3 . . . . . 26, 280, 290, 291, 292, 296, 301, 306, 309, 314, 317, 318, 349, 360, 362, 373, 374, 414, 429, 434, 445
3–4 . . . . . . . . . . . . . . . .329
3–6 . . . . . . . . . . . . . . . .308
3:1. . . . . . . 291, 292, 293, 294, 295, 311, 444, 445, 449, 450, 459, 468
3:1–2. . . . . . . .40, 295, 298
3:1–15. . . . . 291, 294, 295
3:1–32. . . . . 40, 110, 288, 290, 294
3:2. . . . . . . . .293, 294, 295
3:3. . . . . . . . . . . . .292, 300
3:3–5 . . . . . . . . . . .40, 296
3:4. . . . 293, 299, 348, 374
3:5. . . . . . . . . . . . . . . . .296
3:6 . . . . . . . . . . . . .292, 296
3:6–12 . . . . . . . . . .40, 296
3:7. . . . . . . . . . . . . . . . .296
3:8. . . . 294, 297, 300, 310
3:9. . . . . . . . . . . . .294, 297
3:10. . . . . . . . . . . . . . . .295
3:12. . . . . . . . . . . . .294, 297
3:13. . . . . . .292, 296, 297
3:13–15. . . . . . . . . .40, 297
3:14. . . . . . . . . . . . .292, 294
3:15. . . . . . .292, 294, 298
3:16. . . . . . . . . . . . .253, 294
3:16–21. . . . . . . . . . . . .298
3:16–32. . . . . . . . . 40, 291, 295, 298
3:17. . . . . . . . . . . . . . . .294
3:18. . . . . . . . . . . . . . . .294
3:19. . . . . . . . . . . . . . . .294
3:20. . . . . . .294, 295, 298
3:21. . . . . . .293, 295, 299
3:21–22. . . . . . . . . . . . .295
3:22. . . . . . . . . . . . .294, 298
3:22–32 . . . . . . . . . . . .298
3:23. . . . . . .293, 295, 299
3:26. . .294, 295, 298, 300
3:27. . . . . . . . . . . . .295, 299
3:28. . . . . . .294, 295, 298
3:29. . . . . . . . . . . . .295, 298
3:30. . . . . . .299, 348, 374
3:31. . . . . . . . . . . . .294, 295
3:31–32. . . . . . . . . . . . .298
3:32. . . . . . . . . . . . .294, 298
3:33–38. . . . . . . . .291, 309
4 . . . . 279, 280, 291, 292, 293, 294, 308, 309, 317, 325, 326, 329, 342, 344, 347, 349

4–5 . . . 374
4–6 . . . 290, 311
4:1 . . . 309, 312, 313, 331
4:1–3 . . . 33, 40, 309, 320
4:1–5 . . . 312
4:1–6 . . . 291
4:1–14 . . . 86
4:1–23 . . . 40, 307, 308
4:2 . . . 278, 297, 310, 321
4:2–3 . . . 309
4:3 . . . 296, 311, 312, 448
4:4 . . . 311, 313, 323, 448
4:4–5 . . . 309, 311, 312
4:4–6 . . . 40
4:5 . . . 312
4:6 . . . 310, 312, 313, 326
4:7 . . . 309, 312, 313, 331
4:7–8 . . . 33
4:7–9 . . . 40, 312
4:8 . . . 313, 314
4:9 . . . 309, 312, 313, 314
4:10 . . . 309, 314, 319
4:10–15 . . . 40, 314
4:11 . . 33, 309, 314, 315, 342
4:12 . . . 309, 314, 315, 342
4:13 . . . 316, 318
4:14 . . . 309, 314, 315, 316, 319, 348, 362, 446
4:15 . . 31, 309, 314, 317, 318
4:16 . . . 318
4:16–23 . . . 40, 318
4:17 . . . 318
4:18 . . . 319
4:19 . . . 319, 362, 446
4:19–20 . . . 309
4:20 . . . 31, 309, 319, 448, 455
4:21 . . . 319, 320
4:22 . . . 314, 320
4:22–23 . . . 309
4:23 . . . 320, 326, 342
5 . . 255, 266, 270, 273, 291, 320, 324, 326, 328, 376, 378, 418
5:1 . . . 329, 330, 331
5:1–5 . . . 40, 329
5:1–19 . . . 40, 327, 328
5:2 . . . 329, 330
5:3 . . . 329, 330
5:4 . . . 329, 331
5:4–5 . . . 330
5:5 . . . 329, 331, 337
5:6 . . . 331, 461, 462
5:6–13 . . . 40, 331
5:7 . . . 282, 331, 362, 445, 446
5:7b . . . 332
5:8 . . . 332
5:9 . . . 332, 361
5:10 . . . 332, 333
5:11 . . . 333
5:12 . . . 445
5:12a . . . 333
5:12b . . . 333
5:13 . . . 376
5:13a . . . 333
5:14 . . . 76, 272, 281, 297, 329, 377
5:14–18 . . . 329
5:14–19 . . . 40, 328, 334
5:14a . . . 334
5:14b . . . 334
5:15 . . . 283, 334, 361, 363
5:15b . . . 334
5:16a . . . 334
5:16b . . . 334
5:17 . . . 334
5:17–19 . . . 334
5:18 . . . 334
5:18b . . . 334
5:19 . . . 329, 459
6 . . . 26, 283, 287, 317, 333, 372
6:1 . . . 341
6:1–4 . . . 40, 341
6:1–19 . . . 40, 339, 340
6:2 . . . 341, 342, 345
6:3 . . . 342
6:4 . . . 343
6:5 . . . 343
6:5–9 . . . 40, 343
6:6 . . . 343
6:7 . . . 344
6:8 . . . 344
6:9 . . . 344, 345
6:10 . . . 345, 346
6:10–15 . . . 40, 345
6:12 . . . 345
6:13 . . . 346
6:14 . . . 347, 349, 459, 464
6:15 . . . 254, 319, 341, 347
6:15–16 . . . 33
6:16 . . . 31, 41, 347, 348
6:17 . . . 348
6:17–19 . . 41, 281, 348, 362
6:18 . . . 348, 460
6:19 . . . 314, 349
7 . . . 26, 75, 200, 204, 360, 364, 365, 367, 372, 413, 414, 429, 431, 442, 443, 449
7:1 . . . 360
7:1–2 . . . 459
7:1–3 . . . 41, 360
7:1–73a . . . 41, 356, 359
7:2 . . . 253, 255, 361, 431
7:3 . . . 361
7:4 . . . 362, 373
7:4–5 . . . 41, 362
7:5 . . . 362, 364, 446
7:5ff. . . . 73
7:5–73 . . . 73
7:6 . . . 363
7:6–73a . . . 41, 363
7:7 . . . 75, 359, 363, 366
7:11 . . . 360
7:21–26 . . . 363
7:26 . . . 360
7:33–37 . . . 363
7:39–42 . . . 360, 363
7:39–43 . . . 443
7:39–44 . . . 442
7:46–56 . . . 363
7:70–72 . . . 363
7:73 . . . 363, 414
7:73–8:1 . . . 445
7:73a . . . 363
7:73b . . . 107, 364, 372
7:73b–8:1 . . . 360
7:73b–8:8 . . . 41, 372
7:73b–8:18 . . 41, 369, 370
8 . . . 30, 87, 102, 177, 259, 291, 347, 364, 370, 371, 380, 381, 384, 385, 386, 387, 391, 392, 394, 396, 414, 415, 446, 448, 459
8–9 . . . 23, 107, 371, 374, 383, 406
8–10 . . 75, 219, 365, 391, 445
8–11 . . . 26
8–12 . . . 26, 294
8:1 . . 30, 99, 176, 177, 236, 295, 372, 373, 374, 375, 414

8:1–8 . . . 30
8:2 . . . 107, 176, 373, 377
8:3 . . . 373, 374, 375, 377, 378
8:4 . . . 176, 177, 374, 394
8:5 . . . 177, 374, 375
8:6 . . . 333, 375
8:7 . . . 201, 374, 376
8:7–8 . . . 373
8:7–9 . . . 177
8:8 . . . 104, 376, 379
8:9 . . . 26, 176, 256, 371, 372, 377
8:9–12 . . . 41, 377
8:10 . . . 378, 384, 446, 459
8:11 . . . 378
8:12 . . . 378
8:13 . . . 176, 177, 379
8:13–18 . . . 41, 379
8:14 . . . 104, 379
8:14–15 . . . 103
8:14–18 . . . 107
8:15 . . . 102, 379
8:16 . . . 379
8:17 . . . 379
8:18 . . . 30, 177, 380, 391
9 . . . 23, 86, 179, 257, 371, 377, 392, 393, 405, 407, 408, 412, 417, 418, 459, 463
9–10 . . . 380
9:1 . . . 202, 379, 380, 391, 392, 394
9:1–2 . . . 392
9:1–5 . . . 393
9:1–6 . . . 41, 394
9:1–36 . . . 219
9:1–37 . . . 41, 388, 391
9:2 . . . 394
9:2–37 . . . 30
9:3 . . . 394, 404
9:4 . . . 374, 376, 394, 395
9:4–5 . . . 201, 395
9:5 . . . 374, 376, 394, 396, 406
9:5–36 . . . 219
9:5b . . . 395
9:6 . . . 395
9:6–37 . . . 385
9:7 . . . 395
9:7–8 . . . 41, 396
9:8 . . . 396, 397, 413, 461
9:9 . . . 397
9:9–11 . . . 41, 397
9:10 . . . 397, 398, 402
9:11 . . . 397
9:12–15 . . . 41, 397
9:12 . . . 397
9:13 . . . 397, 402
9:14 . . . 397
9:15 . . . 368
9:16 . . . 368, 402
9:16–17a . . . 402
9:16–18 . . . 41, 368
9:17 . . . 402
9:17a . . . 398, 401
9:17b . . . 398
9:18 . . . 398
9:19 . . . 399
9:19–21 . . . 41, 399
9:20 . . . 402
9:21 . . . 399, 404, 408
9:22 . . . 399
9:22–25 . . . 41, 399
9:23 . . . 400
9:25 . . . 400, 401
9:25b . . . 401
9:26 . . . 401, 402
9:26–31 . . . 41, 401
9:27 . . . 401
9:28 . . . 401, 402, 468
9:29 . . . 402, 462
9:30 . . . 147, 401, 402
9:31 . . . 402
9:32 . . . 402, 403
9:32–35 . . . 41, 402, 404
9:33 . . . 403
9:33–35 . . . 393
9:34 . . . 396, 403
9:36 . . . 29, 332, 381, 393, 403, 404, 429
9:36–37 . . . 41, 403
9:37 . . . 393, 403, 414
9:38 . . . 41, 393, 412, 413, 461
9:38–10:39 . . . 41, 410, 412
10 . . . 367, 371, 377, 393, 412, 420, 421, 423, 447, 448, 458, 463
10:1 . . . 26, 412, 413, 421, 459, 463
10:1–27 . . . 41, 73, 412, 413
10:2 . . . 26
10:2–8 . . . 414, 443
10:4 . . . 256
10:8 . . . 421
10:9 . . . 395, 421
10:9–13 . . . 414
10:12 . . . 201
10:14 . . . 421
10:14–27 . . . 414
10:28 . . . 166, 412, 415, 416, 417, 421, 464
10:28–29 . . . 41, 415
10:28–38 . . . 413
10:29 . . . 104, 296, 412, 415, 416, 420
10:30 . . . 105, 417, 420, 458, 462, 464
10:30–31 . . . 41, 417
10:30–39 . . . 412, 458
10:31 . . . 417, 458, 462
10:31b . . . 417
10:32 . . . 418
10:32–33 . . . 418
10:32–39 . . . 41, 418
10:33 . . . 418, 419, 421
10:34 . . . 102, 104, 418, 419, 465
10:34–35 . . . 464
10:35 . . . 418, 419, 465
10:36 . . . 104, 418, 419
10:37 . . . 419
10:37–39 . . . 458
10:38 . . . 419, 442
10:39 . . . 29, 371, 413, 415, 419, 420, 442, 448, 458, 461, 477
11 . . . 290, 371, 413, 420, 428, 437, 458, 460
11:1 . . . 341, 365, 371, 420, 428, 429, 430
11:1–3 . . . 41, 429
11:1–36 . . . 41, 73, 426, 428
11:2 . . . 430
11:3 . . . 430, 444
11:4 . . . 430
11:4–9 . . . 41, 430
11:4a . . . 430
11:4b . . . 430
11:5–6 . . . 431
11:6 . . . 428, 430
11:7 . . . 430
11:8 . . . 430
11:9 . . . 431

11:10 . . . . . . . . . . . . . . .429
11:10–14 . . . . . . . . 41, 431
11:11 . . . . . . . . . . . . . . .431
11:12 . . . . . . . . . . . . . . .431
11:13 . . . . . . . . . . . . . . .431
11:14 . . . . . . . . . . . . . . .431
11:15 . . . . . . . . . . . . . . .429
11:15–19 . . . . . . . . 41, 431
11:16 . . . . . . . . . . . . . . .431
11:17 . . . . . . . . . . . . . . .431
11:18 . . . . . . 290, 428, 431
11:19 . . . . . . . . . . 429, 431
11:20–24. . . . . . . . 41, 432
11:20–35. . . . . . . . . . . .434
11:20. . . . . . . . . . . . . . .432
11:21 . . . . . . . . . . . . . . .432
11:22. . . . . . . . . . . . . . .432
11:23. . . . . . . . . . 413, 432
11:25–29. . . . . . . . . . . .432
11:25–36. . . . . . . . 41, 432
11:30. . . . . . . . . . . . . . .432
11:31–36 . . . . . . . . . . . .432
11:35. . . . . . . . . . . . . . .341
11:36. . . . . . . . . . . . . . .432
12 . .29, 111, 290, 296, 371, 413, 422, 428, 458, 460
12:1. . . . . . . . . . . . 75, 441
12:1–7. . . . . . . . . . . . . .443
12:1–26. . . . . 42, 73, 441, 442, 449, 450
12:1–13:3 . . . . . . . . . .438
12:7. . . . . . . . . . . 441, 443
12:8. . . . . . . . . . . 201, 443
12:8–9 . . . . . . . . . . . . .443
12:8a. . . . . . . . . . . . . . .414
12:10–11 . . . . . . . . . . . .443
12:12. . . . . . . . . . . . . . .443
12:12–21 . . . . . . . . . . . .443
12:22. . . . . . . . . . . . . . .443
12:22–23. . .442, 443, 444
12:23. . . . . . . . . . 441, 444
12:24. . 28, 201, 422, 441, 442, 444, 447, 451
12:24–25 . . . . . . . . . . .444
12:25. . . . . . . . . . . . . . .444
12:25–26. . . . . . . . . . . .442
12:26. . 176, 441, 442, 452
12:27. . . . . . . . . . 370, 444
12:27–39. . . . . . . . . . . .280
12:27–43. . . . . . . . 42, 444
12:27–46. . . . . . . . . . . . .30
12:27–47. . . . . . . 441, 450
12:27–13:3 . . . . . . 42, 441
12:28. . . . . . . . . . . . . . .459
12:29. . . . . . . . . . . . . . .444
12:30. . . . . 445, 449, 450, 458, 460, 464
12:31 . . . . . . .26, 442, 445
12:32. . . . . . . . . . . . . . .445
12:35. . . . . . . . . . . . . . .445
12:36. . . .28, 30, 112, 176, 422, 442, 445, 447, 451
12:37. . . . . . . . . . . . . . .445
12:38. . . . . 300, 442, 445
12:39. . . . . . . . . . . . . . .446
12:40. . . . . .442, 445, 446
12:41 . . . . . . . . . .296, 446
12:42. . . . . . . . . . . . . . .446
12:43. . . . . . 30, 164, 442, 446, 455
12:44. .442, 444, 447, 460
12:44–45 . . . . . . . . . . .464
12:44–47 . . . 42, 447, 458
12:45. . . . . .442, 447, 464
12:45–46 . . . 30, 112, 117
12:46. . . . . . . . . . 422, 447
12:47. . . . . 442, 444, 447
13 . . . . 26, 28, 29, 82, 90, 168, 178, 179, 210, 291, 320, 324, 341, 346, 372, 381, 383, 421, 423, 452, 453, 455, 477
13:1 . . .279, 444, 447, 448
13:1–2. . . . . . . . . . . . . .448
13:1–3. . . . . 42, 247, 442, 448, 452
13:2. . . . . . . . . . . . . . . .448
13:3. . . . . . . . . . . . . . . .458
13:4. . .448, 458, 459, 460
13:4–5 . . . . . . . . . . . . .295
13:4–9 . . . . .42, 458, 459
13:4–31. . . . . . . . . 42, 456
13:5. . . . . . . . . . . . . . . .460
13:6. . . . . . . . . . . 459, 460
13:6–7 . . . . . . . . . . . . .392
13:7. . . . . . . . . . . . . . . .460
13:7–9. . . . . . . . . . . . . .460
13:8. . . . . . . . . . . . . . . .331
13:10 . . . . . . . . . . . . . . .460
13:10–13. . . . . . . . . . . .458
13:10–14. . . . . . . . 42, 461
13:11 . . . . . .458, 461, 462
13:12. . . . . . . . . . . . . . .461
13:13. . . . . . . . . . . 459, 462
13:14. . . . . . 458, 459, 461
13:15. . . . . . . . . . . 462, 463
13:15–22. . . .42, 458, 462
13:16. . . . . . . . . . . . . . .462
13:17. . . . . . . . . . . . . . .462
13:19. . . . . . . . . . . 294, 462
13:21 . . . . . . . . . . . 462, 463
13:22. . . . . . 459, 462, 463
13:23. . . 33, 211, 233, 463
13:23–27. . . .42, 105, 463
13:23–29. . . . . . . . . . . .458
13:23–31 . . 230, 244, 247
13:24. . . . . . . . . . . . . . .463
13:25. . . . . 212, 230, 459, 463, 464
13:26. . . . . . . . . . . 459, 464
13:27. . . . . .233, 464, 475
13:28. . . . . .459, 460, 464
13:28–31 . . . . . . . . 42, 464
13:29. . . . . . . 33, 459, 464
13:30. . . . . . . . . . . 458, 464
13:30–31 . . . . . . . . . . .458
13:31 . . . . . .459, 464, 465

## Esther

1:9. . . . . . . . . . . . . . . . .270
3:6 . . . . . . . . . . . . . . . .135
3:10. . . . . . . . . . . . 135, 157
3:12–15. . . . . . . . . . . . .135
4:3, 16. . . . . . . . . . . . . .202
4:14. . . . . . . . . . . . . . . .271
4:15–16. . . . . . . . . . . . .236
6:1–14. . . . . . . . . . . . . .157
6:11–12. . . . . . . . . . . . .157
7:1–10 . . . . . . . . . . . . . .157
7:8. . . . . . . . . . . . . . . . .331
9:6, 12. . . . . . . . . . . . . .254

## Job

1 . . . . . . . . . . . . . . . . .352
2:13. . . . . . . . . . . . . . . .212

## Psalms

1 . . . . . . . . . . . . . . . . .179
1:1–3. . . . . . . . . . . . . . .179
1:2. . . . . . . . . . . . . . . . .259
2 . . . . . . . . . . . . . . . . .272
2:4. . . . . . . . . . . . . . . . .471
2:10. . . . . . . . . . . . . . . .383

14:2 . . . 383
18 . . . 304
19 . . . 179
19:7 . . . 184
19:10 . . . 180
20:2 . . . 181
22:1 . . . 409
22:2 . . . 408
22:7 . . . 310
22:24 . . . 408
23 . . . 121
23:1 . . . 399
32 . . . 302, 323, 407
32:8 . . . 143, 383
32:11 . . . 407
33:18 . . . 143
33:20 . . . 181
34:15 . . . 143
35 . . . 341
35:13 . . . 202
36:3 . . . 383
41:13 . . . 376, 395
42–43, 74 . . . 54
44 . . . 231
45:9 . . . 270
48 . . . 302
48:1–3 . . . 302
48:2 . . . 306
48:2–3 . . . 299
48:3 . . . 303
48:4–5 . . . 303
48:12–14 . . . 303
51 . . . 302
51:1–2 . . . 403
51:5 . . . 407
51:8 . . . 406
51:12 . . . 406
51:17 . . . 408
51:18–19 . . . 302
55:17 . . . 105
60 . . . 231
63:8 . . . 143
72:19 . . . 376
78:19 . . . 408
89:13 . . . 143
74, 79, 80, 85 . . . 231
78 . . . 396
84:10 . . . 365, 386, 425
89:52 . . . 376
90 . . . 104, 231
90–106 . . . 191
94:22 . . . 303
100:5 . . . 118
105 . . . 396
105:9 . . . 416
106 . . . 118, 396
106:1 . . . 114
106:19–20 . . . 398
106:19–22 . . . 398
106:28 . . . 467
106:28–31 . . . 466
106:30 . . . 467
106:31 . . . 466, 467
106:41 . . . 401
106:48 . . . 376, 395
107 . . . 118
107–150 . . . 193
107:1 . . . 114
110 . . . 378
110:1 . . . 378
111:10 . . . 377
118:1 . . . 114
119 . . . 179, 182, 183, 405
119:9 . . . 405
119:11 . . . 180, 405, 407
119:15 . . . 180
119:31 . . . 180
119:47 . . . 180
119:67–71 . . . 180
119:92 . . . 180
119:97 . . . 180
119:103 . . . 180
119:167 . . . 180
126 . . . 114, 118
126:2 . . . 118
126:5–6 . . . 118
127:1 . . . 455
135 . . . 396
136 . . . 118, 396
136:1–26 . . . 114
137 . . . 29, 54, 117
137:1–6 . . . 436
137:2–3 . . . 117
137:4 . . . 117, 435
137:7 . . . 284, 301
147, 148 . . . 444


### Proverbs


1:3 . . . 383
6:1 . . . 330, 336
11:15 . . . 287
15:3 . . . 143
16:24 . . . 180
22:26 . . . 336
31:10 . . . 430


### Isaiah


1 . . . 179, 331
1–2 . . . 31
1:1 . . . 371
1:2 . . . 374
1:4 . . . 215
1:7 . . . 255
1:11 . . . 449
1:11–15 . . . 473
1:15 . . . 213
1:15–16 . . . 143
1:17 . . . 403
1:19 . . . 218
2:1–4 . . . 382, 429, 433, 473
2:2 . . . 205
2:2–3 . . . 205
2:2–4 . . . 205
2:4 . . . 205
3 . . . 383
5:8–10 . . . 335
5:21 . . . 404
6:3 . . . 376
6:3–4 . . . 467
6:13 . . . 89, 210
7:20 . . . 463
8:18 . . . 472
9 . . . 268
9:2 . . . 215
11:1–3 . . . 399
12 . . . 380
13 . . . 53
13:7 . . . 125
13:20–22 . . . 322
17 . . . 53
19:14 . . . 313
23:15, 17 . . . 53
25:6 . . . 378
30:5 . . . 181
33:5 . . . 472
33:20 . . . 215
35:3 . . . 60
35:10 . . 204, 380, 381, 392
36 . . . 348
36–39 . . . 134
39 . . . 31
40 . . . 65, 89, 238, 272, 284, 318, 321, 371, 434

40–66 . . . 244
40:1–2 . . . 54
40:2 . . . 217, 380
40:3 . . . 205, 206, 380
40:3–5 . . . 392
40:4, 5 . . . 380
40:8 . . . 373, 380
40:31 . . . 378
41:12 . . . 53
41:20 . . . 383
41:25 . . . 53
42:1 . . . 148
42:1–6 . . . 148
42:6–7 . . . 215
44:24–28 . . . 54
44:26 . . . 119
44:26–45:13 . . . 204
44:28 . . . 31, 119, 435
44:45 . . . 38
45:1 . . . 31, 435
45:1–6 . . . 54
45:13 . . . 119
48:2 . . . 428
48:13 . . . 143
48:20–22 . . . 74
49:5–7 . . . 148
49:16 . . . 304
50:1 . . . 234
51:11 . . 204, 380, 381, 385
52:1 . . . 428
52:11 . . . 205
52:11–12 . . . 61
52:12 . . . 205
52:13 . . . 383
52:13–53:11 . . . 148
52:13–53:12 . . . 381, 435
53:6 . . . 450
54:1–4 . . . 215
54:2–3 . . . 434
54:11–17 . . . 304
54:17 . . . 355
55:1–2 . . . 386
55:12 . . . 383
57:15 . . . 472
58:12 . . . 304
59:3 . . . 82
59:21 . . . 65
60:1–3 . . . 215
60:7 . . . 191
60:10 . . . 238
60:13 . . . 191
61:1–3 . . . 399
61:4 . . . 238
65:17 . . . 436
66:1 . . . 450
66:2, 5 . . . 212
66:10 . . . 256
66:22 . . . 436

**Jeremiah**

1–20 . . . 383
2:8 . . . 176
2:11 . . . 398
2:15 . . . 268
3:8 . . . 234
3:14 . . . 204
3:15 . . . 383
7 . . . 109
7:3 . . . 423, 472
7:4 . . . 474
7:7 . . . 472
7:12 . . . 472
7:12–15 . . . 303
9:24 . . . 383
10:21 . . . 383
11:5 . . . 376
14:12 . . . 202
14:19–22 . . . 219
16:18 . . . 235
17:9 . . . 323
20 . . . 341
20:11 . . . 383
21:5 . . . 177
22:28–30 . . . 76, 80
23:5 . . . 344, 383
23:14 . . . 60
23:20 . . . 205
25:11 . . . 53
25:12 . . . 53, 204
28 . . . 285, 353
29 . . . 65, 322
29:10 . . . 54
31:6, 12 . . . 204
31:8–9 . . . 242
31:31–34 . . . 323
31:32 . . . 234
31:33 . . . 379
31:33–34 . . . 381, 382
31:34 . . . 381
32:37–38 . . . 89
33 . . . 32
33:7 . . . 116
33:9 . . . 116
33:10–11 . . . 117
33:11 . . . 116
36 . . . 213
36:1–22 . . . 102
36:6 . . . 202
36:23 . . . 373
38:4 . . . 125
38:4–5 . . . 350
50:5 . . . 204
50:9 . . . 53, 204
51:1 . . . 53, 204
51:11 . . . 53, 204
52:14 . . . 301, 314
52:17–18 . . . 63

**Lamentations**

4:14 . . . 82
5:15–18 . . . 322
5:18 . . . 311

**Ezekiel**

book of, 303
2:9 . . . 212
2:10 . . . 102, 242
3:2 . . . 242
3:14 . . . 212
3:14–15 . . . 242
4:13 . . . 164
7:9 . . . 256, 257
7:20 . . . 218, 235
7:27 . . . 256
8 . . . 109
8:4 . . . 100
9:3 . . . 100
9:8 . . . 219
10:18–19 . . . 222
10:19 . . . 100
11:22 . . . 100
13 . . . 147
13:4 . . . 311
14:6 . . . 242
14:13 . . . 212
16 . . . 216
16–23 . . . 222
16:3 . . . 405
16:8 . . . 235
16:42 . . . 310
16:54, 66 . . . 242
17:18 . . . 240
18:20 . . . 263

18:23, 30, 32 . . . . . . . . 242
20 . . . . . . . . . . . . . . . . 216
20 . . . . . . . . . . . . . . . . 221
20:1–44 . . . . . . . . . . . 101
20:7–29. . . . . . . . . . . . 215
20:7–44 . . . . . . . . . . . 214
20:9 . . . . . . . . . . . . . . 234
20:11 . . . . . . . . . . . . . . 175
20:33–34 . . . . . . . . . . 177
21:28. . . . . . . . . . . . . . 323
22:26. . . . . . . . . . . . . . 176
26:16. . . . . . . . . . . . . . 212
27 . . . . . . . . . . . . . . . . 257
27:9. . . . . . . . . . . . . . . 330
33:11 . . . . . . . . . . . . . . 242
34–38 . . . . . . . . . . . . . 244
34–39 . . . . . . . . . . . . . 242
34:11–16 . . . . . . . . . . . 243
34:12, 22. . . . . . . . . . . . 29
34:25–31 . . . . . . . . . . 243
36:8–11. . . . . . . . . . . . 243
36:24. . . . . . . . . . . . . . 204
36:24–29 . . . . . . . . . . . 29
36:24–38 . . . . . . . . . . 243
36:31. . . . . . . . . . . . . . 243
36:31–32. . . . . . . . . . . 242
37:1–14 . . . . . . . . 216, 243
37:15–28. . . . . . . . . . . 303
37:18–28. . . . . . . . . . . 243
37:23. . . . . . . . . . . . . . 381
37:26–27. . . . . . . . . . . 243
38–39 . . . . . . . . . . . . . 158
39:27. . . . . . . . . . . . . . 204
40:2 . . . . . . . . . . . . . . 429
43:4–5 . . . . . . . . . . . . 473
43:7. . . . . . 471, 473, 474
43:10–11 . . . . . . . . . . . 242
46:12. . . . . . . . . . . . . . . 59

**Daniel**

1–6 . . . . . . . . . . . . . . . 157
1:1–3. . . . . . . . . . . . . . . 54
1:8. . . . . . . . . . . . . . . . . 82
1:21 . . . . . . . . . . . . . . . . 53
2:18. . . . . . . . . . . . . . . . 55
2:28. . . . . . . . . . . . . . . 205
2:37, 44. . . . . . . . . . . . . 55
5 . . . . . . . . . . . . . . . . . . 51
5:1–5, 23. . . . . . . . . . . . 63
6–12 . . . . . . . . . . . . . . 157
6:28. . . . . . . . . . . . . . . . 53
9 . . . . . . . . . . . . . 257, 393
9:1–19. . . . . . . . . . . . . . 53
9:2. . . . . . . . . . . . . . . . . 53
9:3. . . . . . . . . . . . . . . . 257
9:4. . . . . . . . . . . . 258, 375
9:4–19 . . . . . . . . . . . . 219
9:6, 10. . . . . . . . . . . . . 218
9:11 . . . . . . . . . . . . . . . 416
9:24. . . . . . . . . . . . . . . . 53
10:1 . . . . . . . . . . . . . . . . 53
10:2. . . . . . . . . . . . . . . 256
11:34 . . . . . . . . . . . . . . 181
11:45 . . . . . . . . . . . . . . 253

**Hosea**

1:6, 8. . . . . . . . . . . . . . 116
1:9. . . . . . . . . . . . . . . . . 88
2:23. . . . . . . . . . . . . . . . 89
4:6 . . . . . . . . . . . . . . . 374
9:3. . . . . . . . . . . . . . . . 164
9:13 . . . . . . . . . . . . . . . 234

**Joel**

2:28–32 . . . . . . . . . . . 387

**Amos**

1:1 . . . . . . . . . . . . . . . . 296
7:17 . . . . . . . . . . . . . . . 164

**Obadiah**

8–14 . . . . . . . . . . . . . . 285

**Jonah**

1:9. . . . . . . . . . . . . . . . . 55
3:7. . . . . . . . . . . . . . . . 236
4:2. . . . . . . . . . . . 258, 405

**Micah**

3:12. . . . . . . . . . . . . . . 473
4:1–2. . . . . . . . . . . . . . 205
6:16. . . . . . . . . . . . . . . 352

**Nahum**

1:2–3. . . . . . . . . . . . . . 405
1:10. . . . . . . . . . . . . . . 268

**Habakkuk**

2:14. . . . . . . . . . . . . . . 434
3:17–19 . . . . . . . . . . . . 384

**Zephaniah**

1:10. . . . . . . . . . . . . . . 431
3:1. . . . . . . . . . . . . . . . . 82
3:14–17. . . . . . . . . . . . 384

**Haggai**

book of. . . . . . . . . . . . 146
1 . . . . . . . . . . . . . . . . . . 92
1:1 . . . 75, 76, 99, 164, 240
1:1–11 . . . . . . . . . 146, 147
1:1–2:9 . . . . . . . . . . . . 100
1:4. . . . . 38, 125, 146, 305
1:6, 9–11. . . . . . . . . . . 146
1:12 . . . . . . . . . 76, 99, 240
1:12–13 . . . . . . . . . . . . . 75
1:12–15 . . . . . . . . . . . . 142
1:13 . . . . . . . 146, 147, 168
1:14 . . . . . . . . . 99, 147, 148
2 . . . . . . . . . . . . . . . . . 473
2:1. . . . . . . . . . . . . . . . 240
2:2. . . . . . . . . . . . . . . 75, 76
2:3. . . . . . . . . . . . . . . . 115
2:4. . . . . . . . . . . 75, 76, 168
2:5. . . . . . . . . . . . . 147, 168
2:9. . . . . . . . . . . . . 429, 475
2:20–23 . . . . . . . . . . . 146
2:21. . . . . . . . . . . . . . 75, 76
2:23. . . . . . . 344, 366, 429

**Zechariah**

book of. . . . . . . . . . . . 146
1:1 . . . . . . . . . . . . . . . . 164
1:1–6. . . . . . . . . . . . . . 147
1:6. . . . . . . . . . . . . . . . 218
2:7. . . . . . . . . . . . . . . . 204
3–4 . . . . . . . . . . . . . . . 146
3:1. . . . . . . . . . . . . . . . . 76
3:1–5. . . . . . . . . . . . . . 381
3:1–10. . . . . . . . . . . . . 100
3:2. . . . . . . . . . . . . . . . 350
3:6, 8 . . . . . . . . . . . . . . 76
4 . . . . . . . . . . . . . . . . . . 75
4:6 . . . . . . . 306, 321, 455
4:6–10 . . . . . . . . . . . . 305
4:8–10 . . . . . . . . . . . . 145
4:10. . . . . . . . . . . 115, 147
6:8 . . . . . . . . . . . . . . . 399
6:9–15 . . . . . . . . . . . . . 75
6:11 . . . . . . . . . . . . . . . . 76
7:2–7. . . . . . . . . . . . . . 202
7:5. . . . . . . . . . . . . . . . . 53
7:11–14 . . . . . . . . . . . . 147
8:5. . . . . . . . . . . . . . . . 429

8:22 . . . 429
9:9 . . . 344

**Malachi**
1:7, 12 . . . 82
2:10–11 . . . 244
2:13–16 . . . 244
4:5–6 . . . 381

**Matthew**
1:11–12 . . . 76
1:12–16 . . . 366, 367
2:2–3 . . . 135
2:16 . . . 135
5:7 . . . 225
5:44 . . . 323
6:9 . . . 264
6:10 . . . 68, 263
6:13 . . . 138
6:33 . . . 273
8:28–34 . . . 139
9:20–22 . . . 246
9:35 . . . 139
10:16 . . . 287
10:18 . . . 272
11:28–30 . . . 478, 479
12:6 . . . 169
12:15–21 . . . 139
16:13–16 . . . 139
16:18 . . . 304
17:24 . . . 419
18:20 . . . 435
21:23 . . . 138
23 . . . 394, 472, 481
23:1–39 . . . 470
23:4 . . . 479
23:16–22 . . . 470
23:17, 19 . . . 470
23:21 . . . 470, 472, 474
23:23 . . . 470
23:38 . . . 470, 473
24 . . . 473
24:1–2 . . . 470
27:37 . . . 350
27:46 . . . 408
28:18–20 . . . 196, 435
28:20 . . . 275

**Mark**
1:24 . . . 424
5:1–17 . . . 139
5:25–34 . . . 246
8:27–29 . . . 139
8:31 . . . 287
10:18 . . . 121
10:45 . . . 450
11:28 . . . 138
12:30–31 . . . 286, 468
13:11 . . . 272
13:30 . . . 158
15:34 . . . 408

**Luke**
1:17 . . . 381
2:19 . . . 287
2:52 . . . 284
3:27 . . . 76
4:16–30 . . . 91
4:17 . . . 382
4:17–19 . . . 385
4:28 . . . 91
5:27–32 . . . 222
8:43–48 . . . 246, 451
9:18–20 . . . 139
11:37–52 . . . 222
14:1–24 . . . 222
14:15–24 . . . 386
15:20–24 . . . 384
18:19 . . . 121
19:45–48 . . . 467
20:2 . . . 138

**John**
1 . . . 65, 474
1:1 . . . 385
1:1–14 . . . 180
1:12 . . . 95
1:14 . . . 65, 120, 169, 472
1:23 . . . 206
1:29 . . . 449
2:19 . . . 435, 474
2:21 . . . 65
3:16 . . . 481
4 . . . 279
4:21–22 . . . 285
4:23 . . . 285
6:48–58 . . . 408
8:25 . . . 138
8:31 . . . 180
10:1ff. . . . 120
15:5 . . . 479
18:36 . . . 434

**Acts**
1:8 . . . 434
2 . . . 387, 474
2:1 . . . 107
2:1–4 . . . 169
2:14–21 . . . 385
2:17–21 . . . 138, 387
3:1–8 . . . 157
4:1–2 . . . 350
4:3 . . . 157
5:1–11 . . . 467
5:14 . . . 157
5:18 . . . 157
6:1 . . . 157
6:1–6 . . . 364
6:8–10 . . . 157
6:9, 11, 12–15 . . . 222
7 . . . 394
7:48 . . . 168, 169
7:49 . . . 169, 450
7:51 . . . 405
7:51–53 . . . 222
7:57–59 . . . 223
7:59–60 . . . 157
8:1–3 . . . 157
9:31 . . . 157
16:19–21 . . . 350
17:7 . . . 135
17:24 . . . 169
18:2 . . . 135
20:30 . . . 126
21:10–14 . . . 262
24–25 . . . 272
24:27 . . . 262
26:18 . . . 476
28 . . . 272
28:31 . . . 158

**Romans**
1–3 . . . 206
1:3 . . . 89
1:23 . . . 398
2:2–4 . . . 245
2:4 . . . 241, 244, 245, 479
3:10 . . . 404
3:23 . . . 223, 286
3:31 . . . 469
4 . . . 90, 302
4:5 . . . 90
5:10 . . . 223, 286
6:23 . . . 170, 223

7:21–25 . . . . . 223
7:24 . . . . . 476
8 . . . . . 477
8:2 . . . . . 170
8:17 . . . . . 91
8:18 . . . . . 385
8:20 . . . . . 263
8:23 . . . . . 65
8:31 . . . . . 160, 365
8:33, 35 . . . . . 160
8:37 . . . . . 477
9–11 . . . . . 90
9:4–5 . . . . . 91
9:5 . . . . . 89
9:8 . . . . . 91
12:1–2 . . . . . 454, 481
12:1–8 . . . . . 305
12:2 . . . . . 196
14 . . . . . 469
14:5–9 . . . . . 469
14:10 . . . . . 481
15:5–6 . . . . . 127

**1 Corinthians**

1:2 . . . . . 424, 476
1:30 . . . 368, 424, 451, 481
3:16 . . . . . 170, 305
5:7 . . . . . 170
5:7–8 . . . . . 170
6:9–11 . . . . . 476
6:18–20 . . . . . 424, 476
6:19 . . . . . 170
7:1–24 . . . . . 246
7:14 . . . . . 247
7:16 . . . . . 247
10:1 . . . . . 406
10:8 . . . . . 466
10:11 . . . . . 408
11:26 . . . . . 170
12:29 . . . . . 180
15:56 . . . . . 381

**2 Corinthians**

2:11 . . . . . 287, 350
3:1–6 . . . . . 206
5:1 . . . . . 476
6:14 . . . . . 247
6:14–18 . . . . . 453
6:16 . . . . . 170
6:17 . . . . . 453
7:1 . . . . . 453
7:9–10 . . . . . 245
9 . . . . . 336, 423
9:1–5 . . . . . 368
9:7 . . . . . 424
9:15 . . . . . 422
11:26 . . . . . 126

**Galatians**

book of . . . . . 127
1:3–5 . . . . . 436
1:4 . . . . . 65
1:7 . . . . . 353
1:14 . . . . . 481
2:1–21 . . . . . 126
2:4 . . . . . 285, 355
2:20 . . . . . 469
3:7 . . . . . 91
3:10 . . . . . 406
3:26 . . . . . 91
3:29 . . . . . 91
4:4 . . . . . 65
4:6 . . . . . 91
4:7 . . . . . 91
4:26 . . . . . 400, 436
5:2–5 . . . . . 10
5:6 . . . . . 11
5:14 . . . . . 469
6:6 . . . . . 338
6:7 . . . . . 406

**Ephesians**

book of . . . . . 127, 285
1:3 . . . . . 91
1:3–14 . . . . . 264
2:19–22 . . . . . 435
2:21–22 . . . . . 170, 274
2:22 . . . . . 305
3 . . . . . 263
3:6 . . . . . 91
4:3 . . . . . 325
4:11 . . . . . 383
4:26 . . . . . 336
5:5–7 . . . . . 475
5:19 . . . . . 454
6:10–12 . . . . . 137
6:12 . . . . . 138

**Philippians**

1:6 . . . . . 306, 455
1:9 . . . . . 326
2 . . . . . 481
2:9 . . . . . 139
3:1 . . . . . 383
3:2 . . . . . 353
4:2 . . . . . 422
4:4 . . . . . 383, 385
4:10 . . . . . 422
4:12–13 . . . . . 409
4:14–20 . . . . . 367
4:18–19 . . . . . 424
4:19 . . . . . 386

**Colossians**

book of . . . . . 127
2:14–15 . . . . . 65
2:15 . . . . . 65, 169
3:5–6 . . . . . 475

**1 Thessalonians**

1:5 . . . . . 147
1:6 . . . . . 147
2 . . . . . 336
2:2 . . . . . 147, 286
2:13 . . . . . 147
2:14 . . . . . 147
2:18 . . . . . 262, 455
3:10 . . . . . 262
4:3 . . . . . 424, 475, 476
5:2 . . . . . 66

**2 Thessalonians**

2:2 . . . . . 66, 355
2:8 . . . . . 158

**1 Timothy**

book of . . . . . 127
1:12–15 . . . . . 286
2:1–2 . . . . . 68, 261
2:8 . . . . . 155
3:15 . . . . . 304, 436
4:1–5 . . . . . 126
5:17 . . . . . 338

**2 Timothy**

book of . . . . . 127
1:3 . . . . . 275
1:7–9 . . . . . 264
2:15 . . . . . 383
3:8 . . . . . 285
3:16 . . . 23, 180, 383, 406
4:14–15 . . . . . 126
4:17 . . . . . 477
5:7 . . . . . 368

**Titus**
book of . . . 127
1:2 . . . 23
1:10–11 . . . 286, 353
1:12 . . . 23
2:11–14 . . . 127
2:11–15 . . . 449, 454
2:13 . . . 66, 476
2:14 . . . 451

**Hebrews**
1:1 . . . 150
1:2 . . . 180
3:15 . . . 68
4:8–10 . . . 469, 478
4:11 . . . 406
4:12–23 . . . 406
4:16 . . . 264
7:23–28 . . . 449
9:11–14 . . . 449
10:10–14 . . . 449
10:14 . . . 454
11:13 . . . 66
11:31 . . . 450
12:1 . . . 262
12:2 . . . 180
12:14 . . . 475
12:22 . . . 274, 305
12:22–23 . . . 285, 355
12:22–24 . . . 205, 304, 451
12:24 . . . 305

**James**
1:2 . . . 385
1:22–25 . . . 182
2:13 . . . 221
2:25 . . . 450
3:1 . . . 383
5:16 . . . 273

**1 Peter**
1:1 . . . 66, 205
1:4 . . . 91
1:11 . . . 65
1:16 . . . 368, 424, 436, 475
1:19–21 . . . 170
1:24–25 . . . 373
2:3 . . . 479
2:5 . . . 304, 325, 452
2:9 . . . 179, 305, 325, 387, 436
2:10 . . . 223
2:11 . . . 66
2:17 . . . 480
5:8 . . . 325

**2 Peter**
book of . . . 286
1:12–19 . . . 150
2 . . . 352
2:1–4 . . . 353
2:3 . . . 353
3:12–13 . . . 66
3:13 . . . 436
3:16 . . . 406

**1 John**
1:8–10 . . . 262
1:9 . . . 245, 246
2:1 . . . 223, 245
2:15–17 . . . 437
2:19 . . . 127
2:22–23 . . . 286
4:1–3 . . . 286
4:1–6 . . . 10, 127
5:14–15 . . . 263

**2 John**
7, 9 . . . 127

**Jude**
book of . . . 286, 352
3 . . . 127

**Revelation**
1:6 . . . 179
1:10 . . . 478
2:13 . . . 350
2:14 . . . 466
4–5 . . . 396
4:8 . . . 396
5:13 . . . 396
7 . . . 384
7:9 . . . 92, 452
7:9–10 . . . 206
7:9–12 . . . 171, 454
7:10 . . . 92, 171, 172
7:11 . . . 92
7:14 . . . 452
7:15 . . . 171
11:7–10 . . . 158
12 . . . 137
12:6 . . . 408
12:9 . . . 353
12:17 . . . 137
13 . . . 349
13:1–2 . . . 138
13:4 . . . 138
13:6–7 . . . 138
13:10 . . . 138, 159
13:11–14 . . . 349
13:18 . . . 159
14:12 . . . 159
16 . . . 158
16:16 . . . 158
17–19 . . . 66, 158
17:14 . . . 158
18:8 . . . 158
18:9–19 . . . 158
19:2 . . . 158
19:6–9 . . . 386
19:13 . . . 385
19:19 . . . 158
20:7–9a . . . 158
20:7–10 . . . 158
21 . . . 436
21–22 . . . 33, 451
21:2 . . . 92, 171
21:3 . . . 92, 171
21:4 . . . 171, 381
21:9–27 . . . 304
21:18 . . . 452
21:19–20 . . . 452
21:21 . . . 452
21:22 . . . 171
21:25 . . . 452
21:27 . . . 452
22 . . . 285
22:3 . . . 169, 171
22:14 . . . 452
22:14–15 . . . 285, 475
22:15 . . . 481

# Subject Index


Aaron, 79, 175, 443
Abihu, 210n. 4
Abraham, covenant with, 396–97
Achan, 210n. 4, 230n. 1
Ahab, 352
Ahasuerus. *See* Xerxes
altar of burnt offering,
of the God of Israel, 100–101
as manifestation of the goodness of God, 118
purpose of, 98, 100, 101–2
rebuilding of, 97, 98–109, 234
restriction of rebuilding of to only those of Israelite ancestry, 101
responses to rebuilding of, 97, 105–7
unity of community in, 111
worship at, 107–9, 112–17, 118
altar of incense, 100
Amon, 193
Artaxerxes, 25
and Ezra, 177, 178, 187–90, 191, 209
and finances for temple worship, 189
and the God of heaven, 55
and the law of Moses, 187
and Nehemiah, 187, 254–55, 257, 260–61, 262, 266–73, 283, 460
opposition to rebuilding of Zion during reign of, 25, 28, 38, 122, 132–34
and rebuilding of Zion, 25, 132n. 1, 163, 164, 188, 257, 268
and the second return of exiles to Jerusalem, 188–90, 191, 204, 209
and the third return of exiles to Jerusalem, 271–72
timeline of, 38
Asaph, 79
Ashurbanipal, 132, 132n. 2, 133

Babylon, 51–52, 51n. 4, 54, 66, 158
Balaam, 135
Balak, 135
Bani, 394n. 8, 395
Barzillai, 81
Belshazzar, 51, 63

Caleb, 317
Canaanization, 28, 88, 179, 211, 459
confession
Ezra prayer of, 208–9, 213–19, 231, 232
as necessity for restoration of Zion, 30, 241, 242–45, 259, 393
Nehemiah prayer of, 219, 219n. 17, 257–64, 280, 309, 313, 341, 393
returnees' corporate prayer of, 30, 393, 394–403
Shecaniah and corporate prayer of, 231, 232–34, 235, 236–39, 241
significance of in our lives, 407–8
conquest, motif of, 28, 87, 231, 238, 278–79, 399–400, 445
continuity with the past
genealogies and, 360, 366, 368, 371, 414, 443–44
the law and, 108
in rebuilding the temple at Jerusalem, 109–10, 111
religious identity and, 163
in worship, 422–23, 443, 461
Cyrus II. *See* Cyrus the Great
Cyrus Cylinder, the, 52, 53n. 12
Cyrus the Great
as conqueror of Babylon, 25, 51–52, 145
decree of, 25, 31, 50–52, 55–59, 88, 109, 123, 145, 153, 162–64, 415
and fulfilled prophecy, 73, 85
God moving heart of, 13, 31, 52–53, 54–55, 60, 63
opposition to rebuilding the temple in Jerusalem during reign of, 122–25
and provisions for rebuilding the temple in Jerusalem, 13, 56–59, 62–63, 109, 145
and rebuilding of temple, 13, 55–58, 109, 123, 145, 153, 162–64, 204

responses to decree of, 59–62
timeline of, 38
and Yahweh, 56–57

Darius the Great
and the God of heaven, 55
opposition to rebuilding the temple in Jerusalem during reign of, 122, 123
and Persepolis, 25
and rebuilding of the temple, 24, 25, 106, 123, 142n. 1, 146, 153–56, 162, 163, 166–67
and Susa, 25
timeline of, 38
David
and the ark of the covenant, 117, 450, 465–66
authority of, 112, 239
and Barzillai, 81–82
as beloved, 324
and building of the Temple of Solomon, 79–80, 84, 111, 201, 324, 422
and conquest of Jerusalem, 400n. 23
and the gatekeepers, 80, 81, 447
and God's character, 117, 121
and the Levites, 79, 111, 112, 201, 444, 465–66
and praise of the Lord, 406–7
Day of Atonement, 372, 379
divorce, 231, 234, 236, 246–48
Day of Atonement, 98, 99
divine presence, the. *See* presence, God's

Eliashib, 294, 295, 298, 301, 445, 450, 458, 459–60n. 1, 461, 462
Esarhaddon, 124, 132n. 2
Esther, 157, 261. 270–71, 272, 273
exodus, second, 29–30, 77, 108, 165, 205, 231, 238, 380–81, 392, 403
Ezekiel, 54n. 16, 212, 216, 219, 221–22, 242–43, 257, 429
Ezra
arrival of in Jerusalem, 26, 28, 173–74, 177, 199, 203
Artaxerxes and, 177, 178, 187–90, 191
authority of, 103, 175–78, 186
background and commission of, 173–78
and dedication of the walls and gates, 441, 445
and fast for protection, 200, 202–3, 235
and the Feast of Booths, 379–80
and finances for second return to Jerusalem, 200, 202, 203
and God's favor, 177–78, 188, 189, 191–92, 202–3, 204, 205
internal opposition to, 208
and the law of Moses, 28, 103, 175, 178, 189, 193, 205, 209, 241, 373, 382–83
lineage of, 175, 253
mourning of, 212–13, 224, 232, 236
and Nehemiah, 371
personal resolve of, 176–77
prayer of confession by, 213–19, 222, 224–25, 231, 232, 243, 394
as priest, 371, 373
and reading of the law of Moses, 372–77, 380, 382–83, 392
and reestablishment of worship in Zion, 28, 50, 178, 191, 371
and reinstatement of law of God, 28, 30, 32, 188–89, 191, 193
and restoration of sanctity of Zion, 178, 212–19, 371, 467
and returnees' corporate prayer of confession, 396n. 15
and second return of exiles to Jerusalem, 28, 50, 79n. 16, 173–78, 191–92
and unholy marriage alliances, 28, 32, 177, 208–9, 212–19, 229–32, 235–39, 241, 348, 433
worship of God, 191–92, 202–3
Ezra-Nehemiah, book of
as accurate account of events as they occurred, 23, 75n. 5
and answered prayer, 282–83, 284, 287, 306
in Aramaic, 24, 24n. 10, 55, 122, 187
audience of and purpose in writing, 27
authorship of, 25–27
chronology of, 254–57
date of, 25–27, 254–56
in the first person, 26, 174, 191, 199, 209, 212, 229, 232, 462
genealogies in, 75–81, 356–64, 442–44
in Hebrew, 55, 122, 191, 254
inclusion and exclusion in, 31, 85–90, 124–25, 166, 211, 238–39, 285, 360, 452–53

literary and historical setting of, 21–33
as official record of the Persian court, 23
origins of, 24
outline of, 39–42
and prophecies fulfilled, 31, 50–55, 73, 85, 116–17, 119, 162, 204–5
second exodus theme in, 29–30, 77, 108, 165, 205, 231, 238, 380–81, 392, 403
structure and outline of, 27–28
themes of, 29–33
timeline of, 38
in the third person, 26, 174, 203, 229, 231, 232, 290, 309

false prophets, 285, 346, 350, 351–53
fasting, 200, 202–3, 202n. 3
Feast of Booths, 372, 379–80, 392, 393, 395
Feast of Tabernacles, the, 30, 98, 107–8, 107n. 12
Feast of Unleavened Bread, 165, 379
Festival of Trumpets, 98, 372
firstfruits, 419
foundation, temple, rebuilding of
Artaxerxes and, 188
attaining supervision and workers for, 110–11
celebration at completion of, 166, 204
Levitical families and, 111
as manifestation of God's goodness, 113–14, 117–18
opposition to, 124, 188
responses to, 97, 111–16
supplies and personnel for, 109–10
unity of community in, 111

gatekeepers
among returnees, 78, 80, 81, 360, 363
David and, 80, 81, 447
genealogy of, 442
and land apportionment, 429
and ratification of the covenant, 417, 421
role of, 80, 361, 365, 431, 444, 447
support of, 419, 442, 447, 460
and unholy alliances, 240
gates, Jerusalem
Corner Gate, 300
Dung Gate, 292, 295, 297–98, 445
East Gate, 295
Ephraim Gate, 300, 379, 446
Fish Gate, 292, 296, 300, 446
Fountain Gate, 292, 297–98
of the Guard, 446
Horse Gate, 295
Inspection Gate, 295
Jeshanah Gate, 292, 296–97, 446
Sheep Gate, 292, 293, 295–96, 298, 301, 445, 446, 459
Valley Gate, 292, 296, 297–98
Water Gate, 295, 373, 379, 445
Geshem, 340–45
God
character of, 118, 147, 220, 224, 234, 263, 273, 396–99, 404, 405
and destruction of temple in Jerusalem, 144
eye of, 143, 148, 178n. 11
as a fortress, 304–5
fulfilling his promises, 50–51, 53–55, 63–68, 87, 157–59, 216–17, 260, 263, 322, 434
goodness of, 97, 113–14, 116, 117–21, 241, 243, 245, 400, 404
grace of, 147, 209, 213–17, 220
hand of, 143, 177–78, 189, 192, 202, 205, 272, 283, 306, 310
of heaven, 13, 23, 55, 56, 144, 148, 189, 257, 269, 275, 284
*hesed* of, 216–17, 220–21, 258–59, 393, 398, 399, 401, 403, 407, 463
holiness of, 30, 82n. 21
intervening in time and space, 51, 52, 63, 66, 67, 68, 69, 192, 317
of Israel, 56, 100, 163, 219, 285
judging his enemies, 51, 53, 54, 63–66
mercy of. *See* mercy, God's
overcoming opposition to, 33, 156–60, 162, 168
people of, 27, 73, 83, 86–94, 113–14, 115, 116n. 22
presence of. *See* presence, God's
raising up prophets, 147, 148, 150, 156, 192, 216n. 12, 218, 383
as relentlessly pursuing his people, 68, 147, 150, 251
righteousness of, 214, 218, 220, 399, 403, 404, 405
second coming of, 66
sovereignty of, 25, 31–32, 51–53, 92, 143, 148–49, 151, 167, 191, 284, 321

stirring the hearts of people, 13, 52–55, 60, 63, 83, 147–48, 156, 166, 191, 200, 215
Word of, 181–82, 194–96

Hagar, 247
Haggai, 28, 106, 123, 141, 142, 146–47, 156, 162, 163, 164, 305, 429
Hakaliah, 253
Haman, 135, 157
Hanani, 253, 254–55, 255n. 9, 459
*hesed*, 216–17, 220–21, 258–59, 393, 398, 399, 401, 403, 407, 461, 463
Hezekiah, 77, 78, 189, 300, 383
Hilkiah, 76, 175, 193
Hodaviah, 79
Holy Spirit, the
God's presence in, 206
in humans, 169–70
and restoration with God, 66, 69, 275
stirring people to action, 147, 151, 275
Huldah, 193, 405

identity
and bloodlines, 210, 210n. 4, 433
and faith, 88–89, 92, 210, 210n. 4
in God, 148, 377
and inheritance, 94
markers of, 27, 86, 89, 92, 93, 97, 115, 179, 193, 222, 239
national, 50, 84
New Testament conceptions of, 90–93
and obedience to the law, 423
postexilic conceptions of, 85, 86, 87, 90
preexilic conceptions of, 89, 90
and purity, 239
and relationship, 85, 87
restoration of, 98
idolatry, 88, 101n. 5, 109, 116n. 22, 235, 263, 310, 398, 406, 466–67
imprecation, 311–12, 323, 333, 420–21, 464
incarnation, the, 65
inheritance
identity and, 94
in the land, 74–75, 77–78, 84, 85–90
New Testament conceptions of, 90–93
Isaiah, inaugurated restoration of, 435

Ishmael, 247
Israel, people of
conviction of, 232
corporate prayer of confession of, 393, 394–403
defining, 84–90
economic disparity among, 330
external opposition to, 134–39, 148, 157–58, 159–60, 278–79, 283–85, 433
faith of, 88–89
faithfulness of (patient endurance of), 159–60
formal decrees against, 136
instrumental/circumstantial dimensions of, 86, 88, 90, 91
internal opposition to, 328–35
loyalty to God rather than human authorities, 135, 181
personal threat to, 340–49
returnees to Jerusalem as, 76–77, 84–90, 113–14, 259
as servants of the God of heaven and earth, 144, 148
sin-guilt problem of, 220–24, 220n. 18
through bloodlines (primordial traits), 85–86, 87, 90, 115
unity among. *See* unity
use of the term in Scripture, 76–77, 99
Israelites. *See* Israel, people of

Jacob, 163
Jehoiachin, 76
Jehoshaphat, 352
Jerusalem
arrival of Ezra in, 26, 28, 173–74, 177, 199, 203
arrival of Nehemiah in, 26, 28
building of temple in. *See* temple, Jerusalem
building of walls and gates of. *See* walls and gates, Jerusalem, rebuilding of
diagram of city at time of Nehemiah, 37
land apportionment of (resettlement of), 428–32, 433–34
people returning to, *See* returnees to Jerusalem
preserving sanctity of. *See* sanctity of Zion
promise of, 31–32, 50
reestablishment of worship in. *See* worship, renewed

second, 451–52
survey of by Nehemiah, 254–55, 280–82, 281n. 11
Jeshua, 77, 78, 79, 394n. 8, 395
Jesus
charge of sedition against, 350
concealed identity of, 287
condemnation of the Pharisees, 394
cross of, 65
as fulfillment of prophecy, 147, 150
and God's presence in the temple, 470
opposition to, 135, 138–39
as Passover lamb, 170
presence of God in, 169
priestly lineage of, 449
as purifier, 451, 452, 455
reading Scripture, 385
and redemption, 205–6, 406, 469, 481
as revelation of God's goodness, 120, 405
and the Sabbath, 468
as the Word of God, 180, 222, 385
Jezebel, 353
Jezrahiah, 446
Joab, 77, 78
Joseph, 261, 272, 273
Joshua
authority of, 105
call to courage of, 317
covenant of, 393
and first return of exiles to Jerusalem, 27, 32, 75, 441
and Jericho, 450
as Judah's high priest, 76, 76n. 9, 99–100
and rebuilding of temple in Jerusalem, 75, 75n. 5, 76, 99, 100, 101, 105, 106, 111
and reestablishment of worship in Jerusalem, 76
as revealed by the prophets, 146
turning God's anger away, 230n. 1
Josiah, 189, 193–94, 383, 393, 406

Kadmiel, 79, 395
Kasiphia, 201

land apportionment, Zion
gatekeepers, 429, 431
in Jerusalem, 428–32, 433–34
Levites, 429, 430, 431
musicians, 432, 434
priests, 429, 430, 431
in the province, 432–33, 434
temple servants, 430, 432, 434
tribal, 428–29, 430–31

last days, the, 205
law of God. *See* law of Moses
law of Moses
as anchor for the people, 104
authority of, 102–5, 107
eagerness of all people for, 30, 179
Ezra and, 28, 103, 175, 178, 189, 193, 205, 209, 241, 373, 382–83
fixed nature of, 102–3
giving of at Mount Sinai, 397–99
as God-given, 175, 192
importance of, 178–81
and marriage alliances, 28, 32
as marker of identity, 32, 179, 193
obedience to and preserving sanctity of Zion, 423
origin of, 187
public reading of, 372–77, 381–82, 394, 406, 442, 448, 452
and renewal of worship, 28, 30, 103, 108, 174, 187, 187n. 1, 191, 192
restoration of under Josiah, 193–94
Levitical priesthood
among returnees to Jerusalem, 30, 59, 78, 79, 81, 360, 363, 443
and the ark of the covenant, 450, 465–66
David and, 79, 111, 112, 201, 444, 465–66
duties of, 79, 431, 444, 447, 462
and dedication of the walls and gates, 444–45, 449, 450–51
and the Feast of Booths, 379–80
and financial support of the temple, 424
and first return of exiles to Jerusalem, 78, 79, 79n. 16, 200, 201
genealogy of, 442–44
and holy day of celebration, 377
and inheritance, 435
lack of support of, 459, 460
and land apportionment, 429, 430, 431
and ratification of the covenant, 416, 421
and the reading of the law, 374, 376–77, 382–83, 392, 394, 448

and rebuilding of temple of Jerusalem, 111
and rebuilding of walls and gates of Jerusalem, 294, 298, 301
and rejoicing, 384
and restoration of worship, 30, 59, 371, 442, 449
and returnees' corporate prayer of confession, 393, 394–95, 396, 396n. 15
and returnees' covenant with God, 413, 414
and sanctity of Zion, 466
and second return of exiles to Jerusalem, 200, 201, 202
support of, 442, 447
and third return of exiles to Jerusalem, 363
and tithes, 419
unholy alliances of, 210, 240
and worship at the temple of Jerusalem, 112

Luther, Martin, 181, 225, 354–55

Manasseh, 193
marriage alliances, unholy
action taken to resolve, 231–40, 241
and defiling of the land, 233, 234, 237–38
difficulty in avoiding, 433
Ezra and, 28, 32, 177, 208–9, 212–19, 229–32, 235–39, 241, 348, 433
Malachi and, 244
Nehemiah and, 230, 244, 348, 433, 453, 475
New Testament, 246–47
pledge to avoid, 417
restoring sanctity of, 463–64
resumption of, 459
those guilty of, 229, 240–41, 244
mercy, God's
deplorability of unfaithfulness in face of, 209, 214, 217
prayer of Ezra for, 219–20, 235
prophets as visual aid of, 147
restoration as consequence of, 209, 214–15, 241, 405
undeserved, 218, 224, 241, 243, 245
vs. judgment, 221, 222
Meshullum, 296, 299, 348–49, 444
Micaiah, 352
Mithredath, 61
Mordecai, 157
Moses
authority of, 87, 102, 103, 104, 105, 239, 259
and exodus from Egypt, 88
as first lawgiver, 30, 189, 397
and God's glory, 117–18, 120
law of. *See* law of Moses
as man of God, 100, 102, 104
prayer for God's mercy of, 216n. 12, 218, 219, 220, 230n. 1, 232, 257, 262
as prophet, 104, 218, 362
as servant of God, 148
musicians
genealogy of, 447
and land apportionment, 432
and ratification of the covenant, 416, 421
among returnees to Jerusalem, 78, 79–80, 81, 360, 363
supervision of, 432
support of, 419, 442, 447, 459, 460
and unholy alliances, 240

Nadab, 210n. 4
Naomi, 248
Nebuchadnezzar, 61, 62n. 28, 63, 144, 301
Nehemiah
accusation of sedition against, 343–45, 350, 354
addresses to the community, 282–83, 291, 309, 314–18, 319, 329, 332–35, 462
arrival of in Jerusalem, 26, 28, 50
Artaxerxes and, 187, 254–55, 257, 260–61, 262, 266–73, 283, 460
authority of, 104, 266, 283–84
boldness of, 272–73
corporate prayer of, 311–12
as cupbearer to the king, 253, 261, 266
dealing with bullies, 353–54
and dedication of the walls and gates, 441–42, 445–46
defense strategy of, 313, 316, 318–20, 361–62
external opposition to, 278–79, 283–84, 291, 294, 308–20
and Ezra, 371
and famine, 329, 330–34
and the Feast of Booths, 379–80

and financial support of worship, 447–48
generosity of, 334, 336, 337
and God's favor, 284, 312, 335
God's presence with, 275–76
as governor of Judah, 33, 76, 266, 270, 272, 281, 282, 315, 320, 329–35, 346, 362, 366, 414, 447
and holy day of celebration, 377–79
internal opposition to, 354–55, 459–60n. 1
intimidation attempts against, 354–55, 362
lineage of, 253
loyalty to God rather than to human authorities, 281, 283, 334
mourning of, 256–57
and new conquest of the land, 279
participatory suffering of, 325–26, 332–33, 338
personal threat to, 340–49
prayer of confession by, 219, 219n. 17, 257–64, 280, 309, 313, 341, 463
and rebuilding of the city walls and gates, 28, 30, 50, 266, 272, 282, 309, 311–20, 324, 334, 360–61
and restoration of sanctity of the priesthood, 464–65
and restoration of sanctity of Zion, 28, 30, 341, 346, 371, 447, 459, 462–65, 467, 475
and restoration of worship in Zion, 28, 50, 256, 465
and returnees' covenant with God, 413–14
and the sabbath, 462–63, 468–69, 475
as servant of God, 258, 260, 261, 264, 269, 273, 329, 414
and slavery, 332, 336
and survey of Jerusalem, 254–55, 280–82, 281n. 11, 287, 298, 314, 349
and third return of exiles to Jerusalem, 50, 270–71
and Tobiah, 461
and unholy marriage alliances, 230, 244, 348, 394, 433, 442, 453, 475

offerings, 101–2, 418–19
Operation Ezra, 184
Orpah, 248

Passover, 165, 166, 170, 239, 372, 379
Paul, 126–27, 285, 336, 367–68, 437, 453
Persian Empire, 24, 34
Pethahiah, 432
Phinehas, 466–67, 476
presence, God's
anthropomorphically represented, 143, 151
exiles as being without, 74, 88, 238
with Ezra, 177–78, 202
holiness as necessity for, 424, 466, 481
in Jesus, 167–68, 169, 171
necessity of God's forgiveness for, 221, 407–8
with Nehemiah, 275, 276
New Jerusalem as seat of, 171
and rebuilding of the altar, 102, 109
restoration of, 64, 102, 260, 262
and returning of confiscated vessels to the temple, 145
in the temple, 167–69, 168n. 8, 170, 467, 469–75
visible representation of, 167, 168, 169
and willingness of Jews to rebuild temple, 57, 147, 151, 168n. 8, 205–6
priests
among returnees, 78–79, 360
compromising of, 458
genealogy of, 442–44
and land apportionment, 429
and ratification of the covenant, 416, 421
restoring sanctity of, 464–65
support of, 419, 442, 447, 460
and unholy alliances, 240, 464
*See also* Levitical priesthood

Rahab, 453
repentance
as a consequence of restoration, 242–43, 248
corporate, 393, 394–403, 412–13, 422
and God's kindness, 241, 244, 245
and hope that God will withhold wrath, 241, 242, 243–45, 246, 260
Josiah and, 193, 406
peace as a result of, 468
and return from exile, 241, 260, 393
restoration
of Abraham's seed, 73, 89

confession as necessary for, 259
goodness of God and, 114, 116, 118, 215, 241
God as initiator of, 68, 215
Hope of future, 66–68, 264
in Jesus, 244–46, 248
as non-negotiable, 157, 159
repentance as a consequence of, 242–43, 248
time of, 54
returnees to Jerusalem
as captives and exiles, 73–74
corporate prayer of confession of, 393, 394–403, 412–13
covenant of, 412–20
descendants of Israel, 73, 74–81, 360
as divine provision, 201
exclusion vs. inclusion in, 360
first return to Jerusalem, 73–85, 200
gatekeepers. *See* gatekeepers
inheritance in the land of, 74–75, 77–78, 84, 85–90, 364
land apportionment among, 428–33
laypeople with connections by city of origin, 78
laypeople with connections by family of origin, 77–78
leadership team of, 75–76, 75n. 5
Levites. *See* Levitical priesthood
ministers with connections to previous personnel, 78–81
musicians, 78, 79–80, 81, 240, 359, 363, 416, 421, 432, 444, 447
not descendants of Israel, 73, 81–83
people of Israel, 76–77, 84–90, 113–14, 115, 259, 358, 362
personal commitment to covenant of, 393, 394
priests. *See* priests
second return to Jerusalem, 174, 188, 199–201
as servants of the God of heaven and earth, 144, 148
signatories to covenant of, 413–15
temple servants. *See* temple servants
volunteers, 188, 200, 204
Ruth, 248, 452, 453

Sabbath, 423, 459, 462–63, 468–69, 475, 477–79
Sanballat
alliances of Jewish leaders with, 326, 459–60n. 1
as enemy of Nehemiah, 279, 283, 284, 309–15
as governor of Samaria, 278, 278n. 2, 279, 341
not allowed to participate in rebuilding of Zion, 285
opposition to building of walls and gates, 309–15, 318–22, 340–45, 350, 354
sanctity of Zion
compromising of, 459
covenantal promises regarding, 418–20
and exclusion vs. inclusion, 31, 85–90, 124–25, 211, 285
Ezra and, 178, 212–19, 467
holiness and, 423–24
internal opposition to, 354–55
in the modern day, 436–37
Levites and, 466
Nehemiah and, 28, 30, 341, 346, 371, 447, 459, 462–65, 467, 475
obedience to the law and, 423
and rebuilding of the city walls and gate, 28, 30, 292, 293, 294, 295–96, 321
and renewed worship, 28, 30, 31, 101, 168, 174, 247, 321, 418
restoring, 462–63
seventh month as chronological anchor for restoration of, 99, 107–9
Scroll of Ecbatana, 154
Seraiah, 431
seventh month
importance to Jewish worship, 98, 98n. 1, 372
as chronological anchor to restoration of sanctity of Zion, 99, 107–9
Shaphan, 193, 406
Shebaniah, 395
Shecaniah, 232–36
Shelemiah, 461
Shemaiah, 345
Shenazzar, 62n. 28
Sherebiah, 201, 394n. 8, 395
Sheshbazzar, 38, 61–62, 75, 75n. 5, 76, 82, 145
sin-guilt problem, 179, 220–24, 220n. 18, 244, 245, 396, 401, 405, 407

Solomon, 80, 82, 109–10, 145, 257, 262, 324, 422, 459
Solomon's temple. *See* temple, Solomon's
spiritual warfare, 137–39, 137–38n. 14
Stephen, 157, 222–23, 393, 405
Susa, 253–54, 254n. 5, 254n. 7

tabernacle in the wilderness, 167
Tattenai, 143, 148
taxes, 418–19
temple, Jerusalem
- authority for rebuilding of, 100, 101–5, 106, 109, 142, 144–45, 148–49, 153–56, 163
- building resumes on, 142
- celebration of completion of, 162, 164, 165–66, 204
- completion of rebuilding of, 27, 97, 123–24, 134, 142n. 1, 153–54, 162–64
- continuity with the past in rebuilding, 109–10, 111, 164–65
- Cyrus and rebuilding of, 13, 55–58, 109, 123, 145, 153, 162–64, 204
- Darius the Great and rebuilding of, 24, 25, 106, 123, 142n. 1, 146, 153–56, 162, 163, 166–67
- dedication of, 123, 162, 164–65, 168, 169
- destruction of, 144, 293, 301, 424
- disruption of worship at, 459
- Ezra and rebuilding of, 27–28
- funding for rebuilding of, 83–84
- importance of seventh month to, 98–99
- (external) opposition to rebuilding of, 32, 105–7, 122–25, 134, 141–44, 154, 154n. 1, 162
- presence of God in, 469–75
- prophetic word and building of, 142–43, 146–47, 148, 156, 163
- rebuilding of as manifestation of God's goodness, 118, 119
- rebuilding of as prerequisite to renewed worship, 28, 29–30, 56, 57, 97, 105, 107–9, 111, 174
- restoration of support for, 461
- stoppage of work on, 25, 28, 106, 123, 125, 134
- unity of purpose in rebuilding, 98–99, 111
- worship at, 107–8, 112–17, 164, 165–67
- *See also* altar of burnt offering; foundation, temple, rebuilding of

temple, Solomon's, 167, 168, 262
temple servants
- among returnees to Jerusalem, 78, 80, 81, 360, 363
- David and, 80, 81
- and land apportionment, 432
- and ratification of the covenant, 416, 421
- role of, 80, 432

tithes, 419, 425, 429–30, 461
Tobiah
- alliances of Jewish leaders with, 326, 346, 348–49, 459–60n. 1
- as Ammonite, 279, 400n. 21
- as enemy of Nehemiah, 279, 283, 313
- opposition to building of the walls and gates, 311, 313, 320–22, 340, 345–47, 350, 354
- and Sanballat, 311, 313

unity
- importance of maintaining, 324, 325
- Israelite designation as mark of, 84, 99, 112, 259
- in rebuilding the altar, 111
- in rebuilding the foundation, 111
- in rebuilding the walls and gates, 290–91
- in renewing the covenant, 291, 372, 382–83, 415, 418, 421
- seventh month and, 98–99
- as trigger for opposition, 291

Uriah the Hittite, 453
Urim and Thummim, 82–83, 83n. 32
Uzzi, 432

walls and gates, Jerusalem, rebuilding of
- Artaxerxes and, 188
- background to, 299–301
- completion of, 347, 441
- dedication of, 164, 290, 293, 295–96, 383, 441–42, 444–46, 450–52
- diagram of, 36
- and exclusion vs. inclusion, 285
- gate repairs, 294–98
- internal opposition to, 328–35
- Levites and, 294, 298, 301, 305, 450
- Nehemiah and, 28, 30, 50, 266, 272, 282, 309, 309n. 2

(external) opposition to, 33, 106, 122, 131–34, 188, 256, 283–84, 291, 308–20, 347, 433
participants in, 290, 293–99, 305, 309–10
as prerequisite for renewed worship, 30, 31, 168, 174, 292, 321, 422
and preserving sanctity of Jerusalem, 28, 30, 292, 293, 294, 295–96, 301–4, 305, 321, 347
priests and, 294, 295–96, 298, 301, 305
rebuilding vs. repairing of, 292–93
stoppage of work on, 134, 188, 256, 329
temple servants and, 294, 298, 301, 305
unity of community in, 290–91, 305, 315, 318, 332–33
wall repairs, 298
*See also* gates, Jerusalem

worship, renewed
authority for, 107, 108, 112, 441
and confession, 30, 259, 393
disruption of, 459
and eagerness of all people for God's law, 30
and exclusion vs. inclusion, 31, 85–90, 166, 211
financial support of, 189, 418–20, 423, 424–25, 442, 447–48
importance of seventh month to, 98–99
legitimization of, 30–31, 441, 443, 449
Levites, role of in, 30, 59, 112, 210, 247, 371, 381, 444, 447, 449
musicians and, 80
(external) opposition to, 32–33, 105–7, 433
and preserving sanctity of Zion, 28, 30, 31, 101, 168, 174, 247, 292, 321, 371, 418
priests and, 295
prophecies of, 31
and the promise of Zion, 31–32
purity in, 31, 50, 82, 115, 166
rebuilt temple as prerequisite for, 28, 29–30, 56, 57, 97, 105, 107–9, 111, 174
reestablishment of God's law as pre-requisite for, 28, 30, 103, 108, 168, 174, 187n. 1, 191, 192, 381
restoration of support for, 461
at temple of Jerusaelm, 107–8, 112–17, 164, 165–67, 381
unity in, 112, 114–15, 117, 119

Xerxes, 25, 38, 132, 135

Yahweh. *See* God
Yehud, map of, 35
Youth With A Mission (YWAM), 183–84, 224, 274, 436

Zabdiel, 431
Zadok, 175
Zechariah, 28, 106, 123, 141–42, 146–47, 156, 162–63, 305, 306, 429
Zerubbabel
authority of, 105
in Davidic line, 76, 366
and exclusion vs. inclusion, 285
family of, 76n. 8
and first return of exiles to Jerusalem, 27, 32, 38, 50, 75–76, 75n. 5, 441
and the God of Israel, 163, 321
as governor of Judah, 76, 76n. 7, 82, 366, 448
opposition to, 38, 106
and rebuilding of temple of Jerusalem, 38, 50, 75, 76, 99–101, 105, 106, 111, 145, 238, 265
as revealed by the prophets, 146
and sanctity of Zion, 126, 285
timeline of, 38
Zion. *See* Jerusalem

# Author Index


Albertz, Rainer, 269
Alcorn, Randy, 478
Alexander, T. Desmond, 64
Allen, Leslie C., 260
Amzallag, Nissim, 21, 25

Baltzer, Klaus, 258
Barrett, David P., 300, 335
Beale, G. K., 452, 474
Beaulieu, Paul-Alain, 278–79
Belibtreu, Erika, 155
Blenkinsopp, Joseph, 26, 132–33, 155, 382
Block, Daniel I., 28, 243
Boda, Mark J., 21, 168
Boyd, Gregory, 481
Bready, J. Wesley, 196
Breneman, Mervin, 27, 51, 237
Briant, Pierre, 253
Bunyan, John, 206

Carson, D. A., 473
Carter, Charles E., 293
Clines, David J. A., 418
Corey, Barry H., 128, 194
Cowles, C. S., 211
Cunningham, Loren, 194–96, 274
Currid, John D., 300, 335

Dearman, A., 290
De Wette, Wilhelm Martin Leberecht, 415
Dobbs-Allsopp, F. W., 322
Drewery, B., 355
Duguid, Iain M., 243
Dunand, M., 144
Dyer, Jacquelyn, 139

Fee, Gordon D., 146, 286
Fensham, F. Charles, 123, 155, 396
Fishbane, Michael, 174
Forrest, Benjamin, 148
Freedman, David Noel, 27
Fried, Lisbeth S., 256, 279

Gard, Daniel L., 211
Garland, David, 246
Gilbert, Lela, 135, 159
Gill, D., 468
Goldingay, John, 22
Grabbe, Lester L., 56
Graham, Billy, 275
Greene, Joseph R., 168, 470

Hachlili, Rachel, 201
Harper, William, 183
Herodotus, 51, 267
Hill, Andrew, 104

Irons, Charles Lee, 397

Jenson, Philip P., 302
Johnson, M. D., 83
Jones, S., 86, 115

Kaiser, W. C., 254
Keil, Karl F., 255
Khurt, A., 268
Kidner, Derek, 62, 123, 155, 174, 200, 267, 278, 281, 297, 328, 359–60, 362, 371, 374, 377, 395, 414, 419, 429, 431, 443–44
Kitchen, K. A., 23
Klein, Ralph W., 283
Kline, J. Bergman, 397
Kline, Meredith G., 155, 217, 371, 420
Knoppers, Gary N., 279, 452
Kooiman, W. J., 181
Kuhrt, Amélie, 25
Kuniholm, Peter I., 271

Laniak, Timothy S., 260
Laurence, Trevor, 481
Levenson, Jon D., 31
Lints, Richard, 398
Longman, Tremper III, 155, 211, 450

MacDonald, Burton, 466
Marshall, Paul, 135, 159

# *Author Index*


Mazar, Amihai, 297, 299, 300
Mazar, Eilat, 293
McConville, J. G., 51
McRaven, William H., 317
Merrill, Eugene H., 211
Metaxas, Eric, 354
Meyers, Eric, 272
Morris, Leon, 480
Motyer, J. Alec, 257

Na'aman, Nadav, 280
Niehaus, Jeffrey J., 61

Petter, D. L, 473
Petter, T., 86, 210–11, 268, 400, 448, 450, 453
Pierson, A. T., 274
Pittman, Holly, 254
Porten, Bezalel, 55
Pratico, Gary D., 397
Pritchard, James B., 52, 155

Redditt, Paul L., 21
Revell, E. J., 279
Reynolds, R. David, 120
Roden, Chet, 148
Rogers, Janice, 274
Rudolph, Wilhelm, 21
Rupp, E. G., 355
Ryken, Leland, 155

Sakenfeld, K. D., 221
Sanneh, Lamin, 385
Selman, Martin J., 104
Shea, Nina, 135, 159
Shepherd, David J., 115
Shyrock, Andrew, 23
Smith, Gary V., 291, 373–74, 377, 379, 396, 417–19, 431, 442–43
Smith, Ron, 184
Southwood, K., 86, 210
Sparks, K., 86, 210
Steinmann, Andrew, 75, 216, 235, 363
Stuart, Douglas, 146, 286

Taylor, Sophia, 255
Thornbury, Gregory Alan, 195

Van Pelt, Miles V., 397
Vincent, L.-H., 301

Warfield, Benjamin B., 182
Wegner, P. D., 254
Wenham, Gordon J., 364
Wesley, John, 276
Wilhoit, James C., 155
Williamson, H. G. M., 21, 24, 27, 123, 164, 174, 237, 254–56, 270, 278, 282, 292, 298, 300, 315–16, 328, 331–32, 342, 347, 349, 360–61, 371, 392, 395–96, 418, 429, 431, 464
Wills, Garry, 194
Wright, Christopher J. H., 115
Wright, Jacob L., 21, 392

Young, T. Cuyler, Jr., 24